Bible Commentary

by

E. M. Zerr

Volume VI
1 Corinthians—Revelation

© **Truth Publications, Inc. 2018.** All rights reserved. No part of this book may be reproduced in any form without written permission from the publisher. Printed in the United States of America.

ISBN 10: 1-58427-186-8

ISBN 13: 978-1-58427-186-4

Truth Publications, Inc.
CEI Bookstore
220 S. Marion St., Athens, AL 35611
855-492-6657
sales@truthpublications.com
www.truthbooks.com

Foreword: The E.M. Zerr Bible Commentaries

Cecil Willis
Reprinted From *Truth Magazine* XX:26 (June 24, 1976), pp. 3-5

The Cogdill Foundation, which publishes *Truth Magazine*, has obtained exclusive publication rights to the six volume *Bible Commentary* written by Brother E.M. Zerr. . . .

Information About E.M. Zerr

Brother Zerr was quite well-known among a group of very conservative brethren, but he may not have been known among brethren in general. Hence, a little information concerning him is here given. Edward Michael Zerr was born October 15, 1877 in Strassburg, Illinois, but his family soon thereafter moved to Missouri. He was the second of six children born to Lawrence and Mary (Manning) Zerr. Brother Zerr's father was reared as a Catholic, but after he married Mary Manning, he obeyed the gospel. At the age of seventeen, young Edward was immersed into Christ in Grand River, near Bosworth, Missouri.

In June, 1897 young Brother E.M. Zerr received a letter from A. L. Gepford asking him to go to Green Valley, Illinois, and to preach in his stead. His first sermon was entitled, "My Responsibility as a Preacher of the Gospel, and Your Responsibility as Hearers." In the years between delivery of this first sermon on July 3, 1897, and the delivery of his last sermon on October 25, 1959, Brother Zerr preached about 8,000 sermons, from California to Connecticut, and from Washington to Arizona. It is noteworthy that his last sermon was built around Matt. 13:44, and was entitled "Full Surrender." Brother Zerr preached the gospel for a little over 60 years.

Among the brethren with whom Brother Zerr was most frequently associated, it was then common to have protracted periods of concentrated Bible studies, commonly referred to as "Bible Readings." Young Brother Zerr attended a three month "Bible Reading" conducted by the well-known teacher, A.M. Morris, in 1899. During this study which was conducted at

Hillsboro, Henry County, Indiana, Brother Zerr stayed in the home of a farmer named John Hill. After leaving the John and Matilda Hill farm, "E.M." began correspondence with their daughter, Carrie. The following year, while attending a "Bible Reading" conducted by Daniel Sommer in Indianapolis, "E.M." and Carrie were married, on September 27, 1900. The newlyweds took up residence in New Castle, Indiana, where their four children were born, one of whom died in infancy.

In 1911, Brother A.W. Harvey arranged for Brother Zerr to conduct a "Bible Reading" which continued for several months at Palmyra, Indiana. These "Bible Readings" usually consisted of two two-hour sessions daily. Young Brother Zerr's special ability as a teacher was soon recognized, and he continued to conduct such studies among churches of Christ for 48 years. Edward M. Zerr died February 22, 1960, having been in a coma for four months following an automobile accident at Martinsville, Indiana. His body was laid to rest in the little country cemetery at Hillsboro, Indiana, near the church building in which he had attended his first "Bible Reading."

Brother Zerr's Writings

In addition to his oral teaching and preaching, Brother Zerr was a prolific writer. He was a regular contributor to several religious periodicals. Brother Zerr also composed the music and lyrics of several religious songs. Two of these, "The True Riches," and "I Come to Thee," may be found in the widely used song book, *Sacred Selections.*

One of the books written by Brother Zerr is entitled *Historical Quotations*, and consists of the gleanings from 40,000 pages of ancient history and other critical sources which he read over a period of twenty years. These quotations are intended to explain and to confirm the prophetic and other technical statements of the Bible. Another book, a 434 page hard-cover binding, consists of a study course containing 16,000 Bible questions. This book, *New Testament Questions,* has at least 50 questions on each chapter of the New Testament. A smaller book, *Bible Reading Notes,* consists of some of the copious notes which Brother Zerr made in connection with the "Bible Readings" which he conducted. But the crowning success of his efforts was the writing of his six volume commentary on the whole Bible.

These six volumes were published between 1947 and 1955. Brother Zerr has the unique distinction, so far as is known to this writer, of being the only member of the church to write a commentary on the entire Bible. Many other brethren have written excellent and valuable commentaries on various books of the Bible, but no other brother has written on the entire Bible.

Foreword v

The writing of this commentary consumed more than seven years of full-time labor. In order that he might devote himself without interruption to this herculean effort, Brother Zerr was supported by the Newcastle church during this seven year period. It is unfortunate, in this writer's judgment, that other competent men have not been entirely freed of other duties that they might give themselves to such mammoth writing assignments. Through *Bible Commentary*, Brother E.M. Zerr, though dead since 1960, will continue to do what he liked best to do—conduct "Bible Readings" for many years to come. The current printing is the fifth printing of the Old Testament section (four volumes) of the commentary, and the sixth printing of the New Testament section (two volumes).

Many Christians spend but little money on available helps in Bible study. Some own perhaps only a *Cruden's Concordance*, a Bible dictionary of some kind, and then *Johnson's Notes*. It would be interesting to know how many copies of B.W. Johnson's *The People's New Testament Commentary With Notes* have been sold. If I were to hazard a guess, it would be that at least 1,000,000 copies of this superficial commentary have been sold. *Johnson's Notes* contains the printing of the entire New Testament text in both King James Version and the English Revised Version (the predecessor to the American Standard Version), and his comments, all contained in two volumes. In fact, a single volume edition also is available. Thus one is buying two copies of the New Testament, and B. W. Johnson's *Notes*, in one or two volumes. So necessarily, *Johnson's Notes* are very brief.

If brethren somehow could be made acquainted with Brother Zerr's *Bible Commentary*, it is possible that it could be as widely used as has been *Johnson's Notes*, first published in 1889. Brother Zerr printed very little of the Bible text in his commentary. He assumed you would have your own Bible nearby. To have printed in the commentary the entire Bible would have required at least three other volumes. While it would have been helpful to have the Bible text printed by the comments, this unnecessary luxury would have been very expensive, since we all have copies of the Scriptures already. Furthermore, Brother Zerr intended that one be compelled to use his Bible, in order that his commentary never supplant the Sacred text.

A Word of Caution

I am sure that Brother Zerr, were he yet living, would advise me to remind you that his *Bible Commentary* is only that of a man, though a studious man he was. In fact, in the "Preface" to this set of books, just such a word of warning is sounded by Brother Zerr. The only book which we recommend without reservation is the Bible! But Bible commentaries, when viewed merely as the results of many years of study by scholarly men, can be very helpful to one.

Brother Zerr spent his life-time working among those brethren who have stood opposed to "located preachers" and to "Bible Colleges." However, he has not "featured" these distinctive views in his *Bible Commentary*. If one did not know of these positions held by Brother Zerr, he might not even detect the references to them in the commentary. However, I want to call such references to your attention. Along with the opposition to "located preachers," Brother Zerr also held a position commonly referred to as "Evangelistic Oversight." This position declares that until a congregation has qualified elders appointed, each congregation should be under the oversight of some evangelist. With these positions, this writer cannot agree. References to these positions will be found in his comments on Acts 20:28; Eph. 3:10; 3:21; 4:11; 1 Tim. 5:21; 2 Tim. 4:5, and perhaps in a few other places that do not now come to memory. Brother Zerr also took the position that a woman should never cut or even trim her hair. His comments on this position will be found at 1 Cor. 11:1-16.

But aside from a very few such positions with which many of us would disagree, Brother Zerr's *Bible Commentary* can be very helpful. Some restoration period writers of widely used commentaries held some rather bizarre positions regarding the millennium. Brethren scruple not to use *Barnes' Notes*, in spite of his repeated injection of Calvinism, and *Clark's Commentary*, in spite of his Methodist teaching.

Brother Zerr's *Bible Commentary* is far superior to *Johnson's Notes*. Though there are some extraordinarily good volumes in the well-known Gospel Advocate commentaries, there also are some notoriously weak volumes in this widely used set. Viewed from the point of consistent quality, Brother Zerr's *Bible Commentary* is superior to the Gospel Advocate set. Some brethren whom I consider to be superior exegetes of the Word have highly recommended Zerr's *Bible Commentary* and have praised the splendid and incisive way in which he has handled even those "hard to be understood" sections of God's Word.

Our recommendation regarding E.M. Zerr's six volume commentary can be paraphrased from the words of a well-known television commercial: "Try it; you'll like it!"

Bible Commentary

1 CORINTHIANS 1

General remarks. It will throw much light on many passages of this epistle to learn something of the city of Corinth. I shall first quote from Smith's Bible Dictionary: "The situation of Corinth and the possession of its eastern and western harbors, Cenchrea and Lecheun, are the secrets of its history. Corinth was a place of commercial and manufacturing enterprise. Its wealth was so celebrated as to be proverbial; so were the vice and profligacy [extravagant living] of its inhabitants. The worship of Venus [heathen goddess of bloom and beauty] here was attended with shameful licentiousness [immoral thoughts and practices]. "I shall next quote from the Schaff-Herzog Encyclopedia on the city of Corinth: "It soon became one of the most important commercial places on the Mediterranean; but its character was somewhat peculiar. Its population was extremely heterogenous [a mixture]. A numerous colony of Jews settled there when driven away from Rome by Claudius, and among them were Aquila and Priscilla. Everybody went to Corinth to make money or to spend it. All nations were represented there; but nearly the only bonds which held the inhabitants together were their common enterprises and their common debaucheries."

A number of serious defects had come into the church at Corinth when Paul wrote his first epistle to it, which will be commented upon as we come to them in the course of this study. Notwithstanding these evils, the apostle recognized it as a *church of God.* It will help to understand this apparent inconsistency by considering the case of the church at Ephesus as recorded in Revelation 2: 1-5. The Lord had a serious complaint against this church, yet he recognized it as one of His at the time of sending a letter to it. But the candlestick that represented its standing was to be removed if it did not repent. This means that a church (and likewise an individual) does not necessarily lose its standing with the Lord at the mere instance of doing wrong; it loses it when it refuses to correct itself after being admonished. The church at Corinth acted favorably upon the admonition of Paul (2 Corinthians 7: 8-11), hence it continued to be recognized as a church of God.

Verse 1. *Called* is from KLETOS, which Thayer defines at this place, "called to some office," and he explains it to mean, "divinely selected and appointed." *Of Jesus Christ* denotes by whom Paul was thus called unto the apostleship, which also was according to the will of God. Of *Sosthenes,* Thayer says historically, "a Christian, an associate of the apostle Paul, 1 Corinthians 1: 1." Paul chose this brother to join with him in the salutation.

Verse 2. The terms *church of God* and *church of Christ* are both used for the same institution because of their common relation to the Deity. For the meaning of *church* see the notes on Romans 16: 16, in volume 1 of the New Testament Commentary. The various qualifying terms following the phrase of the church do not indicate separate groups, but are qualities belonging to the one institution. *Sanctified* is from HAGIAZO, which Thayer defines, "1. to render or acknowledge to be venerable, to hallow. 2. to separate from things profane and dedicate to God, to consecrate." *Saints* is from HAGIOS, which Thayer defines, "set apart for God, to be, as it were, exclusively his." *With all,* etc., means to apply the epistle to Christians everywhere. For the meaning of *calling on the name of the Lord,* see the notes at Acts 22: 16 in volume 1 of the New Testament Commentary. Lord . . . theirs . . . ours, signifies there is only one God.

Verse 3. *Grace* is from CHARIS, and one part of Thayer's definition is, "kindness which bestows upon one what he has not deserved." This phase of the word explains why the apostle specifies that it is the grace from God he is wishing for his brethren, since all of God's favors upon man are undeserved. Such favors are bestowed upon man only through the Lord Jesus Christ. That is because the sacrifice of Christ provided the way for God to maintain his justice and at the same time extend this unmerited favor to humanity. (See the notes at Romans 3: 26, volume 1 of the New Testament Commentary.)

Verse 4. In his unselfishness Paul was thankful for the favors bestowed upon the brethren at Corinth. In this he was carrying out his own words in Romans 12: 15.

Verse 5. Riches do not always consist of material wealth; the Corinthians had been given the wealth of spiritual blessings in the form of *utterance* and *knowledge*. The first is from LOGOS which is the Greek term for "word," and is applied in a variety of senses. It denotes any expression of thought, whether in single words or in sentences, or even in entire discourses. It is also applicable either to inspired or uninspired speech, so that it would include the gift of tongues. The second word is from GNOSIS and the outstanding definition in Thayer's lexicon is, "intelligence."

Verse 6. This verse shows the preceding one has special reference to the spiritual gifts that were bestowed on the church at Corinth, since that was the primary purpose of those gifts (Mark 16: 20; Ephesians 4: 8-15).

Verse 7. *Come behind in no gift.* Not every member of a congregation was given a spiritual gift, but a sufficient per cent of the membership would be thus endowed to accomplish the Lord's work. The Corinthian church was large in numbers (Acts 18: 8), which would call for a proportionate number of gifted men. *Waiting for the coming.* All persons must of necessity wait literally for the coming of Christ. Strong defines the original word, "to expect fully."

Verse 8. The promise to confirm them *unto the end* does not mean that spiritual gifts will continue that long. The idea is that the Lord will do whatever is necessary for the purpose. After the New Testament will have been completed, spiritual gifts will not be needed and they will cease (chapter 13: 8-10). The grand purpose of all divine means for the confirming of God's people, is that they may be prepared to stand approved by Christ when he comes again.

Verse 9. A part of Thayer's definition of *faithful* is, "worthy of trust; that can be relied on," and this definition is especially applicable to the Lord. It carries the idea that He may be expected fully to fulfill all his promises. God had promised to bless all mankind through Christ, who is the seed promised to Abraham (Genesis 22: 18). In being *faithful* to redeem that promise, God called the Corinthians into the fellowship of his Son.

Verse 10. The apostle now approaches one of the serious defects referred to in the "general remarks," that of *divisions*. This is not a formal or bodily division, but one of sentiment that causes contention and strife. That is why he specifies the *mind* and *judgment* in his exhortation, to the end that all would *speak the same thing*. The *mind* means the faculty of reason, and *judgment* denotes the conclusions arrived at with the mind. The apostle beseeches them all to be united in sentiments.

Verse 11. The name *Chloe* does not appear in any other place, and all we can learn of her is that she was a disciple who was concerned about the conditions existing in the church at Corinth. She passed the information on to the apostle which he repeated in his epistle to the church in that city.

Verse 12. The reader should not be confused over the apparent similarity between *contentions* and "contend," both of which are used in the New Testament. The first means quarrels and wranglings over petty matters of personal opinion. The second is from the vocabulary of contests in the physical exercises, in which a man engages with a contestant under recognized rules of combat. *Every one of you.* That is, each man among them had his preference and was wrangling with the others about it. The four persons named were not literally the subject of their quarrels; chapter 4: 6, 7 shows this, which will be commented upon in detail when we reach that place in this study. But until that time, the apostle reasons as if their contentions were actually over these men (even including Christ), and I also shall make my comments from that standpoint. The idea of Paul seems to have been that, having received the force of the argument before their actual prejudices were aroused, they should be prepared to see the folly of their variances.

Verse 13. The three questions in this verse require negative answers. *In* is from EIS which means "into" the name of another, that was supposed to have been accomplished by the ordinance of baptism.

Verse 14. There was more than one man named Gaius, one of whom belonged to the congregation in Corinth, and was among the few persons whom Paul baptized.

Verse 15. The apostle gives his reason for the feeling expressed in the preceding verse. *In* is from the same word as in verse 15.

Verse 16. Paul did not place much stress on the question of who personally does the baptizing, consequently he seems to have overlooked this case in verse 14. *Household* is from οικος, and in the King James Version it has been rendered by house 102 times, home 4, household 3, temple 1. The first definition in Thayer's lexicon is, "an inhabited house." We know the inhabitants of Stephanas' house were old enough to believe on the Lord, for Acts 18: 8 shows that such were the ones baptized.

Verse 17. *Christ sent me not to baptize.* This statement has been perverted by some who seek to belittle the importance of baptism, and to represent Paul as thinking little of the ordinance. What he teaches in Acts 19: 1-5; Romans 6: 3, 4; Galatians 3: 27 and Colossians 2: 12 indicates the weight that he attaches to the ordinance. But as to what person does the physical act of baptizing a believer, because of the wrong use that might be made of the subject, Paul was thankful he had let others do most of it at Corinth. What Paul could do that others could not was to preach the Gospel, which required more than physical strength. And even that great work was not to be accomplished by the use of *words* or speech that consisted of worldly wisdom, for that would detract from the simplicity of the Gospel of Christ.

Verse 18. The Greek nation was devoted to the importance (as it was considered) of philosophy, or what we would term worldly wisdom. Its people estimated any theory proposed to them in proportion to whether it agreed or disagreed with this philosophy, and it was in view of this truth that Paul wrote as he did in this and several verses following. However, the relation between divine truth and philosophy is somewhat similar to that between it and "science." When this last term is understood, it is found to be in harmony with divine truth. Likewise, when true philosophy is understood, it will be seen that it, too, is in harmony with divine truth. In support of this from the standpoint of history, I shall quote from the Schaff-Herzog Encyclopedia:

"PHILOSOPHY AND RELIGION. Both philosophy and religion must first have had some historical development before their relations could appear for investigation. In fact, they may be said to have proceeded apart until the Christian era, when they openly met as strangers whose mutual interests were yet to be perceived and adjusted. It was not until Christianity had emerged from the symbols of Judaism, that religion stood forth in a mature form, free from philosophic speculation; and it was not until Grecian wisdom had outgrown the myths of Heathenism, that philosophy appeared in a pure state, disengaged from religious superstition. Nor was it strange that the first meeting of the two great powers should have resulted in misunderstanding and conflict. The early Christians, claiming a revealed knowledge from Heaven, could only denounce philosophy as the foolishness of the world; and the philosophers, in their skeptical pride of intellect, were fain to despise Christianity as a mere vulgar superstition. The struggle had its practical issue in the bitter persecutions which prevailed until the triumph of Christianity under Constantine." Corinth was in Greece and the church there was made up in most part of Greeks, hence the occasion of Paul's teaching on the subject of worldly wisdom. The reader should note this paragraph and refer to it frequently as he reads the comments on the following verses. *Perish* and *saved* in this verse refer respectively to the philosophers and Christians described in the quotation from Herzog. Before this development, the philosophers were inclined to judge religion by the standard of their theories, and Paul was opposing that position.

Verse 19. This quotation is in Isaiah 29: 14. What was once called the wisdom of the sages was proved to be not only unwise, but utterly contrary to natural evidences.

Verse 20. *Where is the wise?* etc., means what has become of the theories of these so-called wise and great ones? *Made foolish* means the foolishness has been made apparent by the light of truth. Only one out of the many examples will be cited here. For years the "wise" men of the world taught that the earth is flat, but today the engineers have been compelled to make certain changes in the operation of television in order to compensate for the curvature of the globe.

Verse 21. The world with all its theories that it called wisdom, failed to attain unto that wisdom that would make known to it the true God. *Foolishness of preaching.* Paul is not admitting that the Gospel is foolish, but is using the term expressed by the professed wise men. What they consider as foolishness is the very means God uses to save the believers. But it must be made known in order to save anyone. The third word in italics is from KERUGMA and is defined by Thayer, "that which is promulgated [publicly proclaimed] by a herald or public crier, a proclamation by a herald; in the N. T. the message or proclamation by the heralds of God or Christ." (See Romans 10: 13-18 on the necessity of preaching.)

Verse 22. The Jews professed to believe in a higher form of knowledge than was possessed by mere human beings, but they were critical of any teaching that claimed such a quality unless accompanied with some direct demonstration from heaven. The Greeks were not interested in anything that did not come up to the standard of their own philosophy. (See the long note and historical quotation at verse 18.)

Verse 23. The first clause is virtually the same as the last part of verse 21. The preaching of Christ was always a stumblingblock to the Jews (Romans 9: 32). The story of Jesus did not agree with the philosophy of the Greeks, hence they regarded it as foolishness. This was manifested when Paul was in Athens (Acts 17: 32).

Verse 24. *Them which are called* denotes the ones who respond favorably to the Gospel call. There were persons among both Jews and Greeks (Gentiles) who were sufficiently free from prejudice to recognize the merits of the story of Christ, and to them He represented both the power and wisdom of God.

Verse 25. That which seemed like foolishness in the estimation of the ones clamoring for worldly wisdom, was far beyond the best that the philosophers of the nations could display. The *weakness of God* is used in the same comparative sense as the *foolishness of God*, using the language of the philosophers for the sake of argument.

Verse 26. *Are called* has the same bearing as the words in verse 24, namely, those who accept the call of the Gospel. The classes named are among the philosophers and wise men of the nations. The invitation and promises held out by the story of a slain and risen Lord, do not appeal to *many* of those classes, hence a comparatively small number are willing to accept the favor.

Verse 27. In all of these verses Paul uses such terms as *foolish* and *wise* in the sense attached to them by the so-called leaders of thought among the people of Greece especially, and of the world in general. *To confound* means to confuse and baffle. The unpretentious proclaimers of the Gospel were able to put their adversaries to shame. The case of Stephen in Acts 6: 10 is an outstanding one which states: "And they were not able to resist the wisdom and the spirit by which he spake."

Verse 28. This has virtually the same thought as the preceding verse, with a different set of terms. *Base* and *despised* means the subjects that the philosophers looked down upon. *Things which are not* of any consequence in the eyes of these wise men of the world, were to have such an influence with the sincere believers who hear the sacred story that the *things that are* so important in the estimation of the proud sages would be exposed and shown to be vain.

Verse 29. *No flesh should glory.* The self-exalted accomplishments of fleshly man were to be stripped of their show of wisdom, and leave them without anything of which to boast.

Verse 30. *Ye in Christ* refers to the brethren at Corinth, and Him stands for *God* in verse 28, who had received these brethren in Christ. *Is made unto us* denotes that Paul ascribed to them the qualities named in the verse, even though the philosophers might belittle them.

Verse 31. *As it is written* has such a wide scope of references that it is unnecessary to cite them. The whole teaching of the Bible is that man owes all to God.

1 CORINTHIANS 2

Verse 1. The vanity of worldly wisdom is still the main subject of this part of Paul's epistle. He verifies his attitude on the matter by referring to the work which he did when he brought the Gospel to them, recorded in Acts 18: 1-11. *Speech* and *wisdom* mean the same as "utterance" and "knowledge" in chapter 1: 5.

Verse 2. *Know* is from EIDO, and the definitions and explanations of Thayer occupy nearly two pages in his lexicon, which indicates the wide range of its meaning. In the present verse it has the sense of "to pay attention, observe; have regard for, cherish." It means that Paul determined not to be concerned about anything but the story of the cross, with its offered mercies to the children of men.

Verse 3. Even an inspired man may feel anxious and insufficient for certain tasks. In Acts 18: 9 Paul seemed to have some of these signs of personal weakness, for the Lord saw fit to encourage him and tell him to "be not afraid, but speak." In this great center of worldly learning, he trembled lest he might not do the work justice. However, he determined to depend solely on the Lord's help and wisdom.

Verse 4. *Speech* means the language to be used, and *preaching* denotes the public proclamation of that language. Paul asserts that neither of these items of communication was counted on to persuade the hearer because of its wisdom from man. Instead, he depended on the power imparted to him by the Holy Spirit to be so efficient that its true worth would be *demonstrated* or made to become manifest.

Verse 5. Whatever means that would be used to enlist men in the service of the Lord, would need to be relied on as a motive for remaining faithful. The wisdom of man is changeable, and if this faith was based on such a foundation, it would fall as soon as the wisdom of man was exposed.

Verse 6. The notes at chapter 1: 18 should be consulted again. *Perfect* is used in the same sense as *called* in chapter 1: 24. Those who accept the Gospel from the heart will see in it a genuine wisdom that is beyond all comparison with that of the world. *Princes of this world* means the leaders among the philosophers of Greece.

Verse 7. *Mystery* is from MUSTERION, which Thayer defines at this place, "a hidden purpose or counsel," then explains it to mean, "In the N. T., God's plan of providing salvation for men through Christ, which was once hidden but now is revealed." The word does not necessarily mean something that is complicated and beyond the understanding of ordinary men. As long as anything is not known it is a mystery, regardless of its character. Hence a popular theory that the Gospel is today a mystery and cannot be understood by uninspired persons, is erroneous and calculated to hinder people from studying God's word. *Before the world* denotes that God planned the salvation of man even before the age of human existence. Not that any certain man was *ordained* to be saved, but the scheme by which all men might be saved if they would.

Verse 8. *None of the princes of this world knew* because it had not been revealed. Those who crucified Christ did not realize he was *the Lord of glory* (Luke 23: 34).

Verse 9. This verse has been perverted in song and speech for years, and made to mean that the story of divine love for man, including the reward that is to be given to God's servants, is still a mystery that is to be revealed at some future time. That idea is not even any part of the meaning of the passage. The *eye, ear* and *heart* of man means the natural senses of the human being. No man living, even among the wise sages of the so-called learned world, could discover through his human faculties what the Lord had in store for the faithful.

Verse 10. This verse must be considered in connection with the preceding one. Since the natural mental faculties could not discover these great spiritual truths, it was necessary to give a revelation of them, and that was done by the Spirit bestowed in great measure upon the apostles and other New Testament writers.

Verse 11. The spirit of a man knows what his thoughts are, and likewise the Spirit of God knows the thoughts of Him. Being an intelligent and supernatural being, this Spirit could communicate between God and man and carry the thoughts of the former to the mind of the latter, thus making him acquainted with the truths that his human philosophy and wisdom could not discover.

Verse 12. *Spirit of the world* refers to the matter of human philosophy that has been under consideration through many verses. The spirit which is of God is the source of divine inspiration, and by receiving such a spirit it would reveal the things that are gifts from God. This is the same thought as shown in verses 9, 10.

Verse 13. While the apostle used the language of humanity (Romans 6: 19), he did not form it on the basis of man's wisdom as the philosophers taught it. Instead, he was guided in the selection of terms by the Holy Ghost, so that he would use such of the words of man's language as had a spiritual bearing, in order that they would convey the ideas that were in keeping with the thoughts of the Spirit. *Comparing* might well be rendered "expressing," meaning that Paul expressed spiritual thoughts with such words as would impart the desired ideas.

Verse 14. *Natural* is from PSUCHIKOS, and literally means the animal part of man. In a sentence like our verse, Thayer says it means, "governed by the sensuous nature with its subjection to the appetite and passion." A man thus interested in the things only that will gratify his fleshly desires, will not receive and appreciate the things offered by the Spirit of God, for they are not composed of matters that would give carnal pleasure. Hence they will seem foolish in his estimation so that he will not *know* or realize their real worth. *They are spiritually discerned.* They can be discerned or their true value be recognized only by those who take a spiritual interest in them, seeking only that which will impart spiritual benefits.

Verse 15. He that is spiritual—he who does take such a spiritual view of these subjects coming through the Spirit of God, as set forth in the preceding verse, will be able to realize what they mean, which is denoted by the phrase *judgeth* ["discerneth"] *all things. He himself is judged* ["discerned"] *of no man.* The last word means the natural man described in verse 14. Such a man will not recognize the spiritual truths possessed by the man described in the first phrase of this verse.

Verse 16. No man can know how to instruct the Lord (verse 11), therefore all spiritual information must travel the other way—from the Lord to man. Paul claims that such a flow of instruction had taken place in that *he had the mind of Christ.*

1 CORINTHIANS 3

Verses 1, 2. *Carnal* is from SARKIKOS, and its literal and primary definition is, "fleshly, carnal." Without any qualifying context, therefore, it refers to the material part of man and not his mental or spiritual part. But when it is used in a bad sense, Thayer says it means to be "under the control of the animal appetites; governed by mere human nature, not by the Spirit of God." Paul accuses the Corinthians of being carnal because they were showing a desire for that which was prompted by mere human nature. He also compares them to babes, which is logical because an infant knows only such pleasures as its fleshly body demands and can appreciate.

Verse 3. *Envying, strife,* and *divisions* are prompted by their personal desires, hence the apostle charges them with being carnal. *Walk as men* denotes a conduct that is prompted by the human or fleshly appetites.

Verses 4, 5. See the comments at chapter 1: 12.

Verses 6, 7. The argument in this verse is that the Lord's servants do not all have the same talents or work, even as the production of a crop involves the services of more than one man. Yet all the work of men would avail nothing if God did not give to nature the power of growth.

Verse 8. These men *are one* in the eyes of the Lord. If each will do what he can, he will receive his due reward from God and not from any man.

Verse 9. *We* means Paul and Apollos as laborers in God's vineyard, according to the figure in verse 6-8. God's building is another figure, that of a structure in which various men labor to erect it.

Verse 10. Cooperation or joint labor under God is still the subject of Paul, and he is continuing the figure of a building for his illustration. He gives the grace of God the credit for being able to work as a *wise masterbuilder.* The first thing such an architect will do is to lay the foundation. Paul did this when he introduced the Gospel of Christ to the people of Corinth (Acts 18: 1-11). After he had done this, others came into the community and gave further teaching to the brethren, and that constituted building upon the foundation of truth that he had laid. *Take heed* means that any man offering further teaching should be careful that what he teaches will be in harmony with the original foundation of truth the apostle had laid.

Verse 11. There is but one foundation and that is Christ, which God laid in Zion which is the church, and it was done once for all when He died in Jerusalem and rose from the grave. When Christ was preached to the Corinthians or to any others, that is what is meant by laying the foundation there.

Verse 12. Building upon this foundation means to induce men to accept the Christ as the foundation of their hope. The three degrees of comparison, whether favorable or unfavorable, refers to the different kinds of persons who profess to accept Christ.

Verse 13. No preacher is a mind reader, consequently he may be misled by some who are not acting with sincerity. However, he should heed the admonition given at the end of verse 10, and not use any unscriptural teaching to persuade his hearers to act. The final test of a man's work will come when Jesus is revealed at the last day. But it may be that some of his "converts" will prove unfaithful even while in the life of the preacher, so that he will behold them falling under the fiery trials that are to come before the professed servants of Christ (1 Peter 4: 12).

Verse 14. If a man does his part by teaching the people what is right, and the converts remain faithful, he will have the *reward* that consists of a joyous observation of such steadfastness. This reward is described in 2 John 8 and 3 John 4.

Verse 15. If a man's "converts" fail to stand the test of persecutions or the self-denials required, he will lose this reward described in the preceding verse. But if he has not shunned to declare all the counsel of God, he will be saved from the fire of God's wrath that is to come upon the unfaithful. In other words, a preacher's salvation does not depend upon the steadfastness of those whom he brings to Christ, but on his own faithfulness in preaching and living the truth.

Verse 16. *Ye are the temple of God* means them as a congregation, which was built upon the foundation laid for them by Paul when he preached Christ to them. The church is the spiritual building in which the Holy Spirit dwells (Ephesians 2: 22).

Verse 17. The temple is the church, and such divisions and contentions as were being conducted in Corinth were defiling the temple. Paul is warning the brethren of the wrath of God which they were liable to receive if they continued their variances.

Verse 18. This verse refers to those who were placing undue emphasis on the personal wisdom and special qualifications of certain men in the congregation. Such men were vain and self-deceived, and as long as they maintained such an attitude they would shut themselves off from real wisdom. *Let him become a fool* is an accommodative expression, meaning that if he will admit to himself that he is not a wise man, he will then be in the proper frame of mind really to learn.

Verse 19. The quotation is in Job 5: 13, and is the statement of one of Job's friends. It is an uninspired remark but is the truth, hence Paul gives it approval.

Verse 20. *The wise* means those who boast of their worldly wisdom; all such are vain in the estimation of the Lord.

Verse 21. *No man glory in men.* One man is no more important in God's sight than another, regardless of his apparently great qualifications. *All things are yours* denotes that all of these seemingly great things have been provided for the benefit of the brethren and not for their worldly glorying.

Verses 22, 23. Again referring to the men as he did in chapter 1: 12, Paul takes in more scope in his general summing up of the lesson at hand, including other persons and also other things, both present and future. This all shows that the specific point in view is yet to be brought out, which we will see in the next chapter.

1 CORINTHIANS 4

Verse 1. *A minister* is a servant and a *steward* is an agent. Paul wished that he and his companions should be *accounted* only in that light.

Verse 2. A *steward* or agent is supposed to be honest in handling the affairs of his master, for which he would not deserve any special thanks.

Verse 3. Paul was the agent of the Lord, and it was to Him that he would have to answer. Man might approve of his conduct, but that would be *a very small thing*, for human judges might pass favorably on his case while the Lord would not.

Verse 4. Even though Paul could think of nothing in himself that was wrong if measured by the wisdom of man, yet that alone would not satisfy him, for the Lord was the one who was to have the final word as to his standing.

Verse 5. *Judge nothing* as to the merits of human accomplishments by human standards of wisdom or philosophy. The Lord will come in judgment someday, and then all will be given due reward for any virtue they possessed, whether their brethren appreciated it or not.

Verse 6. The words *figure transferred* are from METASCHEMATIZO, and Thayer's definition is, "to change the figure of, to transform." He then explains the definition at this passage to mean, "to shape one's discourse so as to transfer to one's self what holds true of the whole class to which one belongs, i.e. so as to illustrate by what one says of himself what holds true of all." The reader may refer to what is said about this verse at chapter 1: 12. The four persons named were not really the ones over whom the Corinthians were contending. Paul now explains that he was using the names by way of illustration, in order that they would "see the point" without having their resentment aroused against being personally criticized. The men over whom all these contentions were being waged were right there in the congregation. That is why Paul uses the language that *no one of you* be puffed up for *one against another.* This proves beyond a doubt that the trouble was over men who belonged to the congregation in Corinth. None of the men named in chapter 1: 12 even lived in that city, hence the contention was not over them.

Furthermore, the name of Christ is included with the ones over whom they were contending. It is inconceivable that in their partisan strife, *one of them* would say he was for any teacher as against Christ. No, the men who were the objects of the trouble were those in the congregation with spiritual gifts. The possession of those powers was considered of such importance that it had split the congregation up into groups, not formally but in sentiment, the various sets adhering to the particular gifted man whose gift happened to strike them as the most important. It must be observed that not every member of a congregation would be possessed with a gift, but only a sufficient proportion to accomplish the Lord's plans. This contention over the spiritual gifts was so serious that Paul devoted three chapters—12, 13 and 14—to the subject, which will be commented upon when we come to them in this work. This long note will not be repeated in full, hence the reader should mark it for convenient reference when occasion arises.

Verse 7. The meaning of this verse will be clear when considered in light of the preceding one. The word *another* has been supplied by the translators, so that neither the first nor third personal pronoun is used by the apostle. The entire argument applies to the men of the Corinthian congregation. *What hast thou that thou didst not receive?* This refers to the various gifts that were possessed by members, who were puffed up with pride over such attainments; and it was made worse by the contentions of the groups in the congregation that were arraying themselves as partisans in behalf of their respective "heroes." Paul is rebuking them for this pride by the question just stated. Those gifts were not anything that had been accomplished by them, for they had received them as direct bestowments through the Spirit and hence they had nothing of which to boast, much less to suffer the congregation to be divided up into contentious groups over it.

Verse 8. *Full* is from KORENNUMI which Thayer defines, "to satiate, sate, satisfy." *Rich* is from PLOUTEO and Thayer's definition is, "to be richly supplied." These are such excellent conditions that Paul would surely not seriously attribute them to these brethren after having just given them such a severe rebuke for their pride over gifts that had been bestowed upon them through no personal merit. The only conclusion, then, that we can reach, is that he used it in irony as a further reproof of them for their pride over the gifts. *Reigned as kings without us* (the apostles). Some more irony, referring to their feeling of self-sufficiency, to the extent that they did not feel the need of apostolic help. *Would to God ye did reign* is a serious phrase, expressing the unselfishness of the apostle. He would have rejoiced had the Corinthians been as strong as they felt, for in that case he also could share in the accomplishment, seeing he was the one who put them into the work to begin with.

Verse 9. The apostles really possessed qualifications far beyond all that the Corinthians could rightfully claim, yet Paul was not being puffed up over it. Instead, he wanted them to know that those very peculiar attainments caused the apostles to be placed in an unpleasant position before both angels and men. *Last* means as to personal advantage, the thing of which the Corinthians were boasting. In spite of all their worth-while gifts, the apostles were exposed to the ridicule and persecutions of the world. *Spectacle* is from THEATRON, which Thayer defines, "a public show; a man who is exhibited to be gazed at and made sport of." The illustration is drawn from the Roman practice of the public theatre. When the main show was over, certain men who had been doomed to die, were brought forth into the arena for the "final act"; their clothing was removed and their bodies were exposed to the beasts to devour, for the entertainment of the audience. Thus Paul says the apostles were exposed *as it were appointed to death.*

Verse 10. See the notes on verse 8 where the language is used with a similar meaning to that here. In their own estimation the Corinthians were *wise, strong,* and *honorable.* The apostles were making no pretensions to greatness, but were submissive to the humiliation resulting from the unpopular work of preaching the Gospel.

Verse 11. Being out on the "firing line" and exposed to the hardships of an active soldier of the cross, Paul was made to suffer many things, notwithstanding his many excellencies to which the brethren in Corinth could lay no claim.

Verse 12. Paul often depended on his occupation of tent making to obtain the necessities of life (Acts 18: 3). When he was mistreated he took it in the best of spirit, even enduring all sorts of persecution as long as his character was not challenged. (See 1 Peter 4: 15; Acts 25: 11.)

Verse 13. *Being defamed, we entreat.* This does not contradict the preceding verse. Paul never made any unofficial or personal retort against those who tried to injure his good name, but that did not prevent him from taking the necessary legal steps for his protection. That is what he did when he "appealed unto Caesar" (Acts 25: 11).

Verse 14. The Corinthian brethren were entitled to being shamed, but that was not Paul's motive in writing as he did. His purpose was to induce them to correct their selfish ways, and hoped to do so by calling their attention to his own experiences. Sometimes the example of a loving father will make more of an impression on his sons than will his direct instructions.

Verse 15. There might be no limit to the number of persons who could instruct others, but since a man can be begotten once only, there can be only one person to lead him into primary obedience by making him know what he must believe in order to become a child of God. Paul had done this for the Corinthian brethren, and it is in that sense that he says *I have begotten you through the Gospel.*

Verse 16. Thayer defines the original for *follower* as "an imitator." A son would do well to imitate the example set by a righteous father. If the Corinthians would do that in regard to the life of Paul, they would cease to be puffed up over the comparatively small matter of spiritual gifts.

Verse 17. *Son* is used figuratively, and Thayer explains the original in this and many other passages to mean, "just as in Hebrew, Syriac, Arabic, Persia, so in the N. T., pupils or disciples are called children of their teacher, because the latter by their instruction nourish the minds of their pupils and mould their characters." In chapter 16: 10, 11 is a statement of Timotheus' journey to Corinth, but he had not reached the city when Paul wrote this statement; the apostle wished to have a welcome in readiness for him when he arrived. Paul was not seeking any personal praise for his work, but wished the Corinthians to have the testimony of Timotheus (Timothy) that he was doing all his teaching as Christ would have it done.

Verse 18. *Puffed up* means to "be proud" or act in a boastful manner. The ones who were having that feeling were not especially eager for Paul to come, lest he chastise them orally and severely for their contentious behavior. When they learned that Timothy was coming instead of Paul at that time, they triumphantly asserted that the apostle was not coming.

Verse 19. *Not the speech . . . but the power.* Paul did not propose to be worried by the arrogant assertions of those leaders, but intended to test their real abilities.

Verse 20. Not in word (only), for many loud and boisterous talkers have come into the world, but their real power or efficiency has been exposed as a sham.

Verse 21. This verse is a challenge for them to make the necessary changes in their conduct that would put them in a condition to receive the apostle's approval, and thus receive his spirit of meekness instead of the rod of chastisement.

1 CORINTHIANS 5

Verse 1. *Commonly* is from HOLOS, and Robinson defines it in this passage, "everywhere, commonly," and Thayer's definition is virtually the same. The meaning is that the condition was so well known that the fact was not questioned by anyone. *Fornication* is from PORNEIA, and Thayer gives the one word in our verse as his definition. But he adds the following information historically: "Properly of unlawful intimacy in general. That this meaning must be adopted will surprise no one who has learned from 1 Corinthians 6 how leniently converts from among the heathen regarded this vice and how lightly they indulged in it; accordingly, all other interpretations of the term, such as of marriages within the prohibited degrees and the like, are to be rejected." While on this phase of the subject, it will be well to read the "general remarks" at the beginning of chapter one. Since the ordinary evil of fornication was so prevalent and tolerated so liberally, it makes the attitude which Paul describes all the more significant.

A popular phrase, "living in adultery," is of human coinage, and has no scripture foundation; therefore, we shall examine the word *have* in this verse. It is from the Greek word ECHO, and two full pages are used in the lexicon of Thayer in his definitions and explanations. The definitions (the parts in italics) include, "to have; to hold in the hand; to have possession of; to hold fast, keep; to regard, consider, hold as; to own, possess." Thus the word can be seen to refer to the attitude of a man toward something, without necessarily considering what legal or moral principles are involved. In the present passage, Thayer explains the word to mean, "to have (use) a woman (unlawfully) as a wife." The Lord requires his people to recognize the laws of the land, and they do not regard the fleshly union as constituting the marriage relation as does God (Genesis 2: 24; Matthew 19: 5, 6; 1 Corinthians 6: 16), and that is why Thayer inserts the word "unlawfully" into his explanation. The Gentiles (or heathen), with all their leniency toward immoral conduct, did not endorse such a practice as was being done by this man, and that is the sense in which they would *not so much as name it among themselves. Father's wife* means the man's stepmother. The necessary inference is that his father had remarried, to a younger woman than his son's mother, and the difference in age had induced this woman to become intimate with her husband's son.

Verse 2. *Puffed up* means their pride over the superiority they imagined they had as we saw in the preceding chapter. Even this shameful case of fornication had not moderated their self-esteem. They should have *mourned* or lamented over the wicked character, and resolved that he would be put from among them.

Verse 3. Paul was an inspired man and could speak with authority. This enabled him to form the correct judgment on the present case even though absent and before any hearing had been conducted.

Verse 4. The sentence which Paul is going to pronounce will be in the name of Christ, which means by his authority. The first specification is that the action is to be done *when ye are gathered together*. This teaches that no final act of discipline can be scripturally done except at a meeting of the church. It does not even authorize that a "special meeting" be called for the purpose. The rulers of a congregation may designate the particular meeting at which it will be done, according to their judgment in the case. But when the appointment is made, it must be set at one of the times "when ye are gathered together." Paul informs them that his spirit will be with them in this great and solemn action, which will be true of all congregational actions that are according to apostolic teaching. Moreover, this action would be backed up by the power of the Lord Jesus Christ, so that it cannot be considered as an act of personal revenge on the part of the brethren.

Verse 5. Now comes the verdict of the apostle which must be made that of the congregation also, in order that it may be the action of "the many" (2 Corinthians 2: 6). *To deliver* is defined by Thayer, "to give over into one's power or use." He explains it at this place as follows: "The phrase seems to have originated from the Jewish formulas of excommunication, because a person banished from the theocratic [church and state] assembly was regarded as deprived of the protection of God and delivered up to the power of the devil." *Destruction of the flesh* is explained by Thayer as follows: "Said of the external ills and troubles by which the lusts of the flesh are subdued and destroyed." The idea is that by expelling him from the congregation, it may cause him to realize the terrible condition he is in on account of having lived for the gratification of his fleshly desires, and the result will be his "crucifying the flesh with the affections and lusts" (Galatians 5: 24). That will put him in condition to be restored to the fellowship of the saints, where he can so live that his spirit (his immortal being) may be saved when the Lord comes again. Another serious truth taught in this passage, is that when a person is excluded from the fellowship of the church, he is then in Satan's territory whose inhabitants have no promise of salvation in the world to come.

Verse 6. The Corinthians were so full of pride over their supposed strength, that they seemed to think a single case of wickedness would not hurt them. The illustration of leaven is according to what everyone knows about that product. A woman would not use as much leaven by bulk as the amount of bread she wished to produce, for the small lump deposited in the mass would work until "the whole was leavened" (Matthew 13: 33). Likewise, one bad character who is permitted to remain in a congregation will finally defile the whole body. (See chapter 15: 33.)

Verse 7. Paul has introduced the subject of leaven for the purpose of illustration. There were enough Jews in the congregation to know about the regulations under the law of Moses regarding leaven, and even the Gentiles had seen enough of the Jewish practices to understand something on the subject. At the time of the feast of the Passover and the seven days following, the Jews were required to "put away leaven out of your houses" (Exodus 12: 15), in order that they might keep their feast acceptably. Paul uses the language of that occasion for his instructions to the Corinthians. *Purge out therefore the old leaven* corresponds to "put away leaven out of your houses" with the Jews. The leaven to be purged out of the Corinthian church was the wicked fornicator. *That ye may be a new lump* means the church will be free from the leaven of this wicked man, and in so doing they would become a body fit for the service of Christ, having become *unleavened.* The Jews were to bring about this condition that was free from leaven, because a creature had been slain and prepared to be used in the Passover feast, and it could be eaten only "with unleavened bread" (Exodus 12: 8). Likewise, Christ has been slain and made a passover for us, and we should be prepared to partake thereof with a condition that has been purged from the leaven of sin.

Verse 8. The *old leaven* refers to the case of fornication that had been working in the *lump* or congregation. All other leaven likewise was to be kept out of the body. In naming the various kinds of leaven, Paul includes *malice* which was not present in the case of the fornicator as far as there is any indication. This denotes that the apostle is extending the illustration so as to apply to the entire service of Christ. The *feast* may be said to include all of the activities of the life that Christians are to live under Christ; it is all a rich feast. The passover of Christ's body and blood was consummated but once, it is true, as far as the physical ceremony was concerned, but the spiritual partaking thereof is to be continuous. It will be well at this place to corroborate the idea just set forth by quoting from 1 John 1: 7: "But if we walk in the light, as he is in the light, we have fellowship one with another, and the blood of Jesus Christ his Son cleanseth us from all sin." This walking in the light is equivalent to maintaining a condition described in our present verse as *unleavened bread of sincerity and truth.*

Verse 9. *I wrote* refers to an epistle Paul wrote previously, for up to this verse there has been nothing said on the subject at hand. Colossians 4: 16 speaks of an epistle sent to the Laodiceans, so we know that he wrote some letters that were not intended to become a part of the New Testament compilation. In the epistle referred to here, Paul gave instructions not *to company with* fornicators. We do not know what occasioned that letter nor why that particular instruction was given. The three words come from the Greek word SUNANAMIGNUMI, **and** Thayer defines it, "to mix up together; to keep company with, be intimate with, one." Further comments will be made when we come to verse 11.

Verse 10. This verse is given to clarify a statement in the former epistle as to whom they were to avoid in their associations. The world is so full of such characters as are named, that if Christians were required to avoid all of them, they would have to go out of the world; that is, cease to live in any populated country.

Verse 11. The preceding verse designated who were *not* meant by the restrictions, this one will specify who *is* to be so treated. *Now I have written* denotes that the apostle is giving his latest instruction on the subject. *Man that is called a brother* means one who had been a member of the congregation, but on account of the evils named, had become unworthy of the term "brother," and hence one with whom they should *not keep company.* (See the notes on this phrase at verse 9.) The refusal to associate with this man is to be carried to the extent that they were not even *to eat* with him. Some teach this means eating the Lord's Supper, but the apostle has just explained that his instructions do not apply to men of the world; they apply only to those who had been members of the church. This theory mentioned would mean that people of the world were permitted to partake of the Lord's Supper, but the apostle has just explained that his instructions do not apply to men of the world; they apply only to those who had been members of the church. This theory mentioned would mean that people of the world were permitted to partake of the Lord's Supper, which we know is not true.

To eat is from SUNESTHIO which Thayer defines, "to eat with, take food together with," so the word refers to the physical act of partaking of material food. But such an act itself meant more in old times than it does today; read the following passages. Genesis 26: 30; 31: 46; 1 Kings 13: 15; Proverbs 23: 6; Matthew 24: 49; Mark 2: 16; Acts 11: 3; Galatians 2: 12. From these we may see that the act of eating with others had a social significance formerly that it does not have today. However, the same principle holds good now, and the restriction not *to company with* means any act or association that would indicate a social recognition. If a man has been excluded on such charges as are named in the present passage, others are forbidden to be intimate with him, for such an association would encourage him to continue in his sinful life, thinking himself to be as good as those who associate with him.

Verses 12, 13. *What have I to do* means "I have nothing to do with judging them outside the church." Hence the church was not expected to be further responsible officially for those who were already of the world, or who would become inhabitants of it by being excluded from the church. The Lord would then be the sole judge of them. But those in the fellowship of the church are subject to the discipline of the congregation. The whole discussion of the case is closed with the direct command to put the wicked person from among them. Nothing is said about the woman, hence we must infer she was not a member of the church and so it would not be responsible.

1 CORINTHIANS 6

Verse 1. *Matter* is from PRAGMA and Thayer defines it at this place, "a matter at law, case, suit." The word does not pertain to questions of morals or religion, but to temporal interests between man and man. That is why it is called *things pertaining to this life* in verse 4. Paul tells the brethren they do not have the right to take such disputes to the secular courts.

Verse 2. *Judge* is from KRINO. The outstanding definitions of Thayer are, "To approve, esteem; to be of opinion, deem, think; to determine, resolve, decree; to pronounce an opinion concerning right and wrong." These definitions set forth the idea that the saints (Christians) are to declare the laws by which the world at present is to be ruled religiously, and is to be judged at last. But they could not do this correctly without an inspired law for their guidance which was given by the apostles. That is why Jesus told them (Matthew 19: 28) that they were to "sit upon twelve thrones, judging [KRINO] the twelve tribes of [spiritual] Israel." And after the apostles produced this law by inspiration, the church was to perpetuate the rule under the apostolic teaching. That is why Paul taught in Ephesians 3: 10 that it was "by the church the manifold wisdom of God" was to be made known. The reasoning of Paul is that if the Lord thought his disciples were wise enough to apply His law on the great matters pertaining to the righteous life now and the judgment to come, they should be able to decide such small matters as disputes over temporal transactions.

Verse 3. On the same basis as the preceding paragraph, Christians are teaching and applying the divine law that sets forth the judgment of angels. A part of that law is shown in 2 Peter 2: 4 and Jude 6, that tells of the judgment to be pronounced against those angels that sinned. It is in this sense that *we shall judge angels*, not that any man will literally participate in the procedure at the last day. But the same point is made as that made in the preceding verse, namely, if Christians are entrusted with teaching and applying the law that is to be imposed upon the former inhabitants of Heaven, they certainly should be able to decide matters pertaining to the inhabitants of *this life* or which concern only temporal life.

Verse 4. The original Greek manuscript did not have punctuations, hence the question mark does not show here, but the inflection of the words in the composition does indicate the form of the sentence. It will help in seeing the idea of this verse to quote the version in Living Oracles which is as follows: "If, then, you have the cognizance [decision] of such matters, why do you set those to judge who are of no account in the congregation?" The congregation had very little esteem for the judges in those secular courts, yet these brethren who had some personal dispute over a temporal matter, were going to these courts for settlement instead of letting the church decide it (according to Matthew 18: 17).

Verses 5, 6. This paragraph, following immediately upon the statement of the preceding one, shows that it was not an instruction as to what they should do, but was a criticism in question form of what they were doing, which Paul says was shameful.

Verse 7. Instead of disgracing the church before the secular courts, a brother would better take the loss he thinks the other is trying to impose on him.

Verse 8. It would be wrong to go to law even when a brother was being defrauded, but it is worse when he takes the case to court in order to despoil another of his rights, as some of these Corinthians were doing.

Verse 9. Having dealt with the specific evil concerning going to law, the apostle broadens his teaching to consider various forms of evil. Chief among the corruptions that existed among the people of Corinth was the different forms of immorality that were practiced by many with very little concern as to right or wrong. In fact, much of that was a part of the heathen religious ceremonies of that country, which accounts for the indifferent attitude that even the professed disciples of Christ showed on the subject. The present verse, also some others in the chapter, will show us how much concern the apostle felt over it. The word *effeminate* and the phrase *abusers of themselves with mankind* both refer to sodomites. The second means a male who uses another male in the place of a female, and the first means a male who permits his body to be so used. (See the notes at Romans 1: 27, volume 1 of the New Testament Commentary, on the subject in the italicized phrase.)

Verse 10. Most of the characters named are so well known as not to need detailed comment. *Revilers* are those who use false degrading speech against others, and *extortioners* are men who acquire unjust gain from others on one pretense or another.

Verse 11. Some of the Corinthians had been guilty of these evils, but the Gospel had shown them the way to be redeemed from such practices. Yet they were in constant danger of going back to them if they were not vigilant, hence the apostle is sending them this teaching contained in several of the verses. *Washed, sanctified* and *justified* all refer to the work of becoming a Christian, which was completed by having their bodies washed with pure water (Hebrews 10: 22).

Verse 12. The original word for *expedient* is defined "profitable" in Thayer's lexicon. A thing could not be profitable that was not lawful, but it might be lawful and not profitable. This verse has special reference to foods of all kinds. (See next verse.) There is no direct legislation against any kind of food (Romans 14: 1-3; 1 Timothy 4: 4), but it would not be profitable for a Christian to become a slave to his appetite, and Paul says he will not be brought under it.

Verse 13. A more convenient wording of the first clause would be, "foods for the body, and the body for foods." These two are perfectly adapted to each other, but they are both to be done away with, which is the meaning of *destroy*, and that is why Paul declared in the preceding verse that he would not allow himself to become enslaved by his appetite. This teaching is true independent of any other subject, but Paul is using it to introduce another point about the right use of the body. The same physical use is made of the body in the act of fornication as in lawful intimacy, but the Lord did not intend for man to abuse his body in that way, any more than He intended for him to abuse the use of food for the body. It is easy to see why the apostle is again dealing with the subject of immorality, in view of the prevalence of that evil in Corinth.

Verse 14. The *destruction* of the body mentioned in the preceding verse, did not mean its annihilation, but that its temporal form requiring food would be discontinued. The human body is made in the image of God, and its importance in His estimation is great, so much so that it will be raised from the dead at the last day.

Verse 15. The value of a man's body is still in the apostle's mind, and he declares it is a *member of Christ;* not literally, of course, but a part of that great body of which Christ is a member. In view of such a sacred relation, Paul deplores the sin of using the body to unite with an immoral woman, again referring to the loose morals being practiced by so many in Corinth.

Verse 16. We know the apostle was not using that statement in some special or strained sense, for he supports it by quoting the words of God and Christ where we know the language applies to the intimate relation of the sexes, the only "ceremony" the Lord ever gave as a basis of marriage. (See Genesis 2: 24; Matthew 19: 5, 6.)

Verse 17. The intimate relations of a male and female make them one body, and the faithful joining of a disciple to the person of Christ makes them one spirit.

Verse 18. *Flee fornication.* The prevalence of immorality in Corinth, and its effects on the disciples of Christ, continues to be one of the apostle's chief concerns. To *flee* from a thing means more than merely not partaking; it means to run away as from a poisonous adder. *Every sin* refers to sins of a material or physical nature, not that immorality is the only sin that a man can commit within his own personality, for when he harbors filthy thoughts, that is a sin within his own person. However, they are not bodily sins, while fornication is: it constitutes a sin against his body that was made in the image of God.

Verse 19. In chapter 3: 16 Paul tells the Corinthians that "ye are the temple of God," and it means they as a congregation. In our present verse he tells the same brethren that *your body is the temple of the Holy Ghost.* There is no discrepancy, for the church is made up of individuals, whose bodies must be kept pure in order that the church as a whole may be pure. This is why God claims possession of the bodies of the saints; it is in order that His spiritual body may be right.

Verse 20. If a person wishes to own something he will pay a price for it, and the value of the price will depend on the estimation he has of the thing to be bought. God rated the persons (both fleshly and spiritual) of the disciples so highly, that He paid the price of the blood of Christ for them (Acts 20: 28; 1 Peter 1: 18, 19). It is hence the duty of Christians to use their bodies and spirits (minds) in such a way as to glorify God.

1 CORINTHIANS 7

General remarks. This chapter was occasioned by a condition existing at that time, due no doubt to the activities of the Roman Empire in its military oppression of various religions, which finally affected the church. The general existence of immorality also entered into the teaching of Paul in answer to the letter that was sent to him. The key to many of the expressions of the chapter is in the 26th verse which mentions the "present distress," brought about by the oppression just mentioned. That made it inadvisable to take on further obligations, especially those brought upon a man who begins to organize a family. Under these conditions someone wrote to Paul for advice as to what they should do, and it was that it would be better to remain just as they were, and not take upon themselves the obligations of married life. However, the marriage relation is the Lord's means of meeting the desires of the flesh on this subject, and unless a man is sure that he can resist all temptation to immorality, then he is to discard Paul's advice and enter the state of marriage for the lawful gratification of his desires. While discussing the specific subject brought up by the letter, the apostle will include some teaching on other matters, that are to be observed by disciples today. I urge the reader to become familiar with this paragraph, as it will be helpful for reference at various places, for it will not be repeated in every verse as the comments on the chapter continue.

Verse 1. *Touch* is defined in Thayer's lexicon, "to fasten to, make adhere to," and in this verse it means to have intimate relations with a woman in marriage.

Verse 2. *Nevertheless.* See the paragraph at the beginning of the chapter, about when the advice against marriage was to be discarded.

Verse 3. Since the primary object of marriage (aside from reproduction) is to give lawful gratification of sexual desires, the husband and wife should cooperate with each other to that end.

Verse 4. *Power* is from EXOUSIA, which means authority or control. This verse teaches that neither husband nor wife has exclusive right about the use of his body, regarding whether it should be used for the gratification of the other. This idea, especially as it pertains to the woman, is taught in Genesis 3: 16.

1 Corinthians 7: 5-16

Verse 5. The context shows that *defraud* means to withhold from each other the intimate relation. They are permitted to do so only on condition that both consent, so as to be free for exclusive religious devotions. Even then, they should not stay apart too long, lest they be tempted to seek gratification unlawfully; *incontinency* means lack of control of the fleshly desires.

Verse 6. *I speak this by permission.* Whether the pronoun *this* refers to what Paul has just said, or to what he is about to say, is relatively unimportant. The point to learn is the meaning of *permission.* It is taught by some that Paul was only permitted to write on some things and not commanded to do so, and therefore what he said by permission would have no binding force. I believe the distinction is unimportant, for the Lord would certainly not *permit* Paul to write any instruction that was not right for the benefit of all concerned.

Verse 7. Paul's general teaching on the marriage institution, as well as what he says in this chapter, would show us he does not mean to wish that every man would abstain from marriage as a permanent way of life. But if all men had the self-control over their nature that the apostle had, they would have no difficulty in following the advice during the "present distress." The *gift* means the natural ability to maintain control over the passions.

Verse 8. See the advice explained in the first paragraph.

Verse 9. *Cannot contain* denotes they cannot have complete control over the desires. *Burn* is from PUROO which Thayer explains at this place to mean, "to be inflamed with sexual desire."

Verse 10. *Yet not I, but the Lord.* This teaching was not given to them merely by the *permission* of the Lord (verse 6), but He commanded him to give it. *Let not the wife depart.* Some might think that if it was better not to marry, it would likewise be proper for a wife to relieve her husband of these "added obligations," and Paul is teaching against such an action.

Verse 11. Regardless of what might cause a wife to depart, she would have no right to remarry some other man. The husband had no right to put away his wife on the ground of Paul's advice about the "present distress."

Verse 12. *I, not the Lord* means by Paul's permission and not by command of the Lord. (See the notes on verse 6.) A man might have been tired of married life and thought he could be relieved of the burden by putting his wife away, using as a special excuse that she was an unbeliever. Paul means that he should not do so if the wife is willing to remain with him.

Verse 13. This takes the same comments as the preceding verse.

Verse 14. The unbelieving partner is not sanctified by the other in the sense of religious holiness before God, for in that sense no person can sanctify another. It means that the marriage of one person to another makes their cohabitation moral, since the marriage relation is a fleshly one, primarily for fleshly purposes (see the comments at verse 3). Were this not true, then children born of parents one of whom is an unbeliever would be *unclean,* which means ceremonially improper, whereas, all children of parents who are married to each other are holy as far as their orgin is concerned.

Verse 15. It should be noted in this verse that it is the unbeliever that is determined to desert the marriage, in spite of the willingness of the other to continue even under the "present distress." The believer is told to *let him depart,* which denotes that he is not obligated *(is not under bondage)* to hold the unbeliever with him if it would have to be done under continual strife or "family quarrels," for God is wanting his creatures to live in peace if possible, in which they were called. But that has nothing to do with the question of remarriage for either of them. In truth, verse 11 orders that if the departing wife should change her mind and desire the marriage relation again, she must go back to her husband. And that would mean also that the husband would be required to remain single, else the wife could not obey verse 11 even if she wanted to. All of this is in keeping with Matthew 19: 9 which clearly teaches that no married person may be remarried to another, except upon the immorality of the present marriage companion.

Verse 16. The preceding verse was rather a break into the line of thought being set forth in verse 14. In that Paul was showing that a believing husband or wife need not break up their marriage on account of the unbelief of the other; that the morality of the marriage was not affected by the unbelief of one of them. The present verse continues the thought, and gives another reason why he should remain in the marriage, namely, he might be able to convert his partner. This idea is taught in 1 Peter 3: 1, 2.

Verse 17. Whatever condition may be the lot of a man who has accepted the call of the Lord, let him be faithful to his profession. This command is announced as being applicable to all the churches. (See notes at John 15: 16 on *ordain*.)

Verse 18. *Become uncircumcised.* This refers to a surgical trick whereby it could not be known from appearances whether a man was circumcised or not. The verse means for a Jew not to resort to that if he decides to become a Christian. This surgery is mentioned in Josephus, Antiquities, Book 12, Chapter 5, Section 1.

Verse 19. The teaching of the preceding verse is based on the truth of this. Under Christ it makes no difference whether a man is circumcised or not, just so he keeps the commandments of God. (See Galatians 5: 6; 6: 15.)

Verse 20. This verse is a general application of the preceding several verses.

Verse 21. A great part of the people were slaves in the Roman Empire. The fact that a man was in that "calling" or station in life, need not hold him back from accepting the Gospel call, for salvation is for all classes. However, if his master sees fit to release him, he should accept it for the advantages it would give.

Verse 22. Two kinds of service and freedom are meant here, the temporal under a human master, and the spiritual under Christ. Hence a man can be a servant under the former and yet be free from sin while being a servant of Christ.

Verse 23. This does not contradict verse 21. It means not to serve men as to any religious directions. The temporal masters often bought their slaves, and likewise Christ has purchased his with his own blood. (See chapter 6: 19, 20.)

Verse 24. This is the same as verse 20.

Verse 25. *No commandment* in the same sense as verse 6. *Give my judgment* under the permission of the verse just cited. Paul had shown himself faithful to the Lord, and hence he was given the *permission* to use his judgment in the case.

Verse 26. *So to be* means for him to remain just as he is, on account of the *present distress.* (See the paragraph at the beginning of the chapter.

Verse 27. This repeats the teaching running through much of the chapter.

Verse 28. *If thou marry, thou hast not sinned.* Paul had never forbidden marriage as being wrong, but only advised against it on account of the *present distress.* While not a sin, yet the marriage will bring them *trouble in the flesh* which means the hardships caused by the condition of the country. *I spare you* is a brief way of saying "I wish to spare you these troubles by advising you not to marry while the present conditions prevail."

Verses 29, 30. The original Greek word for *short* is defined by Thayer at this place, "is shortened," and Robinson defines it, "the time is contracted, shortened." The *time* referred to in this passage is the period of the *distress* caused by the oppression under Rome. Naturally the passing days made that period shorter, and the teaching of this verse is that disciples should not be so concerned about these various conditions in their earthly life. Give chief attention to their obligations as Christians until the conflict was over, which was not to be very long in comparison.

Verse 31. The good things of this world are necessary to man's existence as a temporal being, therefore he must make some use of them. *Abusing* is from a word similar to the one for *use*, with a prefix in the Greek composition that makes it mean "to overdo" the use of them. The logical reason the apostle gives for the exhortation is that all these things are temporary; they will pass away.

Verses 32, 33. *Carefulness* means anxiety over the handicaps of the *present distress.* A married man would have to give his attention to the things of the world, such as those necessary to care for his wife. That would really be his duty if he had a wife, but he could avoid such anxiety for the time being if he took Paul's advice and remained single.

Verse 34. The same things apply to women in that a married woman would be obligated to give some attention to the rightful requirements of her husband. If she remained single she would be free to give her sole attention to religious devotions. *Be holy both in body and in spirit* does not mean that her relations with her husband would be wrong, but they would be temporal and would thus require some of the time she otherwise could devote to these spiritual matters.

Verse 35. This verse is a general summing up of several preceding ones. It shows that Paul's teaching regarding the advisability of entering marriage during the *present distress* was not on the basis of right and wrong. It was for their *profit* (advantage) in the services to Christ. Being free from the unavoidable burdens the present conditions would impose on married people, they could devote their time to the Lord's service *without distraction.*

Verse 36. This verse (as here translated) is entirely out of line with the general teaching of the chapter. Note the pronoun *her* is in italics which is because the King James translators did not understand the verse. Some later commentators even insert the word "daughter" after *virgin*, for which there is not the slightest ground in the original. They make this verse refer to a father's willingness for his daughter to marry. What would a man's control over his own passions have to do with his consent to his daughter's marriage? The confusion is caused by a common but erroneous notion that *virgin* always means a woman. A look at Revelation 14: 4 would show that to be wrong, even if one could not consult the original. That passage says the persons were "not defiled by women; for they are virgins."

When the word in question is used as a state or condition in life, it means virginity. The Englishman's Greek New Testament renders this verse as follows: "But if anyone thinks he behaves unseemly [improperly] to his virginity, if he be beyond his prime, and so it ought to be, let him do what he wills, he does not sin; let them marry." It is easy to see this verse means the same as Paul's teaching in the rest of the chapter, namely, that it is best to remain single if one has control of his desires. But if he begins to doubt his ability to remain chaste in an unmarried state, then he should marry, and in so doing he would not commit any sin. It is true it says let *them* marry, which is because any marriage requires two persons.

The word *virgin* is from PARTHENOS, and Thayer gives the following definition as it applies to men: "One who has never had commerce [intimacy] with women." *Pass the flower of her* [his] *age* means a male who has reached the age when his sexual nature has become fully developed and more insistent on gratification. By changing the pronouns from the feminine to the masculine, as the inflection of composition in the Greek text requires, the verse will be easily understood. It will then give the same advice that the apostle has given throughout the chapter, namely, that moral chastity is more important than freedom from the burdens of family life. If a man cannot have sure control over his desires, he should avail himself of marriage which is the Lord's plan for lawful gratification of them. This is directly taught in verse 28, where Paul explains that his purpose in giving the advice was to have them avoid the *trouble in the flesh* that would come to married people in the *present distress.*

Verse 37. This is the same in meaning as the preceding verse.

Verse 38. The pronoun *her* is in italics in both sentences and is not justified by the original. The phrase *giveth in marriage* means to give himself in marriage to another. He that becomes married *doeth well* because he avoids the guilt of immorality, but he that is able to remain unmarried *doeth better* because he not only maintains his moral chastity, but avoids the burdens of married life.

Verse 39. It is sometimes asked if the requirements of this verse would not be on the same proviso of *present distress*, as the advice of Paul about the marriage of those single at the time he was writing. The cases are not the same, for it is expressly stated that if a man married in the first place he would not do any sin (verse 28), since that instruction was given as advice only to avoid the burdens of married life. The present verse plainly says the wife is bound *by the law* (not a temporary condition caused by the *present distress)* as long as her husband lived; not as long as the "distress" continued. Hence the verse involves a matter of right and wrong (not one of expediency as is the other). *At liberty to be married* means she has the right to be married, with the stipulation that it must be *in the Lord.* All marriages are in the Lord in the sense that the Lord is the author of the basis of the physical relation (Genesis 2: 24; Matthew 19: 5), hence the phrase here has a special sense since it is applied only to second marriages. To be *in the Lord*, therefore, can mean nothing else than being in His body which is the church. A Christian widow has no right to marry a man outside of the church. The same principle would logically apply to a Christian man. The woman is mentioned only because the greater part of the other verses have been dealing with the wives.

Verse 40. *Happier if she so abide*, but not more righteous, which again brings in the advisability of any single person entering marriage at that time. *I think* does not mean that Paul was uncertain, for it is from the same Greek word as Jesus used in Matthew 22: 42, where he asked the Pharisees, "What think ye of Christ?" We know Jesus did not wish them to give him any answer on which they were doubtful. It simply means to state some idea or conclusion that a person has. Paul had no doubt as to the source of his idea at this place, for it came from the same One who had given him the "permission" to speak in verse 6. Acting under that privilege, he gave it as his judgment that the woman would be happier were she to remain unmarried.

1 CORINTHIANS 8

Verse 1. Corinth was a Greek city and the sacrificing to idols was common. The flesh of the beasts was not burned, but only put through some routine, then sold in the market for meat. The question arose as to whether it was right for Christians to eat that meat. Some of the brethren understood that it did not make any difference, since the idols were dead objects and meant nothing. Those having this knowledge were being puffed up over their supposed superiority and were discouraging the weaker ones. Paul wanted them who were the better informed to show *charity* (love on behalf of the brethren) and thus *edify* or build up the less informed disciples.

Verse 2. These better informed brethren were correct theoretically, yet their boasted knowledge had caused them to be ignorant of what was more important, namely, the proper attitude toward the others.

Verse 3. The greatest knowledge a man can have is shown by his love for God (and his weaker children). Such an attitude shows that the man knows God, which proves that he has the kind of knowledge that is really great. It may well be worded, "If any man loves God, such a man knows the same God."

Verses 4, 5. Various objects in nature were worshiped as gods, which is why Paul uses the phrase *gods many* *and lords many*. But the apostle agrees with the "knowing ones" that these gods were nothing.

Verse 6. Repeating the idea just set forth, the apostle adds some truths about the God who created all these things which the heathen were ignorantly worshiping.

Verse 7. Not every man (even among the disciples) had been clearly informed on the subject of meats that had been used in the idolatrous service. For the meaning of *conscience*, see the notes at Acts 24: 16 in volume 1 of the New Testament Commentary. When these uninformed brethren were induced to eat this meat, they had a "guilty feeling" because they could not see anything in the act except a form of idolatrous worship. Such an attitude would make them really guilty, because one must have a clear conscience in order to please God.

Verse 8. This is the same as verses 1, 4, 5.

Verse 9. The better informed brethren should not use their privilege in such a manner as to cause the weaker ones to go against their conscience.

Verse 10. *See thee* is a key to the subject, which will be referred to at verse 13. *Idol's temple*. After the religious exercises were over, a temporal meal was served and a visitor could sit down and eat in much the same fashion he would today in a restaurant. There was nothing wrong about it in itself; but if one of these weaker brethren should see it, he would be *emboldened* (encouraged) to eat also. He would reason, "If that brother may eat of that meat, I will also."

Verse 11. But as soon as he had done that, he would have that "guilty feeling" which defiled his conscience. He would *perish;* be in danger of condemnation for defiling his conscience, and it would be through the example of the stronger brother who had no conscientious objections to the meat.

Verse 12. Anything that is done toward the disciples of Christ, whether good or bad, is counted as being done unto Him. (See Matthew 25: 40, 45.)

Verse 13. *Make my brother to offend* means to cause him to stumble or do wrong. *I will eat no flesh;* that is, in his presence (verse 10). If a Christian believes it is right to eat this meat he may do so, but he must exercise that faith or privilege "to himself" (Romans 14: 22).

1 CORINTHIANS 9

Verse 1. *Am I not an apostle?* Verse 2 indicates that some had questioned the apostleship of Paul. He will name some of the reasons for claiming to be an apostle, in both the present and the next verse. *Have I not seen Jesus Christ our Lord?* It was one of the qualifications required of an apostle that he had seen Christ alive after the crucifixion. *Ye my work in the Lord:* Paul started this church (Acts 18: 1-11).

Verse 2. Aside from any work Paul might have done elsewhere, the Corinthians had the evidence in their own experience that Paul was an apostle. *Seal* is from SPHRAGIS, which Thayer defines at this place, "that by which anything is confirmed, proved, authenticated, as by a seal." When a legal paper has an official seal stamped on it, that proves the existence of the seal, just as the letters the reader is now looking at prove the existence of the type somewhere. The bestowal of spiritual gifts could be done only by an apostle (Acts 8: 18). The church at Corinth possessed those gifts after Paul had worked with them, which proved that he was an apostle.

Verse 3. Paul gives an *answer* to the ones who wanted to *examine* him, which denotes the examination consisted of questions as to why he did or did not do some things.

Verse 4. *Power* is from EXOUSIA, which means right or authority. *To eat and drink* means to do so at the expense of those to whom he preaches. (See verse 14.)

Verse 5. Paul means he has the right to do so at the expense of the church, as well as to obtain his own food from it. He abstained from marriage voluntarily, but insists that had he chosen to do so, he would have the right to marry and have his wife travel with him at the expense of the church. His stipulation that his wife would be a *sister* (in Christ) is a strong recommendation that even the first marriage of Christians should be with one in the faith. As an approved example of his right in this matter, he cites that of other apostles including *Cephas* (Peter).

Verse 6. Paul narrows his discussion to himself and Barnabas. *Forbear working* means not to labor with their hands to obtain the necessities of life.

Verse 7. Nobody expects a soldier to support himself while fighting for his country. On the same principle, a man who produces fruit or stock is granted the right to partake thereof.

Verse 8, 9. To show that he was not making these arguments on his personal authority only, Paul quotes from Deuteronomy 25: 4 in regard to oxen. Before the days of machinery, small grain was piled down on a floor and the beast was driven round over it to break the husk from the grain. It was natural for the ox to help himself to the feed, and the command was not to muzzle him to keep him from eating the grain. *Doth God take care for oxen?* The law against muzzling the ox was in force literally, but the circumstance was used as an example for something more important than the comfort of brute beasts.

Verse 10. *For our sakes . . . this is* written. The law indeed was intended as a merciful provision for the dumb creature, but it was *written* as a lesson for men who were to partake of the fruit of their own labors.

Verse 11. Paul is still discussing his right to financial support, not that he is asking for it. *Carnal things* is another term for the temporal necessities of life. The Corinthians had received spiritual things (the Gospel) from Paul, and it was right if they were asked to contribute to his necessities were he to ask for it.

Verse 12. Having shown his full right to the temporal support of the Corinthians, Paul informs them it is not his intention to require it.

Verse 13. The apostle adds another proof for his position by referring to an arrangement under the Mosaic system, in which the one officiating in the altar service got part of his living from that service. (See Leviticus 6: 16, 26; 7: 6, 31, 32.)

Verse 14. To *live of the Gospel* means to obtain a living from those to whom the Gospel is preached. This is taught also in Galatians 6: 6.

Verse 15. Again Paul explains that he is not hinting for favors. In truth, he would even refuse to receive them on account of a special circumstance to be commented on soon. But he wishes to correct a wrong attitude some had on the subject

Verse 16. Regardless of all other considerations, it was the duty of Paul to preach the Gospel, else the *woe* or condemnation of the Lord would be on him.

Verse 17. However, if he preaches independent of his fixed duty, there was a special favor offered to him. If he does not do it under a free motive, then the *woe* mentioned in the preceding verse, here called *dispensation*, would be upon him.

Verse 18. Paul asks and answers the question as to the *reward* mentioned in the preceding verse. That consisted in the privilege of preaching to the Corinthians and not taking any financial support from them. Verse 14 says the Lord ordained that preachers were to be supported by the ones who heard the preaching. Paul was given a special exemption from that law in order to have some satisfaction from the privilege of which he might glory (verse 15). It did not bring all of the enjoyment he expected, for afterward he apologized for it (2 Corinthians 12: 13).

Verse 19. Paul was not legally bound to any man, yet he voluntarily put himself in a position of service to everybody for the good he could do.

Verse 20. The passages from this verse through 22 have been perverted, and made to represent Paul as a timeserver for the sake of peace and friendship, even to the extent of compromising the truth. Nothing could be more unjust toward a man whose integrity was shown in such expressions as, "let God be true, but every man a liar" (Romans 3: 4). There are numberless incidentals in the conditions and lives of people that do not involve any principle of right and wrong. Paul means that in all such circumstances, he conformed to the conditions as he found them, in order to show a friendly interest in the happiness of the people. The customs of the Jews under the law included many items that were not especially of a religious obligation. Jews who were Christians had the right to practice them which Paul did while with them.

Verse 21. When Paul was mingling with those who were not Jews, he did not try to press the Jewish customs upon them, but he did advocate the law of Christ which was and is binding upon all mankind.

Verse 22. *To the weak.* Paul always respected the talents of those with whom he came in contact, and adapted his teaching and practices to their understanding.

Verse 23. By conforming himself to these various conditions, many of which existed in Corinth, the apostle showed a sincere interest in the Gospel. He also placed the whole relation between himself and the Corinthian brethren on a plane that enabled them all to be fellow partakers of the Gospel.

Verse 24. In the foot races that were common in those days, there could be but one successful contestant for the prize. There need be no limitation as to the number of winners in the Christian race. The point is that each man should run as if only one could win, and he was determined to be that one.

Verse 25. Paul is using the various athletic games of the country for his illustrations. The contestants were *temperate*, which denotes that they prepared themselves by a strict schedule of diet and exercise. *Corruptible crown* means the prize to be won in those games was material and subject to decay, while that for which the Christians were contending was "a crown of glory that fadeth not away" (1 Peter 5: 4). For that reason all Christians should make the greater effort to qualify and perform to the utmost of their ability.

Verse 26. *Not as uncertainly.* If only one person could win in the race, then the success of another would mean defeat, and the whole contest would be hanging on uncertainty. But since it is an individual affair and based on faithfulness only, each runner may assure himself of victory. *Beateth the air* is an allusion to a practice of going through the motions of a boxer preparatory to the real fight, in which the performer threw his arms around in the air, similar to the modern practice with dumbbells for the purpose of physical training.

Verse 27. Instead of the actions described in the preceding verse, Paul says he fights with a real person and that is himself. *I keep under* is from HUPOPIAZO, which Thayer defines, "to beat black and blue, to smite so as to cause bruises and livid [black and blue] spots," and he explains it at this passage to mean, "like a boxer I buffet my body, handle it roughly, discipline it with hardships." The great apostle Paul never considered himself to be out of reach of temptation as long as he lived, but believed it necessary to be always on his guard against the wiles of Satan. *Castaway* means one who becomes unfaithful before the end of life's contest.

1 CORINTHIANS 10

Verse 1. The main lesson in several verses of this chapter, is that it is not enough just to get a good start in the service to Christ, but it must be followed by a faithful life to the end. Emphasis should be placed on the little word *all* in these verses. Since *all* of the fathers had the same start, whereas they did not *all* reach Canaan, the lesson mentioned is set forth. The *fathers* means the early ancestors of the Jewish nation who started from Egypt, to go toward the country that had been promised to Abraham and his descendants. The cloud was what guided them, and the sea was the Red Sea, through which *all* passed "without the loss of one."

Verse 2. Notice that both the cloud and the sea were required to accomplish the baptism. That is because the word means a complete burial or envelopment. The sea at their sides and the cloud over the top made a literal surrounding. They are said to have been baptized *unto Moses* because he was their leader, even as Jesus is the leader of Christians unto whom they are baptized.

Verses 3, 4. The meat they ate was literal but had a typical or spiritual significance, because it had to be provided by miracle; it refers to the manna and quails recorded in Exodus 16. The drink also was literal water but had to be produced by miracle (Exodus 17: 6). The rock at Horeb from which the drinking water was drawn was a type of Christ who is the Rock of Ages.

Verse 5. *For they were overthrown in the wilderness* is stated as the proof that God was displeased with them.

Verse 6. *These things* refers to the judgments sent upon the Israelites, and they were to serve as punishments for them, and a warning for Christians not to lust after evil things as they lusted.

Verse 7. The idolatry referred to is recorded in Exodus 32. Verse 6 of that chapter says the people "rose up to play," which is the passage Paul quotes in our present verse. And verse 19 of the chapter in Exodus says when Moses came in sight, the people were dancing. The word *play* in our verse is from PAIZO which Thayer defines, "to play, sport, jest; to give way to hilarity," and he explains it to mean, "by joking, singing, dancing." It is significant that Paul connects *idolatry* with the *playing*, which we now have learned included dancing. That is a serious conclusion, and we are sure the idea is from the truth that in promiscuous dancing, the participants are devoted to the goddess of lust.

Verse 8. The case of fornication referred to is recorded in Numbers 25. The occasion of it was the failure of Balaam to curse Israel in his speeches. Afterward, however, he gave Balak some advice by which the men of Israel were induced to commit fornication with the girls of Moab; this is mentioned in Revelation 2: 14. The secular history of the event is recorded in Josephus, Antiquities, Book 4, Chapter 6, Sections 6-9. It was especially appropriate to warn the Corinthians against fornication, in view of the immorality that was so common in that city.

Verse 9. We know when this temptation took place by the fiery serpents that Paul mentions in connection with it. The case is in Numbers 21: 5, 6, and consisted in the complaints of the people "against God, and against Moses." Christ was not specifically known to the Israelites, but He was with God in all of the dealings with man. If Christians utter words of opposition against Christ, as those Israelites did against Moses and God, it is regarded as a temptation which Paul is warning against.

Verse 10. *Murmur* is from GOGGUZO, which Thayer defines, "to murmur, mutter, grumble, say anything in a low tone," and he explains it at this place to mean, "those who discontentedly complain." The instance Paul refers to is in Numbers 14: 1-4. The word is used of members of the church who manifest an unfavorable attitude toward things in general, yet will not specify anything they can show to be unscriptural.

Verse 11. *These things* means the same as the phrase in verse 6, namely, the judgments sent on the Israelites for their sins. They were thus punished on account of their own deserts, and the account of them is *written* for the benefit of us who are living in the Christian Dispensation; we should profit by their mistakes and the punishment inflicted on them. *Ends of the world.* The last word is from AION and means "age." The word is plural, so the phrase means "the ends of the ages." God has given the world three ages or dispensations, and the Christian Dispensation is here declared to be the last one. The theory that Christ will come and set up another age (the Millennial age) is therefore false, and implies that Paul did not tell the truth here.

Verse 12. This verse is good general advice, appropriate for all people in all ages. No one is in as much danger of falling as the man who is too sure of himself. (Paul showed the opposite attitude in chapter 9: 27.) The Corinthians were so puffed up over their spiritual gifts and other advantages; they had that overconfident feeling, so the admonition was peculiarly needed for them.

Verse 13. The Bible does not teach that God will do something for the salvation of one man that He will not do for another under the same circumstances, therefore this verse does not justify the theory known as "Special Providence." The plan of salvation is completely offered in the New Testament (Colossians 2: 10), and all of the human race have equal access to it. The other passages showing this truth are too numerous to be cited here. No miracle is promised as an escape from temptation that has not been provided for in the Gospel. If such a favor were intended by this passage, Paul certainly would not have written chapter 9: 27, for he would have expected the Lord to provide such an escape for him that he should not become a "castaway." *Will with the temptation*, etc. In the management of the universe, if it is God's will to bring about some conditions that might be too trying for a Christian, then He will so regulate those conditions that nothing will be beyond the protection offered the Christian in the written Word.

Verse 14. Idolatry was frequently mingled with immorality, both of which were common in Corinth. In chapter 6: 18 Paul exhorts the brethren to "flee" from the latter, and in this verse he urges the same action toward the former. To *flee* from a thing means more than merely not partaking; it means to run as from a poisonous adder.

Verse 15. The original for *wise* means one who is intelligent, a man who is capable of forming logical conclusions. Paul believed the Corinthian brethren were able to "see the point" in all of the present reasoning.

Verse 16. In chapter 8 Paul deals with the subject of meat that had been offered in sacrifie to idols. He shows that the mere eating of such meat was not wrong in itself, but that when it was used as a religious performance it constituted a form of idolatry; fellowship (or communion) with idols. On the same principle, to partake of the cup and bread in the Lord's Supper means to have fellowship with the blood and body of Christ. Note that Paul does not call the cup and bread "The Communion," as a familiar but careless saying puts it. In truth, the term is not to be found in a single passage in the New Testament, much less is it applied to the Lord's Supper which is only a part of the communion or general service to Christ under the Gospel system of salvation. *Bless* is from EULOGEO, and Thayer's first definition is, "to consecrate a thing with solemn prayers; to ask God's blessing on a thing," hence it does not mean to confer some miraculous quality on the cup and bread.

Verse 17. *One bread* means that Christians have only one use for bread as a religious act, and that is to represent the body of Christ that was given for the salvation of man. When it is partaken of for that purpose, all who do so are acting as sharers of the same blessing of salvation through Christ.

Verse 18. Ancient Israel not only offered certain articles in sacrifice upon the altar, but the proper ones ate of a part of those animals. In doing so they became participants of the altar service. On the same principle, when disciples eat of the bread in view of the body of Christ, they receive benefits of His body.

Verse 19. In chapter 8: 4 Paul had said that an idol was "nothing," and yet he showed that if a man participated in the sacrifices offered to the idol, it made him guilty of a real sin, that of idolatry. In the present passage he sees that a wrong impression as to the importance of the idols, might have been made of his comparison to the body and blood of Christ. He wishes to prevent such an erroneous conclusion, which he does with this introductory question. It is as if he would say, "Do you think I have changed my mind, and am granting to the idols some important existence?"

Verse 20. In answer to the foregoing question, the apostle affirms that the beings to whom the Gentiles offer their sacrifices are only *devils*, a word coming from DAIMONION. Thayer defines the word, "a spirit, a being inferior to God, superior to men . . . evil spirits or the messengers and ministers of the devil." He then adds historically, "According to a Jewish opinion which passed over to the Christians, the demons are the gods of the Gentiles and the authors of idolatry." With this view of the subject in mind, the idolatrous worship is considered as fellowship with devils.

Verse 21. The thought of this verse is that people cannot be in fellowship with the Lord and with devils at the same time, which Christ taught in Matthew 6: 24.

Verse 22. To be jealous means to be fearful of losing something that may be obtained by another. Paul implies that men might give their devotion to idols and thereby cause God to be jealous, which would actually take place according to Exodus 20: 5. The Corinthians may not have been doing it for that purpose, but Paul shows them that their conduct implies it.

Verse 23. *All things* is said with regard to questions on which there is no specific legislation from the Lord, some of which will be considered soon. To be *expedient* means to be profitable; a thing might not be wrong, but if it would not benefit anyone it would not be expedient.

Verse 24. There is no original word for *wealth*. The verse means that no man should be selfish, but should seek to bring happiness to others.

Verse 25. The *shambles* was a market where they sold meat and other provisions of food. Meat that had been offered in service to idols was taken to these markets for sale. Paul means they need not have any conscientious scruples about partaking of food that might have been purchased at these markets.

Verse 26. All articles that are suitable for food have been created by the Lord and no restrictions need be made as to their use. The law of Moses did make some regulations against certain creatures, but that was for the purpose of ceremonial training and not because of any literal unfitness in them. That law passed away and now "every creature of God is good" (1 Timothy 4: 4).

Verse 27. *Them that believe not* mean one's personal friends who are not members of the church. *To a feast* is not in the original but is implied by the rest of the verse. *Asking no question* means the same as the phrase in verse 25.

Verse 28. *Eat not . . . for the earth is the Lord's,* etc. See the comments on verse 26 for the last phrase. That phrase shows that it would be right in itself to eat of any food, yet he should *not eat* for the sake of one who thinks it is wrong.

Verse 29. Paul explains that it is the other man's conscience he means, not the one who would otherwise eat. *For why,* etc., means as if Paul said, "Why do I give you this instruction? Answer, because my liberty is to be controlled by the other man's conscience with reference to these unlegislated questions."

Verse 30. This verse means the same as the preceding one.

Verse 31. In regulating one's liberty on these matters of eating and drinking so as not to offend a weak brother, it will redound to the glory of God.

Verse 32. *Give none offence* means not to do anything that might cause another to stumble or sin. Some things would be regarded wrong in the eyes of the Jews that would not offend the Gentiles, and vice versa. Also, there might be matters on which neither would have any scruples as far as their nationality is concerned, yet would be objectionable to the brethren. Paul means for the disciples to have regard for the conscience of all these classes.

Verse 33. This is the same as chapter 9: 19-23.

1 CORINTHIANS 11

Verse 1. *Followers* is from MIMETES, which Thayer defines, "an imitator." The word does not require the presence of authority, although an apostle would have that: it may be said of any Christian when the proviso that Paul names is observed, namely, that the person who is imitated is himself an imitator of Christ.

Verse 2. *In all things* is said in the sense of a general statement. The Corinthian brethren were generally favorable to the apostle's teaching, and for that he praises them. But there were some particulars in which they were at fault, and Paul is dealing with them in this chapter.

Verse 3. This verse presents four persons: God, Christ, man and woman, named in the order of their rank. The last two are on earth and are visible to others, which accounts for some regulations of customs that are discussed in this chapter.

Verse 4. *Praying* does not require spiritual gifts, hence the *prophesying* need be no more specific than the description given in chapter 14: 3. The original Greek word for *covered* means to be veiled so as to hide the face. If a man covers his head he dishonors it, because it should be exposed to view due to his position of authority in the social world.

Verse 5. *Praying* and *prophesying* have the same meaning as explained in the preceding verse. The word *shaven* shows Paul is considering the hair as the veil or covering. It was customary for women to veil or cover their face with their hair when praying in the presence of men. To neglect this was a dishonor to her head, because it exposed it and put her in the class of men who are the rulers in the social rank. If she thus keeps her hair away from her face, she is as much exposed to shame as if her hair had been cut.

Verse 6. *If the woman be not covered, let her also be shorn.* This does not endorse a woman's shearing her hair but rather condemns it, for Paul compares it to something else that we know he condemns because it is a dishonor to her. *If it be a shame* is a phrase that takes it for granted that the thing named is commonly thought to be a shame, namely, for a woman to have her hair cut.

Verse 7. God, Christ and man are all rulers in their respective ranks, hence a man should not cover his head and thus put himself in the same subject class as the woman. A woman can be a glory to man only by maintaining an attitude of submission to him.

Verse 8. This verse refers to the fact recorded in Genesis 2: 21-23, which shows the woman was made from a part of the man.

Verse 9. The woman was created for the man because God said it was not good for the man to be alone (Genesis 2: 18).

Verse 10. Submission to authority is the outstanding thought which Paul has been discussing. We have seen that an unveiled head indicates authority, for which reason a woman should be veiled as a sign that she is under authority. Angels are ministering spirits under the authority of God, and are invisible persons in the assemblies of Christians. Some of their class have been rebellious in times past (2 Peter 2: 4; Jude 6), and Paul wishes the woman to show to the faithful angels who are present in the assembly, that they are submitting to the authority that is over them.

Verses 11, 12. Lest the foregoing teaching might make a wrong impression as to the importance of the woman, Paul adds these verses to show that both man and woman are necessary in the general plans of God; the same is taught in verses 8, 9.

Verses 13. *Judge in yourselves* has about the same force as "nature" in the next verse. *Comely* is from PREPO, which Thayer defines, "to be becoming, seemly, fit."

Verse 14. *Nature* is from PHUSIS, which Thayer defines at this place, "nature, i.e., natural sense, native conviction or knowledge," and he adds the explanation, "as opposed to that which is learned by instruction and accomplished by training or prescribed by law." Robinson gives virtually the same definition. The explanation given of the definition is an exact description of the customs discussed in the preceding verses as to what use a woman should make of her hair, and he says it is opposed to (different from) that which nature teaches. Customs change because they are the product of man, while nature never changes because it is the creation of God. As long as nature exists it will be a shame for a man to have long hair, and, as a necessary conclusion, it will be a shame for a woman to cut her hair.

Sometimes a quibble is made by asking just what it takes to constitute *long hair*. In the first place, the statement of Paul remains in the text, and it is as much the obligation of the quibbler to answer the question and prove his answer, as it is that of the one who insists on observing the teaching of the apostle. However, for the benefit of the sincere inquirer, I will state that the Lord has given us a clear-cut definition of what constitutes *long hair*, in the stipulations for a Nazarite which included long hair. The passages that state the law on it are Numbers 6: 5; Judges 13: 5; 1 Samuel 1: 11. These all require that no razor is to be used on the head, hence by *long hair* the Lord means hair that is as long as nature makes it. If a man cuts any of it off he ceases to have long hair, and exposes his head to shame. By the same token, if a woman cuts any of her hair she also ceases to have long hair in the sense the apostle is using the term, and thus she does that which is a shame.

Verse 15. This verse is virtually explained in the preceding paragraph. It has the added thought that by having long hair, which nature teaches her that she should have, she is in a condition to observe also what custom has established in the time of the epistle, namely, using that long hair as a veil when praying in man's presence.

Verse 16. This verse is often pounced upon by the quibblers, like a "drowning man grasping at a straw," in their desperate attempt to find some justification of women in their unnatural and unfeminine act of cutting their hair. I have never yet heard anyone who made a serious effort to show this passage to be related in the remotest degree to the issue at hand. *Any man* is from the one Greek word TIS, which means any person or thing, indefinitely, and would apply to a woman as well as a man. *Contentious* is from PHILO-NEIKOS, which Thayer defines at this place, "fond of strife, contentious." No one would be contentious over anything that was not objectionable to another. It would have to be over something he wished to do that some other one did not want him to do. In the present case it could not be over short hair for women, for nobody was wanting that. Instead, verse 6 shows that there was common objection to that, which was a basis for one of Paul's arguments. The only thing in dispute was whether a woman should cover her face with her hair, or keep it away in a manner that would look as if it were *shorn*, a condition which Paul states would be a shame. Since no person was contending for short hair with women, the contention could not be over that. The point the apostle is making in this verse, is that the custom of all the other churches was for the women to veil their faces with their hair when praying in the presence of men.

Verse 17. In verse 2 the apostle told the brethren there were some things for which he would praise (commend) them. In the present verse there were some things for which he would not praise them, one of which was that their coming together was not for the better but for the worse.

Verse 18. The *divisions* in the church were over several subjects, but Paul is writing of a particular one in the rest of this chapter; and one that is very important because it pertains to the Lord's Supper. A report of the divisions in the church had come to Paul in some manner not stated. *Partly believe it* cannot apply to the degree of his belief, for a man either believes a report or he does not. The idea is that Paul believed the report to be true in regard to a part of the congregation, but that some of them disapproved of the divisions. The argument in the next verse justifies this conclusion.

Verse 19. *Must* is from DEI, which Thayer defines, "it is necessary," and explains it to mean at this place, "necessity in reference to what is required to attain some end." Robinson's definition and explanation give virtually the same thought as Thayer's. It is clear the word means that heresies are necessary for a certain purpose, and that is stated to be, *that they which are approved may be made manifest among you.* This agrees with the conclusion expressed in the preceding paragraph, namely, that a part only of the congregation was guilty of the divisions among them, the faithful ones being "approved" by their opposition to the heresies. But this necessity for heresies should not encourage anyone to promote evil doctrines, for Jesus pronounces a woe on those who cause offences, even though He had just declared that it was impossible for them not to come (Luke 17: 1).

Verse 20. Having set forth some general principles concerning heresies in the foregoing verses, Paul comes to the special subject at hand, namely, the Lord's Supper in the course of their coming together. The Englishman's Greek New Testament renders the last clause, "it is not to eat the Lord's Supper." Of course Paul does not deny the Corinthians professed to come together for that purpose, but he means that under the circumstances what they did could not be rightly called so for reasons soon to be stated.

Verse 21. *Taketh before* means that such persons were so eager to eat that they did so before the others were ready. In the first years of the church it was a custom for the disciples to partake of a common meal before attending to the Lord's Supper. This was somewhat after the order of events occurring at the time Jesus established the Lord's Supper, namely, they had the passover first, then Jesus set forth his memorial supper next. These common meals are referred to in the New Testament as "feasts of charity" (Jude 12; 2 Peter 2: 13). In some way the Corinthians tried to blend the common meal with the Lord's Supper. That corrupted it and caused Paul to say they were not eating the Lord's Supper when they came together. *Drunken* is from METHUO, and primarily means to be intoxicated with drink. But it is used here as the opposite of *hungry*, hence it is in the sense of being filled. Groves defines the word, "to be filled, plentifully fed," and it has that meaning in our verse. Those who *look before* their own supper would be filled, while the ones who waited—the "approved" ones whom Paul's word "partly" in verse 18 included — would still be hungry.

Verse 22. Some might claim they would become too hungry to wait until the rest were ready to eat. Paul tells all such that they should eat at home before coming to the assembly if their appetites were thus demanding gratification. But instead of doing that, they were abusing the purpose of the feasts of charity by their disorderly conduct. By such practices they *despised* (belittled or put to shame) the the public assembling place, and also embarrassed the poor, who are meant by the phrase *them that have not*. I shall quote Thayer's remarks about the feasts as they were related to the poor of the congregation: "AGAPAI, agapae, love-feasts, feasts expressing and fostering mutual love which used to be held by Christians before the celebration of the Lord's Supper, and at which the poorer Christians mingled with the wealthier and partook in common with the rest of the food provided at the expense of the wealthy." Such disorderly conduct of the more prosperous brethren as Paul describes, would confuse the poorer ones and make them feel that they were not welcome to the public feasts of the congregation. This is one of the things for which the apostle said he would not praise them. The poorer sort of the brethren would not appreciate these free meals (feasts of charity) when they saw the corruption practiced by the wealthier classes, and the whole procedure thus made a mockery of the institution of the Lord's Supper, which is why Paul said when they came together they would not eat the supper.

Verse 23. The Corinthians had so corrupted the divine institution that the apostle thought it necessary to describe it to them again, just as he had delivered it to them when he was with them for so long (Acts 18: 1-11). The simple phrase *took bread* states all we need to know as to the article to be eaten in the Lord's Supper. In every place where it is referred to after the church was set up, it is mentioned by the simple word "bread" (Acts 2: 42; 20: 7; 1 Corinthians 10: 16; 11: 23; 27, 28). In all of these places except our present chapter, the word is used independently of any consideration for the Jewish passover. Therefore, to insist on any particular *kind* of bread for the Lord's Supper is to be more specific than the Lord is.

Verse 24. *Brake it*. The term is from the same original Greek word as "brake" in Matthew 14: 19 and it has no more spiritual significance in one place than in the other. The only reason for breaking the bread is that more than one person may partake of it in decency. I have known instances where a group of disciples was so few in number that only one attendant (commonly but erroneously called "deacon") was used. Then if the one presiding at the table happened to forget about "breaking" the loaf in two pieces, it was thought a terrible mistake was made. Such a tradition shows that the real significance of the institution is overlooked almost as much as the Corinthians did it. Whether the one presiding breaks the bread (so as to place it on a number of plates), or the attendants break off a piece to serve to each participant, or he breaks it off himself, the bread is sure to be "broken," and that is all that is required. *My body, which is broken for you* is another expression that is misapplied. It is a common thing to hear the one "presiding" to quote this, then refer to the Roman spear that "broke" the body of Jesus after his death. The mechanical act of piercing His side, or even that of driving the nails through his hands and feet, was only a means to an end, namely, "to be shattered, as it were, by a violent death"—Thayer. Robinson says virtually the same thing. Had it been the Lord's will that Jesus be killed by a violent blow on the head but leaving the surface of the body intact, it would still have been true that his body was broken for us, in the sense the apostle uses the term. When Christians eat of this bread, they are to do so in remembrance of the "violent" death of Christ. It is significant that in Luke 22: 19 where the supper is being instituted, it is stated that the body of Jesus was "given" for his people, which agrees with the idea that the mechanical fact of the spear and nails was not necessary to the word "broken."

Verse 25. *After the same manner* is not a comparison to the form or performance in the procedure, for the phrase is from the same word as "likewise" in Luke 13: 3, and we know Jesus did not mean that all impenitent sinners would perish just as the Galileans did. It means as if it said, "for the same purpose," etc. *Supped* is from the same Greek word as "supper" in Luke 22: 20; it means He took the cup after the passover supper was ended. *New testament* in my blood. In Hebrews 9: 16 Paul says that a testament requires the death of the testator. The beasts that were slain under the Mosaic system constituted the testator for that covenant, which is the reason they were slain. The New Testament (or covenant) also required the shedding of the blood of the Testator (who was Christ), hence we have the phrase italicized here. The expression *is my body* in the preceding verse, and in my blood in the present verse, are used with the meaning that they represent the body and blood of Christ. Partaking of the cup, like that of the bread, is for the same purpose, namely, to be *in remembrance* (a memorial) of Christ.

Verse 26. *Often* is not used in view of the frequency of the observance of the Lord's Supper, for Acts 20: 7 and 1 Corinthians 16: 1, 2 settles that question, and shows it is to be done once each week. The term means that each time the institution is observed it is for the one purpose, namely, to *show* ("proclaim publicly" — Thayer) *the Lord's death*. A common speech that may be heard at the table is as follows: "We now come to the Lord's Supper in which we will commemorate the death, burial and resurrection of Christ." Such a statement is not only unscriptural but is foolish. It is evident that anything that represents the death of Christ could not also represent his life. The life of all creatures is in the blood, and when the body and blood are separated, that body is bound to be dead. Likewise, when the guests see the fruit of the vine in one vessel, and the bread in another place on the table, it represents the separation of the body and blood, and in such a condition it "shows" or represents the *death* of Christ. *Till he come* signifies that the Lord's Supper is to be perpetuated until the end of the world.

Verse 27. The general character of the persons eating and drinking is not under consideration, but the manner or purpose of the act is the subject. (This will be enlarged upon in verse 29.) *Guilty of the body and blood* means to be guilty of sin against the body and blood of Christ.

Verse 28. *Examine himself;* this phrase is perverted many times. The speaker will say, "I cannot examine you nor you me, for I do not know how you have been living." The way a brother "has been living" is not in this text, and such a remark shows that the one making it is in danger of condemnation himself. The manner or purpose of eating and drinking is the point. If a man asks himself why or for what purpose he is about to partake, he will be examining himself in the sense the apostle means. When he does this, and concludes it is for the purpose of showing the death of Christ, he is then ready to eat and drink worthily (an adverb and not an adjective).

Verse 29. *Discerning* is from DIAKRINO, which Thayer defines at this place, "to separate, make a distinction, discriminate." The thought is that the participant should eat and drink with his mind on the body and blood of Christ, *remembering* that the two parts were separated and that He died for us. Unless this is done, the person partaking will bring condemnation upon himself. The Corinthians did not *distinguish* between the body of Christ and food for natural hunger. The same guilt may be brought upon us today without eating to satisfy our hunger. If we partake of the "emblems" while our mind is on some other subject instead of the death of Christ, such as our plans for the day, etc., we will be just as guilty as were the ones at Corinth. Sometimes disciples will be engaged in conversation at the time, and will partake of the bread and/or cup mechanically or as a habit only. When they do so they eat and drink damnation to themselves.

Verse 30. The question is asked at this verse whether it means physical or spiritual sickness, and my answer is that it includes both. In the first years of the church God sometimes inflicted physical punishment upon disciples, even to the extent of putting them to *sleep* (in death). (See the case of Ananias and Sapphira, Acts 5.) But the days of such demonstrations are over, while the guilt of corrupting the Lord's Supper is just as possible, and also just as deserving of being *judged* (condemned) as ever. Therefore, when disciples corrupt the holy ordinance, or commit any other violation of the Lord's spiritual law, it brings upon them the serious condition mentioned here unless they repent.

Verse 31. This verse states a principle that may have an application to other subjects besides the one at hand with the Corinthians. Had they *examined* themselves as directed in verse 28, and then brought themselves under the necessary correction (judgment), it would not have been necessary for the Lord to judge them. Likewise, the New Testament today gives very positive instructions about the conduct of disciples, and they should be able even in themselves to decide between right and wrong. However, if they will not do so, it then becomes the duty of the rulers of the church to make the application for them, and administer such corrective discipline as needed.

Verse 32. In the days of miracles the judgment or punishment was administered directly by the Lord (verse 30). Today the correction has to be delivered by the church, and when it is done it is counted as coming from the Lord (chapter 5: 3, 4; 2 Corinthians 2: 10; 7: 11, 12).

Verse 33. *Tarry one for another.* This is another statement that is often perverted and made to mean that public services should not start until others arrive. Not only does such an application miss the thought intended by the apostle to be conveyed, but it violates other scripture. Romans 12: 11 forbids Christians being slothful or lazy in coming to the services. A soldier who fails to appear at the time he is told to receives the stain of AWOL, and the disciple who is late in arriving at the place of services deserves the same blot. The tarrying of our verse was to be done *after* the congregation was assembled, and it means not to *take before other* (verse 21) his supper, but to wait (tarry) until the others were ready to eat.

Verse 34. *If any man hunger* is explained by the comments on verse 22. It does not mean to rule out the observance of the feasts of charity, but only to correct the abuses of it by those who claimed to be too hungry to wait. *Come together to condemnation* is the same subject that is considered in verse 17. There were other items that needed to be set forth for their instruction, but the apostle thought it well to do that when he made his next journey to them (chapter 4: 18, 19).

1 CORINTHIANS 12

Verse 1. *Spiritual gifts.* The second word has been supplied because it has no separate one in the Greek. The first one is from PNEUMATIKOS, and Thayer explains that it is used both "in reference to things," and "in reference to persons." Paul says he wants the brethren to be informed on the subject, hence this and the next two chapters are written to show the truth concerning such matters; both as to spiritually-gifted men and their gifts. We learned at chapter 4: 6 that the church at Corinth was divided (in sentiment) over the men among them who possessed spiritual gifts. That contention was so serious that the apostle wrote chapters 12, 13 and 14 to discuss the subject. If this is overlooked, any attempt to explain the various parts of the three chapters will likely be a failure.

Verse 2. The Corinthians were Gentiles and worshipers of idols before they received the Gospel. Since the idols were dumb things, to be carried away with them or be devoted to such services was a proof of their spiritual blindness, and no such worshipers could exhibit any fruits of the Spirit.

Verse 3. There were many false teachers coming round in those days, claiming to possess supernatural knowledge. A test of their genuineness was their manner of referring to Jesus. If they pronounced any evil wish or prediction concerning Him, the Corinthians were to know that no such persons were speaking by the Spirit. *No man . . . but by the Holy Ghost.* The idolatrous teachers would never be induced by the dumb idols to confess Jesus; the Holy Ghost only would so inspire them.

Verse 4. Up to this place the remarks of the apostle are general, and are offered as a preparation for instruction on the true spiritual gifts and the disciples possessing them. The dissensions over the gifts previously mentioned are now the direct subject that Paul is considering. *Diversities of gifts . . . same Spirit.* The Corinthians were contending with each other over the comparative importance of their different gifts. The point Paul is making is that since there is but one Spirit, there could be no actual difference as to the value of the various gifts.

Verses 5, 6. *Administrations* and *operations* means the outworkings of the Spirit through the gifts; that all come from the same divine source.

Verse 7. A foreman over a crew of workers knows his men and which tool each can use to the best advantage for the whole project. Likewise, the Lord knows which spiritual gift each disciple can best use to the *profit* of the

Gospel work. Hence not all members of the church received the same gifts, and yet the diversities of the various assignments indicated no partiality as to the different brethren.

Verse 8. *Wisdom* and *knowledge* have much the same meaning in general use, but as spiritual gifts there is a difference. The second one means supernatural understanding, and the first means the special ability to teach it to others.

Verse 9. This *faith* is the miraculous kind such as Matthew 17: 20; 1 Corinthians 13: 2. Miraculous *healing* requires this gift of faith, but the phrase is used as a specification of it, in relieving persons of their physical ailments.

Verse 10. *Working of miracles* is more general, referring to any situation coming before the possessor of the gift that gives an opportunity for demonstration of spiritual power. This *prophecy* is the kind that enables the possessor to make predictions, not that described in chapter 14: 3. Without the complete Word it was not always possible to detect an evil spirit claiming to be of God, hence this *discerning of spirits* was possible through the gift. One man could speak in a foreign tongue, perhaps, but would not know its interpretation. Another man had the gift of interpreting such tongues. (See chapter 14: 27, 28.)

Verse 11. This is virtually the same as verse 7. *As he will* denotes as the Lord willed in directing the Spirit as it delivered the various gifts.

Verse 12. The human body is used to illustrate the church which is the body of Christ, with the unified work of spiritual gifts in that body.

Verse 13. The main thought running through these several verses is that there is only *one* Spirit, hence no difference should be made in the importance of the different gifts of the Spirit. Men would never have been taught the necessity of baptism had not the Spirit given the apostles and other inspired teachers the instruction to pass on to others. The point is that all people who have been baptized have received the instruction as a result of teaching from *one Spirit*.

Verse 14. It takes more than one member to constitute a human body.

Verses 15-17. This imaginary conversation between the different parts of the fleshly body, is written to show the point stated in verse 14. No one of the members of the body can take the place of the other. This reasoning drawn from the fleshly body is continued through verse 26.

Verses 18-21. This paragraph is similar to the preceding one.

Verse 22. Every part of the human body is necessary and should not be removed by surgery, unless it becomes so diseased that medication will not cure it.

Verse 23. *Less honorable* is from ATIMOS, which Thayer defines "less esteem." The comparison is made to the feet and certain hidden parts of the body. According to Thayer, *more abundant honor* means more "preciousness or value." That is true, for the feet and other parts referred to are prized very highly, even though we seek to cover them as not being comely or attractive.

Verse 24. The *comely* or more attractive parts of the body, such as the face and hands, need no special attention, but are able to "take care of themselves."

Verse 25. God has so arranged the human body that there need be no *schisms* (lack of harmony) in the body. For instance, if the feet and hands opposed each other, a man would be constantly hindered in what he wished to do or where to go.

Verse 26. The unity of the members of the fleshly body is demonstrated by this very sympathy of one for the other. If a man injures his little finger, his entire being is concerned and caused to suffer, and the whole person will try to help the wounded member to get well. Of course the point is that the different members of the body of Christ should have a like sympathy for and interest in each other. The spiritual application of the comparison is made in Romans 12: 15.

Verse 27. The apostle now comes directly to the application of his illustration. The church is the body of Christ, and it is composed of disciples who are the members of the body. As the parts of the fleshly body act in harmony with each other, shown in the preceding verses, so the members of the body of Christ should be interested in each other and seek to assist them in the mutual service to Christ. If that is done, the dissensions over the different spiritually-gifted men and their gifts will be stopped.

Verse 28. Every function or office named in this verse still exists in the church except the spiritual gifts. In the early days of the Gospel age the gifts were possessed by each of these officers or workers, in order that they might perform them the better. After the New Testament was completed the spiritual gifts ceased, and these officers and workers continue down to our time, but are working only with the guidance of the Gospel. The apostles are still in authority (Matthew 19: 28), doing their ruling or "judging" through the Gospel which they wrote and left with us. I shall next notice the various officers and functions mentioned in the verse.

First, secondarily, etc., denotes the numerical order in which they were set in the church, the comparative importance of them being denoted as we discuss them. The apostles were first in order because Jesus selected them before the church was set up, and they had charge of the work under the Lord when the divine institution began (Acts 2). They are also first in importance because their inspired word is the permanent law of Christ, and will be until the end of the world. These *prophets* were men who could make predictions by the aid of their spiritual gifts. *Miracles* and *healings* are explained at verses 9, 10. *Help* is from ANTILEPSIS, and Thayer explains it at this place to mean, "the ministrations of the deacons, who have care of the poor and sick." *Governments* is from KUBERNESIS, and Thayer's definition is, "a governing, government." We know from 1 Timothy 5: 17; Hebrews 13: 7, 17 and 1 Peter 5: 1, 2, that the elders are the rulers in the church, hence they are the ones meant by these *governments*. *Diversities of tongues* refers to the men who could speak with various foreign tongues by the help of spiritual gifts.

Verses 29, 30. *Are all apostles?*, etc. All of the questions in this paragraph should receive the negative answer; they are a summing up of the argument that Paul has been making regarding the relation of the different members of the church in the exercise of their spiritual gifts.

Verse 31. *Covet earnestly* is from ZELOO, which Thayer defines, "to desire earnestly, pursue." *Best* is from KREITTON, and Thayer defines it, "more useful, more serviceable." Paul has consistently taught that all of the gifts are important, and he has rebuked the brethren for their contending with each other over their respective gifts. We should conclude, therefore, that he here means their main interest should be in that which will do the church the most good, and not which of them can exhibit the greatest power. *More excellent* way signifies that after all that can truly be said of the spiritual gifts, there is something that is more excellent; that will be shown in the next chapter.

1 CORINTHIANS 13

Verse 1. This chapter continues the same general subject that Paul has been considering, namely, the proper estimate to be placed on spiritual gifts. The Corinthians were so devoted to them that they had fallen to wrangling against each other. This spirit of dissension had caused them to slight the "more excellent way," which is prompted by *charity* or love. The apostle will devote this chapter to showing the emptiness of all their boasted gifts without having this greatest of all virtues, love for each other. *Sounding brass* and *tinkling cymbals* were used in both religious and military exercises. Smith's Bible Dictionary says they were used "as an accompaniment to other instruments." They would therefore not express any distinct note or other useful term in themselves. Paul compares that fact with the use of spiritual gifts when not connected with love.

Verse 2. Some of the most outstanding spiritual gifts are named in this verse for specimens, and even they are *nothing* in the absence of love for the brethren.

Verse 3. Bestowing goods upon the poor is possible even in the absence of what the King James translation calls *charity*, which shows the word does not mean what is commonly called "liberality." The word is from AGAPE, and the common version renders it "love" in 86 places. For further information, see the comments at Matthew 5: 43, volume 1 of the New Testament Commentary.

Verse 4. This and a number of verses following will show some things that charity (or love) will do, and also what it will not do. *Suffereth long* means it will cause a man to be patient and kind. *Envieth not* denotes that one man will not be grieved because some other one has a gift that he does not have. This teaching especially was needed by many of the Corinthians, because they were contending over the respective gifts of each other. To *vaunt* means to make a vain display, and it would be caused by being *puffed up*.

Verse 5. *Unseemly* means unbecomingly, and the Corinthians had certainly been guilty of such behaviour. *Seeketh not her own* signifies that one is not selfish. *Not easily provoked* denotes one who does not become angered at every little provocation. *Thinketh no evil.* If a man loves his brother, he will not hold him guilty of any evil if he has only his personal opinion as an evidence.

Verse 6. *Iniquity* is placed as an opposite of *truth*, which shows that one does not have to commit some outward act of wrongdoing to be guilty of iniquity; his rejoicing in it makes him guilty. Paul taught the same principle in Romans 1: 32.

Verse 7. *Beareth* means to cover or hide the faults of others as far as possible without encouraging sin. *Believeth* and *hopeth* must be understood in the light of other passages. Hebrews 11: 1 tells us that hope is based on faith, and Romans 10: 17 says that faith comes by hearing the word of God. The present phrase means that a man who has the love of God and the brethren in his heart, will believe all that God declares. *Endureth* denotes a willingness to remain faithful throughout all trials.

Verse 8. *Charity* (or love) *never faileth*. A part of Thayer's definition of the original for *faileth* is, "to perish," which means that it will cease to be. That is not true of love, for it will never cease to be, even after the spiritual gifts mentioned in this verse cease to be.

Verse 9. *In part* is said in view of the temporary use and purpose of the spiritual gifts. While the church had such helps only, the knowledge of spiritual things was but partial.

Verse 10. *That which is perfect* (complete) means the completed New Testament, called "the perfect law of liberty" in James 1: 25. When that was given to the church, the temporary and partial information derived through the spiritual gifts was to be no longer necessary.

Verse 11. The illustrations in this and the next verse are to show the difference between the time when the church had to depend on spiritual gifts, and when it would have the complete New Testament. The contrast is likened to the immature activities of a child as against those of a man.

Verse 12. The *glass* means a mirror which was made of polished metal in old times. Seeing a thing as it is reflected against one of these plates is compared to the knowledge attained through spiritual gifts. Seeing the things directly or *face to face*, is compared to the full and direct knowledge to be attained through the New Testament. *Know as I am known.* This is the text usually cited by advocates of "future recognition," meaning that we shall "know each other in Heaven." Of course that has to mean knowing others as we know them now; and that requires that we will be "as" we are now, or the "recognition" will be impossible. The theory is Sadducean, infidel, and a debasing of Heaven. It is Sadducean in that it implies a continuance of marriage as the Sadducees contended. It is infidel in that it contradicts 1 Corinthians 15: 50, which says flesh and blood cannot inherit the kingdom of God, yet which must occur if we are going to be "as we are now." It debases Heaven in that it puts the joys of that eternal place on the basis of fleshly relationship. We know such is the motive for the theory, for its advocates will say, "I would not be happy in Heaven if I did not know my loved ones." Such remarks mean that human beings know better what will be necessary for happiness in that world than does the Lord.

This passage has nothing to do with conditions after this world is ended. It is an item in the same argument Paul has been making since the beginning of chapter 12, namely, the use and comparative importance of spiritual gifts. Before the New Testament was completed, the church had to rely on the spiritually-gifted men and their gifts for information to a great extent. These men could not always be speaking, nor could they be in evidence in every place, due to the many handicaps of human life. As a consequence, some disciples would have knowledge of spiritual matters that others would not. "But when that which was perfect was come" (the complete New Testament), all would have equal chance for such knowledge. The words *know* and *known* are from EPIGINOSKO, which Thayer defines, "to become thoroughly acquainted with, to know thoroughly; to know accurately, know well." Of course this knowledge pertains to our spiritual relationship in the church. On that subject we may "know as we are known," since all members of the body have equal access to the full information offered in the New Testament. Personal recognition is not being considered.

Verse 13. *Now abideth* signifies that after the complete New Testament has been produced — after the spiritual gifts have ceased, there will still be *faith, hope and charity* (or love). That is because the Christian life will always need such graces. *Faith* (which is produced by hearing the word of God) will be necessary to guide the disciple of the Lord aright, and *hope* will be needed to urge him that through perseverance he may gain the reward at last. *Charity* is the greatest of these three, because faith will be changed to sight, and hope will give place to actual possession, after this life is ended. But love is eternal and will exist on into the life with God in Heaven.

1 CORINTHIANS 14

Verse 1. The reader should keep in mind that the subject of the preceding two chapters and the present one, is the spiritual gifts that were possessed by disciples in the first years of the church. Paul is showing the proper purpose and use of the gifts, and is trying to correct the many abuses that had crept into the church in Corinth in the exercise of them. This chapter, therefore, was not written for information concerning 'the duties and privileges of women in the church," as it is so frequently claimed. Such a use of the chapter is a perversion of it, for it has no connection with that subject. Instead, it has to do with the conduct of the church when assembled, showing the proper procedure in the exercise of spiritual gifts. *Follow after charity* is in line with the preceding chapter which shows that charity is the greatest of all graces. If it had been in effect through all of their proceedings, the abuses would not have occurred which the apostle is trying to correct. *Rather . . . prophesy*, because it is "more serviceable" as was stated in chapter 12: 31.

Verse 2. Speaking with tongues manifests miraculous power, but it does not contribute as much benefit to the brethren as does the gift of prophesying, when the latter is done after the manner described in the next verse.

Verse 3. This verse gives the practical form of prophesying, that which edifies, exhorts and comforts men.

Verse 4. Being the possessor of the gift of tongues, this man will be benefited by its use, but the church as a whole would not be benefited as it is by prophesying.

Verse 5. Paul did not begrudge any man his possession of the gift of tongues, and he was not conducting the present discussion from that motive. He had a practical reason, however, for preferring the gift of prophesying, namely, it edifies the church (verse 4). *Except he interpret.* I believe this is correctly translated, and hence that at least some men were given two gifts, that of speaking in a foreign tongue, and also of interpreting it; otherwise he could not "edify himself" (verse 4). Verses 13, 14 also indicates that the same man may possess both gifts.

Verse 6. *If I come.* The apostle uses himself only as an example as if he said, "suppose I come," etc. To speak with tongues would not profit the church unless they were so used as to bestow upon it some of the following results. *Revelation* means a communication of some new truth; *knowledge* denotes the supernatural kind that had not been previously recorded; *prophesying* refers to the kind described in verse 3; *doctrine* means teaching in general.

Verse 7. *Without life, giving sound,* means things that do not have life yet that give off sounds, such as the *pipe or harp. Give a distinction.* These instruments should be so used as to conform to some accepted code, else they would mean nothing to a hearer. The blasts of a locomotive would mean nothing to railroad men, if they were not made according to the code in use by the company.

Verse 8. The same illustration is used in Numbers 10: 1-9, where a nonliving trumpet is used as a signal device. Certain blasts were to indicate a corresponding action. If the "code" was ignored, the soldier would not know whether to line up for action or remain in his tent.

Verse 9. Paul makes the application of his illustration in this verse. He means for them to make such a use of their gift of tongues as will contribute beneficial information to the hearers.

Verse 10. *Voices* is from the Greek word PHONE, and Thayer defines it at this place, "speech, i. e., a language tongue." It is true that several different forms of language are in use in the world, and each has its own significance according to the vocabulary of the people speaking with it.

Verse 11. But unless the hearer knows the meaning of the word when it is spoken to him, he will receive no exchange of thought from the speaker. Barbarian is from BARBAROS, and Thayer's definition in this passage is as follows: "One who speaks a foreign or strange language which is not understood by another." Hence the word does not necessarily mean a term of reproach in the New Testament. But when used with regard to language between different people, it does always mean they are barbarians to each other, if there is not a mutual understanding of the speech that it uttered.

Verse 12. The desire to *excel* merely from the motive of rivalry over others is wrong. The word in this verse is in the intransitive form, and is defined by Thayer "to abound in." The thought is that each member of the congregation should wish to abound in that gift that would best edify the church.

Verse 13. *Wherefore* means a conclusion in line with the exhortation in the preceding verse. *Pray that he may interpret* is commented upon at verse 5, regarding the possession of two gifts by the same man.

Verse 14. *My spirit* refers to the spiritual gift possessed by the one who is praying, while *my understanding* pertains to the one hearing the prayer. If a man prays with an unknown tongue, the hearer who does not understand that tongue will not get any benefit from the prayer.

Verse 15. The first half of this verse is explained in the preceding one. The second half is generally misapplied today. A song leader will arise before the congregation and try to get it in condition for some good singing. He will probably tell the people to wake up and sing as if they meant it, then remind them that Paul said to "sing with the spirit and with the understanding," as if he was conducting a "pep meeting." He may continue his erroneous use of the passage by telling them to study the words of the song so as to understand what they are singing, else they could not "sing with the understanding as Paul commands."

The passage as it reads and is quoted did not apply to congregational singing in Paul's day even, much less does it so apply today. It was a part of the exercise of miraculous gifts, and the spirit that is named is the Holy Spirit, given to Christians in such measure that they could speak and sing with words that had not yet been revealed to others. In selecting his words, the singer was instructed to use those that the *audience* (not himself only) could understand. The term "my understanding" has reference to the ability of the hearer to understand what he hears.

Verse 16. To *bless* means to praise the Lord for his blessings. One man may be expressing thanks in the audience of disciples, which is supposed to represent the sentiments of the hearers. *Occupieth the room* is a figurative expression that means one who is *unlearned*, or not educated in the various languages. It is also defined in the lexicons as a private person in contrast with one who is in public life. *Say amen.* The manner of Paul's question implies that it was taken for granted the audience would use this word after the public prayer of one speaker, thus making his sentiments their own. Doubtless the Lord expects the disciples to do the same thing after a public prayer today. No one can pray with a spiritual gift now, but all should express their prayers in such a manner that the congregation may hear and understand them. If a man mumbles a prayer in an undertone, or drops his chin upon his chest, it will make it impossible for others to know what he says, and hence an "amen" after such a prayer would be as unscriptural as the prayer. I never say amen to a prayer unless I have heard every word of it, and also believe it was a scriptural prayer.

Verse 17. A prayer uttered in a foreign tongue could be well formed, but it would not edify the unlearned man.

Verse 18. Being an apostle, Paul could speak in a multitude of tongues, which was a necessary qualification for one who was to preach the Gospel in various parts of the world. He was grateful for the gift, but also was considerate of the church in the exercise of it in any established congregation.

Verse 19. *My understanding* means the hearers could understand his words (verse 14). Paul's motive for preferring a few of these words to ten thousand of the others was an unselfish one; it was because it would give more teaching to others.

Verse 20. The brethren at Corinth had behaved so foolishly over their spiritual gifts, the apostle likened them to children. He was willing for them to be as free from malice as children, but in *understanding* (activities of the mind) he wished them to be as men. They certainly had shown malice toward each other, when they had become contentious among themselves over their spiritual gifts. It was like children quarrelling with each other over whose mechanical toy would do the best performances. No wonder Paul thought it necessary to give this subject three whole chapters, and parts of some others.

Verse 21. The quotation is from Isaiah 28: 11, 12, which shows that the term *the law* includes the prophetic writings of the Old Testament. The connection shows that Isaiah was writing about conditions just previous to the captivity of Israel by the heathen. Israel had refused to listen to the law of the Lord even when it was spoken to them in their own tongue. Hence He said he would cast them into the midst of a nation speaking a tongue foreign to the people of Israel. Therefore, the use of tongues was not primarily for the purpose of instruction to believers, but as an evidence to unbelievers, to convince them of the existence of supernatural power. In view of this truth, Paul makes the point that the brethren made a mistake in trying to impose their gift of tongues onto the whole church to the extent they were doing.

Verse 22. On the basis of the preceding verse, the brethren should give the use of tongues a comparatively small consideration in the assembly, and make greater use of prophesying since it would edify the church.

Verse 23. We are sure the Bible does not contradict itself; but when the language seems that it does so, there is always a reasonable explanation possible. Verse 22 says tongues are a sign for the benefit of unbelievers, while the present verse says that tongues will cause them to regard the church as a group of madmen. The word *unlearned* is from IDIOTES, and Thayer's definition in this verse is one who is "not a prophet; destitute of the gift of tongues." The key to the question is in the word *all*, for an unbeliever would not require that a whole group in an assembly be able to speak in a foreign tongue to be convinced of the presence of supernatural power; one or two would be sufficient. Therefore, if the whole group did so, it would naturally seem to this "outsider" that the crowd was beside itself.

Verse 24. *All* is the key word again, for it is applied to *prophesying* which was the gift that imparted the most edification or instruction. *Convinced* and *judged* are used in viritually the same sense, meaning that the information imparted by this general display of the gift of prophecy, would have a beneficial influence upon this man who was previously an unbeliever.

Verse 25. *Secrets of his heart* are the thoughts produced by the edifying prophesying just heard. See the note at Matthew 2: 2 for the meaning of *worship*.

Verse 26. *How is it then* is an introductory expression, as if the apostle had said, "How about it, brethren?" *Every one of you* means "each one of you has something to contribute to the services." The general program was approved, with the stipulation that it be so conducted as to edify the church. The items named were to be in the line of spiritual gifts. *Psalm* as used here is defined by Thayer, "a pious song." *Doctrine* is defined, "teaching, instruction." *Tongue* is from the Greek word GLOSSA, which occurs 50 times in the New Testament, and is always translated by this one word. It means the language of any people that is expressed by the natural tongue. *Revelation* is from a word that means a making known some truth that was hitherto not known. *Interpretation* denotes an explaining of a foreign word or sentence that has been spoken by some other person.

Verse 27. *Man* in this verse and the pronoun in the next being singular, indicates the terms *two* and *three* refer to the number of words or sentences that were to be spoken in any given assembling. *By course* means he should utter them in turn with the interpreter. That is, he should speak one of the words or sentences and then let the other man interpret it. Next speak another word and let the other interpret, and after the third word or sentence, he should cease his speaking.

Verse 28. The speaker in tongues was subject to a further restriction, namely, that there be an interpreter present. If none were in the assembly then he was to keep *silence*, and the word is from the very same Greek original as the one in verse 34. So here is an instance where even a *man* was to keep silence, a truth that is ignored by the extremists on the "woman question."

Verse 29. The prophets were a preference as to the gifted men (verses 1, 2), hence the apostle is not as specific in his restrictions on them as he is about the speaker with tongues, where he adds the words *at the most* (verse

27). Two or three would be sufficient for any one gathering, and others were to *judge* or discern the meaning of their words.

Verse 30. Verse 26 shows that certain ones might come into an assembly with a communication to be offered to the church. After coming together, however, the Lord might see fit to make a special revelation to another. In that case the first one was to give way to the one receiving the later revelation.

Verse 31. All of the men who had the gift of prophecy were to be given opportunity to speak in their turn, since prophesying was so highly esteemed (verses 1, 2), so that all might be comforted.

Verse 32. *Spirits of the prophets* means the spiritual gifts that they possessed. These men were not compelled to speak unless they so willed, hence there would be no excuse for their being disorderly in the exercise of the gift.

Verse 33. *God is not the author of confusion.* This is a reason for the foregoing instructions about the proper conduct of the prophets, as well as of other men wtih spiritual gifts. *As in all churches of the saints.* I see no importance in the question whether this phrase belongs with the present verse, or should be attached to verse 34. The point in both verses (as it has been throughout the chapter), is to have the exercises of the assembly so conducted as to edify the church in an orderly way. The Lord desired such a result in all of the congregations but the one in Corinth seemed to be in special need of the instruction.

Verse 34. If the reader has carefully followed the teaching that has been offered from chapter 12: 1 down to this verse, he will see that it has nothing to do with the subject of "woman's duties and privileges in the church," as that is considered today. The extremists on that question will ignore all of the context, and settle upon this one passage, because they think it justifies their unholy restrictions against a part of the body of Christ. Such a use of the verse is as gross a perversion as any sectarian ever committed against Acts 2: 38.

This verse is just another item in the attempt of Paul to restore order in the public assembly when exercising the spiritual gifts. Notice it says *your women*, which shows it was not said to women in general, but to the wives of the gifted men. The perversionists try to dodge this by saying the pronoun refers to the church as a whole. That will not do for the next verse shows these women had husbands, so the attempt at perversion fails again. To say this verse is of general application and in force today, makes it contradict Ephesians 5: 19, where the word "speak" is from the same Greek term as the one in our verse. Yet no one denies that the women have the right to sing, and when they do they are "speaking" according to the apostle's command. *Obedience* is from a word that denotes "subjection," and it does not always require that any specific command has been given. The wives of the gifted men were to be in subjection in that they remain quiet while their husbands were performing their spiritual gifts.

Verse 35. Since it is the wives of gifted men who were commanded to keep silence, it follows that the things they might wish to learn about are those pertaining to the gifts of their husbands; wish to know more details about them. Otherwise they could not hope to obtain such information even at home. Furthermore, we know it does not pertain to information in general, for that was supposed to be obtained in the assembly (verses 3, 5 12, 19).

Verse 36. The Corinthians were so puffed up over their spiritual gifts, that it made them vain enough to regard themselves as a source of divine knowledge. The key to this verse is in the words *from* and *unto*. The word of God had not come out from them— had not originated with them. Instead, all the knowledge they possessed had been bestowed by the Lord, hence they had no ground for boasting.

Verse 37. No spiritual gift is more important nor based on any more authority than the writings of an apostle. If the claimants for spiritual gifts were genuine, they would acknowledge the writings of Paul to be divine commandments. Furthermore, if they go that far, they will be required by the rule of consistency to bring their conduct under the teaching of the same.

Verse 38. No one is ever asked to acknowledge anything that he does not profess to know. The evidences in support of Paul's claim for his writings were so weighty, that everyone should have been in position to recognize them. Therefore, if some man claimed that he knew nothing about what Paul was saying—had nothing to *acknowledge*, it would be prompted by stubborn indifference. In that case the apostle said *let him be ignorant*, which means that he was not worthy of further attention.

Verse 39. *Covet* is from ZELOO, and Thayer defines it, "to desire earnestly." Among the different spiritual gifts, that of prophesying was the one which Paul preferred because it was the more serviceable (verses 3, 19), hence he advised the brethren to desire it. At the same time he instructed them not to slight the other gifts.

Verse 40. This verse is the grand conclusion of the reasoning that Paul has been offering throughout the chapter. *Decently* is from a word that Thayer defines, "in a seemly [becoming] manner." *In order* means for the various items of their services to be done at the proper time, or in a systematic manner so as not to create confusion. (See verse 33.)

1 Corinthians 15

General remarks. This chapter offers a complete change of subject matter from that of the preceding three chapters, and takes up a question involving some of the philosophy of the Greeks. Corinth was one of the chief cities of Greece, and the church in that city was somewhat tinctured with the philosophy of that nation; that accounts for much of the teaching in chapter 2. The Greeks would not have very much interest in any proposition that did not measure up to their ideas of reasonable philosophy. This fact was displayed in Acts 17: 31, 32, where Paul introduced the doctrine of the resurrection, which seemed to the people of Athens as a foolish notion. That same attitude toward the resurrection had crept into the church at Corinth, which called forth the matter contained in this chapter. The false teachers who were agitating that, professed to be believers in Christ, yet denied the resurrection of the body. Paul shows in this chapter that it is inconsistent to profess faith in Christ as the risen Lord, yet deny the truth of the rising of His disciples from the dead. He shows that if one has been raised, we must believe that the other will be also.

Verse 1. *Moreover* is from the little Greek word DE, and in the King James Version it has been rendered by and, but, even, for, further, howbeit, nevertheless, now, then, therefore and others. A part of Robinson's explanation of the word is that "it marks a transition [change] to something else." Thayer's description of the word is virtually the same. Paul uses it because he is passing from the subject of spiritual gifts to that of the resurrection. *I declare* is from GNORIZO, which Thayer defines, "to make known," and at our verse he explains it to mean, "to recall to one's mind, as though what is made known had escaped him." Robinson's explanation is, "by way of putting again in mind." These definitions are appropriate, because the apostle had previously preached the Gospel to the Corinthians (Acts 18: 1-11). It was hence not a new subject, for they had *received* it and professed to *stand* upon it as the foundation of their faith. But some of them seemed to have forgotten it through the effect of the philosophy described in the "general remarks" above.

Verse 2. The mere believing of the Gospel will not save a person, but he must also *keep in memory* the truths concerning it. The phrase is from KATECHO, which Thayer defines, "to hold fast, keep secure, keep firm possession of." But all of these considerations would be *in vain*, according to the teaching of some persons at Corinth. (See verses 13, 14.) It is the purpose of the apostle to show them the logical conclusion that must follow if such a proposition is established, namely, *that there is no resurrection of the dead* (verse 12). By this they meant there would be no future resurrection of the body. They tried to teach some vague kind of theory that would make the word "resurrection" mean only a spiritual event, and that all of the facts concerning a raising of the body had already occurred—that it was "past already" (2 Timothy 2: 18). In that passage Paul declares that such a doctrine was overthrowing the faith of some, which is equivalent to the phrase in our present verse, namely, *believed in vain*. Having advanced the serious conclusion necessarily following their false teaching, Paul repeats the facts of the Gospel to which he referred in verse 1.

Verse 3. Paul did not originate the story of the Gospel; in Galatians 1: 12 he says he was taught it by the revelation of Jesus Christ. The mere death of Christ was not sufficient, for other men had died and even been resurrected. But Jesus is the only man who ever died *for our sins*. *According to the scriptures* means the Old

Testament. One outstanding portion is Isaiah 53, particularly verses 4, 5, 8 and 10.

Verse 4. The burial of Christ was not directly connected with our salvation, for had He not revived, whether in a grave or outside, no one would have been saved. But Jesus had predicted that he would spend three days and there nights in the heart of the earth, and his burial made that prediction true. *Third day according to the scriptures.* Psalms 16: 10 is quoted by Peter in Acts 2: 27, 31, and Paul quotes it in Acts 13: 35. This is the only passage in the Old Testament that directly predicts the resurrection of Christ, and yet it says nothing of the "third day," although Paul so applies it. The conclusion is to be seen by considering John 11: 39 which shows that by the fourth day a body would begin to "see corruption." Jesus must not remain dead that long for his body was not to undergo that change. And yet it must remain the three days in order to fulfill the prediction in comparison with the three days and three nights that Jonah was in the body of a whale.

Verse 5. A few verses are given to cite the evidences of the bodily resurrection of Christ. Cephas was another name for Peter (John 1: 40-42). He was one of *the twelve*, but is mentioned separately because he saw Jesus at a time when he was not with the rest of the apostles.

Verse 6. There is no other direct mention of these *five hundred brethren*, but Matthew 26: 32 and 28: 7, 10, 16 indicates that Jesus saw many of his disciples in Galilee after his resurrection. For additional comments on this subject, see those at Acts 1: 15 in volume 1 of the New Testament Commentary.

Verse 7. This *James* was not one of the twelve apostles, but was the one named in Acts 15: 13 and Galatians 2: 9, and is the author of the epistle of James. *All the apostles* means the eleven (Judas having killed himself), and Luke 24: 33-36 gives the account of their seeing Him.

Verse 8. *Last of all.* From the time of Paul's journey to Damascus (Acts 9: 3-5 and 26: 16), no human being has seen Jesus that we know of. *One born out of due time* is from the Greek word EKTROMA, and Thayer defines it, "an abortion, abortive birth; an untimely birth." Paul uses the term to illustrate his feeling of unworthiness to be called an apostle. Thayer's explanation of the word as the apostle uses it at this place is as follows: "Paul likens himself to an EKTROMA, and in verse 9 explains in what sense: that he is as inferior to the rest of the apostles as an immature birth comes short of a mature one, and is no more worthy of the name of an apostle than an abortion is of the name of a child."

Verse 9. This verse explains the feeling of inferiority that Paul expresses in the preceding verse. He specifies it to mean his record as a persecutor of the church of God. The extent of his persecution is indicated by the relief that his conversion brought to the churches throughout Palestine (Acts 9: 31).

Verse 10. The grace of God is his unmerited favor, and Paul attributed all of his good lot to that source. To show his appreciation for the favor, he labored more than any of the other apostles. But even then he considered the labor as the work of God, using the apostle as an instrument for the work.

Verses 11, 12. Having given proper credit for the work done under God, the apostle settles down upon the argument that is indicated in the beginning of the chapter. He will proceed to show the inconsistency between the professed faith of the Corinthians in the bodily resurrection of Christ, and their denial of a like event for those who die in Him.

Verse 13. This short verse states the major premise for the great argument that Paul intends to present. But the mere assertion of a basis for argument is not sufficient for the support of it, because that would be assuming the very point under discussion. The statement must be either self-evident, or be supported by vital facts or truths. In 1 Thessalonians 4: 14 Paul makes virtually the same statement as the one in this verse. The death and rising again of Jesus is there coupled with the assurance of the bringing of the dead in Christ "with him" from their state of death. Since the body of Jesus (as to its material) was like that of all other men, it follows that it would be as impossible or unreasonable to believe in the resurrection of His body as to expect the same thing of the bodies of other men. Such a proposition is self-evident and needs no further evidence. Reasoning the other direction, therefore, if philosophy denies the bodily resurrection of men in general, then it must deny that of Christ, and hence the professed basis of the faith of the Corinthians, namely, the bodily resurrection of Christ, is disproved, and the major premise of Paul's great argument is established.

Verse 14. Having presented an unquestionable basis regarding the question in dispute, Paul will devote a number of verses showing some of the logical conclusions that must follow, thereby proving to the brethren that their whole program of religious activities and hope is fundamentally wrong. One conclusion is that the preaching of the apostles was in vain or of no avail. That necessarily would mean that their faith was vain, since it was based on the facts that had been preached to them. Reference is made to this "vain" belief in verse 2.

Verse 15. The Corinthian brethren would not intend to accuse the apostles of fraud, yet their theory about the resurrection implied that the preachers were guilty of it. They had preached that Christ was raised from the dead, but Paul has shown that it was false according to the teaching held at Corinth.

Verses 16, 17. This paragraph is covered by comments over verses 2, 3, 13, 14.

Verse 18. The Corinthians had never been taught that eternal salvation was to be actually possessed before the end of the world. But if the dead were never to be raised, then their bodies would be destroyed along with that of the earth. That is why Paul says that those who had died in the Lord were *perished*, which means they had come to their end.

Verse 19. Another conclusion following this false theory advocated by some people at Corinth, is that all benefits to be had from being in Christ must be had in this life—nothing to be received after death. In that case Christians are the most miserable of all men, because they must be denied the pleasures of the world and also undergo many persecutions in behalf of their faith, with no prospect of any joys beyond the grave. While this was true especially of the apostles because of their direct contact with the enemy, it was and is still true of all faithful disciples of Christ. It is true that Christians should be the happiest people on earth, but that is because of their hope of endless bliss in the life to come.

Verse 20. Taking for granted he has proved his point, Paul reaffirms the third fact of the Gospel, namely, that Christ arose *from the dead*. The italicized words are significant in that they specify from what Jesus arose. He previously arose to the cross (John 12:32, 33), and arose from earth to Heaven, but those facts were not in dispute; that from the dead was. The body is the only part of Christ or any other man that dies, hence if the body is not to be raised from the grave, then there will be no resurrection at all. Paul has shown the awful conclusions made necessary by the theory that there is to be no resurrection of the dead. He will next show the glorious conclusions made possible by the truth of the resurrection. The first one is that Christ has become the *firstfruits of them that slept;* that is, he was the first person to rise from the dead to die no more. For detailed comments on this subject, see those on Romans 8:29, in volume 1 of the New Testament Commentary.

Verse 21. Adam was the first man, and after joining with his wife in eating of the forbidden fruit, they were both driven out of the garden and permanently prevented from re-entering it. That cut them and all of their descendants off from the tree of life, so that all had to die whenever their bodies failed through disease or other causes. But none of Adam's descendants were to blame for that condition, hence God arranged it so that through another man's resurrection they could all be raised from the dead without any conditions on their part.

Verse 22. This verse specifies the two men of the preceding verse to be Adam and Christ. The lattter is called a man because he was given a body (Hebrews 10:5) that was like that of other men, in that it was fleshly and was subject to death. That made it possible for Him to die and be raised again, thereby opening the gates of death to all men to come therefrom.

Verse 23. The literal resurrection from the grave will come to all men whether they are good or bad, since they are not responsible for their bodily death. However, that experience is all that mankind in general will receive unconditionally from the resurrection of Christ. What will come to them after the resurrection depends on how they lived on earth (Daniel 12:2; John 5:28, 29). This is why Paul makes the assertion of the words *every man in his own order;* that is, *every man* means of those who are the Lord's own. Some of them were raised immediately after the resurrection of Chirst among whom he was the *firstfruits*, then at His coming the others who are dead in Him will also be raised. While all mankind will be raised whether good or bad (verses 21, 22), yet from now on through the chapter the apostle will be writing only of those who are His and who have been "asleep in Jesus" (1 Thessalonians 4:14).

Verse 24. *Then* is an adverb of time, and refers to the words "at his coming" in the preceding verse. This verse gives the information as to what is to come to end at the coming of Christ, namely, the kingdom or rule of Christ. Paul directly says that the kingdom with Christ as its head will end when He comes, and he will deliver it up to his Father. From this inspired prediction come two other important truths, namely, that the kingdom of Christ will have been in existence before His second coming, and also that he will not be a king after that coming. Therefore, the doctrine that the kingdom is still a thing of the future, and that He will set up a thousand year reign when he comes is false.

Verses 25, 26. When Jesus came from the dead to die no more, he annulled death or gave it the "death stroke" (2 Timothy 1:10). However, not until every human being has been brought back to life, will it be a fact that death is destroyed; Jesus must be king until the great event is accomplished. This does not contradict the statement that He will give up his kingdom "at his coming," for all of the mentioned events, the coming of Jesus, the resurrection of the dead and the transfer of the kingdom to his Father, will take place "in a moment" (verse 52). After the dead have all been raised to die no more (as to bodily death), the triumph will be complete, and Jesus will then be qualified to relinquish the kingdom to God who shall continue to reign endlessly, thus putting the final fulfillment to the prediction that the kingdom of "the God of Heaven" shall "stand for ever" (Daniel 2:44).

Verse 27. The pronouns stand for God and his Son. God has put all things under the feet of Christ except himself. Jesus declared this fact in Matthew 28:18, and it was on that basis that He gave to his apostles the Great Commission.

Verse 28. Eliminating the pronouns, this verse means that after the Son has brought all things under subjection, then that Son will become subject unto God the Father. The grand motive for this consumation is *that God may be all in all.*

Verse 29. *What shall they do.* The pronoun is in the third person, while Paul is writing to the church in general as in the second person. This shows that not all persons in the Corinthian church were practicing this baptism, even as not all were denying the resurrection, as is indicated by the words "how say some among you" (verse 12). This item must not be overlooked in considering this verse, for any professed explanation of it that would apply to all Christians in general would necessarily be wrong. The word *for* is from HUPER and Thayer defines it at this place, "in the place of, instead of." I shall quote Moffatt's translation of this verse: "Otherwise, if there is no such thing as a resurrection, what is the meaning of people getting baptized on behalf of their dead? If dead men do not rise at all, why do people get baptized on their behalf?" Not all of the brethren in Corinth were practicing this inconsistency of being baptized on behalf of their dead, neither were all of them denying the resurrection (verse 12). But Paul considered it necessary to notice them in his epistle to the whole church, even as he deemed it worth while to notice the group that was practicing this "proxy" baptism. The apostle does not endorse the foolish practice, but brings it up to expose their inconsistency.

Verse 30. *Stand in jeopardy* means to be in danger of death from the enemies of Christ. All Christians and especially the apostles were constantly being persecuted (verse 19), some of them even unto death. How foolish, then, to cling to a profession that threatens one with death if there is to be no resurrection.

Verse 31. *I die daily* is figurative, meaning that Paul was daily exposed to the danger of death because of his service to Christ.

Verse 32. *I have fought with beasts.* These words are all from the one Greek word THERIOMACHEO, and Thayer defines it, "to fight with wild beasts."

I believe this was a literal experience of Paul and shall state my reasons. We know it was an action that endangered the physical life of the participant, else Paul would not have connected it with the resurrection in his reasoning. It is certain that he has the same event in mind in 2 Corinthians 1: 8-10, where he relates that he had "despaired even of life." He did not know whether the Lord was ready to release his faithful apostle from his labors through this event, hence he was willing to do his part in the combat with the beasts, trusting in God to help him overcome the beasts if He so willed. Or, if that was not the case, he would meet his fate with his trust in God "which raiseth the dead." Furthermore, had it been vicious men who attacked him, he would not have "resisted the evil" (Matthew 5: 39), but would have submitted to his fate as he did when he was subjected to other threatening brutalities. *Let us eat and drink* is said as representing all the fleshly pleasures of this life. If there is no life beyond the grave, there would be no reason for denying ourselves any of the fleshly pleasures of this world.

Verse 33. The original for *evil communications* is translated "bad company" by James Macknight, and Thayer's lexicon agrees with it. Thayer defines the original of *manners*, "custom, usage, morals, character." We have seen that not all of the brethren at Corinth were advocating this evil doctrine concerning the resurrection. This verse is a warning against others having company with such bad teachers, lest they also be drawn into the heresy. If a man does not believe that he will live again, it is logical that he would be tempted to engage in that which would give him fleshly pleasure, and hence his otherwise good practices would become corrupted.

Verse 34. This is a further warning against being led into the sin of these false teachers. Paul attributes their evil doctrine to ignorance of God, just as Christ charged the Sadducees on the same subject, that of the resurrection (Matthew 22: 23-29). The apostle considers it a shame that some of the Corinthians were so ignorant of the wisdom and power of God.

Verse 35. When advocates of error cannot offer a just defense of their own position, nor show an honest objection to that of their opponent, it is often a trick of theirs to pose a quibbling question which they think will puzzle him. As if a man is required logically to account for all the apparent difficulties that his position may suggest. Nothing could be farther from the truth, nor from the universal practice of reasonable men in accepting a conclusion that has been shown to be fundamentally sound, notwithstanding any incidental items that cannot be explained. Such a subterfuge as herein described was resorted to by the promoters of the heresy that Paul was exposing, when they asked *with what body do they [the dead] come?* Even if Paul could not have answered such a question, that would not have proved that the dead could not come to life again.

Verse 36. *Fool* is from APHRON, and Thayer defines it, "senseless, foolish, stupid; without reflection or intelligence, acting rashly." It does not mean that the person does not have natural mental ability, for then he could not justly be censured. But he is one so devoted to his notion that he will not use his mind to consider other matters with which he is familiar, and which would meet his own quibble in the question at hand. Such a matter is the well known truth that a vegetable grain will never reproduce its kind unless it dies and mingles with the earth in which it was placed.

Verse 37. *Bare* is from GUMNOS, which literally means "naked." The Englishman's Greek New Testament uses the indefinite article "a" in connection with it, making the phrase read, "a bare grain." The verse means that a man puts a mere grain of any kind in the ground from which he expects a crop; not the grain just as he placed it in the soil. And when it dies and decomposes, it partakes of the materials around it and from them a new body is formed with added parts. And while it is another body in one sense, in another it is the same, for the new growth is produced out of the old seed or body. Paul uses this circumstance to illustrate the death and resurrection of the body of a faithful servant of Christ.

According to the theory of the ones in Corinth whose heresy Paul was exposing, and of all others today who say that our bodies will never come from the grave at the last day—according to them, the grain should just all remain in the ground, and in another spot of the earth the farmer would dig up some other grain and consider it as his new crop. No, the bodies of the saints will all come forth, but they will be in another form which will be like that of Christ at his coming (Philippians 3: 21). *It may chance of wheat*, etc. Paul uses the wheat for his illustration, but the same reasoning would be true of any other grain.

Verse 38. The stock with its roots, leaves and fruit, is the new body that God is pleased to give to the original grain. Likewise, He will give to the body of the dead in Christ another form, that will be like the immortal body of his Son, possessed with the new harvest of eternal glory.

Verse 39. To show that it is in keeping with the works of God to have the body of a saint take on another form (although it is the same body), Paul refers his readers to other conditions in the creation, such as the different kinds of flesh.

Verse 40. He uses this as still another illustration of God's wisdom and power. *Celestial* means of the air or sky, *terrestrial* means pertaining to the earth.

Verse 41. The sun and other bodies in the universe all have their own peculiar form and glory, showing that the Creator is not limited in the number and kinds of bodies that He may create.

Verse 42. God's ability to create and change and otherwise manage all of His works has been shown by the preceding verses. The apostle now comes directly to the subject under discussion, the possibility and character of the resurrection. *The dead* is the antecedent of the pronoun *it*, which certainly proves beyond all question that it is the body that is to be resurrected, since it is the only part of man that ever dies literally. *Corruption* means to be subject to decay, and *incorruption* means the opposite.

Verse 43. *Dishonor* is not used in any moral sense, for the same kind of body was possessed by Jesus that Paul is writing about here. It means the state that would be subject to decomposition, which the body of Jesus had which was the reason he must not have remained dead more than three days and nights. *Raised in glory* means more than an existence that is never to end (the wicked will have that; Mark 9: 44, 46, 48), but a state in which the body will be given the same glorious form as that of Jesus in his present condition (Philippians 3: 21; 1 John 3: 2). *Weakness* and *power* are used for the same purpose as the preceding terms because they are opposites.

Verse 44. *Natural* and *spiritual* bodies are applied to the same thing, namely, the human body. But the first applies to it when it *is sown* (is placed in the grave), the second applies to it when it will be resurrected. The false teachers in Corinth, and all others today who deny the resurrection of the body, are disposed to ignore this verse. They say it is impossible for a material thing to be changed into an immaterial one, thus limiting the power of the Creator. Yet in the realm of nature as they must recognize it, there is an indisputable proof of changes virtually as great. For instance; the universe is divided into three distinct classes, namely, the mineral, the vegetable and the animal. The first is inorganic and the others are organic. Notwithstanding these independent and different existences, the inorganic mineral is absorbed into the vegetable, the vegetable is next absorbed and converted into the animal. If there is a Creator who can establish such laws of change within our own knowledge, why doubt His power to lift the animal to one more stage and convert it into a spiritual state? With God all things are possible that are right (Genesis 18: 14).

Verse 45. This statement is written in Genesis 2:7, and Paul calls Adam the first man. This refutes a theory of some visionary followers of a visionary false teacher, that a prior creation of man occurred to that recorded in Genesis. The *last Adam* is Christ according to Romans 5: 14, considered in connection with verse 22 here.

Verse 46. The first Adam did not give us a spiritual body, but instead it is one that was made subject to death and decay by being separated from the tree of life. After that came Christ who has the power to give a spiritual body to all His faithful followers.

Verse 47. This is virtually the same as the preceding verse.

Verse 48. This offers the same thought as that in verse 45.

Verse 49. All men whether good or bad receive their fleshly bodies from Adam. Likewise, all will be brought from the dead through the second Adam, whether good or bad as taught in verse 23. But in addition to this, those who die in Christ will come from the dead with a *heavenly* body. To avoid a misunderstanding, let it be said that every human being regardless of conduct will be raised from the dead, and will continue to exist consciously without end. But only the righteous have been promised a body like that of Jesus. This should not confuse any person, for God is able to preserve the bodies of men continuously in whatever form He sees fit. Hence we read that the bodies of the unsaved will be cast into the lake of unquenchable fire, where their worm dieth not (Mark 9: 44, 46, 48). Those who say that the wicked will have immortal bodies are making an assertion without showing any proof.

Verse 50. *Inherit* is from KLERONOMEO, and Thayer defines it at this passage, "to partake of eternal salvation in the Messiah's kingdom." That is why those to be admitted into the eternal home in the next life must be changed from a body of flesh and blood, to one that is spiritual and like that of the Saviour. But such a change of body is not necessary with the unsaved, for there is no restriction as to what kind of beings can enter into the lake of fire and brimstone, since God is able to preserve all creatures cast therein in whatever state He sees fit.

Verse 51. *Mystery* is from MUSTERION, and Thayer's second definition is, "a hidden purpose or counsel; secret will." It does not necessarily mean something that is complicated or technical in its nature, but only that it has not been hitherto made known. *Sleep* is a figurative term that is defined in the lexicon, "to die." The same truth is stated in 1 Thessalonians 4: 14, 15. In each of these passages the connection shows Paul is speaking only of faithful disciples of Christ. We thus have the precious information that as long as the earth exists there will be those who are true to the Lord, and hence that saving faith "shall not perish from the earth." But though Christians living at the coming of Christ will not die, they will have to *be changed*, as the preceding verse states that a fleshly body cannot inherit the kingdom of God. Here is another point against the heresy that our bodies will not rise nor go to Heaven. These Christians will not die, hence their soul and body will never separate. Yet they are to be taken to be ever with the Lord as Paul asserts in the passage cited in 1 Thessalonians. And if God can and will convert the flesh and blood bodies of these living Christians into a spiritual form that will be fit to "ever be with the Lord," it is foolish to deny His power to effect the same change in the bodies of those who are "dead in Christ."

Verse 52. This verse is virtually the same as the preceding one, except that it adds the information that the resurrection of these saints and the changing of the living ones, will all take place at one instant.

Verse 53. The body is the only part of man that is *corruptible* and *mortal*, hence it is the body that is to be changed into an incorruptible and immortal form. This applies necessarily to both dead and living in Christ when he comes.

Verse 54. When the change just mentioned has occurred, a prediction in Isaiah 25: 8 will be fulfilled, namely, death is swallowed up in victory.

Verse 55. *Where is thy sting?*, etc., is a shout of triumph by the saints, as they rejoice in their victory over death.

Verse 56. *Sting of death* means that because of sin death threatened the human race with the *sting* of God's eternal wrath. The *strength* or effect of sin in bringing about this sting, is through the law against sin, which makes mankind responsible for their conduct.

Verse 57. *The victory* does not mean only the rising from the dead, for all mankind will have that regardless of conduct. But Paul has been writing about the faithful in Christ only from verse 23. Hence this victory means that one over the eternal results of individual sin, which is to be accomplished by faithful service to *our Lord Jesus Christ*.

Verse 58. The grand conclusion to the argument of the chapter is stated in this verse. Since death does not "end it all," but the faithful shall enjoy endless bliss in the world to come, even though death from whatever cause may intervene, they have great reason to press on in their service to Him. There is not much difference between *stedfast* and *unmoveable*. The first means to have a fixed purpose in life, the second means to be determined not to be moved from that purpose. *Abounding* is from PERISSEUO, which Thayer defines, "to be preeminent, to excel." Of course it means for each Christian to excel himself—never to be satisfied with present attainments in the Lord's work, but ever striving to "grow in grace, and in the knowledge of our Lord and Saviour Jesus Christ" (2 Peter 3: 18).

1 Corinthians 16

Verse 1. A great dearth was predicted in Acts 11: 27-30, which came with such force that the disciples in Judea were thrown into a state of want. The condition lasted for some years and it is referred to in Romans 15: 26; 2 Corinthians 8: 1, 2; 9: 1, 2. Collections were made at various times and from different communities for the relief of the saints. It is concerning this matter that Paul is writing in this chapter. We have no record elsewhere of this order given to the churches in Galatia. *As I have given order* indicates that Paul gave those churches the same instructions on the subject that he wrote to the church in Corinth. Such a plan, therefore, should be regarded as the Lord's way for churches to raise money for carrying on His work.

Verse 2. The Englishman's Greek New Testament translates the first clause as follows: "Every first day of the week," and Thayer's explanation of the passage agrees with such a rendering. It was on this day the money was to be contributed for relief of the dearth-stricken saints, and since the disciples came together on that day for the Lord's supper (Acts 20: 7), it was a consideration of convenience on that part of Him to ordain this public collection to come at the same gathering. *Lay by him* has been an occasion for controversy as to where the members were to put their contribution. The pronoun *him* is not necessarily in the masculine gender in the original, but may properly be rendered "itself." *In store* is from THESAURIZO, and James Macknight defines it, "putting it in the treasury." This critical information agrees with the reasoning Paul makes, namely, *that there be no gatherings when I come*. *Gatherings* is from the same Greek word as "collection" in the first verse. If the brethren were to put this contribution some place in their homes, then it would have to be collected when Paul came, and that is what he wished to avoid. Besides, the fact that they were told to do this on the same day the disciples came together, indicates it was to be a public collection. *As God hath prospered him* means each one was to give according to his financial ability.

Verse 3. This advice is on the principle of Romans 12: 17 and 2 Corinthians 8: 18-21. A man who is entrusted with the property of another should wish to protect himself from any suspicions of dishonesty. I have known of cases where brethren who handled the money of a congregation, would resent all inquiries about the amount of funds in their hands. They would probably make some peevish remark such as, "If you think I am not honest, I will just turn the job over to someone else." There is something wrong with a brother who takes such an attitude, to say the least, and he lays himself open to just suspicion.

Verse 4. When Paul wrote this verse he did not know whether he would go to Jerusalem on this mission; Romans 15: 25-27 shows that he did.

Verse 5. Acts 20: 1-3 records this work of Paul in those Greek countries, in which he was threatened with bodily harm from the Jews.

Verse 6. *Bring me on my journey*. The first word is from PROPEMPO, which Thayer defines, "To send before. To bring on the way, accompany or escort." He then explains the word to mean, "To set one forward, fit him out with the requisites [things required] for his journey." Hence when a church furnishes a preacher the things he needs to take him to his "field of labor," it is bringing that preacher on his journey to the Lord's work.

Verse 7. The apostle did not count on seeing the Corinthian brethren in the immediate future, but he was expecting to see them later, subject to the will of the Lord.

Verse 8. The Mosaic system was both religious and secular as a government. When Christ gave his institution to the world it was intended to supplant the old one for religious purposes (Romans 10: 4), but the Jews were still left the privilege of observing their national institutions, as long as they did not try to obtain spiritual benefits from them. That is why Paul planned to continue his work at Ephesus until Pentecost. That being one of the Jewish national feasts, the apostle wished to go to Jerusalem to attend it.

Verse 9. The first part of this verse is somewhat awkwardly constructed by the translators. The words *great* and *effectual* are adjectives, modifying *door*, which means as if it said "a great and effectual [efficient] door." The fact of there being *many adversaries* was the reason Paul wished to remain at Ephesus as long as he could.

Verse 10. Chapter 4: 17 mentions the fact that Timotheus (Timothy) was told to go to Corinth. Paul asks the brethren to give him a friendly reception; as a recommendation in support of the request, the apostle tells them of the work of the Lord in which Timothy was engaged.

Verse 11. To *despise* means to belittle or treat with improper regard. Timothy was supposed to spend some time at Corinth and then return to Paul. He did this, for 2 Corinthians 1: 1 shows him joining in the salutation of that epistle.

Verse 12. Paul was an apostle while A p o l l o s was only an unofficial preacher, yet he was not bound to make the journey to Corinth, for the apostle only *greatly desired* him to go. This indicates that Paul was not inclined to abuse his position by commanding another brother in matters where the legislation of God was not involved.

Verse 13. *Watch ye, stand fast* contains a twofold exhortation. To watch means to be alert for any challenge to their faith, and if it appears it should not be suffered to shake them from their faithfulness. *Quit you like men* is all from one Greek word which Thayer defines, "to show one's self a man, be brave." Such an attitude was necessary to meet the attacks of enemies.

Verse 14. *Charity* is from one of the Greek words that are usually translated "love." For a complete explanation of the word, see the notes on Matthew 5: 43 in volume 1 of the New Testament Commentary.

Verse 15. *Achaia* is another name for Greece, the country in which Corinth was located. The baptism of Stephanas and his household is recorded in Chapter 1: 16. (See the notes on Romans 16: 5.) *Addicted themselves to the ministry of the saints* denotes they were devoted to the service in behalf of the saints or disciples.

Verse 16. Thayer explains the original for *submit* to mean, "to yield to one's admonition or advice." Hence it is not used in the sense of an authoritative command, for even a righteous household like that of Stephanas would have no such authority. The statement of Paul is more in the nature of an advisory exhortation. It is always well to listen to the instructions or exhortations of faithful disciples of Christ. If they are scriptural they should be accepted on the principle of chapter 11: 1.

Verse 17. The lack on the part of the Corinthians, which was supplied by the coming of these brethren, was not in regard to material things as the next verse shows.

Verse 18. These brethren refreshed Paul by their coming to him, and by the message which they evidently brought from the Corinthian church (chapter 7: 1). Paul reasons that such brethren were a blessing wherever they dwelt, and therefore must have been so among the brethren at Corinth; he commends them to the favor of the church.

Verse 19. Revelation 1: 11 names seven churches in Asia, and Ephesus was one of them, where Paul was when he wrote this epistle (verse 8). *Salute* is from ASPAZOMAI, and in the King James Version it is translated by embrace 2 times, greet 15, salute 42, take leave of 1. Thayer defines it, "to salute one, greet, bid welcome, wish well to; pay one's respects to." He explains that it can be done either in person or by letter, and of course it was done by the latter method in the present case. Special mention is made of Aquila and Priscilla because they were outstanding disciples and had been closely associated with the apostle in the Lord's work (Acts 18: 1-3). They were at Corinth at the same time that Paul labored there, but later went to Ephesus and hence gave their salutation to the Corinthian church through the epistle that Paul was writing. *Church that is in their house.* In the first years of the church the brethren did not have regular church buildings in many places. That was due either to their financial limitations, or to the fact that the group in the community was too few in numbers to require it. In such cases the church had its meetings in private homes, and Aquila and Priscilla used their home for that purpose.

Verse 20. *All the brethren* would necessarily mean those in contact with Paul as he was writing the epistle, especially those engaged in public work for the church. *Holy kiss.* I have examined a number of dictionaries and histories, as well as four lexicons, and they all represent the kiss to have been a form of salute between persons of both sexes, the custom dating back to ancient times. The instruction of the apostle, then, was not to start any new form of salutation, for that of the kiss was in existence centuries before he was born. The point is in the word *holy*, and it means for the salutation to be sincere and not hypocritical as was that of **Judas.**

Verse 21. Paul wrote some of his epistles with his own hand (Galatians 6: 11), others he dictated and then signed them to show that they were genuine.

Verse 22. *Anathema* means a curse, and it is pronounced upon a man who does not love Jesus. *Maranatha* is transferred into the King James Version without being translated. Thayer defines it, "our Lord cometh or will come." It denotes, therefore, that such a person will be accursed when the Lord comes. (See 2 Thessalonians 1: 7-9).

Verses 23, 24. Paul wishes that the grace (favor) of Jesus may be with the brethren at Corinth. As a secondary favor upon the church, the apostle assures it of his love for all in Christ Jesus. *Amen* is explained in the notes on Romans 16:24, volume 1 of the New Testament Commentary.

2 Corinthians 1

Verse 1. Much of this epistle will reflect the results of Paul's first letter to the church at Corinth. Because of the conditions in that church due to the habits of the Gentile citizens of the country, it will be well for the reader to reread the "general remarks" offered at the beginning of the first epistle. The apostleship of Paul was supported both by Jesus and his Father. With such a weighty endorsement, the epistle to the church should have the most respectful consideration from those to whom it is addressed. It was sent directly to the church in Corinth, which was the Roman capital of Greece, and the salutation included all the saints (disciples) in *Achaia*, the name the Romans gave to Greece. For comments on *Church of God*, see those on Romans 16: 16, in volume 1 of the New Testament Commentary, and those on 1 Corinthians 1: 2.

Verse 2. For comments on this verse, see 1 Corinthians 1: 3.

Verse 3. A father and son could not be the same individual, and God is declared to be the Father of Christ. This refutes a false teaching in the world that Jesus is "the very and eternal God." It also exposes another heresy known in religious circles by the name of "Jesus Only." God and Christ are one in purpose and goodness, but are two separate persons. Father and God of mercies and comfort simply means that all such blessings come from Him.

Verse 4. Paul regarded himself and all other Christians who were having persecutions for the sake of righteousness as "companions in tribulation" (Revelation 1: 9). The preceding verse says that all comfort comes from God, hence he is the One who enabled the apostle to pass his comfort on to others.

Verse 5. Jesus was in Heaven clothed with a spiritual body when Paul was writing this epistle, hence He could not literally undergo personal sufferings. But the church is His body in another spiritual sense and is subject to sufferings, and in that manner He may well be said to suffer with the faithful disciples. Besides this, Hebrews 4: 15 says that Christ can "be touched with the feelings of our infirmities," and in this sense He is also able to suffer with the saints. By the same token, the faithful disciples will share in the triumph of their Master over all trials and hardships experienced for the sake of righteousness.

Verse 6. The afflictions heaped upon Paul in his defence of the Gospel, should be a source of consolation to the Corinthians, in that they would have an encouraging example of saving faith that is put to the test. That is, it will be thus *effectual* (will have that effect) provided they are willing to withstand that same kind of sufferings if called upon to do so. The assurance that Paul could find consolation in spite of his sufferings, would result in consolation for the Corinthians. This is the same thought that is set forth in verse 4.

Verse 7. Paul's hopefulness in regard to the Corinthian brethren was based on their general attitude toward the Gospel. We shall later learn that they reacted favorably to the first epistle, hence it was reasonable to hope for their continued devotion to the Lord, even though great tribulations might come upon them.

Verse 8. The apostle has been making general references only to his difficulties, but now he makes a more direct mention of them. He names Asia, but the specific place in that district where they occurred was Ephesus, where he "fought with beasts" (1 Corinthians 15: 32).

Verse 9. *Sentence of death.* Paul was so certain that he would die that he resigned himself to his fate. He was enabled to take such an attitude because of this trust in God *which raiseth the dead.*

Verse 10. The event did not turn out as Paul feared, for God took a hand in it and gave him the victory over the beasts. This gave him renewed faith in the power and goodness of God in delivering him from other conditions that threatened him.

Verse 11. Paul believed in the benefits of prayer and asked the brethren to pray for him, that he might continue to overcome all his trials. In that case he would stimulate others to thank God for divine favors bestowed on the apostolic labors.

Verse 12. Among the reasons that would cause Paul to rejoice would be that of a good conscience. *Simplicity* and *sincerity* mean virtually the same thing, except Paul modifies the latter with the word *godly.* A man might be conscientious or honest, and yet not be satisfactory to God. (See Acts 23: 1; 26: 9; Romans 10: 1, 2.) Hence the apostle wished that his motives would all be directed by the will of the Lord. The word *conversation* in the King James Version comes from a number of Greek words, but with the exception of Philippians 3: 20, every instance means "manner of life," and not merely one's speech. Paul desired to live properly toward all men in the world, and such a life had been manifested *more abundantly* toward the Corinthian brethren because of his extended labors among them. (See Acts 18: 1-11.)

Verse 13. In Paul's first epistle to the Corinthians (chapter 2: 1-4), he declared that his oral speech was within the realm of simple language. He here continues that manner in his writing, so the brethren may read with understanding and hence be able to acknowledge the truth conveyed to them.

Verse 14. The reaction of the church to the first epistle shows the brethren had acknowledged its truth *in part* (that is, as far as the epistle had gone in considering the subjects at hand). The result of this respectful attitude was to be a mutual rejoicing over spiritual advancement. *In the day of the Lord Jesus.* Most of the harvest to be received from the "sowing to the Spirit" will not be reaped until the *day* when Jesus comes again.

Verse 15. *This confidence* refers to the state of cooperation mentioned in the preceding two verses. *Second benefit* is said with regard for the spiritual gifts that an apostle can bestow on Christians.

Verse 16. Paul's plans included a visit into Macedonia, another Greek country lying north of that in which Corinth was located. He intended going to Corinth first, then making his journey into Macedonia as a sort of "side trip," after which he would come back to Corinth, from which place he would expect to be assisted onward toward Judea by the church; but 1 Corinthians 16: 5-7 shows he changed his plans.

Verse 17. *Did I use lightness?* The last word means "fickleness," and Paul wonders if the Corinthians would accuse him of that when he changed his plans; the form of his question implies a negative answer. Neither does he admit that he was moved by any fleshly interest in what he was doing. *Yea yea, nay nay* describes a person who is not certain what he wants to do, and the apostle denies being such a person.

Verse 18. *As God is true* is a phrase used for comparison, meaning that what Paul is about to affirm is just as true as the thought in the italicized phrase. *Word . . . not yea and nay.* Paul's preaching was not the wishy-washy kind; when he said "yea" or "nay," he meant it.

Verse 19. Paul was serving and preaching for the Son of God, and hence he could not consistently manifest a fickle spirit in his preaching. *In him was yea.* The promises and other statements coming from Jesus were always positive, leaving no room for doubt that He always meant what He said and would make His word good. *Silvanus* and *Timotheus* are other forms for Silas and Timothy.

Verse 20. This verse is virtually a repetition of the preceding one, with the added information that Jesus is to be regarded as reliable, because He is working in harmony with the Father. The promises are *amen*, which means they are backed up by the authority of Heaven, and are all to the glory of God.

Verse 21. *Stablisheth* denotes to confirm or strengthen a person in his work. Paul gives God the credit for such support which he and the brethren in Corinth were enjoying in Christ.

Verse 22. *Earnest* means a pledge or foretaste of a more complete favor yet to come. Such an assurance was bestowed in miraculous measure upon the apostle.

Verse 23. *Call God for a record.* Paul knew that God was a witness of everything that he or any other man did or thought. He then would certainly not make a statement that was not true. *Came not as yet* refers to Paul's change of plans, commented upon at verses 16, 17. By this change, his visit to Corinth was delayed until they had more time to reflect on the epistle that he had sent to them, which was followed by their correction of many of the evils that were in their practices. By such a reformation, the congregation was "spared" the severe chastisement that he would have thought necessary, had he arrived before they made the corrections.

Verse 24. The severity that is implied in the preceding verse does not mean that the apostle was a tyrant over their faith, but yet he was bound to insist on their adapting their conduct to the will of the Lord however firm it might be.

2 Corinthians 2

Verse 1. This chapter continues the thought introduced in verse 23 of the preceding one. *Heaviness* is from LUPE, which Thayer defines, "sorrow, pain, grief," and he explains it at this passage to mean, "of one who on coming both saddens and is made sad." Paul was always conscientious and would not keep back any unpleasant chastisement that was due his brethren. (See chapter 7: 8.) However, by waiting a while longer before appearing in person, the brethren were given space to profit by the letter which he had sent to them, which caused some grief as we shall see later.

Verse 2. Since the sorrow over wrongdoing would be mutual between the guilty person and the one who chastised him for it, the only way the rebuker could be made glad would be by the repentance of the guilty one. Hence we can understand why Paul delayed his coming to Corinth until they had time to reflect and make adjustments.

Verse 3. This verse has virtually the same thought as the preceding one in its first part. *Having confidence.* Paul believed the Corinthian brethren would rejoice in whatever they saw would bring joy to the apostle.

Verse 4. Like a firm but kindhearted parent, Paul wrote his rebuke of the brethren in Corinth, although it pained him in his heart to do so; he knew they might be grieved also. But the purpose of the epistle was not merely for their grief, but to show them his great concern and love with reference to their spiritual welfare.

Verse 5. Paul is referring to the fornicator reported in chapter 5 of the preceding epistle, although no specific mention is made of him nor his sin. *Not grieved me but in part.* Paul does not claim to be the only one who is grieved over the affair; he is bearing only a part of the burden. *Not overcharge you all.* A part of the congregation at first had endorsed the fornicator, and thus were responsible for the grief that had been brought upon Paul by the circumstance. However, the apostle did not want to make too strong a complaint about it, since the guilty one had evidently repented of his wrong in committing the deed, and the church had taken the right attitude toward the epistle written that included the subject.

Verse 6. The church has no authority to administer physical *punishment*, but the word refers to the rebuke and disciplinary action that was taken against the fornicator. *Inflicted of many.* The last word is from an original that literally means a majority. The New Testament church does not decide religious matters by what is generally known as a "majority vote." In the present case it will be noted that Paul uses the term as a contrast with *a man.* There was just one man who had committed the act, but the chastisement was administered by many more than one, namely, by the church when it was "gathered together" (1 Corinthians 5: 4). No final act of discipline can be scripturally performed except in a general assembly of the disciples. In such a meeting each member of the congregation has the right to offer scriptural objections to what is being proposed. If no such objection is stated, then the action must be regarded as that of the entire assembly; the act *of many.*

Verse 7. This verse considered alone might leave the impression that the church was still holding the charge against the fornicator, but we shall soon see that such was not the case.

Verse 8. Paul would not tell them

to *confirm* their *love* toward the man, if they had not granted him any love at all. But sometimes brethren are too indifferent about certain matters, and expect others to take too much for granted. In as serious a case as the present one, they should not act in that way, but should so conduct themselves that the brother would have no doubt of the love of the church.

Verse 9. *Did I write* has reference to the first epistle to the Corinthians. The Philippians were especially ready to do their duty even when the apostle was not present (Philippians 2: 12), and he concluded to make a test of the faithfulness of the brethren in Corinth, by remaining away long enough to see their reaction to the written instructions of the first epistle.

Verse 10. In 1 Corinthians 5: 3, 4 Paul shows that the act of discipline that he commanded to be done would be by his endorsement and participation, even though he really were not present. By the same token, the action of the church in forgiving the penitent man would be endorsed by him, though absent. *In the person of Christ* means to be acting by His authority. Being an inspired apostle of Christ, Paul could act as His representative in the matter. Not only did he have the authority to share in the act of forgiveness toward the penitent man, but he was personally so inclined.

Verse 11. Verse 7 indicates that if the brethren did not give the penitent one sufficient proof of their love, he would be overcome with sorrow or despair, and might be driven farther out into the world again. Of course that would be an advantage to Satan to have a soul lost to the church and gained for his realm. *Devices* means purposes and plans, and Satan always plans on using every occasion to injure the truth.

Verses 12, 13. Even an apostle feels the need of encouragement from his brethren. When Paul arrived in Troas on this mentioned occasion, he observed an open *door* or opportunity for preaching the Gospel. But he had expected to meet Titus there to report how the church had reacted to his first epistle. Not seeing him at this time, his disappointment cut short the work and the apostle went on to Macedonia, another province made up of Greek people, lying just north of Greece proper.

Verse 14. Paul was induced to change his plans on account of the disappointment. However, a devoted servant of Christ will not permit such an experience to lead him astray, for his trust in the Lord will enable him to triumph. *Savour* means odor or fragrance, and Paul likens the knowledge of Christ to something pleasingly fragrant.

Verse 15. The pronoun *we* refers to any men who preach the Gospel. Such work is a sweet *savour* (taste or odor) in the estimation of Christ, and such is true whether the ones to whom it is preached accept it and are *saved*, or reject it and *perish*.

Verse 16. God does not wish that any soul will be lost, yet if the Gospel is rejected, it will become a *savour* (odor) of something that is deadly. The same Gospel will act as a life-giving odor for those who inhale it with sincerity. Hence the true preacher of God's word has the assurance that whether his hearer accepts or rejects it, the result will be as God expected it, and thereby it will "not return unto Him void" (Isaiah 55: 11). The results of preaching the truth of God will be the same regardless of who does the preaching. However, it was especially true of the apostles since they were the ones who first preached it and did it by direct inspiration. That is why Paul asserts that he *is sufficient* (qualified) *for these things*.

Verse 17. Paul emphasizes his fitness for the aforesaid work, and specifies one qualification, namely, that he is not one who corrupts the word of God. *Sincerity* means a state of being pure or unmixed, and such was the kind of preaching Paul was doing; he gave it to the people unmixed with human traditions.

2 Corinthians 3

Verse 1. In reference to the declarations in the closing verses of the preceding chapter, Paul implies a denial that they were given in the spirit of boastfulness, of which he evidently had been accused by some persons in Corinth. His work was so well known in that city that he did not even need any commendation from outside sources. *As some others* refers to men coming to or going from the vicinity of Corinth who were not so well known, and who had to be provided with letters of commendation as credentials.

Verse 2. *Ye are our epistle;* Paul founded the church in Corinth (Acts 18: 1-11). *Known and read of all men.* That congregation was very strong and became known generally as the work of Paul. Such information was spread not only through the regular channels of news, but the work of the apostle in Corinth was so precious to his heart, that he imparted the information to others. (See chapter 9: 2.)

Verse 3. The gist of Paul's figurative verses is that the lives of the Corinthians constituted an epistle, because they were displaying the principles that Christ taught. The agency through whom the teaching was written to them was the apostle, who was enabled to do such work by the Spirit of God. In contrast with the law of Moses that was written on tables of stone, this epistle was written on the human heart or mind of the Corinthians.

Verse 4. Having described the situation in the preceding verse, Paul affirms his confidence in the correctness of that description in the present verse.

Verse 5. Paul explains the entire qualification for his part in the preceding program, by giving God the honor for the source of such sufficiency.

Verse 6. *Ministers* is from the same Greek word as "deacon." Thayer's general definition is, "one who executes the commands of another, especially of a master; a servant, attendant, minister." Paul was *made able* to administer the commands of Christ by the Spirit of God as stated in verse 3. *New* is from KAINOS, which Thayer defines at this place, "new, which as recently made is superior to what it succeeds." *Testament* is from DIATHEKE, which Thayer defines, "a compact, covenant." In connection with our present passage he says, "we find in the New Testament two distinct covenants spoken of, namely, the Mosaic and the Christian, with the former of which the latter is contrasted." The latter covenant is the one of which Paul was made an able minister. *Letter . . . spirit.* Any document intended for the guidance of human beings would have to be expressed in some language and hence would need to use letters. However, some special sense is here attached to the term which will be seen in the following verses. *Letter killeth.* In Romans 8: 2 Paul calls the first covenant the "law of sin and death," because it inflicted physical death upon those who committed serious violation of it (Hebrews 10: 28). Under the law of the Spirit men are suffered to live physically in spite of their sins, and also may live eternally if they will make the necessary reformation of life.

Verse 7. The Mosaic covenant is called the *ministration of death* for the reason shown in Hebrews 10: 28, together with the comments on the preceding verse. The superiority of the new covenant over the old would not mean much, unless it is known that the old one also was important. Hence Paul reminds the reader that in administering that first one, the face of Moses became so bright with its glory that the children of Israel could not endure looking directly into his face. (See Exodus 34: 29-35.) *Which was to be done away.* This statement refers to the covenant that was written on the tables of stone, namely, the ten commandments.

Verse 8. The original word for *rather* is defined by Thayer, "to a greater degree." Paul justifies his contrast by the fact that the first covenant (though glorious) was written on stone and also it "was to be done away," while the second was a ministration of the Spirit.

Verse 9. This verse refers to the same contrast that is considered in the preceding ones but with slightly different terms. *Ministration of condemnation* alludes to the same thought as that in the words "sin and death" in Romans 8: 2. *Ministration of righteousness* is used of the Gospel or new covenant, because in it is revealed "the righteousness of God" by faith. (See Romans 1: 17.) *Exceed* is used in the same sense as *rather* in verse 8.

Verse 10. *Had no glory* is said in a comparative sense only, for Paul has already shown the first covenant to be very glorious. However, it was nothing when compared with the second; it was glorified by being given through the Spirit.

Verse 11. This verse is an unanswerable refutation of a prominent but perverse doctrine in the world today. Certain followers of a visionary old woman maintain that the sabbath law is still binding on Christians. As an effort to evade the inconsistencies of their heresy, they assume a distinction between what they call the "ceremonial law" written by Moses, and the ten-commandment law written by the Lord. They admit that the law of Moses was to be done away, but maintain that the law of God (the ten commandments) was never to be abolished. But we know Paul is writing about the ten commandments in this chapter, for he says they were written on tables of stone, while Moses wrote his "ceremonial law" in a book. Also, our present verse plainly says the covenant that was written on the stones *IS done away*, while something else (the law of the Spirit) *remaineth*. It would be impossible for language to state a more complete and direct refutation of any theory, than the present chapter does of the Christ-dishonoring heresy of the Sabbatarians.

Verse 12. *Plainness* is correctly rendered "boldness" in the margin of some Bibles. This boldness was caused by Paul's abiding confidence in the perpetuity of the law of Christ. The law of Moses as a religious standard was ended by that of Christ (Romans 10: 4), and His law of the Spirit took its place.

Verse 13. Paul has been showing some contrasts between the old and new laws, and another one is shown here. He does it by making a figurative use of the vail that Moses put over his face. That vail was a literal one and was used as a literal shield for the eyes of the children of Israel. But as the glare on the face of Moses was a symbol of the glory of the old covenant, the hiding of that glare constituted (in Paul's figurative use of it) a concealment of the glory of that covenant. That covenant, though glorious, was destined to be done away, which truth was not realized by the children of Israel. Hence their failure to see the glory of that covenant that was destinued to come to an end, is used by the apostle to symbolize their failure to realize the truth, namely, that it was to be abolished. *And not as Moses*, etc., means that Paul would not try to hide part of the glory of the new covenant, but instead he would "use great plainness [boldness] of speech" (verse 12).

Verse 14. Paul continues his figurative use of the vail, and likens it to the unbelief of the Jews concerning the temporary use of the old covenant, and the permanent use of the new under Christ. As a result, even down to the days of the apostle, when the children of Israel read the Old Testament, that vail of unbelief prevented them from realizing that the glory of that covenant was to be ended under Christ.

Verse 15. This verse is virtually a repetition of the preceding one, with the *heart* being used in the sense of the *mind* as in verse 14.

Verse 16. The pronoun *it* stands for the *heart* in the preceding verse. Of course the heart and mind of a man are the same, meaning the mental faculty by which he either believes or disbelieves a truth proposed to him. Paul here plainly predicts that the heart of the Jewish nation will some day turn to the Lord. That is the same truth that is taught in Romans 11: 26. (See the comments on that passage in Volume 1 of the New Testament Commentary.) The removal of this vail of unbelief is predicted in Isaiah 25: 7, where the connection clearly shows the prophet is making a prediction of the Gospel Dispensation. It all means that the Jews as a nation will finally give up their rejection of Christ, and will recognize Him as the Messiah promised in the Old Testament.

Verse 17. *That Spirit* means the one referred to in verse 3 and others in the chapter. The Lord is that Spirit in the sense that He gave the new covenant to the world through the inspired apostles, and whoever receives that covenant enters into a state of liberty—freedom from the old law.

Verse 18. This highly figurative verse is based upon the incident when the face of Moses was vailed, hiding the glory that was caused by the old covenant. As a contrast, Christians are to look with uncovered faces into the new covenant that was given by the Spirit of the Lord. When they look into it they see the Lord, and his glory is reflected as by a mirror. If I look into a mirror I will see what my appearance actually is. But Paul extends the figure by showing that the Spirit of the Lord is such that when I look into the inspired mirror, it affects my own spiritual appearance so that as I behold the image reflected in that mirror, I will see it change from time to time. Dropping the figurative form of speech, the verse means that the more we "look into the perfect law of liberty" (James 1: 25), admiring the Lord's image that we see therein, the more our own character will become like His. Reasoning from these truths, it may be appropriately said that professed Christians who show the least amount of the characteristics of Christ, are the ones who seldom gaze into the divine mirror, the New Testament.

2 Corinthians 4

Verse 1. Paul calls the new covenant system a *ministry*, which means a service under Christ. He regards it as being so rich and glorious in contrast with that under Moses, that he is determined to *faint not*. It means he will not falter in his service for Christ, since there is so much to be gained by serving Him.

Verse 2. To renounce means to give up and completely turn from a thing.

All *dishonesty* (shame) is wrong, but so much has been said about hiding or covering the face, the apostle specifies that form of wrongdoing in this passage. The servant of Christ should not resort to any *craftiness* (trickery) in his teaching of the truth of Christ. To handle the word of God deceitfully means to pervert it and mix it with human traditions in such a way as to deceive the hearer. He would be misled by the appearance of truth that he would see in the mixture. The Judaizers who had been troubling the Christians were doing that very thing, by mixing a part of the law of Moses with the teachings of the Gospel. *Manifestation of the truth* means to give the plain unmixed and "unvailed" truth to the people. Such teaching would be commended by *every man* who conscientiously desired that which is pleasing to God.

Verse 3. In this verse we have a comparison that results both in a likeness and a contrast, based on the statements of the preceding chapter. The likeness is in the fact that something is *hid* or covered ("vailed"), and the contrast is that the hiding pertains to a different class from those indicated at Sinai.

Verse 4. The Gospel is hid to the people who are *lost*, and yet they are the ones who most need it. However, it is not the fault of the Lord that these people are lost, but it is caused by their own blind unbelief. This condition is caused by a being whom Paul calls *the god of this world*. Luke 4: 6; John 12: 31; 14: 30; 16: 11; Ephesians 2: 2 shows us that Satan is the one referred to by Paul. Certainly he does not want anyone to be influenced by the Gospel, for therein is reflected the spiritual image of Christ, and when men see that and admire it, they will become like Him and hence will reject Satan.

Verse 5. Paul's own personality or importance was not the subject of his preaching, for he claimed only to be the servant of the church for the sake of Jesus to whom the church belongs. The subject of all his preaching was Christ as the Saviour and Lord of all who will believe and obey.

Verse 6. *Light to shine out of darkness* refers to the condition prior to the six days of creation described in Genesis 1. Verse 2 of that chapter says that "darkness was upon the face of the deep" [the sea], and verse 3 states that God said, "let there be light." This material event is used to illustrate the condition of spiritual darkness that all men have before they receive the light of divine truth. This light is displayed upon the divine face of Jesus Christ and is communicated to those who will open their hearts to receive the truth. When that is done the spiritual darkness that enshrouded the heart of the sinner is penetrated, and in the place of that darkness, or "out of that darkness," will shine the glorious light of the Gospel.

Verse 7. The *treasure* means the light of the Gospel, and the *earthen vessel* is a human being. When the effects of the great truth concerning Christ are observed by the world, and knowing that man in his natural ability is unable to accomplish such results, it will be concluded that the power has come from God.

Verses 8, 9. In this paragraph Paul mentions four sets of unfavorable terms, in each pair of which he shows a contrast. The distinction is made between what he is actually experiencing, and what he did not suffer his adversities to do unto him. In other words, what he was forced to endure was bad enough, but the other would have been worse which he would not allow to take place with him; he resolved to surmount all his trials. He did not permit his *troubles* to *distress* him, which means to cramp or hinder him in his work. He was sometimes puzzled and wondered "what was coming next," yet he never gave way to *despair*. In spite of his *persecutions*, the Lord sustained him and he also had the encouragement of some faithful brethren. To be *cast down* means to be prostrated, while to be *destroyed* means to be entirely put out of the contest, and Paul would not let his trials come to that end. He was sometimes "down," but never let himself be counted "out."

Verses 10, 11. A man does not literally die but once, yet Paul was constantly in danger of death. (See 1 Corinthians 15: 30, 31.) The apostle was willing to face all this threat of death, that he might display the kind of life Jesus led on the earth.

Verse 12. On account of his work as an apostle and being on the "firing line," Paul had to face this danger of death constantly. The Corinthian brethren were not thus exposed to death as Paul was, yet they were receiving the spiritual benefit of the sufferings imposed upon the apostle, and it meant spiritual life for them.

Verse 13. *The same spirit of faith* is

a quotation from Psalms 116:10. David's faith was so strong that he was willing to express it in words, regardless of what his enemies might do unto him. Paul affirms that he has that same spirit of faith, hence he is determined to speak the truth of Christ however much it might endanger his life among his enemies. This is a summing up of the attitude described in the verses beginning with verse 8.

Verse 14. Paul's confidence in the resurrection sustained him amid all of his persecutions. *Present us with you.* All men will be raised from the dead regardless of their manner of life, but the righteous will stand together in the group which Jesus will present as his own to the Father.

Verse 15. Paul endured many trials and inconveniences for the sake of his brethren in Corinth. He expected them to react with many expressions of gratitude in their prayers, thus giving God the glory for the *grace* or favor bestowed upon them.

Verse 16. *Faint* is the same as that in verse 1, and means to falter or be heartless, and Paul affirms that he would not suffer such to happen to him. That was because of his abiding faith in the promises of God, and the assurance that some day all "earthly things would cease to be, and life eternal fruit should bear." The *outward man* means the fleshly body that is the subject of persecutions and also is subject to the frailty of age and infirmity. While such changes are going on, the *inward man* (the soul or spirit) is living on and on and growing stronger each day and gaining much of that strength from the very trials that the enemy thought would cast him down in despair.

Verse 17. *Light affliction* and *moment* are used in a comparative sense. The first can affect the outward man only (Luke 12:4, 5), and the second applies to this life only. On the other hand, the glory that shall be given to the faithful will be eternal in its *weight* (or worth) and endless in its duration.

Verse 18. *Look not* means not to be unduly concerned about it. *Things which are seen* means the present physical trials. *Not seen* means the spiritual reward in the next world, and that will be eternal in character and endless in duration.

2 Corinthians 5

Verse 1. *Know* is from EIDO which has a wide range of meanings. In the present passage Thayer defines it, "it is well known, acknowledged." Hence it does not mean knowledge as different from faith, but rather that something is so well established that no doubt can be felt about it. *Earthly house* means the fleshly body that is the victim of persecutions as set forth in the preceding chapter. *Tabernacle* is applied to it because it is the home of the spirit of man while in this world. *Dissolve* denotes that something is thrown down, as a building might be taken down and its use discontinued. *Building of God* means the spiritual body into which the present one of the saints will be changed when Jesus comes *from heaven* (Philippians 3:21).

Verse 2. *In this we groan* refers to the natural desire that every man has for something better than he now has in his fleshly body with all of its tendencies toward disease and decay. (See Romans 8:22, 23.) *House which is from heaven;* the design of this house, and the power of carrying it out, exists in heaven the place of God.

Verse 3. Our spiritual being is not satisfied without a form or immaterial body to be associated with it.

Verse 4. The first clause of this verse is the same as that in the beginning of verse 2. *Being burdened* with the weight of fleshly infirmities creates a desire for relief. The desire is not merely to be relieved of the fleshly weight, but also that we may receive another kind of body for our soul. *Mortality* is from THNETOS, which Thayer defines, "liable to death, mortal," and hence life means the opposite. The saved will have their bodies changed into a form that will not be subject to death, for it will be like that of Jesus (Philippians 3:21; 1 John 3:2).

Verse 5. *Wrought us for the selfsame thing* means that God has worked matters to accomplish this very result. *Earnest* means a pledge or foretaste of a more complete favor yet to come. Such an assurance was given in miraculous measure to the apostle, and is bestowed in a lesser measure upon all Christians. This is done in the church which is the body of Christ, and by the spiritual blessings that come to all faithful disciples of Christ.

Verse 6. Paul was never made uneasy by the threat of persecutions, for if "worst came to worst" and his enemies even slew him, he would then go into the presence of the Lord. On the other hand, as long as his soul was in its *home in the body*, he would be absent from the Lord. Hence the enemy could do nothing to make his condition less desirable. This accounts for his resolute firmness when in the midst of the severest persecutions, or even when it seemed that death was near. (See 1 Corinthians 15: 30-32.)

Verse 7. *Sight* means the appearances of things in the present life, many of which are threatening and otherwise undesirable. *Faith* opens up before the apostle (as well as all other disciples) a vision of the Lord's presence. With such an incentive, the servant of Christ will *walk* or pursue his course while on the earth.

Verse 8. Paul's personal preference is expressed in this verse, which is the same thing that he does in Philippians 1: 23. Were it not for the good he could do while remaining in the world, he would rather die and go to be with the Lord.

Verse 9. Not knowing how nor by what means he would be taken out of the land of the living, the apostle was determined so to live that he would be prepared to stand approved whenever the time came to go into judgment with Him.

Verse 10. *We must all appear* is especially significant because Paul had referred to his responsibility regardless of when or how he would end his life. The thought is in keeping with his discourse delivered in Athens (Acts 17: 31), and with Peter's statement in Acts 10: 42 that Jesus was ordained to be the judge of the quick (living) and the dead. *Receive the things.* The last word has no separate word in the original; the phrase means to receive something from the Judge in view of the *things* that were done while living in the fleshly body. *According.* This word has been perverted by those who wish to defend the heresy commonly called "degrees of reward and punishment." Such a use of it wholly disregards Paul's own application which is in the same verse, namely, whether the things done are *good* or *bad*. There are only two kinds of deeds that can possibly be done, and they come under one or the other of these two words. By the same token, there can be only two kinds of reward bestowed upon man, namely, a crown of life for the *good* or a sentence of death for the *bad*, and it will be administered *according* to whichever a man has done.

Verse 11. *Terror* is from PHOBOS, and Thayer defines it virtually the same as Robinson, but the latter gives a somewhat fuller definition which is, "fear, reverence, respect, honor," and he explains it at our passage to mean, "a deep and reverential feeling of accountability to God or Christ." Paul knew that such a feeling should be had toward the Lord, and it caused him to persuade men to prepare for the judgment day. *Made manifest unto God.* Everything a man does is known to God, which is one of the reasons Paul was constrained to do his duty by warning his fellow creatures against the day of final accounts. He believed that his work was so well known to the Corinthians that they could conscientiously commend him.

Verse 12. *Commend not ourselves.* Paul believes it would be better to let others do the praising of his work, hence he leaves that privilege to the Corinthians. Since self-praise is sometimes criticized, if Paul had indulged in that too much, his friends in Corinth would have been approached by the enemy with criticism of their leader (the apostle). But if the commendations were of their own formation, it would silence those pretenders who were not speaking from the heart.

Verse 13. Festus accused Paul of being beside himself (Acts 26: 24), and it is implied that he was so accused by some at Corinth. He affirms that if it is true, the matter is between himself and his God and so no one else needs be concerned about it, since no information for man would be at stake. On the other hand, his *sober* or serious conduct and speech would be maintained for the benefit of his brethren. Paul does not specifically deny either of the charges, but lets the conclusion be drawn that all of his manner of action and speech is such as to show respect for God and consideration for the needs of man.

Verse 14. The motive for the zeal of Paul was the love of Christ, which was so great that He died for all mankind. The death of Christ was needed by all as was proved by the truth that He died for them, since the death would not have taken place had such an event not been necessary.

Verse 15. The death of Christ was done that all humanity might be brought from the dead (1 Corinthians 15: 22). But it was for the additional and far more important purpose of inducing men to live such lives while in this world, that when they are brought alive from the grave they may live in joy in the eternal world.

Verse 16. *No man after the flesh.* It makes no difference whether a man is a Jew or a Gentile in the apostle's estimation, for such a distinction counts for nothing in Christ Jesus. (See Galatians 6: 15.) It was necessary at one time to consider the fleshly nature of Christ, for that was a part of His qualification as the sacrifice for the sins of the world. But all that is past and He is at his Father's right hand in glory. Hence the time is no more present when such questions should be asked as to whether a man is a Jew or a Gentile, when the matter of his acceptance with God is considered. This fundamental truth was one thing that the brethren in Rome also had overlooked.

Verse 17. *New creature.* Adam was the first man in the first or material creation, and Christ is the first one in the second or spiritual creation (1 Corinthians 15: 45). When a man obeys the Gospel and comes into Christ, he is renewed spiritually and becomes a part of the new creation. *Old things are passed away* denotes that such a man is to follow a new kind of life, not one of sin (Romans 6: 4).

Verse 18. God is the creator of *all things*, whether the material world is being considered or the spiritual one. *Reconciled us* is true of all Christians, but Paul is here considering especially the relation of himself and the other apostles to the great work of the new creation. In order for man in general to be *reconciled* or brought to God in the spiritual creation, it was necessary for some agency to be empowered for the work. Such a service or *ministry* was given to the apostles.

Verse 19. *To wit* is an explanatory term, connecting the preceding verse with the present one. The Englishman's Greek New Testament renders this place, "How that God was in Christ," etc. God accomplishes his work for the salvation of the world through the Son. (See John 14: 6.) *Reconciling* is from KATALLASSO, which Thayer defines, "to receive one into his favor." It should be noted in which direction the reconciling is to be done, namely, from man to God. Man is the guilty party while God is the offended one. He has done nothing that needs to be made right, but man has separated himself from Him by his life of sin. However, God loves the creatures of His great wisdom and power, and desires to have them brought back into a life of righteousness. For this purpose the invitation is given for man to come into Christ by obedience to the Gospel. If he will do this, all his sins will be forgiven or not be *imputed*, which means they will not be longer held against him. The word by which the work is accomplished has been committed unto the apostles.

Verse 20. *Ambassadors* is from PRESBEUO, which is used twice in the New Testament (here and in Ephesians 6: 20). Both Thayer and Robinson give us the simple word that is used in our verse as their definition, which shows they understand the Greek term to mean the same as the English, namely, "the official representative of his own government." Hence there are no ambassadors for Christ living on earth today, for the apostles are still in authority (Matthew 28: 20). *Be ye reconciled.* The Corinthians had already been reconciled to God by their obedience to the Gospel (1 Corinthians 15: 1, 2), but it was necessary to remain faithful in order to continue in the faith or *be reconciled*.

Verse 21. *Be sin for us* means that Christ the sinless one, was made an offering for sin on behalf of mankind. This makes it possible for man to lead a life of righteousness by being in Him.

2 Corinthians 6

Verse 1. *We* has reference to Paul and the teachers associated with him. The important truth is stated that the workers were acting *together;* cooperation is an essential thing in the work of the Lord. *Receive not . . . in vain.* This is an exhortation for his readers to make good use of their opportunities in the cause of the Lord. It is a great favor *(grace)* to be given such an opportunity, but if they are neglectful in their duty, the whole proposition will be fruitless as far as their salvation is concerned.

Verse 2. The present verse is enclosed in parentheses; however, it is directly related to verse 1. In that place the apostle exhorts the Corinthians not to let the offer of salvation to them be in vain. The present one is a quotation from Isaiah 49: 8, and the connection of that passage shows the prophet was predicting the offer of salvation to the Gentiles. The Corinthians were Gentiles and hence were among the ones to whom the prediction applied. That prediction was in effect at the time Paul was writing, hence he informs them *now is the accepted time.* That is why he insists that they make good use of the opportunity.

Verse 3. This verse goes back to the first one and connects the actions with the "workers together" who were Paul and the other preachers of the Gospel. *Offence* is from PROSKOPE, which Thayer defines, "an occasion of stumbling," and explains it to mean, "to do someting which causes others to stumble." One meaning of the original word for *ministry* is "service," and Paul means the service of preaching the Gospel. If the preachers were to set a bad example and cause others to do wrong, then the very truth they were preaching would be blamed for it, though unjustly. But Christians should "practice what they preach," and thus not give others any excuse for doing wrong.

Verse 4. Instead of *giving offence* (see preceding verse), Paul and his co-workers were striving to live in such a way that others would approve them, and regard them as true ministers of God. Such approved conduct was patiently maintained even when conditions were unfavorable. *Afflictions* were sometimes imposed upon them by their enemies. The original for *necessities* is defined by Thayer, "calamity, distress, straits." *Distresses* is similar to the preceding word but not quite as physical. It has special reference to situations where the mind is in a state of perplexity, being anxious about what is coming next.

Verse 5. *Stripes* means blows or wounds inflicted with a heavy rope or leather thong (Acts 16: 23, 33). *Imprisonments* refers to those unjustly imposed on him, such as that in the passage in Acts just cited. *Tumults* means "disturbances, disorders," such as are recorded in Acts 14: 19; 19: 29; 21: 30, which were caused by the presence and teaching of Paul. *Labors* is from an original that means any intense activities, whether in body or mind, that are caused by the service to Christ. *Watchings* and *fastings* pertain to the many seasons of anxiety that Paul was forced to undergo, occasioned by the uncertainties in the activities of the foe.

Verse 6. This and the next verse should be connected with "approving ourselves" in verse 4. The verses are to specify the items in their conduct by which they were to be "approved." *Pureness* literally means "without mixture." Paul endeavored to lead a life "unspotted from the world" (James 1: 27). *Knowledge* denotes the information that had been received from the Lord by inspiration. *Longsuffering* means patience in dealing with the rebellious, and *kindness* indicates a gentle attitude toward those who would mistreat the apostle. *By the Holy Ghost* (or Spirit) means he regulated his work for the Lord by being thus divinely guided. *Love unfeigned* signifies a genuine interest in the welfare of others and not merely a pretended one.

Verse 7. *Word of truth* was that offered in the Gospel, as opposed to the false theories of the Greek philosophers. *Power of God* was given credit for his success and not placing it on his individual ability. *Armor of righteousness*. The strongest protection one can have against any successful attack upon his character that the enemy may make, is a life of constant righteousness. That is why it is called a "breastplate" in Ephesians 6: 14.

Verse 8. Paul reverts to the line of thought presented in verses 4 and 5, with the exception that he states both favorable and unfavorable conditions in contrast with each other. He was shown *honor* by some and *dishonor* by others. *Evil report* means he was slandered by his enemies, but was commended — given *good report* by others. Was accused of being a *deceiver* although he never was guilty of falsehood.

Verse 9. He was *unknown* from the standpoint of worldly fame, yet was *well known* to God and many faithful disciples. *Dying* in that he was threatened with death daily, yet was able to live through the grace of God. *Chastened* with many trials and persecutions, but not suffered to be physically put to death.

Verse 10. *As sorrowful*. The conduct of wicked people and the prospect of their terrible future, caused Paul to be affected with sorrow for them; yet he *rejoiced* over the reward that he believed was awaiting himself and all other faithful disciples of Christ. He was *poor* in this world's goods, yet in giving the Gospel to mankind he bestowed upon them the spiritual riches that cannot be valued in gold (1 Peter 1: 7). The last clause is virtually the same in meaning as the preceding one, except Paul applies the possession of the spiritual riches to himself and his co-workers.

Verse 11. The plural pronoun has been used through many of the passages in this book, because Timothy and other workers were associated with Paul in most of the experiences mentioned. However, they have a special application to the apostle, and some things would have been true of him only. The reader should bear these remarks in mind, regardless of which form of pronoun is used in the comments. *Mouth is open* signifies that Paul spoke freely to the Corinthians. *Enlarged* is from PLATUNO, which Thayer defines, "to make broad, to enlarge," and he explains it at this place to mean "our heart expands itself to receive you into it, i. e., to welcome and embrace you in love."

Verse 12. *Straitened* means to be cramped or restricted, and *bowels* is used figuratively in reference to the affections. Paul is complaining of the lack of affection mainfested by the Corinthians. (See chapter 12: 15.) He means to tell them their lack of affectionate expression for him is not his fault, for his heart was large enough for all their love (preceding verse); the fault is their own restriction.

Verse 13. This verse requests the Corinthians to "loosen up" or enlarge their heart to make room for the apostle's affections, and thus *recompence* (or reward) him for the love he has been showing for them.

Verse 14. Notwithstanding all that can justly be said against Christians marrying those who are not, it is a perversion to apply this passage to that subject. The same subject is under consideration in verse 17, where the apostle commands them to *come out from among them*. If Paul was writing in view of the marriage relation, then the command would require Christian husbands or wives to separate from their companions who were not Christians. But that would contradict 1 Corinthians 7: 12-16 and 1 Peter 3: 1, 2, and we are sure the Bible does not contradict itself. The passage at hand refers to religious organizations, or any such that profess to offer religious benefits to the world. That would include the ones that make direct professions of a religious character, such as the sectarian organizations, also those whose claims for spiritual rewards are only a part of their avowed purpose, such as the various fraternal organizations. The New Testament church is the only organization that has any scriptural right to offer spiritual instructions and other benefits to the world. (See Ephesians 3: 10, 11, 21, and 1 Timothy 3: 15.)

Unequally yoked is from HETERZUGER, and this is the only place the word he is used in the Greek New Testament. Thayer defines it, "to come under an unequal or different yoke; to have fellowship with one who is not an equal." He then explains it to mean, "the apostle is forbidding Christians to have intercourse [familiar association] with idolaters." Robinson's explanation of the word is virtually the same as that of Thayer. The remainder of the verse (and several verses following) shows specific reasons for the command. Idolatrous teaching and practices certainly constitute *unrighteousness*, and Christians can have nothing in common with such a system. *Light* and *darkness* are used figuratively, referring to truth and error as pertaining to spiritual matters. *Communion* means fellowship, indicating a common sharing in the same thing. Christians believe in the truth of the Lord and hence cannot be a partner with those who teach error.

Verse 15. There are several words that have similar meanings, but Paul uses the various ones for the sake of completeness in thought, and also for the sake of being more pleasant to the ear of the reader. *Concord* is virtually the same as "agreement," which is used later in the chapter. Thayer says *Belial* is "a name of Satan," and he is placed as opposed to Christ because there is no unity between them. *Infidel* is the same as *believer* in the Greek with a negative prefix.

Verse 16. *Temple of God* is contrasted with *idols* because those heathen objects of worship were usually boused in buildings. in which the idolaters gathered for their religious exercises. *Ye are the temple* refers to the disciples as a congregation in which God dwells as the "guest of honor." It is true that 1 Corinthians 6: 19 says the bodies of Christians are temples of the Holy Ghost, but there is no difficulty, for the church is made up of individual disciples. *Their God . . . my people*. In the national life of the various groups of people existing in olden times, each group claimed some particular deity as its head or ruling spirit. By the same token, if Christians will be separate from all heathen and other unlawful religious associations, God will claim them as his people, and will allow them to own Him as their God.

Verse 17. *Come out from among them* denotes a complete separation from the thing spoken of, having nothing to do with any of its activities, nor having any interests in common with it. The Gentiles were largely given to the practices of idolatry, and the Corinthians had been mixed up with such relations. *Unclean* means to be foul in a ceremonial as well as literal sense, and the practices of idolatrous nations were defiled in both senses. Their complete separation from all such was a condition on which the Lord would be willing to receive them.

Verse 18. The relation of parent and child is one of the most intimate ones possible to mankind. *Sons* and *daughters* are terms that apply to individuals, but it is true that the church which is the temple of God is composed of individuals, hence the terms are entirely appropriate here. This relation is assured the Corinthians on condition that they maintain a complete separation from all alliances that would corrupt them ceremonially or physically.

2 Corinthians 7

Verse 1. *These promises* are the ones mentioned in the last two verses of the preceding chapter. The prospect of such favors from God should be a sufficient motive for all Christians to do their utmost to obtain them. Since our bodies are made in the image of God (Genesis 1: 26; 5: 1, 2), then a spirit for man was formed within him (Zechariah 12: 1), he should wish to keep that body and spirit clean both physically and spiritually. *Filthiness* is from MOLUSMOS, which is not used in any other place in the Greek New Testament. Thayer defines it by the single word "defilement," then explains it to mean "an action by which anything is defiled." Since this is the only passage where the word is found, we know that by "anything" the author of the lexicon includes both the flesh and spirit of man. In its application to Christians today, therefore, it would include all false religious teaching, which defiles the spirit, and also that which defiles the body, such as narcotics, opiates and alcohol, when used as a habit.

Holiness is commanded here and elsewhere (Hebrews 12: 14), therefore we know it is something that can be accomplished today. The word has been perverted by false teachers, and made to mean something of a supernatural or special attainment, that requires a direct operation of the Lord upon the heart of the disciple after he has come into the church. The term is from five different Greek words in the New Testament, but all of them have virtually the same meaning, which is that relation and practice of a Christian that makes him separate from the worldly life of sin. It has the same meaning as the words "righteousness" and "godliness," and all other terms in the New Testament that are applied to Christians.

Verse 2. *Receive us* is said in the same sense as chapter 6: 12, 13. The three denials of the verse refer to the severe rebukes that the apostle had given them previously; that in so doing he had not done them any injustice.

Verse 3. *Speak not to condemn*. Paul knew that some of the Judaizers had accused him of such treatment toward the Corinthian church, but he was not making the application to all of them. *Said before* refers to the passage cited in the preceding paragraph.

Verse 4. Paul felt *bold* in the sense of being greatly encouraged because of the attitude of the Corinthian church toward his former epistle. It gave him joy and comfort notwithstanding the many tribulations he was suffering for the Gospel.

Verse 5. *Flesh had no rest* denotes that his discomfort was from the standpoint of his temporal feelings, not that his spiritual state of mind was disturbed. (See the comments at chapter 2: 12, 13.) The *fightings* were the conflicts with visible enemies, and the *fears* were from his anxiety over the situation at Corinth.

Verse 6. God uses various means to comfort His faithful children. In this case it was done by sending Titus to Paul with the good news of the attitude of the Corinthian brethren toward the first epistle.

Verse 7. Paul was not selfish in his enjoyment of good news. He found joy in seeing that Titus also was comforted over the good state of the church at Corinth. *Earnest desire* indicates they wish to do their duty. *Mourning* refers to their sincere sorrow over their wrong in the matter of the fornicator. *Fervent mind toward me* denotes a kindly feeling toward Paul, even though he had rebuked them sharply.

Verse 8. A loving parent would regret the necessity of punishing his child, but would not regret having done so. That would be especially true if the punishment produced the desired results. That is the meaning of this verse, for the first epistle caused the Corinthians to be genuinely sorry for their wrongs.

Verse 9. The mere fact that they were made sorry did not cause Paul's rejoicing, but their sorrow was the kind that caused them to repent. *After a godly manner* means their sorrow was the kind that pleased God; hence the letter from Paul had not damaged them in any way, but rather had benefitted them.

Verse 10. Mere sorrow for sin will not cause one to repent, for he may only be sorry he was detected and punished. But if he is sorry for his sin because it is offensive to God, it will cause him to do what he can to make himself right. Such a sorrow is *not to be repented of*, which means it is not to be regretted. To be sorry only because of being taken in sin is a *sorrow of the world*, and such a state of mind *worketh death*, as it did in the case of Judas whose worldly sorrow brought him both physical and spiritual death. (See Matthew 27: 3-5; John 17: 12; Acts 1: 25.)

Verse 11. In the preceding verse the apostle makes only a general reference to the good effect that will be produced by godly sorrow, but in this he specifies a number of fruits of such sorrow. *Carefulness* means concern and diligence in attending to their duty. *Clearing of yourselves* all comes from APOLOGIA, and Thayer's definition is, "verbal defence, speech in defence." Such a speech would be called for only where one is accused of wrongdoing, whether guilty or not. The Corinthians were guilty of wrong in the case of the fornicator, and only by doing their duty could they be able to make their defence. *Indignation* was felt by them when they were made to realize the guilt of the man they had been tolerating in their fellowship. *Fear* means respect for the Lord, and concern over what might result were they not to deal with the guilty man as they should. *Zeal* is virtually the same in effect as *carefulness* used above. *Revenge* means punishment of the guilty man by the proper act of discipline. Romans 12: 19 says that vengeance belongs to the Lord, and when a church inflicts scriptural discipline on a guilty member, it is the Lord's way of administering vengeance upon him. To be *clear* means to be "pure from every fault" according to Thayer. If a congregation fails to exercise corrective discipline upon a guilty member, his guilt becomes that of the congregation also.

Verse 12. The fornicator at Corinth, and the man whose wife he was wrongfully using, were not the only ones concerned in the sad affair. In 1 Corinthians 5: 6 it is declared that "a little leaven leaveneth the whole lump," which refers to this case, and shows that the whole church was affected by the case. Paul wished the brethren to know he had much care on their behalf and hence urged them to do their duty.

Verse 13. Paul found joy in seeing Titus comforted (verse 7), now he has joy over that of the Corinthians, also rejoices that Titus is *refreshed* or encouraged.

Verse 14. Paul had *boasted* (spoken words of commendation) of the merits of the church at Corinth, even before the developments were completed. Now he is *not ashamed* (has no regrets) since his praise of them has been proven true.

Verse 15. Actual obedience is more important than mere professions of agreement. The Corinthians not only showed a friendly attitude toward the epistle of Paul (sent to them by Titus), but confirmed it by doing their duty, and this was also accompanied with friendliness to Titus for having brought the message to them.

Verses 16. Confidence in our brethren is helpful in the struggle against the common enemy, for it strengthens our faith to see that the Gospel has its influence for good upon others.

2 Corinthians 8

Verse 1. *We do you to wit* is an obsolete translation that means, "we will make known to you," etc.

Verse 2. The subject of this and the next chapter is the contribution for the needy disciples in Judea. Paul has referred to it in 1 Corinthians 16: 1, and it is mentioned in Acts 11: 28-30. The preceding verse refers to the contribution of the Macedonians as the grace of God being bestowed upon them. That means that God enabled them to make a liberal gift in spite of their comparative poverty and their own trials as Christians among enemies. What adds to the merits of their giving is their *joy* at being given the privilege of performing such a worthy deed.

Verse 3. No person can actually do more than his *power* to do, but he can have a willingness that goes beyond it, and these churches had that frame of mind.

Verse 4. The sincere interest those churches had in the matter was indicated by their insisting upon Paul to receive their contribution, that he might pass it on to the needy ones. *Fellowship* is from the same Greek word that is used in Acts 2: 42, and means partnership, or a sharing of something with another.

Verse 5. *Not as we hoped.* The liberality of the Macedonian churches went beyond Paul's expectations. He accounts for it by the fact that they *first gave their own selves to the Lord.* When disciples realize that they are actually not their own (1 Corinthians 6: 19, 20), they may be willing to consider "all that they have and are" as belonging to the Lord.

Verse 6. *As he had begun.* Titus began the work of directing the Corinthian brethren in this matter of fellowship (chapter 12: 18), and the favorable reaction of the church caused Paul to urge Titus on to its completion.

Verse 7. The virtues of *faith, utterance, knowledge, diligence* and *love,* pertained principally to spiritual matters. The Corinthian brethren *abounded* in them, which encouraged Paul to exhort them to abound also in the *grace* (favor) of bestowing temporal benefits upon the poor saints.

Verse 8. *Not by commandment.* We know the apostle did not mean the giving was not commanded, for that would contradict 1 Corinthians 16: 1, where he says he had "given order" to other churches on this subject, and passed the same instruction on to this church. The idea is that he wished the brethren to be stimulated unto the work by the good example of others. This shows it is right to refer to the liberality of others when exhorting a congregation to bestir itself in the matter of giving.

Verse 9. Much misplaced sentiment has been expressed at this passage by teachers who wish to show how poor the Saviour was while on the earth. They will even quote Matthew 8: 20 and apply it here, when that passage has nothing to do with the subject of poverty as we commonly use that term. (See the comments on that verse in volume 1 of the New Testament Commentary.) The poverty of Jesus was the opposite of his former riches, which was his possession and enjoyment of the glory of Heaven. He gave it all up that he might come among men to show them how they might come into possession of such eternal riches. He could not have set such an example had He retained his possession of those eternal joys and spiritual wealth continuously, instead of coming to the earth where he would be dispossessed of them.

Verse 10. The *forwardness* or willingness of the Corinthian brethren as to helping the needy ones in Judea, had caused them to begin the collections a year before.

Verse 11. Paul urges the brethren to "speed up" the program so earnestly begun before, carrying their *readiness* of mind into action or actual *performance,* by contributing out of their possessions.

Verse 12. To begin with, in order for the gift to be acceptable to God, it must be prompted by a *willing mind.* The size of the gift that is required in order for it to be *accepted* is based wholly on what they *have,* or, as 1 Corinthians 16: 2 states it, according "as God hath prospered" them.

Verse 13. The actual amount the Lord requires from each disciple is not the same in all cases when stated in "dollars and cents." That would cause the more prosperous to be *eased,* while the less fortunate in worldly goods would be *burdened.*

Verse 14. The *equality* denotes that all members of the body of Christ should be equally interested in the welfare of others. If such were the case, then those in need would be assisted by the ones in better circumstances. (See 1 Corinthians 12: 26.)

Verse 15. This refers to the gathering of manna in the wilderness recorded in Exodus 16: 18, and Paul is making a spiritual application of it. (See the comments on that passage in volume 1 of the Old Testament Commentary.)

Verses 16, 17. Titus was always subject to the instructions of Paul, but his own interest in the Corinthian brethren also prompted him to act.

Verse 18. The original for *praise* is defined by Thayer, "approbation, commendation, praise." This brother had a good reputation among the churches for being true to the Gospel. He was sent with Titus as a moral protection aaginst any suspicion of misuse of the funds he was carrying.

Verse 19. This *brother* was not merely the selection of Paul, but he had been chosen by these same churches among which he had the *praise,* to be with Paul in his traveling to and fro while collecting the *grace* (gift) to be turned over to the needy ones.

Verse 20. These precautionary measures were taken to prevent any questioning as to how the money was being handled. A man who is entrusted with the property of another should wish to protect himself from any suspicion of dishonesty. I have known of cases where brethren who handled the money of the congregation would resent all inquiries about the amount in their hands. They would probably make some peevish remark such as, "if you think I am not honest, I will just turn the job over to someone else." There is something wrong with a brother who takes such an attitude, to say the least, and he lays himself open to just suspicion.

Verse 21. The Lord knows the heart of every man, but human beings do not. It is necessary, therefore, that a man who handles the money contributed by others, should so conduct himself that his *honest things* will be evident to all.

Verse 22. To put the matter beyond all danger of questioning, Paul sent still another brother along with Titus, besides the one mentioned in verse 18. We are not told his name, but he was no stranger to Paul, for he had shown himself diligent in many things. His diligence was strengthened by his confidence in the Corinthian brethren. *(I have in you* should be translated "he has in you.")

Verse 23. This verse constitutes an apostolic recommendation for Titus and the brethren who were going with him. It is somewhat on the same basis as the foregoing statements, namely, an assurance that the men entrusted with the important work at hand were worthy.

Verse 24. Paul had boasted (spoken in complimentary terms) to these brethren, of the good spirit of the Corinthians. They are requested to verify it by their treatment of the messengers upon arrival among them.

2 Corinthians 9

Verse 1. It was *superfluous* or unnecessary to write as far as their general state of mind was concerned, as to giving to the poor ones in Judea.

Verse 2. Their being ready for a year proved the Corinthians had the right attitude on the subject. Paul had *boasted* (spoken in complimentary terms) to the churches in Macedonia of the *forwardness* of the churches in Achaia (another name for Greece in which Corinth was located. *Your zeal hath provoked very many.* (Chapter 8: 8.)

Verse 3. It is easy to forget about a duty, especially if the occasion for doing it is delayed some time. Hence Paul sent the brethren on ahead to remind the brethren at Corinth about it to be ready, lest his boasting should be in vain.

Verse 4. The brethren from Macedonia would be with Paul when he came to take up the money at Corinth. If they had forgotten to get ready it would make the apostle feel as if they had "let him down." *That we say not ye*. Even if such a condition should be found upon arrival, Paul would take the humiliation upon himself only, and he wished to avoid it by this reminder.

Verse 5. Much of this verse is the same as verse 3. *Bounty,* not *covetousness*. The first word means something bestowed as a blessing and therefore as a free gift. If the donation is prompted by the desire to bless another, then the gift will not be so stinted as to show the donor to be covetous, nor that he was making the contribution under the impression that he "had to do it."

Verse 6. This verse is said on the general principle in nature that a man's harvest is regulated in part by the kind of seed that he sows. The harvest in this case consists in the good being accomplished by the fellowship, and the approval of God for their generous contribution toward the needy and worthy disciples of Christ.

Verse 7. *Purposeth* is from PROAIREO, and it is the only place it is used in the Greek New Testament. Thayer defines it, "to bring forward, bring forth from one's stores; to bring forth for one's self, to choose for one's self before another, i. e., to prefer; to purpose." The word gives us two thoughts, namely, that a man should ponder over the amount he is going to give, and also that no one else can do this pondering for him. As to the amount he decides to give, and the spirit in which he does it, that must be determined by the following part of this verse together with verse 6. *Grudgingly* is from LUPE which Thayer defines, "sorrow, pain, grief." After a man decides what he is able to give, it should not be painful to him when he does it. The familiar suggestion that "we should give until it hurts" is therefore unscriptural. *Of necessity* means not to give with the feeling that one "has to."

Cheerful is from HILAROS (similar to our English word "hilarious"), and is the opposite of giving *grudgingly*. As to the amount one should be glad to give, that is to be determined by 1 Corinthians 16: 2 and 2 Corinthians 8: 12, spurred by the exhortation in verse 6 of our present chapter.

Verse 8. In the "days of miracles" it sometimes happened that special literal favors were bestowed upon faithful disciples. But this matter is of too much importance to allow of such an application of the promise. Yet we can believe that the proper grace will be given to those who devote their time and possessions to the Lord.

Verses 9, 10. This paragraph takes the same comments as the preceding one. Matthew 6: 33 also should be considered in connection with the subject.

Verse 11. *Bountifulness* means liberality, and the faithful disciple who is disposed to be generous in his support of the cause of Christ, may expect to be able to perform the worthy service. *Through us*. The apostle was going to take the gifts of the Corinthians to the needy ones in Judea, which would cause them to give God thanks.

Verse 12. This expression of thanksgiving that would be caused by the help bestowed upon the poor saints, was as much valued by Paul as the actual relief of their needs by administration of the financial service.

Verse 13. *Professed subjects*. The Corinthian brethren carried out their profession for the Gospel by doing something practical on behalf of fellow disciples. This caused the recipients of the *distribution* (financial fellowship) to give God the glory, as being the main cause of the whole *experiment*.

Verse 14. The disciples in Judea also prayed for their benefactors. *Long after you* denotes an increasing feeling of interest in these brethren because of the grace or favor of God which they believed to be evident in them.

Verse 15. *Unspeakable* is from a Greek word that means "indescribable." In verse 13 the Gospel of Christ is given a prominent place in the situation, and verse 14 includes the *grace of God*. This wonderful relationship of the Jewish disciples in Judea with the Gentile brethren in Greece and Macedonia, was made possible by the Gospel of His Son. No wonder Paul calls it an *unspeakable* gift, for human language is incapable fully to describe it.

2 Corinthians 10

Verse 1. Up to the present passage Paul has used the pronoun of the first person in both the plural and singular forms. That was because most of his statements could apply to himself and the brethren associated with him, even though some of them may have applied to him in a special sense. (See the comments at chapter 6: 11.) But the words *I Paul* in this verse show he is speaking about himself only, and will be through the rest of the book. That is because certain Judaizing persons in the Corinthian church were opposing the apostle, making various accusations and complaints against him. He meets those charges in some very strong language. Paul refers to the meekness of Christ, and desires to be influenced by it in his approach to the brethren. *Presence am meek . . . absent am bold;* this was one of the complaints.

Verse 2. Paul admits that he is *base* or mild in *presence* or "outward appearance," in his attitude toward most of the brethren. However, he expects to be more *bold* or severe in his dealing with the Judaizing critics. But he *beseeches (you* is not in the original) or desires to avoid showing such an attitude toward the other members of the congregation. One of the accusations the critics were making was that Paul's conduct and teaching were prompted by his fleshly interests.

Verse 3. Paul will show that he is bound to walk *in the flesh* in that he is living in the fleshly body while on the earth, but that his activities are not *after* or according to the flesh.

Verse 4. *Weapons . . . not carnal.* This statement has been perverted to mean that Christians should not engage in warfare in defence of their country. It has nothing to do with that subject, but means that carnal or temporal weapons are not to be used in support of the Gospel. However, the apostle uses some of the terms of such warfare to illustrate that of the spiritual conflict against the enemy of righteousness. In carnal warfare it is necessary to pull down *strongholds* or barricades of the foe, and it means that Christians must attack sin in its strongest forms.

Verse 5. *Imaginations* is defined by Thayer, "a reasoning," and he explains it to mean, "such as is hostile to the Christian faith." There is no element that can do more injury to the cause of Christ than the false reasoning of the self-wise teacher. *Bringing into captivity* is a phrase based on carnal warfare. One objective of a military leader is to capture the soldiers in the opposite army. In some instances such captives have been made to do service for their captors, in which cases it would be better to capture them alive than to slay them in battle. Likewise in spiritual warfare, it is well to subdue the false reasoning of men, and if possible to turn their mental activities into service for Christ.

Verse 6. This *revenge* is the same as that in chapter 7: 11, being the Lord's way of taking vengeance on the workers of unrighteousness. However, it cannot be accomplished without the cooperation of the Christian soldiers in the spiritual warfare. That is why Paul states the condition; *when your obedience is fulfilled.*

Verse 7. Paul is still considering his critics who were boasting of their own importance, which had only some *outward* appearance for their support. But even if such an evidence were to be relied on for the claim of being a servant of the Lord, Paul could lay as much claim to it as his critics.

Verse 8. Paul could actually boast of his authority as an apostle, and he was not ashamed of such qualification were he called upon to resort to it in severe terms. Yet he would prefer to use it for their *edification* (upbuilding) rather than for their *destruction* or severe chastisement.

Verse 9. Regardless of what unpleasant effect the critic might pretend to receive from the letters of Paul, his motive in writing them was not merely to *terrify* them.

Verse 10. The gist of this verse is an attempt of the critic to belittle the work of Paul, by slighting remarks about his personal appearance and his manner of speech. This objector did not like the bold language in the first epistle because it sharply rebuked those at fault. Still feeling the sting of that letter, he pretends to have no fear of the personal appearance of the apostle, since a man so insignificant and *contemptible* (as he thought) as the apostle Paul, could not say or do anything that would humiliate him.

Verse 11. Paul assures this man that whether present or absent, his teaching against error would be the same, regardless of any supposed physical defects. This would be true because the apostle always wrote and spoke as the Holy Spirit guided him, so that his work was not originated with himself.

Verse 12. Paul's critics were inclined to praise themselves, and he was determined not to be like them. The rest of this verse means that the self-appointed judges of Paul formed their own standard of conduct among themselves. *Measuring themselves by themselves.* Each man was satisfied with his own standing if he was as good as his fellows to whom he compared himself.

Verse 13. The reader is again instructed not to be confused by the plural form of the pronoun. The definite phrase "I, Paul" in verse 1, and the subject matter of the closing verses of the chapter, make it certain the apostle is writing about himself only. Webster says the following of the word in question: "*We* is used for the singular *I* . . . by editors and other writers to keep an impersonal character or to avoid the egotistical sound of a repeated *I*. *Without our measure.* Paul had been accused of overstepping his bounds when he came to Corinth. He asserts that the *rule* or commission given to him included that city; that it *reached even unto you.* That was true, for Paul had been especially appointed to preach to the Gentiles.

Verse 14. *As though we reached not.* Had the commission given to Paul not included the city of Corinth, his going that far would have made him chargeable with stretching himself beyond his proper measure. *We are come* is equivalent to saying that his "assigned territory" reached as far as Corinth.

Verse 15. Paul believed in the phrase "honor to whom honor is due," and hence would not boast or take credit for work that was accomplished by another. But Corinth was within his allotted territory, therefore his *hope* was based on developments there. He believed that if the Corinthians made the proper showing of their professed faith, it would enlarge his "field of labor" so that he could do some more work beyond that locality around the city of Corinth.

Verse 16. *Line* is used in the sense of *rule* and *measure* in the previous verses. Paul would not go into another man's field of labor where the foundation work had been done already, then take advantage of it to have something for which to take credit.

Verse 17. *To glory in the Lord* would mean to give Him credit for all good work that might be accomplished. But even such apparently humble glorying would not be justified unless the work had been done in harmony with the Lord's will.

Verse 18. This verse explains why the preceding one is so worded. Self-approval will not count for anything in the great work professed to be done for Christ. (See verse 12.) The Lord will not commend any man on the basis of his comparison with some other man, but only on whether the work is in harmony with His will.

2 Corinthians 11

Verse 1. The original for *folly* is defined in the lexicon as "foolishness," but Paul is not using it in any radical sense. It is somewhat like a case of a doting parent over his child, where it is often remarked, "He is quite foolish about his boy or girl." *Bear with me* is rendered in the margin, "you do bear with me," which is endorsed by other commentators. The Corinthians generally had borne with Paul in his extreme earnestness and anxiety for them, but he wishes them to go along with him still further, because his concern for them is become more and more intense.

Verse 2. In old times the father or other near relative often arranged espousals (engagements) for another. When such an arrangement was made, the one who acted for the parties would be anxious that they be true to each other until the actual marriage time, and if any unfaithfulness should be indicated it would cause him to be jealous. Paul had led the Corinthians in obedience to Christ, which was the time they became engaged to Him, the marriage to be celebrated when the bridegroom comes for that purpose. (See Revelation 19: 7.)

Verse 3. Paul is continuing his comparison with the marriage relation and kindred subjects. A man who wishes to interfere with the engagement of a woman to some other man, will resort to deceptive means in order to seduce her. Likewise, the apostle fears that evil men may seduce the Corinthians by using the deceptive theories of the philosophers of Greece that the false teachers had adopted.

Verse 4. The last word of this verse has been supplied by the King James translators. The marginal reading gives it "with me," which is justified by both the original Greek and the connection in the passage. *If he that cometh*, etc., does not express any ques- as to whether these false teachers came with their evil doctrines, but rather that they actually were doing so. (See verses 19, 20.) Paul is reasoning that since they have been tolerating these unworthy teachers, they certainly ought to listen to him. Moffatt translates the last phrase, "Why not put up with me," which makes good sense and is also in agreement with the context.

Verse 5. In this verse Paul begins to show some reasons why they ought to "put up" with him. He not only was an apostle, but ranked with the *very chiefest apostles.*

Verse 6. *Rude* means unlearned or ignorant in his use of language. Paul is not admitting that he is thus lacking, but his enemies were making the charge and urging it as a reason for belittling his teaching. The apostle is reasoning that even if such a criticism were acknowledged, it would not affect his knowledge which was furnished him by the Spirit on account of his apostolic appointment. This knowledge had been *made manifest* by the supernatural deeds which he had performed at Corinth.

Verse 7. *Abasing myself* does not denote he had done anything improper or undignified, but supporting himself in part by his own labor, his enemies charged that it showed he was not really an apostle.

Verse 8. To *rob* does not necessarily mean to take something wrongfully. A man will say he robbed his bees, and yet he would not have done any unlawful act. Paul means he called upon other churches to support him in his work for the people of Corinth. The church at Philippi was one that supported Paul in his labors in other places (Philippians 4: 15). *Wages* means financial support for work in the Gospel field.

Verse 9. The preceding verse makes a general mention of receiving financial help from the church at Philippi, while this verse cites a more specific case of it. Philippi was in Macedonia, and the brethren from that country came to Corinth with a supply at a time when the apostle was in need; this made it unnecessary to call upon the Corinthians for help. He affirms further that he will continue to relieve them from such service, which was according to a special permit which he had been granted by the Lord (1 Corinthians 9: 17, 18).

Verse 10. By looking to such sources for temporal support, he could still boast of giving the Gospel freely in *Achaia*, another name for Greece, of which Corinth was an important city.

Verse 11. *Wherefore* means, why am I doing this? He then affirms that *God knoweth* it is not through any lack of love for them. (It was rather for an opposite reason.)

Verse 12. This verse tells why Paul pursued the course described above; it was to prevent the enemies from having any occasion for evil claims. *May be found even as we.* The false teachers would like to call upon the church for financial assistance on the ground they were preaching the Gospel. The example of Paul in preaching without charge would shame them out of making such an attempt upon the church.

Verse 13. These false teachers were able to mislead a great many brethren by trickery and other deceptive means, making themselves appear as apostles of Christ.

Verse 14. Satan is a supernatural being, and at times in the history of the world has manifested his power in various forms. He appeared to Eve in the form of a serpent (Genesis 3: 1). Sometimes he assumes the form of a roaring lion (1 Peter 5: 8). In our verse he is said to appear as an angel of light. It will not do to say this merely means evil men who are the agents of Satan, for the next verse mentions those characters as a separate group. We are not specifically told when Satan ceased making his appearance in these disguised forms to men on the earth. Evidently it was at the same time that other miraculous characters (both good and bad) passed out of the land (Zechariah 13: 2). He now does his work through evil human beings, to be mentioned in the next verse.

Verse 15. *Ministers* is from the same Greek word that its rendered "deacon" in other passages. Thayer's primary definition is, "one who executes the commands of another, especially of a master; a servant, attendant, minister." Hence Paul accuses these false teachers with executing the orders of Satan, but doing it under the guise of righteous workers. *Whose end . . . their works;* will reap as they sowed (Galatians 6: 8).

Verse 16. Paul does not admit being a fool to the extent charged; yet, be that as it may, he requests to be tolerated in his feeling. (See comments at verse 1.)

Verse 17. Paul does not put this privilege which he is claiming on the basis of a direct instruction from the Lord. He claims it only as a personal liberty, and on that ground reserves to himself the right to indulge himself in that enjoyment.

Verse 18. *After the flesh* is not said in the bad sense commonly attached to fleshly things. Paul is applying it to his personal experiences, which though they were unpleasant, yet since they were endured for the sake of the Gospel, he found a joy in them and of such an experience he boasts.

Verses 19, 20. These verses are referred to in the comments on verse 4. The argument Paul is making is that he is entitled to the friendly consideration of the brethren for his whim (as they seemed to think his ideas were), when they were giving these other persons such tolerance. Especially since the apostle had nothing questionable in his case, while these other men did have. This paragraph describes what they were doing and the Corinthians were "putting up" with it. The brethren considered themselves wise, yet they endured those they considered as fools; they even tolerated many injustices from these fools. An instance is that of being brought *into bondage* to the ordinances of the old law. Not that they literally were led to adopt those institutions, but suffered themselves to become confused over them. (See chapter 3.)

Verse 21. Paul had been *reproached* because of his bodily *weakness* (chapter 10: 1, 10) but he was not allowing that to humiliate him. Instead, the very weaknesses concerning which his enemies said he was acting *foolishly*, were a valid source for his boasting, for he will now show that he endured untold trials in spite of those supposed handicaps. Through several verses the apostle will state the truly worthy qualifications he possessed, even while undergoing the fleshly inconveniences of which he boasts.

Verse 22. In the Bible there are three terms applied to the same people, namely, Hebrews, Israelites and Jews. However, they were not all derived from the same source. The first came from Heber, a distinguished man in the blood line (Genesis 10: 21). The second is from the extra name given to Jacob by the angel (Genesis 32: 28). Since Jacob was preferred before the elder brother Esau, to be in the blood line for the Messiah, it was an honor to be called an Israelite. The third is derived from Judah, the fourth son of Jacob, through whom the blood line was to flow. A man called by any of these names could boast of being of the *seed of Abraham*, as Paul does in this verse. Since some distinctions could be made between all of these names due to immediate circumstances, some persons might claim an importance out of one or the other according as his personal interests would suggest. Paul shows that none of his critics could boast of any advantage over him, for he could lay claim to all of the names.

Verse 23. See the comments on verse 1 for the sense in which he *speaks as a fool*, also those on verse 21 for the relation between the weaknesses of which he boasted, and the services he was rendering to Christ in spite of those supposed defects. Paul was more of a *minister* (servant) than his critics, and he specifies a number of facts as proof. His *labors* were more in that he carried the Gospel to a multitude of countries, whereas his objectors were located around Corinth. The *stripes* will be noticed at verses 24 and and 25. Acts 16 gives an account of one imprisonment, but secular history relates a great many times at which Paul was placed in prison because of his work for Christ. *In deaths oft* is figurative, meaning he was frequently in danger of death. (See 1 Corinthians 15: 30-32.)

Verse 24. *Forty stripes, save one.* The law of Moses limited the number of lashes that could be inflicted upon a victim to forty (Deuteronomy 25: 1-3). The whip by which it was done was originally single, and the punishment required forty operations of the administrator. For some reason the act was changed, and I shall quote from Prideaux's Connexion, Year 108, for explanation: "This punishment among the Jews was not to exceed forty stripes, and therefore the whip with which it was inflicted [after the change mentioned above] being made of three thongs, each blow giving three stripes, they never inflicted upon any criminal more than thirteen blows, because thirteen of those blows made thirty-nine stripes; and to add another blow, would be to transgress the law, by adding two stripes over and above forty, contraray to its prohibition. And in this manner was it that Paul, when whipped by the Jews, received forty stripes save one, that is, thirteen blows with this threefold whip." The verse means that Paul suffered this treatment on five different ocassions.

Verse 25. Not all of the details of Paul's adversities are recorded, but his tabulation of them in this chapter is authentic, for he is writing under the guidance of the Holy Spirit. One case of his being beaten with rods is related in Acts 16: 22, 23. The one instance of stoning is stated in Acts 14: 19. The case of shipwreck that Paul suffered (Acts 27) was after this epistle was written, hence the three occasions referred to here are not recorded elsewhere. *Been in the deep* means he was forced out by shipwreck to float in lifeboats or on boards, such as Acts 27: 44.

Verse 26. We should bear in mind that Paul is giving a list of his experiences that happened as a result of being a "minister" or servant of Christ (verse 23). *Journeyings* were done on behalf of the Gospel, and that exposed him to the dangers from *robbers* who infested many of the lines of travel. His *own countrymen* were the Jews who often persecuted him (verse 24). *Perils by the heathen* means the mistreatment from the Gentiles, such as were inflicted upon him at Philippi (Acts 16). The perils in the *city*, the *wilderness* and the *sea* include the trials already referred to in the verse and elsewhere in the chapter. An instance of his trouble from *false brethren* is recorded in Galatians 2: 4.

Verse 27. *Weariness and painfulness.* The Englishmen's Greek New Testament renders this, "labor and toil." It refers to the difficult tasks the apostle performed frequently in his work for the Master. Thayer defines the original for *watchings* by "sleeplessness." Paul lay awake for hours, thinking and pondering over the situation, wondering what was coming next. *Hunger and thirst* refers to the times when Paul's friends were prevented from administering to his needs, and he was left to suffer for the things necessary for his bodily comfort. Fastings is similar to the thought just explaind, with the added idea of a more extended abstinence from food. *Cold* was a result of the *nakedness*, or the shortage of necessary clothing, brought about by the conditions similar to those causing the *hunger and thirst*.

Verse 28. *Things that are without.* Most of the trials just recorded affected Paul's body externally, and were the direct result of his work for Christ, and of the activities of his enemies.

On top of all those tribulations, he was daily burdened with the *care* of all the churches. The word means anxiety or worry for the spiritual condition of all the congregations, not only those with whom he was permitted to labor personally. (See Colossians 2: 1.)

Verse 29. This verse is Paul's comment on the preceding verse. *Weak* refers to the disabilities and misfortunes of his brethren; *offended* denotes the mistreatment that is imposed upon his fellow disciples wherever they were located. Paul sympathized with all of them, and that is why he felt such *care* (anxiety) for the churches.

Verse 30. Paul regarded his sympathy for the troubled and tried as a worth-while sentiment. His own *infirmities* and misfortunes would enable him the more to have such a feeling for others, hence he would glory or boast of his own infirmities.

Verse 31. The greatest motive one can have for always telling the truth, is the realization that God knows all about his heart.

Verses 32, 33. Before closing this phase of his epistle, the apostle cites a specific instance of his afflictions that were imposed by his enemies. The significant thing about this case is that it was at the very start of his service for Christ. The account of it is in Acts 9: 23-25, where the Jews were so eager to seize the apostle that they watched the gates day and night.

2 Corinthians 12

Verse 1. In the preceding chapter Paul's boasting refers to the weaknesses and handicaps that were imposed upon him by his enemies, or as a result of his difficult labors for Christ. In this chapter he speaks of infirmities that were placed upon him directly by the Lord. Several verses are used to explain how those infirmities were brought about. *Visions* is from OPTASIA, and Thayer defines it at this place, "the act of exhibiting one's self to view." *Revelations* is from APOKALUPSIS, and Thayer's definition is, "properly [primarily] a laying bare, making naked." He then explains it to mean, "tropically [figuratively], in New Testament and ecclesiastical language, a disclosure of truth, instruction, concerning divine things before unknown." The verse means, therefore, that the Lord appeared to Paul, and while in his presence He revealed some truths to the apostle that had not been known by him before.

Verse 2. The aforesaid truths (or facts) were concerning a *man in Christ* whom Paul says he knew, and these facts occurred more than fourteen years before the present writing. *Caught up* is from HARPAZO, which Thayer defines, "to snatch or catch away," and he explains it to denote, "divine power transferring a person marvelously and swiftly from one place to another." It is the word used in Acts 8: 39 where the Lord "caught away" Philip. The original words for *third* and *heaven* have no specific meaning here as far as the lexicon definition is concerned, hence the connection in which they are used must determine their sense in any given case. Since the first heaven is the region where the birds fly (Genesis 1: 20), and the second is that where the stars are held (Genesis 22: 17), it leaves the third heaven to mean where God's throne is. That will account for some things that are said about the experience of this "man in Christ." *In the body* and *out of the body* is equivalent to "alive" and "dead," and Paul did not know which was the man's condition when he had this experience.

Verse 3. This is the same as verse 2.

Verse 4. *Paradise* is the same as the *third heaven*, because the word is defined in the lexicon as "pleasure gardens," regardless of what specific location may be in the mind of a writer. *Unspeakable* and *not lawful* are accommodative in their meaning. The things heard were in the third heaven, hence the words were not to be repeated by *a man*, although he was permitted to hear them.

Verse 5. *Such an one* and *myself* are different persons, since Paul says he will glory of one and will not of the other. Neither Paul nor any other inspired man has told us the name of the one who was caught up, and I am not disposed to guess at it. Had Paul considered it important for his readers to know it he certainly would have told them; he could have done so since he knew him. There is an important truth made evident by this incident that is often overlooked. Paul says this man heard words while being caught up, yet he did not know whether he was in the body or out, which shows that a human being will be conscious after the death of the body, which refutes the fundamental theory of materialists.

Verse 6. *Fool* does not mean a person without intelligence, but one who does not use it aright, or who goes to extremes in expressing his sentiments. Paul had so much ground for his glorying that he could not be justly accused of going to such extremes as the word *fool* signifies. However, to avoid any misunderstanding, he determined to forbear going as far as the truth would have justified him to go.

Verse 7. To be *exalted above measure* means to be filled with pride or a feeling of self-importance. The Lord wished **to prevent Paul** from being tempted into such a frame of mind. Note it was the *revelations* that might cause the evil effect. Nothing is said of the *visions* in connection with the temptation. It is not shown anywhere who had the visions and hence they do not figure in the consideration of this danger. The *revelations* were what the Lord told Paul, and that alone is stated as being the possible cause of his being too much exalted. Although the English word *thorn* occurs several times in the New Testament, this is the only place where it comes from SKOLOPS, which Thayer defines, "a sharp stake." Robinson defines it, "anything pointed," and he explains it to mean in the New Testament, "something which excites severe and constant pain, probably some bodily infirmity." The only other place where this subject is evidently referred to is Galatians 4: 13, 14. Paul tells the brethren there that they "despised [belittled] not" his temptation which was in the flesh. From what is said in the inspired writings, we know that this *thorn* was some kind of bodily infirmity that was painful and humiliating, but to be more specific would be speculation. *Messenger* (or agent) *of Satan.* Since all human afflictions have come upon man because of Satan's evil work, and since this *thorn* was a bodily ailment of Paul, he calls it the messenger of Satan.

Verse 8. Paul had gloried in his infirmities, hence it was not the humiliating feature of this *thorn* that he wished to have removed. It was therefore the actual physical suffering about which he prayed three times to the Lord.

Verse 9. The Lord did not see fit to remove the thorn, but assured the apostle that he would not be overcome by it. *Strength made perfect in weakness.* There is an old saying that "man's extremity is the Lord's opportunity," and that is agreeable with the passage here. Hence, with the assurance of God's help, Paul was glad to be resigned to the inconvenience of this *thorn in the flesh.*

Verse 10. Paul took pleasure in his infirmities because of the good results they had on his morale. The greater his trials might be the more he would realize the value of the Lord's help. That is why he said when he was weak, then he was strong.

Verse 11. We often hear it said that "overindulgence will result in a spoiled child." That is what Paul is admitting has occurred from his treatment of the Corinthian brethren. They seemed to have taken his kindness for granted, and as a result had failed to recognize the greatness of the apostle; at least they had not expressed their appreciation. That induced him to make up for it with his own glorying, which has been explained in several preceding verses. Their selfish attitude had even implied that he was an inferior apostle, and some of his personal enemies even called in question whether he could rightfully claim to be an apostle. (See 1 Corinthians 9: 1, 2.) Against such an attitude he asserts that he was not only an apostle, but was not inferior to the chiefest of them. *Though I be nothing.* Paul gives all credit to the Lord for what he was accomplishing, otherwise he could not have performed the evidences of his apostleship that they had seen.

Verse 12. These *signs of an apostle* are mentioned also in the passage referred to in 1 Corinthians 9: 1, 2 cited in the preceding verse. *In all patience.* In performing these signs, the apostle was brought into contact with conditions that required much patience on his part.

Verse 13. *Inferior to other churches.* It was the Lord's plan that preachers should be supported by the people to whom they gave the Gospel (1 Corinthians 9: 14), and to accept such support from a group was one important item in recognizing it as a church of the Lord. By preaching to the Corinthians free of charge, they had been deprived of that advantage and so might have complained of a spiritual "inferiority complex." Because of such an unintentional wrong having been done them the apostle asks their forgiveness. However, since he asked permission to make an exception to the rule for support of the preachers of the Gospel (1 Corinthians 9: 18), he proposed to maintain that course toward them **of Corinth.**

Verse 14. *A third time* would imply two previous ones, but Paul's first visit to Corinth as recorded in Acts 18th chapter is the only one that is shown in that book. We need only conclude that the apostle conducted himself on the second visit according to the requirements of the occasion. *Not be burdensome* denotes that he will continue to relieve them of financial obligation to him, just as he has done up to this time. He uses the common rule of provisions being made by parents for their children, to illustrate his feeling for the Corinthian brethren. Of course he is regarding the relationship from a spiritual standpoint. (See 1 Corinthians 4: 14, 15.)

Verse 15. *Though . . . the less I be loved.* Paul would not let the indifference of the Corinthians keep him from continuing his fatherly concern for them. *Spend and be spent* is somewhat figurative. He would go on devoting his time and talents upon them, and also permit them to make use of him for their own benefit.

Verse 16. *Be it so.* It was admitted that Paul did not personally burden them with the duty of supporting him, but some of them were accusing him of getting something from them in a round-about way. The rest of this verse should be understood as a quotation by Paul of what some of his accusers were saying. Moffatt renders this passage thus: "I was not a burden to you, no, but I was clever enough to dupe you with my tricks? Was I?"

Verse 17. In aswer to their implied accusation, Paul asks in general terms if he had taken anything from them through the men he had sent among them.

Verse 18. In chapter 8: 16-22 is an account of the visit of Titus and the "brother" to the church at Corinth. Paul asks if Titus got anything from them wrongfully at that time. Had he done so they would have used it as evidence, which would have been easily proved since Titus was not alone. This other brother who was with him was "praised" or recommended "throughout all the churches." *Walked we not,* etc. Paul's question is really a challenge for them to show any inconsistency in his conduct, in view of what they knew concerning this visit of Titus.

Verse 19. Paul did not make the preceding argument as an excuse (he needed no such defence), but was speaking the truth in the fear of God in Christ. He was speaking for the sake of these brethren whom he loved, and for their edification.

Verse 20. In the preceding verse Paul expresses his purpose to be the edifying of the brethren. That would mean their improvement in spiritual things, so that there would be less to chastise in connection with their conduct. Were such improvement not made, Paul would not be satisfied with them when he arrived and would hence be required to discipline them which would be unpleasant to all. For that reason the meeting would be a disappointment also to the Corinthians. The apostle then gives a list of evil conditions he fears might exist when he came which would need to be corrected. *Debates* are not all alike; some are right and others are wrong. The word here means wrangling and quarreling and that is always wrong. *Envying* means to be indignant because of the good fortune of another. *Wrath* is defined by Thayer, "indignation which has arisen gradually and become more settled." Thayer defines the original for *strifes* as, "a desire to put one's self forward." *Backbiting* means the attempt to defame another's good name. *Whisperings* means secret slanderings for the purpose of injuring the reputation of another. *Swelling* is from a word that denotes one who is puffed up with pride. *Tumults* denotes a state of disturbance that threatens to result in a riot.

Verse 21. *God will humble me.* Not that God would blame Paul for the conditions, for he had done his duty in rebuking them for all their wrongs. But the apostle would be humiliated were he to find the Corinthians guilty of these evils, and it would be chiefly because such practices are displeasing to God. To find them active in these evils when he arrived would be disheartening, but it would likewise be saddening to find those previously rebuked still unrepentant of their corruptions. If Paul should find such a state of affairs when he reached Corinth, he could but bewail the condition and feel the need of administering severe chastisement.

2 Corinthians 13

Verse 1. See the comments at chapter 12: 14 on the meaning of *third time.* In the preceding chapter Paul expresses a fear that he would find conditions undesirable when he got to Corinth the next time. He also expresses a warning intimation that if he found such conditions, he would rebuke them for their sins. Now he emphasizes the warning, but assures them that his treatment of them would be fair and according to a principle already established in the Scriptures (Deuteronomy 19: 15), that a charge must be sustained by two or three witnesses.

Verse 2. *Told you ... as ... second.* This is the more definite information we have of what Paul did the second time he visited Corinth. (See comments at chapter 12: 14.) *Which heretofore have sinned* are the ones designated by *sinned already* in chapter 12: 21, and *all other* means the ones engaged in evildoing right at the time of his third visit which was yet to come.

Verse 3. Paul claimed to be a true spokesman for Christ, but he could not truly make such a claim were he to come short of his duty in rebuking sin. (See Acts 20: 26, 27.) The Corinthians understood that Christ was no weakling when it came to condemning wrongdoing, and therefore they would know that a true teacher for Him would also not *spare* when he was dealing with professed disciples who had become corrupt in their conduct.

Verse 4. *Crucified through weakness.* This has reference to the fleshly body that Jesus took upon himself (Philippians 2: 7) in order that He might become a sacrifice for the sins of mankind. That body was as weak as that of any other man when it was attacked mortally, hence it was the victim of death through the crucifixion. But the power of God was sufficient to unite that body with its soul again and enable Him to live. *We also are weak with him* denotes that Christians will risk their temporal lives if need be, in their devotion to Him who is able to sustain them spiritually. This was especially significant in the case of the apostle who was devoting his services *toward you* (the Corinthians).

Verse 5. *Examine* is from PEIRAZO, which Thayer defines, "to try, make trial of, test," and he explains it in this passage to mean, "for the purpose of ascertaining his quality, or what he thinks, or how he will behave himself." Paul's purpose of the examination is to see if the Corinthians are in the faith; whether they could still be regarded as faithful disciples. DOKIMAZO is the word for *prove*, and it has virtually the same meaning as the word just explained, and it doubtless is used for the sake of emphasis. *Reprobates* is from ADOKIMOS, and the first of Thayer's definition is, "Not standing the test, not approved." The most significant thought is that having Christ in one, and being a reprobate are two opposite conditions, and a man cannot possess both at the same time. The exhortation of the verse is for each man to make this self examination to ascertain what his true condition is.

Verse 6. Paul does not intimate any doubt as to his not being a reprobate. He is concerned, however, over the attitude of the Corinthians on the subject. This concern is justified by the fact of personal enemies among the brethren, which has been referred to in a number of places in this book.

Verse 7. *Not that we should appear approved.* In verse 3 it is shown that Paul's severe chastisement of wrongdoers would prove him to be an acceptable spokesman for Christ. If they *do no evil* it will make it unnecessary for him to exhibit that evidence. Nevertheless, he was more desirous of their not doing evil, even if it did deprive him of such proof, and even though it would seemingly give the enemies of the apostle a pretext for saying he is a reprobate.

Verse 8. This verse is in line with the preceding one. Were the brethren to conduct themselves as they should, Paul could not have exercised his power of discipline against them without doing something *against the truth*, which is a thing he felt that he could not do.

Verse 9. The terms *weak* and *strong* are used somewhat figuratively, referring to the unpleasant experiences of the apostle as against the more fortunate ones of the brethren. If the afflictions must come, he would rather suffer them and let his brethren escape, just so they followed the conduct pertaining to Christian *perfection*.

Verse 10. See the comments at 1 Corinthians 4: 21; 2 Corinthians 2: 3 and 10: 8. Paul was always conscientious and never evaded any duty however unpleasant. Yet he was considerate of the feelings of others, and never used the severest corrections against his brethren if a milder form could lawfully be used. If he could induce them to make the necessary adjustment through the means of his epistle, he would be spared the unpleasant ordeal of invoking his *power* (authority) in person, since his presence seemed to be objectionable to some.

Verse 11. This is a kindly, fatherly admonition with which the apostle approaches the close of his epistle. *Be perfect* means to complete what is necessary by removing the wrongs in their lives, after which they would have the right to feel comfortable in their consciences. In order to *be at peace* it is necessary to *be of one mind*, and that is possible only by each one bending his own mind to that of the instruction delivered to them by the inspired apostle. A man can be at peace with God only by living in peace with his brethren according to the instructions of inspiration.

Verse 12. This is explained at 1 Corinthians 16: 20.

Verse 13. *All the saints* refers to those associated with Paul at this time. They joined the apostle in friendly salutation to the brethren at Corinth.

Verse 14. The three members of the Godhead, namely, the Father, the Son and the Holy Ghost (Spirit), are named in this verse. *Grace* means the favor of the Lord Jesus Christ, and the *love* of God denotes the affection that He extends toward his faithful children. *Communion* is from the same word as *fellowship* in many passages. It means the partnership that all faithful disciples may enjoy with each other through the truth made known by the work of the Spirit. It also includes the blessing of the presence of the Holy Spirit in the church (1 Corinthians 6: 19). For the meaning of *amen*, see the comments at Romans 16: 24, in the first volume of New Testament Commentary.

Galatians 1

General remarks. The preceding three epistles of Paul were written to single congregations, and they were located in Europe. The present one was sent to a group of churches in a certain district called Galatia. It was a part of Asia Minor, which in turn was a part of the continent of Asia. Paul had labored among these churches and at one time a warm personal attachment had been formed between them. There were some Jews in these churches, but for the most part they were Gentiles. The principal reason for the epistle was to counteract the evil teaching of some Judaizers who were troubling the churches. These were Jews who tried to induce Gentile Christians to take up the ordinances of the law of Moses, particularly the rite of circumcision. This disturbance was in evidence in many parts of the Roman Empire where Christianity had been planted (Acts 15: 1, 2; Colossians 2: 16-23, and others), but the present epistle is directed to the territory in Galatia, doubtless because Paul was so disppointed over the reversal of conditions there.

Verse 1. *Apostle* is from APOSTOLOS, and Thayer defines it as follows: "A delegate, messenger, one sent forth with orders." If the word is to have any special application it will need to be determined by the connection in which it is used. For instance, if a man is sent out merely on the authority of men, then such an apostle would have human authority only. Hence Paul considers that point when he says here that his apostleship is *not of men neither by men*. His divine call to the office had been questioned by some of his critics operating in Galatia. The same situation appears to have existed elsewhere. (See 1 Corinthians 9: 1, 2.) *Who raised him from the dead.* This fact gives force to the authority of Paul, for God would not have raised Jesus from the dead had he not been his Son. The apostolic call, therefore, which Jesus gave to Paul, came ultimately from God.

Verse 2. *Brethren which are with me.* These brethren had no authority in connection with this letter; they did not even take part in the writing of it (chapter 6: 11). The phrase means they joined the apostle in friendly salutation to the churches.

Verse 3. This expression of well-wishing occurs at the beginning of every one of Paul's epistles with the exception of Hebrews. It is not a mere sentimental statement but contains some fundamental truths. *Grace* is from CHARIS, and one part of Thayer's definition is, "kindness which bestows upon one what he has not deserved." This phase of the word explains why the apostle specifies that it is the grace from God he is wishing for his brethren, since all of God's favors are bestowed upon man only through the Lord Jesus Christ. That is because the sacrifice of Christ provided the way for God to maintain his justice and at the same time extend this unmerited favor to humanity. (See the notes at Romans 3: 26, volume 1 of the New Testament Commentary.) *Peace* is from EIRENE, and the outstanding definition in Thayer's lexicon is, "peace between individuals, i. e., harmony, concord, security, safety, prosperity." It is significant that Paul ascribes this favor to God and Christ, for they are the only Beings who can assure it to man in the face of unnumbered difficulties besetting an existence on the earth. And such a favor will be granted only to those who model their lives according to the will of the Lord. Such a life will assure one of being at peace with God, though it may not always have such a result with mankind. (See Romans 12: 18.)

Verse 4. The churches of Macedonia were praised for their liberal support of the brethren in Christ (2 Corinthians 8: 5), and their devotion is accounted for partly by the fact that they "first gave their own selves to the Lord." The same motive is ascribed to Christ in his sacrifice for mankind, namely, he *gave himself for our sins.* Many people are willing to bestow some favor upon others if it does not require any personal inconvenience upon themselves. And it is usually even then in a case where the person to be benefitted is "a worthy individual." But Jesus made his supreme sacrifice for the sins of the world. Furthermore, this favor from Christ was not with the motive that the ones benefited might be placed in a condition where they could "return the favor" upon their benefactor; it was to deliver them from *this present evil world;* that is, rescue them from the evil influences and results of the present world or age.

Verse 5. *Whom* refers to the Father in the preceding verse. *For ever and ever* is an emphatic way of saying that God deserves to reecive glory without end. *Amen* is explained at Romans 16: 24, in volume 1 of the New Testament Commentary.

Verse 6. Up to this place the verses constitute Paul's introduction for his epistle. He now begins on the main subject of the letter, namely, the corruptions that had entered among the churches of Galatia through the activities of Judaizers. The reader should again consult the comments on these false teachers in "general remarks" at the beginning of this epistle. *Him that called you* refers to God (1 Corinthians 1: 9), who had called them by the preaching of Paul, to receive the *grace* or favor of Christ. *So soon removed* indicates the fickleness of these brethren, for it had not been such a long time since they had been taught the truth. *Gospel* is always from EUAGGELION, and its primary meaning according to Thayer is, "good tidings," and it can have special applications only by the connection in which it is used. Hence if some pretended good news should be offered to persons, it would be a form of gospel regardless of whether it were true or false. That explains why Paul uses the phrase *another gospel.* The first word is from HETEROS, which means another kind of gospel or supposed good news. The false doctrine was the claim that Christians could obtain salvation by observing the ordinances of the law of Moses, especially that of circumcision; this is clearly shown in Acts 15: 1. But since such "good news" was false, Paul calls it another kind of gospel.

Verse 7. This verse might seem to contradict the preceding one, but the explanation is in the difference between the original words for *another.* (See verse 6 for the meaning of the word in that instance.) In this verse the word is from ALLOS, which means another something of the same kind. As there is but one true Gospel, there cannot be another like it or of the same kind. That is why Paul says this doctrine that the Judaizers were giving was not another Gospel like the one he was preaching; and for a good reason, for there is no other like it. To *pervert* the Gospel means to corrupt it by mixing it with something else. The Judaizers were trying to combine the law of Moses with that of Christ, and in so doing Paul charges them with perverting the Gospel, and it was causing *trouble* for those who otherwise had been faithful.

Verse 8. We have seen that some people questioned the apostleship of Paul (verse 1); on the other hand, some Judaizers charged that he was advocating the practice of circumcision as a religious necessity (chapter 5: 11). A pretext for such a false claim may have been drawn from the fact that Paul had Timothy circumcised (Acts 16: 3), disregarding the fact that Timothy had Jewish blood in his veins, and thus had a right to it from a national standpoint. (See the comments at that place in volume 1 of the New Testament Commentary.) However, even if Paul did preach such a false doctrine, that would not make it right but instead he would be under the curse of God. *Angels from heaven* were never permitted to preach the terms of salvation to any human individual, much less would they dare preach a gospel that contradicted the inspired one given by Paul.

Verse 9. To emphasize his warning

against the false teacher, Paul refers to what he had taught them at a previous time. *Said before* is from PROEIPON, which Thayer defines at this place, "to say before, i. e., heretofore, formerly." Robinson defines it, "to have said before, to have already declared." Hence it could not be intimated that Paul's present warning was some new idea of his. We know Paul had been among them before and had delivered his teaching on the matters of proper living. (See chapter 5: 21.) *Accursed* is from ANATHEMA, and Thayer defines it at this place, "a man accursed, devoted to the direst woes." Robinson says it means to be "separated from God's favor and delivered to destruction." It is easy to see that preaching a false doctrine is one of the worst sins of which a man can be guilty.

Verse 10. *Persuade* in this passage means "to make friends of, win one's favor, gain one's good-will; to seek to win one, strive to please one," according to Thayer. Paul makes his statement in question form, but he really is denying that he is trying to please men with his preaching. The basic reason is that he could not be a servant of Christ while preaching in a way to win the favor of men. He was resolved to be true to God even though he would lose the friendship of the whole world. This was in agreement with his statement in Romans 3: 4.

Verse 11. To *certify* means to make known, and *after man* means to be according to man. Since the Gospel was not composed to suit the wishes of man, Paul could not be true to his call were he to try bending it to suit man in order to win his friendship and good will.

Verse 12. Paul received the Gospel by the *revelation* authorized of Christ. (See the definition of the word in the comments at 2 Corinthians 12: 1.)

Verse 13. *Conversation* means conduct or manner of life, and Paul is referring to what he practiced while he was a worker in the *Jews' religion,* which means that under the law of Moses. His reference to the persecution of the church of God in the past, was to show that his present defense of it was not motivated by a life-long prejudice in its favor. *Beyond measure* is from HUPERBOLE which is defined in Thayer's lexicon as "preeminently; exceedingly." *Wasted* is from the same Greek word as "destroyed" in Acts 9: 21, where the persecution by Paul is the subject. In that place it is stated that he "destroyed them which called on the name" of the Son of God. This explains in what sense the church of God may be destroyed; it is by overthrowing certain members of it. Such individual destruction of the church has always been and always will be possible, but the church as a whole is destined to live for ever. (See Daniel 2: 44.) It was impossible for the powers of darkness to prevent the building of the church (Matthew 16: 18), and the world is given assurance that Christianity will exist on earth until the second coming of Christ (1 Corinthians 15: 51, 52; 1 Thessalonians 4: 15-17).

Verse 14. *Profited* does not have the sense of personal gain as the word usually does. The original is defined in the lexicon, "to go forward, advance, proceed, make progress." *Equals* is from SUNELIKIOTES, which Thayer defines, "one of the same age, an equal in age." It is much like a case in the public schools where it may be said of a boy that "he stood at the head of his class." The point Paul is making is that in leaving Judaism and coming to the Gospel, he was not seeking some balm for disappointment over failure, for he was highly successful before.

Traditions is from PARADOSIS, which Thayer defines, "a giving over, giving up; i. e., the act of giving up, the surrender. A giving over which is done by word of mouth or in writing." The reader should make himself familiar with this word, which is used frequently in the New Testament, but not always in a bad sense. Any doctrine or rule of conduct becomes a tradition when it has once been given over from one person to another. Whether it is good or bad, and whether it is of any authority or not depends upon the persons handing over the doctrine. Hence the traditions Paul was condemning were those that had been given over by the Jewish fathers, and they were not of authority.

Verse 15. *Separated* is from a word that means to "appoint, set apart, one for some purpose." *From my mother's womb* means from the time of his birth. At the time of Paul's birth, God determined to use him as a special messenger of Christ. However, that was not made known to him for many years, and even then He did not put that appointment in effect until He had called him by his grace or the Gospel. That call is recorded in Acts 9.

Verse 16. This verse states the purpose for which God selected Paul, which was to preach His Son among the *heathen,* or nations of the world.

Immediately denotes that Paul did not delay entering into the work for which he had been called. *Conferred not with flesh and blood* indicates he did not seek counsel or information about his duty; not even of his relatives or close personal friends.

Verse 17. Paul did not first try to consult the other apostles, for his call was from God directly and the previous apostles would not have been able to confer any special qualifications on him. Since no other reference is made to this journey into Arabia, we have no way of determining the purpose of it nor how he spent the time while there. But we have the information that after his stay there was ended, he returned to the city of his conversion before going elsewhere.

Verse 18. *After three years* is dated from his conversion, and includes the time spent in Arabia and Damascus. The time spent in the last place was divided between the days immediately after his conversion, and his return from Arabia. (See verse 17 and Acts 9: 19-22.) The special purpose for Paul's journey to Jerusalem was to see Peter. As this was his first visit to that city since his conversion, it is not strange that he had not met Peter before. The words *to see* are from HISTOREO, and this is the only place in the Greek New Testament where the word is used. Thayer defines it, "1, to inquire into, examine, investigate. 2, to find out, learn by inquiry. 3, to gain knowledge of by visiting; to become personally acquainted with, know face to face." All of this was after the three years, in the course of which Paul had been preaching the Gospel elsewhere, hence it does not contradict verse 17. Neither does it leave any room for saying that he went up there to receive the Gospel from Peter (which would have contradicted verse 12). But the importance of the apostle Peter created a desire in Paul to "become personally acquainted with him," and to "know him face to face." He spent fifteen days in the city while visiting Peter.

Verse 19. *Apostles . . . James the Lord's brother.* He was not one of the twelve, but was a very prominent man in the church at Jerusalem, and the term is applied to him in a sort of honorary manner. Regarding such a use of the word, Funk and Wagnalls New Standard Bible Dictionary says the following: "The term came to be used more widely than at first, restricted to its reference to the twelve and Paul. This is confirmed by Paul's reference to James, the Lord's brother, as an apostle (Galatians 1: 19)." Thayer agrees with this thought, for after giving the definition of the Greek word for *apostle,* he adds by way of explanation, "In a broader sense the name is transferred to other eminent Christian teachers."

Verse 20. Paul's apostleship had been questioned by some Judaizers, and his account contained in the preceding several verses is given as factual evidence of his authority. The statement *before God I lie not* is added to show that he is conscientious and serious, for he knows that God understands his heart.

Verse 21. *Syria* and *Cilicia* were provinces north of Palestine, and the latter contained Tarsus, the city of Paul's birth. The immediate occasion for his going there at this time is shown in Acts 9: 26-30. (See the comments at that place in volume 1 of the New Testament Commentary.)

Verse 22. *Unknown by face* means they had not seen Paul personally. This is not strange, for he had spent the years following his conversion in Damascus and Arabia, and was in Jerusalem only *fifteen days* (verse 18) before being driven out by persecution.

Verse 23. *They had heard only.* Even though these churches had never met Paul in person, yet the report of his persecution of the saints had reached their ears and filled them with a state of unrest. Now the opposite report was coming to their ears and it brought great relief to them. Hence the writer of Acts says the churches had "rest" upon the ceasing of oppression from this man. (See the comments at Acts 9: 31 in volume 1 of the New Testament Commentary.)

Verse 24. *Glorified God in me* means they gave God the glory for all of the good results of Paul's conversion. This glorification toward God was not in words only, as may be seen in the passage cited at the close of the preceding paragraph.

Galatians 2

Verse 1. *Fourteen years after* is dated from the same event as "after three years" in chapter 1: 18, namely, his conversion. In Acts 15: 2 where this same trip to Jerusalem is recorded, it says that "certain other of them" went with Paul and Barnabas. In our present verse we are told that the "other" person was Titus.

Verse 2. The English word *revelation* always comes from the same Greek word, and any special part of the lexicon definition that is to be applied must be determined by the connection in any given case. However, its general definition is proper in the present verse, namely, the one word "instruction." So the verse means that Paul was instructed to go up to Jerusalem, hence his move was not merely from a personal desire. *That Gospel which I preach among the Gentiles.* This does not imply that Paul preached one Gospel to the Gentiles and a different one to the Jews. No, it is a declaration that he always preached the same one wherever he went, which is what he teaches in chapter 1: 6-9. The part of this same Gospel that was confused in the minds of the Jewish brethren was that which admits the Gentiles to all the benefits of salvation without requiring them to accept circumcision. (See Acts 15: 1.) Paul knew that the "rank and file" of the Jewish Christians were so perplexed over this subject that he would have difficulty in convincing them if he approached them as a group, hence his plan was first to present the matter to a few of the more able thinkers. The original for *reputation* is defined by Thayer, "to seem, be accounted, reputed," and he explains it to denote, "those who are reputed to be somewhat of importance, and therefore have influence." *Lest . . . in vain.* If the Jewish Christians were to continue in this perverted teaching concerning the Gospel, it would upset the work of Paul among them. To avoid such a result, he used the tactful plan just explained.

Verse 3. Paul's plan accomplished the desired effect as indicated by this verse. Titus being a Greek, belonged to the Gentile nation, but according to the contention of the Judaizers he should have been circumcised to be saved. The statement is made that he was not *compelled* to submit to it. Of course no one thought of using physical force to administer the rite on anyone. The word means to constrain, either by force or persuasion, and the latter means was attempted by the false brethren.

Verse 4. Why was Paul's plan put to the specific test in the case of Titus? This verse answers the question by saying that false brethren had been brought in unawares. The purpose of this movement was to *spy out* ("plot against"—Thayer) the liberty that all Christians have in Christ. Even Jewish Christians are not required to be circumcised in order to be saved, but these Judaizers intended to bring them into the bondage of the law of circumcision.

Verse 5. *Not for an hour* denotes that Paul did not yield to the pressure for a single time. The backing that he had created in verse 2 enabled him successfully to withstand the Judaizers.

Verse 6. Having disposed of the *false brethren brought in,* Paul gave his attention to the men of the city of Jerusalem; doubtless they were the ones referred to in Acts 15: 1. This group might even have included some of the apostles living in Jerusalem who were somewhat confused on the subject at hand. These men *seemed* (were reputed) to be *somewhat* (something) on account of their previous standing with God. But that would not have anything to do with whether they were right or wrong in the present controversy. However, out of respect for their reputation, Paul listened to them but was not told anything that he did not know already. That is the meaning of *in conference added nothing to me.*

Verse 7. The brethren living in Jerusalem, though previously mixed up on the subject of circumcision, seemed to be more fairminded than the *false brethren* who had been imported in verse 4. When they saw the truth of the situation, they sided in with Paul and Peter. *Gospel of the uncircumcision.* This is a brief way of saying that the Gospel does not require circumcision of the Gentiles, and that Paul was to be especially commissioned to preach to them. *Gospel of the circumcision* means that the Jews could still observe the rite of circumcision as a national mark, while depending solely on the Gospel of Christ for salvation.

Verse 8. The pronoun *he* refers to the Lord. This explanatory verse is intended merely to state that the Lord showed no partiality in His qualifying Peter and Paul for the apostleship.

Verse 9. *Pillars* is from STULOS, and Thayer defines it by the same word that is used in the text. He then explains it to mean, "persons to whose eminence and strength the stability and authority of any institution or organization are due." Robinson defines it, "a column, pillar," and explains it to mean, "any firm support; for example, persons of authority and influence in the church." Paul ascribes this character to James (the Lord's brother), Cephas (Peter) and John (brother of James). There is nothing to indicate that any of the group were unfavorable toward the work of Paul and Barnabas, but the three men are named because of their high standing, and because they were the ones who acted in this outward expression of endorsement. *Right hands.* The two words are from the Greek word DEXIOS. Robinson defines it, "right, on the right side or hand, opposite the left," hence it does not mean right as the opposite to wrong. Greenfield explains it at this place, "to give the right hand to any one, as a pledge of sincerity in one's promises." The reason the right hand is used is because most men are right-handed by nature, and hence any gesture that calls for the joining of hands would naturally use the right hand. Thayer explains this feature of the subject as follow: "Property of that hand which is wont [accustomed] to take hold of as well as to point out." The fact that special attention is called to certain persons who were left-handed (Judges 3: 15; 20: 16), shows it is the natural rule to use the right hand.

Fellowship is from KOINONIA and means partnership or joint interest in something. This act of the three "pillars" was to indicate to Paul and Barnabas that they were interested in the work about to be done, and would give it their full moral support. *Heathen* is from ETHNOS, and in the King James Version it is rendered by heathen 5 times, Gentiles 93, nation 64, people 2. As it is used in this verse, it means the Gentiles, and the term *circumcision* means the Jews. We know this does not mean that each one was restricted to the class designated, for Paul preached to all classes. But their assignment as a whole was to be as indicated.

Verse 10. *The poor* were the Christians in Judea, most of whom were Jews. The verse means that while Paul and Barnabas were especially assigned the preaching among the Gentiles in other provinces, they should not forget the poor saints in Judea though they were Jews. Paul was already thus disposed toward them, so that complete harmony existed between them.

Verse 11. *When Peter was come to Antioch.* It is questioned by some whether this was before or after the events of Acts 15. The information as to dates is not clear enough to decide the point definitely. The reason for such a suggestion (that it might have been before) is to clear Peter of the charge of inconsistency in view of his stand on the issue at hand in that meeting in Jerusalem. But that is not called for, since it is not claimed that an inspired man is not capable of personal error in conduct. Paul's teaching in 1 Corinthians 9: 27 shows that it is possible for an old soldier of the cross, an inspired apostle and preacher of the Gospel, to commit a sin so grievous as to cause him to be rejected by the Lord. From these considerations it should not affect our confidence in Peter's inspired teaching, to see him here give way to human weakness. Paul being also an inspired man was able to give the proper teaching on the situation. Hence his statement that Peter *was to be blamed* is an inspired one, and states the truth about the uninspired conduct of the other apostle. Incidentally it disproves all claim that Peter possessed any superiority over Paul or any of the other apostles as the Romanists teach.

Verse 12. *Certain came from James.* There is no definite information available as to whether these men were sent by James, or that Peter was merely intimidated by the fact that they came from the vicinity of that outstanding man, and would doubtless carry a report back to him of what they saw at Antioch. *Did eat with the Gentiles.* On the significance of eating with others, see the comments at 1 Corinthians 5: 11. There was nothing actually wrong in eating with Gentiles, and Peter had done so before (Acts 11: 3); but his feeling for what he imagined was James' exclusiveness on the matter, induced him to act in this inconsistent manner.

Verse 13. *Dissembled . . . with* are from the Greek word SUNUPOKRINOMAI, which Thayer defines, "to dissemble with." Robinson defines it, "to play the hypocrite with any one, to dissemble with." *Dissimulation* has the same meaning, but being a noun it is from HUPOKRISIS, defined by Thayer at this place, "dissimulation, hypocrisy," and Robinson defines it in the same way. Hence we have the sad information that Peter acted the part of a hypocrite; also that his example caused Barnabas and the other Jews to be *carried away* (over influenced) with the unscriptural procedure. But the reader should again see the comments at verse 11 on the difference between Peter's authority as an inspired apostle, and the correctness or incorrectness of his personal conduct.

Verse 14. *Walked not uprightly* means improper conduct whether it concerns the moral or the legal laws.

According . . . the Gospel shows these people were going wrong as measured by that high standard. *Before them all.* Peter was the leader in the defection, but the others were also to blame for allowing themselves to be misled; therefore it was proper to give the chastisement publicity. (This principle is taught in 1 Timothy 5: 20.) *Livest after the manner of the Gentiles.* There were certain customs that both Jews and Gentiles observed as a manner of life socially, which were not a part of their religion. With reference to such, neither was required to cease the observance. Nor was a Jew or Gentile required to take up the customs of the other, although he might do so if he wished. Paul did so in 1 Corinthians 9: 20, 21, and Peter had been doing that in our present case. His inconsistency was shown in his association (socially) with the Gentiles voluntarily for a while, then withdrawing from them unless they conformed (which would not have been voluntarily) to the practices of the Jews. An unfortunate feature of this performance of Peter was the leaving an impression that the Gentiles would be required to go farther than the social customs of the Jews to be saved, and that they also must conform to the ordinances of the Mosaic law to be saved, as was done in the case of Acts 15: 1.

Verse 15. The Jews had always considered the Gentiles to be *sinners* as a class, and so inferior as a class that the term "dogs" even was applied to them (Matthew 15: 26, 27). In this verse Paul is not ignoring the field of history, nor is he denying all claims of superiority for the Jews. However, he reminds Peter that such a rating is from a national standpoint and not due to any moral or personal goodness that they possessed. (He had refuted such an idea in Romans 3: 9-18.) That is why he makes the statement that they were Jews by nature.

Verse 16. The time was past when the national standing of the Jews meant anything to them religiously. No man (whether Jew or Gentile) could be justified or saved by the works of the law. That system had been "nailed to the cross" (Colossians 2: 14), and the observance of the social customs was voluntary only, and could not be forced upon any person of either nation. But all justification before God must be obtained through faith in Christ—by a working faith in Him, and *not by the works of the law.*

Verse 17. *We ourselves are found sinners.* The last word is used in the sense explained at verse 15. By jumbling the two nations together (as Peter was doing by his inconsistent conduct), it would cause the Jews to be *found sinners*, and that, too, right while professing to expect justification through Christ. Such a procedure would imply that Christ had become a minister of sin. Paul puts the challenge to Peter in the form of a question, but interposes his own negative answer by the words *God forbid,* which means "by no means."

Verse 18. Such inconsistent conduct would be like overthrowing a building because it "had served its purpose," then immediately trying to rebuild it with the ruins of the "wrecked" structure. Paul closes this chastisement of the apostle Peter with the severe charge that his inconsistency made him a transgressor.

Verse 19. *Through the law am dead to the law.* The law itself predicted its own end, to be replaced by the law of another prophet who was to be raised up from among the Jews. (See Deuteronomy 18: 18-20.) Hence a Christian was to be regarded dead to the law (for religious purposes), that he might live unto God through Christ.

Verse 20. To be *crucified* means to be put to death, and whether it is figurative or literal depends on how the word is used. Of course we know it is figurative in this case since Paul is living and active in his service to Christ. Chapter 6: 14 shows a practical use of the word, which is that the things of a worldly life had been put to death by the conversion of Paul to Christ. The same thought is set forth in Romans 8: 13 and Colossians 3: 5, where the apostle commands us to mortify (put to death) the deeds of the flesh. Paul was induced to do this by his faith in Christ. Being crucified *with* Christ shows some kind of association with Him in connection with sin. That relation may well be expressed by saying that Christ died *for* sin and Paul died (figuratively) *to* sin. After his life of sin was put to death through Christ, his spiritual being was enabled to live through Him. (See Romans 6: 8-12.) *Live in the flesh* denotes that his life of faith is accomplished while living in the fleshly body.

Verse 21. To *frustrate* means to hinder or set aside. In accepting the law of Christ, Paul did not show any disrespect for God's grace that was given to previous dispensations, but rather he was carrying out the very things that were divinely intended in those ages. (See the comments on verse 19.)

Galatians 3

Verse 1. The original for *bewitched* is defined by Thayer, "to bring evil on one by feigned praise or an evil eye, to charm, to bewitch one," and he explains it to mean, "of those who lead away others into error by wicked acts." The ones who were doing this with the Galatians were the Judaizers who were deceiving them into thinking they should go back to the old law. *Before whose eyes, etc.* The Galatians had seen the evidence of Christ's great sacrifice in the lives of Paul and other true teachers of the Gospel among them, so that they had been given full opportunity for seeing the superior spiritual life in a service to Him.

Verse 2. The argument Paul makes in this verse may be said to be one that has a factual basis. The Galatian brethren knew they were in possession of the Spirit, for whenever and wherever an apostle led men and women into the service for Christ, they were shown evidence of the Spirit by the gifts bestowed upon those receiving the hands of the apostle. And these brethren also knew that they had never received the gifts except through *hearing of faith*, which means the Gospel, though the law had been in existence for centuries.

Verse 3. It is certain that God's dealings with man would not decline in degrees of perfection or completeness, but would advance as humanity became able to receive them. On this principle, the things to be accomplished through the "ministration of the Spirit" (2 Corinthians 3: 8) would be an advancement over that which was possible by *the flesh*, a term given to the ordinances of the law of Moses, because of its consisting of "carnal ordinances" (Hebrews 9: 1, 10). The Galatians were reversing the order and leaving the completeness of the system under the Spirit, in which they had *begun* their religious life, and going backward to finish (be *made perfect)* their religious lives by the ordinances of the law.

Verse 4. *Suffered . . . in vain.* The Gentiles who accepted the Gospel were persecuted by the Judaaizers who wished them to be satisfied with the law of Moses. They could have avoided these persecutions had they yielded to the pressure of the Judaizing teachers. Now, after having stood firm at first in spite of the persecutions, if they backslide and take up the ordinances of the law, it would render all of their past sufferings for Christ to be vain. (See Hebrews 10: 32-35.)

Verse 5. This is the same as verse 2.

Verse 6. In all of the systems of religious conduct that God has offered to man, individual faith was necessary for divine acceptance, even though the system as a whole was not termed one of faith, as the Christian or Gospel system is. Hence we are told that Abraham (in the Patriarchal Dispensation) was regarded righteous because of his faith. Abel belonged under the same dispensation and he also was blessed because of his faith (Hebrews 11: 4). Likewise the Jews who were under the dispensation of the law, did not receive the blessing of God without faith (Hebrews 4: 2).

Verse 7. It was generally regarded an honor to be related to Abraham. (See Matthew 3: 9; Luke 19: 9; 2 Corinthians 11: 22.) In their zeal for persuading the Gentiles to take up the ordinances of the law, the Judaizers tried to make capital of the respect for the great patriarch by connecting him with the law of Moses. Paul does not overlook the greatness of Abraham, but shows that his greatness was due to his characteristic of faith. However, that had nothing to do with the ordinances of the law, for he lived six centuries before the law was given. (See the comments on Romans 4: 1-13 in volume 1 of the New Testament Commentary.

Verse 8. *Scripture foreseeing* denotes that God could see ahead what would be done, and caused it to be written in the Scripture. *Faith* is used in the sense of *the faith*, a term applied to the New Testament system of religion. *Heathen* means the Gentiles, who were not included with the Jews under the law of Moses. (See the comments, at chapter 2: 9.) The Gentiles were going to be offered justification through *the faith*, and hence God revealed this beforehand to Abraham. Not in all its details, of course, but the fundamental truth that Jesus would bless *all nations* (and not the Jews only), was foretold to him in the words *in thee shall all nations be blessed.*

Verse 9. *Which be of faith* applies to all individuals who manifest the same degree of faith in God as was true of Abraham. *Blessed with* him means they will receive the blessing of God as being true servants of Him.

Verse 10. The Bible recognizes a distinction between a literal and a figurative, or a physical and a moral impossibility. Unless we observe such a distinction we will have difficulty with the apparently contradictory passages in 1 John 1: 8 and 3: 9. Peter said the fathers "were not able to bear" the yoke of the old law (Acts 15: 10). That passage is explained in volume 1 of the New Testament Commentary. Yet Paul cites a passage in the Old Testament that says that all who did not do so were *under the curse*. The original for the last word is defined by Thayer, "an execration, imprecation, curse." In severe cases the curse amounted to an unmerciful death (Hebrews 10: 28), but the law of Christ makes one free from such a curse (Romans 8: 2). By going back to the works of the law, the Galatians placed themselves under this curse.

Verse 11. *Evident* means it is clear—the conclusion is unavoidable. The basis for the conclusion is the inspired statement that *the just shall live by faith* (Habakkuk 2: 4). The old law was always considered to be one of outward works as a system, while the principle of faith existed from the days of Abel onward, and the New Testament is the first and only system that is referred to as *the faith*. Since faith and formal works are opposites, it follows that if a man is justified in God's sight by one, it cannot be by the other. This explains why Paul uses the word *evident* as he does in this verse.

Verse 12. *The law is not of faith*. The full significance of this is as if it said, "the law of Moses is not the same system as the faith of the New Testament." *Shall live by them*. The Jew who carefully observed the ceremonies imposed by the law of Moses, was able to live or be contented with the thought that his life was according to the outward forms of that system. Only God would know whether he was "mixing" faith with his work (Hebrews 4: 2), hence as long as he performed the deeds prescribed by the law, he could not be penalized by the congregation, and therefore he would escape the curse of the law.

Verse 13. The particular curse meant here is that of hanging on a tree, which was accomplished by crucifixion. By giving us a system that does not require such physical punishments, Christ took away that kind of curse. And He was able to bring about the change only by going through such a curse himself on our behalf, which is the reason He had to be crucified.

Verse 14. *Blessing of Abraham* denotes the blessing of God that was pronounced on Abraham because of his faith. If such a blessing was possible only through the outward deeds like those imposed by the law, then the great patriarch would have missed the said blessing, for he lived several hundred years before the law. But in adopting the principle of faith instead of the formalities of the law as that on which the blessing would be given, God could include Abraham in the divine blessing. And by the same token, such an arrangement made it possible for the Gentiles (who did not have the provisions of the law) to be blessed with Abraham, provided they manifested the same principle of faith as was shown by the noted patriarch.

Verse 15. *I speak after the manner of men*. For an illustration, Paul is using the usual customs of mankind regarding covenants or legal agreements, and the rules followed in observing them. To *confirm* means to ratify by some formality under the supervision of the proper authority. Hence Paul says that *though it be but a man's covenant*, yet if it has been confirmed it cannot be lawfully disannulled, although it must be confirmed to make it sure.

Verse 16. *Now to Abraham and his seed were the promises made*. This states the first instance that the promise of Christ was ever made to any human individual, notwithstanding a popular notion to the contrary. The reader should see the comments on Genesis 3: 14, 15, in volume 1 of the Old Testament Commentary. *Seed* is a word that may be used in either a singular or plural sense, hence Paul settles which meaning he is attaching to it here by saying *not seeds, as of many; but as of one*. He further specifies the one seed meant by the words *thy seed*, to which the apostle adds *which is Christ*. Thus we have the interesting information that when God made the promise to Abraham of universal blessings through his seed (Christ), He made the same promise to that Seed who was then with the Creator in Heaven. This sheds light on Hebrews 10: 5-7, which represents the attitude of Jesus when he left Heaven and came to the earth. He already knew (having been told at the same time that Abraham was) that He was to come into the world to bless "all nations," and He was submissive to his Father's will. That is why he said, "I come to do thy will, O God."

Verse 17. *Four hundred and thirty years* corresponds with the terms in Genesis 15: 13 and Exodus 12: 40, 41, which is the time the children of Israel were in Egypt. The reader is urged to see the comments on this subject at Genesis 15: 13-15, in volume 1 of the Old Testament Commentary. The present verse also shows that the period of four hundred and thirty years is the time the Israelites were in Egypt. It states that the law was four hundred and thirty years after the covenant was— not first given— but after it was *confirmed*. Psalms 105: 9, 10 plainly says it was confirmed unto Jacob. We cannot interpret that on the general basis that the name Jacob is used as including Abraham and Isaac, they being two of "the fathers" often spoken of, for in this place the writer mentions the three separately, and distinctly says the covenant was *confirmed* unto Jacob. It was in the days of Jacob the children of Israel went down into Egypt (Genesis 46: 1-6), and it was within three months after coming out of that country that they came to Sanai where the law was given (Exodus 19: 1). So the conclusion is clear; they entered Egypt in the days of Jacob, to whom the covenant was *confirmed*, and the law was given at the end of their sojourn, which Paul says was four hundred and thirty years after the covenant was *confirmed*. Paul makes the point that the giving of the law even that many years afterwards cannot disannul the covenant, because it had been *confirmed*. (See the comments at verse 15.)

Verse 18. *The inheritance* means the blessing that was to be offered to all nations of the world through his seed. The argument of the verse is that if the blessing was to come through the law (as the Judaizers were teaching), then it could not have been connected with the promise first made to Abraham, for that was done many centuries before the law. And yet it was well known that God actually did give the promise of universal blessing to Abraham. The grand conclusion, then, is that the blessing intended for all nations (not the Jews only) was not the product of the law.

Verse 19. With the foregoing conclusion before them, it was natural for the readers to ask, *wherefore then serveth the law?* That is, for what purpose was the law given, if the promise of universal blessing through the seed of Abraham had already been given to the world as made known to the patriarch? The question is answered in the rest of this verse. The law *was added* (to the promise); not because God had made any change in His mind about the covenant, but *because of transgressions*. Members of the Patriarchial Dispensation became so unsatisfactory in their conduct, that it was doubtful if there would be a sufficient number of them in line of service to God to receive the Seed when he came. As a supplementary rule of behaviour, the law was given to bolster the nation descended from Abraham in its service to God, pending the final dispensation to come through Christ. But this addition of the law was not to be permanent (as the Judaizers were contending) but was to be in force only until the coming of the Seed to whom (see verse 16) the promise was made. In other words, the law was to be attached to the promise and in force only until Christ came into the world. *Ordained by angels*. God never appeared in person to mankind, but was always represented by angels when speaking to Moses and others. (See Acts 7: 53; Hebrews 2: 2.) *In the hand of a mediator*. The last word is from MESITES which Thayer defines, "a medium of communication, arbitrator," and he explains it as follows: "One who intervenes between two, either in order to make or restore peace and friendship, or to form a compact, or for ratifying a covenant." The mediator was Moses, who acted between God and the Israelties. This is all in agreement with the statement at the beginning of the verse, namely, that the law was added *because of transgressions*.

Verse 20. The very meaning of the word *mediator* indicates that two persons are on unfriendly terms, and the work of a mediator is to get them reconciled. There can be no need for nor work of a mediator in a case where only one person is interested. *But God is one* (only), therefore the presence of a mediator means that another party is involved. God is always righteous and no unrighteous person can be considered as being on good terms with Him. That is why a mediator was employed, and the party who needed to be reconciled to God was the Israelite nation, which had estranged itself from God by its "transgressions," and the law of Moses was the document by which the reconciliation was to be accomplished.

Verse 21. It must be constantly kept in mind that an outstanding evil that troubled the church in the first century was Judaism; the doctrine that the law of Moses was necessary to salvation. Paul is exposing that in the epistle to the Galatians. His argument in the few verses preceding the present one might raise the suggestion that the law was against the promises of God because it was added to those promises. He answers, God forbid, a term frequently used in the New Testament that denotes "by no means." The law could not be regarded as a competitor of the things set forth in the promises, for it did not claim to give (spiritual) life to its followers. It was added to the promises only for the purpose of stabilizing the conduct of the people of that dispensation, so that they would be ready to receive the "life" indicated in the promises when the time of fulfillment arrived. The law given through Moses was never intended in itself or by its merits, to give to its adherents that something regarded as spiritual life. Had such a law been given, then the obedience to it would have been acknowledged by the Lord as *righteousness*, and it would have been continued permanently.

Verse 22. *Concluded all under sin* does not say that God caused them to sin. The truths and facts regarding their conduct by the children of men, disclosed to God that all had sinned, hence He just declared what was true which was that all were sinners, which would make them all the subjects for divine mercy. Since all were actually sinners as a class, all would require the same means of spiritual redemption. The said means could not be by the merits of the law of works, therefore the Lord used that document as a hold-up or preparatory measure (see verse 19), at the same time pointing man to the coming of the promised seed of Abraham, that was to provide all nations with a system to be known as *the faith*, which would be able to assure the believers that they would be justified in Christ.

Verse 23. The thought in this verse is virtually the same as verse 19. *Faith* is a term for the Gospel of Christ, to distinguish it from the law of Moses. *Kept under the law* is the same as "it was added" in verse 19, and shut up unto the faith corresponds with "till the seed should come" in the same verse.

Verse 24. *Wherefore* means the apostle is drawing a conclusion from the facts of the preceding verse, and it is stated in the form of an illustration. *Schoolmaster* is from PAIDAGOGOS, which occurs only three times in the Greek New Testament; twice in Paul's present argument and once in 1 Corinthians 4: 15, where it is rendered "instructors." But neither of these English words is used in the same sense as they are today. The original word is defined by Thayer as, "a tutor," and Robinson defines it, "a pedagogue." Thayer furnishes some historical information on the subject that will be useful as follows: "A guide and guardian of boys. Among the Greeks and Romans the name was applied to trustworthy slaves who were charged with the duty of supervising the life and morals of boys belonging to the better class. The boys were not allowed so much as to step out of the house without them [were "shut up"—E. M. Z.] before arriving at the age of manhood." The apostle likens the law of Moses to this guardian of the child, because it was given charge of the "children of the Abrahamic promise" until such time as the fully-empowered Schoolmaster (Christ) should come, who would take charge of the pupils and administer spiritual education under the curriculum of *the faith*.

Verse 25. Having been brought into contact with the real teacher (Christ), there is no further need for the authority of the guardian (the law).

Verse 26. I again remind the reader that the main object of this epistle is to show that the old law is replaced by the Gospel as a rule of conduct for salvation. In order to be an heir to the estate of God, it is necessary to be a child of His. Paul declares that such a relationship is possible for these Galatians (who were Gentiles) only by *faith in Christ Jesus*.

Verse 27. Continuing the same line of argument expressed in the preceding verse, Paul refers his readers to the event of their obedience in baptism. The force of the argument will be best realized by laying the emphasis on the name *Christ*. It is as if the apostle said that those who had been baptized into Christ had *put on Christ* and not Moses.

Verse 28. *There* is an adverb of place, referring to the position named in the preceding verse of those who have "put on Christ." In Him there is no distinction made between the various classifications mentioned as far as their spiritual relationship with the Lord is concerned. They are all made to compose one group in the sight of God, by their obedience to Christ and not because of any other relationship they previously sustained, either under the one or the other dispensation of religion.

Verse 29. However, the aforesaid statement does not nullify the importance of Abraham, for he was promised a descendant who would be a blessing to all nations (whether Jew or Gentile), and such a blessing was to be acquired through faith in that descendant, who was Christ.

Galatians 4

Verse 1. There is a sense in which all men (whether Jews or Gentiles) were the children of God, namely, in that they were subject to Him either under the Jewish or the Patriarchal dispensatin. Notwithstanding this, all were restrained from enjoying the full benefits of the blessing promised through Abraham, until the time should arrive that the promised Seed came into the world. This period of waiting is here likened by Paul to the years of minority in a child. During that period, even though a man were a child and hence an heir of God, yet he had no more access to the property of his Father, namely, the possessions with Christ, than a servant would have to the estate of his master.

Verse 2. Continuing the line of comparison started in the preceding verse, the world of mankind is considered as minors, and hence under *tutors and governors* (see comments at chapter 3: 24), waiting for the *time appointed of the father*. As far as the disposal of an estate is concerned, a child is a minor until such time as the father has designated, when his child should be released from the rule of these *tutors*, and his share of the estate be turned over to his full use.

Verse 3. *When we were children* is still used in reference to the years before the Gospel Dispensation was introduced. The *bondage* means the preparatory state already described in several preceding verses. *Elements* is from STOICHEION, and Thayer's general definition is, "any first thing, from which the others belonging to some series or composite whole take their rise; an element, first principle." As the word is used in our verse, he explains it as follows: "The rudiments with which mankind, like minor children, were indoctrinated before the time of Christ, or the ceremonial precepts common alike to the worship of Jews and Gentiles." *World* is from KOSMOS, one definition of which is "the inhabitants of the earth, men, the human race." It is used in the present connection in that sense because such elements as pertain to moral and religious conduct could apply only to intelligent beings.

Verse 4. *Fulness of the time* means the time designated by the Father when his minor children (the Jews under the Mosaic Dispensation and the Gentiles under the Patriarchal Dispensation) were to be considered "of age" and ready to receive the full enjoyment of His provision for his children. That event was to be accomplished by the ushering into the world of His "only begotten Son" (see the comments at Luke 1: 35 in volume 1 of the New Testament Commentary). *Made* is from GINOMAI, which has a wide range of meanings in the New Testament. As it applies to an intelligent creature, the proper one of Thayer's definitions is, "to become, i. e., to come into existence, begin to be, receive being." In this verse it means that the Son was brought into being in this world through the use of a woman. (Again see the comments cited in the parentheses above.) *Under the law*. Jesus was born, lived and died while the law was in force, for it was not entirely replaced until Pentecost in Acts second chapter.

Verse 5. As a minor would be *redeemed* or released from the rule of his guardian when he became "of age," so the minors (Jews) were redeemed or released from the authority of the law when Christ brought the Gospel age into the world. *Adoption of sons*. Paul makes a slight change in the use of his illustration. The Jews (as well as the Gentiles, though in a less specific sense), have been referred to already as sons not of age, now they are said to require adoption in order to become sons. But the point of comparison is not so far away after all. Verse 1 says that as long as the heir is a child (a minor), he is virtually the same as a servant. Harking back to that item in his parable, Paul switches from his first use of the servant-heir character, treating him as if he were a servant in the ordinary sense only, and permitting him to become a son of the head of the estate, in order that he might become not merely an heir apparent, but one in fact. However, since this servant cannot be the begotten son of the head of the estate, the relation can be accomplished only by *the adoption of sons* as it is here worded.

Verse 6. *Because ye are sons* has been perverted by religious leaders, and made to teach as if it said, "to make you sons," etc. The sons of God are given possession of the Spirit, to be sure, but it is after they have become sons and not to make them such. However, the possession of this great gift is used in a special sense in this verse, which is evident by the affectionate effect its possession has on the recipients, namely, it causes them to address God as their Father. Hence the term is used to refer to the disposition or attitude toward God that is created in the mind of one who has been adopted into the family of God, through the service of His elder and only begotten Son, Jesus the Christ. *Abba, Father.* Both words refer to the same relationship, but the first is of Chaldean orgin and the second is from the Greek. By using the two, Paul shows that when a man is adopted into the family of God, regardless of his national ancestry, he is led to look upon God affectionately as his spiritual Father. In other words, in Christ Jesus there is no distinction made as to whether the children of God are Jews or Gentiles, learned or unlearned, male or female, bond or free.

Verse 7. This verse is explained by the comments on verse 5, with an added thought as to the advantage of being a son. It entitles one to share in the riches of the Father in Heaven, who is the Creator and owner of all things.

Verse 8. *Howbeit* is an old word, coming from ALLA, which has been translated by "but" 572 times. It has also been rendered "notwithstanding" 10 times. It is used in this verse to introduce a statement about the past conduct of the Galatians, most of whom were Gentiles who had been worshipers of idols. But that was before they had been brought to know the true God, which was done through the preaching of the Gospel. *By nature were no gods.* Most of the objects of worship among the idolaters were articles of their own formation, or were the creatures of their imagination. Even such things as planets and animals, the works in creation, were not made into intelligent beings by nature, and hence were *no gods* in the true sense of the term, since a god is expected to have intelligence enough to plan and power to execute the plan, and thus direct human beings in their religious and moral conduct.

Verse 9. God made himself known to the Galatians, who for the greater part were Gentiles and idolaters, by having the Gospel taken to them. They had never been under the bondage of the law, but under the service to false gods, and the Gospel had delivered them from that bondage. But after their escape from that bondage and introduction to the liberty that belongs to Christians, they were invaded by Judaizers who were leading them in a backward direction toward the ordinances of the Jewish law. The word *again* is rendered "back" in the margin which is correct, since these Gentiles had never been under the law of Moses and therefore could not be taken back to it *again.* In other words, they had been led out of their bondage of idolatry, and were now being turned into another bondage (that of Judaism) that was equally displeasing to God. *Beggarly* literally means to be poverty-stricken, and is here used of something that is not able to bestow any spiritual wealth on one. *Elements* is from the same word that is used in verse 3, and the comments on that place should be read again. The Galatian brethren were acting as if they desired to be in bondage again, only it was the bondage of Judaism.

Verse 10. Paul specifies some of the *elements* to which he referred in the preceding verse, namely, the observance of *days, and months, and times, and years.* This refers to the holy days and seasons that were required of the Jews under the Mosaic law, but which had ceased to be in force for religious purposes even to Jews; the Gentiles had no connection with them at any time for any purpose.

Verse 11. Paul's labors included his preaching the Gospel among the Galatians, in which he induced them to accept Christ and His law as their rule of faith and practice. If the Judaizers should persuade them to take up with the law of Moses, it would make void the work of Paul and thus render his labor *in vain.*

Verse 12. *Be as I am.* Paul, a Jew, had given up his religious devotion to the law of Moses in order to be true to Christ (Philippians 3: 9). The Galatians had similarly given up their worship of idols in order to become a worshiper of Christ. In this respect Paul could say *I am as ye are.* But the apostle had continued in that devotion to Christ, and he wished these brethren also to continue in their faithfulness to Christ. It is in that sense he wishes them to *be as I am. Ye have not injured me.* This is an affectionate statement to show that he did not have any personal complaint to make against them, for they had not shown him anything but kindness when laboring among them. Instead, his reason for the various rebukes he has been giving them is to rescue them from the evil effects of Judaism.

Verse 13. *Through infirmity of the flesh.* That is, in spite of this infirmity, Paul preached the Gospel to these Galatians and they gladly accepted it. For more comments on this infirmity, see those at 2 Corinthians 12: 7.

Verse 14. *Ye despised not.* The Galatians did not belittle the apostle because of this infirmity, which was something that might have suggested such an attitude, since it was placed upon him to humble him. (See the passage cited in the preceding verse.) In spite of it they respected him as if he had been an angel of God.

Verse 15. *Blessedness* means some great favor or good fortune, and the Galatians had congratulated themselves on having Paul in their midst. Their appreciation of him was apparently so great, that had it been possible they would have given him their eyes. This is an illustration drawn from the great value that anyone would place upon his eyes. Now the Galatians had become so changed in their attitude, Paul asks where their good estimate of him had gone.

Verse 16. *Therefore* indicates a conclusion drawn from certain truths or facts. The conclusion, however, is named (in the form of a question) before the basis, which is that Paul had told them the truth. The time when he told it to them evidently was when he was with them in person. Yet his becoming their enemy did not occur then, for we have just seen (verses 14, 15) that all was agreeable while he was in their midst. The change in their feeling for Paul came afterwards, and it was brought about by the meddlesome Judaizers, which is clearly shown by the next verse.

Verse 17. *They* means the Judaizers who have been referred to so many times. *Zealously affect* is from ZELOO, which Thayer defines, "to desire one earnestly, to strive after, busy one's self about him," and he explains it to mean, "to seek to draw over to one's side." Paul says the Judaizers were greatly concerned about the Galatians, but not for their good. *Exclude* is from EKKLEIO, and Thayer's definition here is, "to shut out," and he explains it as follows: "From intercourse with me and with teachers cooperating with me." *That ye might affect them.* The Judaizers hoped that by getting in between the Galatians and Paul, they would turn their attention toward them (the Judaizers), and be zealously affected, or be concerned to be attached to them instead of to Paul.

Verse 18. *Not only when I am present* confirms the comments on verse 16. While Paul was among these Galatians they seemed to be very much attached to him. He reasons that such was the right attitude, but that it should be maintained even when he is absent. (See Philippians 2: 12.)

Verse 19. *Little children* is from TEKNION which is used only 9 times in the Greek New Testament, and is always rendered by this term. Thayer explains that "in the New Testament it is used as a term of kindly address by teachers to their disciples." Robinson defines and explains it in virtually the same way. *Travail in birth,* etc. The sentence is used figuratively, and no figure or other illustration can be applied literally in all of its items. The main thought should be considered, and the over-all application of the figure be applied accordingly. An expectant mother will be concerned and at times will feel some uneasiness (travail) over the child that is being formed within her. Paul uses the circumstances to illustrate his concern for the Galatians. He is anxious that the spirit of Christ be formed in their minds, and given birth by proper devotion to Him and not to Moses in their lives.

Verse 20. *Desire to be present.* Since the Galatians seemed to be better inclined toward Paul when he was in their midst personally, he wished to be with them again. *Voice* is from a word that means speech, either written or spoken. The apostle believed that if he were with these brethren personally, this better attitude would permit him to be milder in his spoken words than he was in his written words. *Stand in doubt of you* corresponds with "I am afraid of you" in verse 11. (See the comments at that place.)

Verse 21. The very document (the Old Testament) that the Judaizers professed to respect so much, predicted in numerous places that there was to be a new prophet come into the world, who would give another system of religious government. Paul is challenging them to hear that law, which means for them to respect its predictions, and cease disturbing Gentile Christians with their subversive teaching.

Verse 22. To avoid confusion, it is well to keep in mind that no parable or other illustration is big enough to include every detail of the subject to which comparison is made. As a result there may be some items in one illustration that do not apply to the subject at hand, and may even seem to contradict some parts of another illustration on the general subject. But the whole story has to be told in order to make it understood at the point where it does apply. Furthermore, the same facts or truths may be used at different times to represent different subjects, or different phases of the same subject. It is generally understood that Christians are under the law of Christ, which was given at Jerusalem in Palestine, while the Jews were under the law of Moses that was given at Sinai in Arabia. Yet in this and the following verses, Sarah is represented as the mother of Christians, notwithstanding she was an ancestor of Moses by whom the law for the Jews was given. All of this will clear up by simply remembering that Abraham and Sarah were not only the parents of Isaac as the one from whom the Jewish nation was derived, but also were the parents of Isaac as the one from whom was to come the seed (Christ) that was to bless "all the families of the earth" by giving them the Gospel to take the place of the law of Moses. It is in the latter sense that the present use is made of the two sons of Abraham.

Verse 23. *After the flesh*. Ishmael was conceived and born according to the established laws of fleshly reproduction; the account of it is in Genesis 16. The mother of Isaac was barren and a miracle was needed to enable her to conceive. But God had promised her a son, hence He performed the miracle upon her so that she could become a mother, and that made him a son *by promise*. (See Genesis 16: 1, 2; 21: 1, 2.)

Verse 24. *Allegory* is another word for illustration or figure. The events concerning these two women were literal and actually happened, but Paul is showing how the facts illustrate some other truths pertaining to God's dispensations of religion among mankind. An illustration does not prove a point under discussion unless it has been selected by some acknowledged authority. That is what Paul has done in the present case, for he cites Isaiah 54: 1-6, where the context plainly shows that a spiritual use is made of the experience of Sarah. And this was an appropriate authority to quote, for the Judaizers professed to have great respect for the prophets. *The two covenants* means the law of Moses and the Gospel. In the illustration the apostle connects *Agar* (Hagar) with the law of Moses. *Gendereth to bondage* means to bring forth children who are destined to bondage under rites and ceremonies of the law.

Verse 25. The literal fact is that Sinai (represented by Agar) is in Arabia, and was the place where the law of Moses came forth, with all of its burdens of ordinances, which are termed the *yoke of bondage* in the next chapter. The location of Jerusalem in Palestine is another literal fact, but Paul makes a figurative use of the fact because of the conditions of servitude involving the city in his day. That is why he says that Agar and Sinai *answereth* (meaning to correspond with or be in the same rank or condition) *to Jerusalem which now is*. It is true that Jerusalem was the place, geographically, from which the Gospel was given to the world. But at the time of Paul the city was still clinging to the law of Moses as far as the Jews were concerned, and hence was yet under the bondage imposed by the Sinaite law.

Verse 26. This *Jerusalem* is figurative and means the church that was started in that city. Hebrew 12: 22, 28 connects the name of this city with the church, which is the institution through which Christians obtain their spiritual relation with Sarah, the mother of the great Seed that was to bless all nations.

Verse 27. Some comments on this verse are offered at verse 24. The barren woman is Sarah who *travailest not* (does not have pains of childbirth) for the most of her life, and hence was *desolate* in that she had no child over which to rejoice until near the end of her life. *Many more children*. Isaac was the only son whom Sarah ever bore, but he was the person through whom Christ came into the world, by whom "all nations" were destined to furnish spiritual children for God. *Hath an husband.* Hagar was but the handmaid of Sarah, yet she was permitted to receive Abraham in the relation of husband and wife. However, the descendants from this union though numerous, were people of the heathen world and not spiritual children of God, as were the descendants of Sarah through Christ.

Verse 28. *As Isaac was.* The comparison is in the fact that Isaac was promised to Abraham and Sarah, and God performed a miracle so that the son could be produced. From that child of promise came the Seed that was to bless all nations (whether Jew or Gentile) by giving them the Gospel plan of salvation. Whoever, therefore, accepted this plan became children of God. They are termed *children of promise* because it is through the noted Seed that was given the world as promised to Abraham.

Verse 29. *Persecuted him.* The account of this is in Genesis 21: 9, but all that is said in that place is that Sarah saw Ishmael "mocking." It was on the occasion when the weaning of Isaac was celebrated with "a great feast." The original for "mocking" has several renderings in the Old Testament, some of which are more severe than others. But Paul says that Ishmael *persecuted* Isaac, hence we must conclude that some of the more severe definitions are applicable. (See my comments on Genesis 21: 9, in volume 1 of the Old Testament Commentary.) *Even so it is now.* In the comparison that Paul has been making, the descendants of Ishmael represent the Jews, and those of Isaac stand for Christians. As Ishmael persecuted Isaac, so the Jews were persecuting Christians, especially those from the Gentile nation.

Verse 30. *Nevertheless.* The idea is that the persecutor was stopped, and Paul quotes the passage that proves it; the statement is in Genesis 21: 10. Sarah was acting purely because of her motherly resentment against the envious treatment being accorded her son by Ishmael. However, her performance proved to be a prediction of another important one, namely, the rejection of the Sinaite covenant as a religious system for God's people.

Verse 31. The grand conclusion of this unusual argument is that Christians are spiritual children (or descendants) of the freewoman and not the bond. It means they are not under the bondage imposed by the law of Moses.

Galatians 5

Verse 1. Continuing from the thought in the closing verse of the preceding chapter, Paul exhorts his readers to maintain the freedom from the burdens of the old law. While that system was in force, it was commendable for those under it to be loyal to its requirements. But since Christ has given them liberty under His law through the Spirit, it is foolish for them to go back and try to take up the *yoke of bondage.* The word *again* might leave the impression that the Galatians had all formerly been under the law of Moses. That was not the case, for most of them were Gentiles and not under it. But many were now being induced by the Judaizers to take up that system, and thus entangle themselves with that yoke, which would be as severe a bondage as was that of idolatry from which they as Gentiles had been delivered. (See the comments on chapter 4: 9.)

Verse 2. *I Paul* is a phrase that is used to impress the Galatians with the seriousness of the matter at hand, and the authority that was behind the teaching being delivered. The general subject of this epistle is the issue between the law of Moses and the Gospel of Christ. Circumcision was only one item of the Mosaic system, but the Judaizers made more ado over it than any other part, so that accepting or rejecting it was virtually the same as thus treating the whole system as far as the logical requirements were concerned; indeed, Paul brings out that conclusion in the next verse. Since the Galatians were Gentiles, the only reason they could have for adopting circumcision was for its religious use, because only the descendants of Abraham had any right to if from a national standpoint. Hence, in adopting that rite, the Galatians would be going to the law for their religious rule of life. In so doing they would be bypassing Christ and his religious system, since He and Moses were never in authority at the same time.

Verse 3. In adopting circumcision as a religious rite, it committed them to the entire law if they were to be consistent. (See comments on the preceding verse.)

Verse 4. *No effect* is from KATARGEO, and in the King James Version it is rendered abolish 3 times, bring to nought 1, cumber 1, deliver 1, destroy 5, do away 3, loose 1, make of none effect 2, make void 1, make without effect 1, put away 1, put down 1, become of no effect 1, be to be done away 1, cease 1, come to nought 1, fail 1, vanish away 1. The Englishman's Greek New Testament translates the first part of this verse as follows: "Ye are deprived of all effect from the Christ." *Justified* is a key word in the present discussion, meaning to obtain spiritual or religious benefits from the law. A Jew was never deprived of the observances of the law if he did it only from the national standpoint, but he had no right to use it for any other purpose after Christ came. (See Romans 10: 4.) *Fallen from grace* means to lose out in the divine favor. This statement of the apostle completely overturns the doctrine labeled "once in grace always in grace."

Verse 5. *We* means Christians whether Jews or Gentiles, who have been taught by the law of the Spirit and not the law of Moses. *Righteousness by* (the) *faith* gives hope to those who *wait for* (rely on it and live and abide by its instructions) the reward held out to be given at the end of the race.

Verse 6. Circumcision was given to Abraham and his immediate family descendants, to be observed as a national mark as long as the world stands. When the law of Moses was added to the promise of Christ that was made to Abraham, it incorporated circumcision within its other rites as a part of that system of religion. When Christ gave the Gospel to the world as the final "rule of faith and practice," He left circumcision out of his system, which meant that the rite was again where it was at first, namely, a national mark only and restricted to the fleshly descendants of Abraham. Having lost all religious significance, it was of no avail in Christ whether a man was circumcised (being a Jew), or uncircumcised (being a Gentile). Instead, all works of the law were rejected for religious purposes, and a man's acceptance depended on the *faith which worketh by love*. That phrase means that a man's faith in Christ is such that he will work for Him from the pure motive of Love. (See John 14: 23.)

Verse 7. *Ye did run well.* This refers to the time before the Judaizers got among them and did their evil work. *Not obey the truth* means they failed to hear the requirements of the Gospel to the rejection of the works of the law.

Verse 8. The present attitude of the Galatians did not come from Christ, who had called them by the Gospel. Neither does Paul believe they had of themselves formed such a conclusion as was bringing about so much confusion. He is certain that some busy person is responsible for the trouble, by injecting himself among Gentile brethren.

Verse 9. There might be only one or perhaps a few men who were making all the trouble, but the apostle wants them not to be misled by the smallness of number among the disturbers. He illustrates the idea by the well known truth that a small amount of leaven is all that is necessary to affect the whole mass. This same truth is used in the case of the fornicator at Corinth (1 Corinthians 5: 6).

Verse 10. Paul still has confidence in the "rank and file" of the Galatian brethren that they will finally adjust themselves in conformity with the mind that he has expressed to them. But he warns that it will be unpleasant for the one or ones who are troubling them.

Verse 11. Some Judaizers charged that Paul was practicing or advocating circumcision as a religious rite. A pretext for such a false claim may have been drawn from the fact that he had Timothy circumcised (Acts 16: 3), disregarding the fact that he had Jewish blood in his veins, and thus had a right to it from a national standpoint. In our present verse Paul shows the foolishness of such a claim. Circumcision was the main issue between him and the Judaizers, and they were also the ones who were persecuting the apostle. If he was advocating the practice of circumcision, then nothing would be left in connection with the religion coming from the cross that would be so offensive to the Jews.

Verse 12. *They were even cut off* all comes from the Greek word APOKOPTO, which Thayer defines, "to cut off, amputate," and he explains it to mean, "I would that they (who urge the necessity of circumcision would not only circumcise themselves, but) would even mutilate themselves (or cut off their privy parts)." Robinson defines the word as does Thayer, and also gives the following explanation: "Would that for themselves they would (not only circumcise but) even cut off the parts usually circumcised, i. e. make themselves eunuchs." Strong defines and explains the word virtually the same as Thayer and Robinson. The idea of Paul is that the Judaizers were making so much of circumcision that they deserved "an overdose of their own medicine."

Verse 13. From here to the close of the epistle Paul will make only a few references to the law, the main argument of the letter having been given a thorough treatment. Matters of interest to Christians in their personal lives will receive attention. This verse warns that the liberty of which Paul has said so much, must not be abused and made an occasion to gratify the desires of the flesh. *Serve one another* is said in the sense of rendering loving service to each other in the work of Christ.

Verse 14. The Judaizers would claim that giving up the law would be losing an important rule of conduct for one another. Paul shows that no principle that was required under the law is given up, for the Gospel requires its believers to *love thy neighbor as thyself*, which virtually incudes every command contained in the Mosaic law. *All the law* means all of the commandments that pertain to the proper conduct between man and man. Exodus 20: 12-17 gives the six of the ten commandments that pertain to this subject. In the very nature of the case, if a man loves his neighbor as himself, he will observe all things required by these six commandments. The *one word* is Paul's term for the one commandment about love for one's neighbor.

Verse 15. *Bite, devour* and *consume* are used figuratively, referring to the treatment the Galatians were giving to each other. The main difference in the meaning is the degree of intensity with which they pursued their campaign of opposition. The apostle means to show them that a continuation of such a course would finally destroy their unity in Christ. One of the effects of such evils as Judaism when it is injected into a congregation, is to work up bitterness among the members, so that they get into a state of mutual conflict such as described by the three words italicized.

Verse 16. This verse clearly indicates that such conduct as described in the preceding one is prompted by **the** *lust* or desires of the flesh. The opposite would be that prompted by the Spirit, which gives to God's people the "rule of faith and practice" that belongs to the religion of Christ, as against that contained in the law of Moses, which the Judaizers were urging among the Gentile Christians.

Verse 17. *Lusteth against* means the desires of one are opposite of the other; their desires are not the same. This thought is treated at length at Romans 7: 15-21, in the first volume of the New Testament Commentary. It is true that the teaching for the guidance of Christians has been given through the work of the Holy Spirit, but in this verse the word should not be capitalized as it is used for the spirit or inner part of man, as against his outer or fleshly part. *Cannot do the things that ye would*; cannot follow both at the same time. (See again the passage just cited.)

Verse 18. The Spirit here has direct reference to the Holy Spirit, since He was the instrument by which the New Testament system of religion was given to take the place of the Mosaic law.

Verse 19. *Works of the flesh are manifest* on the principle that a tree is known by its fruits (Matthew 7: 15-20). *Adultery, fornication*. The difference between these words is only technical and legal. The laws of the land define adultery as the unlawful intimacy between married persons, and fornication is that between the unmarried. The Bible does not require such a distinction, but uses the words both as applying to a married person as well as to another. In Matthew 19: 9, Jesus gives fornication on the part of a wife as the only ground for divorce and remarriage of the innocent husband. And in Matthew 5: 32 where the same subject is considered, if the wife is innocent and her husband puts her away, he "causeth her to commit adultry." That is, such a woman would be tempted to marry another man, and in so doing she would be guilty of adultry. The two passages together show us that in the estimation of Jesus, a married woman can be guilty of either fornication or adultery, and hence there is no actual difference. But the distinction is thought of in some cases, and the apostle makes sure of eliminating any possible excuse by naming both words in the same condemnation. *Uncleanness* is from a word that means impurity of either mind or body. *Lasciviousness* is from ASELGEIA, and it must have been a strong word in the Greek language, for Thayer defines it as follows: "Unbridled lust, excess, licentiousness, lasciviousness, wantonness, outrageousness, shamelessness, insolence."

Verse 20. *Idolatry* being a word that belongs to religious activities, it might be wondered why it is named as a work of the flesh. The general explanation is that all activities not prompted by the law of the Spirit must be classed with those suggested by the flesh. (See verse 17.) The special explanation is in the definition of Thayer for the original word, and his comments on it as it is used in the New Testament; he defines it, "The worship of false gods, idolatry," and he explains it, "used of the formal sacrificial feasts had in honor of false gods." Since a feast would be interesting from the standpoint of the appetite, we can see why it is classed with the works of the flesh. A similar explanation will apply to a number of other things to be seen in this list, which, though not consisting literally of physical activities, yet are prompted by evil motives and hence must be attributed to the flesh. *Witchcraft* is from PHARMAKEIA, and its first definition is, "the use or administering of drugs." The next definition is, "sorcery, mgaical arts." It means any attempt to accomplish a result by means of pretended supernatural power or knowledge, such as fortune telling, palm reading, astrology, etc. Thayer defines the original word for *hatred* as, "cause of enmity." It means that attitude toward another that would tend to cause trouble between the two. *Variance* is a disposition to wrangle or quarrel. *Emulations* is from ZELOS, and Thayer defines it at this place, "envious and contentious rivalry, jealousy." Thayer defines the original for *wrath* as "passion, angry heat." *Strife* is from ERITHEIA, which is a very strong word. Thayer defines it, "a courting distinction, a desire to put one's self forward, a partizan and factious spirit which does not disdain [object to] low arts." It describes one who is determined to win, "by fair means or foul." *Sedition* means the disposition to bring about cliques and parties in the congregation, which might result in confusion and disunion of the whole body. *Heresies* is from HAIRESIS. Thayer's definitions are, "1. act of taking, capture. 2. choosing, choice. 3. that which is chosen; chosen opinion, tenet. 4. a sect or party. 5. dissensions," and according to his comments in connection with the word, it means something that a man chooses and uses, not because it is right, but because it happens to suit his personal taste.

Verse 21. The simple word *envy* is the only definition the lexicons give for the original Greek word, hence we are left to the English dictionary for information. Webster defines it "Chagrin or discontent at the excellence or good fortune (of another); to begrudge." Such a state of mind is a violation of Romans 12: 15. *Murder* literally means the unlawful slaying of a human being, which all will admit to be a work of the flesh. However, one can be guilty of murder in God's sight without the literal performing of it (1 John 3: 15). *Drunkenness*. Thayer gives the simple fact of intoxication as his definition of the Greek. Robinson gives a somewhat fuller definition, "strong drinking, drunkenness, a drunken-frolic." *Revelings* is from KOMOS. I have consulted seven lexicons, including Thayer and Robinson, and they all give virtually the same definitions and explanations. However, I shall quote from Groves because his definition is more concise and will require less space: "Festivity, feasting, revelry, riotous mirth; dancing and song; wantonness, dissoluteness, debauchery; luxury, indulgence, voluptuousness; a company of revelers, troop of bacchanals; any company, society, party." The definitions, together with the connections in which the original word is used in the New Testament (Romans 13: 13; Galatians 5: 21; 1 Peter 4: 3), clearly indicates loud or boisterous conduct, which should not be any part of the conduct of Christians.

Such like is rendered by the Englishman's Greek New Testament, "things like these." Thayer defines the word for *like*, "like, similar, resembling; may be compared to." The phrase is very significant in that Paul knew that as time passed, men would be originating new forms of sin, and he thus includes all such in the condemnations, even though a person might deny guilt of the ones specified. Any conduct, therefore, that resembles or may be compared to any of the evils named would be wrong for Christians. The question arises, who is to decide in any given case, whether it comes under the classification? Hebrew 5: 14 shows that such ability should come from use or practice in the Christian life. But if a disciple refuses to use his ability thus acquired, then 1 Corinthians 11: 31, 32 shows that some other person must exercise the judgment in the case. Hebrews 13: 17 says the rulers (elders) watch for the souls of the flock, hence the sheep are commanded to obey them. Elders must be the final judges on the unspecified things, as to whether they are to be considered "such like" or compared to the works of the flesh enumerated in this passage. The importance of this teaching is seen in the words that *they which do such things shall not inherit the kingdom of God.*

Verse 22. *Fruit of the Spirit* is said on the same principles as was stated about the *works of the flesh*, namely, a tree is known by its fruit. Many extravagant claims are made by some people about their being in possession of the Spirit. The sure way of determining the question is to observe the kind of lives they are showing. If they are truly living within the line of conduct prescribed in the New Testament by the inspiration of the Spirit, the things named in this and the following verses will be produced in their conduct. *Love* in this place is from the Greek word AGAPE. A full explanation of this word as indicated by the Greek is given in comments on Matthew 5: 43, volume 1 of the New Testament Commentary. *Joy* is defined in the lexicon also to mean "gladness." Certainly a Christian has much for which to be glad, and the connection in which the word is used in this passage, indicates that the rejoicing is over the proper things. (See 1 Corinthians 13: 6.) The general meaning of *peace* is a state of harmony between individuals, but whether that condition is pleasing to God depends on the terms of the agreement. If they are those authorized by the Spirit (as implied by the present passage), then the peace will be pleasing to Him. *Long-suffering* is from MAKROTHUMIA, and Thayer defines it at this place as well as at a number of other places, "patience, forebearance, long-suffering, slowness in avenging wrongs." It does not apply to cases pertaining to principles of right and wrong, for in such matters it is not expected that Christians will agree to any compromise. But where it is only a question of one's personal treatment, he should be slow in maintaining his "rights." *Gentleness* is another word for kindness, and a Christian can manifest it without any compromise of righteous principles. *Goodness* is general in application, being defined in the lexicon, "uprightness of heart and life." The idea is that a person wishing to bear the fruit of the Spirit, will regulate his life by the teaching that comes from that divine source. *Faith* is from PISTOS, and in the King James Version it is rendered assurance 1 time, belief 1, fidelity 1, faith 239. The lexicon gives it a wide range of meanings, depending on the connection in which the word is used. The main thought is that Christians will accept the testimony of the Spirit as given in the New Testament, and fashion his life accordingly.

Verse 23. *Meekness* is virtually the same as mildness or gentleness in one's attitude toward another. One who is meek will not be severe or harsh in his approach to another, even though the latter may be in the wrong. *Temperance* is from EGKRATEIA, and Thayer defines it, "self-control," and explains it to mean, "the virtue of one who masters his desires and passions, especially his sensual [fleshly] appetites." In popular usage, the word is made to have direct application to the use of intoxicating liquor as a beverage. It cannot be properly so used, because no amount of indulgence in drunkenness, however limited, is permitted for Christians. The scripture term for such things is "abstain" (1 Thessalonians 5: 22). *Temperance* can be used only in reference to things that are not wrong except when carried to excess. *Against such there is no law.* Paul has had much to say about the law of Christ as against that of Moses, because that was the most outstanding issue in the church at that time. The statement here means that the Lord has never had any law in force that would have been violated by the virtues just mentioned in this and the preceding verse.

Verse 24. *They that are Christ's* means the same people described by the words "led of the Spirit" in verse 18, and the ones who bear the "fruit of the Spirit" in verse 22. They became His by obeying the Gospel, given by the inspiration of the Spirit. *Crucified the flesh* denotes that the works of the flesh were killed or put out of action. *Affections* and *lusts* are virtually the same in principle, meaning the passions and evil desires of the flesh.

Verse 25. It is actually impossible to *live in* the Spirit and not *walk in* the Spirit, hence the thought is that our daily life should harmonize with our profession; it is about the same in thought as verse 16.

Verse 26. *Not be desirous* is rendered "not become" by the Englishman's Greek New Testament. *Vain glory* is defined as "self-esteem" in the lexicon. Such a spirit is not only wrong in the person himself, but it has an evil effect with his influence over others. *Provoking* is from PROKALEO, which Thayer defines, "to irritate," and a spirit of self-esteem will have that effect upon others. *Envying* is explained at verse 21, and such an attitude will be a logical result when one permits himself to become controlled by the spirit of self-esteem.

Galatians 6

Verse 1. The word *overtaken* is from PROLAMBANO which Thayer defines at this place as follows: "To take before; to anticipate, to forestall; to take one by forestalling him, i.e. surprise, detect." The word does not apply to a man who deliberately goes in the direction where he knows he may be tempted. Such a person could not truthfully say he had been "surprised" into doing wrong. The word means a case where a man is brought unexpectedly into contact with a strong temptation and under the "spur of the moment" yields to sin. *Spiritual* is from PNEUMATIKOS which Thayer defines, "One who is filled with and governed by the Spirit of God." Hence it means any faithful member of the church, not the elders only as is generally thought. It is a duty of every member of the congregation to act in trying to restore the one who has been overtaken. *Restore* literally means to mend or repair, which denotes that the man has been damaged by sin, and the effort should be made to repair the damage. *Meekness* is the same as in chapter 5: 23, and the explanation offered there should be applied here. In approaching a brother who has been surprised into sin, the would-be restorer should not have a feeling of self-esteem, as if such a misfortune could "never happen to him", for he does not know what effect an incident of "surprise" might have on him.

Verse 2. To *bear* means to take up and carry a load. *Burdens* is from BAROS which Thayer defines, "heaviness, weight, burden, trouble." It means the hardships and trials of this life, and Paul instructs Christians to help each other in such experiences. *Fulfil the law of Christ.* His teaching all through life was that the disciples should love each other, and that would be shown by lending a helping hand in the hardships of human existence.

Verse 3. *For* carries the thought back to verse 1 where self-esteem is condemned. If a man felt so conceited that he had no fear of being overtaken in a fault, the truth might turn out to be that he would have no background of character at all, when it came to meeting the tests of life. Such a man is here described as one who thinks himself to be *something* when he is *nothing*. The first word is from a neuter pronoun of very indefinite meaning as to degree or amount. The second is properly translated, and means absolutely *nothing* as far as any claim of any importance is concerned. The difference between *something* (however small) and *nothing* is infinite, yet Paul implies that a self-deceived man is that far off from the truth.

Verse 4. One of the common weaknesses of man is to feel justified because he thinks his life compares favorably with that of others. Paul condemns that in 2 Corinthians 10: 12, and he is again dealing with that subject here. *Prove* is from DOKIMAZO, and in the King James Version it is rendered allow 2 times, approve 3, discern 2, examine 1, like 1, prove 10, try 4. Thayer defines it, "To test, examine, prove, scrutinize; to recognize as genuine after examination, to approve, deem worthy." Of course such an examination cannot be made without the use of a proper standard. 1 Peter 4: 11 (and many other passages too numerous to cite) shows that the true standard of right and wrong is the word of God. The important thought in this verse is for each man to prove his *own* work instead of another's. Whether he would do better than the man he is supposed to be trying to "restore" is not the issue at stake, for being better than some other brother does not prove that one is what he should be. But if he tests his life by the divine standard of God's word and finds it in harmony therewith, he will then have the right to rejoice. And that rejoicing will not be because someone else has done his duty, but because he *himself alone* has measured up to the divine rule.

Verse 5. This verse might seem to contradict verse 2, but they are in perfect agreement for they are speaking of *burdens* that are altogether different; the word in this verse is from PHORTION. Thayer explains that the burdens in the Greek word indicated are, "the obligations Christ lays upon his followers," and it is clear to all that no man can discharge the "obligations" of another. He can help others in the trials and hardships of life, but each man is individually responsible to God. That is the reason he should test his life by the word of God, and not by comparing it with the lives of others.

Verse 6. In 1 Corinthians 9: 14 it is said that "they which preach the gospel should live of the gospel." No preacher can literally live on the word of God, hence the passage means he is to get his living from those who receive the preaching; such is the meaning of the present verse. To *communicate* denotes the act of giving, and *good things* means the things necessary to life. The man who devotes his time to the preaching of the Gospel, should be financially supported by those who get the benefit of the preaching.

Verse 7. *Mocked* is from MUKTERIZO, and both Thayer and Robinson define it, "To turn up the nose or sneer at; to mock, deride." This is the only place where the word is used in the Greek New Testament. The term is used in connection with the thought of a man's responsibility to God, which will finally require him to answer for his conduct in this life. God has commanded his creatures to follow the proper course; to do that which is spiritual and not that which is dictated by the flesh. Moreover, He has told man that he will reap the kind of harvest that he has been producing. Paul is warning his readers not to be deceived or misled into thinking he can ignore (snub or by-pass) God and avoid the undesirable consequences of an unrighteous life. God will not suffer any man to "get by" with such an attempt, but will sustain His law already established on the relation of "cause and effect." On that basis the apostle affirms that a man will reap as he sows, a truth that is taught by nature.

Verse 8. The word *to* is from EIS, and Thayer uses three and a half pages of his lexicon in defining it in its various shades of meaning. However, his introductory paragraph gives the general meaning of the word as follows: "Into, to, towards, for, among." We should use the word that is best adapted to the connection in which it is found. When a man sows a field, he does it (or is supposed to) *for* the purpose of raising a certain kind of crop, hence the word italicized would be the proper one of the definitions for our use here. In temporal matters no man thinks he can sow his field with weeds and expect to raise wheat. Yet in moral and spiritual matters man seems to think he can ignore that law, sow the seeds that are qualified for the production of a fleshly crop, and then gather a spiritual harvest from it. The apostle warns that it will not be so, but that a man will reap as he has sown. There are only two kinds of seed and hence only two kinds of harvest possible. The fleshly seed will produce *corruption* which Thayer defines, "the loss of salvation, etrnal misery." The opposite is *life everlasting* to be reaped at the harvest which will be at "the end of the world" (Matthew 13: 39). The two kinds of seed are described as the kinds of human conduct in verses 19-23 of chapter 5. Every man is sowing just one or the other of these kinds of seed, and he will reap accordingly at the day of judgment.

Verse 9. God never commands that which is impossible, nor forbids that which is unavoidable. *Weary* does not pertain to the body or material part of our being, for if we exercise ourselves we cannot avoid becoming tired; such a result is beyond our control. The word is from EKKAKEO, and Thayer defines it, "to be weary in anything, to lose courage, flag, faint." Robinson defines it, "to be fainthearted, to faint." Hence it is clear the word refers to the mind and not the body. A man may become literally worked down or "worn out" by his toils for the Master, but if he has the proper interest in the work he will never become tired in mind, but will always feel keen and alert in the duty for Christ. (See 2 Corinthians 4: 16.) This all agrees with the reasoning of the latter part of our present verse.

Verse 10. *Good* is from AGATHOS, which has a wide range of meanings, including both material and immaterial subjects. Among the definitions given by Thayer are the following: "Excelling in any respect, distinguished, good; useful, salutary; pleasant, agreeable, joyful, happy; benevolent, kind, generous." It is right for the church or an individual Christian to bestow a favor upon those of the world, but where the opportunities are limited, preference must be given to members of the church.

Verse 11. According to several lexicons, the original word for *letter* has two meanings; first, the size of the characters that make up an alphabet; second, the size or length of a composition formed by the letters. There is nothing in the connection here to indicate that Paul was making any point out of the size of the characters he was using, hence the conclusion is that he uses the second meaning. As a rule the apostle dictated his epistles and then signed them to make them authentic (2 Thessalonians 3: 17); but because of his great concern for the interests of the Galatian brethren, he wrote this entire epistle with his own hand. Considering the rule of not doing the writing of the body of his letters, it would make the present one comparatively *large*. Robinson defines the original for the last word as meaning "of dignity." Strong defines it, "figuratively, in dignity." Thayer defines it, "how distinguished."

Verse 12. *As many* refers to the Judaizers among the disciples. *Fair show in the flesh* means they wished to make a favorable impression on the unbelieving Jews who were jealous lest the law of Moses should be neglected. By constraining the Gentile Christians to become circumcised, they thought it would please the unbelieving Jews, and hence they would not be so apt to persecute them (the Judaizers) for their association with the Gentile Christians.

Verse 13. *Neither they . . . keep the law.* These Judaizers were like the Sabbatarians of our day, who make a great ado about the law and pretend that it is still in force. Yet they spend most of their energy in condemning Christians because they do not "keep the sabbath holy." The inconsistency of these modern Judaizers is shown in that they violate the very commandment they pretend to observe. (See Exodus 20: 8-11.) This forbids working the beasts of service on the sabbath, yet it is not uncommon to see these pretenders drive their horses to the "sabbath school" on Saturday. This puts such false teachers in the same class with the Judaizers of Paul's day. They did not keep the law, but wished to induce the Christians to accept circumcision, so that they (the Judaizers) could boast about it.

Verse 14. *God forbid.* There is no word in the original for the name of God, and it has been supplied by the King James translators by way of comment. The American Standard Version renders this as follows: "But far be it from me to glory," etc. *The world is crucified unto me.* When *crucified* is used figuratively, it denotes that something has been killed or put out of action. Paul became dead to the sinful things of the world, and that spiritual state was caused by his devotion to the cross, or the spiritual service made possible by Christ's death on the tree.

Verse 15. This verse is the same in thought as chapter 5: 6; *a new creature* being equivalent to "faith which worketh by love"; please see those comments again.

Verse 16. *This rule* means the one stated in the preceding verse, namely, being a new creature in Christ Jesus. *The Israel of God.* None but those who believe in Christ Jesus would walk according to the *rule* mentioned, hence the first consideration is given the Gentiles who have accepted the Gospel. That places the italicized phrase with the believing Jews. The Jews were formerly the people of God before Christ was offered to the world, hence they are referred to here as being the *Israel of God* in this special sense. (See James 1: 1.)

Verse 17. Paul's apostolic authority had been questioned by some of the Judaizers. They made great claim on the ground of the fleshly mark of circumcision. In that respect they had no advantage over the apostle since he was circumcised also, but he had that mark as a Jew and a lineal descendant of Abraham. However, he was not claiming any special connection with Christ on that account, for the time had come when being in Him did not depend upon whether a man was circumcised or not. (See verse 15.) But Paul had other marks in the flesh that were significant, and that proved his close relationship as a servant (slave) of Christ. *Marks* is from STIGMA, and Thayer defines it, "a mark pricked in or branded upon the body." He then gives the following historical information: "According to ancient oriental [eastern] usage, slaves and soldiers bore the name or stamp of their master or commander branded or pricked (cut) into their bodies to indicate what master or general they belonged to . . . hence the marks of (the Lord) Jesus, which Paul in Galatians 6: 17 says he bears branded on his body, are the traces left there by the perils, hardships, imprisonments, scourgings, endured by him for the cause of Christ, and which mark him as Christ's faithful and approved votary [one devoted], servant, soldier." If a man was suspected of being a run-away slave, or for any other reason his identity should be questioned, the matter could be settled by unclothing him and looking for the brands. Paul is making the point that it is unnecessary for any man to *trouble* about examining him; he freely adimts that he is a servant of Christ, and that the brands could be seen on his body. As in many illustrations, there are some points that are exceptions. In the case of temporal slaves, the brands were stamped on their bodies by their masters, while Paul's marks were inflicted by the enemies of his Master. Also, Paul was not a run-away slave but was happy to admit his relationship of service to Jesus Christ.

Verse 18. Paul wished that the grace (favor) of Christ would be with the *spirit* of his brethren; if so, their temporal needs would be supplied also.

Ephesians 1

Verse 1. Unlike the preceding epistle, this one is addressed to a single congregation, which was located in the city of Ephesus. It is the same congregation that is mentioned in Revelation 1: 11, which had its start in Acts 18: 19. *Saints* and *faithful in Christ Jesus* are not different people. The second term is just one description of the first.

Verse 2. *Grace* and *peace* are commented upon at Galatians 1: 3. In every instance of this kind of passage the point is emphatic that God and Christ are the source of these good things.

Verse 3. When man blesses God it means he gives Him the credit for all blessings or happiness. It is important to note that God is called the Father of Christ. This refutes the doctrine of Rome which is followed by most of the denominational world, that God and Christ are one and the same person. It is foolish to imply that a father and his son could be the same person. *All spiritual blessings* denotes that no blessings of that kind can be obtained from any source but God and Christ. *Places* has no word in the original and and it is not useful in this connection. *Heavenly* is an adjective and used to describe the kind of blessings that are enjoyed *in Christ*. They are called *heavenly* because they originated in Heaven, and are unlike the favors produced on earth.

Verse 4. From this verse through 12, the passages have special reference to the apostles. This truth should be kept in mind in order to avoid confusion on the subject of predestination. God never decreed that any certain person should be saved, but He has predetermined what kind of character would be given salvation, then left it to the individual to qualify for the favor. However, God has predestinated certain official facts to be accomplished, and has selected certain ones to be His instruments in bringing about the predestined results. Among the persons who were chosen beforehand for special work were the apostles, referred to here by the pronoun, *us*, whom Paul says God has chosen *in him*, meaning Christ. This foreordained plan was formed before the foundation of the *world*, which means the inhabitants of the earth. The work for which they were previously selected will be named in the next verse, but this one tells the kind of character the apostles must have before they would be permitted to go on with the work. They must be *holy* and *without blame*, which pertains to their personal character. This may sound like the doctrine of salvation by predestination, but it is not since they were left as their own agents as to those qualities. If they chose not to qualify for the work they were put out of the plan as was done in the case of Judas.

Verse 5. The pronoun *us* stands for the apostles, whose work (not personal destiny) had been foreordained by the Lord. That work is designated by the phrase *adoption of children*. The term *adoption* is proper, since becoming children by birth can be accomplished only by the actions of the prospective parents. But it is possible for "outside" parties to work upon the individuals concrened, in persuading and arranging for them to be adopted into a family. The apostles did such work through the prospective Elder Brother, Jesus Christ. *Good pleasure of his will*. Sometimes a man will adopt an orphan from a humane motive or feeling for an unfortunate. But God has a pleasure in adopting the needy ones hence He *willed* it to be done according to the divine plan.

Verse 6. The *grace* or favor of being adopted into the family of God is a glory to Him as well as a credit of praise for His great benevolence. Receiving men into the close relationship of members in the divine family is an unspeakable blessing to man, but the Lord ordained that such a situation was to be fully acceptable to all parties concerned, and not merely one that was tolerated through a spirit of pity.

Verse 7. *Whom* is a pronoun that stands for *the beloved* in the preceding verse, who is Christ. The blood of Christ not only made men free from the bondage of the old law, but it brought forgiveness of sins to all who appropriated it through obedience to the Gospel. It is true that the servants under the law received forgiveness of their sins when they offered their sacrifices or animals, but that favor was given them on the merits of the one and final offering of the body of Christ. Hence when a man obtains the forgiveness of sins under the system put forth by Christ, that favor is done by virtue actually invested in the blood so applied. That is why Paul says it is *according to the riches of his grace*.

Verse 8. At verse 4 it is stated that many of these verses have special application to the apostles and their official work. It is also noted that even they had to develop certain personal qualifications in order to be retained for that special work. If they chose to maintain such traits (all of whom did except Judas), then the special and miraculous powers necessary for the work were given to them. Hence we have the statement here that God *hath abounded toward us* [the apostles] *in all wisdom and prudence*.

Verse 9. A *mystery* is anything not known, whether that is due to its never having been revealed to anyone, or that the story has not yet reached the ears of those to whom it is said to be a mystery. Hence the word does not necessarily mean something that is complicated or made up of ideas that cannot be understood by the human mind. The Gospel is a plain document, and its terms of salvation are within reach of the most ordinary understanding. But it was a mystery as far as the complete system is concerned, until it was made known by the Lord. He chose the apostles as the ones through whom the revelation was to be made, and it was done by giving them the Holy Spirit in great measure. All of this was according to God's *good pleasure*, and it was a purpose which He formed in himself long before it was revealed to man.

Verse 10. *Dispensation of the fulness of times* means when the time has fully come for the final dispensation of religion. *Gather together in one all things in Christ*. God has always had people on earth that were His from a religious standpoint, some of them under the Partriarchal Dispensation and some under the Jewish Dispensation. It was the divine plan to discontinue both of these systems and form a new one in Christ. *Which are in heaven*. Angels are not required to obey the commands of the Gospel as men are, but they are called upon to recognize Christ as the King and spiritual Ruler through the centuries of the final Dispensation; in this way they are a part of the body of Christ and in that sense are *in Christ*. (See Matthew 28: 18; Philippians 2: 9; Colossians 1: 20; Revelation 5: 13.)

Verse 11. The *inheritance* has special reference to the honorable work of extending the knowledge of the Gospel to all mankind. This was the work for which the apostles were predestinated. *Worketh all things*. God is powerful enough to accomplish anything that is right, hence whatever he predestines he can bring to pass. *Counsel* means purpose and advice, and when God formed his purpose concerning the plan of salvation through his Son, *his own will* was that it should be carried out.

Verse 12. The pronoun *we* represents the apostles, who were chosen beforehand to be the instruments of God in making known to the world the Gospel. Even the decree that the apostles were to be these special agents of God, would not have been completed through them had they not personally become believers in Christ to begin with. This explains why Paul was not given the commission as an apostle until he had *first trusted* in Jesus, (See Acts 9: 6; 26: 16-18.)

Verse 13. *Ye also* refers to the Ephesian brethren in general, to whom the apostle is writing this letter. What he says to them as Christians applies to all others in contrast with the apostles. This italicized phrase is proof that what has been said so far in this epistle applies to the apostles officially, and hence does not teach predestination of any man's personal salvation. There are some truths that can be said of all Christians, whether they are apostles, elders, deacons or unofficial members of Christ's body. That is why it will be well for the reader to go back and again take note of all that has been said in the comments on this chapter from the first verse on, then resume his study of the present verse, etc. *Trusted* has no word in the original at this place, but it is implied in the preceding verse and is therefore justified here. Note the brethren trusted *after* they heard the truth of the Gospel. This shows that becoming a disciple of Christ is not done by any miracle, except that the whole scheme of salvation is a miracle. *In whom* is a pronoun standing for Christ (last word of verse 12), in whom only is a Christian *sealed* (furnished with assuring evidence) by the Spirit which reveals the truth of salvation, by having dictated to the chosen writers (the apostles) the revelation of the Truth. The outward proof of being in the Spirit is the fruit borne by disciples (Galatians 5: 22).

Verse 14. This verse is an illustration drawn from a familiar business transaction involving a considerable value, in which one party makes a "down" payment as an evidence of good faith. It binds the parties to the contract until the time when full payment is to be made and the contract completed. God has promised eternal life to all who enter into this covenant with Him, which is to be bestowed in fact at the day of judgment. This, of course, is on condition that both parties fulfill all the terms of the agreement until the final time comes. This "down" payment is here called the *earnest*, which literally means a pledge. The pronoun *which* means that God's *earnest* or pledge payment is the favor bestowed through the Spirit as shown in verse 13. When the time arrives and God delivers the crown of eternal life to all the faithful "signers" of the agreement, all *praise* and *glory* will go to Him.

Verse 15. *Heard of your faith* does not indicate that Paul had never had personal knowledge of these brethren, for Acts 18: 19 shows he was present when they began their service to Christ. But some time had passed since he saw them, and hence his present knowledge of their continued faithfulness would come through some reliable report. *Love unto all the saints*. Faithfulness to Christ includes love for his people (John 13: 35). *Saints* is another name for disciples or Christians, because the word means those who have been made holy or spiritually clean by obedience to the Gospel.

Verse 16. Paul was thankful for the encouragement of faithful brethren, for that was of more value than temporal favors. *Making mention of you*. It is a common thing for brethren to specify to God the "objects of their prayers" when asking for divine favors on their behalf, but it is seldom that personal mention is made of those for whose services we should be thankful. Paul's example should have our careful consideration, in which he not only thanked God for the faithfulness of these brethren, but also prayed for the continued favors of the Lord upon them as we shall soon see.

Verse 17. This verse states some of the things Paul requested of God on behalf of the brethren at Ephesus. The Almighty is called the *God of our Lord Jesus Christ*. This statement is not favorable to the heresy that God and Christ are the same person, for it would be nonsense to say anyone could be his own god. *Father of glory* means that God is the originator and protector of all true glory. *Spirit of wisdom*. Those were the days of spiritual gifts (chapter 4: 7-11), and the gift of wisdom was one of them (1 Corinthians 12: 8). *Revelation* was another gift (1 Corinthians 14: 26), and Paul wished the brethren to receive it to the extent that it would increase their *knowledge of him*, meaning God.

Verse 18. *Eyes* is used figuratively because the physical body gets its light through those organs. It is used to compare the *understanding* or mental man as being enlightened by the sources of information mentioned in the preceding verse. With such enlightenment the brethren would *know* or realize the value of their *hope* that was held out for them by *his calling*, which means the Gospel call to salvation. On the same principle, they would see how *rich* is the glory that the *saints* (this word is explained at verse 15) may inherit in Him.

Verse 19. A fundamental thought in this verse is that God's power is great *to usward who believe*. The power of God does not mean anything to a man who is an unbeliever in the Gospel, which rests upon the resurrection of Christ; but it has saving power to one who does believe (Romans 1: 16).

Verse 20. The particular *working* to which the preceding verse refers is here explained to be the resurrection of Jesus from the dead. But the mighty work did not stop with the resurrection; others had been raised from the dead previously. In the case of Jesus, he was raised to die no more (Romans 6: 9; Acts 13: 34), and then was placed in a position of great honor and power at the right hand of his Father.

Verse 21. *Principality* is from a Greek word that has virtually the same meaning as our word "seniority," and is used of Christ because he existed before all other beings or things except his Father. *Power* especially means "authority," and Jesus said in Matthew 28: 18 that all "power" (same Greek word) was given to him in heaven and in earth. *Might* is a little stronger word in the original than the one for *power*, meaning not only the right or authority to do things, but also the ability to accomplish them. *Dominion* has special reference to the extent of territory over which one may rule. The statement of Jesus just cited in Matthew 28: 18 shows that His territory is heaven and earth. *This world* means this age or the Gospel Dispensation. Jesus will not rule as king after this age closes (1 Corinthians 15: 24, 25), but He will always be exalted above angels and men while the eternal ages roll.

Verse 22. This verse is virtually a repetition (in different words) of the thoughts expressed in the preceding verse. *All things under his feet* means that Christ was made superior to all things. The original word for *head* is used both for fleshly and spiritual things. When used for the latter, Thayer defines it, "supreme, chief, prominent, master, lord." *All things* is from one Greek word that is equivalent in meaning to "everything." *All things* that rightfully is connected with the church is subject to or is regulated by Him. Any movement or work or organization that cannot be shown to be directed by Jesus, has no scriptural relation to His church.

Verse 23. *Which is his body.* This is a fundamental statement, showing that the church of Christ and the body of Christ are one and the same. *Fulness of him* means that all the spiritual blessings of God are offered to man through the body of his Son.

Ephesians 2

Verse 1. *Hath he quickened* is in the Greek text in verse 5, and the King James translators have inserted the words in this verse to clarify the thought. To *quicken* means to make alive, whether used figuratively or literally. It is in the former sense here as the last part of the verse indicates, for the Ephesians had been *dead in sins*, which is a figurative phrase. When two things are separated they are dead to each other. Hence when men are living in sin they are separated from God, for sin cannot have any connection with Him. (See Isaiah 59: 2.) This is the same kind of death and life that Jesus meant in John 5: 25, which will be noticed further in verse 5.

Verse 2. Absolute sinless perfection does not exist in any man (1 John 1: 8), but to *walk* in sin which is referred to here means to lead a life whose general practice is one of sin. Such a walk was done by the Ephesians prior to their obedience to the Gospel. Such a life is *according to the course of this world*, which means that when a man lives daily in sin he is "running true to form" for those following the ways of the world. *Prince . . . the air.* Many of the words of human language have their origin in the opinions of the people using the language. Thayer says in connection with this place: "in the air, i. e., the devil, the prince of the demons that according to Jewish opinion fill the realm of the air." Paul recognizes this popular impression and uses it to describe the former manner of life that was practiced by the Ephesians. *The spirit* means the spirit of the evil *prince*, who is considered as the leader of all who are living in sin. *Children of disobedience.* The first word is from HUIOS and is used figuratively; it is explained by Thayer to mean, "one who is connected with or belongs to a thing by any kind of close relationship." Before the Ephesians became Christians, their life as a whole was one of disobedience against the law of righteousness. Such a life would produce a class of offspring *(children)* of like character, hence Paul calls them children of disobedience.

Verse 3. The pronoun *whom* refers to the *children of disobelience* who are mentioned in the preceding verse. *Conversation* is from ANASTREPHO, which Thayer defines, "to conduct one's self, behave one's self, live." So the term means the Ephesians formerly behaved themselves after the manner of disobedient children. The apostle specifies by saying it was the desires and lusts of the flesh that they were gratifying. *By nature the children of wrath.* By following the desires of their fleshly nature they did wrong, and that threatened them with the wrath of God.

Verse 4. *Rich in mercy.* Riches do not consist solely in the amount of one's possessions, but also in the character of them. The richness of God's mercy was indicated by the kind of love with which He regarded mankind while in the bondage of sin. This is the same thought that is the outstanding subject of the familiar but underestimated verse in John 3: 16, where the word "so" has reference to the *kind* of love God had for the world.

Verse 5. The first part of this verse is explained at verse 1, and the reader is requested to see that place again. This verse adds the information that the quickening is done *with Christ,* which means that it is through Him that we are made free from sin (Romans 6: 11). *By grace are ye saved.* This may be understood by the meaning of the second word. See the comments at 1 Corinthians 1: 3.

Verse 6. *Places* is not in the original as a separate word; it is explained at chapter 1: 3. The association of Christians with each other in the church of Christ is heavenly, because the entire arrangement originated in Heaven.

Verse 7. *Ages* often is used in the sense of eras or dispensations, but it is here more general and only means that "in the years to come," etc. Through the years, God was to show how rich is His grace in the form of kindness, and it was all to be accomplished through Christ Jesus.

Verse 8. The matter of being saved involves two parties; the one being saved, and the one doing the saving. God is the latter and is indicated by the word *grace;* man is the former and is represented by the word *faith.* Since grace is the unmerited favor of God (see comments at 1 Corinthians 1: 3), it includes the entire plan of salvation as far as the Lord's part is concerned. *Faith* is on the part of man, and it includes all of the things a man must do to prove his faith. *Not of yourselves.* Man could not have provided any plan whereby he could be saved. *It is the gift of God.* The subject under consideration is salvation, therefore it is the gift of God. A father might promise his son an automobile on condition that he work for him long enough to plant a crop. No boy can earn such an article in a few weeks, therefore the car would rightfully be considered a gift. Likewise, a lifetime of service to God could not merit eternal life, and therefore it will truly be the gift from God.

Verse 9. *Not of works.* See the illustration in the preceding paragraph drawn from a father and his son. The merits of our work for Christ would never have obtained salvation for us; had they done so, then man could have boasted that he had earned his salvation by what he had done.

Verse 10. *Workmanship* is from POIEMA, which Thayer defines, "that which has been made." When a man makes a piece of mechanism, he does so with the intention of getting certain things done with it, and he so forms it that it will be equipped to turn out such work. When it is accomplished, the mechanism would not be entitled to any credit for the work, for its maker has formed it for that particular production. Likewise the *good works* a Christian may perform are but the products that God had in mind when He created or formed him in the great Assembly Plant, the Lord Jesus Christ. The word *ordain* has such a great variety of meanings that I request the reader to see the complete definition of it at John 15: 16, in the first volume of the New Testament Commentary. In our verse it is defined, "To prepare before, to make ready beforehand." It means that God in his wisdom foresaw what would be the best kind of works for His children to follow, and so prepared a plan in His Son whereby they would be furnished with all the necessary equipment for such work.

Verse 11. *Gentiles in the flesh* denotes that the Ephesians were in the class of mankind that was distinguished from the Jews, and that the distinction was a fleshly one. *Called circumcision.* This rite was the fleshly mark that designated the classification as to which nation a man belonged. Hence the terms *circumcision* and *uncircumcision* were used to identify Jews and Gentiles.

Verse 12. *At that time* means the time before the Gospel Dispensation was brought into the world. *Without Christ* because the Patriarchal Dispensation did not specifically show any connection with Him, even though the spiritual benefits which God bestowed upon the faithful members of that dispensation, were done in view of the part that Christ was to play in the salvation of any man in any age. The Gentiles were *aliens* or foreigners from the *commonwealth,* nation or government, of Israel or the Jews. *Strangers* is from XENOS which Thayer defines, "without knowledge of, without a share in." Although the promises made to Abraham applied to the Gentiles (since Christ was to bless all nations), yet it was not known to them, hence in that sense they were *strangers* to the promise of Christ. *Having no hope* as far as the commonwealth or government of Israel was concerned. *Without God* is from ATHEOS; it is the origin of our English word "atheist." The Gentiles were without God as far as the provisions of the law of Moses were concerned, in the same sense that they were *without Christ* as explained earlier in this paragraph.

Verse 13. The ones *far off* were the Ephesians and all other Gentiles; they were far off as far as the Jewish Dispensation was concerned. *Made nigh by the blood of Christ.* This is said in contrast with the animal sacrifices that were offered under the Mosiac system, which were done for the benefit of the Jews only. It also is in contrast with the sacrifices that were offered upon the family altars under the Patriarchal Dispensation. It is to be understood that those sacrifices which were made under both the former dispensations, gave to the members thereof the favor of God, including the forgiveness of sins. But that was because God knew that the blood of Christ was to flow at the cross as a ransom, to make good the pledge of forgiveness that He had made to every Jew or Patriarch when he had performed his duty at the proper place of sacrifice. This is clearly shown in Hebrews 9: 15, which the reader should see in connection with the present verse.

Verse 14. *He is our peace.* The first word is a pronoun that stands for Christ, and the third is one that means the Jews and Gentiles. These two groups had been separated religiously by the partition wall of the Mosaic law which was given for the Jews only. This wall was removed by cancelling the religious function of the Jewish system, and giving a new one through Christ, adapted to the needs of Jews and Gentiles.

Verse 15. *In his flesh* refers to the crucifixion of Christ, whereby He nailed the old law to the cross and opened the way for the new law of the Gospel. Paul explains *enmity* to mean the "ceremonial" *ordinances* and *commandments*, which kept the Jews and Gentiles separated religiously. *Twain* means the two nations just mentioned, and *one new man* is a figurative name for the church, in which all men of every nation may be united in Christ.

Verse 16. The original word for *reconcile* is defined by Thayer, "to reconcile completely," and he explains it to mean, "to bring back to a former state of harmony." A significant word is "back," which indicates that a state of harmony had existed before. That is true, for man was at peace with God until Satan persuaded him to sin. That separated him from God and made it necessary for something to be done before he could be received into the divine favor again. The *one body* is the church (chapter 1: 22,23), and the death on the cross made it possible for both Jews and Gentiles to serve God in one religious system. *Slain the enmity.* (Enmity is explained at verse 15.)

Verse 17. Jesus did this preaching through the apostles first, and then by other devoted evangelists. The *peace* applies to the relationship of mankind in general to God, and the Jews and Gentiles to each other, who had been separated by the Mosaic law. *Far off* were Gentiles and *nigh* were the Jews; explained at verse 13.

Verse 18. *Him* means Christ and *both* denotes Jews and Gentiles. *Access* means the privilege of approaching the Father to receive the divine favors. *By one Spirit.* The Holy Spirit gave the apostles their instruction for setting up the church, and also to fill that body (the church) as a divine Guest (the original form for Ghost). The same apostles were also enabled to furnish the members of the church the necessary information for their service to God, including their *access* or approach to Him for his favors.

Verse 19. *Strangers and foreigners* means the same as "aliens" and "strangers" as explained in verse 12. *Fellowcitizens* means they are all citizens of the same government. This government is composed of *saints* which means those who have been made righteous by obedience to the Gospel, and it is called a *household* because the group called the church is regarded as a great family of God and Christ.

Verse 20. *Foundation of the apostles and prophets.* It has been thought by some that these prophets were those of the Old Testament, who prophesied the coming of the church. It is true they did make such predictions, and in that figurative manner could be referred to in connection with the church when thinking of the basis of truth upon which the divine institution was founded. However, Paul declares these prophets were a part of the foundation itself, hence they were the spiritually-gifted prophets that the church contained in the first century. This is specifically stated in Acts 13: 1 and 1 Corinthians 12: 28. That these prophets in the church were among those who received spiritual gifts is declared in Ephesians 4: 8-11. *Chief corner stone* is from the one Greek word AKROGONIAIOS which Thayer defines, "placed at the extreme corner." He also gives the historical information, "For as the corner-stone holds together two walls, so Christ joins together as Christians, into one body dedicated to God, those who were formerly Jews and Gentiles."

Verse 21. Most of the buildings in old times were built of stones, and Paul is using such as an illustration of the church. *Fitly framed together.* We generally think of wooden buildings only as being "framed," whereas the church is here likened to a stone structure. The three words in italics are from one Greek word which Thayer defines, "to join closely together." The statement means that all of the building, composed of both Jews and Gentiles, is fitted into the structure of which Christ is the binding stone at the corner. Such a building becomes a holy temple in (or on behalf of) the Lord.

Verse 22. Every building is erected for some special purpose. This divine structure is no exception, and the present verse tells us the purpose. It is the dwelling place of God on the earth. Not that He is dwelling in it personally, for in that sense God dwells only in Heaven (Acts 7: 48, 49); but He dwells in the church *through the Spirit*, or in a spiritual sense. (See 1 Peter 2: 5.)

Ephesians 3

Verse 1. *For this cause* means as if Paul said, "in view of what I have told you concerning what God has done for us through Christ," etc. What the apostle intends to say *for this cause*, he does not mention until he gets to verse 14 which begins with the same three words, where he goes on and completes the thought he has in mind. All the other verses from these first three words at the beginning of the chapter through verse 13, are put in as explanatory information. As Paul was writing this epistle he was actually a prisoner in Rome, and it was brought about by his preaching the Gospel to these and other Gentiles. (See Acts 21: 33; 28: 17, 20; Ephesians 6: 20.) Christ had taken possession of Paul or "apprehended" him for the very purpose of doing such work and receiving such treatment (Acts 9: 16; 26: 16-18; Philippians 3: 12).

Verse 2. *If ye have heard* has the sense of saying, "I take it for granted ye have heard," etc., yet Paul considers it well to give them further information on the important subject. *Dispensation* is defined in Thayer's lexicon, "the management, oversight, administration, of others' property; the office of a manager or overseer, stewardship." The phrase means that the apostle had been given charge of administrating the *grace* or favor of God unto the Gentiles.

Verse 3. According to the lexicon, the word *revelation* means "a disclosure of truth, instruction, concerning divine things before unknown—especially relating to the Christian salvation—given to the soul by God himself, or by the ascended Christ." An outstanding thought in the meaning of the word is that the communication was done by addressing the intelligence of the apostle, and not by some impression made upon his emotions. By this intellectual method, God made known to Paul the truths of the Gospel, that he might be able to tell them to the Ephesians and others. It is called a *mystery* because that word merely means anything not known, whether that be something that is complicated or simple in its nature. (See the definition of the word at chapter 1: 9.) *Wrote afore* refers to chapter 1: 9 and 2: 11-13, where the apostle wrote about the call of the Gentiles to share in the benefits of the Gospel.

Verse 4. *Whereby* denotes that when the brethren would read what Paul had written, they also might understand his knowledge of the subject. All that Paul or any other inspired writer knew of the Gospel was what had been revealed to them through the Holy Spirit. Therefore, when an uninspired man reads what has been thus written, he may have the same knowledge of the subject as does the inspired writer. This completely disproves the notion that people today cannot understand the Bible when they read it unless they have some miraculous assistance of the Spirit.

Verse 5. The promise made to Abraham in Genesis 12: 3 and 22: 18 really meant that both Jews and Gentiles were to be blessed by the Gospel of Christ. That same truth was repeated in various forms by many writers in the Old Testament. But the system as a whole was never revealed by them, hence Paul here declares that it was not made known to men in those years *as it is now revealed* by the Spirit. That revelation was made through the services of the *apostles and prophets*. (See the comments on chapter 2: 20.)

Verse 6. This verse states the specific feature of the Gospel that was not realized by the people in Old Testament times, namely, that the Gentiles were to be placed on an equal footing with the Jews in the Gospel.

Verse 7. *Whereof* refers to the Gospel of which Paul was made a *minister*. This word is from DIAKONOS, and it is elsewhere translated "deacon." Thayer's general definition is, "one who executes the commands of another, especially of a master; a servant, attendant, minister." The word does not necessarily denote an official, and when it is so used, the connection in which it is found will determine it so. In the present verse it has a special appplication because it refers to Paul who was an inspired apostle, and possessed with that measure of the Holy Spirit that enabled him to execute his official position. Such is the meaning of *effectual working of his* [God's] *power*.

Verse 8. *Less than the least* is described by both Thayer and Robinson as a double comparison that is permitted on the principle of what today is called "poetic license." Paul uses it for the sake of emphasis, to describe his feeling of unworthiness in being entrusted with the Gospel. He regards it a great honor to be selected by the Lord to be the one to preach the Gospel to the Gentiles, who had for generations past been "aliens from the commonwealth of Israel." *Unsearchable* is defined in Thayer's lexicon, "that cannot be traced out, that cannot be comprehended." It is the *riches of Christ* that is unsearchable, not the terms on which a man may obtain them. A person could completely understand all of the conditions on which he would obtain possession of a fine automobile, without fully realizing all the wonderful perfection of its mechanism.

Verse 9. The *mystery* again is the truth that the Gospel was to be given to the world for the benefit of both Jews and Gentiles. *Fellowship* means the mutual enjoyment of all nations in their equal relationship to Christ as their Saviour. *Been hid in God* is the same thought that is expressed by verse 5. *Created all things by Jesus Christ*. This was true of the creation of the material world (John 1: 1-3), but it is true also that all spiritual blessing are provided through Him. (Colossians 1: 16.)

Verse 10. *To the intent* denotes that God's intention in keeping the "mystery" hid through the past ages, was to let it be made known by the church. *Heavenly places* is from EPOURANIOS, which Thayer defines at this place, "the heavenly regions," and then explains his definition to mean, "heaven itself, the abode of God and angels." It is true that men in various ranks on earth were kept uninformed as to the complete system of righteousness to be brought into the world through Christ (Luke 10: 24), who would be benefitted by the fuller revelation. But even the angels in Heaven also were not given the information notwithstanding their desire to know about it. (See 1 Peter 1: 12.) *Might be known* is a verb and comes from the Greek word GNORIZO, which Thayer defines, "to make known." *Manifold wisdom of God* denotes that the many items of wisdom that God had in store for the world, were to be made known by the church. This wisdom includes all the religious instruction that mankind needs for proper service to God. He kept the full plan for such instruction from men and angels for four thousand years, in order that it might fully be made known by the church. It is the height of folly, therefore, for men to think they can establish educational and other organizations that can give this information "better than the church." Any human organization that pretends to give spiritual or moral benefits to man, is an infringement upon the exclusive rights of the church, for which God was making preparations through the centuries, and which He finally established through the blood of his Son.

Verse 11. *Eternal* is from AION, which means age or ages. Throughout the ages since the beginning of the world, God was planning for the complete plan of redemption for man, and that planning is here called the *eternal purpose*. It was to be perfected through Christ Jesus, who was promised to Abraham (Genesis 12: 3 and 22: 18).

Verse 12. *In whom* refers to Christ, who was foreordained of God to be the one through whom this eternal purpose was to be accomplished. *Boldness* does not mean a spirit of self-importance, but a feeling of abiding faith because of one's confidence in Christ. This confidence is produced by our faith in Him, and it bids us enjoy access to the Father through the Son.

Verse 13. To *faint* means to falter or become downhearted. Paul bids the brethren not to become thus affected over his tribulations caused by being a prisoner at Rome. *Which is your glory.* It should be regarded as an honor to be the brethren of a man whose faith causes him to keep cheerful under such conditions. The disciples in Acts 5: 41 rejoiced in the honor of suffering such treatment because of their service to Christ.

Verse 14. *For this cause.* This phrase is commented upon at length in the first verse of the chapter; please read that again. The apostle now proceeds to tell what he will do on the basis of the wonderful story of Jesus as just described in the foregoing verses. *Bow my knees* is mentioned incidentally as far as the posture of the body is concerned. We know it is not intended as a binding example for general practice, thus disfavoring other positions of the body while in prayer. Such a theory would contradict too many instances where prayer was offered while in some other position, and where the prayer is recorded in a favorable connection. In Matthew 26: 39 Jesus "fell on his face" and prayed; the publican's prayer was acceptable though he prayed "standing" in Luke 18: 13; Jesus gave thanks while sitting (Luke 22: 14-17). The validity of prayer depends upon the condition of the heart and not the position of the body; a hypocrite could pray as well in one position as another. God is again called the Father of Christ, which disproves the foolish notion that God and Christ are the same person.

Verse 15. *Of* is from EK, which means the source or authority by which the naming is done; that source is mentioned in the preceding verse, namely, the Father of our Lord Jesus Christ. *Family in heaven and earth* includes saints on earth and angels in Heaven. (See comments on chapter 1: 10.) As to what name or names are meant is not the question. The point in this verse is that a father of a family has the right to name the members of it. That truth rules out all of the multitude of names that have been applied by men to the professed children of God.

Verse 16. This verse begins the prayer that Paul proposed to offer to the Father. *According to the riches of his glory.* It would not be reasonable to ask a favor of anyone that is greater than the possessions of that person. The glory of God is so rich that Paul is encouraged to ask for enough of it to strengthen his brethren. God does his favors for the members of the divine family by the agency of the Spirit that fills the church. This is for the benefit of the *inner man,* which means the spiritual being, which can be affected only by spiritual help.

Verse 17. With two or three exceptions, the word *heart* in the King James Version comes from the Greek word KARDIA, and it is not translated by any other word, which occurs 158 times in the New Testament. I shall quote Thayer's various definitions of the original, which will give the reader a fair view of the range that it covers: "The heart; the vigor and sense of physical life; the soul or mind, as it is the fountain and seat of the thoughts, passions, desires, appetites, affections, purposes, endeavors; of the understanding, the faculty and seat of intelligence; of the soul so far forth as it is affected and stirred in a bad way or good, or of the soul as the seat of the sensibilities, affections, emotions, desires, appetites, passions; the middle or central or inmost part of any thing, even though inanimate."

In this quotation I have copied only the words in italics, which means they are the direct definitions of the author of the lexicon. In this vast list of definitions, the reader can see just two real general meanings of the heart as used in the New Testament, namely, the literal or fleshly as one, and the mental or spiritual as the other. The one to be taken in each given case must be determined by the connection in which it is used. Since Christ does not dwell literally or personally in any place on earth today, we know this verse does not use the *heart* in the fleshly or literal sense. This is also shown to be correct by the phrase *by faith* which Paul uses. Faith comes by hearing the word of God (Romans 10: 17), and when a man receives that word into his heart, he has the teaching of Jesus constantly with him, which is the meaning of the apostle's thought that He is to *dwell in your hearts by faith. Rooted and grounded.*

There is virtually not much difference between these words, and they could well be used interchangeably. In a techincal sense, the first means for a plant to take deep root, and that will give it a solid groundwork as a basis from which to make its growth. The soil in which this rooting is to take place is love—the love of God and Christ for this "plant" that was predicted in Ezekiel 34: 29. With such ever-fertile soil from which to grow, this divine plant is prepared to bring forth much fruit for the Keeper of the vineyard.

Verse 18. *Comprehend* is from a word that has different shades of meaning. In the present instance the first two definitions of Thayer are the most appropriate. "1. to lay hold of so as to make one's own, to obtain, attain to. 2. to seize upon, take possession of." Our word, therefore, does not mean that the human mind may fully know all about the greatness of God's loving system, but that it can take full possession of it under the terms that are offered by the Lord. The reader should see the comments on the word "unsearchable" in verse 8. *With all saints* (or Christians) means that no partiality is shown by Christ for any portion of His followers, but each has the same privileges to enjoy the great love exhibited in the Gospel. All solids have only three dimensions literally, so that *depth* and *height* would be the same. However, in the illustration Paul is thinking of a building which is the divine structure. Its *length* and *breadth* are important because it takes in the entire territory of human existence, both Jews and Gentiles. And its *height* signifies that it towers above all other institutions in dignity and efficiency. Also its *depth* means that its foundation is laid deep, even down to the rock of Truth.

Verse 19. *To know . . . which passeth knowledge* may seem to be a contradiction, but it will be clear in the light of the comments on the preceding verse and those on verse 8. The love of Christ is indeed so great that it surpasses all human knowledge. However, that need not prevent man from having some knowledge of it. *Filled with all the fulness* is a phrase so formed for the purpose of emphasis. When a man complies with the terms of salvation, he becomes the possessor of all that God has provided for him in this life. There is nothing lacking in his spiritual needs (Colossians 2: 10), even though he does not fully understand all its divine greatness.

Verse 20. This verse should be regarded as an inspired comment on Romans 8: 26, as they mean virtually the same thing. It does not say that God will do for us all that we ask, for He knows better than we what is good for us. The thought is that God *is able* to do whatever He deems best; also, God will even do us such favors in a better form than we are able to express it. *Power* is from DUNAMIS, one of the strongest words in the Greek language for the thought of might or ability. That power is used by the Lord as he answers our prayers, and it is *in us* or on our behalf.

Verse 21. The pronoun *him* stands for God, whose name is mentioned in verse 19. *Glory is from* DOXA, which occurs about 163 times in the Greek New Testament, and is rendered by "glory" 144 times. The outstanding definition in Thayer's lexicon as it applies to God, is expressed by the three words, "praise, honor, glory." Men are expected to honor God, but they are not left to follow their own devices in offering honor to Him. Unless they proceed in the way that God has directed, their pretensions of honor will not be recognized by Him. It is stated by the apostle that the glory (or honor and praise) that is offered to God is to be done *in the church*. This decree rules out all other attempts, devised by man. Even admitting that the show of honor performed by men outside the church are as expressive as any that are done in the church, yet it will not be accepted because He has ruled that it must be done through the divine organization. This is in agreement with the divine purpose that all religious instruction must be done by the church (verse 10). The further stipulation that the glorying must be done *by Christ Jesus* is not done arbitrarily, but is logically necessary if it is to be done *in the church*, for chapter 1: 22 declares that Christ was given to be head over all things to the church. Therefore, anything that is done in the church is done by Christ Jesus, and vice versa. *Throughout all ages*. There are men who teach that the church was sufficient for the Lord's purposes in the beginning of the era, but that modern conditions make it necessary for new methods to be used. This italicized phrase disproves that heresy, for it declares the honor given to God in the church must be so done throughout all ages. As a matter of further emphasis Paul adds *world without end* which is the same as saying "to the end of the world." *Amen* is explained at Matthew 5: 18 in volume 1 of the New Testament Commentary.

Ephesians 4

Verse 1. *Therefore* means that a conclusion is being drawn from the truths stated at the close of the preceding chapter. *Prisoner of the Lord* is explained in the comments on chapter 3: 1. To *beseech* means to entreat very earnestly. To *walk worthy* is to walk or conduct one's self in a manner suitable to his *vocation*. The last word technically means first the divine call or invitation to serve the Lord, and next it denotes that service itself. The same Greek word is used in 1 Corinthians 7: 20, where it is rendered "calling" and where the connection clearly shows it means a man's chief occupation. A Christian's chief occupation or *vocation* is service to the Lord.

Verse 2. *Lowliness* and *meekness* are virtually the same in meaning, but when used in combination, the first pertains to the state of mind and the second denotes the manner of approach. The phrase as a whole denotes a spirit of humility, which is indicated by the rest of the verse. *Longsuffering* does not indicate the least degree of compromise where principles of right and wrong are involved. It means patience in dealing with those who are uninformed and who thereby are led to make things unpleasant for others. *Forbearing* means about the same thing, and the apostle names the motive that will cause Christians to treat each other as he has been instructing them to do, and such motive is accounted for by the fact they have love for each other.

Verse 3. The "seven units" as they are so familiarly termed will be itemized soon, and in view of that combination the apostle gives a significant exhortation in this verse. All who are in the church are partakers of the one Spirit that animates the spiritual body. (1 Corinthians 12: 13; Ephesians 2: 18.) In this formal sense all members of the body of Christ are a unit since they are in the one and only institution that has been organized by the Lord. However, members of the church sometimes make their unity "doctrinal" only, and while maintaining a "united front" against the encroachments of false teachings and organizations of men, they may not observe the degree of love for each other that they should. As a result, there will not be the *peace* with that organic unity that is so necessary for the welfare of the cause of Christ.

Verse 4. Having introduced the subject of unity in the preceding verse, Paul now names the items involved in the setup, consisting of six or seven, depending on the classification named in verse 6, to be considered when we come to that verse. *One body and one Spirit*. This is logical, for it is universally admitted that there is but one Spirit, hence if there were more than one body (which is the church) then all but one would be without a Spirit and hence would be dead, since a body without a spirit is dead. There can be but *one hope* because God has called us with only one purpose in view, namely, the life eternal beyond this age.

Verse 5. The primary meaning of *Lord* is "ruler," and God is generally thought of as the Ruler of the universe. At the same time we commonly think of Christ as Lord; why, then, does Paul say there is *one Lord?* There is a special sense in which Christ is Lord, in that he is "head over all things to the church" (chapter 1: 22); hence He is this *one Lord*. Faith comes by hearing the word of God (Romans 10: 17); since there is but one inspired Word there can of necessity be but *one faith*. We frequently hear people speaking about the various "faiths" in the world. Doubtless there are many systems of religious doctrines in the world, but they can only be those produced by human wisdom, and are thus vain beliefs since the apostle definitely declares there is *one faith*. *One baptism*. The simple meaning of this word is "immersion" or "an overwhelming," regardless of who is baptized, the element in which it is done or the purpose for the act. The New Testament tells us of four different baptisms; that of suffering (Matthew 20: 22, 23), of fire (Matthew 3: 11), with the Holy Ghost (same reference), and with water (Acts 10: 47, 48). We are sure that Paul was aware of all these, yet he says there is *one baptism*. The apparent difficulty will clear up by observing that the first three are not commanded of sinners while the fourth one is. Whatever the Lord wished to take place by His action, whether that be some kind of baptism or anything else, was sure to happen without the cooperation of man. But something that must be done in response to a divine commandment, requires the willing act of needy mankind. Of such kind of baptism there is but one, and that is water baptism. Hence we find it here in a list of things that pertain to man's *endeavoring* in response to the apostolic command. More information on the meaning of the word *baptism* is given at Acts 8: 38, in volume 1 of the New Testament Commentary.

Verse 6. God and the Father are actually the same person, and hence give only one item of the "units" referred to at verse 4. The first term refers to Him as a deity, a fact applying to him regardless of all other persons in the universe. The second states His relation to other individuals as the Heavenly Parent. The words *above*, *through* and *in* are used for the purpose of emphasis. Paul wishes us to think of God as the one supreme Being who is superior to all others in existence.

Verse 7. Several verses following this one deal with the spiritual gifts that Christ caused to be given to disciples in the first years of the church. This verse refers to them as *grace* because the possession of them was certainly a favor, which is the meaning of *grace*. *According to the measure* denotes that not all disciples received the same kind or amount of this spiritual favor. (See 1 Corinthians 12: 4-7.) But whatever degree of this grace that was bestowed upon the various members of the church, it was all a part of *the gift of Christ*.

Verse 8. *Wherefore he saith* indicates a quotation is about to be made, which is from Psalms 68: 18, and it is a prediction of the ascension of Jesus to Heaven, which is the meaning of *on high*. *Captivity* is from a Greek word that is translated "a multitude of captives" in the margin of many Bibles. This rendering agrees with the definitions and comments of both Thayer and Robinson. The fact that Jesus did this leading of the captives *when he ascended up on high* indicates it applies to some special group. Evidently that consisted of the saints who are mentioned in Matthew 27: 52, 53, who came from their graves after the resurrection of Jesus. It will be well for the reader to see the notes on Romans 8: 29, 30, in volume 1 of the New Testament Commentary. These saints had been prisoners (captives) in Hades, but they were released from their "narrow chambers of death" by the resurrection of Jesus, who then led them with Him *when he ascended* to the Eternal Abode of those who are never to die again. As soon as Jesus arrived in the presence of his Father, he prayed that the Holy Spirit (Comforter, John 14: 16, 17) would be sent down upon the apostles. That was done, enabling them to bestow spiritual gifts upon them who had obeyed the Gospel (Acts 8: 15-18). The purpose of these gifts will be explained a little farther on in this chapter.

Verses 9, 10. These verses are a break into the direct line of thought that the apostle is discussing. However, are related to it in that they show the importance of Him of whom so much is being said. Having just referred to the ascension of Jesus, the apostle deems it well to say a few words about that subject. There have been two persons who have ascended to Heaven before: Enoch (Genesis 5: 24) and Elijah (2 Kings 2: 1, 11). But these persons were natural men prior to their ascension, hence that experience would not prove them to be divine. Paul at once meets that situation by declaring that this one who was said to have *ascended*, had before that time *descended*, and of necessity we would understand the descension to have been from the same place to which he afterwards ascended, which was Heaven, and that proves the divine origin and character of Jesus. *Lower parts of the earth.* Some explain this to mean the grave; it could not mean Hades since that is no part of the earth. Others teach that it refers to the lowly state which Jesus took upon himself and the humble life that he lived. I believe the statement embraces all of these and any other facts that were true of His stay on this earth. As proof that Paul has these great facts in mind, I will use the space to quote as follows: "Who, being in the form of God, thought it not robbery to be equal with God. But made himself of no reputation, and took upon him the form of a servant, and was made in the likeness of men. And being found in fashion as a man, he humbled himself, and became obedient unto death, even the death of the cross" (Philippians 2: 6-8). The first half of the tenth verse virtually repeats the statement of the preceding one, and then adds the phrase *above all heavens*. Since the heavens were all created by Christ in cooperation with God, it follows that in going back to his

Ephesians 4: 11-13

Father, Jesus would be raised above those things he had assisted in making. *Fill all things* is said in the sense of fulfilling all things that He had promised to do, including the bestowal of the Comforter (promised in John 14: 16) to give to the apostles miraculous power, and the work of conferring spiritual gifts upon others, which gifts will be discussed soon.

Verse 11. *And he gave some.* Many translators and commentators insert the words "to be" after this italicized phrase. But the grammatical inflection does not require nor justify it, so that the words must be regarded as an insertion upon no inspired authority. On the other hand, the word "unto" is in the text in verse 8, where the subject matter is the same as it is in our present verse, and thus the word may be inserted after the phrase with inspired example. It is true that bestowing the office of apostleship and the other offices mentioned, could be regarded as an honor and hence as a gift. But if that is the gift Paul meant, then we are confronted with the thought that the apostleship and eldership were to be discontinued after the first ages of the church, for verse 13 shows the gifts were not to be permanent. In truth, that very heresy is today advocated by some extremists. No, it means that Christ bestowed some of the spiritual gifts upon the various persons named. That is not strange, for even the apostles needed miraculous qualifications while the New Testament was in the making. But the office of the apostleship itself was not to cease after the miraculous gifts ceased, but they (the apostles) were to continue in authority unto the end of the world (Matthew 28: 20).

These *prophets* were the ones referred to in chapter 2: 20. *Evangelists* is from EUAGGELISTES, which Thayer defines, "a bringer of good tidings, an evangelist," and he adds this comment: "This name is given in the New Testament to those heralds of salvation through Christ who are not apostles." Robinson defines it, "In the New Testament, an evangelist, a preacher of the Gospel," and adds the explanation, "not fixed in any place, but travelling as a missionary to preach the Gospel and establish churches." Groves defines it, "an evangelist, preacher of the Gospel." Greenfield gives the definition, "one who announces glad tidings, an evangelist, preacher of the Gospel, teacher of the Christian religion." I have quoted from a number of lexicons because of the confusion that some are under concerning this word. The general trend of the various definitions, together with the connections in which the word is found in the King James Version, gives us the conclusion that it means a preacher whose special work is to preach the Gospel in new fields, then call the converts into assemblies for regular services, take charge of their development until men have been qualified for the eldership, then after appointing the elders to take himself from the management of the congregation and go on to other fields of labor. (See Titus 1: 5; 2 Timothy 4: 5; 1 Timothy 5: 19-21.) *Pastors* is from POIMEN and Thayer's definition is, "a herdsman, especially a shepherd; the presiding officer, manager, director, of any assembly." It applies to the elders of a congregation. This is shown in 1 Peter 5: 1-5 where the elders are mentioned in connection with Christ whom the apostle calls the chief Shepherd, thus representing the elders as shepherds, that being one of the words in the definition of our word *pastors*. *Teachers* is indefinite and applies to any disciple engaged principally in giving instruction to others.

Verse 12. This verse is a general statement of the purpose of spiritual gifts mentioned in the preceding verse. *Perfecting* means the strengthening of the saints (or Christians). *Work of the ministry* denotes the service of Christ in general. *Edifying* means upbuilding or making firm and being braced against attack.

Verse 13. *Till* is a preposition and denotes the termination of something. As used in this place it means that the things named in the preceding two verses will cease at the accomplishment of those mentioned in the present verse. *In the unity.* The first word is from EIS and may more properly be rendered "into.". *Of the faith.* Verse 5 declares there is *one faith*, hence it is always a unit, and the statement of Paul does not mean that something was to be done to bring the faith into a unit, for it is already so. The thought is that *all* professed disciples would come into or embrace that unity. *And of the knowledge.* The word *unity* has already been introduced in connection with *faith*, and it is implied in connection with the phrase about knowledge. That would make it mean as if it said "and into the unity of the knowledge," etc. Since not all kinds of knowledge is desirable, Paul specifies the kind he is writing about, namely, that of the Son of God. *Perfect man* is a figure of speech and means a full-grown man in contrast with an immature child. The illustration is to show the difference between the time when the church had to depend on spiritual gifts, and when it would have the complete New Testament. The contrast is likened to the immature thoughts and activities of a child, as against those of a man. *Stature* is from HELIKIA, which Thayer defines, "age, time of life; adult age, maturity; stature." It refers both to the age and size of a person, hence is a fitting illustration of the subject at hand. *Fulness of Christ* denotes that completeness of spiritual advancement that Christ makes possible through the complete revelation of the New Testament. I shall urge the reader to consider again the comments on 1 Corinthians 13th chapter.

Verse 14. The preceding two verses and several following the present one, show what is to be accomplished affirmatively by the complete New Testament. The present one states some of the things to be avoided by the complete volume. The original word for *children* is defined "untaught, unskilled," in Thayer's lexicon, and it is used to illustrate the unreliable standing of disciples who have no complete volume to guide them. *Tossed to and fro* is another figure for the same purpose, representing the untaught disciples as a frail raft tossed about by the waves. Waves are usually caused by *winds*, and the ones Paul has in mind are the false doctrines of men. Without the help of special guidance, the disciples would not be able to detect the false doctrines. *Sleight* and *cunning craftiness* refers to the trickery and deceptive language that false teachers use to mislead the untaught.

Verse 15. *Speaking the truth in love.* It is possible for one to be very strict in his compliance with the demands of truth from a "doctrinal" or technical motive, and yet not manifest the proper spirit toward those whom he addresses. Paul speaks of certain ones who received not the *love* of the truth (2 Thessalonians 2: 10). Those people would outwardly admit the truth because it is so evident they could not deny it, yet they had no real love for it and hence did not profit by it. In our passage the apostle teaches that full-grown Christians will love to speak the truth. Truth is the substance upon which the disciple of Chirst may grow—*grow up into Him in all things*. Physical bodies will not thrive unless they are under the control of the head where all the directing impulses originate. Likewise it is necessary for the spiritual body (the church, chapter 1: 22, 23) to have its growth and activities controlled by Christ its head, which will be considered in full detail with the next verse.

Verse 16. This verse as a whole may be regarded as a compound-complex sentence, but the central thought is expressed by the words *the whole body maketh increase.* All the rest of the verse is related to these words, enlarging and explaining how the body (the church) makes this increase. It is one of the most informative passages in the apostolic writings on the subject of "mutual edification," otherwise and more accurately termed mutual ministry; let us analyze the verse very carefully. *From whom* means from Christ who was named in the preceding verse as the head of the body. *The whole body.* If any part of a human body is thrown out of connection with the head, a state of ill health will result. Likewise the entire body or church must be subject to Christ the head, or spiritual illness will develop. *Fitly joined together.* In 1 Corinthians 12: 18 Paul is using the fleshly body as an illustration where he says: "But now hath God set the members every one of them in the body, as it hath pleased him." The same is true of the spiritual body or church, of which he is writing in this verse. *Compacted* is similar in meaning to the last italicized phrase, only it is a stronger term. The phrase means the members are so constructed that they fit each other, while the word *compacted* denotes a closer knitting of the parts as if they were welded together to compose this body of which Christ is the head. *Every joint supplieth.* The joints are the members of the body, and the phrase clearly teaches that each member of the church is expected to contribute something toward the edification of it. Any discrimination that is made against a member of the body is wrong, and any member who fails to contribute whatever he can to the advancement of the church is a dead joint that is a detriment to the body of Christ. This *effectual working* must be according to *the measure* or ability of the parts, since the members do not all have the same talents. When all of this process is observed, it will result in the increase or growth of the body, and it will be edified or built up in love for the Head and for each other as members.

Verse 17. *Testify in the Lord.* The first word means to exhort, and Paul is doing it in the Lord or by His instruction. The Ephesians were Gentiles mainly and had previously walked after the ways of the ungodly world. Having accepted Christ and started in His service, they were exhorted to discontinue their life of sin. *Other Gentiles* means those who had not become Christians.

Verse 18. This and the following verse describes the unrighteous way of life that the Gentiles practice who are still under the darkness of heathenism. It is much like the description of them in Romans 1: 18-24. *Understanding* means the mind, and it was darkened by their being *alienated* or separated from Him. The situation is accounted for by the fact of their *blindness* of heart. The other word for blindness is hardness of heart, or stubbornness.

Verse 19. *Being past feeling* all comes from the one Greek word APALGEO, and Thayer defines it, "to become callous." They were so hardened by sin that the truth had little or no effect on them, until they were even not concerned whether a thing was right or wrong. Such a state of mind would cause them to abandon themselves to the grossest kind of practices. LASCIVIOUSNESS means vile and vicious thoughts and desires. *All uncleanness* would include both physical and mental kinds. These people not only practiced such things, but did it *with greediness*, which denotes an active appetite for that kind of life.

Verse 20. *But ye have not so learned Christ.* The thought of this verse is as if it said, "you did not learn such practices from Christ." The Ephesian brethren had evidently become tinctured with such corruptions, for the exhortations so common in the rest of this chapter, as well as in many other places in the epistle, indicates such a conclusion. We recall this is the same church that is accused by John of having "left its first love" (Revelation 2: 1-4).

Verse 21. *If so be* is not said in the sense of any doubt, but it means that it really was true they had heard about Christ, and had been given the truth concerning Him. That being true, the apostle would repeat what he had said in the preceding verse, then go on and give his readers some exhortations concerning righteous living in Christ.

Verse 22. To *put off* means to cease doing things that belong to men of the world. *Conversation* refers to the general conduct including the speech used with their fellowmen. *Old man* is a figurative name for the fleshly desires that people of the world try to satisfy. It is the same "old man" that is described in Romans 6: 1-6. *Deceitful lusts.* Such lusts are deceitful because they lead a man to think he is enjoying genuine pleasure, and yet they will be disappointing in the end.

Verse 23. *Spirit* and *mind* means virtlally the same thing in a sentence like this, but the two are used for the purpose of emphasis. Paul wants them to realize that he is not writing about things that the fleshly body desires, but of those that are higher, and of a spiritual character. To be *renewed* denotes a change in their mind from an interest in carnal things, to desire the things that are spiritual.

Verse 24. *Put on* is the opposite of *put off* that is used in verse 22, and *new man* is the opposite of *old man* in the same verse. In ordinary language it means to cease doing worldly things and begin doing those that are spiritual. God is the creator of the material universe and also gives man his fleshly body. And He also is the creator or originator of the spiritual life that is to be practiced in Christ. *True holiness* does not imply there could be such a thing as false holiness. The phrase means that holiness is that kind of life that is according to truth.

Verse 25. Genuine repentance means a reformation of life, and it includes both the ceasing of practices that are wrong, and the doing of those that are right. Hence Paul teaches that lying should be put away, and truthful speaking be done instead. *Members one of another* is true because all Christians are members of the one body, namely, the body of Christ. (See Romans 12: 5:) It would not be good for the different parts of the physical body to oppose each other, for that would have a bad effect upon the whole body (1 Corinthians 12: 26). On the same principle, the members of the church should be interested in each other to such an extent that they would not do each other any harm by being untruthful in their dealings together.

Verse 26. The mere fact of being angry does not constitute sin, for

Jesus looked upon the people with anger (Mark 3: 5), and God is angry with the wicked every day (Psalms 7: 11). The sin consists in what one allows his anger to lead him into doing. That is why the apostle adds the warning not to let the sun go down upon one's wrath. That is, do not harbor the angry thoughts, but banish them before the day comes to a close, lest they finally tempt us into committing some sin.

Verse 27. *Neither give place to the devil.* Do not furnish the devil any room in your heart, for he will be sure to occupy it and go to work with his schemes. If a person harbors wrath from day to day, he is making an opportunity for the devil, and that is the same as giving him place.

Verse 28. Many of the admonitions throughout these verses deal with the two sides of practices, namely, the wrong and the right. The reader is instructed to avoid the first and do the second. The thief must cease obtaining property by stealing, then go to work that he may obtain it in an honest way. This is not only to supply his own needs, but also those of others. There are persons who are unable to support themselves, and that makes it the duty of the strong to help them in their need.

Verse 29. *Corrupt* is from SAPROS, which Thayer defines, "Of poor quality, bad, unfit for use, worthless." Robinson defines it, "Bad, decayed, rotten; corrupt, foul." *Communication* is from LOGOS, and it has been rendered by "word" in the King James Version at least 220 times. Hence the first sentence of this verse means that Christians should not use any language that is filthy and useless. Paul gives his explanation of what constitutes *good* language, namely, that which will edify or build up and strengthen the hearer. Such speech will further help the hearers by ministering or serving them with *grace*, which means favor of a spiritual kind.

Verse 30. A part of Thayer's definition of the original of *grieve* is "to offend." The Bible was given to the world through the guidance of the Holy Spirit. If we show any disrespect for the Sacred Volume, then, we will *grieve* or offend the Spirit. *Whereby ye are sealed* means they are furnished with assuring evidence by the Spirit which reveals the truth of salvation through the apostles. *Day of redemption* refers to the day of judgment when all faithful servants of God will receive their eternal crown of redemption from sin.

Verse 31. *Bitterness* is the same as strong hatred. The three words, *anger*, *wrath* and *malice* are used in this one verse, indicating that there is some distinction between them, although they have a similarity of meaning and may generally be used interchangeably. The three words are used in immediate succession in Colossians 3: 8. The difference is chiefly in the degree of their intensity. *Anger* is the temper when stirred up, but which should not be retained beyond the sunset. If it is so retained it may develop into a more fixed state and then it is *wrath*. If it is still cherished against another it will become *malice* which is a form of hateful spite. *Clamor* means a disorderly outcry or noisy demonstration against someone whom we consider as being in the wrong. *Evil speaking* refers to unfavorable remarks against another that are made from the motive of injuring him. All of the evils named in this verse must be *put away* or avoided by those who have become Christians.

Verse 32. *Kind* and *tenderhearted* does not require any compromise of the right, but it means that we should be considerate in our criticism of others in view of our own weaknesses. (See Galatians 6: 1.) *Forgiving one another, even as.* The point is that God has given us a divine example of the act of forgiveness, and we should be influenced by that example also to forgive our brethren.

Ephesians 5

Verse 1. *Dear children* means beloved or favorite children. If a child could think of his father only as a tyrant, and a man who regarded his offspring merely as subjects whom he could rule with a cruel hand, it would be an unpleasant task to obey his commands. On the other hand, if he believed that his father was directing his conduct because of a deep love for his child, it would certainly be a joy to obey such a parent. God has given numerous evidences of His love for the children in the divine family, and Paul asks the Ephesian brethren to obey Him from that motive.

Verse 2. *Walk in love* is along the same line as the preceding verse; love to walk so as to please the loving Father. An additional motive is in the fact that Christ as well as God loved us—even before we loved Him. The

Ephesians 5: 3-9

love of Christ for us was proved by the supreme sacrifice that He made for us by the death on the cross. *Sweet-smelling savor* is said in view of some sacrifices that were offered to God under the law of Moses, in which sweet incense was burned as an odor that was sweet.

Verse 3. *Fornication* is the unlawful intimacy of the sexes. For a detailed explanation of the word in its relation to "adultery," see the comments at Galatians 5: 19. *Uncleanness* means impurity in general, whether of the body or the mind. *Covetousness* is from PLEONEXIA which Thayer defines, "greedy desire to have more." A reasonable desire for the good things of the world is not wrong, for they are necessary to man's existence in this life. But a greedy desire for them will take a man's mind away from spiritual matters and may lead him back into a life of sin. *Not be once named.* We should not interpret any statement in the Bible in such a way as to contradict some other plain one. The fact that Paul just named these things shows he is not forbidding his brethren even to mention them, for that would be condemning himself. The explanation is in the last three words of the verse, namely, *as becometh saints.* Hence he means these things should not be mentioned with approval.

Verse 4. The Greek word for *filthiness* in this *passage* does not appear in any other place in the New Testament. It means something that is low grade in character, either in word or deed. *Foolish talking* and *jesting* mean virtually the same thing, but the two are used for the sake of making a stronger impression. Christians are not required to be glum and unhappy, yet they should not indulge in conversations that are undignified and meaningless. *Not convenient* means unbecoming; anything that would be out of place in a Christian. *Rather giving of thanks.* The children of God have so much to be thankful for, that such a frame of mind should influence their speech.

Verse 5. Even one single act of unlawful sexual intimacy constitutes fornication or adultery, but a *whoremonger* is a man who makes it a common practice; especially one who patronizes a woman who receives men for money. *Unclean person* means one who is corrupt either in body or mind. *Covetous* is explained in the comments at verse 3. Paul does not say that such a man is merely as bad as an idolator, but says he is one. That is because idolatry consists of being devoted to any thing or person except the one true God. A man who is greedy for the temporal things of this world will be chiefly interested in them, and will give his greatest devotion along that line, hence is an idolator. An *inheritance* is a share in the property of another either through a relationship with him, or by some provision in his will. God has offered to adopt any person who will, into His family, and thus make him an heir of the Heavenly Estate. Paul states that such evil characters as the ones just mentioned will be denied any share in the good things of God. It is called the kingdom of Christ *and* God, because both the Father and the Son are one in spirit and purpose. Christ is the active king, ruling under his Father, but at the last day he will give up the rule that the Father may be the exclusive King. (See 1 Corinthians 15: 24-28.)

Verse 6. *Vain words* are those that sound very well on the surface, but which are deceptive in reality. Some men might be able to speak in such a way as to make it seem that the things Paul had just mentioned were not wrong; he is warning his brethren against such false teachers. God's wrath is never shown against anything that is right, yet it has been expressed concerning these practices; therefore they must be wrong. *Children of disobedience* is a figurative term that means a group of persons who do not have enough faith in their professed father to obey Him.

Verse 7. A *partaker* with a person is one who either actually joins with him in doing the same things, or who encourages him in it by friendship with him.

Verse 8. *Were sometimes darkness* refers to the time when these Ephesians were in the darkness of heathenism. Having been led into the light of divine truth in Christ, their *walk* or general conduct should be in harmony with such divine truth. *Children of light* is a figure similar to the one in verse 6 except that it applies to truth instead of unbelief.

Verse 9. A tree is known by its fruit (Matthew 7: 16-20), and the kind of character a man maintains can be known only by the fruit or outward deeds in his life. The Spirit cannot produce anything but that which is *goodness and righteousness and truth.*

This important subject is treated also in Galatians 5: 22, 23.

Verse 10. When men walk according to the truth that has been given to them by the Spirit (through the inspired writers), it produces the good fruit of righteousness just mentioned. That will *prove* (make a practical demonstration) the Lord's way is best.

Verse 11. To *have fellowship* has the same meaning as being a partaker, which is commented upon at verse 7, but Paul adds another command in this verse, namely, to *reprove* the evil. The word is from ELEGCHO, and Thayer defines it at this place, "by conviction to bring to light, to expose." According to the laws of the land, even, "to conceal a crime constitutes another crime." If the servants of God know of the existence of sin and do not condemn it, they thereby become partakers thereof. All active things whether good or bad produce some kind of fruit (Matthew 7: 17), hence the word *unfruitful* in our verse means that it does not bear any proper fruit. *Works of darkness* refers to the evil practices that are performed under the cover of the darkness of error and the absence of spiritual light of truth.

Verse 12. The workers of darkness mentioned in the preceding verse are the persons meant by "them" in this verse. *To speak of* cannot mean the mere reference to the things done, for Paul has just done that very thing. The word *speak* is from LEGO, and one part of Thayer's definition is, "to enumerate, recount, narrate, describe." *In secret* denotes that the things they were doing were not open to the public, not that no people knew anything about it. Paul had to know about it, else he could not have spoken of it as he did. Neither is that because he was an inspired man, for some historians have given accounts of such proceedings. But they were often so vile and immoral that it would be a shock to the decent mind to describe them in detail.

Verse 13. *Reproved* means to be exposed or made known to all, and that would be done by turning on the *light* of truth. That is why those deeds were done "behind closed doors." This subject is treated in John 3: 19-21, which shows the same spirit of men who do not want their actions to be known, because they fear that good people would refuse to have any fellowship with them.

Verse 14. The terms used in this verse are figurative or spiritual, and pertain to the proper conduct of Christians. Divine truth is referred to as light, because it makes known many things that could not be known otherwise. Isaiah 60: 1-5 is a passage that deals with the subject of light, and our verse evidently refers to that. Paul is exhorting the brethren to bestir themselves from their spiritual slumber, and arise from their spiritually-dead condition so as to be ready for the light that Christ offers.

Verse 15. The original for *circumspectly* is defined by Thayer, "exactly, accurately, diligently." To *walk* in such a manner, it is necessary for one to *see* or take heed to the divine law that is given to direct his steps. Jeremiah 10: 23 says "it is not in man that walketh to direct his steps." Hence it is necessary for the Lord to give the directions, which He has done in his word of truth. The sentence may well be expressed by the familiar phrase appearing in many public places, "watch your step." The original for *fools* does not appear in any other place in the Greek New Testament. It does not mean a person without intelligence, for such an individual would not be responsible and hence should not be given any religious commands. The word is defined in the lexicon, "unwise, foolish," and Robinson explains it, "without true wisdom in Christ." This shows the word means a person who does not consult the Lord's instructions as to the proper way to walk; the *wise* person is the one who does give them heed.

Verse 16. *Redeeming* is from EXAGORAZO, and Thayer's definition (the part in italics) at this place is, "to make a wise and sacred use of every opportunity for doing good." *Time* is from KAIROS, and Thayer defines it at this place, "opportune or seasonable time," then adds the comment, "with verbs suggestive of the idea of advantage." This definition fits in well with the meaning of redeeming just explained. We should make use of every advantage that comes before us for doing something good. If that is done, it can be said that the time we spend is not in vain. *Days* is from EMERA, and has such a wide range of meaning that Thayer uses two pages of his lexicon in defining it. Paul means there is much evil present in these days, and Thayer's definition of *evil* at this place is, "bringing toils, annoyances, perils."

To overcome these *evils* and make the time count for good, we are exhorted to "redeem the time."

Verse 17. This verse is related to the preceding one in that it recognizes the contrast between wisdom and the lack of it. The man who understands the will of the Lord is regarded by the apostle as a wise man, and vice versa. Such wisdom is necessary to enable one to walk in the ways of righteousness.

Verse 18. *Excess* is from ASOTIA. Thayer and Robinson agree on the meaning of this word, but I shall quote the definition of the latter because he uses a more common language. "Debauchery, revelry, riot." The American Standard Version also renders it "riot." The heathens generally filled themselves with wine and then engaged in their idolatrous performances, which often were disorderly even to the extent of being immoral. In contrast to that, Paul instructs his brethren to be filled with the Spirit. That can be done by drinking deep from the fountain of truth as it is produced by the Spirit through the preaching and teaching of the apostles. Instead of making them drunk and leading them into riotous actions and filthy conversations, it will produce the kind of thought exchange that is indicated in the next verse.

Verse 19. There is so much misunderstanding in the religious world over the proper kind of "music" to be used in the services of the Lord, that I believe it will be well to go into much detail at this verse. I shall first give the meaning of the different words in the passage. *Speaking* is from LALEO, which means words uttered by mouth, regardless of whether it is done merely as expressions of speech, or performed by singing. In the present verse it is used only in the form of singing. *Psalms* is from PSALMOS, which Thayer defines, "a pious song, a psalm." *Hymns* is from HUMNOS, and the same lexicon defines it, "a sacred song, hymn."—*Songs* is from ODE and Thayer defines it, "a song, lay, ode," and explains it to mean, "in the Scriptures a song in praise of God or Christ." *Making melody* is from PSALLO. This word originally referred to a musical instrument and is defined in Thayer's lexicon, "to cause to vibrate by touching, to twang; to touch or strike the chord, to twang the strings; to play on a stringed instrument, to play the harp; to sing to the music of a harp." Many words in the old classical language came later to have a more restricted meaning, and that is the case with PSALLO. Hence, Thayer defines it further as follows: "In the New Testament, to sing a hymn, to celebrate the praises of God in song." Since the word literally has reference to a musical instrument, but Paul uses it figuratively, he tells us what instrument Christians are to play, namely, the heart. *Spiritual songs* means those exhibiting the effects and character of the Holy Spirit as taught in the New Testament. Any composition that combines the qualities of PSALMOS, HUMNOS and ODE would be a scriptural song, and such a composition is possible according to a footnote in Thayer's lexicon.

Verse 20. In Colossians 3: 16 Paul writes a passage on the same subject as the preceding verse at this place, but there is some difference in the wording as to what is to be accomplished by the singing. The brethren are to teach and admonish each other, and in the next verse they are told to give thanks to God, after having told them to do everything in the name of Jesus. We should consider our present passage in the same light as the one in the letter to the Colossians. *Whatever ye do* is directly connected with the command in the preceding verse to "teach" themselves in song, hence they were to speak on the subject of doing things for the Lord's cause, just as the instructions are given in our present passage. *In the name* means by the authority of Jesus, and all of the deeds performed for Him will prompt the true disciple to offer thanksgiving for the privilege of doing things for the Lord.

Verse 21. Whatever the New Testament says in one place must be considered in the light of what it says elsewhere on the same subject. We know there are certain men in the church who have ruling authority over others (1 Thessalonians 5: 12, 13; Hebrews 13: 17). By this we must understand our present passage does not teach a promiscuous exercise of rulership, for that would be devisive in its results. Thayer explains the original for *submitting* in this place, "to yield to one's admonition or advice." Such an explanation is correct since Paul adds the proviso *in the fear of God*. If a brother fears or reverences God, he will not give another disciple any admonition that is not in harmony with God's will. Therefore, if any member of the body of Christ, whether official or private, gives another some admonition that is according to the will of the Lord, it is the duty of that person so admonished to heed the advice. Such an attitude if manifested by the various members of the church would prevent much of the confusion that so often divides the body.

Verse 22. This verse should be understood on the principle set fourth in the preceding one. A wife must *submit* to the authority of her husband as long as he requires nothing that is contrary to the will of God. When she does that, she is doing so *as unto the Lord*, for He has willed the husband is the head of the wife.

Verse 23. A comparison is made between a husband as head of his wife, and Christ as the head of the church. No institution or organization or body, whether temporal or spiritual and whether physical or moral, can prosper without a head, and the body must be under the control of the head. *Saviour of the body.* Chapter 1: 22, 23 says the body of Christ is his church. Hence, unless a person is a member of the body or church of Christ, he has no promise of salvation.

Verse 24. All normal human bodies are subject to and controlled by their head, and likewise the church is subject to Christ its head. Since the husband is the head of the wife (verse 23), she is to be subjected to him. *In every thing* is modified by the proviso mentioned and explained at verse 22.

Verse 25. When a man asks a woman to become his wife, it is presumed that he loves her; but too often he ceases to have the affection that prompted his proposal, and he may even become "bitter" against her as the companion passage in Colossians 3: 19 expresses it. The love of Christ for his church is cited as an example of the love a true husband has for his wife. Christ proved his love by giving his life for the church, and a devoted husband will do all he can for the sake of his wife.

Verse 26. The comparison between a husband and wife on one hand, and Christ and the church on the other, is used for the purpose of illustration as far only as the two are similar. However, the case of Christ is far more extensive than is required of a husband. Christ literally died to produce the cleansing blood for the purification of the institution that was to become His bride. *Washing of water* refers to the ordinance of baptism, by which men and women are made members of the divine body. (Acts 2: 38, 41, 47; Titus 3: 5.) *By the word.* Baptism will mean nothing to a man unless he submits to it in obedience to the word of the Lord (Romans 6: 17).

Verse 27. *Present it to himself.* When a man looks upon a woman who is to become his bride, he delights in seeing her properly attired, with garments that are suitable for the occasion, being unsoiled and free from wrinkles. Jesus wished his bride (the church) to be thus qualified, and the phrase in italics first applies to the way the church appears to Him in this world if it is what it should be. But the actual marriage is to take place at the judgment day, and Christ desires that when the time comes, the bride will have adorned herself properly, in character and appearance (2 Corinthians 11: 1, 2; Revelation 19: 7, 8). To enable her to be so adorned, He has provided her with garments that have been cleansed from all blemishes by his own blood. *Spot* or *wrinkle.* A wedding garment should be free from stains, and be smooth in its physical form. The figure means the church should be "unspotted from the world" (James 1: 27), and free from such evil blemishes as *wrinkles* that may be caused by contact with the pressure of sin. To be *holy* denotes a life that is righteous according to the rules that have been left by the bridegroom.

Verse 28. The apostle continues his comparison that was started at verse 22, because there are so many points of likeness between the family and the church, the two and only divine organizations on earth today. *Wives as their own bodies.* When a man joins himself to his wife they become one flesh (Genesis 2: 24; Matthew 19: 5, 6). That is why it is said that *he that loveth his wife loveth himself.*

Verse 29. Self-interest will cause a man to be concerned about his own body, and if he is neglectful of his wife's welfare, it indicates that he does not realize she is a part of him. Christ never forgets the relationship between Himself and the church, hence he has always been mindful of its needs.

Verse 30. The terms of this verse are literal as they pertain to the members of the fleshly body. That is why the blood of Christ is not mentioned, for He did not have any blood even after coming from the grave (John 19: 34; Luke 24: 39). However, the application is to our relationship with

Christ and with each other (Romans 12: 4, 5; 1 Corinthians 12: 27).

Verse 31. *For this cause.* Since the union of a man and woman makes them one flesh, the man should *leave his father and mother*—consider himself no longer under their authority as a specific part of their group—and should give undivided faithfulness to the new union he has formed with his wife.

Verse 32. A mystery is anything that is not known, whether complicated or simple in its character. It is also something that could not be discovered by human investigation alone. No uninspired man would have thought that the joining of a male and female in sexual intimacy would actually merge their bodies into one. But the word of God has declared it so, and the fact will be acknowledged by all who respect Him. Paul recognizes the great reality, but says he is referring to it as an illustration of Christ and the church.

Verse 33. *Nevertheless.* Because of his statement as to why he was referring to the great *mystery* of the marriage relation, some people might conclude that what the apostle said on that subject was of minor importance. He here avoids such an error by direct instructions on the duties of a husband to his wife, repeating what he said in several preceding verses on that subject. He then adds instructions for the wife in her proper attitude toward her husband. *Reverence* is from PHOBEO, which Thayer defines at this place, "To reverence, venerate [regard with respect], to treat with deference [courteous regard] or reverential obedience." It does not have the sense of regarding her husband as a superhuman or divine being, as the word "reverend" generally (but erroneously) is thought to mean.

Ephesians 6

Verse 1. The fundamental commands by which one becomes a Christian are the same for all persons, regardless of their place in society and the nation. But there are various duties assigned to Christians that are adapted to them in the different relations of life. The preceding chapter deals with husbands and wives, while the present one starts with the special duties of children toward their parents. The original word for *children* means offspring, regardless of age or sex, and whether temporal or spiritual. But the connection here shows it means fleshly children of either sex, but old enough to have become Christians and thus subject to the religious instructions from the apostle. We learn also that a son or daughter may be old enough to obey the Gospel while still under the control of the parents. *In the Lord* means they are to obey as long as the parents do not require them to do something contrary to the word of the Lord. The proviso is similar to "in the fear of God" in chapter 5: 21. *For this is right* states the highest motive that can prompt anyone in obeying the commands of the Lord.

Verse 2. *Honor* does not contradict the preceding verse. If a parent asks his child to do something that is contrary to the word of the Lord, then he is not required to obey it. But while refusing to obey the request of his parent because it is unscriptural, he should do so in a manner that does not show disrespect for the parent. The overbearing attitude that so many boys and girls manifest toward their parents is never right under any circumstances. *With promise.* (See next verse.)

Verse 3. This is the promise referred to in the preceding verse. It pertains to a temporal reward consisting of long life on the earth, particularly that part given to the Lord's ancient people. The promise is not literally extended to Christians, but it is mentioned to indicate the importance of the command. If children obey this command (together with all others given to Christians), they have the promise of sharing in the new earth promised the righteous. (Matthew 5: 5; 2 Peter 3: 13.)

Verse 4. *Provoke not . . . to wrath* all comes from PARORGIZO, which Thayer defines, "to rouse to wrath, to provoke, exasperate [vex bitterly], anger." Parents who fail to control their children sometimes try to find justification by this passage. The rest of the verse shows they are wrong in such a course. The phrase means for a father to correct his child firmly, but in a spirit that shows he is doing it for his good. *Bring them up* refers to the supporting and rearing of one's children. *Nurture* is from PAIDEIA, and in the King James Version it has been rendered by chastening 3 times, chastisement 1, instruction 1, nurture 1. Thayer defines it, "the whole training and education of children." He adds by way of explanation, "which relates to the cultivation of mind and morals, and employes for this purpose now commands and admonitions, now reproof and punishment." Robinson's definition and comments are virtually the same as Thayer's. The correction that is included in the word *nurture* is to be accompanied with *admonition* or exhortation, which means an earnest plea for the children to give heed to the correction administered by the parent. *Of the Lord.* The third word is in the possessive case, and makes the phrase mean, "such as belongs to the Lord or proceeds from him." This would apply to a father's duty to discipline his children (including minors) in a way acceptable to the Lord.

Verse 5. The word *servant* in the King James Version comes from a number of Greek originals. The one in this verse is the most frequently used, and it means a slave or servant as we commonly use the term. It is from DOULOS, and Thayer defines it, "a slave, bondman, man of servile ["slavish"] condition." In the time of Christ and the apostles the Roman Empire contained millions of slaves. These were not all inferior persons as to intelligence, but were the victims of war or other conditions over which they had no control. The prevalence of these persons explains why so many references are made to them in the New Testament. Jesus did not intend to interfere with the relation of master and servant, but He did give many instructions about the duties of each to the other when either became a Christian. Hence our verse commands the servants to obey their masters. *According to the flesh* denotes they were their masters in temporal things only. *With fear and trembling.* Not fear of punishment from the master, for that would be equivalent to "eyeservice" which is condemned in the next verse. Following his definition of the original for *trembling*, Thayer gives the following comment: "Used to describe the anxiety of one who distrusts his ability completely to meet all requirements, but religiously does his utmost to fulfill his duty." *Singleness* means with sincerity from the heart. *As unto Christ.* A faithful servant of Christ will strive to do his duty because it is right, and a slave also should be conscientious in serving his master.

Verse 6. Both Thayer and Robinson explain *eyeservice* to be "service performed only under the eye of the master." Such service would not spring from a conscientious motive, and would indicate that if the master were absent the servant would come short of his duty. *Doing the will of God.* It is the Lord's will that all men who are employed by others shall fulfill their obligation with a pure motive.

Verse 7. *As to the Lord* is the same as the preceding verse.

Verse 8. Earthly masters may not always reward their slaves fully for their services, nor even give them due credit for the good work done; but one wrong act does not justify another. The slave who does his duty from the heart will not be forgotten by the Lord, and will be duly rewarded in the day of Final Accounts.

Verse 9. *Do the same things.* The masters were to conduct themselves as the servants were exhorted to do, namely, remembering their obligation to the Lord. *Forbearing threatening.* The first word means to cease using threats as a means of forcing the servant into obedience. This would not bar all reference to possible punishment for disobedience, for the apostle makes direct reference to the Heavenly Master in connection with the subject, and we know He has threatened to punish all of the disobedient servants. (See 2 Corinthians 5: 11.) The phrase is clarified by the one at the close of the verse, namely, *neither is there respect of persons with him.* Doubtless there were masters who felt superior because of their relation as masters, and took advantage of it to frighten their slaves. Also there were certain slaves for whom they had a personal dislike, and would be influenced thereby to utter spiteful threats against them. Paul instructs them that the Master in Heaven will not make any distinction between any *persons* in the exercise of His judgments, whether between masters and slaves, or between one slave and another.

Verse 10. *Finally.* In this and the preceding chapter Paul gives special instruction to husbands and wives, parents and children, masters and servants. He now addresses his words to them all as his brethren, and the instructions he is about to deliver will apply to them all, as well as to other disciples of Christ. *Be strong in the Lord.* The apostle is about to introduce an illustration from a soldier in the Roman army. One of the first things to be considered when a war is being planned or expected, is to make sure that every possible preparation has been made to strengthen the forces soon to engage in battle. Accordingly, Paul tells his brethren to obtain such a strength from the Lord. *Power* and *might* mean virtually the same thing, being items added to the general instruction to obtain strength from the Lord. It is as if the apostle had said, "equip yourselves for the war by calling upon the Lord, for he is powerful and mighty."

Verse 11. A few verses are devoted to general remarks about warfare, after which Paul will specify the parts of equipment that make up the armor and fighting implements for the conflict. It is necessary to put on the *whole* armor, not merely the parts that may be the most agreeable to wear. *Wiles* is from a Greek word that Thayer defines, "cunning arts, deceit, craft, trickery." The *devil* (from DIABOLOS) uses all sorts of tricks in his warfare against Christians, hence it is necessary to have on the whole armor, for there is no way of knowing just which piece will be needed most.

Verse 12. Paul likens the Christian warfare to a wrestling contest which was a common form of athletics in those days. In that bout the winner was required not only to throw his rival, but must hold him down with his hand upon his neck. A Christian must not only "win a point" against the devil, but must continue his victory until the antagonist acknowledges his defeat. "Resist the devil and he will flee from you" (James 4: 7). *Not against flesh and blood* means the warfare is not a temporal one, but one in which the issue is religious or spiritual. (See 2 Corinthians 10: 3-6.) *Principalities* means rulers with seniority, and *powers* denotes that these rulers have authority from some effective source. The source is denoted by the phrase *darkness of this world*, which is a figure for the doctrines of error taught by false leaders. *Spiritual wickedness* is rendered "spiritual powers of wickedness" by the Englishman's Greek New Testament. *High places* is rendered "heavenly" in the margin. The Greek word OURANOS is the word for the three heavens — the air, the starry region, and the dwelling place of God. In our verse it means the first heaven, because the devil and his angels were said to have that region for their dominion. Hence we read of "the prince of the power of the air, the spirit that now worketh in the children of disobedience" (chapter 2: 2).

Verse 13. After describing the kind of warfare the Christian is to fight, the apostle repeats his exhortation for taking on the *whole* armor, which is necessary for him to withstand the enemy. *Evil day* means any day in which the enemy appears. *Having done all* comes from the Greek word KATERGAZOMAI, and it is defined by Thayer, "to perform, accomplish, achieve; to work out, i.e., to do that from which something results." Hence the last five words of the verse means, "having taken on the whole armor and thus made full preparation, then make good the use of it and *stand* firm against the enemy." The Christian soldier who avails himself of this complete armor, then follows up with faithful use of it, is assured of final victory (Romans 8: 31, 37).

Verse 14. *Girt* is from PERIZONNUO which Thayer defines, "to fasten garments with a girdle," and he explains it to mean, "to fasten one's clothing about the loins with a girdle." Robinson defines it, "to gird oneself around, to be girded around," and his explanation is, "spoken in reference to the long flowing garments of the orientals [people of the East], which they gird up around them while engaged in any business." Further light will be shed on the passage by a similar word in 1 Peter 1: 13, which Thayer explains by the following information: "A metaphor [illustration] derived from the practice of the Orientals, who in order to be unhampered in their movements were accustomed, when about to start on a journey or engage in any work, to bind their long and flowing garments closely around their bodies and fasten them with a leathern girdle. Robinson gives the same definition and explanations. It explains the words "loins girded" in Exodus 12: 11, and "cast thy garment about thee" in Acts 12: 8. Paul uses the circumstance as an illustration; that truth will help the Christian to "get himself together" and be unhampered for the service at hand. The *breastplate* was a piece made of metal, covering the body from the neck to the hips, thus protecting the heart and other vital parts of the body. If a Christian's life is one of *righteousness*, the attacks of Satan cannot harm him. O, he might be put to death physically, but that will not injure his soul. (See Romans 8: 31, 38; Philippians 1: 20.)

Verse 15. *Feet shod*. The Israelites were told to have their shoes on their feet as they ate the passover. That was in order to be ready to travel on a moment's notice (Exodus 12: 11). The Christian is to be *prepared* to travel as a spreader of the Gospel (Isaiah 52:7) by means of the story of peace—peace in the great warfare for all the forces in the enemy's ranks if they will surrender to Christ.

Verse 16. The *shield* was a protective instrument supplementary to the breastplate, but smaller, and was carried by one hand and could be turned toward various danger spots independent of the general movements of the body. Firebrands in the form of darts were hurled by the hand in the close-up conflict. The shield was made of metal and could receive the *fiery darts* without any harm. The shield of the Christian is his faith in the great Commander, who has given assurance of victory. When a disciple of Christ gives up to the attacks of the enemy, it is because his faith is weak, and he acts as if the experience had come upon him as an unforeseen incident. Such is not the case, for 1 Peter 4:12 warns Christians not to look upon the circumstance as some strange thing that has happened to them.

Verse 17. The *helmet* was a cap for the head, made of metal as a protection from the darts of the enemy. The term is more definite in 1 Thessalonians 1:8, where it is called "the hope of salvation." A Christian can face any foe and even rejoice in the presence of death, because of his hope for salvation after death. Mohammed inspired his soldiers to "fight to the finish" by his assurance that faithful servants who died on the field of battle, would be taken to a land filled with the things that gratify the lusts of the flesh. Christ promises that faithful soldiers of the cross will live after earthly death in a country that will give unending enjoyment of spiritual pleasure. This completes the armor, all of which is for the forepart of the body, indicating that Christ expects his servants to be always facing the foe.

The only weapon that is furnished the Christian soldier is a sword, which denotes that the struggle is to be one of close contact — no long distance fighting. The sword consists of the word of God, which Paul declares is "sharper than any twoedged sword" (Hebrews 4:12). It is the sword that Jesus used against Satan in the wilderness (Matthew 4:4, 7, 10). Paul calls it the *sword of the Spirit* because the word of God is inspired by that source. Since the days of the apostles the Holy Spirit operates and speaks to man only by means of the Bible, hence the Christian soldier can "fight the good fight of faith" only if he knows what that Volume teaches.

Verse 18. *Praying always* is a general phrase, denoting that the soldier of the cross must never cease to be a praying man. *With all prayer* is rendered "with all manner of prayer" by Moffatt, and the lexicons agree with it. That is because the addresses offered to God are of various kinds and degrees of intensity, and Paul mentions some of them here. The simple word *prayer* is general and means any request or plea. *Supplication* is a more intense pleading for the thing desired. *In the Spirit* denotes the prayer must be spiritual, which means it is in harmony with the teaching of the Spirit in the word of God. *Watching.* Jesus taught his disciples to "watch and pray" (Matthew 26:41). The soldier of the cross must always be on the alert against the tricks of the enemy. *Perseverance* means patient continuance in the service of Christ, even when conditions might seem to be un favorable. *For all saints.* We should pray for ourselves and likewise for our brethren everywhere.

Verse 19. *And for me.* If an inspired apostle needed the prayers of his brethren, it is certain that other disciples need them also. However, Paul was not so much concerned about his personal welfare in the present instance. He was in Rome and was a prisoner, having been taken there upon his appeal when in the court of Festus (Acts 25:9-12). He was anxious that *utterance* (opportunity to speak) might be given him to preach the Gospel boldly. *Mystery* is explained at chapter 1:9.

Verse 20. *Ambassadors* is from PRESBEUO, which is used only twice in the New Testament (here and in 2 Corinthians 5:20). Both Thayer and Robinson give us the simple word that is used in our verse as their definition, which shows they understand the Greek term to mean the same as the English, namely, "the official representative of his own government or sovereign." The term is never used in reference to any person but the apostles in the New Testament. Hence there are no ambassadors for Christ living on earth today, for the apostles are still in authority (Matthew 28:20). *Bonds* is from ALUSIS which Thayer defines "a chain, bond," then adds the explanation "by which the body, or any part of it (the hands, feet), is bound." It is an apparent contradiction that an ambassador would be shackled with a prisoner's chain. But we need to observe that the chain attached to Paul was not placed there by the government of which he was an ambassador. Hence, while bound in a literal chain by an enemy government, he might be able still to represent the sovereign in a foreign land. "The word of God is not bound" (2 Timothy 2: 9). Paul's mouth was still free, and he wished the brethren to pray for divine help that he might speak the Gospel of Christ with boldness.

Verse 21. Thayer says TYCHICUS was "an Asiatic Christian, friend and companion of the apostle Paul." Funk and Wagnalls New Standard Bible Dictionary gives the same information, with additional notes that he carried the epistle of Paul to the Ephesians.

Verse 22. Tychicus was near Paul much of the time and was acquainted with the state of affairs concerning the apostle. He could comfort the hearts of the brethren by the information that Paul was standing firm in his faith.

Verse 23. Paul's manner of salutation was not always the same as it pertained to the persons addressed. Sometimes he singled out certain individuals, at others he made it general as he does in this verse. Hence there is nothing significant in the form used.

Verse 24. Paul wishes the *grace* (favor of the Lord) to be with the brethren; that is, with those who professed to love Him and who were sincere.

Philippians 1

Verse 1. The account of starting the church at Philippi is given in Acts 16, and the reader should now take time to study that entire chapter before going further with these comments. This epistle was written in Rome, under circumstances similar to those connected with the one to the Ephesians, for Paul was a prisoner in chains on account of the persecution of the Jews in Palestine (Acts, chapters 22 to 26). *Timotheus* is another form for Timothy, who was a faithful companion of Paul in his travels (Acts 16: 1-3), and hence with whom the brethren at Philippi would have some acquaintance. Paul mentions him as joining in the loving salutation to the church. The epistle is addressed *to all the saints*, which means all the Christians in Philippi since the two words mean the same. The salutation includes both official and unofficial members, because the quality of being a saint is not an official one. However, the apostle makes special mention of the two and only classes of officials in the New Testament church. *Bishops* is another name for the elders or rulers over the congregation, which will be fully discussed at 2 Thessalonians, chapter 2. *Deacons*. The work of these officials is explained at Acts 6: 2, in the first volume of the New Testament Commentary.

Verse 2. *Grace* is from CHARIS, and one part of Thayer's definition is, "kindness which bestows upon one what he has not deserved." This phase of the word explains why the apostle specifies that it is the grace from God he is wishing for his brethren, since all of God's favors are bestowed upon man undeserved by him. They are bestowed only through the Lord Jesus Christ. That is because the sacrifice of Christ provided the way for God to maintain his justice and at the same time extend this unmerited favor to humanity. *Peace* is from EIRENE, which is used 90 times in the Greek New Testament, and is rendered by our present word 88 times. As it applies to individuals, Thayer defines it, "peace between individuals, i.e., harmony, concord." As to disciples and the Lord he defines it, "the tranquil state of a soul assured of its salvation through Christ, and so fearing nothing from God and content with its earthly lot, of whatever sort it is."

Verse 3. The original Greek word for *remembrance* is so rendered 3 times in the King James Version, and by "mention" 4 times. The various translations and commentaries differ as to their preferred rendering. The truth is that the difference between them is slight. However, I believe the connection favors the marginal rendering, namely, the word "mention." In Romans 1: 9 and Ephesians 1: 16 this Greek word is used in virtually the same kind of connection, and in each of those places it is rendered "mention." The verse could well be understood as if it said: "Every time I have occasion to mention you in my prayer, it is with thanksgiving for what you have meant to me in my service to Christ." Several verses following bears out this thought.

Verse 4. *Request with joy*. The record of helpful service extended to Paul by the Philippian brethren enabled him to expect further good work by them. Hence his requests were made with the joyful feeling that God would grant his requests for them.

Verse 5. One of the things for which Paul believed God would bless the church at Philippi was their *fellowship in the Gospel*. The first word is from KOINONIA, which means anything by which one person shares with another the same experience. This can be done either by direct joining with him in the activities concerned, or by support of the same by contribution of money and other necessities of life. *From the first day* means the first of their acquaintance with Paul in his work among them, in which he got them started as a church of Christ. *Until now* indicates they did not cease their support of him as soon as he left their community. Chapter 4: 16 shows they sent contributions to him more than once when he was in Thessalonica.

Verse 6. The pronoun *he* refers to the Lord, to whom Paul gives the credit for all the good work accomplished at Philippi. *Will perform it*. The apostle's confidence in the faithfulness of the brethren prompts him to say this, for as long as disciples are faithful, He will continue to help them in their good work. *The day of Jesus Christ* literally means the coming of Christ, but it is equivalent to saying that He would be with them as long as they lived.

Verse 7. In the preceding verse Paul expresses his confidence in the perseverance of the Philippians to the end of life, thereby obtaining the continued favor of the Lord. He now affirms that such a feeling about them is *meet* or natural, and then gives his reason for the statement, namely, that they were constant in their fellowship with him under the *grace* or favor of God. *I have you in my heart*. The marginal rendering of this is, "you have me in your heart." I have consulted a number of translations and they are about equally divided between the two renderings. However, the Englishman's Greek New Testament gives the same as the margin. Since that work is a literal word-for-word translation I would prefer its form of the rendering. The difference, though, is not great, for the thought is that Paul and the brethren had a heartfelt interest in each other with reference to the great work of the apostle. *Bonds* refers to the chain that made Paul a prisoner, but which did not keep him from making a *defence* of the Gospel, which refers primarily to the first proclamation of it. *Confirmation* means the assurances which the apostle gave of the truth of the preaching, which he accomplished through his inspiration and miraculous power.

Verse 8. *Record* means a witness; the apostle means that God knows all about what is in his heart with reference to the brethren at Philippi. *Bowels* is from SPLAGCHNON, which Thayer defines, "bowels, intestines." But it is used figuratively in the New Testament, which Thayer explains as follows: "In the Greek poets the bowels were regarded as the seat of the more violent passions, such as anger and love; but by the Hebrews as the seat of the tender affections, especially kindness, benevolence, compassions; hence is equivalent to our heart, tender mercies, affections, etc." As the apostle uses the term, it means that he longs after the brethren with a tender affection like that of Christ.

Verse 9. A meaningless love would be of no avail for any persons concerned. Paul wishes the love of his brethren to grow according to knowledge. *Judgment* means discernment or recognition of what is morally proper. The apostle prayed for such progress to be made by the brethren, and he wrote this epistle as a help along that line.

Verse 10. *Approve* means to try or test (by the scriptural standard of right and wrong). *Excellent* denotes things that differ from others for the better. The complete thought is that they may be able to recognize what is better after making the lawful test. Such a course would prove them to be sincere, which would also keep them approved by Christ until he came again.

Verse 11. The same thought as the preceding verse is expressed in this, but in different words. *Being filled* means the brethren were working in the Master's vineyard faithfully, and the result was a full crop of righteousness. *Which are by Christ Jesus* denotes that no good works can be done except as are authorized by Him. Such works will always reflect glory and praise to God, for he has willed that all service must be done through the Son.

Verse 12. *The things which happened unto me*. This includes Paul's entire experience of persecution, beginning with his arrest and binding with a chain, and the unfavorable events being thrown around him since being in Rome. He did not wish his brethren to be unduly disturbed over the report of his situation, hence he made the present explanation which might well be expressed by a familiar phrase, "evils are often blessings in disguise." Such is the meaning of his statement that the happenings had *fallen out rather unto the furtherance of the Gospel.* The several verses following give the details of his remarks.

Verse 13. *Bonds* refers to the chain by which Paul was made a prisoner, and it was *manifest* literally since he had an actual metalic chain fastened to his body. *In Christ* is said because the apostle's persecution was on account of his service to Him. *Palace* is from PRAITORION, a military term, and is defined by Thayer at this place, "the camp of praetorian soldiers." Paul was under guard of the soldiers, even though permitted to occupy a house which he hired for himself (Acts 28: 30-31). Under these circumstances he would come in contact with a great many persons of various ranks, and to those who came within the sound of his voice he preached the Gospel, the subject because of which he was wearing the chain.

Verse 14. *Waxing confident by my bonds.* The brethren coming and going could see the chain attached to Paul's body, and could also behold his unwavering faith in Christ. Yes, they could see the chain and also hear him as he preached the Gospel to those who came near him. Such an example had the effect of strengthening their own faith, and causing them to go out among the people and repeat the sweet story of the cross. In this way Paul meant his persecutions had produced the good effect of *furtherance* (advancement) of the Gospel.

Verse 15. *Some* is general, but cannot apply to the persons mentioned in the preceding verse, for Paul speaks of them in a favorable way. Doubtless they were the Jews who had professed Christianity but who were inclined to Judaism. Such characters would naturally envy Paul's great work among the people who had heard him. *Preach Christ.* This is indefinite as to how much of the Gospel they preached. We are sure, however, that what was preached was correct, or else Paul would not have *rejoiced* in it as he does in verse 18. But these Juda-

izers spread the word that this Christ whom Paul was preaching was the Messiah of the Old Testament. This would be objectionable to the Romans since the predicted one was coming into the world as a king. With the mistaken idea that it was to be a temporal kingdom, the Romans would resent having such a king advocated among their people.

Verse 16. *The one* refers to those of the preceding verse who preach Christ from *envy and strife.* Paul adds a word to their motive which is *contentions,* and according to Thayer this word has the idea of such activities as are practiced by what is familiarly called a "politician." It is easy to see why they would do that kind of public teaching, for it would rouse the opposition of the Roman citizens. That in turn would bring forth an inquiry as to who had introduced such propaganda into the community. Upon being informed that it was Paul, it would enrage the Roman leaders (as the Judaizers thought), and cause them to do something that would *add affliction* to the bonds already fastened upon the apostle.

Verse 17. *The other* means the ones in verse 15 who preached Christ *of good will.* Seing that Paul was *set* (determined) to proclaim and defend the Gospel, these brethren were encouraged to join in the good work.

Verse 18. *What then?* This denotes that Paul is about to draw a conclusion from the foregoing facts, namely, that in either case he is glad that Christ is preached. Great abuse has been made of this circumstance by some who wish to apologize for the erroneous methods that are used in the religious world for the spreading of the Gospel. It is claimed that if Paul would rejoice in the work of these evil persons, then we should rejoice in what is done even by unscriptural organizations for the spreading of truth. It should be noted, however, that what these envious preachers proclaimed was the truth — their motive only was what was wrong. Also, no unscriptural organization or methods were used in their work, while the modern use of this case is to justify the institutions of men in their professed teaching of the Scriptures.

Verse 19. The pronoun *this* means the same as *the things* in verse 12, with the additional items pertaining to Paul's conduct under the circum-

Philippians 1: 20-25

stances. *Shall turn* [out] *to my salvation.* The last word has a wide range of meaning, and the primary definition of the original is given by Thayer, "deliverance, safety, preservation, salvation." The word can apply to physical or spiritual deliverance, and to the present or eternal age. The connection in each case must determine the particular application of the term. In Paul's case it may well be taken in both the physical and spiritual sense. The epistle was written when Paul was a prisoner the first time, and we know that he was actually delivered from his chain and permitted to go out among the churches. *Through your prayer.* No doubt the brethren prayed for his deliverence as the church did on behalf of Peter (Acts 12: 5). *And the supply of the Spirit of Christ Jesus.* Of course the prayers of Christians would avail nothing except they were offered in connection with the Lord's plan. The spiritual salvation of the apostle would also be on condition that he be true to Christ regardless of how the situation might terminate

Verse 20. *Earnest expectation* is from one Greek word, and it means virtually the same as *hope* that is used here, except that it is a more intense word, implying some anxiety. The whole statement means that it is Paul's earnest expectation and hope, etc. He means to conduct himself in such a way that he would have nothing of which to be ashamed. Instead, he is determined to continue his present boldness in preaching the Gospel, regardless of whether he was permitted to live, or would be put to death by his persecutors. By submitting his body to whatever his enemies might decree against him, whether it be life or death, he would be doing honor to Christ. *Magnified* is from MEGALUNO, and Thayer's explanation of the word in this passage is that Christ would "get glory and praise" from the service that Paul's body would be rendering by this devotion.

Verse 21. If Paul is permitted to live in the flesh, he will use his time for the service of Christ. But if his earthly life and service are cut off by the enemy, he will not be to blame for it because he will die in a good cause. That is why he says in the last phrase, *to die is gain.* If a man loses his physical life for the sake of the kingdom of heaven, he will gain the reward of spiritual life (Matthew 16: 25).

Verse 22. The pronoun *this* refers to the service for Christ mentioned in the preceding verse. On the basis that if he lives he will serve Christ, he will expect the *gain* also mentioned as the fruit of his labor for Him; said gain to come after death. Since both parts of the proposition—life of service and gain after death—are important, Paul is undecided as to which he prefers. *Wot not* is an old expression meaning "know not."

Verse 23. *Strait* means Paul was under pressure from two different desirable experiences, which were of such a character that he could not have both at the same time. One of these is stated in this verse, which was *to department and to be with Christ.* Of the two desirable experiences he says this would be *far better.* This gives us a very significant truth. We know that Christ was not personally on earth, and hence to be with Him it would be necessary for Paul to leave this earth. That would require him to leave the fleshly body as the next verse clearly shows. This disproves the materialistic theory which claims that man is wholly mortal, and that when he dies, everything about him dies and hence would remain wherever the body does. The passage teaches also that after a man's body dies, the part of him that *departs* from this world is conscious. Furthermore, if such a man was a faithful servant of the Lord until death, he will have an enjoyable consciousness after death, else it would not be *far better* to depart.

Verse 24. This verse states the other thing that was causing the *strait* or pressure in which Paul found himself. *To abide in the flesh* is equivalent to saying he would continue to live on the earth in his fleshly body. *More needful for you* expresses the reason why this side of the *strait* was regarded as something that was desirable in the mind of Paul. He knew that after death he could not continue to serve his brethren personally, for the only assistance they could receive from him would be the good example and teaching that he would leave in their memory. Of course such a benefit would be available to all true disciples as long as the world stands.

Verse 25. *Having this confidence.* That is, being confident of the truth of the statement in the preceding verse. Things that were "more needful" for the church would be more important than something desirable to

Paul personally. For that reason he was sure that he would remain a while longer for their *furtherance* (advancement) in the faith, and the joy that such advancement would give them.

Verse 26. Paul was made a prisoner in Rome two times (2 Timothy 4: 16), and this epistle was written when he was there the first time. He was released and permitted to go out among the churches for a while. I shall quote from Smith's Bible Dictionary as follows: "In this epistle [the one to the Philippians] Paul twice expresses a confident hope that before long he may be able to visit the Philippians in person. (Chapter 1: 25; 2: 24.) Whether this hope was fulfilled or not has been the occasion of much controversy. According to the general opinion the apostle was liberated from imprisonment at the end of two years, having been acquitted by Nero in A.D. 63, and left Rome soon after writing the letter to the Philippians." The release of Paul would be regarded as an answer to the prayers of the church. This would cause their *rejoicing* to be *more abundant. In Jesus Christ for me* denotes their rejoicing would be in regard to Paul and his victory through Jesus Christ over his enemies.

Verse 27. *Conversation* means conduct or manner of life, and *becometh* is defined to denote that which is becoming or suitable to a thing. The sentence means for them to conduct themselves in a way that shows respect for the Gospel of Christ. Such conduct would become known to others, so that Paul would learn about it even though he never got to see them again. The apostle did not write this in a spirit of doubt, for these brethren had already shown such kind of faithfulness (chapter 2: 12). The subject is mentioned as a kindly exhortation from a loving apostle. *Stand fast in one spirit* has the same meaning as *unity of the Spirit* in Ephesians 4: 3. *With one mind* denotes that each mind is being guided by the same rule, and that rule is the one provided for them by the inspired word. *Striving together* is from one word that Thayer defines, "to strive at the same time with another." The idea is that all the brethren would join their forces in the contest for one cause. *Faith of the Gospel* means the "one faith" Paul mentions in Ephesians 4: 5, which is made known through the Gospel.

Verse 28. A glance at the next verse will help in arriving at the meaning of this one. The verse starts with *for*, which indicates that a reason is about to be given for the statements of the preceding passage. Since the servants of Christ are the ones who are *given* the honor of suffering for Him, the very fact that they are having such an experience, and are holding firm under it, is proof that they are the accepted of the Lord. That is why it means so much to these Judaizing enemies of the Philippians, to observe that they are *in nothing terrified* by the persecutions. It means that they (the Philippians) are the Lord's faithful servants and hence are heirs *of salvation.* By the same token it means that they (the adversaries) are threatened with perdition for their enmity against the true disciples of Christ.

Verse 29. It would be foolish to pretend that any physical enjoyment can be had from persecution, for the bodies and sensibilities of Christians are like those of all other human beings. Their joy comes from what such experiences indicate on their behalf. The thought is well stated in Acts 5: 41 where the disciples rejoiced because "they were counted worthy to suffer shame for His name" All of this supports the comments on the preceding verse.

Verse 30. *Conflict* is from AGON which Thayer defines, "a contest." The Christian life is likened to the athletic contests that were so common in old times. Paul means these brethren were engaged in the same contest that he had encountered in their presence (Acts 16th chapter), and in which he is now engaged as they had been informed.

Philippians 2

Verse 1. *If* does not mean Paul had any doubt of the things he is about to mention. It is used in the sense of "seeing there be," or "inasmuch as there does be," etc., then he names the things he believed assuredly to exist. All true consolation is to be found only in Christ through the kingdom (Matthew 5: 4). All who love Christ and his disciples, will find untold comfort in their fellowship with each other. *Fellowship* is from a word that means the sharing of something with another. The Spirit, through the divine law which He has dictated to the inspired writers, creates a partnership in spiritual things not to be found in the world. *Bowels* is used with reference to the affections, because the people in old times believed that part of the body was the seat of those sentiments. See a detailed definition of the word at chapter 1: 8. The primary meaning of the original for *mercies* is pity or compassion. It will lead us to be considerate of another's misfortunes (1 Corinthians 12: 26).

Verse 2. The epistle to the Philippians contains no rebukes nor reproofs, but it has admonitions and exhortations, and much instruction intended to improve their already excellent state of spirituality. The present verse is one passage of this kind. It would make Paul's joy full for them to be *likeminded*, which means to be united in their work for the Lord. (See chapter 1: 27.) *Having the same love* denotes their love for each other was to be mutually complete. *Of one accord* means to work together harmoniously for the "faith of the Gospel."

Verse 3. *Strife* is an attempt to put oneself ahead of others for the purpose of being pre-eminent. *Vainglory* is the same as self-esteem, which would cause a man to seek the pre-eminence just mentioned. In contrast to all this, the apostle would have his brethren show *lowliness of mind*, which is the same as humbleness. Instead of considering oneself worthy of special honor, he should think of his brother as being better than himself. That would cause him to push the other person forward instead of seeking to be prominent for his own gratification. (See Romans 12: 10.)

Verse 4. Christians should not be concerned in their own things only, for that would be selfishness. Instead, they should be interested in the welfare of others.

Verse 5. *This mind* does not mean that the mind of man can be equal to that of Christ. The original word is PHRONEO, and a part of Thayer's definition at this place is, "to seek one's interests or advantage; to be of one's party, side with him." As Jesus was unmindful of himself and thoughtful of others, we should be likeminded.

Verse 6. *Form* is from MORPHE which occurs only three times in the Greek New Testament. *Robbery* is from HARPAGMOS. I shall give Thayer's definition and explanations of this word first. "A thing seized or to be seized, booty," and he explains it to mean, "to deem anything a prize—a thing to be seized upon or to be held fast, retained." In his definition and explanations of MORPHE, Thayer includes some statements pertaining to verse 7. I shall quote his definition of the Greek word, also his explanations (the parts in parentheses). "The form by which a person or thing strikes the vision; the external appearance . . . (this whole passage is to be explained as follows): who, although (formerly) he bore the form (in which he appeared to the inhabitants of heaven) of God, yet did not think that this equality with God was to be eagerly clung to or retained, but emptied himself of it so as to assume the form of a servant, in that he became like unto men, and was found in fashion as a man." My comments on the verse, based on the connection and the lexicon definitions of the words, is that Christ was willing to underestimate the great honor of being equal in form with the Father, and condescend to becoming even lower than the angels, so that He could suffer and die as a man.

Verse 7. *Made himself of no reputation* all comes from two Greek words, and they are rendered "emptied himself" by the Englishman's Greek New Testament, and four other translations that I have consulted render it the same. Paul means that Christ divested himself of the glorious form He had before he came to the earth. (See the comments on the preceding verse.) Christ became like a servant in form only, because all slaves in the various ranks were men (not angels), in order that He might be capable of death for the sake of mankind.

Verse 8. *Being found* or appearing on earth in *fashion* (form and manner of life physically) *as a man. Humbled himself* means Christ subjected himself to voluntary humiliation, which will be made clear by further comments on this verse. *Obedience* implies a commander giving law to be obeyed, and Jesus was subject only to his Father. Unto means "as far as, to the extent of," and it is used here to denote that Jesus obeyed his Father to the extent of submitting to death. *Even* used in connection with *death of the cross* is more significant than is generally realized. Jesus not only submitted to die in obedience to his Father and for the benefit of sinful man, but to die the most horrible and humiliating form of death. Smith's Bible Dictionary gives a description of this performance, which I shall quote for the information of the reader:

"Crucifixion was unanimously considered the most horrible form of death. Among the Romans [by whom Jesus was crucified] the degradation [disgrace] was also a part of the infliction, and the punishment if applied to freemen was only used in the case of the vilest criminals. The one to be crucified was stripped naked of all his clothes, and then followed the most awful moment of all. He was laid down upon the implement of torture. His arms were stretched along the cross-beams, and at the center of the open palms the point of a huge iron nail was placed, which, by the blow of a mallet, was driven home into the wood. Then through either foot separately, or possibly through both together, as they were placed one over the other, another huge nail tore its way through the quivering flesh." A little farther on in the article the author says: "A death by crucifixion seems to include all that pain and death can have of the horrible and ghastly,—dizziness, cramp, thirst, starvation, sleeplessness, traumatic [shock] fever, tetanus [spasm caused by infection], publicity of shame, long continuance of torment, horror of anticipation, mortification of unattended wounds . . . the unnatural position made every movement painful; the lacerated veins and crushed tendons throbbed with incessant anguish," etc. Besides this historical description of the physical suffering, we have the statements in the Bible of the shame attached to crucifixion (Deuteronomy 21: 22, 23; Galatians 3: 13; Hebrews 12: 2). From all the foregoing information, the reader can realize the reason for Paul's use of the word *even* in connection with Christ's death on the cross.

Verse 9. God rewarded the humility and obedience of his Son by exalting him with a name that denotes authority. Matthew 28: 18 states that all power (authority) is given Him in heaven and in earth. Our present verse makes the general statement that His name is above every name. Of course it is to be understood with the exception shown in 1 Corinthians 15: 27.

Verse 10. The preceding verse gives a general declaration of the authority vested in the name of Christ; this one names the three regions in which that authority is to be recognized. The three regions include all intelligent creatures that are in existence, namely, heaven, earth and under the earth which means Hades or place of departed spirits and demons. For a full explanation of the last place, see the comments at Matthew 5: 30, in first volume of the New Testament Commentary. A foretaste of the recognition of His authority by creatures from these three regions was accorded him when on the earth. Matthew 4: 11 shows the angels *(things in heaven)* paying their respects and serving Him. The instances of *things in earth* (men) are too numerous to need special citation. *Things under the earth* (demons) acknowledge Him (Mark 5: 1-6).

Verse 11. This verse expresses the same recognition of authority by means of the tongue, that the preceding verse does with the bended knee. An added thought is that it is all to be to the glory of God the Father. That will be true, whether the acknowledgement is made willingly by friends of the Lord, or unwillingly by enemies. But if it is by the enemies, they will get no reward for it, while the friends will have themselves confessed in the presence of God (Matthew 10: 32).

Verse 12. In chapter 1: 27 Paul exhorts the brethren to be faithful whether he is present with them or not, and in this one he acknowledges just such faithfulness on their part. Brethren cannot do more than obey, hence the words *much more* only means an expression of degree. It is more commendable for them to be obedient in his absence, for that is proof that their work is not "eyeservice" (service performed only under the eye of the master), which is condemned in Ephesians 6: 6. *Work out* comes from one Greek word which Thayer defines, "to do that from which something results." They were to do the work under Christ that would result in their *own* salvation; no person could do it for them. *Fear and trembling*. The first word means reverence and the last means anxiety. Christians should have reverence for God and be anxious to obey His law.

Verse 13. God works in his children through the inspired word. That word instructs them not only to profess the *will* to serve the Lord, but also *to do* His will; such a life will be pleasing to God.

Verse 14. *Without murmurings* means to do one's duty cheerfully, not secretly resenting the task required. The original for *disputings* is defined by Thayer, as "hesitating, doubting." Disciples should not question the right of the Lord to command them, nor be curious as to why He has given them the duty.

Verse 15. *Blameless* denotes a life against which no charge can be truthfully made. *Harmless* is rendered "sincere" in the margin, and the lexicon agrees with it. The fuller definition would be "without mixture" with the evil things of the world. The sons of God should be *without rebuke*, which they will be if they comply with the forepart of the verse. *Crooked* and *perverse* mean virtually the same, and are used for the purpose of emphasis. It refers to people who will not walk in the straight path of righteousness, but stubbornly persist in doing that which is evil. Christians must live *in* such a nation while in this world, but they should not live *as* such a nation lives. Instead, their lives should reflect the light of divine truth by practicing the good works directed by Christ (Matthew 5: 14-16).

Verse 16. *Holding forth the word of life* means to hold the Gospel up before the world so it will be seen as the truth coming from the apostle. In 1 Timothy 3: 15 Pauls says the church is the pillar (or support) of the truth, and the Lord does not permit any other organization to offer His word to mankind. Paul gave the Gospel to the Philippians, now he expects them to continue the good work by holding it up in their lives and teaching. *Labored in vain*. No preacher's salvation depends on the faithfulness of his converts if he is himself faithful in teaching them their duty. But if they do not carry out their part of the great plan, their salvation will be a failure. Such a result would make Paul's work among them *in vain* as far as they are concerned. If they are faithful to the end, it will give Paul a cause a rejoicing on their behalf, and such rejoicing would constitute the "reward" such as 2 John 8.

Verse 17. This verse contains a very beautiful thought concerning the unselfishness of Paul. *Offered* is from SPENDO which means literally "to be poured out." Paul did not know how his present situation would terminate (verse 23), or whether he would have to give up his blood on the executioner's block (as he finally did after the second arrest according to 2 Timothy 4: 6). However that may be, he was willing to make such a sacrifice if called upon to do so. But even such a service was regarded by him as small in comparison with the services of the church at Philippi. The figure of being *offered* ("poured out") is drawn from a service under the law of Moses. (See Exodus 29: 40, 41; Leviticus 2: 1, 6; 23: 13, 18, 37.) These liquid offerings were "poured" upon the main sacrifice to combine a service to God. They might well be called a minor offering or sacrifice, and that upon which they were poured a major one in comparison. Paul was willing to represent himself as a minor sacrifice, poured upon the major one of the faithful service of the Philippians. Even that humble service would cause him to *joy and rejoice* with the brethren.

Verse 18. Paul bids the Philippian brethren to share his joy with him, which would constitute one of the finest examples of fellowship in Christ that is possible.

Verse 19. *Trust in the Lord* is equivalent in thought to "if the Lord will" in James 4: 15. Everything Paul expected to do was subject to the will of the Lord. Timothy had been with Paul as a "companion in tribulation," and the apostle desired to send him to the church at Philippi to get first hand information concerning conditions there. Paul's general confidence was strong, but he craved the satisfaction that comes from a direct report. That would be especially true when coming from one who would take sincere interest in the welfare of the brethren, as he believed Timothy would.

Verse 20. *Likeminded*. Paul means he had no other person with him with a mind like that of Timothy, namely, would *naturally* (sincerely) care about their state.

Verse 21. *All* is used in the sense of the general rule; there were exceptions, such as Timothy. But most people were self-concerned and not much interested in the things that belong to Jesus Christ. This is an instance that shows that when a man is concerned with the welfare of the church, it is counted as for Christ. (See Matthew 25: 45.)

Verse 22. *The proof of him*. The conduct of Timothy gave the proof of the correctness of Paul's estimate as just stated, namely he had been as near and attentive to Paul as if he had been his father. And all this service was on behalf of the Gospel for which they both were devoting their lives.

Verse 23. Paul did not plan to send Timothy at once; not until he saw how it went with him. This means the case that was pending before the Roman authorities.

Verse 24. This verse indicates one reason Paul wished to retain Timothy until his case was decided. If he should be released, he might find it possible to make the journey to Philippi with him; at least he hoped to make the trip soon after.

Verse 25. He did not retain *Epaphroditus* for further developments as he did Timothy. That was because he was in Rome as a personal messenger between the church at Philippi and Paul, sent to take him necessary supplies. It was appropriate to send him back home to report on his mission.

Verse 26. Here is an unusual case of worrying; that is, the cause for it. As a rule a person worries over his own situation. But here is man who is very sick (or has been), and yet he is not concerned about himself. Instead, he knows his brethren back home have heard about his sickness, and he is grieved for fear they are overly worried. It is a striking case of unselfishness and suggests 1 Corinthians 12: 26.

Verse 27. *Sick nigh unto death.* The question might arise why Paul did not heal him since he had miraculous power. Such a query overlooks the primary object of miracles, namely, the making of believers (John 20: 30, 31). Unless some good reason for using miraculous healing existed in a given case, it was the Lord's will to let it depend on the provisions of nature; hence a miracle was not always resorted to. A similar case of this kind is mentioned in 2 Timothy 4: 20.

Verse 28. To relieve the tension was another reason for sending Epaphroditus back to Philippi at this time, besides the one mentioned at verse 25. When the brethren saw their messenger in their midst again, recovered from his serious illness, they would have the load of anxiety lifted and all parties concerned would rejoice together.

Verse 29. *Receive him* does not imply any doubt about their attitude toward this messenger, but rather it is a friendly recommendation from Paul, induced by his appreciation for the good services that the messenger had rendered to him while in Rome. *Hold such in reputation* means give him the honor that his faithful services deserved.

Verse 30. This verse tells the cause of the serious sickness of this messenger. After arriving in Rome, he was detained for some time because the supplies from Philippi were not sufficient to care for Paul, and he had to do some kind of secular work to obtain the needed things. Just what caused the situation is not revealed, but we know it was not through any fault of the brethren at Philippi, for chapter 4: 10 says they "lacked opportunity." And we know this has reference to the temporal necessities of life, for several verses following the one just referred to show clearly that Paul was writing on that subject in this part of his epistle.

Philippians 3

Verse 1. *Finally* is from LOIPOS and one term Thayer uses in his definition is "moreover," signifying that Paul has something more to say; or, that he is going to repeat what has been said previously. *Rejoice in the Lord.* There are two important thoughts in this expression. One is in the first word, and indicates that Christians should be joyful. The other is that it is in the Lord that rejoicing may be had. *To write the same things.* To repeat what has been said at various times, giving such wholesome exhortation as this one about rejoicing in the Lord. Such a repetition was not any unpleasant task for Paul, and besides it was a safe kind of advice for the readers.

Verse 2. *Dogs* is from KUON, and Thayer defines it at this place, "a man of impure mind, an impudent man." The editor of Thayer's lexicon says the word is always used in a reproachful sense when it is used figuratively. Robinson gives the same definition, and says it is used figuratively in Philippians 3: 2, "where it is spoken of Judaizing teachers." Paul literally calls them *evil workers.* The original for *concision* is KATATOME which Thayer defines with the one word "mutilation." We know Paul is writing about the rite of circumcision, but he designates it by the other word because of the unlawful use that the Judaizers were making of it. Circumcision was given to the descendants of Abraham as a national mark, and later was included in the Jewish system as a religious ordinance. When that was replaced by the Gospel system; the religious feature of circumcision was taken away and the rite was left just where it was in the beginning, namely, a fleshly mark for the Jews only. The Gentiles were never given the rite for any reason, hence it is unlawful to perform it on any of them. When a doctor circumcises a new born infant he violates the law of Christ, and Paul would accuse him of mutilation.

Verse 3. *We are the circumcision.* The original word for the rite in this phrase is the one for the fleshly act, but Paul is using it in a spiritual sense. The Judaizers taught that fleshly circumcision was necessary to make one a part of God's true people. The apostle is teaching that since physical circumcision has lost its religious significance, true circumcision is of a spiritual kind. It is the action of those who *worship God in the Spirit*, or according to the "law of the Spirit of life in Christ Jesus" (Romans 8: 2), and not after "the law of sin and death," which called for fleshly circumcision, and which was the system the Judaizers were trying to impose upon the Gentile Christians. (See Romans 2: 29; Colossians 2: 11.)

Verse 4. *Confidence in the flesh.* This phrase occurs in the preceding verse as well as the present one. Such an expression usually refers to the evil desires of the carnal mind. However, such desires have been regarded as wrong all through the Bible. But Paul is using the phrase in a special application, based on the fleshly relation the Jews bear to Abraham, which is indicated by the rite of circumcision, a fleshly performance. The Jews laid much stress on this relationship and even felt such a "confidence" in the time of John the Baptist (Matthew 3: 9). The Judaizers might say that Paul's attitude against them was from envy, or prompted by the feeling that is familiarly expressed by the figure, "sour grapes." He asserts that such is not the case, but that instead, he could truthfully boast of greater accomplishments while professing the religion that included this fleshly rite, than others; he then proceeds in two verses to enumerate them. (See also the comments at Galatians 1: 13, 14.)

Verse 5. *Circumcised the eighth day* (Leviticus 12: 3). The parents of Paul had attended to this rite according to the detail as to the exact age when it should be done. Even Moses was not that faithful (Exodus 4: 24-26). *Stock of Israel* or Jacob. He was the descendant of Abraham who was selected even before he was born to be in the blood line for the Messiah. (See Romans 9: 7-12.) *Tribe of Benjamin.* He (Benjamin) was the son of Rachel, of tender memory, and his tribe gave the nation its first king (Acts 13: 21). *Hebrew of the Hebrews.* Both parents of Paul were of that race, whereas some members of the nation were not full blooded (Acts 16: 1). *Touching the law, a Pharisee.* Among the various sects of the Jews, the Pharisees were regarded as the most exacting in their demands of religious duty. (See Acts 26: 5.) There is a lengthy comment on this sect at Matthew 16: 12, in the first volume of the New Testament Commentary, which also includes information concerning the Sadducees.

Verse 6. The Greek word for *zeal* is used in both a good and bad sense in the New Testament. When used in the former, it means ardor or enthusiasm, and that is its meaning in this verse. The reader may be surprised that I would say this, when Paul used his zeal in *persecuting the church.* Yes, he had the right *kind* of zeal, but made a wrong use of it, even as a man might have the right kind of money but make a wrong use of it. Paul believed the church was an unscriptural institution, and to be consistent, he was required to oppose it. *Blameless.* This means Paul lived up to all requirements of the law, which proves that it was not physically impossible to do so as some teach. The parents of John the Baptist lived up to them according to Luke 1: 6.

Verse 7. In the lexicon the original for *gain* is defined "advantage," and that for *loss* is defined "damage." There was a time when Paul thought it was a great advantage to have all of the fleshly accomplishments named above to his credit. But after learning what it means to have Christ, he could realize that it would have been a disadvantage or *loss* to him, had he clung to them. Indeed, the "damage" would have been to the extent of losing the grace or favor of God (Galatians 5: 4).

Verse 8. The first half of this verse repeats the thoughts of the preceding one, and Paul extends it to include *all things*, not only those Jewish claims which he once trusted. He became aware of this great advantage through *the knowledge of Christ Jesus his Lord. Suffered the loss of all things.* This denotes a complete sacrifice by Paul of whatever would hinder him from wholehearted service to Christ, regardless of how near and precious they may have seemed. Yea, he did not count his own life valuable enough to sacrifice Christ for it (Acts 20: 24). *Do count them but dung.* The last word is used figuratively, meaning something that is worthless and objectionable. It is not enough for a disciple of Christ just to "ease up" or lessen his interest in the things of the world, he must spurn them as he would a vessel of filth.

Verse 9. *Be found in him;* now or at any time the Lord calls him to account. Paul's desire was to be found acceptable to his Lord, in that he would not be having or holding on to the form of *righteousness* that was prescribed by the law. He designates this form as *mine own righteousness,* although he says it *is of the law,* a document that came from God. Here is set forth a very significant principle. When God changes his own law and calls upon man to receive the new one, if that man persists in clinging to the old one, he is guilty of wanting to have his own way.

Verse 10. The word *know* means more than a mere acquaintance of one's identity; it includes a personal realization of whatever is being considered. Paul wanted to know what it means to have experimental knowledge of Christ by serving Him wholeheartedly. *Power of his resurrection.* That power first demonstrated itself by inducing man to repent of sin and follow a spiritual life in Him. It will be finally demonstrated when it brings the "dead in Christ" from the grave to die no more. *Fellowship of his sufferings.* A faithful Christian will suffer persecution for the sake of Christ, and in so doing he is a partner (having fellowship) with Him in his tribulations. *Conformable unto his death.* Christ died for sin, and if Paul serves Him faithfully even with the possibility of dying in the Cause, his experience would partake of a like death.

Verse 11. *Resurrection of the dead.* The resurrection of all mankind whether good or bad, is clearly taught in John 5: 28, 29; Acts 24: 15. Since this will not depend on the kind of life a man has lived, we know Paul is using the word in a special sense. He therefore means the resurrection of the just as mentioned in the passages cited in this paragraph. In order to take part in that kind of resurrection, one must die in Christ; and that will be true only of those who have been faithful until death.

Verse 12. The *gain* or advantage that Paul obtained immediately upon his becoming a Christian, was not considered as the complete experience he expected. Lest his readers might get the wrong impression, the apostle explains that he had not yet attained to it, or that he was *perfect* which means complete as regards the good things to be enjoyed through Christ. *Follow after* is from the Greek word DIOKO, and the Englishman's Greek New Testament renders it, "am pursuing." *Apprehend* is from KATALAMBANO, and Thayer defines it at this place, "to lay hold of so as to make one's own, to obtain, to attain to." Christ Jesus had laid hold upon Paul, and through the obedience to the Gospel, He wished that the convert would finally "lay hold on eternal life" (1 Timothy 6: 12). Paul is declaring that his reason for this "pursuing" is that he may lay hold upon the reward for which Christ had laid hold on him.

Verse 13. The first sentence of this verse is a repetition in thought of the preceding verse. The apostle makes no claim to a victory he has not won, but he can and does affirm what are his determinations. *Forgetting* means to cease cherishing a memory of the things he once loved, not that his memory would become a blank on the subject. The apostle now adopts the ancient foot race for an illustration of the Christian life. *Reaching forth* is from EPEKTEINO which Thayer defines, "to stretch out to or towards." A runner in a race will lean toward the goal for which he is contesting.

Verse 14. *Press* is from the same word as *follow after* in verse 12, and is a somewhat stronger word than the one for *reaching forth* in the verse preceding our present one. That term indicates the direction toward a man's goal, while the one here denotes that he will use pressure in progressing toward that goal. Every foot race has a goal which the contestant wishes to reach in time to win the prize or stake. That is what is meant by the *mark* in this verse. Needless to say that no literal thing or specific date constitutes that mark or goal in the Christian race. It may well be expressed by the words, "be thou faithful unto death, and I will give thee a crown of life" (Revelation 2: 10). This passage states the goal (death), and also the *prize* which is the crown of life. A *calling* is a man's chief occupation in life, and the one Paul had chosen was the service for Christ. It is called *high* because it came from God through Christ. This occupation does not promise any temporal prize or reward, but assures every "faithful" (not successful) worker a prize that is fadeless.

Verse 15. *Perfect* means mature in spiritual matters, such as those described in Hebrews 5:14. Paul believed such disciples were able to be *thus minded;* that is, were prepared to make the same resolution that he just declared for himself. *Otherwise minded.* If some among them had not yet reached that point in their Christian growth, they need not despair; if they will continue partaking of the truth of God, this advanced thought possessed by Paul will finally be *revealed unto them.*

Verse 16. *Nevertheless,* as to those who have not attained that degree of *perfection* or maturity of thought that Paul has, they should use what knowledge they have to guide them in their *walk. Same rule* and *same thing* means that their conduct must differ in degree only, and not in kind.

Verse 17. To be a *follower* means to be an imitator. Paul told his brethren at Corinth to be followers (imitators) of him as he was of Christ (1 Corinthians 11:1), and the same restriction holds good on our present verse. *Mark* means to take note of certain ones who were walking *so*—were following the pattern set by Paul—*as ye have,* or since ye have the apostles as examples.

Verse 18. Not all professed Christians were walking after the example Paul was setting before them. The conduct of some was so evil that it caused the apostle to weep as he told them about it. It was not because of any personal loss to him that he wept, but because such characters were *the enemies of the cross of Christ.*

Verse 19. *End* means fate or final outcome, and that which is awaiting those characters described in the preceding verse is eternal destruction. The word *god* should not be capitalized, for it refers to a wrong object of devotion, namely, the *belly.* The original Greek word has different shades of meaning, but it is here used in reference to the fleshly desires. Some people are more devoted to such interests than they are to the true God, who wishes His children to make their devotion to Him first in their lives, and all other matters (even those that are right of themselves) secondary. *Glory in their shame.* Not that they admit having pride in their shame, but Paul is asserting that the things these evil workers take glory in, are truly shameful. The reason such people act as here described is due to the fact they *mind* (care) *earthly things.*

Verse 20. *Conversation* is from POLITEUMA, which is not used anywhere else in the Greek New Testament. Thayer defines it, "a state, commonwealth." Robinson defines it in virutally the same way, then adds the following explanation of his definition: "Figuratively, of Christians in reference to their spiritual community, the New Jerusalem in heaven." The idea is well expressed by some words of an old hymn: "I'm but a stranger here; Heaven is my home." (See Hebrews 11:13-16; 13:14; 1 Peter 2:11.) Our stay on the earth should be used in preparing for the eternal residence in our true Home, for this world is to pass away. *From whence* denotes that Jesus is now in that Country, but will come from it sometime to call His own from the earth.

Verse 21. Flesh and blood cannot inherit the kingdom of God (1 Corinthians 15:50), hence the fleshly bodies of faithful children of God must be changed from a fleshly to a spiritual form. This will apply to both the living and the dead when Christ comes (1 Corinthians 15:51-54; 1 Thessalonians 4:14-17). *Change* is from META-SCHEMATIZO, which Thayer defines at this place, "to change the figure of, to transform." The original for *vile* is defined by Thayer, "lowness, low estate"; it is applied to the body because it is fleshly and subject to decay. Let it be noted that *it* (the body) is to be changed and fashioned like unto that of Christ. The possibility of making such a change is accounted for by the fact that He has been able *to subdue all things unto himself.*

Philippians 4

Verse 1. *Therefore* indicates a conclusion, and it is drawn from the wonderful truths expressed by the closing verses of the preceding chapter. This verse is in the form of a kindly exhortation, but really it is telling the Philippians that they have much reason to *stand fast in the Lord*. The record of Paul's work in starting this church, also the constant devotion the brethren had shown him, will fully explain the words, *dearly beloved and longed for*. They were a *joy* to him because of their faithfulness in the cause of the Lord. *Crown* is from *stephanos*, and Thayer defines it at this place, "that which is an ornament and honor to one." Paul felt honored by the faithfulness of these brethren, since they were the product of his labors, and their continued devotion was due to their respect for the truth he had delivered to them.

Verse 2. To *beseech* means to plead earnestly, hence it is a stronger word than a mere request, but not as strong as an admonition. *Be of the same mind in the Lord* means they should be united in their work for Him, regardless of any personal difference they might have. *Euodias* and *Syntyche were* sisters in the church at Philippi.

Verse 3. *Intreat* has practically the same meaning as "beseech." The *yokefellow* evidently was Epaphroditus, for in chapter 2: 25 he is referred to as Paul's "companion in labor." This man was sent to Philippi with an epistle which contained a request for himself. *Those women* are the ones named in the preceding verse. In some way they had assisted Paul in his work of the Gospel, but just when or how they did it is not revealed. Young calls *Clement* "A fellow laborer with Paul at Philippi." He is not mentioned elsewhere in the New Testament. *Names are in the book of life*. No literal book is meant here, but whatever and wherever the book is, we know it is possible for man to do something to get his name written in it, since it is mentioned in a manner that implies responsibilities. See Luke 10: 20; Hebrews 12: 22, 23; Revelation 3: 5; 13: 8; 20: 12.

Verse 4. See the comments at chapter 3: 1 for the explanation of this verse.

Verse 5. Thayer defines the original Greek for *moderation* as follows: "equitable [just], fair, mild, gentle." An act might be technically right according to the knowledge of a Christian, but it would not appear so to the public. This instruction means for a person not to do that which would raise doubts in the minds of others. The same thought is expressed in Romans 12: 17 and 2 Corinthians 2: 21. *The Lord is at hand* means that He is always near, beholding all that is done by His disciples.

Verse 6. *Careful* is from MERIMNAO which has a variety of meanings. Thayer defines it at this place, "to be anxious; to be troubled with cares." Paul does not mean that Christians should be indifferent about the responsibilities of life, but they should not permit such things to absorb their minds so that it will detract them from useful activities. Instead, they should trust in the Lord and make their troubles a matter of prayer. (See 1 Peter 5: 7.)

Verse 7. *Peace of God* denotes the peace that He grants to those who are faithful to the divine law. Man will not be the judge in the last great day, hence it is unimportant whether a disciple is at peace with him or not. *Passeth* is used in the sense of "surpasseth," because the peace that comes to those who form their lives according to the law of God, is far beyond anything the mind *(understanding)* of man ever thought of. Such a state of contentment will keep the servants of God in a settled attitude. *Hearts* and *minds* refers to the same part of the human inner man, but to different characteristics of his being when used as separate terms. The first refers to the sentiments and the second to the reasoning faculty.

Verse 8. The words *true, honest* and *just* are not used with any new meaning, the point being as to the standard by which they should be measured. (That will be shown in the next verse.) *Pure* means "unmixed," and requires that the principles of right living should not be adulterated with the things of the world. *Lovely* has reference to things that a Christian has the right to love, too numerous to name here. *Of good report* is from one Greek word, and Thayer defines it, "sounding well; uttering words of good men," and this also is subject to the next verse. *Virtue* means "moral excellence" according to Thayer's lexicon. *Praise* applies to things worthy of being commended. *Think on these things* means to consider them; meditate on them; give them serious attention.

Verse 9. This verse completely rules out the idea that man is to decide for himself as to what comes under the list of things named in the preceding verse. They are restricted to and bound by what has been received from Paul (or any other inspired man). They may have been received either by his example *(seen in me)*, or by his words *(heard)*. *God of peace* means the peace described in verse 7, which is promised only to those who comply with the conditions just stated.

Verse 10. *Care* and *careful* are from the same Greek word, and have a different meaning from "careful" in verse 6. (See the comments at that verse.) In the present verse it means to be mindful of the welfare of others. Something had interfered with the support the church at Philippi was giving Paul (chapter 2: 30), but the hindrance was removed, whatever it was. As soon as they had the opportunity, they *flourished* or revived their support of the apostle. He rejoiced *in the Lord* because he regarded all good things as coming from Him.

Verse 11. Paul's expression of joy in the preceding verse might leave an impression that his motive was a temporal one; he hastens to explain that such is not the case. He had already become accustomed to the various circumstances of life, so that he was contented with whatever came upon him. The cause of his rejoicing in this case will be explained at verse 17.

Verse 12. The apostle would not pretend to see something favorable where nothing of the kind existed. The terms *abased* and *abound; full* and *hungry; abound* and *need,* are sets of opposite terms that are used figuratively, intended to enlarge upon the thoughts of verse 11.

Verse 13. Human strength alone cannot surmount the difficulties that one may encounter in life's pathway, hence Paul explains he does the things of his experience *through Christ which strengtheneth me.*

Verse 14. Paul's life and even his comfort did not depend upon the contributions of the Philippians. For their own sakes, however, it was the right thing for them to come to his aid, for in so doing they *communicated* (had fellowship) with him in his affliction, and it entitles them to the favor of Christ as in Matthew 25: 40.

Verse 15. *Beginning of the Gospel* refers to its beginning in Macedonia, recorded in Acts 16. Before leaving that province, some other churches were started, as may be seen in Acts 16 and 17. *Communicated* means to have fellowship with another, and it could apply to any subject in which both were interested; hence Paul explains that he is applying it to the subject of financial support. Many churches think their obligation on this matter pertains to their own locality only. Here we see that none of the Macedonian churches supported Paul beyond their borders, but the Philippians.

Verse 16. *Thessalonica* was Paul's next field of labor after leaving Philippi (Acts 17: 1). We do not know how long he remained in that city, but it was long enough to require extra supplies for his living. He did manual labor in order to relieve the brethren of the burden (1 Thessalonians 2: 5-9; 2 Thessalonians 3: 7-9). But even with his own toil, he was unable to secure sufficient for his needs. That is the reason the Philippians *sent once and again unto his necessity.*

Verse 17. This verse repeats the statement in the forepart of verse 11, then adds the reason for Paul's attitude. He wished the brethren to receive credit from the Lord for having done something for His disciples. While Paul was the one who received the temporal benefit from the *fruit* of their liberality, yet it would *abound* (add to) the *account* or record of good deeds done by the congregation at Philippi.

Verse 18. Paul would have been satisfied, as far as his personal interests were concerned, had he not received any provisions from Philippi. Yet he wished to have the contribution from them for the reason shown in the preceding verse. Now that a full supply was sent from them, the apostle wishes to make full and grateful acknowledgement of it. Epaphroditus was the messenger by whom the supplies were sent, and the disciple who personally contributed to the apostle's needs by his manual labor (chapter 2: 25-30). *Odor* and *sweet smell* are used figuratively, based on the use of sweet incense that was offered to God under the Old Testament system (Exodus 30: 1-8). Paul calls it a sacrifice *wellpleasing to God.* Since the apostle is writing about the necessities of life that were given to him, why does he speak of it as if it were given to God? It is on the principle mentioned before, namely, Matthew 25: 40.

Verse 19. This verse is similar in thought to Matthew 6: 33. The Philippians were chiefly interested in the kingdom of God, which is the reason they gave of their means to Paul, so he could continue to advance that kingdom. In turn, he assures them that God will take care of their needs. He teaches the same principle in 2 Corinthians 9: 8-10, where he is exhorting those brethren to contribute for the relief of the needy ones in Judea. *Riches in glory.* God is the giver of all good things (James 1: 17), and He bestows the divine favors through Christ Jesus.

Verse 20. *God* and *Father* are the same person; the first refers to His e t e r n a l, self-existent and infinite power. The other to His affectionate relation to the creatures of His care. The term *for ever* actually covers as long a period as *for ever and ever.* The words are used for the sake of emphasis, and the significance is that God is worthy of endless glory. For an explanation of *amen,* see the comments at Romans 16: 24, in the first volume of the New Testament Commentary.

Verse 21. *Salute* and *greet* are from the same Greek word. It has a wide scope of meanings, but the central thought is that all Christians should manifest a friendly attitude toward others, whether it be by word of mouth on personal meeting, or by a friendly word in writing; a *saint* is the same as a Christian. The brethren that were with Paul (personally) requested him to *greet* the brethren at Philippi for them.

Verse 22. This is the same kind of salutation as in the preceding verse, but is more general in its source. It comes from the *saints* (Christians) throughout the area where Paul was located since coming to Rome, and is based upon expressions he had heard from them in various conversations. He was especially impressed with what he had heard from the group he calls *Caesar's household.* The last word is so general that it could mean either the immediate members of Caesar's family, or his servants or attendants. In any case, it means persons closely connected with the emperor of Rome. It indicates the good influence and standing Paul had, in spite of his humiliating situation.

Verse 23. This verse is a kindly wish that the *grace* (favor) of Christ would be with the brethren at Philippi. The word *amen* is explained at verse **20.**

Colossians 1

General remarks. The date and by whom the church at Colosse was planted is uncertain. I have consulted a goodly number of reference works, and nothing more definite than "perhaps" or "maybe" was found in any of them. We know it was not by Paul, for chapter 2: 1 indicates he had not even seen those brethren when he wrote this epistle. A little information about conditions in Colosse as it pertains to religion and social life, will help to understand the various passages in the epistle. The Colossians were mostly Gentiles, but some Judaistic teachers had come among them. In addition to this, some theories of philosophy had been injected among them. Smith's Bible Dictionary refers to such a condition in the following words: "The main object of the epistle is to warn the Colossians against a spirit of semi-Judaistic and semi-Oriental philosophy which was corrupting the simplicity of their belief." Summing up, a mixture of Judaism, philosophy, idolatry, and a form of extreme bodily self-denial, had to be encountered when Paul wrote this epistle.

Verse 1. An *apostle* means one who is sent by another on a mission. Paul was sent into the world by Jesus Christ on the mission of preaching the Gospel, hence he was His apostle. The entire arrangement was according to the authority of God, which caused it to be by His will. *Timotheus* is another form of Timothy; he was with Paul and joined in the salutation to the Colossian church.

Verse 2. *Saints* and *faithful* are not different people. The second term is just one description of the first. A saint is a person who has accepted the Gospel through obedience to its commands, and who has promised to continue in the service consistently. The term *faithful* is added to show that these brethren were actually making good their promised loyalty to Christ. *Grace* is the unmerited favor of God, and *peace* is that state of mind that is made possible by accepting the salvation coming from God, and bestowed upon man through the *Lord Jesus Christ.*

Verse 3. It is important to note that God is called the Father of Christ. This refutes the doctrine of Rome, and most of the denominational world, that God and Christ are one and the same person. It is foolish to imply that a father can be his own son, or vice verse. In the beginning of the verse Paul says *we give thanks*, and in the close he says he is *praying* for the brethren. This is because there are various forms of addresses to God; thanks being offered for past favors, and prayer being requests for future ones.

Verse 4. *We heard of your faith.* According to chapter 2: 1, Paul had not seen these brethren (see "general remarks"), but had received a report of them through others. It is significant that their faith in Christ Jesus is coupled with their love for all the saints. This agrees with 1 John 3: 14; 4: 7, 8; it is morally impossible to love God and not love His children.

Verse 5. *For* is from DIA which means "on account of." It is connected with the preceding verse which asserts the love the Colossians had to all the saints. The idea is that the hope for heaven they had, was an inducement for them to act the part of true brethren in Christ by showing genuine love for them. *Heard before* refers to the fact that they had heard these great truths in the beginning of their contact with the Gospel, by the ones who brought the good news to them.

Verse 6. *World* is from a Greek word that means the people of the earth. It is sometimes limited to the people of the Roman Empire by various commentators, yet that is rather insignificant, since virtually all the civilized world was under the rule of that Empire at the time the New Testament was written. Besides, verse 23 of this chapter says the same Gospel was perached "to every creature which is under heaven." It all gives the conclusion that the commission that Christ gave the apostles in Matthew 28: 19, 20 and Mark 16: 15, 16, had been fulfilled in the time of Paul's writings: the same fact is taught in Romans 10: 18. *Bringeth forth fruit* refers to the effect that was produced by the hope given to those who believed the Gospel. *Grace of God in truth* means the favor of God is for those only who accept the truth.

Verse 7. *Epaphras* had been associated with the church at Colosse, but when this epistle was written, he was in Rome and a prisoner on behalf of the Gospel. This is indicated in Philemon 23, where Paul calls him his "fellowprisoner." *A faithful minister.* The last word is from DIAKONOS, and in the King James Version it is rendered deacon 3 times, minister 20, servant 7. Thayer defines it, "one who executes the commands of another, especially of a master; a servant, attendant, minister; deacon; a waiter, one who serves food and drink." It is never used to designate a preacher as a separate class, for the preachers of the New Testament church are never called "ministers" in that sense. Epaphras is called a *minister*, because he faithfully served the interests of the church at Colosse, which included his preaching of the Gospel.

Verse 8. Epaphras had been associated with the church at Colosse, and could give a first hand report of its conduct to Paul and the other brethren in Rome. *Love in the Spirit* denotes their love was spiritual because it was prompted and directed by the teaching of the Holy Spirit.

Verse 9. *For this cause* refers to the good things that Paul (and his companions) had heard about the Colossian brethren. Ever since he heard about it, the apostle had continuously prayed for them. Such good disciples are worthy of further encouragement and assistance, hence he desired that they might be filled with knowledge of the Lord's will. For all practical purposes, *wisdom* and *understanding* may be used with the same sense, but when a distinction is made by using them in one sentence, the first refers to the mind or intellect, and the second to the proper use of it in applying the truths at hand. Paul specifies that he is speaking of truths that have been revealed by the Spirit.

Verse 10. To walk worthy of the Lord means to walk in a way befitting a servant of His. *Unto all pleasing:* walk in a way pleasing to the Lord. *Being fruitful* or producing *every good work*, which consists in doing the good things required by the Gospel. *Increasing* indicates that a Christian should not be satisfied with his present degree of good works. However, his growth must be in accordance with the knowledge of God; this knowledge is to be obtained through Christ (chapter 2: 2, 3).

Verse 11. When used as distinguishing terms, *might* means strength or ability, and *power* means dominion or authority to use that ability. All authority in heaven and earth was given to Christ (Matthew 28: 18), and He gives his disciples the right to operate under that power; this is what will *strengthen* them in the service. The special meaning of *patience* in this passage is endurance or perseverance, and *longsuffering* refers to the unresentful attitude of one's mind while under difficulties.

Verse 12. Thayer defines the original for *meet*, "to make sufficient, render fit." No human being can ever be worthy of the salvation provided by the Lord, if measured by the strict rule of justice. But He has made it possible for the faithful disciples to be "sufficient" or entitled to it through the merits of Christ. The passage in Romans 3: 24-26 should be considered in connection with our verse. It should be understood that no man will ever enter into eternal reward unless he has a right to it (Revelation 22: 14), but he may obtain that right through Jesus. *Saints in light* means those who have fashioned their lives after the light of divine truth as revealed in the Gospel.

Verse 13. *Power* means authority or rule, and *darkness* is explained by Thayer as "ignorance respecting divine things and human duties." It applies to all who have renounced their interest in things of the world and taken the proper steps to get out of such a situation. Our verse, continuing the thought in the preceding one, tells us that it is the Father who can deliver men from such a state of darkness. *Translate* signifies to move something from one place or condition into another, and Paul tells us that the disciples had been *translated* (moved) into the kingdom of his dear Son. It is impossible to move a person into anything that does not exist. Therefore, the kingdom of Christ was in existence when Paul lived, thus disproving the heresy that the kingdom is still in the future.

Verse 14. The pronoun *whom* refers to the Son, whose blood redeems men from the bondage of "darkness" as stated in the preceding verse. No man is free from the bondage of sin until something is done that can satisfy God, against whom all sin is regarded as being committed. That satisfaction can be accomplished only through the merits of the blood of Christ. When a sinner "obeys from the heart" (Romans 6: 17) the doctrine or commandments of the Gospel, he is "then made free from sin," which is what our present verse declares.

Verse 15. No man can see the face of God and live (Exodus 33: 18-23), yet he needed to be shown how to conduct himself. The situation was met by having Christ come into the world in the nature of man, but in the form or image of God. That is why Paul calls Christ the *image of the invisible God. Firstborn of every creature* means that Christ existed before all other persons or things in all creation. That enabled Him to take part with the Father in the creaiton of the universe, and it accounts for the plural form of the pronoun (us) in Genesis 1: 26; 3: 22; 11: 7. (See also John 1: 3; Ephesians 3: 9; Hebrews 1: 2).

Verse 16. The existence of Christ before all other things in the universe (God, of course, being excepted) is still the subject under consideration. Paul is dealing thus particularly with this matter because of the pretensions of philosophy that were being injected into the Colossian community. (See the comments in "general remarks.") This verse is more specific, mentioning things both material and spiritual, and both visible (to man) and invisible.

Verse 17. *Before* is used in the sense of time or order of existence, and it denotes that Christ existed before anything else in the universe of creation. *Consist* is the same as "exist," and it means that all things were created through Him, but also they continue to be through Him. This is the same thought that is expressed in Hebrews 1: 3 which says of Christ, "and upholding all things by the word of his power."

Verse 18. The *church* is declared to be the *body*, which is taught also in Ephesians 1: 22, 23. In Ephesians 4: 4 Paul declares there is one body, so that is equivalent to saying there is one church; our present verse says Christ is the head of that one church. All of this is not only scriptural, but is logical or reasonable. A body with more than one head in nature would be a monstrosity, likewise a head with more than one body would be one. Hence it is easy to understand that, since there is but one Christ (which is admitted by all professed Christians), there can be but one church recognized by the Lord. *Who is the beginning.* This is true of Christ in many respects, but here it means he is the beginning of the new creation or age of the *one body. Firstborn from the dead* does not mean Jesus was the first person to die and rise again, for there are numerous cases in the Bible where it occurred before the time of Christ. It means He was the first person to come to life never to die again. (See Romans 6: 9.) The chief purpose of making Christ to be the first person to come from the dead never to die again, was that He might have the *preeminence*. That means to be above all other persons who would go through death and rise to die no more, in that He was the first to have that honor.

Verse 19. The word *fulness* means that nothing is lacking in Christ that is necessary for the spiritual welfare of mankind. *The Father* is not in the Greek text directly, but is of necessity implied. This "preeminence" of Christ was accomplished through His resurrection, and that event was made possible by the Father. (See Acts 2: 24; 10: 40; 1 Corinthians 15: 15.)

Verse 20. *Made peace* pertains to the satisfaction which Christ gave his Father by shedding His blood on the cross. In other words, such a supreme sacrifice was enough to answer the demands of God, and that opened up the way so that the Son could bring about reconciliation between God and the forces arrayed against Him. *Or things in heaven* would necessarily be the good angels, since an angel who sins is cast out (2 Peter 2: 4). Good angels, however, have never offended God, and hence they do not need reconciliation in the strict sense of the word. But they are called upon to recognize Christ as King and spiritual Ruler through the centuries of the final dispensation. In this way they are a part of the body of Christ, and thus participate in the grand plan of reconciliation through Christ. (See Matthew 28: 18; Hebrews 1: 6; Philippians 2: 9; Revelation 5: 13.)

Verse 21. *Alienated* is from APALLO-TRIOO, which Thayer defines, "to be shut out from one's fellowship and intimacy." Paul tells the Colossians they were once in that condition with God, but that it was caused by their own wicked works. Such a state of mind and conduct rendered them the enemies of God.

Verse 22. The condition of enmity mentioned in the preceding verse was overcome *(reconciled)* by the fleshly body of Christ. This work of reconciliation was accomplished through death, thereby making the "supreme sacrifice" that took the place of all those offered under the Jewish law (Hebrews 10: 1-9). This great plan made it possible for Christ to present his followers *unblameable* and *unrebukeable* in His (God's) sight. Not that men can become "as sinless as angels," but the blame will be removed by the blood of Christ, so that when they are presented to the Father, there will be nothing for which He will reprove them.

Verse 23. The blessings promised in the preceding verses are based upon an important *if*, which is that they must *continue in the faith*. This requires that they be *grounded and settled*, which means to be fixed in their determination to serve Christ, and hence are steadfast in their service to Him. Such a life will prevent them from being *moved away from the hope of the Gospel* which they had heard. The Colossians were not the only ones who had heard the Good News, for it *was preached to every creature which is under heaven*. This fact fulfilled the commission that Christ gave his apostles in Matthew 28: 19, 20 and Mark 16: 15, 16, and it is also declared to have been accomplished in Romans 10: 18. This teaching refutes those who quote the "great commission" and apply it to preachers of the Gospel in our day. No uninspired man can "preach the Gospel to every creature," for there are too many languages in the world.

Verse 24. The afflictions which Christ personally suffered were complete so that God was satisfied (Isaiah 53: 10, 11), hence this verse does not mean there was anything *behind* on His part. But Christians are expected to have fellowship with Jesus in his sufferings (Romans 8: 17; 2 Timothy 2: 12; 1 Peter 4: 1), and if Paul had shrunk from suffering for the sake of Christ, then he would have been the one to be *behind* as to his duty. But in undergoing tribulation in service to the brethren, he would be credited with doing so on behalf of Christ, since the church is His body. This great truth caused Paul to "rejoice in my sufferings for you."

Verse 25. Paul calls himself a *minister* because the word means a servant, whose duty it is to administer the affairs of his master. Such ministration is to be done according to the directions of the master. God had commissioned Paul to dispense (dispensation) His word by preaching (or writing) it to the Colossians and to all others where opportunity appeared.

Verse 26. A *mystery* is anything unknown, regardless of whether it is complicated or simple in its form. The mystery Paul is referring to had been kept back *from ages and from generations*. Not that the Old Testament writers were entirely silent on the subject, but it was couched in prophetic passages to such extent that the New Testament preachers had to explain the subject in light of the Gospel. (See the following verse.)

Verse 27. The pronoun *whom* refers to the "saints" in the preceding verse. All Christians are saints, but the ones to whom the *mystery* was to be directly made known were the inspired preachers and writers of the New Testament. After such revelation was made known, others would also be able to understand it. That is why Paul writes in Ephesians 3: 4, "when ye read, ye may understand my knowledge in the mystery of Christ." The particular part of the great mystery was that which pertained to the Gentiles, namely, that they were to be given the same privileges as the Jews. Of course this is to be enjoyed through Christ (not Moses), and it is *in you* (the Gentiles), extending to them *the hope of glory*. For centuries the Jews overlooked the predictions of the Old Testament, which pointed to the final acceptance of the Gentiles.

Verse 28. *Whom* refers to Christ who is the subject of Paul's preaching. *Warning* is from NOUTHETEO, which Thayer defines, "to admonish, warn, exhort." It has a somewhat milder meaning than it generally has, and signifies an earnest piece of advice to accept Christ (in the place of Moses), as the lawgiver who is in authority now. *Teaching every one.* It would not be of much use to exhort people to follow Christ unless they know what Christ wishes them to do, hence Paul states he is teaching them. *In all wisdom* means the instructions that the Holy Spirit would impart unto the apostle. *Perfect* means complete or rounded out in knowledge of divine things. By giving full information to them concerning the Gospel for the Gentiles (which was not fully known before), they would have their knowledge advanced as *perfect* (complete) *in Christ Jesus*.

Verse 29. *Whereunto* denotes the purpose for whch Paul was laboring, as described in the preceding verse. *Striving* is from AGONIZOMAI, and the lexicon of Thayer defines it, "To enter a contest; contend in the gymnastic games; to contend with adversaries, fight; to contend, struggle with difficulties and dangers; to endeavor with strenuous zeal, strive." Paul uses the athletic contests of his day to illustrate the struggles connected with his labors for Christ and his disciples. *His working* refers to the use that Christ was making of the apostle in the great conflict against sin. *Mightily* is from DUNAMIS, which is one of the strongest words in the Greek New Testament for power or ability. Paul uses it to indicate the help his Trainer is giving him in the contest going on in the arena of life.

Colossians 2

Verse 1. Much of the thought in the last verse of the preceding chapter is continued in this verse. The Greek word for *conflict* means virtually the same as "striving" in the close of the preceding chapter. It refers to the great care and anxiety Paul felt for the Colossians, and he wishes that they knew about it; this feeling was extended to the brethren at Laodicea (a city near Colosse). *As many as have not seen my face in the flesh.* This clause indicates that Paul had not been personally in the presence of the Colossian brethren, hence he could not have been the one who started the church there nor at Laodicea. (See the comments under "general remarks.")

Verse 2. Paul connects the comfort of the brethren with their being knit together in love. Such a state is a great source of satisfaction, for if the disciples of Christ are thus bound together, they will be of mutual help and can meet the trials of life as a unit. David expressed this thought in Psalms 133: 1. This condition will result in the *riches of full assurance* that comes from *understanding*. Of course all of this blessed state will come only after their *acknowledgement of the mystery*. The last word refers to the mystery that is explained in chapter 1: 26. God the Father and Christ are named together because they are both concerned in the subject. The relation between the names *God* and *Father* is explained at Ephesians 4: 6.

Verse 3. *In whom* is supposed to refer to Christ, who is last named in the preceding verse. However, some confusion might come from the marginal rendering which gives "wherein," making it apply to the *mystery* mentioned in the preceding verse. But the following verses all show that Christ is especially meant and hence the text as we have it is correct. That does not do any injustice to God, for everything He does for mankind is done through the Son. This verse is a direct denial of the theories of philosophy that were mentioned in "general remarks." Whatever wisdom and knowledge there is in the world that is worthy of the attention of man, all is found in Christ.

Verse 4. Paul is saying the present things as a warning against false teachers. To *beguile* means to deceive, and *enticing words* are those that sound well and are of a persuasive nature. These false teachers used a mixture of philosophy and Judaism in such a way as to mislead unsuspecting disciples away from the simplicity of the Gospel of Christ. Most of this chapter is written to expose both philosophy (so called) and Judaism, especially the latter.

Verse 5. The Colossian church had not yet departed from the faith, but it was in danger and the apostle is warning them. For the present, he is pleased with their excellent devotion to Christ, and wishes to have them continue in the same status. He was not in their midst bodily but was there in spirit or mind, and took joy from what he could behold through the things he had "heard" (chapter 1: 4). *Order* is from TAXIS, which Thayer defines at this place, "orderly condition." It does not mean any set routine to be followed in a mechanical order, but denotes that the church at Colosse had some system in its procedure. It is the same thought expressed in 1 Corinthians 14: 40, "Let all things be done decently and in order."

Verse 6. *As* is used in the sense of "since"—*since ye have received*, etc. Having *received* or accepted Christ as the Lord (which means Ruler), to be consistent, they should also *walk* or conduct their life *in Him*. That can be done only by doing His will.

Verse 7. *Rooted* and *stablished* have vritually the same meaning, namely, to be firmly fixed in something. In this passage it means to be established *in the faith* or in the Gospel. Of course if something has taken firm root in a fertile spot, it will be able to produce a stalk or body above the ground. Likewise, Paul says the brethren will be able to grow or be *built up* as a stalk of righteousness in the world. And as a plant thus rooted and developed will be able to produce fruit, so the brethren would be able to *abound* (grow and produce), being thankful for the opportunity of being of service to Christ.

Verse 8. The apostle again comes to the subject of the Judaistic philosophers, who claim to have something to offer the brethren that is better than their simple belief of the Gospel. They would make them think that something of value was being lost if they did not accept the ideas of philosophy as a part of their religious life. Paul is warning them to *beware* of these false teachers. To *spoil* means to take from a man that which is his valuable possession. The simple faith of the Gospel is the most valuable thing one can possess, and if he permits the false teacher to cause him to give up that faith, he will be robbed of a costly treasure. A thief accomplishes his work with instruments adapted to his evil work, and likewise this false teacher has his instruments which are named in this verse. *Vain deceit.* The ideas offered by these philosophers were not only deceitful, but they were empty *(vain)*. They were *traditions* or things handed down from man and not from Christ. *Rudiments* denotes elements and *world* means the people of the earth. These deceitful philosophies were elements produced in the minds of men and not by Jesus Christ.

Verse 9. *Godhead* is from THEOTES, which Thayer defines, "deity; Godhead," then explains it to mean, "the state of being God." *Bodily* refers to the form in which Jesus appeared while on earth, so that the entire *fulness* or virtue of the Deity was represented in Him. That is why Jesus said to Philip, "he that hath seen me hath seen the Father" (John 14: 9). Not that Jesus was the Father personally, but he was a full representation of God in human form.

Verse 10. Since the entire Godhead is represented by Christ, nothing of value will be lacking to those who are in Him. *Principality* is the same as seniority or priority, and *power* means authority. He is senior because he is the "firstborn of every creature" (chapter 1: 15), and He is head of all power or authority because it was all given to Him after his resurrection (Matthew 28:18). If we believe the teaching of Paul in this verse, we will not clamor for things in our religious life that Christ has not authorized.

Verse 11. I have consulted several translations, and they put the word *are* in the past tense, showing it refers to a specific event of the past. The occasion when it was accomplished will be noted in the following verse. *Circumcision* means a cutting round or off, and when used figuratively it refers to the separation of a man's sins from his life by his obedience to the Gospel. It was *without hands* because while its outward form was done by a human act (see next verse), the real performance was spiritual or inward. (See Romans 6:17.) *Circumcision of Christ* denotes that the whole transaction was accomplished by His authority.

Verse 12. The final act of the spiritual circumcision is by baptism, and men are said to be *buried with him*, that is with Christ. This phrase is used because in baptism the person is placed under the water and then raised again, thus going down and up in the form of a burial and resurrection. It is said to be with Him because he commands it, and also because he died and was buried in the tomb, from which he rose again. Such a like burial and resurrection is recognized as an act of faith in Christ and God. *Operation* means the energy or divine activity by which God raised Christ from the dead. Much has been said as to what constitutes "valid baptism," and we have some direct information in this passage. If a man believes that God raised Christ from the dead, and he is baptized in view of his faith in that act, then Paul declares that such a man has been *risen with him*, which certainly would prove that his baptism was valid. This thought is given also in Romans 10:9.

Verse 13. All statements in this verse except the last one are figurative. Death means a separation, and as long as these people were living in their sins they were separated from God and hence were dead to Him. They likewise were uncircumcised during that time since their sins had not been cut off. To be *quickened* means to be made alive, or have the condition of death just described, reversed by obedience to the Gospel.

With him means with Christ, which was done when they were "buried with Him" in baptism. When all this was done, God forgave them all trespasses.

Verse 14. *Blotting out* is from a word that denotes something has been erased or canceled. However, since this refers to the Old Testament, we know it means that the enforcement of it as a religious law only was canceled, for the document is still in print and its national customs were still permitted to the Jewish Christians in Paul's day (Acts 21:21-24). It is called *handwriting* from the fact that God wrote it with his own fingers on the stone, then authorized Moses to write it all in a book with his hand. *Against* and *contrary* literally means to be an enemy, but it is not used in that sense here, for the law of Moses should not be thought of in that light. The idea is that no one could form his religious life by that law and be under the law of Christ at the same time. (See Galatians 5:1-4.) *Nailing it to his cross*. As long as a note or bond is in force or unsatisfied, it stands as an obligation "against" those who are under it. But when its demands have been met, it is canceled and its debtors are no longer held. Then such a document is rendered void by having a punch make a perforation through it, as a ticket is punched. This was done to the law when Jesus suffered himself to be punctured or nailed to the cross.

Verse 15. To *spoil* anything means to take away its valuables. The most valuable possession of a power or government is its authority. Jesus took that away from the law, as far as religious obligations were concerned, when He died on the cross and gave to the world another law and government. *Make a show of them openly* by being crucified in the view of the world. In this great event, though Jesus died and apparently was overcome, yet he came forth again from the dead to die no more. In so doing, Jesus triumphed over them (all other powers) *in it*. The last two words are rendered "in himself," which is correct since He was the one who triumphed.

Verse 16. The law of Moses had certain regulations concerning what they might eat and drink, and how (Leviticus 7:10-27). It had various days that had to be observed as holy days. Among these were the new moons (2 Chronicles 31:3; Numbers

28: 11), and all the sabbath days (Exodus 31: 13). Since that law has been replaced by the Gospel, no man should be allowed to *judge* the Christians concerning these regulations, by trying to force their observance on them.

Verse 17. The lexicon explains the original for *shadow* to mean, "an image cast by an object and representing the form of that object," and *body* is from SOMA, which the same lexicon of Thayer defines as, "the thing itself which casts the shadow." The ordinances of the Mosaic law were types or shadows of those to be given through Christ, and that is the reason He is said to be the body that casts the shadow. By insisting on the ordinances of the old law, the Judaizers were preferring the shadow of something to the thing itself.

Verse 18. *Beguile you of your reward* is from a Greek word that is used literally in reference to the athletic contests, where a judge or umpire would decide who is the winner. Thayer defines the word, "To decide as umpire against one, to declare him unworthy of the prize; to defraud of the prize of victory." As Paul uses it the meaning is, not to let the Judaizers cheat the disciples out of their reward from Christ by means of the evil things mentioned in the rest of this verse and the next. *Voluntary humility* means a pretended or self-imposed show of humility that is outward only. *Worshiping* is from THRESKEIA, which Thayer defines, "Primarily fear of the gods; religious worship, especially external, that which consists in ceremonies." It is used here in reference to some formalities that were claimed to be pleasing to the angelic hosts or beings in the unseen world, which Paul describes as an *intruding into those things which he hath not seen*. These Judaistic philosophers did all this because their *fleshly* or carnal mind had puffed them up over their imaginary importance.

Verse 19. The head of a body is that which directs its movements, hence if the body should become disconnected from the head, its performances would become disorderly (such as a fowl when its head has been severed by an ax). These deceptive teachers are likened to a body thus disconnected from its head, because they have rejected Christ who is "the head of the body." *Joints and bands* refers to the parts of the body, which must depend upon the head for proper control. When that is done, it will result in *having nourishment ministered*, and hence will be *knit together* into a well ordered body. The grand result will be a proper development and *increase* (growth), because it will be *the increase of God*. (See Ephesians 4: 16.)

Verse 20. In his deunciation of false teachers, the apostle has reference to both Judaism and so-called philosophy in the rest of the chapter, but chiefly the former. *Rudiments of the world* means the elements or ordinances of the law that were types of the Gospel. Since Christ has released them from their obligation to the former *rudiments*, why (Paul asks) are they still subjecting themselves to them as if they were still under them.

Verse 21. Paul did not give this verse as his command, but quotes it as one of the human ordinances from which Christ has made men free. The restrictions of the law, such as *touch not, taste not, handle not*, referred to the eating and drinking of certain things. Those regulations had been lifted by the Gospel, so that trying still to fasten them upon Christians was considered as forcing upon them a human regulation.

Verse 22. *Perish with the using*. The things the Judaizers insisted that Christians should "touch not; taste not; handle not," were the articles of food and drink that were restricted by the law. Paul is reasoning that the restrictions were not made because of any bad effect such things would have on the body, for they perished with the using. That is, as articles of food, they were soon cast out of the body, leaving it unharmed. (See Mark 7: 15-19.) The ordinances against them, therefore, were purely ceremonial, and when the law was canceled, the said restrictions were canceled also. After that was done, any continuance of them would be regarded as being *after the commandments and doctrines of men*. Paul taught the same idea in Philippians 3: 9, where he designates the righteousness of the law "mine own righteousness," after the law had been replaced by that of Christ.

Verse 23. *Show of wisdom* denotes that these unauthorized theories and practices have an appearance of wisdom only. This verse has special reference to the items of so-called philosophers, and the practices of people called ascetics. Such extremists believed it was a virtue to torture the body in the name of religious philosophy. *Will worship* means that which is suggested by the human will instead of by the will of God. *Humility* is the same as "voluntary humility," and it is explained at verse 18. *Neglecting of the body* is defined by Robinson as "harsh bodily discipline." *Not in any honor* denotes that these things are of no real value, and *to the satisfying of the flesh* means they are prompted by the fleshly or human notions.

Colossians 3

Verse 1. Some translations render the first part of this verse as follows: "Since, then, ye have been risen with Christ." That is correct, for the first word is from the Greek term EI which is defined in the lexicons as a conditional term. It means a condition that something is based upon, and the condition in this case is that the Colossians had been risen with Christ. However, there is no doubt implied, for chapter 2: 12 plainly states that they had done so, and says it was when they were baptized. That act entitled them to the things mentioned in our verse. The preceding chapter shows them the folly of depending on human elements, hence they should look elsewhere for something worth having and seeking for. The instruction is to seek the things which are *above*, and the word is defined by Thayer, "in a higher place." But the apostle leaves no place for uncertainty as to where that is, for he says it is *where Christ sitteth on the right hand of God*. Baptized believers, then, have a right to these things, but they must *seek* for them. Romans 2: 7 and Revelation 22: 14 will tell us how the seeking is done.

Verse 2. *Set your affections* are from the Greek word PHRONEO, and Thayer defines it, "to direct one's mind to a thing, to seek or strive for." The verse is virtually the same in meaning as the preceding one.

Verse 3. Death means a separation, and when the disciples turned from a sinful life, they were separated from sin and thus died to it. The life or activity that had been devoted to a worldly practice then became devoted to Christ and so was *hid with Him*. Of course it was *in God*, because everything pertaining to righteousness and salvation, m u s t be accomplished jointly with the Father and the Son.

Verse 4. *Christ who is our life.* To be hid with Christ gives assurance of enjoying the provisions that He has made for his faithful servants. Those provisions include eternal life; and all of the interests of Christians that have been *hid* with Him will be revealed—will come out of hiding—when Christ appears at the last day. "When that illustrious day shall rise," it will be in a halo of eternal glory, betokening victory over the sinful world.

Verse 5. In the preceding chapter Paul condemns the extremists who considered it a virtue to torture the body. In the present passage he instructs the disciples to *mortify* (put to death) certain evil things that are often practiced in the *members* or parts of the body. *Fornication.* According to Thayer's explanation of this word, it means unlawful intimacy in general, between the sexes, whether married or not. *Uncleanness* is a general term and applies to any kind of defilement whether of body or spirit. *Inordinate affection* is from PATHOS, which Thayer defines, "depraved passion;" it is the word for "vile affections" in Romans 1: 26. *Evil concupiscence* is a term for evil desire, and it is described by Thayer as, "desire for what is forbidden, lust." *Covetousness* is from PLEONEXIA, and Thayer defines it, "greedy desire to have more, covetousness, avarice." *Idolatry* is from IDOLOLATREIA, and its primary meaning is as the King James Version renders it. Thayer explains it at this place to mean "avarice [greed], as a worship of Mammon." The last word is derived from the Chaldean lagnuage, and means "what is trusted in," which shows us why Paul says that covetousness *is* (not just as bad as) *idolatry.*

Verse 6. The theory of predestination that many human creeds teach, is disproved by this verse. It shows that the wrath of God comes on people only who are guilty of the evils described in the preceding verse. Such conduct puts them in a class called *children of disobedience.* The first word is described in Thayer's lexicon as, "those who are connected with a thing by any kind of close relationship."

Verse 7. The Colossians were once living in sin but are now disciples of Christ, having been baptized into Him. The words *walked* and *lived* are used in the same sense, showing that a man's walk is classified by the way he lives.

Verse 8. When they obeyed the Gospel they were made free from all guilt and stood pure before God. However, being in the beginning of their service to Him, they were like children and would need to make further advancement in their contest against sin. *Anger, wrath, malice.* If used alone, these words would have virtually the same meaning. When used in one sentence, they represent a growing of intensity of evil temper, finally becoming fixed in a deep feeling and evil intention called *malice.* *Blasphemy* is any kind of evil speaking, especially that which is prompted by the kind of heart just described. *Filthy communication* is foul and indecent language.

Verse 9. *The old man* is a figurative name for the kind of life the Colossians had lived, which was *put off* when they ceased such a life of sin. One of the evils they formerly committed was falsehood, which is to be replaced with truth.

Verse 10. When a person puts off one suit of apparel, it is usually for the purpose of putting on another. In like manner, after discarding their old garb of sin, the Colossians had *put on* the new one that was *renewed* (modeled) after a divine pattern like Christ who *created* or designed it.

Verse 11. This verse does not mean that the groups named cannot be in Christ, but that in Him no distinctions are made for or against any of them. When *Greek* is used in contrast with *Jew* it means a Gentile. *Circumcision* and *uncircumcision* also mean Jew and Gentile, because that rite was a distinguishing mark between the two from a national standpoint. *Barbarian* means a foreigner, and *Scythian* means a class of people considered below the average in culture and intelligence. *Bond* and *free* refer to slaves, and those not under slavery. All of these classes have equal right to be in Christ upon obedience to the Gospel, and when they comply with it, they are united as one religious group in Him.

Verse 12. What the Colossians had *put on* is mentioned in general in verse 10, and this verse gives some items of that new attire. *Elect of God* means people who have obeyed the law of God and therefore are elected or chosen by Him, and are regarded as *holy* and *beloved. Bowels* is used figuratively in the New Testament, which Thayer explains as follows: "In the Greek poets the bowels were regarded as the seat of the more violent passions, but by the Hebrews as the seat of the tenderer affections." Paul partly gives the same definition by adding the rest of the words of this verse. *Humbleness* and *meekness* are about the same in meaning, and *longsuffering* denotes patience under trials and unjust treatment.

Verse 13. *Forbearing one another* is virtually the same as "longsuffering" in the preceding verse, denoting a spirit of patience with the faults of others. This will be manifested by a willingness to forgive one who has trespassed against us. *Quarrel* means complaint that one feels he has against a brother. *Even* comes from KATHOS, which Thayer defines, "according as, just as, even as." The idea is that we should be willing to follow the example of Christ in forgiving those who have offended us.

Verse 14. *Charity* is from AGAPE, which means love that is prompted by a genuine interest in another, which is manifested by a willingness to contribute to his welfare. *Above all these things* means that love is more important than all the other things that were mentioned in the preceding verses. That agrees with 1 Corinthians 13: 13, where the last word is from the same Greek term. *Bond of perfectness* signifies that charity (or love) will make a perfect (complete) bond between brethren.

Verse 15. *Peace of God* would be that calmness of mind provided by Him. To *rule* in their hearts means for such a state of mind to predominate in their minds. Such a condition can be had only in the *one body* which is the church (Ephesians 1: 22, 23). Such a blessedness with God is enough to cause them to *be thankful.*

Verse 16. The body of this verse is the same in thought as Ephesians 5: 19; a full explanation is given at that place, which the reader should see; some additional comments will be offered here. The *word of Christ* is recorded in the New Testament, hence a knowledge of that book is necessary for it to dwell in one's mind richly and *in wisdom.* Such a knowledge will enable the disciples to *teach* and *admonish* each other. To teach means to impart instruction, and to admonish means to insist on doing one's duty, with an intimation of danger in neglecting it. *Singing with grace* indicates that the service is prompted by the grace (favor) of God.

Verse 17. *Word or deed.* According to Luke 6: 43-45, a man's words are the fruit of his heart or thoughts. Therefore, the phrase in italics includes one's entire conduct, and the command is that it must be all *in the name* of the Lord Jesus, otherwise it will be wrong. That cannot mean that merely professing the name of Christ in connection with a thing will make it right. Matthew 7: 22; 24: 5 shows persons doing things "in the name" of the Lord, who we know were not doing right. The phrase can mean only to do all by the authority of Christ. Since His authority is known only in the New Testament, it follows that Christians have no right to any thought, word or deed, that is not authorized by that volume.

Verse 18. The relationship between God and Christians is a religious and spiritual one, yet He gives certain regulations regarding conduct of the disciples, in all of their relations and dealings with each other, in their various connections with social, political and industrial activities. The general law that should always prevail when a question is raised as to right and wrong in the cases to be mentioned soon, is stated in Acts 5: 29 as follows: "We ought to obey God rather than men." That is why our present verse instructs wives to submit themselves unto their husbands *as it is fit in the Lord.* As long as a wife can obey her husband without violating any law of the Lord, it is her duty to do so.

Verse 19. *Love* is from AGAPAO, which Thayer defines, "to have a preference for, wish well to, regard the welfare of." It does not necessarily include the "romantic sentiments," although such a feeling should exist for a woman before a man seeks to make her his wife. *Be not bitter* means for him not to show an angry or irritated feeling toward his wife in ruling over her.

Verse 20. *In all things* should be understood with the same proviso as "in the Lord" at Ephesians 6: 1. A full explanation of this subject is given in that passage which the reader should consult. As long as the commands of parents are not in conflict with the law of the Lord, children must obey them, even though they are old enough to have obeyed the Gospel.

Verse 21. The words *to anger* are not in the primary definition given by the lexicon. *Provoke* means to irritate one's children in a way that will discourage them. It does not oppose proper disciplining of them, even though such correction may be unpleasant. It should be considered in the light of Hebrews 12: 11.

Verse 22. It was not the purpose of the Lord to interfere with the relation of master and servant, for that is a temporal one. But He gave regulations for their conduct toward each other when either or both became disciples, which frequently occurred. *Eye service* means "service performed only under the master's eye."—Thayer. *Singleness* is another name for sincerity, and such service here termed *eye service* would not be sincere, and would not be prompted by the fear or respect for God.

Verse 23. They were to serve their masters with the same sincerity that they do their service to the Lord. In truth, since He requires servants to obey their masters, such service could well be considered in a sense as having been done for the Lord.

Verse 24. *Reward of the inheritance* merely denotes the Lord will see that a faithful servant will receive his due reward. The last clause is the same as the preceding verse; Lord Christ means the anointed ruler.

Verse 25. As surely as the Lord will see that a faithful servant will receive his due reward, so He will see that an unfaithful one will be punished. *No respect of persons.* No unfaithful servant will be shown any partiality on account of some personal preference, as earthly masters sometimes do. (See the comments at Ephesians 6: 9.)

Colossians 4

Verse 1. Masters who become disciples were under the authority of Christ as well as were their servants, hence were given instructions as to the proper treatment to be accorded them. *Just and equal* means they should furnish their servants with such wages as their labor deserved and their needs required. Remembering that they have a Master in heaven should prevent them from being unduly severe with their own servants, and cause them not to withhold from them their just dues.

Verse 2. To *continue in prayer* denotes a life that is devoted to God, and that makes all activities for Him the subjects of Prayer. Prayer has to do with one's attention to the Lord, and watching pertains to the care a disciple will have as to his own conduct. *Thanksgiving* is appropriate because of the consideration God gives to the faithful child of His.

Verse 3. *Withal* is defined "at the same time" by Thayer, which connects this verse with the preceding one. As they "continue" in prayer for themselves, Paul wishes them to include a prayer for him. Not for his personal benefit, but for the work of Christ in which he is engaged. He wished for a *door of utterance*, meaning an opportunity for speaking the *mystery* (Gospel) *of Christ. For which* refers to this mystery or Gospel, meaning that his *bonds* or chain was upon him because he wished to preach the Gospel, which was displeasing to so many Jews and others.

Verse 4. A mystery is anything that is not known, whether complicated or simple in its character. Paul refers to the mystery of the Gospel in the preceding verse, now in this he wishes to be able to make it *manifest* or known to those with whom the "door of utterance" would bring him into contact.

Verse 5. *Walk in wisdom.* Let the conduct be according to good judgment, considering the effect it will have upon *them that are without*, meaning the ones who are not in the church. The people of the world often have a better knowledge of how Christians should live than we realize. *Redeeming the time* means to make good use of our time, by devotion to the things that will build up a character acceptable to God.

Verse 6. The instructions in the preceding verse have special reference to the bodily conduct of disciples, and the present one pertains to their language in conversation with others. *Grace* is from CHARIS, and it is used in the New Testament with reference to both the Lord's dealings with man, and to the dealings of men with each other. When used in the latter sense, it is defined by Thayer as follows: "Sweetness, charm, loveliness; goodwill, lovingkindness, favor." Salt has the quality of preserving that with which it comes into contact, and also of rendering it more agreeable to the taste. Our verse means that by proper talk with people on the outside of the church, disciples may be true to the Gospel teaching, and yet not give unnecessary offense. Such a rule or attitude towards others will show that a disciple *knows how to answer every man*, and thus his good influence may be preserved as *with salt*.

Verse 7. Thayer says Tychicus was "an Asiatic Christian, friend and companion of the apostle Paul." Funk and Wagnalls New Standard Bible Dictionary gives the same information, with additional notes that he carried the epistle of Paul to the Ephesians, and the same would apply to the present letter. It should be kept in mind that all Paul's epistles were sent by messengers, since there were no postal arrangements for carrying private letters such as exist in our times. When delivering the epistle to the Colossians, Paul expected Tychicus to give information as to the personal circumstances that his work in the Gospel had caused.

Verse 8. *Same purpose* refers to the subject of welfare mentioned in the preceding verse. Tychicus was to inform the Colossians of the state of Paul, and he wished also to learn that of them. *Comfort your hearts.* Thayer defines the Greek for the first word, "to encourage, strengthen." In spite of the restricted situation surrounding the apostle, there was much in which to rejoice, because of the great amount of good that he was doing for the Gospel's sake.

Verse 9. Onesimus was the runaway slave of Philemon (Philemon 10-16) who got in company with Paul in Rome and was persuaded to obey the Gospel. His master being a resident of Colosse, he was sent back there with Tychicus as the epistle of Paul was sent to the church in that city. *Who is one of you* pertains both to his being a resident of the city, and also a brother in Christ. He was expected to join with Tychicus in reporting on the state of Paul.

Verse 10. A number of brethren were in Rome when Paul composed this epistle, and many of them joined in sending friendly greetings to the Colossians. *Aristarchus* was a citizen of Thessalonica (Acts 27: 2), who became a traveling companion of the apostle (Acts 19: 29; 20: 4). He became a fellow-laborer with Paul (Philemon 24), and because of his zeal in the work he was finally taken captive by the authorities and made his fellow-prisoner as our verse states. *Marcus* is another form for Mark, who was in Rome, having been restored to the confidence of the apostle (2 Timothy 4: 11). *Sister's son* is from ANEPSIOS, which Thayer defines, "a cousin." The Englishman's Greek New Testament renders the phrase, "Mark, the cousin of Barnabas." *Ye received commandments.* We are not told what those orders were, but the necessary inference is that they pertained to the attitude that was to be shown toward Mark. That accounts for the instruction to *receive him* if he came to Colosse.

Verse 11. This *Jesus* is distinguished from others of the same name by giving us his surname; *called* [surnamed] *Justus. Of the circumcision* means they were Jews converted to the Gospel. *These only* refers to the Jewish Christians mentioned in this and the preceding verse. They were the only ones of that nationality who were *fellow-workers* with Paul, and who thus had been a comfort to him. Certain Gentile converts also co-operated with him, some of whom have been already mentioned, and others will be named later in this chapter.

Verse 12. *Epaphras* had been associated with the church at Colosse, but when this epistle was written, he was in Rome and a prisoner on behalf of the Gospel. This is indicated in Philemon 23, where Paul calls him his "fellow-prisoner." He joined in sending salutations to the Colossian brethren. *Laboring . . . . in prayers* for the "home congregation" was a natural thing because of his personal interest in those brethren. *Perfect* and *complete* mean about the same if used separately in various places. In the present use of the words, the former means to be fully developed, and the latter shows why; that it is because they would be fully supplied with necessary spiritual principles.

Verse 13. Laodicea and Hierapolis were cities not far from Colosse, and Epaphras had expressed a fervent interest in the disciples at those places.

Verse 14. Luke was a physician by profession, but became a devoted companion of Paul, both in his travels and also in his tribulations at Rome. He is also the writer of the Gospel record bearing his name in the heading, and of the book of Acts (Luke 1: 3; Acts 1: 1). Demas was yet in Rome and devoted to the apostle also at the time this letter was written; he deserted him afterward (2 Timothy 4: 10).

Verse 15. The salutations of this verse are general as a whole, but Paul makes some specifications. Laodicea is mentioned in verse 13, and Nymphas was a disciple in that city. The original for *house* sometimes means "the inmates of a house, the family." This disciple had a group of others in his house who composed the church in that city, and Paul sends greetings to it through the Colossian brethren.

Verse 16. Laodicea was not far from Colosse, and Paul directed the brethren to read this epistle among themselves first, then pass it on to the brethren at Laodicea to be read by them. There is some uncertainty as to what epistle is meant that was to come *from Laodicea*, but whatever it was, the brethren at Colosse were instructed to read it. The common conditions in these two churches were such as to make the two epistles appropriate for both.

Verse 17. *Archippus* is described by Thayer as, "a certain Christian at Colosse." He was a teacher in the church there, and Paul sends this exhortation to him to be expressed by the brethren on behalf of the apostle. *The ministry* means the service of teaching that the Lord had delivered to him.

Verse 18. Paul occasionally did the writing of his epistles (Galatians 6: 11), but as a rule he dictated them to someone else, then signed his name to them which made them authentic. *Remember my bonds.* This was not written to obtain sympathy, for the apostle was not the kind of disciple to complain. The reference was for the benefit of the brethren, to stimulate their zeal on behalf of the Gospel.

1 Thessalonians 1

Verse 1. The planting of the church in Thessalonica is recorded in Acts 17th chapter, and soon afterward Paul wrote this epistle to it. According to Thayer, Silvanus is another form of the name for Silas, who was chosen to travel with Paul in his second journey (Acts 15: 40). When they reached

Lystra they met a disciple by the name of Timotheus (same as Timothy), and Paul took him along on this journey. These brethren were with Paul and joined their salutations to his as he composed this epistle to the church of the Thessalonians. God and Christ are not the same person, but they are one in spirit and purpose, and no relation can be had with either that ignores the other; hence the church is said to be *in* them both. In their specific relations to the church, God is the Father and Christ is the ruler, that being the meaning of *Lord;* this is in agreement with Matthew 28: 18 and 1 Corinthians 15: 24, 25.

Verse 2. *Making mention of you in our prayers.* Here is a specific example of direct or personal mention of those for whom we wish to pray to God, and not the unnecessary and indefinite request for Him to "bless all for whom we should pray."

Verse 3. This verse states the reason for thanksgiving as mentioned in the preceding verse. It contains three distinct items in the conduct of the Thessalonians which Paul remembered with thanksgiving. *Work of faith.* Romans 10: 17 tells us that faith comes by hearing the work of God. Hence no work can be done by faith unless the word of God authorizes it. But there is another item in this phrase that is often overlooked, namely, it must not only be according to the word of God, but it must be put to *work* in order to please the Lord. *Labor of love.* Christians should not only do those things that are authorized by the word of God, but they must love to do them, else their labor will not be acceptable. (See Galatians 5: 6.) *Patience of hope.* The two parts of this phrase cannot exist separately in the life of a Christian. If he does not have any hope for the reward, he will not have the patience to labor for it (Romans 8: 24, 25). Likewise, if a man does not have the patience to continue in a faithful life, he will not have a right to hope for the reward promised to the faithful.

Verse 4. *Election* is from EKLOGE, and Robinson defines it with the words, "choice, election, selection." The term refers to those who are selected by the Lord to be the ones upon whom He will bestow the divine blessings. The selection, however, is not made independent of the conduct of man. It is from the same word used in 2 Peter 1: 10 where the apostle exhorts the disciples to "make their calling and election sure," which shows that the selection is determined by their conduct.

Verse 5. *Not in word only* denotes that it was not the word of Paul as a man only. It was in *power* (Greek DUNAMIS) because the source was the Holy Ghost (or Spirit). With such a foundation for his teaching, Paul could come to the Thessalonians *in much assurance.* The *manner of men* refers to the teaching and conduct that was manifested among them by Paul and his companions. One motive they had for such conduct is revealed by the words *for your sake,* and it had the desired effect as the next verse shows.

Verse 6. The original Greek for *followers* is defined "an imitator" by Thayer, and it is connected with the thoughts in the close of the preceding verse, regarding the conduct of Paul and his companions while in Thessalonica. It is noteworthy that the apostle says they imitated *us and the Lord,* which is according to his instruction in 1 Corinthians 11: 1, to follow him as he followed Christ. *Received the word in much affliction;* this experience is recorded in Acts 17: 5-9. *With joy of the Holy Ghost.* The Gospel which these disciples received was given by inspiration of the Holy Ghost (or Spirit), and the joy was due to their assurance that they were suffering for the sake of the Gospel of Christ. (See Acts 5: 41.)

Verse 7. The example of righteous living set by Paul did not stop with the people in Thessalonica, for it was taken note of by disciples in other places. *Macedonia* was the province in which Thessalonica was located, and *Achaia* was a name given to Greece by the Romans after they got possession of the country.

Verse 8. *From you sounded out the word.* The effect of a good example is still the subject uppermost in the mind of the apostle. These brethren did not actually preach the word by mouth in all these areas, but their good lives spread a report for the good cause. That is why Paul says their *faith is spread abroad,* to such an extent that he did not feel the need of publishing it in those parts.

Verse 9. *Manner of entering in* is the same as "manner of men" in verse 5, and the meaning is that the teaching and conduct of Paul's group was reflected by the brethren in different places. This reflection did not consist in indefinite compliments only, but they specified some of the good things that resulted from their example. Among them was their conversion from idolatry (the Macedonians being Gentiles and worshipers of idols) to the worship of the true God. He was *living* and not made of wood or stone.

Verse 10. *Wait for* is from ANAMENO which Thayer defines, "to wait for one," then explains it to mean, "to await one whose coming is known or foreseen." It is true that all people must wait for the coming of Christ in the sense that nothing can be done by them to hasten His coming. The idea is that Christians are waiting with confidence that He will come again. The interest in Christ's second coming is in the truth that he overcame death when in this world and thereby provided deliverance from the wrath of God that is to come upon the disobedient. His coming will be the time when those who have accepted this deliverance will be gathered to Him.

1 Thessalonians 2

Verse 1. The coming of Paul and his companions to Thessalonica resulted in the conversion of some of its citizens, which proved that it was not in vain.

Verse 2. The shameful treatment mentioned is recorded in Acts 16: 19-24, after which they came to Thessalonica. But the persecution did not keep them from continuing their good work of preaching the Gospel. Instead, it made them *bold* ("confident"—Thayer) in speaking it to them. *Contention* means earnestness and anxiety, which describes the attitude of Paul on account of the opposition that had been waged against him. In other words, Paul regarded the issues as being a contest between truth and error, and he was determined to perform his part of the struggle with the same zeal that men showed when they entered the arena of the athletic games.

Verse 3. Paul could not have had any wrong motive when he was exhorting the Thessalonians, for his conduct under persecutions while at Philippi showed that he had nothing to gain by practicing *deceit* or *guile* which means trickery. His conduct and teaching also had nothing unclean either physically or spiritually as he labored among them.

Verse 4. *Put in trust* is rendered "be entrusted" by The Englishman's Greek New Testament, which expresses the idea better. It denotes that even an apostle was to handle the word of God as a faithful agent, and not as if he were managing his own business. As long as he or any other disciple holds the law of the Lord in that light, he will not violate Revelation 22:18, 19. That is why Paul says he was speaking *not as pleasing men, but God. Trieth our hearts.* The first word is defined to mean "to examine" or "scrutinize." If Paul should handle the Gospel with a view to pleasing men, that motive would be seen by the Lord when He examined his heart (or mind).

Verse 5. *Flattering words . . . . nor a choke of covetousness.* Paul did not use flattery to hide a motive of covetousness, for he was not covetous, but was interested in their spiritual welfare and not their wealth.

Verse 6. Paul did not seek the praise of men when he was preaching the Gospel among them. This was true, whether he was with the Thessalonians or with others. *When we might have been burdensome as the apostles of Christ.* Paul could have used his authority as an apostle, but he did not burden them for his own advantage.

Verse 7. Instead of using the stern attitude of authority, Paul manifested that of an affectionate nurse toward the children under her care.

Verse 8. The word *souls* is from PSUCHE which has a wide range of meanings. Sometimes it refers to the inner man as distinguished from the body, and at others it means the part that makes one a living creature and not a dead one. It is used in the latter sense in our verse, and Paul means he and his companions would have been willing to die for the brethren at Thessalonica, had it been necessary for their welfare. He explains that the cause of it was their affectionate desire on behalf of these disciples, who had shown such courage after hearing the Gospel.

Verse 9. *Labor* and *travail* mean very much the same, and are used for the purpose of emphasis. When taken together, the idea is to show hard bodily toil, performed in connection with an intense concern for the comfort of the brethren. The apostle worked at his trade of tentmaking (Acts 18: 1-3), in order to relieve the

Thessalonian brethren from the burden of supporting him. Being inspired, he did not have to spend time in reading and meditating as did other preachers of the Gospel (1 Timothy 4: 13-16).

Verse 10. It is certain that God knows everything that is going on, and the fact is mentioned in connection with the knowledge of the Thessalonians to signify the unity of interest between God and his people. *Holily* and *justly* both mean virtually the same thing, but the first has special reference to one's responsibility to God, and the second toward his fellowman. In being unblameable on both counts, Paul could claim to have a conscience "void of offence toward God and man" (Acts 24: 16).

Verse 11. The tender attitude of Paul toward the Thessalonian brethren was due to his close association with them in the beginning of their service to Christ. There was so much opposition from the enemies that it bound the apostle and his converts with a nearness that was like that between a father and his children. That relationship of feeling caused him to exhort them toward their duty and to encourage them in their work for Christ.

Verse 12. To *walk worthy of God* means to walk or conduct themselves in a way befitting those belonging to God. This is especially true, since their call from Him was not into a work of a temporal nature, but was *unto his kingdom and glory*.

Verse 13. Paul was thankful for the respect shown the word of God that the Thessalonians manifested. Although it was delivered to them by the mouth of man, they regarded it as of divine authority. *Effectually worketh* means to work with energy and power in those who believe it; it has no effect on those who disbelieve it.

Verse 14. *Followers of the churches.* Not that the churches were looked to for authority, but as good examples of right living in Christ Jesus. Judea was the place where the first churches were planted, amidst persecution, and the Thesslonians imitated them by enduring opposition brought by the Jews. (See Acts 17: 5-9.)

Verse 15. The Jews did not directly kill Jesus, because they did not have that authority (John 18: 31), but they caused it to be done, and for that reason they were charged with His death. Jesus and Stephen accused them of killing the prophets before them (Matthew 5: 12; 23: 27-36; Acts 7: 52). *Persecuted* is rendered "chased us out" in the margin. That is correct, for the original word is defined by Thayer as follows: "To drive out, banish; to pursue; to persecute, oppress with calamities." Paul was virtually chased out in Acts 16: 39, 40. *Contrary to all men.* The Jews were forbidden to participate with the heathen in their false worship, but they were told not to oppress them (Exodus 23: 9). These instructions were observed for many years, but in later times, especially after the Greek and Roman Empire took control of the world, the Jews became suspicious of the Gentiles in general, and became bitter in their treatment of all who would not submit to their religious bigotry.

Verse 16. The feeling of the Jews toward the Gentiles as described in the preceding verse, will help to explain why they forbade the apostle to speak to the Gentiles, to offer them salvation through the Gospel. An example of their jealousy against any favor shown to them is recorded in Acts 13: 42-45. *To fill up their sins alway.* Such an attitude of the Jews toward their fellowmen was so evil that Paul used the phrase in italics, meaning that it rounded out or completed a very sinful character, which was destined to bring upon them the wrath of God *to the uttermost*. This was brought to pass when the nation was rejected and their temple destroyed by the Romans.

Verse 17. *Being taken from you for a short time.* In Acts 17: 10 is the account of Paul's departure from Thessalonica, and his pause at Berea. He was still present with them in heart (or mind), and he desired and planned to return to them in body soon.

Verse 18. Acts 17: 13, 14 tells how *Satan hindered* Paul's return to Thessalonica. When the Jews persisted in their opposition to Paul's work, by even pursuing him to Berea, it was regarded as the work of Satan that hindered him from his plan.

Verses 19, 20. No man's salvation depends on the faithfulness of his converts if he has done his duty in teaching them. However, there is an added joy in seeing them remain true, and this is the *crown of rejoicing* meant in this verse. They must be faithful until Christ comes again (or until death). This is the reward that is meant in 1 Corinthians 3: 14, 15; 2

John 8 and 3 John 4. While the reward will not be given to the converts until Christ comes, yet the *hope* that it will be done was possible for Paul to enjoy in this life, by observing the faithfulness of his brethren.

1 Thessalonians 3

Verse 1. *Left at Athens alone.* This means the time when Paul had Timothy sent from him to go and visit the Thessalonians and inquire after their condition. Acts 17: 15 states that the brethren who conducted Paul from Thessalonica to Athens, were to return with a command for Silas and Timotheus (Timothy) to come immediately to him. However, when the apostle went to Corinth, both Silas and Timotheus joined him, coming from Macedonia (Acts 18: 5). This indicates that only Timotheus really went to Athens, the reason for which is not stated.

Verse 2. The notes on the preceding verse will explain why our present one mentions Timotheus only as being sent from Athens back to Thessalonica (in Macedonia), there to be rejoined by Silas when he came back from Athens; then together they left and went to Paul who was in Corinth. Paul calls Timotheus a *minister*, which is from DIAKONOS. Thayer's general definition of the word is, "one who executes the commands of another, especially of a master; a servant, attendant, minister." It is the word for "deacon" in every place in the King James Version. The word "minister" is never used in the New Testament as applying to preachers as a special class. *Fellowlaborer* means one who labors with another for a cause in which they both are interested; in the present case it was *the Gospel of Christ.* To *establish* denotes that they were to be further strengthened by being *comforted* through the message sent to them by Paul.

Verse 3. *Moved* is from a Greek word that means "to agitate, disturb, trouble," and Paul did not want the brethren to be disturbed by their *afflictions* or persecutions. *Are appointed* means to be destined to a thing, and it denotes that opposition is bound to come against those who are true servants of God. The reason is that such a life is a rebuke against the people of the sinful world, and they show their resentment by persecuting the doers of the righteous life. (See 2 Timothy 3: 12.)

Verse 4. "To be forewarned is to be forearmed" is as true on this subject as on any other. Paul wished that the brethren in Thessalonica would not be surprised by persecutions, lest they might thereby be "overtaken in a fault" (Galatians 6: 1). To prevent such a result, he told them to be prepared for the trials awaiting them.

Verse 5. In spite of the precaution mentioned in the preceding verse, Paul wished to reassure himself of their steadfastness, and hence he sent Timotheus to them (verse 2) to strengthen them in the faith.

Verse 6. Paul was not disappointed by sending Timotheus to inquire into the state of the Thessalonians, for he brought back a good report of their *faith* and *charity.* The first word has special reference to their service to God. The second is from one of the words that are elsewhere translated "love," and it is the form of love that is manifested in service to the brethren. *Desiring greatly to see us, as we also to see you.* This sentence shows the close feeling that existed between Paul and the brethren whom he had led into the service of Christ. When men and women are sincere disciples of Christ, they will prize each other's company above all others.

Verse 7. Paul's afflictions were not removed by the service of the Thessalonians, but their example of steadfastness made it easier for him to bear them.

Verse 8. *We live* is a figurative or comparative term, not that Paul's physical life actually depended on the faithfulness of the brethren. Robinson defines the original in this place, "to live and prosper, to be happy, blessed." It is somewhat like the familiar expression of one whose circumstances have been changed from unfavorable to favorable; he will remark, "now this is more like living."

Verse 9. *What thanks can we render* means Paul thought he could not be thankful enough for the joyful feelings their faithfulness had brought him. *For your sakes* means Paul was rejoicing because of the benefit that would result for the Tessalonians for them to be true to God, before whom or in whose sight all conduct is known.

Verse 10. Having been so favorably impressed concerning the Thessalonians, it was natural that Paul would desire further association with them.

He offered daily prayers that he might have that privilege. There was nothing wrong about their faith, but they were still but babes in Christ, and Paul wished to impart more inspired information to them, to strengthen and build them up, and in so doing to *perfect* (make more complete) their faith.

Verse 11. There are just two persons named in this verse, but each of them has more than one name. *God* is the supreme ruler of the universe, and he is *Father* to all who will become His children by obedience. *Lord* means ruler, *Jesus* means saviour, and *Christ* means anointed. Paul invoked the help of these two great Beings in making a way for him to revisit the Thessalonians.

Verse 12. All good things can be made better; that is what is meant by spiritual growth. The good brethren at Thessalonia loved each other, and had an interest in the welfare of all men. The apostle exhorts them to increase in all such qualities.

Verse 13. *Stablish* is from the same word as "establish" in verse 2, and the meaning is to strengthen or confirm. *Unblameable in holiness* signifies a life of righteousness that avoids the evils of the world to such an extent, that they cannot be truly blamed with committing them.

1 Thessalonians 4

Verse 1. The gist of this verse is that the brethren in Thessalonica had been informed by Paul about how they should live. To please God, it was necessary that they grow or *abound more and more* in that good manner of walk.

Verse 2. Paul always made it plain that he was not preaching on his own authority. He had learned that nothing would be acceptable to God that did not agree with his Son. He understood that the former system under the law was replaced by that under Christ. (See Philippians 3: 9.)

Verse 3. The Thessalonians were Gentiles in the flesh, and had formerly lived in the indulgences of carnal pleasure, prominent among them being that of fornication; some even mixed it with their idolatrous exercises. *Sanctification* is from HAGIOSMOS, which Thayer defines, "consecration, purification." Acts 15: 9 says that the hearts of mankind are purified by faith, and Romans 10: 17 says that faith comes by hearing the word of God. All of this shows that sanctification is the result of hearing (in the sense of heeding) the word of God, thus giving another name for righteousness.

Verse 4. *Possess* is a key word in this verse. It comes from KIAOMAI, which Thayer defines, "to acquire, get or procure a thing for one's self." The sexual desire is a natural one, and God has provided a lawful means of gratifying it, namely, the marriage relation. A wife is called a vessel (1 Peter 3: 7), and Paul means for a man to *possess* (acquire) a wife as the means of lawful gratification, instead of finding satisfaction by committing fornication. The same thing is taught in 1 Corinthians 7: 2 as to the proper means of sexual gratification.

Verse 5. The original Greek word for *concupiscence* is defined by Thayer, "desire for what is forbidden, lust." The verse means the opposite of the preceding one. To commit fornication would be to obtain that which is forbidden by the Lord. The Thessalonians were Gentiles, but they had been made acquainted with God, and hence were expected not to do like the Gentiles who do not know Him.

Verse 6. *Defraud his brother.* When a man commits fornication, he has the relation with a woman who is another man's wife or some other man's unmarried daughter. To do so is "to gain or take advantage of another, to overreach," which is Thayer's definition of the word *defraud* in our verse. God will revenge all who do this, and Paul gives warning in this epistle, even as he had done previously when among them.

Verse 7. This verse gives us a clear meaning of *holiness*. The subject being discussed is fornication, which is still under consideration in this verse. Hence the conclusion is that refraining from the uncleanness of fornication would be to show a quality of *holiness*.

Verse 8. Thayer defines the original for despiseth, "to reject, refuse, slight." When a man commits fornication he rejects the law against that evil and does wrong against *man;* that is, a human being. However, Paul means that it is not only a sin against man, but it is also against God, the giver of law against the evil act. It is just that God should restrict us in our bodily practices, since

1 Thessalonians 4: 9-16

He has given unto us his holy Spirit. The practical use of this Spirit with us is the teaching which He offers through the inspired word, that shows man a higher life in the use of his body.

Verse 9. The duty of mutual love is not new to the New Testament teaching. Leviticus 19: 18 commanded, "thou shalt love thy neighbor as thyself," and the same thought is expressed in Psalms 133: 1. But the command is given new meaning for Christians by the unspeakable example of love that was shown to the world by Jesus.

Verse 10. These remarks were not in the nature of criticism, for the brethren in Thessalonica had shown their love for others in that they displayed the good example to the other Macedonians (chapter 1: 7). The point is that Paul wishes them to increase in the good spirit.

Verse 11. To *study* means to be concerned, and *be quiet* denotes to be settled and not meddlesome. It is explained by the apostle in the same sentence where he says *to do your own business*. To *work with your own hands* means to engage in some manual labor or occupation that will bring them an income. Paul had given these instructions orally when he was in their midst. (See 2 Thessalonians 3: 10.)

Verse 12. To *walk honestly* means to walk in a becoming manner. To be dependant upon others for the necessities of life is not always a fault, but it is so if one brings the condition on himself by a spirit of idleness. *Them that are without* refers to the people of the world. If they see Christians who are not willing to work for their own living, they will have an unfavorable opinion of the Gospel. In 2 Thessalonians 3: 10, Paul teaches that if a man will not work when he is able, he has no right to the good things of life. It is very plain that a lazy man is not a true Christian.

Verse 13. *Would not have you to be ignorant* simply denotes that Paul did not wish the brethren to be uninformed on the subject he was about to discuss. *Them which are asleep* means the Christians who had died, the last word being a figure of speech based on the apparent condition of those who are dead. The term is used with reference to death in the following passages. Acts 7: 60; 13: 36; 1 Corinthians 15: 6, 51; 2 Peter 3: 4. Sorrow over the death of loved ones is natural and right, which Jesus showed by his attitude toward the sisters of Lazarus (John 11: 35). But there is a difference between the sorrow when it is for those who "sleep in Jesus," for in that case there is a hope of a happy life after the resurrection.

Verse 14. *If we believe*, etc., means that it is as reasonable to believe one part of this verse as the other. The resurrection of Christ is a fact, hence the same God who brought his Son from the dead and up to Heaven, is able to bring others from death into Heaven. The same thought is expressed in other words in Hebrews 2: 10, where it is said that God will be "bringing many sons unto glory." It should not be overlooked that it is only those who *sleep in Jesus* who are being given such a prospect. All the dead will be resurrected at the last day (John 5: 28, 29; Acts 24: 15), but the resurrection of the unsaved is not being considered at all in this chapter.

Verse 15. Paul, speaking on authority of *the word of the Lord*, takes it for granted that there will be Christians living when the resurrection day arrives. The same is taught in 1 Corinthians 15: 51, and hence we have the assurance that no matter what may happen among the people of the world, true Christianity "shall not perish from the earth" while it is permitted to exist. *Prevent* is from PHTHANO, which Thayer defines, "to precede." The faithful disciples who are living when Christ comes will not precede the ones in their graves in going up to meet Him to be taken to heaven.

Verse 16. *Shout* is from KELEUSMA, which occurs only once in the Greek New Testament. Thayer defines it, "an order, command, specifically a stimulating cry." He then explains that by which animals are roused and urged on by man, as horses by charioteers, hounds by hunters, etc., or that by which a signal is given to men, such as to rowers by the master of a ship; to soldiers by a commander; with a loud summons, a trumpet-call." The Englishman's Greek New Testament translates it, "a shout of command." Matthew 16: 27 shows that when Jesus comes again, he will be "with his angels." They will be accompanied by the archangel (whose name is Michael, Jude 9), whose voice will announce the coming of the great Master and Judge. Trumpets have long been used to signal the approach of important events, especially those of conquest (Exodus 20: 18; Numbers 10: 1-9; Joshua 6: 1-5; Judges 6: 34, 35; 1 Samuel 13: 3; and many others). The second coming of Christ will mark his final victory over all his enemies (1 Corinthians 15: 24-26); it will be fitting, therefore, that the event be signaled with the *trump of God. Shall rise first.* This cannot mean the first resurrection numerically, implying a second, for there will be only one literal resurrection; everybody will rise in the same hour (John 5: 28, 29). The word is explained in Thayer's lexicon to mean "before anything else is done." The idea is that the dead in Christ will be raised before the living in Christ are changed and taken up to meet Christ.

Verse 17. *Alive and remain* refers to the Christians who will be living on the earth when Christ comes. *Caught up together* means that after the dead in Christ have been raised incorruptible (1 Corinthians 15: 52), and the living in Christ have been changed (same verse), then all will ascend in one group to meet the Lord in the air. *So shall we ever be with the Lord.* The first word refers to the condition just described, namely, the righteous changed into an incorruptible body, and living in the constant presence of the Lord. This denotes that no sin will ever be committed by the righteous after the resurrection. The same grand truth is taught in Revelation 22: 11.

Verse 18. *Comfort* is rendered "exhort" in the margin, and that is one of the definitions given in the lexicon. However, verse 13 indicates that Paul wrote these verses for the comfort of those who were sorrowing over the dead, hence the word in the common version is correct.

1 Thessalonians 5

Verse 1. *Times* and *seasons* refer to the events described in the closing verses of the preceding chapter, namely, the second coming of Christ and the resurrection. *No need that I write.* Paul could not write the date of these events for no one but God knows that (Matthew 24: 36). Neither was there any *need* to write as a warning, if they are living as they should, for in that case they would be prepared to meet Him when the day arrived. (See verse 4.)

Verse 2. Jesus had taught the world that His second coming would not be announced beforehand (Matthew 24: 42-44). There could be no advantage for the faithful disciples to know the exact date when Jesus is to come. In truth, it might be an incentive to carelessness if they knew the date, for they would act on the impression that "there is plenty of time yet." *As a theif in the night* applies to the arrival of *the day of the Lord,* and not a comparison of the Lord himself. A thief does not give any information of his plans, neither will there be any previous announcement of the coming of the last day.

Verse 3. *Shall say, peace and safety* is a figurative expression, representing the state of indifference that the people of the world will be indulging regarding the day of judgment. They will have scorned the warnings of the Lord, spoken to them through the teaching of the Word, and settled themselves in the false *peace and safety* of their life of sin. The pangs of a woman with child are sharp and sudden, throwing her into a state of fear or dread that can be fully uderstood only by one who personally has such an experience. (See Psalms 48: 6; Jeremiah 6; 24; 49: 24.) Paul uses it to illustrate the terrible state of mind into which the hordes of sinners will be thrown when they suddenly realize that they are faced with the doom of the judgment day. *Shall not escape.* When that awful day comes, it will be impossible to find a hiding place from the wrath of God, for the earth and all things therein will be melting with fervent heat, leaving them in the grasp of Him whose righteous law they have despised. (See 2 Peter 3: 10.)

Verse 4. *Not in darkness.* The brethren had been warned of the surety of the coming of Christ, although the time was not known. They had manifested confidence in the apostolic teaching by accepting it and living according to its precepts; in this sense they were not in the dark to be surprised as by a thief.

Verse 5. *Light* and *day* are figurative names for the truth, and are opposite night and darkness.

Verse 6. The hours of night are the natural ones for sleeping in the temporal realm. By the same token, the disciples were expected not to be asleep (indifferent) concerning these spiritual matters, since they were living in the light and day of the truth. They should *watch* (be on the alert) and *be sober*, which means to be thoughtful and take life seriously.

Verse 7. Those who *sleep* (are indifferent) are in the night of spiritual darkness, which means they are lacking in understanding of the things that concern their soul. But that shortage of knowledge is not the Lord's fault, for He has offered full opportunity for the necessary information. *Druken in the night.* With the increase of indulgence in intoxicating drink, this phrase would not have the same application as in former times. When there was such an abhorrence for the practice that most people literally chose the cover of darkness for the shameful vice. (See Acts 2: 15.) The principle is true, also, in the spiritual realm, for those who hate the truth, prefer to shun the investigation of their teaching.

Verse 8. *Who are of the day* is the opposite to the ones who sleep in the preceding verse, meaning that they have taken advantage of the light of truth that has been offered by the Lord. Paul exhorts all such to make good their advantage and their profession, by *being sober* which means to be seriously minded concerning the great affairs of the soul. The parts of a soldier's equipment are mentioned with greater detail in Ephesians 6: 11-17, taken from those used by the Roman soldier. The *breastplate* was a piece made of metal, covering the body from the neck to the hips, thus protecting the heart and other vital parts of the body. No greater protection can be provided a Christian than his *faith* in the Lord and his *love for* his brother. The former will prevent him from going into error, since faith comes by the word of God (Romans 10: 17), and the latter will keep him from making the fatal mistake of harming his brother. The *helmet* was a cap for the protection of the head. A Christian can face any foe and even rejoice in the presence of death, if he has the *hope of salvation* in his heart.

Verse 9. *Not appointed us to wrath.* If people come under the wrath of God, it is not because He prepared them for that purpose. Instead, the plan of the Lord is that men might be saved through the Lord Jesus Christ. The cause why the wrath of God comes on men and women is shown in Ephesians 5: 6 and Colossians 3: 5, 6.

Verse 10. Christ showed his interest in the salvation of man in that He was willing to die for him. *Wake* or *sleep* means alive or dead when Jesus comes. (See 1 Corinthians 15: 51; 1 Thessalonians 4: 15-17.) *Live together with him* will take place after the second coming of Christ and the resurrection, referred to in the last-named passage.

Verse 11. *Comfort yourselves* is the same exhortation that is stated in 1 Thessalonians 4: 18. *To edify one another* means to build each other up in the faith by mutual support in spiritual instruction. These brethren had been doing this, hence the instruction of Paul is not a complaint against them, but rather an encouraging word for them to continue in the good work.

Verse 12. *Know* is from EIDO, and Thayer defines it in this passage to mean, "to have regard for one, cherish, pay attention to," *Labor among you* is indefinite and could refer to any friends of truth if nothing specific had been added by the apostle. But he shows of whom he is speaking by the words *over you in the Lord.* Acts 20: 17, 28 and 1 Peter 5: 1, 2 plainly teaches that the elders are the ones who have rule over the congregations. *Admonish you* is one of the duties of the elders, and they do it for the sake of the souls of the flock (Hebrews 13: 17).

Verse 13. To *esteem them* has about the same meaning as to "have regard for" as defined in the preceding verse. *Be at peace among yourselves.* If the members of a congregation would always endeavor to "keep the unity of the Spirit in the bond of peace" (Ephesians 4: 3), it would simplify and lighten the task of the elders in their rulership.

Verse 14. To warn always implies a possible danger or unpleasant experience; and since it is the *unruly* (disorderly) who are warned, it denotes that the unpleasant experience would be brought on them by their own conduct. The unpleasant experience might consist either of disciplinary action by the church (2 Thessalonians 3: 6), or the sentence of punishment at the last day (Matthew 25: 46), or both. *Feebleminded* does not mean folks who are irresponsible mentally, for such would not be in the church. The word means "faint-hearted" according to Thayer; disciples who are inclined to be easily discouraged in the presence of trial. *Support the weak.* Some members have less ability than others, and Paul would have the stronger ones to support them. (See Romans 15: 1.) In all the various conditions of human society, it is a gracious attitude to be patient or longsuffering.

Verse 15. *See that none render* is the same as saying "let none render" *evil for evil.* The so-called golden rule (Matthew 7: 12), and Paul's teaching in Romans 12: 21 also will agree with the present verse. *Follow that which is good* is opposite rendering evil for evil. This kind of conduct was to be practiced among the disciples, and also was to be done toward all others. A Christian does not have the right to return evil for evil at all, whether to his brethren or to men of the world.

Verse 16. *Rejoice evermore.* We need to look elsewhere to learn what it is that Christians may and may not rejoice in. (See Romans 5: 2; 1 Corinthians 13: 6.)

Verse 17. *Pray without ceasing.* This would not mean that Christians are to spend every minute of their waking hours in prayer, for that would not leave them any time for other duties. It means for them never to cease being praying disciples, in the same sense we would say a man should not cease to partake of food or he would die.

Verse 18. This verse gives one specific form of prayer, namely, giving of thanks for *every thing.* Of course it means things that are good, and we should give thanks to God for them, since all such gifts come from Him (James 1: 17). Paul is still more specific in 1 Timothy 4: 5, where he shows we should give thanks to God for our food. Since this is *the will of God,* it follows that if disciples fail to give thanks for their necessities of life, they are failing to do the will of the Father.

Verse 19. *Quench* is from SBENNUI, which Thayer defines, "to suppress, stifle." The Spirit guided the writers of the New Testament (John 16: 13), hence to quench or try to hinder the word of God would be to quench the Spirit.

Verse 20. To *despise* means to belittle or treat with indifference. Prophesyings refers to the speeches of the inspired prophets in the church in those days. Sometimes such were predictions of events still in the future, and at other times they consisted of exhortation and edification (1 Corinthians 14: 3). Verses 21-24 of the same chapter would indicate the importance Paul attached to prophesyings, and hence why he exhorted the Thessalonians not to treat them with indifference.

Verse 21. *Prove* is from DOKIMAZO, which Thayer defines at this place as follows: "To test, examine, prove, scrutinize," and he explains, "to see whether a thing be genuine or not." The passage applies to the various doctrines that were being offered by the teachers in religion. Disciples were warned not to take the mere word of any stranger, but to test his teaching by comparing it with the truths that had been delivered to them by inspired men. The same kind of warning is given in 1 John 4: 1, 2. After the disciples have applied the scripture test, they are to accept and hold fast to everything that passes inspection.

Verse 22. *Abstain* is from APECHO, which Thayer defines in this passage, "to hold one's self off, abstain." Hence it means that we should wholly refrain from the thing being considered. *Appearance* is from EIDOS, and in the present passage is defined by Thayer with the simple words, "form, kind," and he explains it to mean, "every kind of evil or wrong." Robinson defines it, "form, manner, kind." It therefore does not mean "resemblance of evil" as a popular theory claims. It is true the scriptures elsewhere teach that Christians should not indulge in anything that is doubtful or that might possibly be wrong, but that is not the meaning of our present verse. Nor does this explanation lessen the responsibilities of Christians in avoiding evil, as some fear, but rather does it make it more strict and far-reaching. Some professed disciples would cheerfully give up a number of evil practices, but insist on retaining some others on the ground that they are not in the same class, or that they are not as bad a "kind" of evil as the others. Our passage allows no distinction to be made between the so-called worse and lesser of evils. They are all— "every kind"—forbidden to Christians.

Verse 23. Every good thing is of God, but he is here said to be *of peace* because that is an outstanding result of being wholly *sanctified*. The word means to be devoted to the service of God, and such a condition is accomplished by the word of God (John 17: 17). As a general statement, the rest of this verse is a prayer of Paul that the entire being of the brethren be kept blameless, which means in obedience to the truth of God that has sanctified them, and that such a condition would exist until Christ comes again. *Spirit* and *soul* and *body*. This is the only place in the Bible where the three parts of the human being are named in one sentence. There is not much difference between the first two, for they are used interchangeably at various places in the sacred writings. However, since Paul uses them together in the present passage, there must be some difference, although they both refer to the inner or immaterial part of man, in contrast with the material or bodily part. Genesis 2: 7 states the origin of the body and soul of man. But God did not stop with the creation of those two parts. Zechariah 12: 1 states that God formed the spirit of man within him, thus completing the three parts of the human being. From the forgoing considerations, I will give to the readers the three parts of man as follows: The body is that part that is composed of the ground, made in the form of an animal (not a vegetable or mineral); the soul is the part that makes him a living animal; the spirit is the part that makes him a human, living animal. It should be added that God intended this being to have an endless existence, beginning with his stay on the earth, during which he was to be given opportunity to serve his Creator intelligently and spiritually. Because of this exalted purpose, God gave to this being a superior personality over all other living creatures, both as to his material and to his immaterial formation.

Verse 24. We usually think of the term *faithful* as applying to one who is true and obedient to another unto whom he is obligated. Yet it would not be appropriate to regard the Lord in that light; hence it means that He will make good all of the promises he has made to man. Such promises were made when He *called* man by the Gospel and promised him spiritual benefits in this life, and endless joys in the life to come. *Who also will do it*. God not only has always been faithful, but always will be.

Verse 25. It is interesting that the apostle Paul felt the need for the prayers of the brethren, although he was an inspired man. That was because inspiration was not any special protection against misconduct in one's personal life; it guaranteed only that he would not make any mistake in his teaching. An inspired man could go wrong in his life, even though he had done his duty in his teaching (1 Corinthians 9: 27).

Verse 26. Paul was not starting any custom by this command. The salutation of a kiss was a common one in that age, and still is in some countries. The emphasis should be placed on the word *holy*, and the thought is for the brethren to be sincere when they greet each other.

Verse 27. There were no duplicating devices known in old times, whereby multiple copies of an epistle could be made and sent to all individuals of a congregation. The inspired documents were sent in care of some responsible person, who was expected to see that the other members would learn of their contents; hence the command to read this epistle to them. *Holy brethren* simply means righteous men and women of the congregation, since holiness and righteousness are names for the same quality.

Verse 28. Grace is the unmerited favor of Christ, which Paul wishes for the Thessalonians. It was a benediction with which he closed most of his epistles.

2 Thessalonians 1

Verse 1, 2. These verses are the same in thought as the opening verse of the first epistle to the Thessalonians. See that place concerning *Silvanus* and *Timotheus*.

Verse 3. In the preceding epistle Paul expressed thanks for the good report of the brethren in Thessalonica. He repeats it in this place, and adds the word *bound*, meaning he is urged toward his attitude by the great truths connected with the work of that congregation. *It is meet* denotes that it is proper because the good influence of their work made them deserving of such consideration. *Faith groweth* means they were increasing their good works as a result of their faith. (See

1 Thessalonians 1: 3.) This growth included their *charity* (love) for each other, which is the meaning of the word *aboundeth*.

Verse 4. *We ourselves glory in you* is not said in the sense of vanity or puffed-up boasting. It means that Paul spoke very commendably of their good work, when he had any contact with other churches. *Churches of God* is the same as "churches of Christ" (Romans 16: 16), because God and Christ are one in spirit and purpose. *Patience and faith* are very logically coupled together, for a Chrisitan's patience will be no greater than his faith. These brethren were put to a special test of these qualities by their enemies among the Jews (Acts 17: 1-9). *Persecutions* and *tribulations* are virtually the same, the former having special reference to the disagreeable treatment of the body, the latter to its effect on the mind by way of worrisome concern.

Verse 5. It is God's judgment that the faithful servants shall prove their faith by enduring persecutions (2 Timothy 3: 12), such an experience being a proof that they are true disciples. Knowing that such persons will actually endure their trials, He has regarded such a truth as rendering them worthy of the test. (See Acts 5: 41; James 1: 2, 4; 1 Peter 4: 12-14.) This is why Paul refers to the matter as a *manifest token of the righteous judgment of God.* The Lord knows how much the true disciples can withstand, hence He will not suffer them to be tried beyond that (1 Corinthians 10: 13); and when they come out of their trials as victors over evil, it proves the righteousness of His judgment.

Verse 6. God will suffer evil men to persecute His children in this world, knowing they will withstand the test and thus prove their worthiness to be counted as heirs of the kingdom. But these evil doers will get their just dues after a while, and such a dealing with them is declared to be a righteous thing. *Recompense* means to repay or "deal out"; *tribulation* denotes trouble or punishment. The verse means that God will deal out punishment to the ones who have been troubling His children.

Verse 7. The word *rest* is a noun (not a verb), and it is the object of the verb "recompense" in the preceding verse. The two verses contain a sentence that has two objects. God is the actor or subject; *recompense* is the verb or predicate; *tribulation* and *rest* are the objects. Since these objects are opposite in kind, it follows that they will not be recompensed to the same people. The preceding verse says the *tribulation* will be recompensed to the troublers of God's children; this verse says the *rest* will be recompensed to the ones who are troubled by these evil workers. *With us* means that faithful Christians will join with the apostles in enjoying this rest—the rest that "remaineth to the people of God" (Hebrews 4: 9). The time when all this is to take place will be *when the Lord Jesus shall be revealed from heaven with his angels.*

Verse 8. *In flaming fire.* The first word is from the Greek EN, and Thayer's general definition is, "in, on, at, with, by, among." In the King James Version it has been rendered through 37 times, by 142, with 139. In Luke 21: 27; Acts 1: 9-11; Revelation 1: 7 it is shown that Jesus will actually be accompanied with clouds when he comes, yet there is no teaching that clouds will be used as instruments for the punishment of the unrighteous. On the other hand, there is plenty of scripture that teaches us that fire will be the element used in their punishment. (See Matthew 3: 12; 25: 41; Mark 9: 43-48; 2 Peter 3: 7; Revelation 20: 15; 21: 8.) From this information the conclusion is that when Jesus comes he will be prepared to administer the fire upon the unsaved. All fire will burn, but a flame is more active and penetrating, so the phrase *flaming fire* is used to indicate the intensity of punishment that is to be inflicted upon the wicked. *Vengeance* is not used in the sense of spitework or the "get-even" spirit as men often do, but it is from an original that means legal and judicial punishment on one who has shown disrespect for some law. *Know not God* means those who refuse to recognize Him, and that attitude is manifested by their refusal to obey the Gospel of Christ who is the Son of God.

Verse 9. The preceding verse names the element the Lord will use in punishing the disobedient. This verse shows the nature or extent of that punishment, that it will be everlasting. The unrighteous will first be sentenced to this fate, which is one meaning of the word for *punished.* It is the same Greek word translated "judgment" in Acts 25:15, where Festus says he was asked to have *judgment* (meaning a sentence) against Paul. So our verse means Jesus will pronounce the sentence when he comes, and the verdict will begin to be served on that day. The punishment to which the unsaved will be sentenced is described next. *Destruction* is from OLETHROS, which Thayer defines, "ruin, destruction, death," and he explains it to mean, "the loss of a life of blessedness after death, future misery." The word does not mean total annihilation as certain false teachers claim. The wicked will not cease to be, but their right to happiness will be totally destroyed. Hence they will be driven from the presence of God, and the separation will be everlasting.

Verse 10. The nature and extent of the punishment to be pronounced against the unsaved are set forth in the preceding two verses, and the occasion when such a sentence will be announced is stated in this verse, namely, when Jesus comes again. *Glorified in his saints*. Other believers are mentioned in addition to these *saints*, hence these are the "ten thousand of his saints" mentioned in Jude 14. Their presence with Him at that time will be a glory to him, in the same sense that a person of great dignity is honored upon his entry into a place, by a vast escort of other persons of high rank. This distinction is indicated further by what is said of others who are called *believers* who will admire Jesus when he comes. It is made definite by the words *among you*, in direct connection with the fact of the testimony of the apostles having been delivered to them, and believed by them. Another conclusion is justified by these several verses, namely, that the sentencing of the wicked, and the resurrection and ascension of the righteous (1 Thessalonians 4:16, 17) will occur at the same time, although the entire story is not told in any one place.

Verse 11. In Ephesians 4:1 Paul exhorts brethren to walk worthy of their calling, and in this verse he expresses the same thought in a different wording. He prays that God would *count* or consider the Thessalonians worthy, which would require that they live as they should, since God will not favor any unworthy persons. God is perfectly good, and will not take pleasure in the disciples unless they *fulfill* the conditions on which such grace is promised. Those conditions must be a work of faith, and that means according to the Gospel, since it is the *power* that directs men and women into salvation (Romans 1:16).

Verse 12. When Christians prove their faith by their works, they will thereby glorify the Lord. By the same token the glory of the Lord will be given upon them, for both Lord and servant are to work together (1 Corinthians 3:9). This entire workmanship is *according to the grace of our God and the Lord Jesus Christ.*

2 Thessalonians 2

General remarks. The background of most of this chapter is historical, involving the original government of the church as it was established by Christ and the apostles. The ruling men were called by three different names as rendered in the King James Version; they are elders (Acts 20:17), overseers (Acts 20:28), and bishops (1 Timothy 3:1). There is some difference in the meaning of the words, because the duties of the men are so various that one word will not cover them. However, no distinction is made between their authority because of these names; each of them wore all the names. This is proved by the two verses in Acts 20 referred to above, where the same men are called elders and overseers. Incidentally I will add that bishop and overseer come from the same Greek word which is EPISKOPOS, and elder comes from PRESBUTEROS. The qualifications and work of these men will be explained when we come to 1 Timothy 3 and Titus 1. For the present their authority and function as governors or rulers is what is to be considered. There was a plurality of elders in each congregation (Acts 14:23; Titus 1:5), and their authority did not extend beyond their own congregation. As proof of this it is well to consider the case recorded in Acts 15. When the dispute arose in Antioch over circumcision because of the teaching of some from Judea, a group of them went to Jerusalem to consult the church. While the decision arrived at was sent to the brethren at Antioch, it was concerning the agitation among them caused by these who came from Jerusalem. Besides, this matter was enforced by the apostles, and they had authority everywhere.

The time came when some of the elders became thirsty for more power than the others had, and they worked it around so as to dominate them in the affairs of the congregation. This was one thing that Paul had in mind in Acts 20: 30, where he says "of your own selves shall men arise, speaking perverse things, to draw away disciples after them." This ambition for power continued until in most of the congregations, one elder became virtually the head over the others, assuming the exclusive right to the title "bishop" and leaving the simple role of "elder" to the others. But human nature is such that when a man becomes desirous of more authority than he is supposed to have, he will not stop until he tries to obtain the rule outside his allotted realm. Hence these dominating bishops reached out and gained control over other churches in their general area. Such a movement as I have just described was going on in many parts of the world, until the government fell into the hands of the bishops in such centers as Antioch, Corinth, Ephesus, Jerusalem, Rome, and others. The next struggle was among the bishops, to obtain superiority over all the other bishops, with a hungry mind upon a possible attainment of universal rule of one bishop over the brotherhood.

But this concentration of power among the bishops was held back by another mighty force, which I will now describe as briefly as I can. The Roman Empire was the secular government in power, which was the fourth one of the "world powers" predicted in Daniel 2: 31-45. These world powers made their religion a state affair, so that whatever the state religion was, it was regarded as a mark of disloyalty to the government to oppose that religion. The religion of the Roman Empire was the pagan or idolatrous system, and its presence presented an obstacle to the growing ambition of these bishops in the church, for if they went too far in their activities, they were apt to run into trouble with the government. But a change took place in the Empire which turned out to the advantage of the bishops. Constantine became emperor and was pursuing a military course in behalf of his government. On his way to what proved to be one of the "decisive battles of the world," he claimed to see a cross in the sky, with an inscription that said, "by this sign conquer." He won that battle which he professed to believe was caused by the influence of the cross, the emblem of Christianity. On the basis of that victory and its causes, Constantine (as emperor) announced his support of Christianity with the weight of the empire in support of his decision. After that the Roman Empire presented no obstacle to the enlargement of the power of the bishops, since their religious professions were the same. That circumstance virtually united church and state, bringing on the apostasy and the Dark Ages, called by Paul the "falling away." With the foregoing paragraphs to consult frequently, the reader is now asked to consider the several verses in order.

Verse 1. *By* is from HUPER, which Thayer defines at this place, "concerning, of, as respects, with regard to." It is the word for "concerning" in Romans 9: 27. Paul beseeches the brethren concerning some very important events to occur in the future. One is the coming of Christ, and the other is our *gathering together unto him*. These events are prophesied in 1 Thessalonians 4: 16, 17.

Verse 2. There seemed to be a state of unrest among the disciples over the coming of Christ, thinking that it was "just around the corner," to use a familiar figure of speech. This doubtless was suggested by Paul's words in 1 Thessalonians 4: 17, "we which are alive and remain." It might seem to teach that Paul and some others would be living when Jesus comes, and hence that the event was due and might occur at any hour. As a result of such a notion, business and religious activities were at a standstill. Why should anything be done when the end was just at hand? To correct that error, the apostle takes occasion to make the famous predictions of this chapter, to tell them that all of this revolution will take place before the Lord comes. *Soon shaken in mind* refers to the unsettled condition which I have just described. To add to this disturbance, certain false teachers made claims of having "first hand" information on the subject, just as Jesus said some would do at the time preceding the destruction of Jerusalem (Matthew 24: 5, 24). Paul mentions three sources of false information that might deceive the disciples, and he wants them to know

2 Thessalonians 2: 3-6

that any theories claiming to come from such sources, that predicted the immediate approach of Christ, were false and not according to truth. Those three so-called sources were *spirit, word*, and *letter*. The first refers to those who claimed to have a gift of the Spirit. The second claims that they had received word from the apostles on the subject, and the third refers to some letters that had been forged as coming from the apostles. *At hand* is from ENISTEMI, which Thayer defines, "to stand in sight, stand near, to be upon, impend, threaten." This is commented upon at the beginning of this paragraph.

Verse 3. All who accepted this disquieting teaching were being deceived, and Paul bids them not to be deceived *by any means*. The words in italics denote that any information, from whatever source, that claims to teach this disquieting theory, is false. The second coming of Christ will not occur until after the *falling away*. Those words are from the Greek word APOSTASIA, which Thayer defines, "a falling away, defection, apostasy," which is a name for the formation of centralized rule in the church, described in "general remarks" at the beginning of this chapter. *Man of sin* would be a term of general application, were it not for the description that follows through several verses. It shows it means the bishop who finally got to the head of the church as it came to be, and he was finally known as the Pope of Rome. He is called the *son of perdition*, because the first word means "one who is worthy of a thing" (Thayer).

Verse 4. *Opposeth and exalteth himself above* is the same as saying, "he exalts himself in opposition to all" of what is to be named next. *That is called God.* Any person or thing that might be related to God or be claimed to be so related, would come under this phrase. *Or that is worshipped.* This is an extension of the thought expressed in the preceding phrase in italics. The thought is that this *man of sin* (the pope) will not recognize any being or object of worship as his equal, regardless of whether it pertains to the One in heaven or the many earthly rulers who receive homage from men. *Sitteth in the temple* means in the church, for it is said to be the temple of God (1 Corinthians 3: 16, 17; 2 Corinthians 6: 16). It is true that the institution called the church in history at this period of development, was so corrupt that we could not acknowledge it to be the true church. But the pope and the system of centralized power over which he was head, was professed to be the church, and Paul is speaking of the subject historically, and from the standpoint of the pretensions of the Romish institution. At this point it will be well to state that all through these centuries that the apostasy was forming, there were some exceptions where congregations would not join in the departure, so that during the entire time of the Dark Ages there were faithful congregations here and there, which kept the pure church in existence, although as a woman persecuted for righteosness' sake, she had to flee to the wilderness of comparative hiding or obscurity, caused by the apostasy, to preserve her existence. (See Revelation 12: 1-3 and verse 14 of that chapter.) *Showing himself that he is God.* No man can actually *show* or display proof that he is God, but he can claim such a high rank, and display himself under such a guise, hence the pope is presented to his people as "Lord God, the Pope."

Verse 5. *I told you these things.* Since signs of the apostasy, namely, desire for power were being manifested in those early years of the church (3 John 9), it was natural that Paul would warn his brethren about it when laboring in their midst. He also instructed Timothy to remind the brethren where he preached, of this very defection that was to come into the world. In 1 Timothy 4: 1-3 is such a prediction, and verse 6 directly advises the evangelist to do this service of remembrance for the brethren.

Verse 6. *Withholdeth* (likewise *letteth* in next verse) is from KATECHO, which Thayer defines, "to restrain, hinder, "and he comments on it as follows: "That which hinders, namely, Antichrist [the pope], from making his appearance; the power of the Roman empire is meant." I urge the reader to consult "general remarks" again, to learn why the Roman emperor was a hindrance to the coming of the pope into universal power over the church. In verse 5 Paul refers to previous information which he had given to the Thessalonians, to the effect that certain men were already showing signs of wanting this great power, and who finally would come out in the open and strive for it. The brethren might wonder why such a development did not then come to the fore, and he is explaining that this Roman power (which then professed the heathen religion), was withholding or hindering such a movement. *Revealed in his time* means when the time came that the religion of Rome would not be any hindrance, then would be the *time* for the pope to be *revealed* or come out in the open.

Verse 7. This verse virtually has the same thoughts that have been already explained, but in different words that give additional points. *Mystery of iniquity* means the concentration of power described in "general remarks." *Doth already work.* The thirst for power was already manifesting itself in those days (3 John 9). *He who now letteth* (hindereth) *will let.* He (the Roman heathen religion) will continue to be a hindrance to the growing movement in the church for universal power. *Until he be taken out of the way.* This means until the pagan or heathen religion of the Roman Empire is replaced by the professed Christian religion that was claimed by the ambitious bishops. Again, let the reader consult "general remarks" at the beginning of comments on this chapter.

Verse 8. *Then* means when the pagan religion is replaced by the profession of the Christian, which finally resulted in the union of church and state. *That wicked be revealed* refers to the bishop who was to succeed over all the others in obtaining supremacy at the head of the church, and who later took the title of Pope of Rome. He was *revealed* or came out in the open after the hindrance of the pagan or idolatrous religion had been removed. *Consume* and *destroy* mean virtually the same if either of them is used alone. When both are used in one sentence, the former means a gradual using-up of something, and the latter denotes the final result of that consuming, namely, the complete canceling out of the thing spoken of. *Spirit of his mouth* is a figurative term for the truth spoken by the Lord through the apostles and others who were proclaimers of the inspired word. *Brightness of his coming* is the same as saying "the appearance of his presence." This does not mean that Christ was to appear in person, but would be present in the world or represented by the teachers of divine truth, which was finally to counteract the power of the pope, by breaking up the union of church and state. This great event was accomplished by the Reformation, when the Bible *(the spirit of his mouth)* was given to the people in their own languages.

Verse 9. *Even him whose coming.* When the predicted *man of sin* does come, it will be like the coming and working of Satan. He is compared to Satan in that his power will consist of *signs and lying wonders.* The first italicized word is used in both a good and a bad sense in the New Testament, and it means an omen of something to come, or a supposed proof of something already in existence. It is used in a bad sense in this verse, since the signs are coupled with lying wonders. That refers to the deceptive means the pope and his associates will use, whereby the unsuspecting subjects of the Romish institution will easily be deceived.

Verse 10. *Deceivableness and unrighteousness.* All kinds of unrighteousness are to be condemned; but some kinds are naked and open so that everyone can understand them. However, the kind that this *man of sin* will use is such that his followers will be misled into doing it, with the notion that they are doing the right thing. *In them that perish.* The pope will not be able to deceive every individual on whom he tries his trickery. He will succeed only on those who are not honestly disposed to eternal life, and they are the ones who are destined finally to perish. The explanation for such an attitude is in the fact that they do not have enough *love of the truth* to obey it and be saved. In other words, since they do not love the truth, they will be "easy marks" for the agents of the pope, and consequently they will not be saved.

Verses 11, 12. *And for this cause.* Because of the conditions just described, these people who are devoted to the pope and his system, will receive some deserved punishmnet. *Strong delusion.* This phrase is rendered "a working of error" by the Englishman's Greek New Testament. A correct and short term would be "active errors." The word *that* is a poor translation for it is from EIS, and that word has the idea of "unto" or "to the end that" or "with the result that." It is a statement of what results from the thing spoken of, and

2 Thessalonians 2: 13-15

not intended as a term to show any motive on the part of God. Also, God *sends* things in other ways than by direct force; sometimes it is done merely by suffering a thing to happen. In Romans 11: 8 it is stated that "God hath given them the spirit of slumber," yet we know it only means that He had given them over to their own determination to be blind to the truth. So in our passage it is preceded by the statement "they received not the love of the truth." For that reason God determined to "let them have their own determined way," and in so doing He sent them these errors that were so active that it resulted in their believing the lies of the leaders of the pope's system; this agrees also with verse 12. It does not say that they all would be damned because God had arbitrarily decreed it so, but it was because they "believed not the truth, and had pleasure in unrighteousness." That is the principle upon which God has always dealt with mankind. The Bible in no place teaches that God ever forces a man to sin, then punishes him for the wrong-doing. Neither does He compel man against his will to do right, but has always offered him proper inducements for righteous conduct, then left it to his own responsibility to decide what he will do about it.

Verse 13. With the preceding verse, Paul concludes his great prophecy of the apostasy and formation of the church of Rome. He now comes to matters more directly pertaining to the Thessalonians. He is thankful for their standing with God, which was brought about by their acceptance of the truth. This is far different from the characters described in the foregoing verses, who were condemned because they did not accept the truth. *From the beginning* is both general and specific. It was always God's plan to choose any who would accept the truth. The Thessalonians did so at the first opportunity, or *from the beginning* of the preaching of the Gospel among them. On the Lord's side of the plan, they were chosen through sanctification, which means a setting apart for a holy purpose, and it was by the Spirit because the truth that sanctified them (John 17: 17) was given by the Spirit. But this alone would not have caused them to be chosen; it required also the *belief of the truth* on their part.

Verse 14. *Called you by our gospel.* God does not call people into His service from the world, for the sake of their personal salvation, by any direct contact with them. In every case of conversion recorded in the New Testament, there was a third person or other means used for the purpose. The people of Samaria heard the word through Philip (Acts 8: 5, 6). The eunuch heard the Gospel from the mouth of Philip (Acts 8: 35-38). Saul was instructed to go where he could be told what to do (Acts 9: 6). Cornelius was to be told "words" whereby he could be saved (Acts 11: 14). The Philippian jailer became a saved man by hearing the word of the Lord (Acts 16: 30-33). All this is in keeping with 1 Corinthians 1: 21, which says it is by the foolishness of preaching (called foolishness by the critics) to save them that believe. Hence our verse says the Thessalonians were called by the Gospel. Paul calls it *our gospel* in the sense that it was the Gospel which he preached. The word is not used with the meaning of possession, but to show relationship. When a man speaks of "my country," he does not mean he owns it, but that he is related to it and not to some other. The result of having been called by the Gospel was that the Thessalonians might obtain the glory of our *Lord Jesus Christ*. Stated in other words, the italicized phrase means that the salvation coming from Christ is the most glorious or praiseworthy thing a man can obtain.

Verse 15. *Stand fast* denotes that they were to remain firm in their belief of this Gospel, and not be deceived by the tricky teachers of the Romish system. *Traditions* is from PARADOSIS, which Thayer defines, "a giving over, giving up; i.e. the act of giving up, the surrender. A giving over which is done by word of mouth or in writing." The word is used in both a good and a bad sense in the New Testament. Any doctrine or rule of conduct becomes a tradition when it has once been given over from one person to another. Whether it is good or bad, and whether it is of any authority or not, depends upon the person or persons handing over the doctrine. Hence the traditions Paul is recommending to the Thessalonians are of authority since they come from him, either "by word of mouth" (oral preaching), or by his epistle.

Verse 16. God and Christ are again named in a manner that proves they are two separate individuals, although they are a unit in spirit and purpose. The title of *God* denotes his supreme deity as head over all creation, while that of *Father* pertains to his spiritual relationship to all who will become members of the spiritual family through obedience. *Lord* is a title that means ruler, and the Son has been given the rule over the church (Matthew 28: 18). *Jesus* means saviour and is given to him because he is the Saviour of the world (Matthew 1: 21). The title *Christ* belongs to him because he was anointed (figuratively crowned) to be over the kingdom (Acts 10: 38). *Everlasting consolation* is thus named because the consolation that comes from God and Christ is not temporary. *Good hope* simply means that the things for which Christians can hope are good in the highest sense. *Through grace* denotes that the entire benefit is a gift from on High, and not a return for labor, since that cannot earn or merit eternal life.

Verse 17. The preceding verse gives a general statement of the provisions or spiritual benefits possible for man, and this verse expresses Paul's wish for all such good things to come upon the Thessalonian brethren. One result of such comfort would be to *stablish* (make firm) them in *every good word and work;* no other kind of works will be blessed of God.

2 Thessalonians 3

Verse 1. *Finally* is defined "moreover" in Thayer's lexicon. It merely indicates that the apostle has some additional instructions to give the brethren, and not that it was to be the final or last of his remarks. *Pray for us.* In 1 Thessalonians 5: 25 Paul makes this same request. (See the comments at that place.) It is sufficient here to say that not even an inspired man has any special immunity against temptation. *Us* is the plural form of the first personal pronoun. It is true that all of the apostles needed the prayers of the faithful, and Paul could properly include them in his request. However, this use of a plural pronoun is like that of "we" which is a form of "editorial modesty" with reference to one's personality. In this verse the request is not for some favor to Paul especially, but for the *word of the Lord. Have free course* means that it may not be obstructed by any foe. *Be glorified* denotes that it would receive its proper recognition from those who heard it. *As it is with you.* The Thessalonians had given such respectful attention to the word of the Lord, and it was the wish of Paul that others accord it the like treatment.

Verse 2. *Be delivered.* Be rescued or be protected from falling into the hands of them. *Unreasonable* literally means "out of place"; men who do not keep their place in society. *Wicked* has the regular meaning, referring here to the men who do not stay in their proper places nor mind their own business. *All men have not faith.* Paul regards this as the explanation of why some men are *unreasonable and wicked.* If a man does not believe the word of the Lord, he will not have any motive for respecting righteous people.

Verse 3. *Lord is faithful.* We usually think of the term *faithful* as applying to one who is true and obedient to another to whom he is obligated. Yet it would not be appropriate to regard the Lord in that light; hence it means that He will make good all his promises. Among the things God has promised to do for his obedient servants is to *stablish* or make them firm. A means of doing so is to protect them *from evil,* by not suffering them to be tempted beyond endurance (1 Corinthians 10: 13).

Verse 4. *Confidence in the Lord touching you.* This phrase combines Paul's estimate of the steadiness of the brethren, and his feeling of assurance that the Lord will perform his part of the relationship as the preceding verse states. The outward proof of the truths the apostle here expresses is the present life of obedience among the Thessalonians, which he is sure will be continued.

Verse 5. This verse is a prayer of Paul for the Lord's direction of their hearts. Under His guidance, they will come under the enjoyment of God's love, which can never be obtained except by faithful service to Him (John 14: 23). Such a degree of devotion to God will beget in the mind of a true disciple the quality of *patience* as the apostle desires him to have. The word is from HUPOMONE, and Thayer defines it at this place, "a patient, steadfast waiting for." It means that while faithful disciples will be eager for the coming of Christ

(2 Peter 3: 12), they will not become fretful and wavering because of their desire for it.

Verse 6. The command is in the name of Christ which means by his authority; hence to disobey would constitute disobedience against Him. *Disorderly* is from ATAKTOS, which Thayer defines as follows: "disorderly, out of ranks; irregular, inordinate, deviating from the prescribed order or rule." The word originated in the conduct of soldiers who got out of line in the march. When used in religious affairs, it applies to any kind of misconduct, although Paul is here specifically dealing with indolent persons, who are neglecting to perform the manual labor necessary for a living. But he states the rule by which any conduct may be classified, namely, the *tradition* that had been delivered by him. This word is explained by the comments at chapter 2: 15. Any conduct that is not in harmony with apostolic tradition is disorder; and when such is continued it constitutes *walking disorderly. Withdraw yourselves* is from the single Greek word STELLO, and Thayer's definition at this place is as follows: "To remove one's self, withdraw one's self, to depart; to abstain from familiar intercourse with one." It would be impossible to obey this command without excluding the guilty one from the congregation. Opponents of formal discipline claim this command can be obeyed without excluding the party; that it only requires the faithful to abstain from friendly association with him. But that would be out of the question if he is retained in the fellowship of the congregation, for that would entitle him to partake of the Lord's supper and other parts of the congregational services. It is certain that such an association would require great intimacy, the very thing that the command for withdrawal forbids.

Verse 7. The apostle now comes to the specific case of disorderly walking that he introduced in the preceding verse. There were some brethren who would not perform manual labor to obtain the necessities of life, and all such were guilty of disorderly conduct and subject to final discipline. The apostle reminds the congregation of his own example that he set when among them, saying they ought to *follow* (imitate) him—be willing to perform labor.

Verse 8. This verse is another reference to Paul's practice when he was among the brethren in Thessalonica. The subject is mentioned in the first epistle to the Thessalonians, chapter 2: 9, which shows that he labored for his own support very diligently, in order to relieve the brethren of that burden.

Verse 9. *Power* is from EXOUSIA which also means right or authority. Paul had the right to live from the support of the brethren, since the Lord has ordained that "they who preach the Gospel should live of the Gospel" (1 Corinthians 9: 5, 14). However, he had voluntarily refrained from using that privilege, in order to set an example of getting one's living from his own labor.

Verse 10. *When we were with you* refers to the time after coming from Philippi. The teaching now put in writing in this epistle, was given to them in person when among them, which is referred to in his first epistle, is very severe on people who are lazy; such have no right to the provisions produced by others. Of course we know the apostle does not expect these idlers to go on a "hunger strike" and die of starvation. However, he does lay the command before them that they go to work, and as a means of enforcing the order, he states that if they are not willing to work, they have no right to eat. This brings the brethren into the command, forbidding them to feed those who are not willing to work.

Verse 11. In this verse Paul makes it plain whom he especially means by the ones *walking disorderly* in verse 6, namely, the idlers. One might wonder why Paul would call an idler a *busybody.* The term is from a Greek word that Thayer defines as follows: "To bustle about uselessly, to busy one's self about trifling, needless, useless matters." Our own observation will verify this definition. Men who will not work, are often seen intruding into the affairs of those who are willing to work, even to the extent of trying to interfere to prevent them from working.

Verse 12. The idlers are first given a *command* which makes the thing under consideration a positive obligation. Then the *exhortation* is given which is an appeal to the conscience, to persuade them to do their duty in the case. This command and exhortation did not come from the personal impulse of the apostle, but it was *by our Lord Jesus Christ. Quietness* is from HESUCHIA, and the one word "quietness" is Thayer's definition of the Greek word. He then adds by way of explanation at this place, "descriptive of the life of one who stays at home doing his own work, and does not officiously meddle with the affairs of others." *Eat their own bread* shows Paul means for them to work at something to earn a living.

Verse 13. *Weary* does not pertain to the body or material part of our being, for if we exercise ourselves we cannot avoid becoming tired; such result is beyond our control. God never forbids that which is unavoidable; the original word refers to the mind and not to the body. A man may become literally worked down or "worn out" by his trials for the Master, but if he has the proper interest in the work he will never become tired in mind, but will always feel keen and alert in the duty for Christ. This thought is treated by Paul in 2 Corinthians 4: 16-18.

Verse 14. When Paul was with these brethren he gave them instructions about the evils of idleness, but we are not told what commands, if any, he gave the congregation as to how the idle persons should be treated. Here the information is given that the same command is delivered in this epistle and that it must be obeyed as if the apostle delivered it in person. *Note that man* means to pay particular attention to him, to make sure that he comes under the classification of men whom Paul has been condemning. If it is seen that he does, then the brethren were to *have no company with* him. Since the apostle is writing about the same case that he has been for several verses, we know the words in italics have the same meaning as "withdraw yourselves" in verse 6. Let the reader consult the comments at that place in connection with the present one. The purpose for the discipline upon the disorderly one is *that he may be ashamed.* Indeed, the first object of discipline is the salvation of the guilty one (1 Corinthians 5: 5), and the second is to save the church (verses 6, 7 of the same chapter).

Verse 15. In a sense, every person who does wrong is an enemy of righteousness and of the church. The idea here is that this man is not an enemy in the same rank as an outsider who has always been in the army of the foe. He has been in the congregation, but had to be dealt with on the principle of discipline, hence he should be regarded in the light of a member of the family who has gone wrong. By such a token, the admonition should be as to a wayward brother and not as to a member of a foreign family. The word *admonish* implies that some undesirable result may follow if the wayward member does not return to the government of the Father's family.

Verse 16. *Peace* is from EIRENE. As it pertains to individuals, Thayer gives a very complete definition of the word, and it is in full agreement with the teaching of the New Testament; the defintion follows: "The tranquil state of a soul assured of its salvation through Christ, and so fearing nothing from God and content with its earthly lot, of whatsoever sort that is." This certainly describes something that is good; and since all good things come from the Lord (James 1: 17), it is appropriate for Paul to refer to Him as *the Lord of peace.* He adds his wish that the Thessalonians be given such peace from Him. *The Lord be with you all* is another form of the wish for His peace to be with them.

Verse 17. Some impostors had forged the name of Paul to their letters, and thereby had deceived the brethren. (See chapter 2; 2, 3.) However, the uniformity of his handwriting would finally make them acquainted with his genuine signature. As a safeguard against further deception, Paul states that his signature would be seen at the the end of every one of his epistles, and it was to be understood as a *token* or sign of the genuineness of the epistle. *So I write.* This is to call their attention to his style of writing, for his signature would be done in the same manner, which would help them to recognize it and know it to be genuine. For a discussion further into the subject of the actual writer of his epistles, see the comments at Galatians 6: 11.

Verse 18. This is a closing benediction to indicate Paul's personal concern for the happiness of the brethren. The grace of the Lord is his favor to be given to them as a gracious gift, for the word means something that is not received upon the principle of merit. For the significance of *amen*, see the comments at Romans 16: 24, in volume 1 of the New Testament Commentary.

1 Timothy 1

Verse 1. Thus far in the New Testament, according to the compilation in the King James Version, all of Paul's epistles have been addressed to congregations in cities that are named, or in other designated areas. He now changes his plan and will address some to individuals. He calls himself *an apostle of Jesus Christ*. The significance of the phrase will be appreciated more by considering the meaning of the word *apostle*. It is from APOSTOLOS which Thayer defines, "a delegate, messenger, one sent forth with orders." Hence the italicized expression means Paul was sent forth with orders from Jesus Christ. The weight of authority behind his apostleship is increased by the fact that God commanded it to be so. God is called *our Saviour* because he is the one who provided a sacrifice that could save mankind. *Our hope* means that all hope of eternal life is in the Lord Jesus Christ.

Verse 2. *Son* is from TEKNON, which occurs more than 75 times in the Greek New Testament, and it is always rendered by child, with a few unimportant exceptions. Its various shades of meaning have to be determined by the connection in which it is used. Paul did not have any family of his own begetting, hence we know the word is used in a figurative sense in this verse. With reference to such a meaning, Thayer says of it historically, "With the possessive, it is used of a person who depends on another or is the follower; one who is connected with or belongs to a thing by any kind of close relationship; pupils or disciples are called children of their teachers." *In the faith* means the close connection between Paul and Timothy, just described by these historical statements of Thayer, which was brought about by their common faith in Christ. Paul had instructed Timothy in the faith of the Gospel, hence he is here called his *son* according to the phrase "pupils or disciples" as cited above. *Grace, mercy and peace*, etc., is the same kindly salutation by which Paul begins many of his epistles. (See the comments on such a salutation at 1 Corinthians 1: 3).

Verse 3. Timothy was selected by Paul to travel with him (Acts 16: 1-3), and he was in his company much of the time. However, at times the apostle appointed him to certain tasks, while he went on to other territories. Such special journeys were made by Paul on more than one occasion, hence we are not informed when the one occurred referred to in this verse. But this item is not essential to our study and conclusions upon the matters mentioned. When Paul was ready to depart from Timothy, he requested him to remain at Ephesus for the purpose of defending the truth against false teachers. And now in this epistle he refers to the matter and repeats the program he expects the evangelist to follow. This repetition of the instructions constitutes them virtually as an order. *Teach no other doctrine* than what was taught by the apostles. The false doctrine has special reference to that being circulated by the Judaizers, namely, that the law of Moses was binding on all Christians. There was also a mixture of traditions from the pretenders of learning that was injected into the ordinances of the law, and pressed upon disciples as items necessary to salvation.

Verse 4. *Fables* has the same meaning as myths, and the ones spoken of here are those put forth by the Judaizers. They were a part of the commentaries that were composed with the claim that they were necessary to understand the law of Moses. It was easy to use such a notion as an opportunity for devising all sorts of speculative theories, and Paul's instruction is to pay no attention to them. *Endless genealogies*. The Jews laid much stress upon their descent from Abraham (Matthew 3: 9), yet many of them were not content with the literal line from that patriarch, but ran off into some vague notions of an immaterial or mystic ancestry. However, in their wild speculations upon such a line of genealogy, though still professing much interest in their relation to Abraham, such unreasonable mixtures of genealogies would cause persons to become unsettled. As a result, the patriarch Abraham was left behind as the speculations went on and on into the dim past without any certain conclusion. That is why Paul calls them *endless genealogies*. It is evident why he says they *minister questions*, meaning they raise disputes among the people that will be of no edification since they are not *in faith*. *So do*. These words have no originals at this place in the Greek text, but the King James translators thought they were justified by the repetition in the epistle of the exhortation Paul had given Timothy in person when he was with him. The idea is as if Paul said: "When I was with you in person I besought you to see after how certain ones taught. Now I am more particular about it, and insist on your doing as I requested."

Verse 5. *End* is from TELOS, and Thayer defines it at this place as follows: "The end to which all things relate, the aim, purpose." *The commandment* refers to the charge that Paul had given Timothy regarding the kind of teaching he was to require among the people at Ephesus. The *end* or purpose of the charge was that it would produce *charity* or love. *Out of a pure heart* denotes that it was to be a sincere love and not a mere pretended one. Such a pure love would be in harmony with a good conscience; it could be professed conscientiously. *Faith unfeigned* means a genuine faith and not an empty pretense for personal advantage such as the evil Judaizers displayed.

Verse 6. *From which* refers to the good things mentioned in the preceding verse. To *swerve* means to deviate from some established path or way of life. If a person gets off of the proper road, he generally gets mixed up in some uncertain situation. Hence if a disciple departs from the road marked out by an unfeigned faith, it is no wonder if he falls into *vain jangling*. This term means "idle talking" according to Thayer's lexicon, and certainly the fables and endless genealogies mentioned in verse 4 would fall into that class.

Verse 7. *Desiring to be teachers of the law* could not of itself be wrong. However, these teachers were not motivated by the right principle, or they would not have swerved from the faith in search of an opportunity to do their teaching. Besides, they were not qualified to teach the law, because they did not understand it themselves. *Affirm* is a stronger word than *say*. The latter merely means to speak without any special emphasis; even that should not be done about something that one does not understand. The former denotes a strong utterance in which the speaker is positive about his declarations. It is the height of folly to behave in such a manner concerning something which the actor does not understand.

Verse 8. The pretended teachers of the law would try to justify their activities by saying that law is a good thing. Paul does not deny that claim, but explains that in order for the law to bring good results, it must be used *lawfully*. One word in Thayer's definition of the original word is "properly." The correctness of the definition is evident, for we know that the best of things in any of life's relations will work harm if misused.

Verse 9. *The law is not made for a righteous man.* 1 Peter 2: 14 says that governors are not only for the punishment of evildoers, but also for the praise of them who do well. Also in Romans 13: 3, 4 it is clearly shown that the same ruler who is to punish them who do evil is also expected to praise the righteous. Hence we know that Paul is here speaking only of the penal section of law. *Lawless and disobedient* refers to the members of society who are disturbers of the peace. *Ungodly* and *sinners* could well be used interchangeably if taken separately, but when combined in one phrase there is some distinction. The Greek word for the former has special reference to the personal attitude toward God. Such a person practices a life of sin, but he does not even have any concern whether such a life is displeasing to God or not. The Greek word for the latter term has chief reference to the kind of life the man is living, without any consideration of his mental attitude about God; that idea is not in the word. *Unholy* is a general term applying to all people who are unrighteous, since holiness is another word for righteousness. *Profane* means those whose lives are such that they can scarcely be distinguished from men of the world who make no profession of righteousness. *Murder* is a capital crime no matter against whom it is committed, but when perpetrated against one's parents, it also violates all the laws of affection that are intended to keep families united. *Manslayers*. The law of the land makes a distinction between manslaughter and other degrees of killing. Murder strictly consists of the unlawful taking of human life which is performed intentionally, while other instances of killing may be designated only as manslaughter. Yet if that is done as a result of carelessness, or in other ways that could have been avoided, it is also wrong and the law of God as well as of man provides some penalty for the act.

Verse 10. Even one act of unlawful sexual intimacy constitutes fornication or adultery and is a grievous sin. But a *whoremonger* is a man who makes it a common practice; especially one who patronizes a woman who receives men for money. In some extreme cases the original word applies to a man who engages in the business for money (such as described in Ezekiel 16: 30-34). Some lexicons define the original word as "a male prostitute." Regardless of whichever phase of the crime is considered, it is one against God and man, surpassed perhaps only by that which is named by the words *defile themselves with mankind*. These italicized words are all from the one Greek word ARSENOKOITES, which Thayer defines as follows: "One who lies with a male as with a female, a sodomite." The wicked character that is described just preceding this one sometimes is defined "a sodomite." However, when that is the case it is a man who permits another to use him instead of a female. The one now being considered is the man who so uses this other man instead of a female. The reader should see the comments on these two characters at 1 Corinthians 6: 9. *Menstealers* is from ANDRAPODISTES, and Thayer defines the word as follows: "a slave-dealer, kidnapper, man-stealer." He refers to the historical origin of the word and gives the following information: "As well one who unjustly reduces free men to slavery, as one who steals the slaves of others and sells them." *Liars, perjured persons.* All perjured persons are liars also, but they are those who falsify under oath, or other form of legal testifying. The last clause of the verse is a generalization of the subject introduced at verse 3. Hence anything that is contrary to the doctrine taught by the apostles would be *contrary to sound doctrine*.

Verse 11. This is Paul's explanation of the term *sound doctrine* in the preceding verse. To be such, it must agree with the glorious Gospel. *Blessed* in the original is defined also as "happy," but when it is applied to God it means he is the source of true happiness. He is the giver of the *glorious Gospel*, and that is the reason He is credited with that which will make men happy. *Committed to my trust* denotes that Paul was entrusted with the preaching of this holy document.

Verse 12. This verse is related in thought to the previous one concerning the trust that the Lord had in Paul. Christ counted the apostle as a faithful servant, hence was worthy of being put into the *ministry* or service of preaching the Gospel.

Verse 13. One of the strongest evidences of Paul's sincerity was the radical change in his conduct toward the cause of Christ. A *blasphemer* is one who speaks with strong and bitter language against another, and a *persecutor* is a man who puts such bitterness into action against the object of his blasphemy. *Injurious* is from HUBRISTES which Thayer defines as follows: "An insolent [overbearing] man, one who, uplifted with pride, either heaps insulting language upon others or does them some shameful act of wrong." We have no information that Paul ever saw Christ personally, much less that he could have injured him directly. But in persecuting the disciples of Christ he was mistreating Him. (See Matthew 25: 44, 45 and Acts 9: 4, 5.) *Obtained mercy* does not say that he was excused for what he did. A jury may recommend mercy for a defendant, although it has found the man guilty, because there are circumstances that justify an easier punishment than strict application of the law might demand. This is the case in Paul's instance, so the Lord showed him mercy because he was an unbeliever —had made no profession toward Christ—and was ignorant of the facts in the matter.

Verse 14. *Grace* is the unmerited favor of the Lord, which explains why Paul was accorded mercy after his opposition to His people as just stated in the preceding verse. *With faith and love.* Even the "unmerited favor" of Christ will not be given to a man unless he does his part in the transaction. Paul accepted the testimony of the divinity of Christ which produced *faith*. He then began at once to labor for the new-found religion, which showed his *love* for the cause.

Verse 15. *Faithful saying.* The first word is defined "that can be relied on" by Thayer; it means that it is true. Of course if a saying is true, it is *worthy of all acceptation*. The *saying* Paul has in mind is that *Christ Jesus came into the world to save sinners*. It could not be untrue, for He made the same declaration himself (Matthew 18: 11; Luke 19: 10). *Chief* is from

PROTOS, which means "principal" in the sense of being outstanding and noted. This again refers to his former activities against the cause of Christ.

Verse 16. In verse 13 the apostle says he obtained mercy because of his misunderstanding of the case. In our present verse he repeats his statement and adds the Lord's other motive for extending the favor to him. It was that he could be used as a pattern for the encouragement of other believers. When they learn of the great long-suffering that Christ showed toward such a "chief" sinner as Paul, they will be induced to depend upon Him for grace to assist them toward a working belief that will bring them to eternal life.

Verse 17. *Eternal* is from two Greek words at this place, which are TON AIONON. In the composition they are plural in number and in the possessive case, and the Englishman's Greek New Testament translates them "of the ages." There have been three ages or dispensations of religion given into the world, namely, the Patriarchal, the Jewish and the Christian. God has been and is the supreme ruler or King over each of them, although the Son has been placed in charge of the third. *Immortal* means He is not subject to decay as were the idols that were worshiped as gods by some. *Invisible* is another distinction between the true God and those made of "gold or silver or stone," which could be seen literally with the eyes of man. *Only wise God* has the sense of saying: "He is the only God, and he is wise." *Be honor and glory* means these qualities should be attributed to this one true God. *For ever and ever* is an emphatic form of expression, meaning these virtues wil be possessed by Him endlessly. *Amen* is defined by Thayer, "so be it, so it is, may it be fulfilled."

Verse 18. *This charge* refers to the one recorded in verses 3 and 5. The term *son* is explained by the comments on verse 2. *Prophecies* is from PROPHETEIA. Thayer does not define the word at this passage, but he does for chapter 4: 14 where the same Greek word is used "on" Timothy, which means concerning him. His explanation of the word for that passage is as follows: "Specifically of the prognostigation [prediction] of those achievements which one sets apart to teach the Gospel will accomplish for the kingdom of Christ." Robinson explains the word at our verse as follows: "'Refers to prophetic declarations respecting the labors and success of Timothy, made by those having the gift of prophecy, on occasion of his being sent forth." This verse means as if Paul said, "it was predicted at the time of your appointment to the work, that you would be able to 'war a good warfare,' now I repeat my charge already made, that you make good the prediction."

Verse 19. *Holding* means to keep a firm grip on a thing because of its necessary use. *Faith and a good conscience*. This phrase involves the entire conduct of a Christian. Faith is the result of testimony, hence divine faith requires divine testimony (Romans 10: 17). A subject, then, on which the word of God furnishes no information, is one on which a man cannot have any divine or scriptural faith. A man can have faith in anything that is authorized by the word of God, and such a matter is bound to be right. However, a man can be sure that a certain act is right if done at all, yet he might not be concerned about whether he did it or not, and there is where a good conscience comes in. Thayer's main definition of the Greek word for *conscience* is as follows: "The soul as distinguishing between what is morally good and bad, prompting to do the former and shun the latter, commending the one, demning the other." A good conscience is that part of a man that "prompts" him to do that which is right. However, a man's conscience might be mistaken as to what is right (as Paul's was when he was persecuting Christians). Because of this, it is necessary also that a man be guided by the word of God, then he will be acting by faith. To sum up; the conscience will prompt a man to do something, and his faith (produced by the word of God) will assure that what he does is right. *Shipwreck* is a figurative reference to what happens if the steering apparatus becomes defective; the ship will be misguided with the result of a wreck. If either faith or good conscience is lacking in a mans life, he will fail to be guided aright and will wreck his soul.

Verse 20. According to 2 Timothy 2: 17, Hymenaeus was a false teacher. We have no certain information concerning Alexander, but he was a blasphemer according to Paul's statement in this verse. *Delivered unto Satan* means they were excluded, as the same thing is said in 1 Corinthians 5:5 of the fornicator who was excluded.

1 Timothy 2

Verse 1. *Therefore* indicates a reference to some former considerations. They especially are to be found in chapter 1: 3 and 18, where the apostle reminds the evangelist of what was expected of him after being given his charge. Resuming his directions for the carrying out of the great work in the "warfare" amid the various conditions of the world, he instructs the evangelist that he will *begin* the details *(first of all)* with the subject of prayers in their various forms. Some commentators think this instruction has reference to the public services of the congregation. Doubtless it includes that, but verse 8 commands that men pray *every where*, which makes the exhortation general. Any address made to God may be called a prayer generally speaking, but there are various forms or classes of the addresses, and they are specified in this verse which I shall define briefly. *Prayers* are requests of any degree of intensity that may be chosen. *Supplications* are the more earnest requests made under intense necessity. *Intercessions* are prayers on behalf of others who are in need of the mercy of God. *Giving of thanks* are expressions of gratitude for favors that have already been received from the Lord. *For all men* is a general statement as to "the subject of our prayers."

Verse 2. In this verse the apostle specializes on the ones for whom Christians should pray, namely, for those who are in positions of authority, and whose rule may have some effect on the liberties to be enjoyed by the citizens. The object of such prayers is that Christians be undisturbed in their desire to lead a godly life. We know Paul did not expect these prayers to affect the rulers directly, for they would not hear them. The only conclusion possible is that if the prayers are scriptural, then God will take some hand (in His own divine way) to see that the rulers govern aright as to our liberties. If that is not the intention, then He would certainly not require the disciples to pray for the rulers. This is not a new doctrine, for Nebuchadnezzar had to eat grass seven years to be convinced "that the most High ruleth in the kingdoms of men" (Daniel 4: 25). It may be replied that it was in Old Testament times that this was said. Well, we will come to the New Testament, to Romans 13: 1-4, where the temporal ruler is declared to be "the minister of God," and we can see how the subject is treated, and that God has never repealed what he told the king of Babylon.

Verse 3. See comments at chapter 1: 1 as to God being titled Saviour. The immediate occasion for the term in this verse is what follows in the next verse. *This is good* refers to the results of a life of honesty and godliness that may be practiced by the disciples, when not hindered by improper legislation. God is desirous that rulers as well as private persons may be saved, and a godly life displayed before them by faithful servants of God will be a help in showing them the value of the plan of salvation as provided by the Father. (See Matthew 5: 16.)

Verse 4. It should be noted that the salvation of men is connected with *the knowledge of the truth;* the latter is necessary for the former.

Verse 5. Idolatry and the worship of many gods was a common condition in the world when the Gospel was first proclaimed. Kings and other rulers knew something about hearing the causes of their subjects. The dignity of the office was such that a citizen had to be represented by an agent who could act between the ruler and his subject. These same rulers were often among the believers in many gods, and they (like their own subjects) approached some one of their many objects of worship by means of a priest officiating for them at the heathenish altar. It was appropriate for them to learn that if they are saved through the doctrine preached by the Christians, they must abandon the idea of many gods and realize that there is only one God and hence only one mediator, who is the *man Christ Jesus*. He was a *man* in order to represent fairly the human seeker after God, and he was Christ Jesus in order to be good enough to receive recognition before the throne of this God.

Verse 6. Being man as well as God, it was possible for Christ to be used as a ransom in the form of a sacrifice. *For all* is in contrast with the sacrifices offered under the law, for they were on behalf of the Jews only; Christ died for both Jew and Gentile. *To be testified.* The fact that Jesus died as a ransom, and then came back to life that He might complete the plan of salvation, was to be proved and testified or borne witness to by the chosen proclaimers. *In due time.* When the fact of His resurrection had been accomplished, and the Holy Spirit came upon these chosen proclaimers to qualify them to speak, it was then only that the *due time* had come. That is why Jesus gave the instructions recorded in Luke 24:48, 49 and Acts 1: 7, 8.

Verse 7. *Whereunto* refers to the testifying to the truth of Christ's ransom mentioned in the preceding verse. For the purpose of engaging in this testimony, Paul was *ordained a preacher*. The first of the italicized words is from TITHENI at this place, and Thayer's definition is, "To set, put, place." For the complete information of the word "ordain" as given in Thayer's lexicon, see comments at John 15: 16, in the first volume of the New Testament Commentary. Paul was not only ordained a preacher but also an apostle. Any Christian may preach the good news (Acts 8: 4), but only an apostle could speak with miraculous inspiration and have power to bestow the Holy Spirit on others (Acts 8: 15, 16). *I speak the truth in Christ and lie not.* Paul could say this because he had been ordained as an apostle, hence the things he preached were bound to be the truth. *Teacher of the Gentiles.* Any disciple had the right to tell the story of the cross to the Gentiles as well as to the Jews, but Paul was given the special commission to be "the apostle of the Gentiles" (Acts 9: 15; Romans 11: 13). *In faith and verity.* Paul was to lead the Gentiles into the faith of the Gospel, and out of the myths of heathen errors. This could be done only by giving them the divine truth that he as an inspired apostle could do; *verity* is a Greek word for the truth.

Verse 8. *Lifting up holy hands* means hands of men who are living holy or righteous lives. The lifting up of the hands is merely an allusion to the ancient practice of presenting the uplifted hands in respectful petition to God (Nehemiah 8: 6; Psalms 141: 2; Lamentations 3: 41). The command pertains to the kind of hands being lifted up, and not as to the posture of the body during prayer; the Lord is not concerned about that matter. That the men were to pray *every where* shows the apostle was not especially writing of prayers in the public assembly of the church. *Wrath and doubting.* The first word means anger that would be disposed to inflict punishment on someone. The last word denotes a disposition that is given to questioning. Not that discipline or discussion should be done without prayer, but the outstanding thought of the apostle here (as will be seen in several following verses) is a time of earnest but calm approach to the throne of grace. A man under the impulse of the italicized phrase would not be in a frame of mind suitable for such a season of prayer.

Verse 9. *In like manner* is all from the Greek word HOSAUTOS, and one word in Thayer's definition is "likewise," and that word does not necessarily mean a repetition of some previous action, but rather that the writer has something more to say. It is as if the apostle said, "furthermore, I have something to say about the women." Neither does the use of the words *men* and *women* in these verses support those who take extreme views on the "woman question." If the fact that Paul mentions the *men* in verse 8 means that they only are the ones who may pray, then the women are prohibited entirely from that act of devotion. It will not do to say that it is in the public assembly where they are thus forbidden, for the apostle said the prayers were to be offered "every where," and even the most radical objectors will admit that women have the right to pray outside the public assembly. What proves too much proves nothing, hence we must conclude that Paul was not writing about which sex could pray, but what *kind* of men might do so, and that they might do so in every place.

The proper general demeanor of women, especially as it respects her relationship to man in all walks of life, is the subject of the rest of this verse and of the rest of the chapter. Neither does it apply to the public assemblies any more than to the social life. Therefore it is a perversion of this chapter to make it a regulation of "women's duties and privileges in the church," for the passage was not written for that purpose. It is God's intention for woman to be attractive in the eyes of man (1 Corinthians 11: 7-9), but He instructs her as to what shall constitute her attractiveness. *Apparel* is from KATASTOLE which Thayer defines, "a garment let down, dress, attire." It is evident that *modest apparel* means a woman's clothing should not be such as would expose her body in a way to suggest evil thoughts. *Shamefacedness* means womanliness; the opposite of brazenness. The Greek word for *sobriety* is also defined "self-control" in Thayer's lexicon. This restriction will serve as a regulation in the things named in the rest of the verse. Immodest women braided their hair as a means of holding more of their showy jewels here enumerated, in order to excite the attention of the opposite sex. They likewise depended on the costliness of their clothing to attract the men. A woman who possesses this *sobriety* (self-control), will not use these things to such an extent that she will suggest improper thoughts in the minds of men. Hence a controlled use of these feminine trinkets is not forbidden as far as this passage is concerned.

Verse 10. The adornment of women is introduced in the beginning of the preceding verse, and the subject has not been changed. That shows the present verse is in line with the same subject, for it closes with the phrase *good works*. We know Paul has not been writing exclusively of the public assembly; in truth, he has not been considering that subject as much as in other places, for we do not regard the assemblies as the places for the practice of *good works* as that expression is commonly used. Furthermore, the matter of feminine adornment pertains to the social sphere of human life, in which the question considered is what is the proper and what the improper means a woman should use in order to interest the opposite sex. If a woman who professes to be godly in life will back it up with *good works*, she will be making herself attractive in the highest sense of the word. These remarks are not restricted to unmarried women in the matter of being adorned in the eyes of men, for the success and happiness of the married state is dependent to a great extent upon the regard the husband can have for his wife. If she maintains the same modesty of bodily adornment after marriage that attracted the man and induced him to obtain her for his wife, he will continue to be happiest when in her society.

Verse 11. *Learn in silence.* Even the extremists must admit from this phrase that the woman has a right to learn. However, they insist that she must be silent while learning, making a literal use of the word. But it is a principle universally recognized by all courses of learning throughout the world, that the best method of imparting and receiving instruction is by the question and answer system. Jesus used it in the temple (Luke 2: 46, 47). Even in the case of 1 Corinthians 14: 35, Paul permits the woman to learn about the special matters her gifted husband knows about; she may "ask her husband." It may be replied that she is to do so "at home." Certainly, and the chapter we are studying applies to the home more properly than any other place. She is not very silent while asking a question. Are we to suppose that she must keep her ears open and her mouth closed? Certainly not if she is to "ask" her husband for the information.

The apparent difficulty is caused by misunderstanding the word *silence*. It is from the Greek word HESUCHIA, and Thayer's first definition is the word "quietness," and his explanation is, "descriptive of the life of one who stays at home doing his own work, and does not officially meddle with the affairs of others." It is the word for "quietness" in 2 Thessalonians 3: 12. Paul surely does not expect a man to work for a living and at the same time maintain silence in the literal sense that is attached to the word by many well-meaning disciples. But this is not all the apostle says in the same sentence about the way a woman is to learn, for he says she is to do so *with all subjection*. The last word is from HUPOTAGE which Thayer defines, "obedience, subjection." It is the word for "subjection" in 1 Timothy 3: 4, and we know that a child can be in subjection to his father, even while using his tongue for conversation. The verse as a whole means that a woman has the right to speak and ask questions of men, but it should be in the spirit of humility and not forgetting that she is not to act as one in authority.

Verse 12. This verse very properly follows immediately after the preceding one, since the outstanding thought in that place is the subject of authority as it pertains to the relation between men and women. *I suffer not a woman to teach.* I am quoting this much of the verse only for the present, because it is the part that is usually relied upon by the extremists on the "woman question," to prove their notion on the subject. These same disciples will condemn the denominational world for taking a part of the scripture out of its connection in order to make a point. But for the sake of the widespread argument, let us consider this so-called prooftext as it is quoted, which makes no exception or provision for one. It is an established principle that an explanation of a passage that makes it contradict another passagee, is bound to be wrong since the Bible does not contradict itself. Well, the extremists' use of this clause makes it contradict Colossians 3: 16 where we know the women are included, and the verse says for them to teach one another, and the same Greek word is used in both passages. It is true that "everybody" joins in the singing, even tnose wno are not members. That is no valid argument since two wrongs do not make one right. Furthermore, if the underscored clause is to be taken generally, then the women members of the congregation should be forbidden to participate in the singing, also the people of the world should be informed not to sing, in the same manner that we notify the audiences that only faithful members have any right to the Lord's supper. The foregoing remarks would be appropriate even though the italicized clause had been written with regard to the public assembly only, which would be impossible to prove. So then, since "what proves too much proves nothing," it follows that the words marked do not prove that women are entirely prohibited from teaching.

Now let us give this subject fair treatment and see what else the apostle has to say about it. The next word is *nor* and it is properly translated. It is from the Greek word OUDE which Thayer defines, "and not," and he explains by saying "continuing a negation" [something denied or forbidden]. Webster defines the word *nor* as follows: "Likewise not; and not; or not," so that what is said of the words preceding *nor* is on the same proviso as what follows the next negation, namely, *usurp authority over the man.* If a woman presumes to teach over the man and hence act in an authoritative way, she violates this verse, whether it be in the public assembly or in the social circle. The case in Acts 18: 24-26 is in point here. A preacher of the Gospel was in error on an item and *they* (both the man and the woman) took him unto themselves and expounded or taught him in the way of the Lord more perfectly. Thus a woman helped to teach a preacher in the doctrine of the Gospel. But nothing indicates that she assumed an authoritative attitude, in desregard for the authority of her husband or the presence of the other man. Had she done so she would have violated the teaching of this passage. *Silence* is the same in the original as in verse 11, explained at that verse which the reader should see.

Verse 13. In this and the following verse, Paul gives two reasons for his restrictions upon the woman, which are not identical but are related. The one in this verse is based upon the prestige one has by reason of priority; *Adam was first formed.* The man was not created for the sake of the woman, but it was the other way around, which indicates that the man possessed some precedence or importance over the woman.

Verse 14. Eve was deceived but Adam was not. Both of them sinned, but the statement is made with regard to their talents or reliability, more than to their moral character. The main object with Paul still is to show why the man and not the woman is to be entrusted with authority. Since a woman is more easily deceived than a man, she is restricted from authoritative teaching, and when she teaches it must not be over the man, but under his supervision; and such a work may be edifying to others even though it is not the expression of authority. *Was in the transgression.* It is a sin to transgress the law of the Lord, even though one is induced to do so by being deceived. Jesus taught this same truth in Matthew 15: 14, and it proves that the mere fact of being honest (all deceived persons are honest at the time) will not save a person.

Verse 15. While Eve was the first woman, and the one who brought transgression into the world, all women bear the same relation to God as to responsibility. We know Paul means to include them in the argument, for he has been writing to women of his day, and referred to Eve only to show the reason why he placed the restrictions on her—on women in general. However, such restrictions as he placed on woman need not endanger her salvation as we shall see. *She shall be saved in childbearing.* This cannot mean the woman is given assurance of passing safely through childbirth, for the salvation is made conditional that she *continue in faith*, etc. It would be foolish to say a woman will live through childbirth provided she lives right afterward. Neither can it mean she will be saved through the birth of Christ, for that is true also of man, if he is saved at all. But it is replied that a woman was chosen to bring the Saviour into the world, hence she and her kind have the promise of salvation through her act. Again, that is just as necessary for the man as for the woman. The part that Mary performed in nurturing and bringing forth Jesus into this life was just like the experience of all mothers. It was the conception that was different, and that was not anything done by her personal choice. The italicized words are preceded by the word *notwithstanding*. Although the first woman transgressed, and as a result all her daughters down through the ages are destined to suffer the increased inconvenience and added sorrow of childbirth, yet that very thing will be one of the conditions on which she can save her soul. There are regular terms of salvation set forth in the Gospel, and all men and women must observe them regardless of their station in life. But there are special duties that apply in particular to those who are parents or children; husbands or wives; and neither of them can take the place of the other, and no two of them have the same obligations. The special duty of woman is to bear children, which is one of the conditions on which she may be saved. Of course, motherhood alone will not assure a woman of salvation, but she must follow it up with a life of *faith and charity and holiness with sobriety*. In 1 Timothy 5: 14 Paul commands women to marry and bear children. It is therefore one of the conditions of salvation imposed upon woman. A woman who is able to bear children and refuses to do so, will find herself in trouble on the judgment day.

1 Timothy 3

Verse 1. For the meaning of *bishop*, see "General remarks" at 2 Thessalonians 2. *The office of a bishop.* These words all come from EPISKOPE which Thayer defines, "inspection, visitation; oversight, i.e. overseership, office, charge, since the words are two terms for the same men. Paul calls this office a *good work*, which shows that a bishop (or elder) has something on his shoulders besides "holding down an office." *Desire* and *desireth* are from different words but have virtually the same meaning. The word is used both in a good and a bad sense in the New Testament. Strong's definition is, "To set the heart upon, i.e. long for (rightfully or otherwise)." It is possible, then, for a man to desire the office with proper motives. However, if the wrong kind of man pretends he wishes the office for the right purpose, the qualifications immediately following, when he is examined under the requirements, will expose his unworthiness for the office, thus proving his desire for it is improper.

Verse 2. *Blameless*. This word has been distorted out of its true meaning by saying it requires a bishop to be free from sin or any other defect. Such a definition would make it impossible to have scriptural elders, since the scripture clearly teaches that no man is perfect in that sense. The word is from ANEPILEPTOS which Thayer defines as follows: "Not apprehended, that cannot be laid hold of; hence that cannot be reprehended, not open to censure, irreproachable." It is plain that the word has reference to the standing a man has among men. That no one is able to make any specific accusation against his character or conduct. That is, no one must be able to make such accusation and support it with the truth. This item is shown by the words in the lexicon definition, namely, "that cannot be laid hold of." The foregoing is a general statement of the character required of a proposed candidate for the office, as it pertains to disqualifications. The particular items required, both positive and negative, will follow in this verse and extend through verse 7. But before considering the detailed list of qualifications, it should be remembered that all of them are preceded by the word *must* in the beginning of this verse. That term is from the Greek word DEI, which Thayer defines, "It is necessary, there is need of, it behooves, is right and proper." Strong defines it, "It is (was, etc.) necessary (as binding)." Robinson defines it, "In N. T. it behooves, it is necessary, it must needs, one must or ought." From these definitions it is clear that the requirements of qualifications for bishops (or elders) are positive, and that no man can be scripturally appointed to the office who lacks any one of them; the *degree* to which he must have them will be discussed when we come to Titus 1: 9-11.

Husband of one wife. Some people say this means that he has never been married but once, and that the word *be* in the beginning of the verse should be rendered "having been," making the word include the past as well as the present tense. I have six translations and they all render it the same as the King James Version, namely, by the single word "be," which restricts it to the present tense, at the time of appointment. Another theory is that it means "one wife only." But the third word is added without any authority from the original, for there is no word in the Greek that justifies it. Besides, that doctrine would imply that the church had in its fellowship men who were polygamists, and such a character is not permitted in the church concerning any of the men. The necessary conclusion is, then, that a man who is appointed to the office of bishop must be a married man at the time of his appointment. *Vigilant* means he must be watchful for the spiritual safety of the flock; must "watch for their souls" (Hebrews 13: 17). *Sober* is from SOPHRON which Thayer defines, "Curbing one's desires and impulses, self-controlled, temperate." A man lacking self-control would certainly be unfit to be placed in control of a congregation. *Of good behavior.* It would seem that many of the qualifications for a bishop already requires good behaviour in him, so why this phrase? It is a somewhat general expression, meaning that his life as a whole is orderly; one that is commendable in the eyes of his fellowmen. *Given to hospitality.* This does not require that an elder must keep "open house" constantly, so that he cannot have the satisfaction of home privacy, and that the general public may feel free to run in and out at will. Such a condition would often interfere with one of his own obligations about maintaining government over his household. But if the relations between him and the members of his flock are as they should be, they will wish to counsel with him over their troubles and trials in the Christian life. It should be understood that the home of the elder is one to which all worthy persons will be welcome. *Apt to teach.* Titus 1: 9 requires that elders must be able to expose false teachers who have become unruly. This cannot be done privately in many cases, therefore an elder must be able to teach publicly.

Verse 3. *Not given to wine.* In old times wine was used as a medicine (1 Timothy 5: 23), and that was before the discovery of means for preserving it sweet. Hence the kind used was necessarily the fermented, except in the grape-growing season. But the amount needed for medical purposes ("a little wine") would not make a man drunk. Thus if a person manifested drunkenness, it was evidence he was not using it for purposes of health. *No striker.* This word is from PLEKTES which Thayer defines as follows: "Bruiser, ready with a blow; a pugnacious [like a pugilist], contentious, quarrelsome person." Groves defines it, "A striker, smiter, disturber; a reviler, calumniator [false accuser]; a boxer, pugilist; quarrelsome, turbulent; impetuous [rash], violent." It means a man who wants to settle his arguments with his fists. *Not greedy of filthy lucre.* All but the first word is from AISCHROKERDES, which Thayer defines, "eager for base gain." It is similar to the last word of the verse, except that our present word specializes on the idea of making money by any means, good or bad, while the other considers only the eager desire for money. A man who is so intent on making money that he shows he loves it, will not likely give proper attention to his duties as elder of a congregation. *Patient* means the elder should be mild and gentle in dealing with the members of his flock. He can do this without compromising the right or encouraging the wrong. A *brawler* is one who is contentious over matters that come up. This does not contradict the command to contend for the faith (Jude 3), but one should not insist in a quarrelsome spirit. *Not covetous* is explained in the forepart of this paragraph under *lucre.*

Verse 4. *House* is from OIKOS which Thayer defines as follows: "The inmates of a house, all the persons forming one family, a household." A man might not rule his own household because he does not know how, or because he is not willing to exert enough moral and/or physical force to do so. In either case he is unfit to be appointed as a ruler over the household of God (the church). *Having his children in subjection.* In specifying this part of the household, the apostle shows where a man may need to use both moral and physical force. *Having children* must still be considered in connection with the word "must" in verse 2, hence a man who has no children cannot be scripturally appointed to the eldership. Does this necessarily mean that he must have a plurality of children? No, the form of the language does not so require it if it is taken in the same way that a like expression is understood. A captain of a sinking ship gives orders, "women with children to be placed in life boats first." Yet if a woman with one child should be present, she would not be denied the favor. Sarah remarked in Genesis 21: 7, "Who would have said unto Abraham, that Sarah should have given children suck? for I have borne him a son." We know that Sarah never had but one child, yet she used the plural form of the word in the same sense that Paul uses it. And must an elder's children be his own bodily offspring? The language does not require it, for it is said in direct connection with the mention of his *house*, which we have seen is composed of "the inmates of his house." Rulership and not fatherhood is the point in question, and that can be shown whether the children are his own flesh and blood dependents, or are orphans or otherwise persons who are placed lawfully in his charge. *Gravity* means the children must be taught to obey and respect him as the head of the house.

Verse 5. See comments on the preceding verse.

Verse 6. A *novice* is one who has recently become a Christian, regardless of his age in years. A man of seventy-five years would be a novice if he had become a believer at that age. *Lest being lifted up with pride.* If a man were placed in the eldership who had only lately come into the church, it might give him a wrong impression of his importance. This would puff him up until his conduct would make him deserve being condemned the same as was the devil. This passage incidentally tells us the motive (pride) which prompted Satan to make war in heaven (Revelation 12: 7), so that he was cast out and fell as lightening (Luke 10: 18).

Verse 7. *Good report* denotes that he has a good reputation among people outside of the church. *Lest he fall into reproach*. Not that the questionable reputation would cause the reproach, but if a man's standing is in doubt, it will indicate that his conduct has not been the best in the eyes of the world. If that is the case, then he might again be caught in some of his former irregular habits and thus be *snared* by the devil. And if such a man had been put into the eldership, it would present an embarrassing and damaging problem for the church. Hence the warning of Paul means that such a man should not be appointed, "lest" this unfortunate situation might develop.

Verse 8. *Likewise* does not necessarily mean that all of the foregoing items are to be said of the deacons. The word is used as a kind of notice that the writer has something to say, somewhat along the line that he has been considering. It is from the same Greek word as "in like manner" which is explained at chapter 2: 9; the reader should see the comments at that place. While many things will be repeated as to personal qualifications, that were said regarding the bishops or elders, yet the subject as a whole is changed to another official that the Lord placed in the New Testament church; they are called *deacons*. The work of these officials is not stated in this chapter, except as it may be indicated by some of the qualifications required of them. That subject is explained in detail by the comments on Acts 6: 1-3, in the first volume of the New Testament Commentary.

The word *deacon* is from DIAKONOS, and in the King James Version it is translated by deacon 3 times, by minister 20, servant 7. When the word is in verb form it is from DIAKONEO, which has beeen translated by administer 2 times, minister 7, minister to 1, minister unto 15, serve 10, use the office of deacon 2. Thayer's general definition of DIAKONOS is, "One who executes the commands of another, especially of a master; a servant ,attendant, minister." His specific definition is, "a deacon" and he explains it to mean, "one who, by virtue of the office assigned to him by the church, cares for the poor and has charge of and distributes the money collected for their use." Considering all of the foregoing information, we should understand that the word "deacon" could apply to any member of the church. However, if it is to be used officially (as it is in the present chapter), then the connection will show that it has such a meaning. There is a case where the word has an unofficial meaning and that is the one concerning Phebe. It is explained at the Romans

16:1, in the first volume of the New Testament Commentary.

Grave is from SEMNOS which means honorable and dignified. *Doubletongued* is from DILOGOS which Thayer defines at this place, "doubletongued, double in speech, saying one thing with one person, and another with another." In familiar language it means a man who tries to "be on the fence" or who wants to "carry water on both shoulders." Such a person would certainly not be fit to have such a responsible office as that of a deacon. *Not given to much wine.* This is explained at the first clause of verse 3. *Not greedy of filthy lucre* is commented upon at the same verse.

Verse 9. The work of deacons pertains to the temporal things of life (see Acts 6:2), yet they are expected to be interested in spiritual matters also. *Mystery of the faith.* Anything is a mystery until it is made known, regardless of whether it is something complicated or only a simple matter. Hence *the faith* (another name for the Gospel or salvation through Christ) was a mystery for ages, but was made known fully by the apostles. The deacons are required to maintain a *pure conscience* on the subject, which means they will be true to its teaching while administering their duties with the temporal needs of the poor members.

Verse 10. *Proved* is from DOKIMAZO and Thayer defines it is follows: "To test, examine, scrutinize; to recognize as genuine after examination, to approve, deem worthy." It is understood that some rule or standard is necessary by which a thing may be tested. The rule in this case consists of the qualifications required of the man who is to be appointed to the office. The apostle says for the deacons to be proved *also*, which indicates he applies the requirement (of being proved or tested) in the case of elders as well as of deacons. It does not mean, then, that the men are to be "put in office on trial" as some people teach. They are to be placed therein only after examination, and even not then unless they are *found blameless*, which means they are found not lacking any of the required qualifications. *Use the office of a deacon* all come from DIAKONEO, and this is one of the places referred to in the comments at verse 8; the other place is in verse 13 below.

Verse 11. *Even so* is from the same Greek word as "likewise" in verse 8 and takes the same comments. The pronoun *their* is not in the original, also the Greek word for *wives* is the same as for "women" in general. Because of these facts, some commentators say that Paul is giving instructions for all women in the congregation. It is true that all women should manifest the qualities described here, but it is especially important that the wives of these officials should do so, since without them the work of their husbands would be hindered. *Grave* means their conduct is such that others will respect them. *Slanderers* is from the same word as "devil," and the word is also defined as a false accuser. It is easy to see that a woman who is free with her tongue in falsely accusing others, will make it difficult for her husband to perform his official duties. *Sober* means to have self-control regarding all of the things permitted for a Christian; does not apply to things that are wrong of themselves. *Faithful in all things* is a summing up of the items mentioned or implied, showing a life devoted to the service of the Lord.

Verse 12. *Husbands of one wife* is to be understood in the same way as a like expression in verse 2. *Ruling their children* corresponds with "children in subjection" in verse 4. *Houses* are composed of the same persons defined in the fourth verse.

Verse 13. *Used the office of a deacon* is the other expression coming from the Greek word DIAKONEO, referred to in the comments at verse 10. *Well* is from KALOS, which is a word describing the kind of service the deacons have rendered in their office. Thayer defines it at this place as follows: "Good, excellent in its nature and characteristics, and therefore well-adapted to its ends." *Purchase to themselves* means they acquire or secure for themselves, etc. Thayer explains the word for *degree*, "of a grade of dignity and wholesome influence in the church." *Good* is from the same word as *well* in the beginning of this verse. *Great boldness* means courage and assurance of the things that are right. Nothing can give a man more moral support than the knowledge of having discharged his duty in the best possible manner. It strengthens his faith in Christ, when he sees the good fruit of serving Him on behalf of the disciples. This work is performed in connection with the funds of the church, but the disposition to **use** them for the benefit of poor but worthy disciples, springs from the same spirit that would prompt him to do so out of his own possessions (Matthew 25: 40).

Verse 14. Timothy was at Ephesus and Paul was at Laodicea when he wrote this epistle. Hoping to be with him before long, he would have waited to instruct him personally. However, due to the uncertainty of making the journey for quite a while, he thought it best not to risk the welfare of the church too far, hence he wrote the instructions we have been considering.

Verse 15. This verse states the reason for writing the foregoing instructions as they might affect Timothy's own responsibility with reference to the church. It was to inform him of his proper conduct in the *house of God*. That term is immediately explained to be the *church of the living God*. The words thus far would clearly identify what institution the apostle meant, but he adds some important truths about the position of it in the great plan of God's truth. There is virtually no difference between the *pillar* and the *ground* of the truth. The figure is taken from the architecture of ancient buildings. Many of the structures were largely supported by a few main pillars (Judges 16: 26, 29), but of course the pilars would need to be resting on a good base. Paul means the church is both of them, and hence that God expects the church to be the sole means (on the human side) of propagating and defending the truth. This great principle is taught also in Ephesians 3: 10 and 21. No other organization, whether it be religious, fraternal or educational, has any right to offer moral or religious instruction or other benefits concerning the Bible, and any such activities that are so professed among men are competitors of the institution for which Christ gave his blood.

Verse 16. *Without controversy* denotes something concerning which no one would express any doubt. That which is so evident that all must admit it, is the truth about to be stated, namely, *great is the mystery of godliness*. The last word means the system of faith given to the world through Christ, to take the place of the Patriarchal and Jewish religions. It is called a mystery because it was not revealed to mankind for many centuries, even though God had it planned in his mind. *God was manifest in the flesh*. We should bear in mind that the word *God* is a family name, and that each member of the Deity or Godhead is entitled to the name. Hence the present passage means God the Son, for he it was who was on the earth in the flesh. He is called "God" in Acts 20: 28 where Paul is talking to the elders of the Ephesian church. Before coming into the world He was called the Word (John 1: 1), and verse 14 of that chapter says "the Word was made flesh and dwelt among us," which is the same declaration that is made by our present verse. *Justified in the Spirit*. To justify one means to declare and prove him to be what he claims to be, and to disprove all false accusations that may be made against him. Jesus claimed to be the Son of God, and his enemies accused him of being an imposter and put him to death. But the Spirit enabled Him to be raised from the dead (Romans 8: 11), and that fact proved he was the Son of God (Romans 1: 4), which is what he claimed to be, and hence He was *justified* as our verse says. *Seen of angels* (Matthew 4: 11; 28: 2; Mark 16: 5; Luke 22: 43). This is very significant considering the importance of angels as agents of God in serving those who are heirs of salvation (Hebrews 1: 14). *Preached unto the Gentiles*. This was not true of the system that had been used under the law of Moses. It was restricted to the Jews while Jesus was offered to all mankind. Had no one believed the Gospel, it would not have been perpetuated after the death of the apostles, for no others were inspired to preach it to the people of the world. *Received up into glory*. This was done when he ascended from the earth to go back to his Father (Luke 24: 51; Acts 1: 9). The ascension of Jesus is predicted in Psalms 24: 7-10. In view of these wonderful facts about the story of Christ, it is no wonder the apostle says it is great and above all doubt as to its reality.

1 Timothy 4

Verse 1. *Speaketh expressly* means to speak in express or exact words. This is what is known as verbal inspiration, where the Spirit gives the apostle or other hearer the message in the exact words to be received and communicated to others. That is not the usual method of inspiration, but instead, the Spirit reveals the truth on the subject being considered, but leaves it to the one being inspired to use his own words in handing the message over to others. This accounts for the fact that the various writers can be distinguished from each other by their own peculiar manner of speech; such as that of Paul or Peter or John, etc. But since the Spirit supervises the whole revelation, it assures us that the writings of all these men are inspired and hence what they say is divine truth. *Latter times* represents an indefinite date, only that it is in the future from the time the apostle is writing. *Depart from the faith* denotes a foresaking of the true faith in Christ as it is revealed in the Gospel. While the original Greek word is not the same as that used in 2 Thessalonians 2 regarding the apostasy, the meaning is the same. It is a prediction of the false doctrine of Rome, that came out from those headquarters after the "man of sin" (2 Thessalonians 2: 3) came into being in his full power. *Seducing spirits* refers to the deceiving men who pretend to speak by inspiration, such as the clergy of the church of Rome. *Doctrines of devils.* The last word means demons, spirits in the intermediate state, which is usually translated by the word "devil." The Romish church makes great claim of having communications with beings in the unseen realm, and the doctrines (or teaching) that were claimed to have come from the intermediate state were put out by Rome as of great significance, and were believed by the disciples of the "man of sin."

Verse 2. *Speaking lies in hypocrisy.* The last word is from HUPOKRISIS, and its primary definition in Thayer's lexicon is, "the acting of a stage-player." When a person goes on the stage to act the part of a certain character, he and everyone else knows he is not really that person—that he is only acting. The word has been appropriated by composers of moral speech to mean a man who pretends to be what he knows he is not. The speakers of Rome, then, know they are expressing lies when they put forth their false doctrine. The question arises, why will these teachers express what they know to be false? The answer is in the rest of the verse, namely, their conscience has been *seared with a hot iron.* This is figurative, as we understand, but is used because when a part of one's body has been seared over, it becomes dull to pain, so that it will not even flinch from a contact that would at other times cause much resistance. At this point I insist that the reader see the comments at 2 Thessalonians 2: 11.

Verse 3. *Forbidding to marry.* This is a specific prediction of the doctrine of Rome, for no one of the clergy of that institution, from the pope down to the ordinary priest is permitted to marry. It makes no difference to them that Paul declares that "marriage is honorable in all" (Hebrews 13: 4). The edict of the "man of sin" is of more weight to them than a declaration of an apostle. *Abstain from meats.* The last word may include anything that is used as food, but in this passage it refers to the flesh of animals. Even in our day the members of the church of Rome are told not to eat the flesh of animals on any Friday. They make an exception by permitting the use of fish on that day. Their inconsistency is proved by Paul's statement in 1 Corinthians 15: 39, that the bodies of fishes is flesh also. This is another one of their "lies in hypocrisy." Paul declares that every creature that God made is good for food, and is so regarded by them which *believe and know the truth.* This gives us the conclusion that the devotees of Rome do not believe the truth.

Verse 4. Paul is not posing as an authority on diet, or presuming to decide on what might be liked or disliked as an article of food. He means there is nothing that is wrong from a religious standpoint. There were certain things forbidden by the law of Moses, but that system as a religious course of conduct, was taken away by the Gospel and therefore no one has the right to impose restrictions on the people of God concerning what they may eat. (See Colossians 2: 16.) The privilege of eating the various articles of food is on condition that they be received with thanksgiving. It is an obligation upon all disciples to give thanks for their food (Ephesians 5: 20; Colossians 3: 17). The writer has been in homes of disciples where the practice of offering thanks for food was evidently not done. This was indicated by the embarrassment manifested by the host in requesting the guest to "please ask a blessing."

Verse 5. To be *sanctified* means to be set apart or devoted to a righteous use. The word of God says it is right to use these creatures as food, and the thanksgiving prayer gives the disciple a right to eat it; the two factors thus sanctify the food.

1 Timothy 4: 6-12

Verse 6. Brethren need to be told over and over again the things they have known as the truth (Hebrews 2: 1; Peter 3: 1). Timothy was an evangelist and would be in various places to work with the Gospel. The present verse states a qualification that would make him a *good minister*. That term is not a title as the present day usage of religious language would express it. The word *minister* is not used in any place in the New Testament as a special class of public speakers. It comes from the same Greek word as servant, and may apply to any member of the church. Paul shows that doing one's duty toward his brethren, in reminding them of their obligations, will constitute him a good minister (servant) of Jesus Christ. Being equipped with the wisdom of the world does not constitute one a good minister, although such seems to be what is demanded by the popular notions of the day. Instead, being *nourished up* (informed) in the words of faith which constitutes *good doctrine*, will equip him for acceptable service to the Lord. *Whereunto thou hast attained.* This denotes that Timothy was not lacking in these qualities, and other passages indicates the same accomplishments in him (1 Timothy 1: 18, 19; 2 Timothy 1: 5; Acts 16: 1, 2). But Timothy was no exception to the rule that servants of Christ need to be reminded of their obligation to Him.

Verse 7. *Profane* means something that is common or worldly; heathenish and useless. *Old wives* fables refers to myths originating with foolish old women who have no substantial basis for their shallow stories. Timothy had no time to waste on such useless subjects. The kind of exercise worthy his attention was godliness or piety.

Verse 8. *Bodily exercise* refers to the gymnastics or training that the Greeks and other ancient nations practiced, in order to get themselves prepared for the combat in national games. *Profiteth little.* Those performances brought some advantages of a temporal nature, but the benefits were small and did not last very long. The exercise that counts most is of a spiritual kind, consisting of a godly or pious mode of conduct. Such training did not restrict its benefits to this life, although it included that in the highest sense. That is, such a life helped the body to have a healthy condition, which has many advantages even in this world. But that kind of training prepared one to win in the combat against evil in the world, and also developed a character that will be acceptable to the Lord in the life to come. The man who performs bodily training only, gets nothing out of it but a victory over another like contestant, with nothing to look forward to after this life ends.

Verse 9. *Faithful saying* means that what Paul has been saying is true, and hence is worthy of being fully accepted. Of course, if a man does accept it wholeheartedly, he will regulate his life accordingly, and prepare himself for the greatest possible usefulness in this world, and for eternal happiness in the world to come.

Verse 10. Paul's confidence in the principles that he had just expressed, induced him to labor (spiritual exercise or gymnastics of the inner man), even though it would bring reproach upon him from the enemies of righteousness. The apostle was so certain of the promises of the living God, that he looked upon the mistreatment coming from the enemies as a "light affliction," and that as a result it would work for him " a far more exceeding and eternal weight of glory" (2 Corinthians 4: 17). *Saviour of all men, especially,* etc. If one man is saved at all, how could another be *especially saved?* The idea involves the sense in which *all men* are saved, which is that God provided salvation for the whole world (John 3: 16), but only those who believe (and obey) will actually get the benefit of the plan; in that sense they will be *especially* saved.

Verse 11. *Command* and *teach.* Not being an inspired man, Timothy could not speak with authority. However, he could deliver the communications as the express commands of the apostle, then explain their meaning and urge their observance.

Verse 12. Moffat translates the first clause, "Let no one slight you because you are a youth." Timothy could avoid being belittled (the meaning of despise) or his teaching underestimated by proper conduct. Otherwise it might be said that he was but a youth, and it would not be necessary to take him very seriously. When he would insist on others leading a life of devotion and self-denial, they would be convinced he was in earnest if he led the way by an example in his own life. *In word.* His speech should be pure and respectful towards God and man. *Conversation* means conduct or manner of life. *Charity* means a sincere interest in the welfare of others. *In spirit.* By the proper kind of conduct, Timothy would show that he was mindful of the teaching of the Spirit; that his own spirit was being regulated by the influence of the Spirit of Christ. *In faith.* His manner of life should be such as that of one who believed from the heart in the Saviour he professed to serve. *Purity de*notes a life unmixed with the evils of people in the world who care not for the Lord.

Verse 13. *Till I come* is a repetition of Paul's expressed purpose, which he stated in chapter 3: 14 . Timothy was not an inspired man, and hence needed to obtain his instructions by hearing another or by reading what was written for him. Likewise, when he preached to others, he had to give them what had been written in the law of Moses or by the apostles. Furthermore, he needed to make a personal examination of all such reading matter, so that he could make the proper application to others. (See 2 Timothy 2: 15.) To exhort another means to insist on his doing what he has learned to be his duty. Teaching includes the impartation of truths hitherto not known, and/or the explanation of those truths after having been communicated to others.

Verse 14. *Given thee by prophecy.* This refers to the prediction of those achievements which one set to teach the Gospel wil accomplish for the kingdom of Christ. The prediction was made by those having the gift of prophecy, at the time hands were laid on Timothy and he was about to be sent forth. We do not know just what the gift was, but we do know that it was not the gift of inspiration as that term is usually taken, for such a gift could not be *neglected,* which Timothy was told not to do. (See the comments at chapter 1: 18.) *Presbytery* means the group of elders over the congregation. Acts 8: 14-18 shows us that it required the hands of an apostle to confer the spiritual gifts. However, when such a performance was to take place in a locality where there were elders, it was fitting that it be done in conjunction with them, in respect for the dignity of their office. In such a circumstance, the laying on of the elders' hands would only be a formality to show their approval, in much the same spirit that the "right hands of fellowship" were given to Paul and Barnabas in Galatians 2: 9.

Verse 15. Thayer defines *meditate,* "to care for, attend to carefully, practice." The definition agrees with the rest of the verse, for it emphasizes the thought by the instruction to *give thyself wholly to them,* which is to result further in his improvement as a teacher. *Profiting* refers to the good fruit that would be borne of his meditation, and it would be so practical that all people could see it.

Verse 16. This verse sets forth an idea that is couched in a familiar saying, namely, "practice what you preach." Timothy was to take heed unto himslf (his practice) and unto the doctrine or teaching (that which was preached). This sort of conduct was not to be observed occasionally only, but he was to *continue in them.* This kind of life would benefit two groups; himself and his hearers. That is because such a life would be carrying out the conditions on which a man may be saved, and it would be convincing to the hearers of the righteousness of the doctrine, to the end they would also accept it and be saved.

1 Timothy 5

Verse 1. The word *rebuke* occurs twice in this chapter, but they are from Greek words with very different meanings, so that no real disagreement exists between them. In this verse it is from EPIPLESSO and Thayer defines it, "to chastise with words, to chide, upbraid, rebuke." The word *elder* is always from the same Greek word, but it does not always mean an official elder; it may even refer to a woman, as it does in the next verse. The connection will have to be considered each time in discovering which sense of the word is to be applied. Since Paul mentions both men and women, and those of different ages, we know he means the older men, and that it would not be right for a young evangelist to chide an older man. That does not mean he should overlook what he conscientiously believes is wrong in the life of older men. No, he may show his disapproval, but should do it with such language as is befitting a young man when entreating an older one. On the same principle he should show an attitude toward the younger men that recognizes their equality in years.

Verse 2. The elder women were to be given the consideration proper for their age, on the same principle as that expressed for the elder men in the preceding verse. Timothy was a young man, hence it was especially appropriate to mention the subject of *purity* or chastity in his conduct toward the younger women in the congregation.

Verse 3. It would not be right to show dishonor to anyone of any age or either sex, to use the word in its ordinary sense, hence the term is used with some special meaning in this passage. The verses following through 16 indicate the meaning of it as Paul uses it, namely, to give them the honor of being supported out of the funds of the church. (See Acts 6: 1, 2.) The bestowal of temporal needs is spoken of as an "honor" in Acts 28: 10, and it has that meaning in our verse. Some commentators say that the widows were appointed by the church to teach the younger women in the principles of the Christian faith, and were given this financial support to care for them as they discharged their work. I am not in possession of the history on this matter, but am not disposed to doubt it. We may be certain that Paul is not writing of incidental misfortune or distress that is to be cared for, because the scripture teaches that any person in distress, whether young or old, and whether women or men or whatever their social situation, if necessity calls for it, the church must come to their relief. But in such cases there would not be required such a train of qualifications as is described in this chapter. But to place a widow in the permanent appointment as teacher of other women, to be supported out of the funds of the church, would call for these items as to her worthiness as a teacher, and the genuineness of her personal needs. *Widows indeed*, then, means those who are actually unable to furnish their own living while giving their time to this ministry of teaching. Moffat renders this verse as follows: "Widows in real need must be supported from the funds."

Verse 4. The original word for *nephews* includes descendants in general, so that the phrase *children or nephews* means children or other descendants. *Let them learn first* denotes that these descendants should learn that the duty of supporting the widows is first upon their shoulders. *Show piety* means to manifest proper respect concerning their rightful obligation toward the *parents*, which means near ancestors. To *requite* denotes the performance of that service that is needed for these relatives. Such service is what God desires and hence it will be acceptable to Him.

Verse 5. *Widows indeed* is the same as in verse 3 as to her actual condition of need, but her worthiness to receive it is also considered in this verse. She is *desolate* because her husband is dead and she is lonely. However, if she is a worthy disciple and puts her trust in God, she will spend her time in prayer to God, and not in the frivolous pleasures of the world. It would certainly be a good work to lift the burden of her living needs from her, and give her the valuable employment of teaching the young women. This would not only relieve her of the strain of temporal necessities, but it would give her the spiritual joy of associating with her younger sisters, as well as be a benediction to them.

Verse 6. This verse is a specific instance of one's being dead and alive at the same time. It means she is living in sin and hence is alive to pleasure. But that knid of life separates her from the favor of God which causes her to be "dead in trespasses and sins" (Ephesians 2: 1).

Verse 7. *Give in charge* means to insist gravely upon the rules described, lest the cause of Christ be blamed for corruptions in the membership.

Verse 8. *His own, and especially*, etc. A man might have a widowed mother or sister or aunt, living alone and desolate; or they might be residing within the group that he calls his own household. In either case it is his duty to see that their needs are taken care of so that the church will not be charged. *Denied the faith*. The faith is the system of righteousness under Christ, a part of the obligations of which is to care for the worthy poor. To refuse doing this duty is equivalent to backsliding from the religion he professes to practice. *Worse than an infidel* because this man makes no profession of believing in the teaching of Jesus, and hence is not committing any inconsistency when he refuses to observe these obligations in his conduct of life.

Verse 9. *Taken into the number* means to be placed with the widows who were to be supported out of the funds of the church. *Under threescore years old*. These widows were to be placed on the permanent list of dependents of the church. It was supposed that they were lonely and in the declining years of life. Some line needed to be drawn to show when they had reached that period, and no mere human judgment could have been certain when that was. Hence the apostle, writing by inspiration, directed it to be set at this age. *Having been the wife of one man.* In the case of an elder (chapter 3: 2), it was shown that the verb "be" was used purely in the present tense, and that the requirement was merely to show he must be a married man at the time of his appointment. There is an apparent similarity in the language of the case of widows, yet the circumstances are different. A person can be a man without being married, while one cannot be a widow who has not been married. Hence the requirement in this case means to restrict the number of times she has been married, which is once. The Lord did not limit the number of times a woman might be married (if lawfully; 1 Corinthians 7: 39), hence the restriction in this case was not because of moral considerations. The matter was one of inspired judgment, very much on the same principle as the age limit. If a widow was sixty years old and had been satisfied with one marriage, it would indicate a control over her nature that is not the most usual. Such a person, coupled with the list of good points in life to be mentioned next, would be a "safe risk" to be put on the permanent support and employment of the church.

Verse 10. *Well reported of for good works.* It should be noted that this verse begins and ends with a general statement of good works. It indicates that the items in the body of the verse are classed as good works and not ordinances for the public services of the church. To be well reported of means she has been so generally engaged in doing various good deeds that it has gained her a favorable reputation among the people where she has lived. *Brought up children.* These may have been her own and also any others who were in need of home care. It was never the Lord's plan for children to be reared in human organizations, but they should be given the influences and joys of the family life. (See Psalms 68: 6.) When orphans are kept out of family homes and herded as groups in human institutions, they are deprived of the training that can be given only in a private home. Hence when this widow has performed such a service for children, she has done a good work and done it in the Lord's way. *Lodged strangers.* In the days before she was needy and lonely, she bestowed hospitality upon the wayfarer, including disciples who might have been fleeing from persecution. (See Hebrews 13: 1.) Now she is unable to perform such services, but must herself have her needs provided by others. *Washed the saints' feet.* This was another good work and not a church ceremonial performance. The subject of feetwashing is treated in detail at John 13: 5, in the first volume of the New Testament Commentary. *Relieved the afflicted.* This could be done by nursing the sick, or by extending comfort and sympathy to those in sorrow, etc. *Diligently followed.* She did not merely perform these good works incidentally or half-heartedly, but gave her best attention to all opportunities for doing good. Now that her age and financial circumstances make it impossible to continue such services, she is entitled to be cared for by the church, if she has no relatives who can do so for her.

Verse 11. *Younger widows refuse* means not to take them into the list of those who are to be supported by the funds of the church. *Begun to wax wanton* is all from KATASTRENIAO, which Thayer defines, "to feel the impulses of sexual desire." *They will marry.* This phrase if taken by itself would not state any sin, for it is the Lord's own plan for the lawful gratification of the desire (1 Corinthians 7: 2). But in the case of these women, they would have been rceived among those who were supposed to be past the ordinary age when marriage would be thought of, and were lonely and ready to give their entire attention to the work of the Lord and dependent on the church.

Verse 12. *Having damnation* denotes they are worthy of being condemned. *Cast off their first faith* means they have reversed their former claim of being alone, and ready to be devoted exclusively to the work of the Lord; they have gone contrary to the claim.

Verse 13. It would be a natural outcome for such women who had lost their spirit of devotion, but who were still on the financial support of the church, to cease their activities on behalf of the disciples. Such persons would not be quiet on account of their restless emotions, and would become what are familiarly called gadabouts. Neither might such characters be expected to have much care about their conversation, for they would naturally see things to talk about and thus become *tattlers*. Such a person would also not be satisfied merely with talking "out of turn," but Paul says they would become *busybodies*. That is from PERIERGOS which Thayer defines as follows: "Busy about trifles and neglectful of important matters, especially busy about other folks' affairs, a busybody."

Verve 14. There is no word in the Greek at this verse for *women*, but there is in verse 11 where the translators give us "widows" for the word CHERA, where we know the apostle is speaking of the same class of persons. Hence we should conclude that in the present verse, Paul means to say for the younger widows to marry, bear children, etc. The restrictions for widows who may be taken into the number of dependents of the church, clearly describe one who is past the childbearing age. Hence it is consistent that the ones "refused" are expected to be still able to bear children, and the apostle commands them to marry and do so. In so doing they will not only be cured of the frivolous habits described in the preceding verse, but will be doing one of the conditions on which women may be saved. Since childbearing is a condition of salvation for women in general (chapter 2: 15), there is no disagreement with that for Paul to make special references to young widows in this verse. His occasion for doing so is the fact that he has been writing on the subject of widows in relation to the funds of the church. *Guide the house*. We know the Bible does not contradict itself, and it teaches that the husband is to have rule over his wife and the household (1 Corinthians 11: 3; Ephesians 5: 22; 1 Timothy 3: 4, 12). The apostle's meaning, then, is that a wife should take charge of the work of her home, exercising discipline over her children and thus being a good homemaker (Titus 2: 5), and doing all this subject to the authority of her husband. Such a life will not give the adversaries, enemies of the cause of Christ, any excuse for reproaching her manner of life. Vicious critics may wag their tongues in slanderous remarks in spite of the godly life of such a "mother in Israel," but let it not be truthfully said she gave them room for it.

Verse 15. *Some* necessarily refers to widows who had unfortunately been employed by the church, and had proved the very things Paul warns against in verse 11. When their fleshly desires became active, they forsook the consecrated work they had espoused, and broke out into the disorderly conduct, proving the mistake that was made by taking in the younger widows. Since Satan is the sponsor of all evil, this backsliding of the young widows is attributed to that great enemy of righteousness.

Verse 16. This verse is virtually a repetition of verses 3 and 8. It concludes Paul's teaching in this chapter about widows.

Verse 17. *Elders* are the same rulers who are called bishops in other places. The meaning of the three names applied to the rulers over the churches of Christ is explained in detail by "general remarks" before 2 Thessalonians 2. *Rule well* denotes a lead or management of the flock that is very efficient. *Double honor*. The first word is from DIPLOOS, and both Thayer and Robinson define it, "twofold, double," and the latter also explains it. "put for any greater relative amount." Then it is not a precise mathematical figure, such as saying that two is double of one, etc. *Especially* designates one item that entitles this elder to the double honor, and the argument in verse 18 clearly shows that financial support is included in the honor. This is not the only place where temporal support or favors is referred to as an honor. (See the comments at verse 3.) *Labor in word and doctrine*. This cannot mean merely that they are teachers over the flock, for chapter 3: 2 shows that all of the elders must do that. Hence the phrase is bound to mean those elders who give their whole time to "the ministry of the word" (Acts 6: 4); the next verse confirms this conclusion.

Verse 18. In immediate connection with the preceding instruction about double honor for certain elders, Paul here cites an Old Testament scripture pertaining to the reward of a laborer. Furthermore, in 1 Corinthians 9: 1-14 the apostle refers to the same passage, then applies it to temporal support for those who preach the Gospel. Hence our verse (together with the preceding one) means that if an elder devotes his entire time to his work as ruler and in teaching the word, he should be "honored" by being financially supported by the funds of the church.

Verse 19. The eldership is very important, and because of its public character of rulership, bringing it into contact with all classes of persons, it is exposed to the suspicions and little jealousies of those who might desire to injure the good name of the men in office. On the other hand, these officials are human and might fall a victim to their own unrighteous ambitions. (See Acts 20: 30.) As a safeguard, then, both to the eldership and the congregation, Paul directs that at least two witnesses be available before the evangelist may *receive* (which means to consider) an accusation against an elder. The word *before* is from the Greek word EPI, which occurs several hundred times in the New Testament, and Thayer uses five pages of his lexicon in defining the word. Among its many renderings in the King James Version, I shall list some as follows: Before 14 times, in 51, on 71, upon 158. It is clear that whether we render the word by "before" or by "upon," the thought is that unless there are at least two witnesses to support an accusation against an elder, the evangelist must not act in the matter.

Verse 20. *Them that sin* is often made to apply to the congregation in general. There is teaching elsewhere that indicates the necessity for every person who sins (publicly) to be exposed publicly. But the whole connection in this passage shows Paul means the elders who have been accused to the evangelist and found guilty. *Rebuke* is the same English word as the one in the first verse, but comes from an entirely different original. It is from ELEGCHO, and I will quote Thayer's entire definition (the words in italics), including that for our verse and several other passages: "To convict, refute, confute; by conviction to bring to light, to expose; to find fault with, correct; to reprehend severely, chide, admonish, reprove; to call to account, show one his fault; to chasten, punish." From the various shades of meaning in the word at hand, it is evident that the evangelist in charge is to hear the testimony of the two or more witnesses. If he believes the accusation is true, he should so state it in the hearing of the congregation. What final disposition he makes of the case will depend on the reaction of the elder to the public rebuke. If he refuses to make the adjustment, then he must be "punished" (one part of the definition of the original word) by removal from office, which will conclude the official work of the evangelist in the case. The reason this is to be done before all is *that others also may fear*. They would be impressed with the seriousness of public exposure of sin, and thereby be induced to watch their own conduct.

Verse 21. *I charge thee before God*, etc. Timothy was to realize the seriousness of the charge by knowing that Paul was not the only one who was concerned in the matter, and that others would be witnesses of the way he conducted the duties of his work as an evangelist in charge. *Elect angels*. The first word is from EKLEKTOS, and Thayer's general definition is, "picked out, chosen." He offers the following explanation of the phrase in connection with this verse: "Those whom God has chosen out from other created beings to be peculiarly associated with him, and his highest ministers in governing the universe." (See Hebrews 1: 13, 14.) *Doing nothing by partiality*. There might be a temptation to prefer one person or perform one act instead of another under pressure of prejudice. Timothy is charged to be fair and execute his duties unpleasant though they may be, "without fear or favor," regardless of who may be involved in any case coming up.

Verse 22. *Lay hands* could not refer to the laying on of hands literally for the purpose of conferring a spiritual gift; that required the hands of an apostle (Acts 8: 14-18; 19: 5, 6). The rest of the verse, which is the opposite of laying hands *suddenly*, indicates the meaning of the phrase. Paul had just dealt with the disciplining of elders, hence this verse means for Timothy not to be hasty in laying hands of discipline on any man. Neither should he be indifferent or unduly tardy in handling the charge, for that would encourage such a man in his wrong, and the evangelist would thereby become a *partaker of other men's sins*. By avoiding both extremes, Timothy would *keep himself pure* as regards the evil at hand.

Verse 23. Travelers through the territory of Ephesus testify to the unwholesomeness of drinking water available there. And this verse directly mentions that Timothy had oft-recurring infirmities, involving a condition of his stomach. It is generally known that wine is a good tonic in ailments of the stomach, satisfying both to the demands of thirst, and soothing to the delicate tissues of this digestive organ. But the amount of wine necessary for such medical and nourishing purposes would not meet the craving of one who wished to drink it as a beverage. Hence Paul tells him to *use a little wine*, on the same principle he requires elders and deacons to be "not given to much wine" (chapter 3: 3, 8; Titus 1: 7). Some commentators think this verse is misplaced as to its appearance in the epistle here, since it seems to be an abrupt change of subject. But the evangelist was working under difficult and trying tasks, and it was especially necessary, therefore, for him to take the best care of his body and conserve his strength for the responsibility.

Verse 24. The Englishman's Greek New Testament renders the first clause, "The sins of some men are manifest" [are plainly seen]. *Judgment* is from KRISIS which Thayer defines, "opinion or decision given concerning anything." *Going before* denotes that people can form their judgment as to whether the man's conduct is right or wrong before much time passes. *Some men they follow after.* Their sins are so unapparent that people will not realize the man's real character for a long time after he has committed them; sometimes not until after he is dead.

Verse 25. This verse has the same meaning as the preceding one, except that it is about the actions of good men instead of evil. A righteous man's good deeds are not always realized at first, but they will become known finally; they cannot always be hid. The truths of these two verses show why an evangelist should not be too hasty in forming his verdict concerning an accused elder.

1 Timothy 6

Verse 1. A great portion of the people in the Roman Empire were slaves when the Gospel was brought into the world. Neither Christ nor his apostles tried to interfere with the status of master and slave, but only to regulate the proper conduct of each to the other. The salvation through Christ was offered to slaves as well as to masters, and this verse is addressed to the slaves who had accepted it. *Yoke* is used figuratively, and Robinson says the word means "an emblem of servitude." Some slaves might think more highly of themselves than they should on account of having been given the privilege of becoming Christians. Such conduct would be blamed by their masters on the name and doctrine (teaching) of God, which would cause them to blaspheme (speak evil) of the divine cause. On the other hand, since the Lord requires servants to obey their masters, if they are careful to manifest all the more respect for them after becoming Christians, it will speak well for the religion which their servants have embraced, and possibly might even induce them to become Christians also, being thereby convinced that the faith which the servants have espoused is bound to be desirable, seeing it has improved the service and disposition of their slaves.

Verse 2. Masters sometimes were among those who became Christians. A slave might think that when his master became a believer, that he (the master) would not be as particular about requiring good service of his slaves, and so he would become indifferent about his duties and services. Instead, the servant was not to *despise* (belittle or think lightly of) his master, but must recognize him in even a higher relationship, that of a brother. *Partakers of the benefit.* Master and slave alike, after becoming Christians, become partakers of the benefit of the improved service of the Christian slave. *Teach and exhort.* This is a significant phrase as the words are arranged. To exhort means to insist that one perform his known duty. It was in order, then, to insist on the brethren that they do their duty, after being taught what it was.

Verse 3. *Teach otherwise* means to teach contrary to that stated in the preceding two verses. Naturally, if a man was disposed to go contrary to this teaching of the apostle, it would be because he did not want to agree with *wholesome* (spiritually sound or healthy) words. *Even the words of our Lord Jesus Christ.* The man being described would be opposed to this apostolic teaching, notwithstanding it was the doctrine of Christ. It also was *according to godliness*, yet this contrary man would reject such holy doctrine.

Verse 4. *He is proud* means he is conceited and puffed up over his pretended learning, when in truth he knows nothing of any account. *Doting* is from NOSEO and defined by Thayer, "to be sick"; it is similar to the English word "nausea." The word is used in a figurative sense, and means about the same as when we speak of some person acting like a man in his dotage. The object of this man's dotage is his extreme love of strife over unimportant words. Not only is such a contention fruitless of any good, but it produces a number of harmful results which the apostle names. *Envy* is the spirit that begrudges another his prosperity or other success. *Strife* is a contention for the sake of being different from another. *Railings* consist of severe and unjust expressions against others, and such expressions as would not be justified even against a person in wrong. (See Jude 9.) *Evil surmisings* means evil suspicions about the character of another, without any evidence to support them. A self-conceited person might be expected to be guilty of such thoughts against those whose sound teaching he did not like.

Verse 5. *Perverse disputings* is defined by Thayer, "Useless occupation, empty business, misemployment," and Robinson defines it in virtually the same language. *Men of corrupt minds* would very naturally come under such a description as the foregoing. *Destitute of the truth* denotes a mind that never has any truth for its wild outbursts such as the apostle has been describing. *Supposing that gain is godliness.* These people evidently came into the church for the personal advantage they thought it would be to them. They reasoned that if a person obtained some gain after professing an interest in religion, that would prove that such gain was to be considered as a part of godliness or piety. Such characters are not worthy the association of righteous men, therefore Timothy was told to withdraw himself from them.

Verse 6. Paul reverses the foolish notions of the vain characters he has been describing. Instead of temporal gain being the object of godliness, true gain is godliness itself, if a person is contented with it, for it is a form of wealth that will not pass away when this world comes to an end.

Verse 7. In this verse Paul enlarges on the thought of the preceding one, and shows why godliness is real gain while the temporal wealth of this world is not. *We brought nothing into this world.* This is expressed by Job, chapter 1: 21 as follows: "Naked came I out of my mother's womb, and naked shall I return thither," and David says in Psalms 49: 17, "For when he dieth he shall carry nothing away." All of this shows the folly of making material things of the world the chief interest in life.

Verse 8. Food meets the internal needs of the body, and raiment the external. These facts have originated the familiar phrase *food and raiment*, used not only in this verse, but it is one of almost universal use, and is really meant to cover all of the actual temporal needs of this life. (See Genesis 28: 20.) *Let us be therewith content.* Not that we should limit our secular activities to what is absolutely necessary at the moment, for such a conclusion would contradict other statements of the New Testament (Acts 20: 35; Ephesians 4: 28). But while we are doing what we can to obtain the good things of this life, let us be thankful for what we have, even though we may not be as successful as some others.

Verse 9. *Will be rich* is not a mere statement of a fact that is to come to pass, meaning that someone is going to be rich, but it is a stronger term. It means those who eagerly intend to become rich and who exert themselves to that end. There is no sin in the simple fact that one is rich, for Joseph of Arimathea was a rich man and a disciple of Jesus, yet he is never referred to in any unfavorable light (Matthew 27: 57-60; Mark 15: 43-47; Luke 23: 50, 51; John 19: 38). In verses 17-19 of our present chapter, the rich are not told that their wealth is an evil, but only that they must not trust in it and that they should make the proper use of it. It is not a question of how rich a man is, but how did he obtain his wealth and how is he using it? If he obtained it by his own determination, urged by an eager desire to be rich, he will be tempted to engage in wrongful conduct that will *snare* him in sin. *Hurtful lusts* means foolish desires that are injurious to one's moral and spiritual character. *Drown* is used figuratively because a drowning man is one who is sinking into the water until he is overwhelmed and finally dies. These evil practices of the man so eager to become rich will cause him to be overwhelmed by them until his soul will meet *destruction of perdition*, which means eternal condemnation.

Verse 10. This verse is similar to the preceding one (which the reader

1 Timothy 6: 11-14

should again see in connection with the present one). *Love of money* corresponds with "will be rich" in the other verse. And again, the love of money is where the sin comes in, not the mere possession of it. A man might have that love and yet never become rich because he is not a "financial success." But the "eager desire" is there, and that is what leads him into sin. By the same token, a man might possess money without having the *love* of it in the unfavorable sense used in this verse. (See again the case of Joseph in the preceding verse.) *The root of all evil.* The Englishman's Greek New Testament renders this phrase, "a root of all evils," and Thayer renders *all evil*, "all kinds of evil." These renderings are correct from the very truth of the case. Love of money is not *the* root because there are many other motives for doing evil. On the other hand, there is no kind of evil that cannot be induced by the love of money, as well as by other unrighteous motives. The latter half of this verse is virtually the same in thought as that in the preceding verse; to *err from the faith* will bring to a guilty man the sorrow of perdition.

Verse 11. *Man of God* is in the possessive case, denoting that Timothy belonged to God. However, that is true of all true disciples (1 Corinthians 6: 19, 20), hence it is not a title that applies to Timothy only. Furthermore, the same phrase is used in 2 Timothy 3: 17, where Paul is writing of those who are completely furnished by the inspired word unto all good works, and we know that is true of all servants of God. It is true also that Timothy had some special duties to perform, that were peculiar to his place in the great system of the kingdom, but that also is true of various disciples. So it leaves all as men of God, seeing they belong to Him and are doing his service. *Flee these things* means more than a mere negative attitude towards evil; it means to abhor it and lose no time or effort in getting away from it. (See Romans 12: 9; James 4: 7.) Fleeing away from evil denotes only the proper attitude towards it. The man of God must also follow the proper course that is opposite the evil. *Righteousness* and *godliness* are really the same in effect. They mean to do that which is right when measured by the law of God. *Faith* requires that one not only profess a belief in the word of God, but also to be faithful in keeping its precepts. *Love* is from a word here that denotes a sincere interest in the welfare of others. *Patience* is another word for endurance or steadfastness in service to the Lord. *Meekness* signifies a spirit of humility in all of one's activities for God.

Verse 12. It is a *good fight* because it is on behalf of a good cause and against an evil one (2 Corinthians 10: 3-5; Ephesians 6: 10-12). It is the *fight of faith* because the Christian soldier does not fight according to his own strategy, but goes on into battle because of his faith in the great Commander, who will not fail to obtain final victory. The soldier of the cross is not fighting to gain any temporal property or worldly possessions, but is expecting to win the crown of *eternal life*. Timothy, like all other warriors in the Lord's army, was called to enlist voluntarily in the army, for there are no draftees in this conflict. When a man goes into the army of his country, he is expected to declare allegiance to that country and help to defend it against the enemy. *Hast professed* [confessed] *a good profession* [confession]. Every person wishing to become a soldier of the cross (become a Christian), is required to make a public confession (Matthew 10: 32; Romans 10: 10). *Many witnesses* include whoever were present when Timothy made his confession, also the invisible (to him) witnesses mentioned in the next verse.

Verse 13. These are some of the witnesses referred to in the preceding verse who knew of Timothy's confession of faith. To *quicken* means to give life to anything, and all life originates with God. *Before Pontius Pilate.* The first word is from EPI, which is rendered "in the days of" two times, and "in the time of" once, in other places in the New Testament. Jesus actually made the confession of his divine Sonship in the Sanhedrin (Matthew 26: 63, 64; Mark 14: 61, 62; Luke 22: 70); this was "in the time of" Pilate which would be a more accurate translation. However, Jesus made virtually a like confession directly before Pilate (Matthew 27: 11; Mark 15: 2; Luke 23: 3), hence either translation is correct. An important conclusion upon the argument of Paul is, since Jesus made this good confession and died for it, Timothy should live for Him for whose sake he had made the same confession.

Verse 14. *Without spot, unrebukeable* means for Timothy to be wholehearted in his obedience to the command of the apostle. *Until the appearing.* Neither Paul nor any other man knew whether Christ would come in the lifetime of Timothy or not. But when a man dies, his record is complete and will remain as it is until Christ comes. Hence to be "faithful until death" is equivalent to being so until He comes. (See Revelation 2: 10.)

Verse 15. *In his times* means the time for Christ to make his second appearance on the earth, the date of which no man knows. *He shall show* denotes that Christ will then display or give evidence of the facts about to be mentioned. God is said to be *blessed* because he is the source of all true blessings or happiness. (James 1: 17.) The word *potentate* means a ruler of great and unusual power. God is here said to be the *only* such ruler, because all other rulers in the universe are subject to Him. There are many *kings* and *lords* among the various intelligent creatures in the universe, but God is the King and Lord above all of them. Jesus is "acting" as potentate now (Matthew 28: 18), but he will give that up to his Father again (1 Corinthians 15: 28), and that is when and how He will *show* that, after all, God is the *only* final and supreme Ruler.

Verse 16. *Who only hath immortality.* This should not be taken to mean that no person but God may ever have immortality, for that would contradict 1 Corinthians 15: 53, 54, where the same Greek word is used, and where Christians are promised immortality at the resurrection. But in their case it will be something bestowed upon them. When anything is bestowed upon a person, someone has to be the giver of it, and that someone can only be an individual who did not have to receive it from another. God is the only being who has that peculiarity. He always was immortal, which means endless existence both past and future, hence a personality incapable of decay in any sense. *Dwelling* is from a word that means to have a permanent and uninterrupted residence. Whether considered figuratively or literally, *light* denotes a condition where nothing is obscured or impure or undesirable in any way. Such a condition is that where God has the *dwelling* just described. *Man* is from ANTHROPOS, and Thayer's primary definition of it is, "a human being, whether male or female." It therefore means man in the natural state since that is the only time that a human being has any sex (Matthew 22: 30; 1 John 3: 2). Being human and mortal is why he cannot even approach unto the infinite light that haloes the Eternal One. Of course when the righteous receive their glorified bodies, they will be able to dwell with God in glory in the glory world. *No man hath seen nor can see* is to be explained in the same way as just described. *Honor and power* will belong to God without end. *Amen* is added by the apostle as an expression of emphasis for the foregoing declarations concerning God.

Verse 17. The rich are not criticized for being rich, nor told they must dispose of their wealth. A man can be rich and at the same time be a good man (Luke 23: 50, 51). The rich were charged not to be highminded (proud) over their possessions, nor to put their trust in them. Jesus taught the same thing on the subject (Mark 10: 24). Riches are called *uncertain* because there are so many things that can happen, often beyond the control of the owner, that can cause them to be lost (Proverbs 23: 4, 5). If a man's trust for the future is based on earthly riches, such a hope will be disappointed if the wealth is lost. The trust that never can bring a disappointment, is that which is based on God, for he is *living* (always), hence the hope that is in Him is bound to be sure. A logical reason for the surety of such a hope is in the fact that all good things come from Him (James 1: 17).

Verse 18. *That they do good.* A rich man can do some good that cannot be accomplished by one who has no wealth. If there were no "capitalists" in the world, very few of the advancements in the industrial department of human endeavor could be made. The command in Genesis 1: 28 for man to subdue the earth would be difficult if not impossible of obeying were it not for men of great capital, hence the popular prejudice against that class of men is not justified. It is significant that the fundamental principle of communism is its cry against "capitalism." Men of wealth are told to be *rich in good works*, and that is supplemented by the words *distribute* and *communicate*. Not that they must give their wealth all away and render themselves without possessions, for that would make it impossible for them to continue in the requirement to be rich in good works. The only thing that men with an abundance of means are required to do in the way of distributing or giving to others is to "give to him that needeth" (Ephesians 4:28). Further than that they are permitted to use their wealth in promoting such "good works" as will be beneficial to mankind in general. Of course if the rich men are Christians, they should use their wealth in advancing the cause of Christ in such situations that require financial support.

Verse 19. If a rich disciple will use his wealth as described in the preceding two verses, he will be "laying up for himself treasures in heaven" (Matthew 6:20), in that by such use of his earthly possessions he will gain the friendship of God and Christ, who will admit him into their home at the judgment (Luke 16:9). Such a preparation for the future is figuratively called a *good foundation*, and it promises an actual reward of *eternal life*.

Verse 20. Timothy had been entrusted with the Gospel, and he is exhorted to *keep* (guard) it by avoiding *profane and vain* (empty and useless) *babblings*. Science is from the same word as "knowledge," hence there is no such thing as false science, but error is often falsely called science.

Verse 21. If a man professes to believe this falsely-called science, it logically will lead him from the faith, which is based on the truth from the Lord.

2 Timothy 1

Verse 1. Paul began his first epistle to Timothy by saying his apostleship was by the commandment of God and Christ. This one begins by saying it is by the will of God; hence a command of God is an expression of His will. In the other he says Christ is our hope, and in this he says it is according to the promise of life in Christ. The general thought in each place is the same as in the other.

Verse 2. *My dearly beloved son.* The last word is from HUIOS, and it is explained in detail at 1 Timothy 1:2. The salutation or good wishes expressed here are virtually repeated in all of Paul's epistles, and are commented upon at 1 Corinthians 1:3.

Verse 3. *Serve from my forefathers* means he had been a servant of God all his life, and that he had served Him according to what they had taught him. *Pure conscience* denotes that Paul had always done what he thought was right. Since we know that he did grievous wrong when he was persecuting Christians, we should understand that it is not enough just to be conscientious, but the conscience must act in harmony with faith which is produced by the word of God. (See Romans 10:17 and 1 Timothy 1:19.) Paul *thanked God* for his favorable remembrance of Timothy, so that he offered daily prayers concerning him.

Verse 4. *Mindful of thy tears* refers to some occasion when they had to separate. Since no definite information is available as to when it was, we must be satisfied with the thought that Timothy had a tender feeling for Paul as his father in the Gospel. The memory of those tears made Paul likewise to have a longing to see again his own "beloved son."

Verse 5. *Unfeigned faith* means one that is sincere and not merely a pretended one. Faith cannot be inherited, but it can be induced by righteous parents or other relatives. Paul attributes the faith of Timothy (at least in part) to the influence of his mother and grandmother. There is a lesson in the case for all parents, to encourage them in training up their children in the way they should go.

Verse 6. Timothy is here told to *stir up the gift*, and in 1 Timothy 4:14 it is "neglect not" the gift. Both phrases mean the same, for if a man stirs up a gift, he certainly will not neglect it. This was not the gift of inspiration, for such a gift could not be stirred up. An inspired man speaks or writes "as the Spirit gives him utterance" (Acts 2:4). This gift, whatever it was, came to Timothy by the laying on of the hands of Paul, with endorsement of elders. (See Comments at 1 Timothy 4:14.)

Verse 7. The word *fear* is from an original here that is always used in a bad sense, meaning "timidity, fearfulness, cowardice."—Thayer. Christians do not need to have such feelings, for God wishes them to be "strong in the Lord and the power of his might" (Ephesians 6:10). The *love* considered in this passage is a sincere desire to do that which will be beneficial for others, even though it might require some unpleasant reproof. Such service would call for good judgment or discretion, which is the meaning of *a sound mind*.

Verse 8. Timothy was still at Ephesus where there had been much encountering with false teachers. Under such conditions it was appropriate that Paul exhort him not to be ashamed to bear *testimony* (declare the evidences in favor of) for Christ. *Nor of me his prisoner.* Paul was in Rome when he wrote this epistle, having been arrested and brought into the jurisdiction of Nero Caesar the second time. Timothy was urged not to be backward about pressing the claims of the Gospel upon the people, even though the great apostle was at the time a prisoner for that very Cause. *His prisoner* means that Paul was being held in chains because of his devotion to Christ. To be a *partaker* denotes that he should be willing to endure similar persecutions for the sake of Christ, and in so doing he would be having fellowship with the apostle. *According to the power of God.* Romans 1: 16 says that the Gospel is the "power" of God unto salvation, and it is from the same Greek word as the one in our verse. Hence a sincere belief in the Gospel will enable one to meet and overcome all persecutions for His sake.

Verse 9. *Who hath saved us* refers to God, because he is the source of all good things, and who arranged this salvation through his Son. *Before the world began.* The Englishman's Greek New Testament renders this phrase, "before the ages of time." Moffatt renders it, "ages ago." The idea could well be expressed by saying that God had the plan of salvation decided upon before anyone else even heard about it. The plan did not predestinate any certain persons to salvation, but God did determine to save all who would accept the *holy calling* when it was given to them. And while all who accept the call on its divine terms will be saved, it will not be on the merit of works performed, for man cannot do anything to "earn" salvation. The whole arrangement is based on the grace (unmerited favor) of God, and made possible through the sacrifice of Christ upon the cross.

Verse 10. The plan of salvation through Christ was not fully revealed to man for ages, even after some of its preliminaries were being arranged with certain special servants (Matthew 13: 17; Ephesians 3: 5; 1 Peter 1: 12). But when Jesus came to the earth he opened up the complete plan, which began with His death and resurrection. These are the facts of the Gospel (1 Corinthians 15: 1-4), and when they occurred, the hope of *life and immortality* was brought to light—was revealed to the world.

Verse 11. After the facts of the Gospel had taken place, they had to be made known to mankind, in order that they might be heard of and believed (Romans 10: 14). For this purpose Paul was appointed as one of the preachers as stated in the passage just cited. But a mere preacher could not spread the good news without being sent with power to speak with inspiration, as Romans 10: 15 declares, hence Paul now states that he was appointed to be an *apostle,* which is defined in the lexicon as, "a delegate, messenger, one sent forth with orders." *Teacher of the Gentiles.* All nations were to be offered the blessings of the Gospel, but Paul was chosen by the Lord to be sent especially to the Gentiles (Acts 9: 15; Ephesians 3: 8; 1 Timothy 2: 7).

Verse 12. *For the which cause I also suffer.* It might seem strange that a man would be persecuted for preaching the good news of salvation. The mere fact of offering salvation was not what brought persecution to Paul, but it was because he claimed that it was obtained through Christ. The Jews were the ones who caused the persecutions, because they had rejected Christ and disliked all men who professed faith in Him. In Acts 4: 2 the Jews did not all object to the preaching of a resurrection (some of them professed to believe in it themselves), but it was because it was being preached "through Jesus." *I am not ashamed.* Paul's confidence amidst persecutions is because of the knowledge he has of Christ in whom he believes. Paul had committed his entire interests of soul and body into the care and keeping of Christ, and he firmly believes that it is all in good hands. *Against* (or until) *that day* means the day of judgment. It is often referred to in such indefinite language because of the unequalled importance of it, for which reason it needs no other specification.

Verse 13. *Form* means pattern or example, and *sound* denotes a condition of good health. The verse means for Timothy to adhere to the pattern of (spiritually) healthy words which he had received from Paul. He was to maintain such a course in *faith* and *love.* He should do so because he believed them and because he had *love* (interest in the welfare of all) in his heart. All of these motives were desirable and possible *in Christ Jesus.*

Verse 14. *That good thing* refers to the "faith" that is mentioned in the preceding verse. Timothy was to *keep* it by *holding fast* to it and exposing any false teaching that might be attempted against it. The Holy Ghost (or Spirit) is in the church or body of Christ, and all faithful members of that body are made strong by the comforting influence of the divine Guest.

Verse 15. Regardless of whether this refers to residents of Asia, or former professed friends of Paul, the significant fact is that he was deserted in the midst of his persecutions for the cause of Christ. Such treatment was to be expected, for Jesus taught his disciples while he was with them that they would be hated for His sake (Matthew 10: 22; 24; 9), and Paul teaches the same thing in chapter 3: 12 of this epistle. Nothing more is known of Phygellus and Hermogenes than is stated here. Paul's specifying them among the large number who had turned against him, indicates that they had been especially active in opposing the apostle's work.

Verse 16. According to Funk and Wagnalls New Standard Bible Dictionary, Onesiphorus was a former resident of Ephesus, but his household only is mentioned directly in this verse, also in chapter 4: 19. This indicates that he was dead at the time this epistle was written, but his memory was to be honored by well-wishing for his family. While he was living he often *refreshed* the apostle. That word is from ANAPSUCHO, which Thayer defines, "to refresh," then he explains it to mean, "one's spirit, by fellowship, consolation, kindnesses." Robinson defines it, "to refresh, to cheer." Such ministrations could be accomplished by either the bestowal of bodily needs, or by words of cheer, or both. *Not ashamed of my chain.* Paul was literally fastened by a chain and was under sentence of death. But Onesiphorus did not let that keep him from showing friendship for the apostle, as some others might do according to Mark 8: 38; being ashamed of a disciple of Christ is counted as being against Him (Matthew 25: 45).

Verse 17. Onesiphorus "proved his faith by his works" in that his interest in Paul was not profession only. He could have contributed material refreshment to him while absent, by sending necessities of life to him. Such a service would not have exposed him to danger for his life or to shame of being a friend to a prisoner in chains, had he been unwilling to suffer any inconvenience to himself. But his interest in and devotion to Paul was more intense than that as we shall see. When he had occasion to be in Rome, he made diligent inquiry until he contacted the apostle, so as to give him the comfort of his presence.

Verse 18. *That day* is commented upon at verse 12. The reward prayed for on behalf of the faithful brother was to be given at the day of judgment. This is especially significant if he was dead at the time of this epistle according to verse 16. Paul refers to some kindnesses that he bestowed upon him while he yet lived and the apostle was at Ephesus, Timothy also being in that city at the same time.

2 Timothy 2

Verse 1. See comments at 1 Timothy 1: 2 for explanation of *son*. Being a pupil of Paul, his teacher was desirous that he do the good work that was entrusted to him (1 Timothy 1: 3, 4). Grace is the unmerited favor of the Lord, but it may be obtained by faithfulness to His cause. Timothy is directed to be strong in that favor, and that can be accomplished by properly handling the inspired truths that His apostle has communicated to his "son."

Verse 2. Timothy was not an inspired man, but had to receive instructions from Paul or others who were inspired. The *witnesses* evidently included those referred to in 1 Timothy 4: 14 and 6: 12. It is true also that the truths about the divinity and authority of Jesus that Paul had declared to Timothy, had been attested by many who could speak from personal knowledge. With such an array of basic support, Timothy should be fully persuaded of their genuineness, and of their right to be transmitted to others. Hence Paul instructs him to commit them to *faithful* or trustworthy men, not to men of ambition for prominence but perhaps lacking in sincere interest. These faithful men thus equipped with the truths coming to them from Paul through Timothy, would be able to teach others in the principles of the Gospel.

Verse 3. A good soldier is one who is willing to endure *hardness* or hardships on behalf of his country. He cannot always be resting in the comfort of his own camp, but must be out on the firing line before the enemy. Likewise the soldier of the cross must face the many persecutions as he battles against the enemies of the Lord.

Verse 4. There are two applications of this verse, a specific and a general one. The former is concerning a person like Timothy who has gone into the special "work of an evangelist" (chapter 4: 5). Such a person must give his entire attention to that work, not being involved in temporal affairs. The latter is applied to all Christians, and pertains to matters that would interfere with the kind of personal conduct a true disciple of Christ should practice. Specifications would be too numerous to mention in this space, but any kind of occupation, whether it is right or wrong of itself, that will prevent a disciple from doing his duty, would constitute the entangling affairs mentioned in this verse.

Verse 5. The apostle takes up another subject for the purpose of illustration, and that is the athletic performances that were popular in those days. *Strive for masteries* is rendered "contend in the games" by the Englishman's Greek New Testament. It is the same exercise mentioned in 1 Corinthians 9: 25 and commented upon in that place. In those games there were certain rules that the contestants were required to observe, and if they did not *strive* according to the rules, they were denied the prize even though they appeared to have outdone their rivals. The lesson is that in the great contest where the crown of eternal life is the goal, no one will receive that prize uness he complies with the rules. Of course those regulations have been laid down by the Lord, and they are recorded in the New Testament (John 12: 48; Matthew 7: 21). As in the case of the temporal contests, no matter how earnestly a professed contestant labors for the prize of salvation, his earnestness will not count unless it is guided by the law of Christ. Such "zeal" will be unavailing because it is "not according to knowledge" of the authorized rules prescribed by the "righteousness of God" (Romans 10: 1-3).

Verse 6. According to the Greek text, the words of this verse should be arranged as follows: "The husbandman must labor before partaking of the fruits." This is both scriptural and logical, for no man can expect to partake of the fruits of the ground, until after he has labored to produce them. Likewise no one may expect to reap eternal life unless he first sows the proper seed for such a harvest (Galatians 6: 7, 8).

Verse 7. The Lord gives things in various ways; sometimes direct and sometimes through the agency of another. In the present case, He will give Timothy understanding of the proper application of his duties by considering what Paul says to him. *Consider* is defined by Thayer, "to think upon, heed, ponder, consider." The simplest statement may convey no proper meaning to one if he treats it with indifference. For this reason Timothy was also told to "give attendance" to reading, etc. (1 Timothy 4: 13). The ancient Israelites failed to know what they could have known, because they did not "consider" what the Lord said unto them. "Israel doth not know, my people doth not consider" (Isaiah 1: 3). Furthermore, Paul named a large number of important subjects, then exhorted the brethren to "think on these things" (Philippians 4: 8).

Verse 8. Among the things Timothy was to *consider* and *remember* was the great fact of the story of Christ. He was of the seed of David—was a lineal descendant of the ancient patriarch, yet that relationship did not keep Him from dying. In truth, He was predestined to die in harmony with the aims of that lineage. His death was not permanent, however, for his resurrection was accomplished which was the final fact of the Gospel. Paul calls it *my Gospel* with the meaning of saying "the Gospel which I preach." He words it in that very way at 1 Corinthians 15: 1.

Verse 9. *Wherein* means for which cause Paul was in trouble, being falsely accused as an evildoer. *Even unto bonds* is literal, for he was fastened to a real chain as a prisoner held for execution. *Word of God is not bound.* The exact date set for the slaying of Paul is not stated, and we do not know whether he was informed of it. However, he was still able to tell the story of Jesus to those who came within the sound of his voice, and to write it as he is doing in this epistle, which is the reason he said the word was not bound. That is not the only sense in which the word of the Lord cannot be bound. Others who received it, and especially those who learned that Paul was being persecuted because of his devotion to it, would be thereby roused to speak out boldly on its behalf (Philippians 1: 12-14).

Verse 10. The over-all meaning of *elect* is given in Thayer's lexicon as, "picked out, chosen." All special meanings, such as who does the choosing and on what condition the choice is made, must be determined in each case by the connection in which it is used. In the present passage it means those whom God has chosen as heirs of salvation, because they have complied with the terms that He has made known to man. Each disciple must work out his own salvation (Philippians 2: 12), but he can be greatly assisted in that conflict by the co-operation of others who likewise are engaged in the struggle. Such encouragement is especially helpful when it comes from one who has "borne the brunt of battle" as Paul has been doing. Hence he says he is enduring his sufferings for their sakes, to the end they may win the reward of salvation made possible only through Christ. *Eternal glory* signifies that which will be enjoyed by the residents of Heaven, in contrast with the glitter and tinsel of this world which will soon fade away.

Verse 11. *A faithful saying* is one that is based on the truth. An example of such a saying is that now expressed, namely, that the dead in Christ shall also live with him. Of course this means in a figurative or spiritual sense, for all mankind whether good or bad will live bodily at the resurrection (John 5: 28, 29). But those who die to sin by obedience (Romans 6: 7, 11, 17, 18), will enjoy the life referred to.

Verse 12. *Reign with* is from SUMBASILEUO, which Thayer defines, "to reign together." Since Christ is the sole king in the realm of religious government (Matthew 28: 18; Ephesians 1: 22, 23), we know this reigning is not in the sense of sharing in His authoritative rule. Thayer explains his definition as follows: "Figuratively to possess supreme honor, liberty, blessedness, with one in the kingdom of God." But Christians are expected to "take the bitter with the sweet." Christ had to suffer to establish his kingdom, hence the citizens must be willing to share in the persecutions heaped upon the kingdom by the enemy. To refuse to endure sufferings for the sake of Christ, is equivalent to denying or disowning Him. Those who do such an unworthy thing will be disowned by the Lord; not only in this world but in that to come (Mark 8: 38).

Verse 13. Unbelief on the part of man is here put as a contrast with the faithfulness of God. This is hardly a clear presentation of the subject, for it is inappropriate to speak of God either as believing or disbelieving; He *knows* everything. When the faithfulness of God is mentioned it means that He is always true to his word. This verse means, then, that regardless of whether man believes on the Lord or not, he will maintain his divinity and will make all divine declarations come true. Since God cannot lie (Titus 1: 2), it would be impossible for Him to deny or disown his personal divinity and eternal existence.

Verse 14. Timothy was left in Ephesus to guard the truth against false teachers (1 Timothy 1: 3). He is still there and the same kind of instruction is repeated in this verse. *These things* are the facts and truths in the preceding verses. *Charging them* means he is to insist earnestly and religiously *before the Lord*. Let them know that all they do and say is known to Him. *Strive not* denotes they should not spend their time disputing over unprofitable words. Such contentions do no one any good, but rather result in *subverting* the hearers. The italicized word is from the Greek word KATASTROPHE which Thayer defines, "overthrow, destruction." We know how serious a catastrophe is considered as the English word terms it, and Paul considers the result of heeding unprofitable words as a happening amounting to a calamity.

Verse 15. *Study* is from SPOUDAZO, and Thayer's definition at this place is as follows: "To exert one's self, endeavor, give diligence." Robinson defines it, "To give diligence, to be in earnest, to be forward." Hence the word does not especially apply to the mental process of investigating a literary subject, although it includes that. The general meaning is to be diligent in trying to show one's self approved unto God, whether in the actions of the body or the mind. If one's work is the kind that God will approve, the workman will have nothing of which to be ashamed. One important task for a workman employed in the service of God, is to make the proper application of *the word of truth*. *Rightly dividing* is from ORTHOTOMEO, and Thayer's definition at this place is as follows: "To make straight and smooth; to handle aright." The familiar use of this passage, that it means to divide rightly between the Old and New Testament is correct as a human comment, but it is not what the original word means, for the New Testament had not been composed when this epistle was written. Hence the word covers all phases of one's treatment of the word of God, and requires the teacher to give it the respect due a document coming from the Lord.

Verse 16. *Shun profane and vain babblings* is the same instruction that is stated in 1 Timothy 6: 20, and refers to empty and foolish talk that has no good use. But any kind of activities on the part of human beings is bound to produce some kind of results. Paul says these vain babblings will advance along the wrong lines, namely, *more ungodliness*. Thayer defines the last word, "want of reverence towards God." That is logical, for everything pertaining to God and the speech originating with Him, is full of helpful principles. Hence if one is concerned with such foolish lines of thought as are here described, it can be only from lack of respect for God.

Verse 17. *Canker* is from GAGGRAINA which Thayer defines, "a gangrene." He explains the word as follows: "A disease by which any part of the body suffering from inflamation becomes so corrupted that unless a remedy be seasonably applied, the evil continually spreads, attacks other parts, and at last eats away the bones." An evil influence, whether it is in the form of false teaching or sinful conduct, is sure to spread and increase. This truth is illustrated by various figures in the Bible. The spread of bad leaven is used in 1 Corinthians 5: 6, and the eating of a gangrenous infection is the illustration in our verse. Hence it should be attacked and destroyed as soon as it is discovered. Hymenaeus is mentioned in 1 Timothy 1: 19, 20 as one who had given up the faith, but nothing is specified. In our chapter (verse 18) his false doctrine is revealed. Philetus is called a heretic by Thayer.

Verse 18. *Concerning the truth have erred*. The last word means to wander from the path, and the men just named had departed from the truth concerning the resurrection. They taught that no resurrection was to come in addition to what had already occurred. That same hersy was taught at Corinth, and the fifteenth chapter of Paul's first epistle to that church deals with the subject. *Overthrow the faith of some*. The most cherished item of a Christian's faith, is that of the resurrection from the dead at the day of judgment. This heresy of the false teachers, that no future resurrection was to occur, naturally destroyed the faith of all who received the false doctrine.

Verse 19. *Nevertheless*. The preceding verse states that the faith of some men was being overthrown by false teaching. A man's faith must be resting upon some foundation or base, and the faith in God is based on the facts of the Gospel. If a man is seduced by false teaching to forsake that divine foundation, it will be the ruination of his faith, yet he cannot take the foundation along with him into ruin. In spite of the desertion of some professing believers, the foundation remains unmoved. Because of these precious truths, the ones who remain faithful need not be discouraged, for the Lord *knoweth* (recognizes and cares for) his own. That is, amid the turmoil and confusion of the backsliders, the Lord will not lose sight of those who are remaining on the unmoveable foundation. A *seal* is an inscription attached to a book or other document or any other important article, that signifies the approval of an authority concerned. This is used figuratively to denote the surety of acceptance for all who will remain true to God. However, to receive and keep such a seal, each man must keep himself apart from *iniquity*. The last word is from ADIKIA, which Thayer defines, "unrighteousness of heart and life." But in order to be free from it, the professors of faith (those who *nameth the name of Christ*) must *depart from* such a life, and not expect God to perform a special miracle to rid them of sin.

Verse 20. *A great house* literally refers to the material structures made by men, but it is used to illustrate the church which is also called a house (1 Timothy 3: 15). In the material buildings there are various kinds of *vessels* (defined "house-hold utensils" in Thayer's lexicon). These vessels will be made of different kinds of material, depending on the service expected to get from them. *Honor* and *dishonor* in a material building means only that the use of some utensils is more special or particular than that of others. When such a service is wanted, the householder will use the utensils that are made of the best materials, and those most in keeping with the dignity or importance of the occasion. A utensil made of gold or silver could be used on occasions when those of wood or clay would not serve the purpose.

Verse 21. In the illustration, a vessel is whatever kind its owner decrees for it. But in the house of God every man may be an "honorable" vessel if he will. Hence *if a man therefore purge himself from these*, meaning the objectionable principles referred to in the preceding verses, he can be the kind of vessel that is desirable. *Sanctified* means he is cleansed from *iniquity* by obedience to the truth, and set apart for a righteous use, namely, that of the Master's. Such a reformation in his life prepares him for the work that is designed by his Owner. Note that nothing is said about doing great or highminded work, but *every good work*.

Verse 22. *Youthful lusts*. Thayer defines the first word, "peculiar to the age of youth, youthful." The phrase means those desires that are more common in one who is young. The Lord will not overlook a misdeed of one on the ground of his "early years." Joseph was scarcely out of his "teens" when his mistress tried to seduce him, yet he was able to resist her advances by the faith he had in God. In 1 Timothy 4:12 the evangelist is told not to let anyone despise or belittle his youth. Our present passage is similar in its purpose, and he is to maintain the respect of others by practicing the things that both young and old should do in order to please God, and be an example to others. *Righteousness* is a general term and always means the practice of that which is right. To *follow* after it requires that one make it his daily conduct, not merely when it is covenient. *Faith*, when used with reference to one's manner of life, means the conduct of one who is true or faithful to the will of the Lord. *Charity* in this passage denotes a sincere interest in the welfare of others. *Peace* must be in accord with *the wisdom that is from above* (James 3:17). Such a peace is not always agreeable to others, hence Paul specifies that Timothy may have it with those who are pure in heart in the sight of the Lord.

Verse 23. *Unlearned questions* means subjects that are not instructive. Many times we hear brethren worrying and laboring over matters that are not set forth in the scriptures, and often it is concerning inquiries that would not be of any profit even if they could be solved. Such conversations are foolish, and Timothy is directed to avoid them. They not only are without any lawful result, but rather will they *gender* (beget) *strifes*. The last word is from MACHE which Thayer defines, "A fight, combat; quarrel." Sincere contention on behalf of a revealed principle is right and is commanded (Jude 3), but an argument over useless words is always wrong.

Verse 24. The Bible does not contradict itself, and when there seems to be a disagreement there is always a proper explanation. This verse says a servant of the Lord must *not strive*, while other passages show he may (verse 5). But it is from a different original in the present verse which Thayer defines, "to quarrel, wrangle, dispute." The connection shows Paul is writing about Timothy's work among those who are out of the way because of being uninformed; he should be gentle and patient toward such. *Apt to teach*. This phrase is from DIDAKTIKOS, which occurs only twice in the Greek New Testament. Thayer's definition is, "apt and skilful in teaching." The other place where the word is used is 1 Timothy 3:2 where it is applied to the elders, while in our verse it is applied to anyone who is a *servant of the Lord*, which might not always be an evangelist even. In one place it is applied to a man with authority in the church, in the other the connection does not indicate authority. Since the definition does not state *how* skilful he must be in teaching, we must consult some other passage for that. Titus 1:9 is considering the qualifications and work of a bishop (or elder), and it shows he must be able by "sound doctrine" (teaching) to convince the gainsayers. Unless a man is able to do that kind of teaching, he is not qualified for the eldership, while a man without that degree of teaching ability might be an acceptable servant of the Lord.

Verse 25. *Meekness* means humbleness and is about the same in effect as gentleness in the preceding verse. *Oppose themselves* refers to those who place themselves in opposition to the truth that Timothy was teaching. *Peradventure*. God wishes every person in sin to repent (2 Peter 3:9), and never prevents him from so doing if he becomes penitent in mind. Hence the uncertainty expressed by the word is on the question of whether these people in error will be persuaded by the means that God will be using through the services of Timothy. Such repentance or reformation must begin by *the acknowledging of the truth* that was offered to them.

Verse 26. These people engaged in opposition to the truth are compared to a victim caught in a snare or trap. The trap has been set by the *devil* (from DIABOLOS), who uses various means to capture the people of the Lord. Sometimes he is overt and vicious after the manner of a roaring lion (1 Peter 5: 8), at other times he captures them with his wiles or snares. *Taken captive* is from ZOGREO which Thayer defines, "to take alive." The last clause is a very interesting use of an illustration. It pictures a scene where the Lord finds a human being who had once been His servant, but was caught in the trap of the devil. The victim is released and taken captive by the Lord, who originally had possession of him anyway, and who now will again be turned into the kind of service that is in harmony with His will.

2 Timothy 3

Verse 1. *Last days.* I shall explain these words separately, then comment on the phrase as a whole. The first is from ESCHATOS, and Thayer's general definition is, "Extreme, last in time or in place," and some variation in shades of meaning must be determined by the connection in which it is used. The second is form HEMERA, and Thayer uses two pages of his lexicon in defining its various meanings. I here give his three outstanding definitions (the words in italics), followed by his explanations of the definitions. "Of the natural day," then explains. "the interval between sunrise and sunset, as distinguished from and contrasted with night." "The civil day," and explains, "the space of twenty-four hours (thus including the night)." "The last day of the present age," and he explains this to mean, "the day in which Christ will return from heaven, raise the dead, hold the final judgment, and perfect his kingdom." By the last three words is meant the completion of Christ's personal reign and his delivering it up to his Father (1 Corinthians 15: 24). We should conclude from the various meanings of the separate words, that when combined into a phase, no absolute date or dates can be affirmed as the nesessary application. The term *shall come* indicates that Paul is making a prediction and that he is writing of things then in the future. (How far into the future is not shown.) Since about all of the evils named in the chapter have always been committed, we must conclude that they were to become worse, and therein lies the prediction phase of the passage. (See verse 13.) *Perilous* is from CHALEPOS, and Thayer defines it as follows: "Hard to do, to take, to approach; hard to bear, troublesome, dangerous; fierce, harsh, savage." Of course these *times* means certain periods then in the future when the conditions about to be named were to increase upon the world. They were not to come by any decree of God, but would be caused by the actions of men according to the items now to be listed.

Verse 2. *Lovers of their own selves.* They will be selfish and interested chiefly in that which gives themselves the enjoyments of life. Such characters will often insist on such gratification even when it causes discomfort to others. *Covetous* is from PHILARGUROS, which Thayer defines, "loving money, avaricious." It is easy to understand how such characters would make it hard for others to get along. *Boasters* is from ALAZON and Thayer defines it, "an empty pretender, a boaster." It is unbecoming for a man to manifest the spirit of a boaster, even when he has accomplished something worth while. It is more so when one boasts of some merit that he does not actually have. *Proud* includes much of the same spirit as the word just explained, and goes further to include an exalting of one's self above others. It means a person who is overbearing and shows a "holier-than-thou" attitude toward others. *Blasphemers.* I can do no better at explaining this word than to quote the definition of the original given by Thayer as follows: "Speaking evil, slanderous, reproachful, railing, abusive;" and that of Robinson, "Hurtful to the good name of any one, detractive." *Disobedient to parents.* The simple fact of disobedient children was nothing new when Paul wrote this epistle, as may be seen by reading Deuteronomy 21: 18; Proverbs 19: 18; Hebrews 12: 9-11. Hence it is well to consider again the comment at verse 1, that is was the increase of the evils that was predicted. We do not know how soon after Paul's day this predicted increase began, but we do know that disobedience and other forms of disrespect to parents are rampant today. However, the children are not the only ones who are responsible for this condition; parents also are to blame. They will throw up their hands in a gesture of despair, and wonder what is to be done about the "problem of the young people," as if a radical change had come into the natural relation between parents and their offspring. Nothing of that kind has happened, for the children have always been just as they are now, except that their natural tendency toward disobedience has become worse according to the prediction. The change has come on the part of parents, in that they are too indolent to exercise the discipline they should. This situation is made worse by the modern teaching of public schools, where it is said that the youth should be left to form their own conclusions regarding their personal conduct. They have always wanted to do that, hence it is no new idea. Another thing that encourages this increased rebellion is the daily public press. Many of the "columns" in the papers advocate such notions as "proper handling" of our children. In some instances, this "advice" comes from persons who never had any children of their own, and may even never have been married. The world would be better off if these features were ruled out of the papers. *Unthankful.* Ingratitude is one of the worst characteristics manifested by humanity. Many people will grasp the favors that come within reach, and act as if such things were to be taken for granted, and that the obligations all traveled in one direction. *Unholy.* This is a general term, and applies to all forms of evil conduct considered in this passage. Any form of unrighteousness may truly be described as unholy.

Verse 3. *Without natural affection.* These words all come from the Greek word ASTORGS, and the only other place it is used is in Romans 1: 31, and in each place the translation is the same, which is also according to Thayer's lexicon. The word is derived by inflection from the Greek word STORGE which means "love of kindred," the inflection giving it a negative meaning. The thought is that children should be inclined to obey their parents from the motive of the close kindred if from no other. But if they do not have such love, that will help to explain their disobedience to parents mentioned in the preceding verse. *Trucebreakers* is from the same word as "implacable" in Romans 1: 31, and Thayer defines it. "without a treaty or covenant; that cannot be persuaded to enter into a covenant." Such people are so unwilling to be at peace with others that they will not even talk about "terms" of agreement. *False accusers* is from DIABOLOS which is one of the names of Satan, and is elsewhere translated "devil." This is an appropriate name since he is the father of lies (John 8: 44). *Incontinent* means "without self-control, intemperate." *Fierce* is from a Greek word that is defined "savage" in the lexicon of Thayer. Such a characteristic does not necessarily mean bodily attacks, but is a vicious attitude toward those who oppose their unrighteous ways. *Despisers of those that are good.* There is no personal pronoun in the original, but the statement means they despise or belittle anything that is good. Not being good themselves, they pretend to have no respect for anything that is good.

Verse 4. *Traitors* are those who will turn against their best friends if they oppose their evil ways, using underhanded means to overcome them. *Heady* means to be rash, inclined to plunge forward without "thinking twice before the leap." *Highminded* is another word for "proud," and it is used for those who are puffed up over some imaginary personal merit. *Lovers of pleasures.* The last word does not occur here as a separate term, hence we cannot give a specified definition of it as we can in other passages. It is also true that the simple word "pleasure" is not definite as to whether lawful or unlawful enjoyment is meant; the context in each case must determine that. But regardless of this distinction, the sin in our passage consists in loving pleasure *more than* loving God. Even things that are right in themselves will become evil if they are preferred above God. (See Matthew 10: 37.)

Verse 5. *Having a form of godliness.* They make a profession of some form of religion that is supposed to cause a man to do right. *Denying the power thereof.* These people claim that they have a system of religious conduct that is adapted to the right kind of life, yet they will not let that system have any effect upon their own lives. They *deny* the system the chance to have the said good effects upon their own conduct. Timothy not only must not join with these empty pretenders in their inconsistent course, but he must *turn away* from them.

Verse 6. *This sort* refers to the characters described in the preceding verses. Such persons might be expected to accomplish their unrighteous schemes by means of this kind. *Creep into houses.* According to the Greek sense of the words, they mean men who manage to get inside the houses after the manner of an insistent salesman. They make their approach to the *silly women* ("little women"—Thayer) who are already in a state of uncertainty on account of their many sins. Since they are already *led away* with their various lusts, they would be easy prey for these intruding men who will capture their attention for evil purposes.

Verse 7. *Ever learning* means these silly women are always curious to hear something different, hence they eagerly listen to these corrupt men. But while they are thus *ever learning*—are always seeking to hear something—it is not the truth they obtain.

Verse 8. Jannes and Jambres were the magicians who stood against Moses and Aaron in Exodus 7: 11, 12. According to Thayer, their names were given in the Jewish commentaries. Paul is making the comparison of the simple fact that both sets of evil workers resisted the principles of truth that would have been accepted of the Lord. Out of the heart the mouth speaks (Matthew 12: 34), and since these were *men of corrupt minds,* is was in line for them to act against the principles of righteousness. *Reprobate* (unfit or useles) *concerning the faith.* There was nothing in the character of these men that was of any use for the faith.

Verse 9. The first two pronouns *(they* and *their)* refer to the men being considered in this chapter, the third one *(theirs)* means Jannes and Jambres. The magicians finally were exposed as frauds, and likewise these evil men in Paul's case were destined to be brought to shame.

Verse 10. *Hast fully known* all comes from PARAKOLOUTHEO which Thayer defines as follows: "To follow faithfully, namely, a standard or rule, to conform one's self to." Robinson defines it, "To follow, to conform unto." I have consulted four translations which also render the word according to these lexicon definitions. So that Timothy not only learned the truth from his father in the Gospel, but he imitated the example of faithfulness that was shown amidst various trials. *Doctrine* refers to the teaching, and *manner of life* is the putting of that teaching into practice. (See 1 Timothy 4: 16.) *Purpose.* Timothy had heard and seen enough from Paul to learn his sincere motive in life; that it harmonized with his conduct. It also was a practical demonstration of his *faith* which was according to the Gospel. *Longsuffering* means a submissive spirit under persecutions, and *patience* denotes that submission to his lot was enduring or followed with perseverance. *Charity* in this passage means sincere interest in the welfare of others.

Verse 11. *Persecutions* and *afflictions* denote the same experiences referred to in the preceding verse, but are repeated in connection with the places where the apostle had the experiences. At *Antioch* (Acts 13: 14, 50), at *Iconium* (Acts 14: 2), at *Lystra* (Acts 14: 6, 19). Paul does not mention these things out of a desire to "feel sorry for himself," but to give force to his next declaration that *out of them all the Lord delivered me,* which is added for the encouragement of Timothy and others.

Verse 12. This verse is Paul's comment on the preceding two verses, to the effect that his experience was no exception to the rule of the faithful in Christ. Persecutions are caused by people who are enemies of the Lord. They generally do not make much ado over the mere fact that a man is not a bad character in his personal life, hence to *live godly* means more than merely abstaining from evil practices; it includes activity against the things that are evil. A Christian must not only "have no fellowship" with the sinful conduct of others, but he must "rather reprove it" (Ephesians 5: 11). When this is done it will arouse the anger of evil workers, and their usual procedure is to persecute the one who opposes them. It is no real compliment to say of a man that "he never had an enemy," as we frequently hear. Jesus said, "Woe unto you, when all men shall speak well of you" (Luke 6: 26). This is why the apostles in Acts 5: 41 could rejoice over the shame they were enduring for His name.

Verse 13. *Evil men* is general and could apply to all persons who are not righteous, while *seducers* specifies one of the evil things such men will do. The word is from GOES, a Greek term which originally meant "a wizard, juggler," according to Robinson, and a "juggler, enchanter," according to Thayer. Such a word is appropriate, because in verse 8 the apostle makes reference to the magi-

2 Timothy 3: 14-17

cians in Egypt. Both lexicons give the word also the meaning of "impostor," which would apply to any of the means these evil men might use to mislead the people. *Deceiving and being deceived.* It is possible for a man to formulate and utter false doctrines so persistently, that he will come to believe in them himself and thus be deceived. The magicians in Egypt evidently were devoted to their witchcraft until a shameful defeat convinced them that they had been misled, for they admitted that "this [the work of Moses and Aaron] is the finger of God" (Exodus 8: 19). Paul says that all of this *shall wax worse and worse*, which is really the prophetic phase of this chapter.

Verse 14. This verse is an exhortation for Timothy not to be swerved from the course of truth that had influenced him all his life. The assurance of being right is based on the reliable source of his information, of which he was fully aware. His mother and grandmother had taught him the scriptures, which is the subject of the rest of this chapter. (See chapter 1: 5.)

Verse 15. *From a child* has the same meaning as "from my forefathers" (chapter 1: 3). The thought is that he had been reared in the spiritual surroundings that are mentioned here and in chapter 1: 5. *Holy scriptures* refers to the Old Testament, for the New had not been written when Timothy was growing up. *Able to make thee wise.* The Old Testament was the law for salvation with the Jews, it being the one that was in force during that age. And its use as a source of wisdom or information was still available for the evangelist, even though he had become a disciple of Christ; and that is one reason that volume was preserved unto the Christian Dispensation (Romans 15: 4). However, the wisdom that was possible through the Old Testament would not alone bring salvation, now that Christ has put an end to that law "for righteousness" (Romans 10: 4). Hence Paul adds what is necessary for Timothy (and all others) to do that he might be saved, namely, accept the faith (the New Testament system) *which is in Christ Jesus.*

Verse 16. *All scripture.* Having proceeded to include the faith in Christ in the general subject of divine law, the term *scripture* here means both the Old and New Testaments as to their divine source. *Given by inspiration of God.* All of these words are from the Greek term THEOPNEUSTOS, which Thayer defines, "inspired by God," and which Robinson defines, "God-inspired, inbreathed of God." When an author puts his ideas in a book, the volume is said to be inspired by the said author. That is true whether he does the writing bodily himself, or dictates it and has some other person to do the writing. Likewise, God dictated (by means of the Holy Spirit) to the writers of the Bible what He wished to go into the Sacred Text, and for that reason it is said to be a volume inspired of God. *Profitable* means it is useful or serviceable for the following purposes. *Doctrine* is the same as teaching, stating what is the truth about the whole system of "the faith," and *instruction in righteousness* is the information that shows how to put the above *doctrine* into practice. All *reproof* is *correction*, but not all correction is reproof; the difference is mainly in the degree of intensity. If a man is in error through weakness or lack of information, he needs correction only. But if he is wrong when he knows better or could have known better, then he deserves to be reproved. (See Jude 22, 23.)

Verse 17. *Man of God.* This phrase is used of the evangelist in 1 Timothy 6: 11, and I wish the reader would turn back and see the comments at that place, for they include a reference to our present passage. *Man* is from ANTHROPOS, and the universal meaning as given in Thayer's lexicon is, "A human being, whether male or female." Any human being, therefore, who has given himself to God may truly take the phrase underscored. It is expected that a servant of God will work for Him, and to do so he needs the kind of equipment that is adapted to the work that his Master will approve. The inspired scriptures will provide such an equipment, making him *perfect* which is another word for "complete." With the word of God, a Christian has the complete outfit necessary in his service for the Lord. The rest of the verse is along the line of emphasis, specifying what Paul means by being perfect. *Thoroughly furnished* means completely prepared unto *all good works.* It is evident, then, that if a man attempts or desires to do something in his religious life for which the scriptures do not furnish the authority and instruction, he is seeking to be active in something that is not a good work.

2 Timothy 4

Verse 1. To *charge* means to make an earnest plea to the evangelist; and to do so *before God*, etc., signifies that He is a witness to the charge, and that to Him the preacher will have to give an account. The name of Christ is connected with the charge because He is the one who will have direct handling of the judgment, at which all men will receive the final sentence that will announce their eternal state. The *quick* and the *dead* mean the living and dead when Jesus comes. *At his appearing* tells when the final judgment is to take place. This completely sets aside the notion that Christ is first to appear, and that the judgment will be a thousand years later. *And his kingdom.* Not that the kingdom will then begin, for 1 Corinthians 15: 24-26 shows that Christ is now reigning in his kingdom, but will cease to do so after the judgment. The phrase means that the authority of Christ as head of the kingdom will fully appear, when He is shown executing final judgment on the world.

Verse 2. *Preach the word.* This is consistent with the declarations in the closing verses of the preceding chapter. Since the word is inspired and complete, it is logical that it should be preached. *Be instant* means to be at hand and ready for the work when any opportunity occurs. *In season, out of season.* There are times when the prospect is apparently more favorable than at others, but the true preacher of the word should not wait until he finds it more convenient (for himself) to press the claims of the Gospel. *Reprove* and *rebuke* are virtually the same in effect, and means to disapprove of the wrongs committed by professed disciples of Christ. *Exhort* means to insist on one's doing what he has learned to be his duty, and in order that men may be ready for exhortation, the preacher must first deliver the *doctrine* (teaching) that is applicable in the case. He will need to be *longsuffering* or patient in all this work, because of the conditions to be described next.

Verse 3. Among the things predicted to get worse (chapter 3:13), was the growing dislike for the teaching of the word, especially that part of it that condenms a sinful life. When the term *sound* is used with reference to the physical body, it means to be in good health. When used of doctrine or teaching, it signifies the kind of instruction that will result in good moral and spiritual health. But evil men are not interested in that kind of health, hence they will not *endure* or put up with such teaching. They want the kind that will allow them to feel comfortable in the midst of their corrupt practices. To do so, they seek to obtain men who will give them that kind of teaching. A faithful proclaimer of the word will not try to tickle the *itching ears* of these lustful pretenders, hence they seek for the kind of teachers who are as bad as they—men whose lives are also fashioned after the lusts like those of the hearers with itching ears. This verse might seem clearer if the construction would be arranged as follows: "They will not endure sound doctrine; but, having itching ears, they will heap to themselves teachers who practice their own lusts."

Verse 4. These teachers with lusts like the people who employed them, would naturally be disposed to furnish the kind of speeches that were acceptable. Hence *they* (the lustful teachers) *will turn away their* (the people with itching ears) *ears* from the truth. In place of the truth, they will entertain them with *fables* or fictions.

Verse 5. *Watch thou* is a kindly warning for Timothy to maintain his composure under all circumstances, for many tests of his perseverance were likely to come. Encouraged by the example of Paul, he should be equal to the occasion even when persecutions come. *Do the work of an evangelist.* We may learn two important items of information by this statement. One is that Timothy was an evangelist, which has sometimes been questioned. Paul certainly would not tell anyone to do a work that did not belong to his position in life. The other is that an evangelist has a work to perform that is peculiar to his office. By consulting 1 Timothy 3 and Titus 1, we will learn that an evangelist is the one to appoint elders and deacons, and in 1 Timothy 5 it is shown that an evangelist is the one to discipline an elder when charges are preferred against him. It is also taught in Titus 1: 5 that an evangelist is to take charge of churches that have not been established, and hold that charge until matters are set in order and elders are appointed to take oversight of the congregation, at which time the evangelist is to go to other fields of labor.

2 Timothy 4: 6-11

Make full proof of thy ministry is rendered "fully carry out thy service" by the Englishman's Greek New Testament.

Verse 6. *For I am now ready to be offered.* The Englishman's Greek New Testament renders this as follows: "For I already am being poured out," and the Greek text justifies the translation. The word for *offered* is defined "poured out" by Thayer, and Paul used it because he knew he was actually to have his blood poured out of his body on the executioner's block. Of course the execution was not actually started, and was not to start at once, for Paul still expected to do some writing (verse 13). But he was a captive in chains, condemned to die for the Gospel's sake, and he regarded his sacrifice as having been started. One item in the Mosiac system consisted of pouring blood out about the altar of sacrifice (Exodus 29: 12; Leviticus 4: 7), and Paul compares the pouring out of his blood, to those sacrifices. In other words, here is one instance where an act (pouring out) is used in both a literal and a spiritual sense, since his death was to be occasioned by his religious devotion to God. *Departure* is from ANALUSIS, which Thayer defines, "An unloosing, a dissolving, departure." The unloosing refers to the separation of the soul from the body, and departure pertains to the flight of the soul to the intermediate region after it leaves the body. *At hand* denotes it is comparatively near only, for the apostle expected still to do some more work for the Lord as the chapter will later show.

Verse 7. A *good fight* is one that is waged on behalf of a good cause and against a bad one. A *course* means one's career or race of life, and *finish* means to complete or make full. Paul's active work was over because of his chains, and in that sense his race was run. But the teaching of the scripture is that Christians must be faithful until death in order to gain the crown (James 1:12; 1 Peter 5: 4; Revelation 2: 10). That is true, but a man can be faithful even when prevented by unavoidable circumstances from further activity in the work. Paul's activities were stopped by the enemy, and in that sense his course was *finished*. *Kept the faith.* The law of God, which is the basis of the faith, will live until it has accomplished its divine purpose, hence it is not left for man to "keep" the faith in the sense of preserving its existence. So the phrase means that Paul had kept himself true to the law of divine faith, always advocating it whenever he had the opportunity.

Verse 8. *Henceforth* means "hereafter" or "from now on." It is equivalent to the preceding thought that the prospect of a crown is held out only to those who complete a life of *righteousness.* The last word denotes that the crown is a "medal of honor" to be bestowed upon a person who has lived a righteous life. *Lord, the righteous judge* is significant, because in earthly contests the judges are sometimes influenced to decide with partiality, while He will decide strictly on the basis of faithfulness. *That day* refers to the day of judgment, and it is often referred to in such indefinite language because of its unequalled importance, for which reason it needs no other specification. *Love his appearing.* The first word is defined by Thayer, "To welcome with desire, long for." If a man has not been living a righteous life, he will dread to see the Lord come. But a faithful servant (Luke 12: 41-46) will be glad to look forward to the coming of Christ (Revelation 22: 20).

Verse 9. Though he was an apostle, Paul had the same craving for companionship that any Christian will have for another. He knew he was not to live much longer (how much longer is not stated), and he wished to have his son (in the Gospel) with him again before he left this world.

Verse 10. According to Colossians 4: 14 and Philemon 24, Demas had been associated with Paul in his travels, and for a while even after the apostle was taken to Rome in chains. But he failed to stand the test when persecution threatened, being more interested in the pleasures of this world than in the cause of Christ. No unfavorable comment is made about the departure of Cresens and Titus, hence we may conclude they left with Paul's consent. Such a conclusion is reasonable since verse 12 expressly says that the apostle sent another disciple away for some purpose (not stated).

Verse 11. *Only Luke is with me* means of the ones who had traveled with Paul, for verse 21 shows that several brethren were still associated with him in his trials and labors for the Lord. *Mark* is the disciple who deserted Paul, recorded in Acts 13: 13; 15: 36-41. But he seems to have reclaimed himself in Paul's confidence, for he calls for him that he might be of use in the *ministry* or service.

Verse 12. This is referred to and commented upon at verse 10.

Verse 13. A *cloke* is a loose outer garment, especially needed in winter. *Books* means the documents already composed and the *parchments* are writing materials. His calling for all these articles indicates that while death was "at hand," yet he expected to be able to do some more reading and writing, and as a faithful servant (even "unto death"), he determined to "die fighting."

Verse 14. *Alexander the coppersmith.* The last word is given merely to identify the one Paul means, as there were several men with the same name. We have very little information about him except what is given here, that he did the apostle much harm. The last sentence denotes that Paul expects Alexander to receive punishment from God.

Verse 15. Alexander evidently was going about since Paul warns Timothy about him. This verse indicates that the "evil" he was doing against Paul was to oppose his teaching; he was doubtless a Judaizer.

Verse 16. *First answer* means Paul's first defense before Caesar's court. It may be learned by history as well as by Acts 28: 30, that when Paul arrived in Rome from Caesarea, he was turned over to the Roman authorities who placed him in chains, but permitted him to live in a house which he rented. After this two-year period he was released, and traveled out among the churches a short while, then came back to Rome and was again arrested and brought before the court and made his own defense (called his *first answer* in our verse), but was not further punished as yet. (See next verse.) He was still held in chains and was soon to be condemned to die. It was at this *first answer* that all his associates deserted him or failed to stand by him. He was unresentful over it, though, and prayed God not to hold it against them.

Verse 17. The Lord stood by Paul as he faced the Roman court, and for the time being prevented him from being slain. The purpose was that the apostle might round out his work of preaching to the Gentiles of that city, thus making *fully known* the Gospel for which cause he was there in chains.

Christians were sometimes thrown to the lions, literally, to die for their faith. That fact is used figuratively of Nero, who threatened to have Paul executed immediately. But he was given a temporary respite, and in that sense he was *delivered out of the mouth of the lion.*

Verse 18. *Shall deliver me.* Not that he was to be prevented from being slain at last, but that his death would not keep him from enjoying the *heavenly kingdom*, which is the same as the "everlasting kingdom" of 2 Peter 1: 11.

Verse 19. *Prisca* is another form for Priscilla. She and her husband Aquila had been faithful friends of Paul, and he is here "speaking a good word" for them. See chapter 1: 16 for comments on the *household of Onesiphorus.*

Verse 20. Erastus had been with Paul (Acts 19: 22), but later came to Corinth to reside (Romans 16: 23). On his way back to Rome, Paul left Trophimus at Miletum because of his being sick. Not that the apostle was unable to heal him miraculously, but neither Christ nor his disciples were to perform miracles when there was no question of testimony at stake.

Verse 21. *Come before winter.* (See the comments at verse 9.) It might have been an additional reason for this instruction in the fact that sailing was difficult in the winter season. The other persons named were friends and disciples who joined with Paul in sending their greetings to the evangelist.

Verse 22. This verse is Paul's affectionate benediction to his "son in the Gospel."

Titus 1

Verse 1. Paul mentions his relation to God as *servant* before that of apostle, which is a mark of humbleness. *Faith of God's elect.* God elects or chooses as His own, all men who fully embrace *the faith* or New Testament system of religion. This service of Paul was *according to that faith* which embraced *acknowledging of the truth.* The *truth* meant here is that which is *after godliness* or piety.

Verse 2. The motive for such service as the preceding verse describes, is the hope of eternal life; nothing pertaining to the world. *God cannot lie.* These words are from the Greek term APSEUDES, which does not occur in any other place in the New Testament. Thayer and Robinson define it just as it is rendered in the King James version. It is to be understood on the basis that God is able to do that which is right only, but is not able to do wrong. *Promised before the world began.* The first recorded promise of eternal life is that made to Abraham (Galatians 3: 16). But that was after man began to live upon the earth, hence the *world* which is from a Greek word that means "age," must mean the Jewish age or Dispensation. Such an explanation clarifies the apparent difficulty as to when the promise was made. It was after man began living on the earth, but *before* the period when the organized "age" (the meaning of *world)* or the Jewish Dispensation began.

Verse 3. The promise of salvation through Christ (the seed of Abraham) was made to the patriarch in prophetic language, but was revealed in its fulness by preachers.

Verse 4. Titus was Paul's son in the same sense as was Timothy (1 Timothy 1: 2), and it was after (or according to) the *common faith,* which means the faith adapted to all people who will accept it. Paul expresses the familiar salutation that has been commented upon sufficiently before this.

Verse 5. Between the first and second imprisonment of Paul, he traveled among the churches in a few places, and Titus was with him a part of the time. When they came to Crete (a large island off the coast of Greece), they found the churches on the island somewhat out of order and without rulers. Paul went on his journey, but left Titus there as evangelist in charge to bring the work to a scriptural establishment. This consisted in whatever was necessary to bring conditions into line, and then *ordain* (or appoint) elders. Note that he was to appoint a plurality of elders and it was to be in every city. The plan of human practice is to have a plurality of churches under one elder, while the scriptural plan is a plurality of elders over one congregation. It was the duty of Titus under the instruction of Paul, to remain in Crete until he had completed this evangelistic work. For more detailed explanation of the work of an evangelist, see the comments at 2 Timothy 4: 5.

Verse 6. In order that Titus might know whom to appoint as elders (also called bishops here and elsewhere), the apostle devotes several paragraphs to describing their qualifications and work. *Blameless, the husband of one wife.* This is fully explained at 1 Timothy 3: 2. *Having faithful children.* This phrase has raised a question among students of the Bible, and two different views have been maintained. One is that it means children who are faithful to the Lord, or who are believers in Him to the extent of having become members of the church. The other is that it means children who are faithful or obedient to their fathers. I shall first give the reader the benefit of information I have in support of the first position, which is as follows. The word *faithful* is from the Greek word PISTOS and Thayer defines it, "One who has become convinced that Jesus is the Messiah and the author of salvation." Robinson defines it, "A believer, Christian." I have consulted four other lexicons, and they define it virtually the same as the two just quoted. I have consulted also five translations that render it "believing." I shall now give the other view, and state that I am not fully convinced that it is required that an elder's children be faithful members of the church, and shall give my reasons for saying so. It is true the lexicons and various translations generally render the word as "believing," but that would still leave unsettled the question whether the child is to be a believer in Christ or in his father; for if he believes in his father, he is likely to be obedient to him. That would show that the father has control over his child, which is really the point that Paul was making. In 1 Timothy 3: 4, 12, where the same point is under consideration with reference to children of elders and deacons, there is no intimation of their religious relation to the Lord, but that the father is to have control of them. Therefore, my conclusion is that "faithful children" in Titus 1: 6 is equivalent to controlled children in 1 Timothy 3: 4, 12, and hence that they are to believe in and be faithful to their father, regardless of whether they are members of the church or not, or even that they are old enough to be members. *Not accused of riot or unruly.* This is significant in view of the foregoing comments. *Riot* is from ASOTIA, which Thayer defines, "an abandoned, dissolute, life; profligacy [wastefulness], prodigality [extravagance in expenditure]." *Unruly* is from ANUPOTAKTOS, which is defined by Thayer, "that cannot be subjected to control, disobedient," etc. The fact that a son is not a member of the church cannot be blamed upon his father, for a man cannot use his parental authority to bring his children into it. But he does have authority as a father to control his son against the above described conduct.

Verse 7. *Blameless* is from the same word as that in the preceding verse, and takes the same general definition. But it is given a special significance here by calling the bishop (or elder) the *steward* of God. That means one who has charge of the affairs of another, which is true of a bishop, since he has charge of the flock of God. A steward or agent is expected to be faithful in the administration of his employer's property. The qualifications, both affirmative and negative, are next given. Those in the rest of this verse are negative; that is, qualities that he must not have. *Not selfwilled* means he must not be selfish, insisting on having his own way regardless of the rights of others. *Soon angry* denotes one who becomes angered at the slightest provocation. *Not given to wine.* This is explained by the comments at 1 Timothy 3: 3. *No striker.* This also is defined at the passage in Timothy just cited. It can be seen that it means one who does not generally resort to physical assaults whenever he is opposed; that it does not refer to some incidental or isolated act. *Given to filthy lucre* is defined by Thayer to mean, "eager for base gain." It means one who not only covets money, but who is willing to gain it in any kind of way, whether it be right or wrong.

Verse 8. *Lover of hospitality.* It should be known that the elder's home is one in which any worthy person is welcome. *Lover of good men.* The last word is not in the original as a separate term, although it may be included in the phrase. The meaning of the phrase concerns a man who loves that which is good. *Sober* is defined as one who curbs his desires; he is self-controlled. *Just* signifies one who is considerate of the rights of all, in his exercise of rulership over the flock. *Holy* is another word for righteous. If an elder does not live rightly himself, he can have but little influence over others. *Temperate* has virtually the same meaning as *sober*, and it is added for the sake of emphasis.

Verse 9. This verse should be considered as an explanation of the phrase "apt to teach" in 1 Timothy 3: 2, in that it shows *how apt* or able a man is as a teacher. *Holding fast* means he holds to the *faithful* (truthful) *Word.* The elder is not an inspired man, but he *hath been taught* what is the truth by those who are inspired. *Sound doctrine* literally means wholesome teaching; and when used of spiritual matters, it denotes the kind that will result in spiritual health. When a disordered condition comes or threatens to come into a human body, a treatment must be used that will counteract the threatened disease. Likewise, an elder must have the ability to *exhort* those who are threatening the spiritual health of the body. Then if exhortation does not stop them, he must use a stronger remedy, namely, *convince* them. That word is from ELEGCHO, which Thayer defines, "To convict, refute, confute." Elders are required to be able to convict and expose false teachers, called here *the gainsayers.*

Verse 10. *Unruly and vain talkers* are those who will not submit to the apostolic rules, and who deal in useless conversation for the purpose of misleading unsuspecting disciples. *They of the circumcision* means the Judaizers, who were the most prominent trouble makers in Paul's day.

Verse 11. *Mouths must be stopped.* Neither the evangelist nor an elder can use force literally to close the mouth of a false teacher. But he can use the means stated in verse 9 to expose him, and thus counteract the evil effects of his mouth. *Subvert whole houses* denotes that they sometimes mislead whole families with their false teaching. *Filthy lucre's sake.* By their perverted use of the law of Moses, they sought to please their hearers, in the hope that it would bring them some money as a sort of "tip" from the dupes for their good feeling.

Verse 12. *One of themselves* means one of the natives of the island of Crete. One of their own writers accused the people of that region of being habitual liars, which would account for their disposition to pervert the truth when they had hopes of gain from it. *Evil beasts* is a figure of speech to indicate the low type of character the islanders possessed. *Slow bellies* is rendered "lazy gluttons" by the Englishman's Greek New Testament. If a man's chief interest is his animal appetite, and he is too lazy to obtain wherewith to satisfy it honorably, he would naturally take the unprincipled course that has been described in these verses.

Verse 13. Paul agrees with the Cretan prophet who said the accusing things about his countrymen. Such people do not deserve much compassion, hence the apostle bids Titus rebuke them sharply. *That they may be sound in the faith* states the motive for the sharp rebuke, not that it is certain to have that result.

Verse 14. The mention of Jewish *fables* or myths, confirms the remark at verse 10 about their being Judaizers who were disturbing the brethren in Crete. *Commandments of men* signifies doctrines that have no divine authority behind them. Such teaching cannot be true, hence it will cause all who accept it to *turn from the truth*.

Verse 15. *Unto the pure all things are pure.* This is said because of the agitation being made by the Judaizers. The law of Moses had certain regulations regarding the eating of the flesh of animals. But those rules were not based on any actual impurity of the meat, for "there is nothing unclean of itself" (Romans 14: 14). The uncleanness was ceremonial only and was a part of the law. But that law has been cancelled, so that no reason exists any more for regarding the meats as impure. But these pretenders were impure in life themselves, hence they professed to believe that it was still wrong to eat the meats. If a man is pure in heart, he will see nothing wrong in eating these articles, since the only thing that ever did make it wrong, namely the legislation of the law, has been taken away.

Verse 16. While these Judaizers were busying themselves in disturbing the churches, they professed it was because of their love of God and their knowledge of His law. But, like many other religious frauds, their personal life was a contradiction of the purity of doctrine which they professed. *Abominable* pertains directly to the corrupt practices they were performing, and *disobedient* designates the relation of their practices to the law of God; they were in rebellion against it. *Unto every good work reprobate.* The last word means "useless," denoting that the conduct of the Judaizers had nothing good in it.

Titus 2

Verse 1. Instead of doing false teaching as the Judaizers were, Titus was to counteract it by speaking that which *becomes* (is befitting to) *sound doctrine.* That means teaching that will cause spiritual health to all who accept it.

Verse 2. The apostle then specifies what will constitute *sound doctrine*. The items are appropriate for the persons in the various age groups and other places in the walks of life. The *aged* or elderly men were to "act their age" by being *sober* or watchful, *grave* or sober-minded, *temperate* or self-controlled. *Sound in the faith* means to be true to the word of God which is the basis of faith (Romans 10: 17). *In charity* requires them to be interested in the welfare of others. *Patience* means for them to be constant in their devotion to the Lord, enduring whatever it brings without complaining.

Verse 3. *Aged* is from the same Greek word as that for the men in the preceding verse, and signifies that the women are to keep in mind their years of life and behave accordingly. *As becometh holiness* means that a righteous life requires that they realize their responsibility in view of their age. *False accusers* is from the same word as "devil," and when used to describe character it means slanderers. *Given to much wine* is explained at 1 Timothy 3: 3. *Teachers of good things* is general, and they will be specified in the next two verses.

Verse 4. *Teach* is from a Greek word that has a general meaning, and is defined by Thayer, "to make or cause one to come to his senses; to moderate, control, curb, discipline; to hold one to his duty; to admonish, to exhort earnestly." When the young women are *sober* or self-controlled themselves, and then exert such influence upon others of their age class, it will cause them to love their husbands and children. They will show that love by the proper kind of behaviour.

Verse 5. They will be *discreet* or moderate, and *chaste*, which means to be pure in heart and life. *Keepers at home* is from OIKOUROS which Thayer defines, "The (watch or) keeper of a house. Keeping at home and taking care of household affairs, domestic." A woman cannot display the kind of character and conduct as this and the preceding verse describes, if she follows the example of many modern wives, who spend much of their time running round in the neighborhood, or devoting their attention to clubs and other social gatherings. *Good* has virtually the same meaning as *chaste*, except that the apostle adds the specification that they be *obedient to their own husbands.* Ephesians 5: 22-24 teaches that the husband is the head of the wife, hence she is required to be subject to him. *That the word of God be not blasphemed.* The world in general understands that a wife is supposed to be subject to her husband; but if she is otherwise while making a profession of being guided by the Bible, it will reflect unfavorably on that profession. To *blaspheme* means to speak evil, and hence such inconsistent conduct on the part of a married woman will give occasion to speak against the Book she claims to love.

Verse 6. *Sober minded* means having a mind of self-control.

Verse 7. Since Titus was himself a young man, as may be gathered from the fact of his being Paul's "son after the common faith" chapter 1: 4), it was proper that he show an example of righteous living before other young men by practicing good works. *In doctrine showing uncorruptness* denotes that his teaching was to be pure. *Gravity* denotes dignity and seriousness. *Sincerity* is from an original term that means especially a continuous life of pure conduct.

Verse 8. *Sound speech* is that which will have a good effect on those who accept it. *Cannot be condemned.* Such speech may be opposed and misrepresented, but it cannot be shown to be wrong. The opposers will therefore be put to shame when they are unable to say anything (truthfully) against it.

Verse 9. See the comments at 1 Timothy 6: 1 on the subject of servants. *Not answering again* means to refrain from "talking back" to their masters, but to do what they are told without arguing the matter.

Verse 10. *Purloining* means the taking of the property of another in a secret or underhand manner. A slave would have many opportunities for doing that, in connection with the services he has to render with the possessions of his master. *Showing all good fidelity* means for them to be honest and faithful with the goods of their masters as they go about their work. *Adorn* is from a Greek word that means to honor. In its details, it denotes that use of or handling of anything that recognizes order and harmony. If a slave is faithful in his service to his master, at the same time he is professing a belief in the doctrine or teaching of Christ, it will show that a man can be such a believer, and at the same time be under the yoke of servitude. The result will be to make a favorable impression on the mind of the master.

Verse 11. All of the words in this verse are correctly rendered, but the order in which they are arranged is different from the original. In its present form it means that the Gospel has appeared to all men. That is true, which may be seen also at Romans 10: 18 and Colossians 1: 23. But that is not the particular truth the apostle is stressing at this place. The order of words according to the Greek text should read as follows: "For appeared the grace of God which brings salvation for all men." This brings out the important truth that the Gospel is for all men, not for the Jews only as was the law of Moses.

Verse 12. *Teaching us that,* etc. This denotes that something more than the favor of God is involved in the salvation of man, and that he is required to do something in order to obtain this salvation. *Denying* does not mean to question the existence of the things mentioned, but that we must deny them the opportunity of affecting our lives. *Ungodliness and worldly lusts.* There is not much difference between the meaning of these terms. The first is a somewhat stronger word in the original, meaning a life that is wrong because it is vicious and wicked. The second concerns chiefly things that are wrong in that they conform to the world, and hence are interested in this life instead of that which is to come. *To live soberly* means to use judgment and wisdom such as that which is "from above" (James 3: 17). *Righteously* signifies a life that is patterned after the law of righteousness which is the Gospel. *Godly* is so termed because it requires a man to live in the way that will be pleasing to Him.

Verse 13. Christians may have the blessed hope in this life even, but they are *looking for* the fulfillment of it in the future. The glorious appearing of the *great God* and that of *our Saviour* refers to the same person. The Deity (Godhead) is composed of three persons, namely, the Father and Son and Holy Ghost (or Spirit), hence God is a proper term to be applied to either of them.

Verse 14. *Gave himself for us* shows that Christ is the particular one of the Godhead who is meant in the preceding verse, since He is the one who was given as a sacrifice. To *redeem* means to rescue something from a state of bondage. A condition of *iniquity* or sin was that from which Christ offered himself as a ransom. After being rescued from iniquity, we are purified and are ready to become the Lord's *peculiar* (special possession) *people*. Such a people are expected to have the distinction of being *zealous of good works*.

Verse 15. Titus was to *speak* so as to inform them of their duty. He was then to *exhort* them, which means to insist on doing what one knows to be his duty. If they refuse to perform their duty, the next thing is to rebuke the disobedient ones. *With all authority* means that Titus was fully authorized to speak all these things. To *despise* means to belittle, and Titus was to conduct himself in such a manner that people would look with respect upon him.

Titus 3

Verses 1, 2. *Put them in mind* means for Titus to remind the brethren in Crete of the following obligations. *Principalities and powers* refers to the units of authority in the civil government in force over the country. *Magistrates* are the particular officers who execute the government referred to in the preceding sentence. This obligation of Christians to the law of the land is taught also in Romans 13: 1-7. *To be ready to every good work.* If the country calls upon Christians to perform some kind of service, they should be ready to serve. All of this is with the proviso expressed at Acts 5: 29. *Speak evil of no man* does not prohibit us from condemning a man who does wrong, but we should not use evil expressions that are not founded upon facts. To be *no brawler* means not to be contentious, or dispute merely for the sake of opposition. *Gentleness* does not mean we need compromise with evil, but in our approach to persons in error, let us use language that is appropriate. *Meekness* is the same about as humility.

Verse 3. The separate items of this verse have been considered in many places. The main point the apostle is making is one of consideration for others. If we think back over the time before we became Christians, we will the better realize what it means to "turn round" and give up the practices that have been followed a great part of our life.

Verse 4. This verse is similar in thought to verse 11. In that place the grace of God is given credit for the offer of salvation to man. In the present passage it is the *kindness and love of God* that appeared in behalf of sinful man.

Verse 5. Man must perform the works of righteousness in order to be saved, but it was not such works that caused God to bring forward the plan. It was because of God's mercy that the offer of salvation was made for poor fallen humanity. *Washing of regeneration* refers to the same act as that in Hebrews 10: 22. *Renewing of the Holy Ghost* refers to the spiritual nourishment that children of God need to sustain their life of service to Him. That nourishment is the *sincere milk of the word* (1 Peter 2: 2). This word was given by men who were inspired by the Holy Ghost (or Spirit).

Verse 6. The pronoun *which* stands for the favor of salvation that is mentioned in the preceding verse and in chapter 2: 11. This salvation was *shed on us* or was brought within our reach by Jesus Christ.

Verse 7. The original word for *justified* has a great many shades of meaning, depending on the connection in which it is used. In this place the definition of Thayer is, "To judge, declare, pronounce, righteous and therefore acceptable." No man can be called just on his personal merit, but by the grace or favor of God, a sinner can be pardoned upon obedience to Christ, and then he will be "pronounced acceptable." After being thus freed from sin, he becomes an heir to eternal life toward which he may hope.

Verse 8. *This is a faithful saying* means it is a truthful one, referring to that in the following words, namely, that believers should follow up their conversion with good works. They will be *profitable* because they will bring much spiritual gain to man.

Verse 9. *Foolish questions* are those which are unprofitable. *Genealogies.* This subject is treated at length by the comments at 1 Timothy 1: 4. *Contentions* means useless arguments conducted merely from a motive of opposition. *Strivings about the law* refers to the disturbances caused by the Judaizers. Titus is told to avoid all these because they are *unprofitable* (bring no gain) and *vain* (or useless).

Verse 10. A *heretic* is a false teacher according to Thayer's lexicon. When

Titus came in contact with such in his work on the island, he was to admonish him to cease his false teaching because it was divisive. He was to be given a second opportunity to cease his heretical teaching, and if he persisted in it, Titus was to *reject* him, which means he was to avoid all association with him.

Verse 11. *Subverted* means to be turned aside from the proper course. Since nothing outside the proper course can be right, it follows that when a man leaves that course he *sinneth* as it is here stated. *Condemned of* himself. Not that he acknowledges his wrong, but is condemned by the things he *himself* is doing.

Verse 12. Chapter 1: 5 states that Titus was "left" in Crete for some extensive work. Hence this instruction for him to meet Paul at Nicapolis (of Macedonia), was for consultation. *Artemas* and *Tychicus* were friends and companions of Paul, whom he was planning to send to Crete, at which time Titus was to come to the apostle as instructed. That particular meeting place was designated because Paul had decided to pass the winter there.

Verse 13. Zenas was a *lawyer*, meaning an expert in the law of Moses. He and Apollos were to be escorted by Titus to the presence of Paul, and be provided with all things necessary for their transportation.

Verse 14. *Ours* refers to the disciples in Crete, who are commanded to *maintain good works*. This is rendered "profess honest trades" in the margin, which is a correct translation. The reader should see the comments at 1 Thessalonians 4: 11, 12 and 2 Thessalonians 3: 10. The subject is the importance for disciples to work for a living and not be a parasite upon others. A man who is too lazy to work has no right to eat. If he is unable on account of things beyond his control, that makes him a just object for the care of others. But all men are expected to contribute to the maintenance of himself and all who are depending on him lawfully for support.

Verse 15. Paul usually had brethren and friends with him who were interested in the work he was doing, and who also were kindly disposed towards the disciples to whom he wrote his epistles. When the apostle wrote them, it was common for them to join in sending salutations to the brethren thus separated from them. Such expressions indicated the love and interest they had for their fellow disciples. In turn, Paul asked for like greetings for those who were his friends in the island. Grace or favor was wished by the apostle for all the saints in the island. *Amen* means emphasis on the things that have been written.

Philemon

Verse 1. According to Thayer and Strong, and some commentators, Philemon was a resident of Colosse, and was converted to Christianity by Paul. Timothy is not mentioned as of any authority, but as an associate of Paul. His name is joined by way of friendly interest in Philemon and endorsement of the epistle. Paul calls himself a *prisoner of the Lord* because his imprisonment was caused by his service to Him. Philemon is designated *fellowlaborer* because he was working for the Lord in the same cause as was the apostle.

Verse 2. Apphia is described by Thayer merely as "name of a woman." Some commentators say she was the wife of Philemon and that Archippus was his son. The suggestion is given by the next phrase, *church in thy house*. In early times the congregations in some places were small, and had their services in the homes of the brethren. Or, the whole congregation may have consisted of the members of one household, if there were as many as two disciples in it (Matthew 18: 20). If Philemon's wife and son were disciples, they might well have composed the *church in his house*.

Verse 3. This is a familiar salutation of Paul, which he used in most of his epistles. See the comments on it at 1 Corinthians 1: 3.

Verse 4. The next verse shows what it was for which Paul thanked the Lord. Since the faithfulness of Philemon was a help to the apostle, he would consider it as a blessing, and it is stated in James 1: 17 that all good things come from God.

Verse 5. *Love* as used here means a sincere desire to help in the welfare of others in the work of the brethren, and an interest in the progress of the cause of the Lord. *Faith* means one's practice of the ordinances of the Lord's commandments.

Verse 6. The fellowship that Philemon had with others concerning the faith, had the effect or was tending to have a good effect on them. It would be manifested by their acknowledgment of the good example that he set before them.

Verse 7. *Love* in this passage is from a Greek original that means to be interested in the welfare of others. This is borne out by the rest of the verse, for it speaks of the refeshing that Philemon had brought to the *saints*, which means the Christians. *Bowels* is used to mean the intellectual part of the saints, from the ancient theory that the affections were seated in the intestines.

Verse 8. Paul was an apostle and had the authority to *enjoin* (or order) Philemon to do what was desired for him to do, had he thought it necessary to use that strong a form of speech.

Verse 9. Because of his love for Philemon, the apostle preferred to use a milder basis for his instruction, namely, his age and also his situation. Respect for age should incline Philemon to heed the request of Paul. Also, his imprisonment would indicate his sincerity which should prompt Philemon to heed the request.

Verse 10. The special request referred to in the preceding verses was concerning Onesimus. He was a slave of Philemon, but not the most satisfactory kind of one. (See next verse.) He had run away from his master, and in some way had come to Rome and fallen into the company of Paul. The apostle taught him his duty to the Lord and induced him to obey it. On this principle he calls him his *son*, in the same way he referred to Timothy as his son (1 Timothy 1: 2).

Verse 11. Servants are commanded to obey their masters (Ephesians 6: 5; Colossians 3: 22). The teaching Paul gave Onesimus, therefore, would include his duty to his master. That would explain why he would be *now profitable* to Philemon, and also to Paul because of being in fellowship with him.

Verse 12. In keeping with his duty as a part of the life of a Christian slave, Onesimus returned to his master at the instruction of Paul. *Thou therefore receive him* is a kindly commendation. *Mine own bowels*. A child is brought forth from the bowels of his parents, and since that part of the human anatomy is used figuratively of mental and spiritual matters, Paul uses it here to signify that Onesimus had been begotten by him in the sense that he had brought him to obey the Gospel.

Verse 13. *I would have retained*. Had Paul felt free to follow his personal desires, he would have kept Onesimus with him as a helper in his struggles for the Gospel under the handicap of imprisonment. Had such a thing been done, Paul would have considered the service the same as if it was coming from Philemon.

Verse 14. Such a service, however, would have been equivalent to taking some benefit from Philemon without his consent, and the apostle would not do anything like that.

Verse 15. This could not mean that Onesimus left his master with the motive of some advantage to him. A slave who had been *unprofitable* would not likely be that much interested in the welfare of the man from whom he was fleeing. The meaning is as if it read, "Perhaps it will turn out to be an advantage to you, after all, for him to leave, for now the way that things have happened, he will be a better servant than ever."

Verse 16. *Not now as a servant*. Onesimus was to continue as a servant to Philemon, but not in that relation only. He was to be regarded as a brother also, which was a spiritual relationship, and far above that of an earthly servant. *Especially to me* is said because Paul was the one who converted him to Christ. Yet because of prior relations, he was to be appreciated by Philemon all the more, both as a servant in *fleshly* or temporal matters, and as a brother in the Lord.

Verse 17. On the ground that Philemon would agree to all these considerations of relationship, Paul asks him to indicate his recognition of the partnership by accepting Onesimus back into his love the same as if he were the apostle.

Verse 18. *If he hath wronged thee*. A slave would have many opportunities for doing wrong to his master by taking some of his possessions (Titus 2: 10). Whether that is meant here, or only the wrong he did by his "unprofitable" service (verse 11), we do not know. But in either case, Paul was offering to make it up to Philemon. *Put that on mine account*. Whatever was the obligation that Onesimus owed his master, Paul agreed to have the debt transferred to his account against Philemon.

Verse 19. This obligation or account of Paul against Philemon was not a material one, but a moral one due to what he owed the apostle for having led him into the service of salvation. *Albeit I do not say*, etc. This unusual sentence is a sort of explanation, to assure Philemon that what he said was not for the purpose of reminding him of his indebtedness (morally) to the apostle for his conversion to Christ.

Verse 20. *Let me have joy of thee.* This he could do by receiving Onesimus in the way that Paul requested. Such an act of cooperation would constitute a *refreshing* or encouragement for the *bowels* or heart of the apostle.

Verse 21. *Do more than I say.* Not that Philemon would go beyond and add to the inspired word of the apostle, for that would be wrong (Revelation 22: 18). But it means he would even be more thoughtful in good deeds than Paul was requiring.

Verse 22. Paul had hopes of being released and permitted to go out among the churches, and the testimony of history indicates that it was accomplished. In view of such an experience, he asked that Philemon make provision for his lodging.

Verses 23, 24. The names mentioned are of some brethren who were with Paul. They were either in chains also, or were otherwise engaged in defence of the Gospel. As Paul was writing this letter, these brethren joined in friendly greeting to Philemon.

Verse 25. *Grace* is the favor of Christ, which Paul wished to come to Philemon. *With your spirit.* This is significant, for a true Christian is bound to have unpleasant experiences as it pertains to his body (2 Timothy 3: 12); yet he may be comfortable and refreshed in spirit all the while. (See 2 Corinthians 4: 16.)

Hebrews 1

General remarks. Much has been said on the subject of whether Paul, or some other person, is the author of this book. I shall offer a few statements in view of the importance of the question due to the general agitation. I believe Paul is the author because it has the same logical form of reasoning shown in his other epistles. Also, 2 Peter 3: 15, 16 declares that Paul had written an epistle to the brethren, and his discription of it ("some things hard to be understood") indicates one consisting of logical discussion. It is true also that many of the Nicene writers (known as Apostolic Fathers) ascribe the epistle to Paul. These men lived only a few centuries this side of Christ, and hence had access to evidences that were well founded. Furthermore, there is no negative reason for ascribing it to any other writer, for the whole epistle contains nothing that differs in a single feature from the manner of Paul's language or reasoning.

Verse 1. The principal subject of this book is the law of Christ over that of Moses and the prophets. The revelation of God's will was made known through Christ in the place of all other means in former times. The most outstanding disturbance of the first century of the Gospel Dispensation was caused by Judaizers. That means Jews or any others who insisted that Christians should conform to the Mosaic system in connection with their profession of faith in Christ. This book was written to show the errors in such a teaching. *Sundry times and in divers manners* refers to the many instances and various plans under which God used to give his revelations of truth to the prophets, to be given on by them to the heads of the units of His people.

Verse 2. *Last days* means the closing days of the Jewish Dispensation, since that was when Jesus lived in his personal ministry. The Son gave the words of the Father to the apostles (John 17: 8) and they to us, and that is the way in which we of this age have been spoken to of God. *Appointed heir of all things.* Heir is used in the sense of possessor (John 17: 10) because God turned all things pertaining to the new dispensation over to Him (Matthew 28: 18). *By whom also he made the worlds.* This refers to the cooperation which Jesus showed in all of God's works. See the plural "us" in Genesis 1: 26; 3: 22; also read John 1: 3.

Verse 3. Thayer defines *brightness* by "reflected brightness," meaning that when Jesus was on earth he reflected the glory of his Father. *Express image* is from CHARAKTER which Thayer defines at this place, "A mark or figure burned in or stamped on, an impression; the exact expression (the image) of any person or thing, marked likeness, precise reproduction in every respect." God is not composed of substance as that word is commonly used, hence the word *person* as in the King James Version is a good translation. It means that when Christ was on earth, he had the form or image of his Father. That is one reason why He said, "he that hath seen me hath seen the father" (John 14: 9). All of this agrees with the words of God that the man was to be created in "our" (God's and Christ's) image (Genesis 1: 26). *Upholding all things by the word of his power.* All power (or authority) being given to Christ (Matthew 28: 18), the arrangement of all things pertaining to the new system of salvation was disposed of according to His will and direction. *By himself purged our sins.* This took place when He died on the cross, thereby making the supreme sacrifice that was sufficient to purge all men from their sins who would accept it. By the death on the cross, the plan was made completely efficient, which is why He said "it is finished" (John 19: 30). By coming alive from the grave, Jesus validated the purchase price of man's salvation, and then He was ready to return to his Father. He did so and was seated at the right hand of the throne of God, having been welcomed by the angelic hosts in the city of everlasting glory. (See the wonderful reception given Christ in Psalms 24: 7-10.)

Verse 4. *Better* does not apply to the personal character, for the angels who are living in heaven are perfect in that respect. Thayer defines the original word, "It is more advantageous." The meaning of the phrase is that Jesus was given a greater advantage in the great plan of God than the angels. The word *excellent* is to be understood also in the sense of advantage. *By inheritance* means that Jesus received this mentioned advantage through his relationship with God. It was not merely given to him as a man might see fit to give something to a stranger, but this was his by right of being the Son of God; he inherited it. While the favors or honors that the angels enjoy were given to them by the Creator of all things.

Verse 5. The *more excellent name* mentioned in the preceding verse is that of Son, as we may observe by the argument of this verse. God never said *Thou art my Son* to a single one of the angels, as he did to Jesus. *This day have I begotten thee* occurred when Mary conceived of God by the services of the Holy Spirit (Luke 1: 27-38). The angels were not brought into being by any personal relations between God and another being as was Jesus, but was created directly by the power of God. The rest of this verse restates the same relationship already mentioned.

Verse 6. When Jesus was born of the virgin Mary, God directed all the angels to *worship him.* That word in the Greek New Testament comes from several different words, and has a variety of meanings, depending on the connection in which it is used. In the present passage it means to "do homage" or manifest great respect for one. There are myriads of angels, and all of them were told to render homage to the babe in Bethlehem. The argument the apostle is making is that if such great beings as the angels were commanded to acknowledge the superiority of the babe that was laid in a manger, He certainly is to be ascribed a great giver of law. (If angels worshipped the humble babe thus posed in the city of David, common mortals like us should regard it an honor to be permitted the act of worshiping him today, when He is sitting at his Father's right hand, reigning as King of kings and Lord of lords.)

Verse 7. But even this contrast with angels would not mean so much, unless the angels themselves were important beings. Accordingly, Paul says God makes his angels ministering spirits, thus being very important personages in the great scheme of grace.

Verse 8. The superiority of Christ over all other beings (except his Father) is still the main subject. *Thy throne O God.* Jesus is called God because that is the family name of the Godhead. He is called God in Acts 20: 28, where his blood is mentioned as the purchasing price of the church. The throne of Christ is declared by his Father to be *for ever and ever* because He is to reign to the end of the age (1 Corinthians 15: 24-26). A scepter is a rod or instrument that a ruler holds that is a token of his authority. The scepter connected with the kingdom of Christ is a righteous one, because it requires the citizens of the kingdom to live a life of righteousness only.

Verse 9. *Loved righteousness and hated iniquity.* This phrase expresses two completely opposite terms. *Hated* is from a Greek word that sometimes has a milder meaning than it does here. In the present passage it is defined by Thayer, "To hate, pursue with hatred, detest." Because Christ had these qualities, He was given the great honor that the verse states. The specification, *God, even thy God*, is made because the name "God" is the family name of the Deity, and Christ had that name by virtue of his being a member of the family. But in the work assigned to Him as head of the kingdom, He was to be a king and the Father was to be God over him (1 Corinthians 11: 3). In old times it was customary to anoint kings with oil at their coronation. Christ was figuratively anointed with the *oil of gladness* or exultation. *Above thy fellows* means that Christ was exalted higher than any other ruler that had ever been on earth.

Verse 10. This and the following two verses are quoted from Psalms 102: 24-27. David was the famous ancestor of Christ, yet he recognizes him as his Lord (Matthew 22: 43-45). The work of creation is ascribed to Christ because he was associated with his Father in that work. It is so taught in John 1: 1-3, and it is indicated likewise by the plural pronoun "us" in Genesis 1: 26; 3: 22.

Verse 11. The main subject of this epistle is the superiority of Christ over all other persons or things (except his Father). The works of creation, in the making of which He had a part, will cease to be even though He will continue. *They* means the things of creation mentioned in the preceding verse. *Wax old as doth a garment* is an illustration drawn from a garment that has reached the end of its usefulness. When a garment gets into that condition, it is discarded and treated as the next verse states.

Verse 12. A *vesture* is a covering piece, to be folded up or discarded when no longer useful. *Changed* is from ALLASSO which Thayer defines, "To exchange one thing for another." This is said with reference to the earth and the other parts of the material universe related to it. They are finally to be discarded and dissolved, and other things will be used in their place. (See 2 Peter 3: 10-13; Revelation 21: 1.) *Thou art the same*. Not that Christ will never change his position in the great plan of God, for He will cease to be the king after the judgment day (1 Corinthians 15: 24-27). But He will never cease to be (as will the material universe), and in that sense His years *shall not fail*.

Verse 13. The second part of this verse is a quotation from Psalms 110: 1, in which David states something that God said of Christ. The point that Paul is making is that since nothing like this was ever said to any one of the angels, Christ is to be regarded as superior to them. Making His enemies his footstool is equivalent to subjecting all things to him, which is the thing predicted in 1 Corinthians 15: 25, 26.

Verse 14. Unless the angels also are important beings, there would not be much significance in being made superior to them. Paul recognizes this point by the statement made here in question form. Angels are among the instruments or agencies which God uses, in his treatment of and care for His own. (Read the following passages. Genesis 24: 7; Daniel 6: 22; Matthew 2: 13; Acts 12: 11; 27: 23.)

Hebrews 2

Verse 1. *Therefore* means in view of the things set forth in the preceding chapter, the following conclusions should be observed. *More earnest heed* signifies that we should be all the more concerned about it, since we have heard our duty taught by the Son of God and his spokesmen. *Slip* is from PARARREO, which Thayer defines, "To flow past, to glide by; lest we be carried past, pass by." He then explains his definition to mean, "Lest the salvation which the things heard show us how to obtain slip away from us." Thayer also quotes from Greek literature to show the word to mean, "A thing escapes me, slips away from my mind." Even if Christians do not deliberately discard the sayings of Christ, they may forget about them unless they give earnest heed to them.

Verse 2. *Spoken by angels*. There were times when God delivered some special messages to individuals through the services of angels (Genesis 16: 9; 19: 17, and others). But the main thing Paul has in mind is the use God made of the angels in delivering the Mosaic law to the people (Acts 7: 53; Galatians 3: 19). *Was stedfast* means it was fairly established on the authority of Christ. *Transgression* denotes a going over and beyond an established law; not only the doing what it expressly says must not be done, but also the doing of what it does not give any authority to do. *Disobedience* means the simple failure to do what the law requires, regardless of the cause or motive for such failure. *Recompence of reward* is all from one Greek word that means the treatment one receives on account of his conduct. *Just* signifies that what was done to those who transgressed or disobeyed the law of Moses, given through the services of angels, was proper and what they deserved.

Verse 3. *How shall we escape* our just fate? *If we neglect* is fully as dangerous as to be guilty of active wrongdoing. *So great salvation* is said because of the greatness of the means by which it was made known to us, which means will now be described. *Began to be spoken by the Lord.* Jesus spent more than three years in the personal work of preparing the foundation or fundamentals of His kingdom among men. *Was confirmed unto us by them that heard him.* This refers to the apostles who were chosen by Christ to be with him all of the time between His baptism and ascension (Acts 1: 21, 22). The apostles had first-hand information from Christ when he was on earth, and they afterward received "all truth" pertaining to the Gospel as the plan of Christ for salvation (John 16: 13). This word was *confirmed* by the miracles which they and their converts were enabled to perform (Mark 16: 20).

Verse 4. These miracles are to be attributed to God also, because He bestowed the Holy Ghost (or Spirit) on the apostles in answer to the prayer of Christ (John 14: 16). *Gifts according to his own will.* The miraculous gifts which the disciples were enabled to perform in the early years of the church were regulated by the Lord in the best way for the good of the work of salvation (1 Corinthians 12: 7).

Verse 5. Paul is still considering the superiority of Christ over the angels, and of His law over that which was "spoken by angels." Those beings were inferior even to all men that they were not to have dominion over the earth at the time of creation, while it was given to man. (See Genesis 1: 26-28.) The *world* means the inhabited part of the universe, and *to come* is said because when the dominion was given to man, the population of the earth was still in the future.

Verse 6. *One in a certain place* means David in Psalms 8: 4-6. *Testified* is a strong word in the original, and denotes a solemn and earnest declaration, as if the speaker felt surprise and admiration over something. *What is man* is not meant to lower the importance of man, except as a contrast with so great a Being as the creator of all things. That God would be mindful of such a creature to the extent of the facts referred to, caused David to express himself as it is in this passage. *Son of man* is virtually the same as the simple term *man* above, except that it indicates a being that is reproduced by another like himself, and hence that he is inferior to his Creator. *Visitest* is from EPISKEPTOMAI which Thayer defines, "To look upon in order to help or to benefit, equivalent to look after, have a care for, provide for."

Verse 7. *Little lower than the angels* This same thing is said of Jesus in verse 9, and the sense in which it is said is explained, namely, *for the suffering of death.* Hence we understand that this inferiority of man to the angels in the present verse refers to the nature of his body, that it is possible for him to die which the angels cannot do (Luke 20: 36). Notwithstanding this humble status of man, God did crown him with the glory and honor of being placed over the works of His hands.

Verse 8. *Thou hast put all things in subjection under his feet.* This is said in reference to what is declared in Genesis 1: 26-28. From here on the apostle extends his remarks to include Jesus, which is not considered in the original passage in the Psalms. This is not the only instance where a New Testament writer makes a second or extended use of an Old Testament passage. Hosea 11: 1 is said regarding the departure of ancient Israel from Egypt, but Matthew 2: 14, 15 quotes it and applies it to Christ. Likewise Matthew 1: 23 cites Isaiah 7: 14 and applies is to Christ, yet the passage in Isaiah first referred to an infant born to the prophet and his young wife. *See not yet all things put under him* is said of Jesus, and the next two verses will indicate what it is that is not yet *put under* or been conquered by Jesus, and what he must first suffer before His final victory over all except his Father.

Verse 9. Jesus was made lower than the angels in regard to his body only, as explained in verse 7; it is further explained in the present verse. In order to be able to taste death for every man, He must himself be able to die, which required such a body. It was by the grace or favor of God for mankind, that Jesus was enabled to die (and live again) for humanity.

It was a *glory and honor* for Jesus to be crowned with such an exalted privilege as that of dying for the salvation of man.

Verse 10. The pronoun *him* refers to God, and it *became him* or was befitting that He should do the things mentioned in the verse. *Whom* also is a pronoun standing for God, because all things were originally for and by Him. He planned to bring many (as many as would) persons unto the glory of spiritual service in this life, and eternal glory in the life to come. For such a grand accomplishment it was necessary to have a captain who could lead them in the manner. Such a captain was to be Jesus, and he was made *perfect* (completely qualified) by suffering. Such an experience was all that Jesus lacked before he came to the earth, and hence He was given a fleshly body that was capable of suffering and death.

Verse 11. This verse and on through the chapter, carries the main subject of the oneness and fellowship that was designed to exist between Jesus and those whom he planned to save. To be *sanctified* means to be devoted to the service of God. Such a state of devotion is accomplished through Jesus who is *he that sanctifieth*. They are *all of one* in that both Jesus and his disciples are united in reverence for God who makes all good things possible that exist. In this sense they are all brethren and Jesus is not ashamed in the happy relationship.

Verse 12. Paul verifies his statement of the preceding verse by a quotation from the Psalms 22: 22, which is a part of a chapter composed of predictions about Christ. *In the midst of the church.* In Matthew 18: 20 Jesus promises to be present in every scriptural assembly, and in such a meeting He will be joining in the praises.

Verse 13. This verse is a quotation from some Old Testament sayings, parts of them from David, pertaining to the close fellowship between the Lord and his disciples.

Verse 14. The fellowship is continued in this verse. The motive for sharing in a nature of flesh and blood is the same as indicated in verse 9. *Destroy* is used in the sense of counteract, for the devil will never be literally destroyed. But he had the *power* of causing death to come upon mankind, and Jesus died and rose again in order to bring all men to life again.

Verse 15. *Bondage* is from DOULEIA which is literally defined by Thayer as follows: "Slavery, bondage, the condition of a slave." He then explains it to mean, "The slavish sense of fear." With no prospect of living again, mankind would have a feeling of dread for death that would be like the terror caused by a harsh master over his slaves. Such a fear of death would indeed be a cruel bondage, but the resurrection of Christ dispelled that fear in the minds of all who believe in Him.

Verse 16. *Nature* is not in the original text because angels are not natural beings. The thought is that Jesus did not come into the world with a body like those of the angels, for then He could not have died (Luke 20: 36). He came instead as a fleshly descendant of Abraham.

Verse 17. It was necessary for Jesus to be like his brethren with regard to His body, in order to have a sympathetic interest in their trials and other tests. Being so formed, He could have a feeling of mercy toward them in their transgressions. One meaning of *faithful* is to be "worthy of trust; that can be relied on." Christ became such a high priest by partaking of the nature of fleshly man, while not surrendering His divine character and likeness to God. This qualified him to make *reconciliation* (satisfaction with God) for the sins of the people.

Verse 18. Jesus was clothed with the flesh and was actually tempted (yet never yielded; chapter 4: 15) as we are. This made Him able to *succour* (support) others who were taken in their sins, or who are in danger of being so taken.

Hebrews 3

Verse 1. Let the reader keep constantly in mind the leading thought in this book, namely, the superiority of the system of Christ over that of Moses. *Holy brethren.* Not that worshipers under Moses were not holy, for they were required to be so (Leviticus 11: 44, 45). But they did not become brethren by their holiness; they were born into that relationship regardless of their knowledge of God. (See 1 Samuel 3: 7.) To be brethren of Christ requires a life of righteousness (Matthew 12: 50), hence Paul calls these people by the term italicized. *Heavenly calling* is used mainly as a mark of superiority for the service under Christ over the old one. The word *apostle* means one who is sent on a mission with authority to speak and act. Jesus was sent from Heaven to earth to carry out a mission of salvation. After shedding His blood in a supreme sacrifice, Jesus was qualified to reenter the court of eternal glory, there to act as the High Priest for the Christians on the merits of His shed blood, even as the high priests in the Mosaic system entered the second court of the tabernacle and temple with the blood of animals.

Verse 2. *Who was faithful . . . as also Moses*. All of the good points about Moses were equalled and some of them were excelled by Christ. They were equal as to being faithful over their own houses or religious institutions.

Verse 3. *This man* means Christ, and a point in which he excelled Moses is stated, namely, that He was the builder of his own house (the church). The house over which Moses presided was the Jewish nation of which he was not the originator.

Verse 4. The word *man* is not in the original and *some* is an indefinite pronoun. The idea is that as a rule, each house has its own particular builder whose activities are limited to the one house. On the other hand, God is the Master builder whose architectural powers include everything in the universe.

Verse 5. Moses did not build the house (Jewish nation), but he was given the honor of being a servant over it. Since he was a faithful servant, his behaviour and teaching became a *testimony* or background for the *things which were to be spoken afterward*, meaning the ordinances under Christ. (See Romans 15: 4.)

Verse 6. Christ was even more than a faithful servant; he was a son, and was given the honor of presiding over His own house (the church), which his Father gave to him. *Whose house are we* refers to Paul and all others who are faithful. The faithfulness consists in maintaining our *confidence* or trust in Christ, which causes us to rejoice in the hope that such a divine house contains. It is necessary that our conduct in these matters be continued *unto the end* (of life).

Verse 7. Paul now makes a quotation from Psalms 95: 7-11, but strengthens it with the declaration that it is the Holy Ghost (or Spirit) that says it. That means that David was inspired to make the statement. *Hear his voice* means to hear God who speaks to us through his Son (chapter 1: 1).

Verse 8. *Harden not your hearts* is a warning not to set their minds against the teaching of Christ. *As in the provocation* refers to the disobedience of ancient Israel by which they provoked God into punishing them. Paul specifies the circumstance to which he refers by mention of the days they were going through the wilderness.

Verse 9. The apostle gives further explanation of his preceding warning by the words of this verse. *Your fathers* means the first heads of the Jewish nation. *Tempted* and *proved* occurred when the disobedience of the Israelites put the patience of God to a test. Such conduct on their part was without cause, for they had abundance of evidence that He was able to care for them under all conditions, and also that He would punish them for their rebellion. All of this was manifested to them during the *forty years* in the wilderness.

Verse 10. To be *grieved* means God was "wroth or displeased with" them according to Thayer's lexicon. *That generation* has reference to the heads of the nation who were leaders in the rebellious actions. Their misconduct was due to a heart or mind filled with error. As a result of such an attitude toward God, they failed to become acquainted with *His ways* or the ways the Lord wished the people to follow.

Verse 11. God *sware* or made a solemn decision against the disobedient people. This was caused by His wrath or *grief* as mentioned in verse 10. The decision was that they should not be permitted to *enter into my rest*. This rest refers to their settlement in the promised land, which the Lord had designed should come to his people after the weariness of the wandering. God calls it *his* rest because he designed it to be an antitype of the rest on the seventh day from His works of creation.

Verse 12. *Take heed* is the same warning made in verse 8, for these Christians not to make the same mistake their Jewish forefathers made in the wilderness. *Unbelief* is shown to cause man to have an *evil heart*. Such a heart will cause a man to *depart from the living God*. This is the same warning Paul gave in his epistle to the church at Corinth (1 Corinthians 10: 1-11). We should profit by the mistakes of others and thus avoid a like falling from the favor of the Lord. The record of these things is placed in the Old Testament for our benefit (Romans 15: 4).

Verse 13. To *exhort* means to insist on doing what we know to be our duty. These brethren knew it was their duty to listen to the teaching given by Christ, for they just had the instruction in this epistle. They were told to do the exhorting *daily* which would require frequent contact with each other. Such an intimacy was expected of the people of Christ, and it was even predicted that it would be so. In Malachi 3: 16 we may read, "Then they that feared the Lord spake often to each other." *While it is called to day* is equivalent to saying, "While the days are going by." This teaching of Paul is not very favorable to the notion of half-hearted disciples who insist that Christians have no need to assemble except on Lord's Day to "partake of the communion." *Hardened through the deceitfulness of sin.* The Lord knew that frequent contact with each other was necessary to prevent disciples being deceived by sin.

Verse 14. This verse is virtually the same as verse 6. To be a partaker of Christ is to have part in the good things He has in store for his faithful disciples.

Verse 15. *While it is said* signifies that the admonition will not always be given, hence while it is *to day* is the time to heed the admonition given by the apostle.

Verse 16. Again the apostle wishes his readers to profit by the mistakes of their forefathers. *For some* indicates that Paul has reference to a certain part of the Jewish people in the wilderness. We may often hear some such a remark as the following: "Of the vast congregation that left Egypt only two ever reached the promised land." This will be said in spite of the positive statement that the failure to go through did not happen to *all that came out of Egypt by Moses.* This kind of statement would indicate a greater number of exceptions than only two.

Verse 17. This verse explains that the forgoing sad fate pertained only to the sinners—those able to be responsible for their actions. Those were the ones only *whose carcases fell in the wilderness.* The identity of the class that fell is made still more definite in Numbers 14: 22-31. By considering these several verses it may be seen that only the men of war are considered when just two were to be permitted to enter the land of promise. We have no definite information as to how many women and children made the entire journey from Egypt to Canaan.

Verse 18. The ones who were to be unable to enter the land of promise are again mentioned under the general description of *them that believed not.*

Verse 19. All of the shortcomings the Israelites committed in the wilderness are charged up against *unbelief.* This is significant and teaches the fundamental truth that whenever professed disciples fail to do their duty, it may be laid to their lack of faith.

Hebrews 4

Verse 1. The word *fear* in this verse means anxiety or extreme caution, not to make the same mistake the Israelites made. There is a promise made to the disciples of Christ, to be considered a few verses below, and they might *come short* or miss it.

Verse 2. The simple meaning of *gospel* is "good news," hence any announcement of good news or promises may rightly be termed gospel. The Israelites had good information that they were to be given a land of rest from their wanderings. The disciples of Christ are given the promise of a rest from their worldly cares after this life is over, provided they are faithful to the end. The promise did not profit the Israelites under consideration because they did not believe it. (See chapter 3: 18, 19.)

Verse 3. *We which have believed* are the only ones who are promised the privilege of entering into rest. *As I have sworn,* etc., God deals with all people on the same principle. That is that He declared to ancient Israel that their unbelief would keep them out of the promised land. *Although the works were finished.* A rest period implies a preceding one of work, and that took place in the beginning of creation. Hence the rest after the labor was established, which was to serve as a type of the next rest; the one in Canaan after the wandering in the wilderness.

Verse 4. The *certain place* where this is spoken is Genesis 2: 2, 3, and that is where the Lord set the pattern of rest after labor that was to be a foreshadowing of another rest far into the future.

Verse 5. But the ones whom God planned to enjoy that second rest made themselves unworthy of it, hence He sware that they should not enter into it.

Verse 6. *Remaineth that some must enter therin.* God is sure to "have His own way" at last, even though certain ones may be rebellious and thus lose the benefits that He intended for them. Even if unbelief cuts off the ones first intended to have been favored, the Lord will find another outlet for the divine mercy.

Verse 7. *Limiteth* is from a Greek word that means "to determine, appoint" according to Thayer. *Saying in David* means it is said in the writings or David, namely, in Psalms 95: 7, 8. The thought of this verse is that God "determined" to have another rest and caused David to write about it, and to exhort the ones living before it not to make the mistake the former ones did.

Verse 8. The Greek word for Jesus is also defined "Joshua" in the lexicon, and should be so translated in this verse. Joshua led the few faithful ones across the Jordan into the Canaan rest, but God had already determined upon another rest, seeing so many of the candidates for the rest in Canaan had proved unworthy. In justice to the fathful ones at that time, they were permitted to be led by Joshua into the land of Canaan, but that circumstance was not to be regarded as the final arragement of the Lord for a better rest. That is why our verse states that Jesus (Joshua) did not *give them rest*, meaning he did not give them the third and final rest. This truth is further indicated by the Lord's statement afterwards that there was to be *another day*.

Verse 9. This verse is the climax of the reasoning in the preceding verses. *There remaineth* signifies that the final rest is still in the future, and that is the one which Christians are warned not to miss on account of unbelief. It may be well to observe that three rests have been discussed by Paul, and he shows that God speaks of them as "my rest." That is because He originated them and determined the conditions affecting them. B r i e f l y stated, the three rests are the seventh day after the creation, the national rest in Canaan, and the rest in Heaven after the judgement.

Verse 10. This is a comment on the relation of the rest to work. The mere mention of *rest* implies a preceding period of *work* to be followed by the rest.

Verse 11. Verse 9 states the grand conclusion upon the line of reasoning the apostle has been giving. The present verse states the exhortation that would logically be given upon such a conclusive background. Since the term *rest* implies a preceding one of *labor*, the apostle makes his exhortation upon that basis. Disciples who are not willing to labor for the Lord, should not expect to share in His rest. If they at last "come short of it," the cause will be attributed to their disobedience or *unbelief*.

Verse 12. The orginal Greek word for *quick* is defined in the lexicon as "alive" and that for *powerful* is "active." The meaning of the clause is that the word of God is alive and active. When it is absorbed as spiritual food its effect should be to make one a living and active servant of the Lord. A *twoedged* sword is extra sharp because such instruments are made of the best material. Likewise the word of God is composed of the best material, namely, the wisdom of divine inspiration. It would not indicate any unusual keenness for a knife to sever between things that do not resemble, or that are not closely adhering to each other. The ability of the "sword of the Spirit" to distinguish between the *soul and spirit* of man is mentioned as a proof of its keennesss. This indicates that there is not much difference between them, and yet that some difference exists. This subject is explained in t h e comments at 1 Thessalonians 5: 23. *Joints and marrow* are other parts of the human system that pertain to the flesh, and are used figuratively for the same purpose as the preceding illustration, showing the sharpness of the divine instrument. *Discerner* is from κριτικος which means a measuring rule or standard, by which things are measured and judged. The statement means that the word of God is the standard by which all our thoughts and intents are to be regulated. It is sometimes insisted that Christians may think whatever they please as long as they keep it to themselves. This verse condems such a notion, and it is contradicted also by Philippians

4: 8, 9 which tells Christians the subjects on which they have a right to think.

Verse 13. The foregoing verse and remarks have special reference to the Word of God as an inspired volume. But if God can produce a book that has such qualities, then He certainly has a mind that is likewise able. Everything that we think (or do) is seen by the eyes of the Infinite One, because his "eyes are in every place, beholding the evil and the good" (Proverbs 15: 3).

Verse 14. Jesus is a *great high priest* because he is the Son of God. Another item of His greatness is his entrance into *the heavens* or the place where God is, whereas the high priests of the Mosaic system entered into the buildings on earth, which were only the figures or types of the ones above. Paul uses this truth as a basis for our holding *fast* or firm to our profession of faith; not going back to Moses.

Verse 15. In taking on a body with the same nature as ours, Jesus was able to have the same experiences as we. *Touched with the feeling* means to sympathize with our infirmities. Whatever would be a temptation to us would be likewise one to Him, and he came in contact with all kinds of temptations which are on the earth, yet never yielded once to them.

Verse 16. *Come boldly* denotes a feeling of confidence that we may have on account of such a sympthetic Intercessor. The Israelites came near the tabernacle or temple, relying on their high priest to officiate on their behalf, by making intercession for them before the mercyseat in the most holy place, which was a type of the *throne of grace.* Accordingly we as spiritual Israel may approach by faith unto this throne where Jesus is acting as our High Priest. Our prayers through Him will reach the ears of God, calling for *grace* or favor to help us in the *time of need* while in this world of temptation.

Hebrews 5

Verse 1. The superiority of the system of Christ over that of Moses continues to be the subject of this book. The discussion is especially formed around the priesthoods, making comparison to show wherein they are alike as well as where they differ. This and a number of verses following will deal (generally) with many of the points in which they are similar. The high priests of the Mosaic system were men—human beings—who were *ordained* (appointed) to act on behalf of the nation's relation to the things of God. These priests acted in these things by offering the *gifts* and *sacrifices* for their sins. The two words are much alike in many respects. The first means the offerings that were made voluntarily, consisting of money or fruits that could be used for the living of the priests or the maintenance of the temple. The second has reference to animals that were to become victims on the altar; the blood of some of these was taken by the high priest into the most holy place.

Verse 2. The *ignorant* means those less informed than the priests who were better aquainted with the matters of the service. (See Leviticus 10: 8-11; Deuteronomy 17: 8-13; John 11: 49-52.) Out of the way denotes those who err in their ways on account of their lack of knowledge. *Can have compassion* means the same as "being touched" as was explained by the comments on chapter 4: 15. *Compassed with infirmity* means those priests had the same fleshly tendencies as others of the nation.

Verse 3. This can apply to the high priests under the old law only, since Jesus had no sins to be atoned for.

Verse 4. The apostle again takes up the points in which the high priests of both systems were similar. Numbers 16 and 18 will clearly show that Aaron did not seek the office of high priest, but that he was called into that service by the Lord.

Verse 5. Thou art my Son, etc., was not what made Jesus the High Priest of the Christian Dispensation. It is quoted as an identification of the One who did call Christ into that office. David is the one who wrote the statement by inspiration, and it was written many centuries before Christ was born.

Verse 6. This verse cites another passage in David's writings (Psalms 110: 4) that predicts the priesthood of Jesus, even specifying one of the particulars in which He was to be superior to the Levitical priests (which is another of the points of difference referred to above); being like Melchisedek in that it was not to be changeable as were the Levitical priests. Having been determined upon and predicted of God long before he was born, Jesus could not be accused of usurping the office.

Verse 7. *Days of his flesh* means while Jesus lived on the earth before his crucifixion. He often prayed to his Father, but we are not always told what was the subject of the prayers. The one in the garden (Luke 22: 41-44) is an instance of *supplications with strong crying and tears*. Our present verse indicates one subject of His prayers was to be saved from death. This could not mean that when He prayed in the garden he was asking God to shield him from death on the cross. Peter was rebuked for trying to shield his Master from death (Matthew 26: 51-54; John: 18 10, 11). But the prayer of our verse received a favorable answer, for it says He *was heard*. *Save* is from the Greek word sozo which Thayer defines. "To bring safe forth from." Jesus was saved from death in the sense that He was brought "safe forth from" the grave, hence the conclusion is established that He prayed for that favor from his Father, intensifying the prayers with the *supplications* and *tears*.

Verse 8. *Though he were a Son*, Jesus was not excused from undergoing the program his Father planned for him. Jesus learned by practical experience what it means to obey his Father, when the trials of His life led up to his suffering and crucifixion.

Verse 9. The word *perfect* means complete and fully qualified or equipped. The experience of suffering is what gave Jesus this completion. *Author* is from a Greek word that p r i m a r i l y means "cause." Jesus suffered many trials and finally went to His death on the cross. This qualified Him to cause a plan of eternal salvation to be effected for mankind. *Eternal* is from AIONIOS, which Thayer defines at this passage, "Without end, never to cease, everlasting." The salvation offered by Christ will go on endlessly after the world ceases to be. However, the important condition on which men may obtain this salvation is that they obey Him.

Verse 10. Melchisedec had no successor in his priesthood, neither will Jesus have any, for He is now and will continue to be High Priest.

Verse 11. *Of whom* has direct referenec to Melchisdec because he was the last person named. But the apostle concluded his readers were not ready for the fine points in the comparison between this man and Christ. He drops that line of argument for the present, and will take it up again (in chapter 7) after giving them other instructions that may prepare their minds for the further study of types. *Hard to be uttered* means "difficult of explanation" according to Thayer's lexicon. *Dull of hearing* denotes a mind that is slow in apprehending what is said.

Verse 12. These disciples had been in the church long enough *time* to have become teachers, but were still in need of being taught by others. There is no criticism to make merely because someone needs to be taught— all people need that. The fault is in being so indifferent as not to advance beyond the "kindergarten grade." The word *first* means "beginning," and *principles* denotes "steps or elements." The phrase means the beginning steps of the oracles of God. These steps include the types revealed in the Old Testament, that pointed forward to the institution of Christ. The system of the Levitical priesthood and that of Melchisedec were steps or elements that looked forward to Christ. Being unable to grasp the comparisons, Paul described them as being like babes who can partake of milk only.

Verse 13. *Unskilful* is defined "inexperienced" by Thayer's l e x i c o n. This does not mean that the lack of experience is due to their babyhood, but it is the other way around. They were still babes because they had not launched out after further activities or experiences, such as a normal babe will do.

Verse 14. The E n g l i s h m a n's Greek New Testament renders *strong meat* as "solid food." *Of full age* means those who are adults instead of babes. *By reason of use* denotes the experience a Christian has in practicing the things taught in the "oracles of God." *Senses* is defined "Faculty of the mind" by Thayer, and he explains it further, "For perceiving, understanding, judging." The Bible is like an appliance that has been obtained for the home; it must be used to be understood and appreciated. But in order to make the proper use of it the owner must observe "instructions" that are given by one who furnished him the appliance. Likewise the Lord has provided instructions in the "oracles" for the proper use of the items making up the system of Christian living. By following these instructions the disciples will learn to make correct distinctions between the various situations in life, accepting the right and rejecting the wrong. (See 1 Thessalonians 5: 21.)

Hebrews 6

Verse 1. *Therefore* signifies that a conclusion is being drawn from the truths set forth in the preceding chapter. *Leaving* does not mean to desert or disregard, but not to remain with the beginning steps thus making no advancement. A builder *leaves* the foundation and goes on with the building. He should not find it necessary to *lay again* the foundation, for that was done in the "beginning" of the project. Likewise Christians should advance beyond the *principles* ("beginning") of their service to Christ and become *perfect* or full grown. *Not lay again the foundation.* These Jewish disciples had begun their service to Christ (had laid the foundation) by turning from the things on which they had been relying all their lives. Some of those things consisted of items commanded by the law of Moses, while others were the erroneous notions taught by some of their leaders. These disciples had begun their new life—had laid the foundation—by no longer adhering to the former practices or observances. A number of these items are considered in this and the next verse. *Dead works* means the works of the old law which are no longer able to impart spiritual life; they have become dead works. *Faith toward God.* Christians are not told to turn away from faith in God, for then they could not please Him (Hebrews 11: 6). The Jews had faith in God only, not including Christ since they had not been taught concerning Him. This verse means that disciples must have faith in both the Father and the Son.

Verse 2. *Baptisms* is from the Greek word BAPTISMOS which Thayer defines "A washing, purification effected by means of water." It refers to the washing of animals prescribed by the Mosaic law. (See Exodus 29: 4,17: Leviticus 1: 9; 9: 14.) The word is never used for the ordinance of Christian baptism. *Laying on of hands.* Under the Mosaic system the priests or others laid their hands on the animals that were to be offered in the service (Leviticus 3: 2; 4: 4, 13; 16: 21). *Resurrection of the dead . . . eternal judgement.* These phrases must be considered together, for they are connected with one of the erroneous theories that were maintained in those days, and were shared in by the Jews. The theory was false but Jesus never bothered about exposing it in His day. However, when the apostles came to induce the Jews to accept the Gospel, it was necessary to tell them they must give up such notions; that they must do "repentance from" such errors. The false theory referred to is known in historical literature as "Transmigration of souls." The doctrine taught that when a man dies his soul passes into the body of another, thus enabling him to live again or experience a resurrection. If the person had been unrighteous, he would be punished by being sent into some other being who was afflicted, or into an abnormal child then being born. (See John 9: 1-3.) If necessary this form of punishment or *judgement* would be repeated again and again. (a form of "eternal judgement") as here expressed.

Verse 3. *If God permit.* No passage should be interpreted so as to contradict another in the Bible. 2 Peter 3: 9 says that God is "not willing that any should perish, but that all should come to repentance." The italicized phrase, then, does not imply that God will prevent any man from doing what is right. The thought is as if Paul would say, "We who are determined to be right, will go on unto maturity in the spiritual life, God being our helper."

Verse 4. *It is impossible.* The thing that is impossible and the reasons for it will require a number of lines of the text to explain. After the simple announcement of an impossibility, the apostle drops the subject and gives a description of the characters concerning whom it is said, then tells what it is that is impossible. We shall carefully study this description before attempting to state the conclusion. *Enlightened* is from PHOTIZO which Thayer defines, "To enlighten spiritually, imbue with saving knowledge." Thayer defines the orginal for *taste* as follows: "To feel, make trial of, experience." It means to have experienced enough of the *heavenly gift* of Christianity to know how precious it is. The Holy Ghost (or Spirit) was bestowed upon the church (Romans 5: 5; 14: 17; 1 Corinthians 6: 19), hence when people become Christians they are *made partakers of the Holy Ghost.*

Verse 5. *Tasted the good word of God* means to have "experienced" the help of that word enough to know what its benefits are. When a person knows by experience what effect for good the Gospel will have on one in preparing for the *world to come*, he may truly be said to have tasted of that coming *power* even in this life.

Verse 6. To *fall away* means to desert or purposely turn away from a thing. It here applies to those who have had all the experience just described, then deliberately pull away from such a manner of life. Now we are ready to see what it is that is impossible, namely, to *renew such a person to repentance*. The impossibility is upon the part of the would-be restorer and not on the one who falls away. It does not say he cannot repent, but it is impossible for anyone else to iduce him to. The reason is that the apostate already knows as much about the subject as the one who wants to renew him, and hence the exhorter cannot offer any new arguments or reasons. On the basis of the foregoing statements of the apostle, it is proper to say that if persons fall away after all those experiences, then "It is impossible . . . to renew them again unto repentance." If they ever come back to Christ it will be on their own change of heart, which will always be possible for them. Paul describes this falling away as another crucifying of the Son of God, since it puts them outside the church and in the class of the enemies who actually did crucify Him. It is an *open shame* because the radical turning from a life of righteousness is apparent to the world about the apostate.

Verse 7. Paul is making an illustration out of the earth and its products. Not all ground is desirable as the parable of the sower in Matthew 13 teaches. The blessing of moisture will fall on the earth regardless of the character of some particular spots. If any portion responds by producing useful herbs, it will be blessed of God and be worthy of additional showers.

Verse 8. On the same basis as the preceding verse, if some spot receives the rain but yields only the thorns, such products will be burned, and that spot will be rejected by the owner as unprofitable.

Verse 9. Paul expected his readers to understand the general lesson in the parable, but he does not mean for them to make a personal application of it as yet. Hence he makes the kindly remark that he is counting on a better showing from them than was indicated by the thorny ground. However, we are sure the apostle intended the illustration as an exhortation for them to be thoughtful and not fail at last. It is similar to the warning given in chapter 3: 12 and 4: 1.

Verse 10. This verse is consistent with the preceding one. The Hebrew brethen were given credit for the good work they had done. We are not told the particulars of what they were doing, but it has the highly commendable credit of being a *labor of love*. An important part of their motive for the work is indicated by the statement that it was *toward his name*. Such a motive corresponds with Matthew 25: 40.

Verse 11. It is not enough to be doing one's duty just at intervals and then stop, but it must be persisted in until the end of life.

Verse 12. To be *slothful* means to be sluggish or indolent. A *follower* is an imitator, but a person cannot imitate those who are patient (persistent) if he is indolent.

Verse 13. Persistence was the outstanding characteristic of Abraham, and he manifested it because of his faith in the promises of God. Until the Christian Dispensation there was no command against taking oaths. God made use of an oath in the promise to Abraham, but it was necessary to swear by himself because He is the greatest Being in existence. In making such a personally-supported oath it was similar to the statement of a man who says, "I give you my word of honor."

Verse 14. The particular blessing promised to Abraham meant in this verse was that he was to have a son with whom the covenant was to be established (Genesis 17: 19).

Verse 15. He finally obtained that son as a reward for his patience (Genesis 21: 1).

Verse 16. The usual practice of men as to oaths is cited by the apostle by way of illustration. If a contract is bound under an oath it will prevent any dispute.

Verse 17. God had no one greater by whom He could swear, yet he wished to provide some means of assurance to those interested in His *counsel* or promise. *Immutability* means that it is unchangeable—nothing can be done to change it. God accomplished the assurance by adding His oath to the promise thereby *confirming* it.

Verse 18. The *two immutable* (unchangeable) *things* were the promise and the oath of God. It was impossible for God to lie concerning either the promise or the oath, and hence by applying both for the sake of the heirs, it gave them the *more abundant* evidence. As a further result, the heirs of that promise (meaning all who believe in Christ as the seed of Abraham that was promised) have a *strong consolation* for the future, because that is the direction toward which hope must look. *Fled for refuge.* This phrase is based on a provision under the Mosaic system whereby persons accused of crime (whether guilty or not) could "flee" to a place called a city of *refuge.* (See Numbers 35.) Today men are all under accusation, justly, of being sinners and in danger of punishment at the hands of the avenger of sins. But a city of refuge (the church) has been built and those who will hasten (flee) to enter this institution may be saved from their past sins. And if they will remain in that city as faithful citizens, they have the promise of salvation in the world to come.

Verse 19. This prospect of eternal salvation is the *hope* that stimulates Christians in this work for Christ. It is fastened, like an anchor, to Christ who is our High Priest. He has entered *within the veil*, the phrase being based on the veil in the temple that enclosed the most holy place, which was a type of Heaven.

Verse 20. Jesus is called the forerunner because he has gone on before us to be the intercessor for His people. For this purpose He was made a High Priest like the order of Melchisedec. The advantage of being after that order instead of the order of the Levitical form was predicted in the Old Testament (Psalms 110: 4), and it will be discussed in the next chapter.

Hebrews 7

Verse 1. This epistle was written for the special benefit of the Hebrews (or Jews) who had become Christians. The Judaizers in those days were very busy in trying to force the Mosaic system upon Christians, claiming it to be still in force. The argument of this book is based on both contrasts and likenesses between the two systems. But a special argument is made in connection with the priesthood of Melchisedec. All readers of the Old Testament know it was predicted that the "other priest" (verse 11) was to be more like Melchisedec than Aaron. The present argument, therefore, is concerning that remarkable character. Salem is a short name for Jerusalem (Psalms 76: 2), where this man was located as both king and priest. The Jews made great claim of being related to Abraham, yet this verse (citing Genesis 14: 18-20) shows that Melchisedec blessed Abraham. And since a person would need to be greater than another in order to be able to bless him (verse 7), this circumstance shows that even their father Abraham was not as great a person as Melchisedec. Proper nouns in Bible times often had distinctive meanings, and Thayer says that the name Melchisedec means, "King of righteousness," which is the statement in our verse. *Salem* is defined in this verse as *King of peace*, and the brief information given in Thayer's lexicon does not contradict it. Melchisedec is set forth as a type of Christ, hence it was fitting to connect him with a place signifying "peace." (See Isaiah 9: 6.)

Verse 2. Another fact showing Melchisedec to have been greater than Abraham, is that the latter paid tithes (a tenth) of his personal property to the former.

Verse 3. The key to this misunderstood verse is in the meaning of the phrase *without descent*. It is from the Greek word AGENEALOGETOS which Thayer defines as follows: "Of whose descent there is no account." This was no accident nor is it due to a lack of custom or facilities for recording *descent* which means a record of family names. Many other persons of those times had their pedigrees or family names recorded in the Bible. (See Genesis 10.) This shows that God had a purpose in leaving out all record of Melchisedec's family, namely, so that he would appear in that sense to be like that "other priest" who actually was not to have any descendants. (See Isaiah 53: 8; Acts 8: 33.) In other words, the verse describes the situation of Melchisedec as God permitted it to *appear* in history, in order to form a type of Christ whose situation as to family relationship was to be *actually* that way. *Without father and without mother* means he did not obtain his priesthood from his ancestors as did the Levitical priests (Exodus 29: 29,

30; Numbers 20:28). The *beginning of the days of Melchisedec* and the *end of life* are all kept from the record for the purpose of carrying out the type, and it is to be understood on the same principle as "without descent" explained above. In this way he was *made like unto the Son of God*. This shows they were two separate persons, but were *like unto* each other in certain respects. If no record is given of the death or replacement of Melchisedec, then logically his priesthood was continous. This was true of him *apparently*, as it was true of Christ *actually*.

Verse 4. Paul did not underestimate the greatness of Abraham; he emphasized it. However he used that fact in support of his reasoning, since it was made clear that notwithstanding his greatness, he was inferior to Melchisedec who was declared in so many points to be like Jesus in the priesthood order.

Verse 5. This verse continues the argument based on likenesses and contrasts between important characters. It is evident that he who *pays* tithes is less than the one to whom he pays them. Abraham paid tithes to Melchisedec hence was of less importance than he. But the Levite priests (who descended from the great man Abraham) took tithes from the people. The argument is that although the Levitical priests were great enough to *receive* tithes from the people, yet their great ancestor was not great enough to receive tithes from Melchisedec, but rather had to *pay* them to him. All this is according to the teaching, that the priestly order of this great man Melchisedec being more like that of Christ than was that of Levi, it follows that the priesthood of Christ should be accepted over all previous ones.

Verse 6. The reasoning of this verse is virtually the same as the several preceding ones. There is one additional point on the greatness of Abraham, namely, he was the one to whom God made the first promise of Christ.

Verse 7. *Without all contradiction* means it is so evident that it cannot be successfully disputed. *Blessed* is from EULOGEO which Thayer defines at this place, "To invoke blessings." In order for a good wish to have any assurance of fulfillment, it must be uttered by someone endowed with special knowledge and authority. Melchisedec had such qualification since he was the *priest of the most high God*.

Verse 8. The word *here* stands for the Levitical priesthood, and *there* refers to that of Melchisedec. *Men that die* is said because the priests under the Levitical order ceased to serve because of death and the event was recorded. Whereas there is no record of the death of Melchisedec, and as far as the historical account is concerned he is still living. The point is that while the priests designated by *here* had tithes given them, yet they were subject to death. The priest designated by *there* also received tithes, but there is no account of his death. This makes him superior to the other priests notwithstanding both orders received tithes.

Verse 9. Another contrast between Melchisedec over Levi is that the latter (though being given tithes), himself paid tithes to Melchisedec while in Abraham's body.

Verse 10. *Was yet in the loins*, etc. Paul takes advantage of a common theory believed by the Hebrews concerning the seat of the reproductive function. The word for *loins* is OSPHUS which Thayer defines. "A loin . . . the (two) loins," and then explains it by, "The Hebrews thought the generative powers resided in the loins." Strong defines it, "The loins (externally), i. e., the hip; internally (by extension) procreative powers." There was a pure blood line from Abraham to Levi, who was only the fourth generation from his great ancestor. In this sense Levi was represented by Abraham as he paid the tithes to Melchisedec. This is a phase of the argument based on the superiority of Melchisedec over Levi.

Verse 11. The law of Moses was inspired and served the purpose of the Lord, but it was not intended to be permanent as to the duration of its force. (See Galatians 3:18-25) The Judaizers (Jews who tried to force the law of Moses on Christians) maintained that it was to be permanent. Paul reasons that since the law was received under the Levitical priesthood, such law would necessarily be c h a n g e d whenever the priesthood was changed. But it was well established that *another priest* was to arise like Melchisedec more than like Aaron (father of the Levities), therefore the point is made that the law was not longer in force.

Verse 12. This is a repetition of the argument in verse 11.

Verse 13. *These things* refers to the statements about *another priest* who was to bring a change in the law. That priest belonged to *another tribe*, which had nothing to do with the altar service.

Verse 14. *Evident* denotes something that is plainly established and understood. *Juda* is a short spelling of Judah, the tribe from which Christ *sprang* or was produced. The genealogies of Matthew 1 and Luke 3 show Christ to have descended from David, who all readers of the Bible know was a descendant of Judah the fourth son of Jacob. And the writings of Moses concerning the system of priesthood were completely silent about the tribe of Judah.

Verse 15. *Yet far more evident* means the testimony on behalf of the priesthood of Jesus is still more clearly shown. Paul refers to the comparison made between Melchisedec and Him, and the point is made stronger by the fact that Melchisedec lived several centuries before the Mosaic system was started. And it was concerning Melchisedec that *another priest* was to arise; that is, another besides him.

Verse 16. *Carnal* means pertaining to the flesh; the Levitical priests received their office through their fleshly birth. Melchisedec was made a high priest by the Lord independent of any fleshly relationship to anyone. *Endless life* is used in the sense set forth in verse 3, namely, his life is still continuing as far as any record of his death is concerned. This makes Melchisedec's priesthood more like that of Christ than was that of the priests in the Levitical order.

Verse 17. The pronoun *he* refers to God, who *testified* or declared that the Son was to be priest *for ever* (unchanging, throughout the age) after the order of Melchisedec.

Verse 18. To disannul signifies to cancel the force of the law which *went before*. God declared that such an act would be done by changing the priesthood and also the *commandment* (law of Moses). The reason for this annulling was the *weakness and unprofitableness thereof*. This weakness was not through any failure of God, for it was not brought into the world with the idea of its being final and complete. (See Galatians 3: 18-25.)

Verse 19. *Law made nothing perfect*. The last word means something complete regardless of the quality of the thing spoken of. Since the law was added for a limited time only (see reference in Galatians cited above), it follows that God did not equip it with the entire requirements of a spiritual life. *Better hope* is a term used to designate the hope that is held out to those who serve under the priesthood of Christ in the place of the Levitical one.

Verse 20. Another contrast in favor of Christ is that he obtained the priesthood under the oath of God (verse 21).

Verse 21. *Without an oath* is a negative statement, based on the truths that are recorded in the books of Exodus and Leviticus. In all those passages where so much is said about the priesthood of the Levites, the reader will not find one instance of an oath in connection with their office. On the other hand we find a positive declaration (Psalms 110: 4) that an oath was made in reference to the priesthood of Christ. *Will not repent* means that the Lord will never change his mind concerning the priesthood of Christ, namely, that it is to be after the order of Melchisedec.

Verse 22. *By so much* refers to the oath by which Jesus was made a High Priest, and it enabled Him to make a *testament* (or covenant) that was *better*. The last word does not infer that the first one was not good as to its qualities or principles of righteousness. Paul elsewhere (Romans 7:12) declares the law to be good and holy, but the second is better in the sense of having more advantages and being more useful.

Verse 23. The first system was served by priests whose terms were terminated by death, which made it necessary for it to have many priests.

Verse 24. *This man* refers to Christ who *continueth ever* because He never died after becoming a priest. *Unchangeable* means the priesthood did not pass or change from one man to another, hence it necessarily was a stronger system.

Verse 25. An advocate or representative may start pleading for a client, and be getting the case in good shape. Then if something makes it needful to change representatives, he may be unable to do as satisfactory a service as the previous one because of the break in the procedure. Christ never died and hence he is always on the case and is at all times "up to date" on the conditions.

Verse 26. *Became us* means it was fitting that we of the last dispensation should have a High Priest having the best of qualifications. *Holy, harmless, undefiled* all means a character that is perfect, and Christ has such because He is *separate from sinners;* has no association with them. *Higher* refers to rank or importance rather than bodily position; Jesus is more lofty as a High Priest than all the heavens.

Verse 27. There are two contrasts between Christ and the Levitical priests, namely, they had to offer sacrifices *daily* and also needed to atone for their own sins. Christ had to offer a sacrifice only *once* for the people, and not one time for Himself for he had no sins for which to make atonement.

Verse 28. The priests made under the law were infirm in that they were subject to death. *Word of the oath* came after the law since David (to whom the oath was made) lived some centuries after Moses (through whom the law was given). The point is that since the oath came after the law, it proves that document was not considered absolutely perfect. This later act (the oath) *maketh the Son* (High Priest). The grand total conclusion is our High Priest has a service that continues *evermore*.

Hebrews 8

Verse 1. *Sum* is from KEPHALAION which Thayer defines, "The chief or main point, the principal thing." It refers to what Paul said in the preceding chapter, together with what follows in the present one, concerning the priesthood of Christ. *Such an high priest* has virtually the same significance as *sum*. The Levitical priests served in Jerusalem while Christ is at the right hand of his Father. *Majesty* pertains to the greatness of the throne of God. *In the heavens* has the same significance as "higher than the heavens" in chapter 7: 26.

Verse 2. The building used in the Mosaic system was regarded as a sanctuary (holy place) and a tabernacle as truly as is the one in the service under Christ. The difference is in the description given in the rest of this verse. *True tabernacle* means that of which the first one was a type. *Pitched* is defined by Thayer as follows: "To make fast, to fix; to fasten together, to build by fastening together." The Lord directed the building of the Old Testament tabernacle, but it was made of literal material and the work was actually done by human hands (See Exodus 36-40.) The last tabernacle employed the services of man also, but the materials were not literal and the formation of the system was the handiwork of God.

Verse 3. *Every high priest* refers to those under the Old Testament line. Thayer defines *ordained,* "To appoint one to administer an office." *Gifts and sacrifices* were in the same general class, but the first refers especially to articles that were not intended to be used as victims on the altar. *This man* means Christ who was called upon to make a *somewhat* offering. That is, Christ offered many contributions to the New Testament service, and then made the "supreme sacrifice" of himself on the cross just before ascending from earth to his Father in Heaven.

Verse 4. *If he were on earth.* This means as long as Christ was on earth he could not act as a priest. That is because the law was in force all the time He was on earth, and it already had its priests to offer according to that law.

Verse 5. The institutions of the Mosaic system were *examples* and *shadows* (patterns or types) of the *heavenly things* (the institutions under Christ). *Who* means the priests mentioned in the preceding verse. In Exodus 25: 40 is the instruction that God gave Moses to make all things according to the "pattern" shown to him in the mount. The idea is that when God mentioned this pattern for the tabernacle service, He had in mind that it was to be a type or pattern of the greater things to come, as well as to serve the purpose of that first dispensation.

Verse 6. Several words of comparison in the second degree are used in this verse which should not be misapplied. God never made any mistakes and all that He ever did was good from the standpoint of being righteous. But the purposes to be accomplished by His plans were not always considered as final. He had a terminal to be reached in the preparation of mankind for the Hereafter, and until the final plan had been reached (that which was "perfect" 1 Corinthians 13: 10), each step in the unfolding of the divine plan may be considered as looking forward to something *more excellent* and *better.*

Verse 7. A part of the *fault* of which the Lord complained was concerning the shortcomings of the people. They did not do even as well as they could with the system which God had given them. However, God has always been inclined to give His creatures every opportunity for developing a desirable character. In view of this, He regarded the old law as not the best that could be accomplished in the future, and in that sense He would not consider the old covenant to be *faultless*.

Verse 8. *Finding Fault* is explained at the preceding verse. It should be constantly borne in mind that most of this book, as well as many parts of the New Testament, was called for by the disturbances from Judaizers (Hebrews trying to bind the Jewish law on Christians). Had all people understood and been satisfied with the New Testament as the fulfillment of the law and the prophets, these books would not have been needed. But they maintained that the Mosaic system was intended by the Lord to be permanent. That made it necessary for the apostles to cite many places in the Old Testament (being disregarded by the Judaizers) that clearly predicted a change in the whole religious system. *The days come* has reference to the days of the New Testament. *Saith the Lord* is citing Jeremiah 31: 31-34 where the prophet plainly declares that He was going to make a new covenant. *Israel* and *Judah* are mentioned because at the time of Jeremiah the nation was divided, the ten tribes being called *Israel* and the *two* tribes called *Judah* (recorded in 1 Kings 12). The tribes were destined to be reunited after the captivity, but the two parts are named to show that every Jew (as well as the Gentiles) was to be included in the new covenant.

Verse 9. *The day* refers to the period in general when Sinai was the principal place of interest. (See Jeremiah 34: 13, 14.) The shortcomings of the Israelites was the reason on the human side for a change. (See verse 7.)

Verse 10. This verse states one of the main differences between the old and the new covenant. When a male child was eight days old he was circumcised, and that made him a full member of the covenant, notwithstanding he had no mind to receive anything; the law was put in the flesh instead of the mind. The new covenant laws were to be put in the mind (or heart) instead of the flesh.

Verse 11. Samuel was a full "brother" to Eli although he "did not yet know the Lord" (1 Samuel 3: 7); his circumcision introduced him into the brotherhood (Genesis 17: 9-14). That is why it was necessary for Eli to make his brother Samuel acquainted with the Lord. It was done in verse 9 of the same chapter where he told Samuel to say, "Speak, Lord; for thy servant heareth," which is the same as *know the Lord* in our present verse. Such an introduction in the brotherhood under Christ will not be necessary because *all shall know me from the least to the greatest*. That is because under the New Testament system a person cannot become a member until he is old enough and has mind enough to receive the law of Christ intelligently. This would completely rule out all such conditions as "cradle rolls" or infant church membership in the New Testament church. All must have mind enough to "know the Lord" through the law of the Gospel before they can come into the church.

Verse 12. This verse contains a likeness and a contrast between the two covenants. God showed mercy under the old, and the passages that show it are too numerous to mention. (It should be stated what was overlooked at verse 10, that another likeness between them is that in each case the relation of *God* and *people* holds good.) The contrast in this verse is that the sins would be remembered *no more. The word* "against" is often added in quoting this subject which is incorrect, for God never did remember a sin against a man after he had been forgiven. This point will be dealt with in detail by the comments on chapter 10: 3.

Verse 13. The main point in this verse is a conclusion based on the term *new covenant;* it proves that the other one was considered old. Since old things are expected to disappear, the conclusion is that the old covenant was to be replaced by the New Testament.

Hebrews 9

Verse 1. The apostle now enters into more of the typical features of the Mosaic system, occasionally pointing out some of the places in which it differed from the one under Christ. *Ordinances* means ceremonies that were ordained to be observed in the service. *Worldly sanctuary* is used because that part of the tabernacle was a type of the church that is in this world, and not in Heaven where God lives.

Verse 2. This verse names what was in the *first* part of the tabernacle, the part called "worldly sanctuary" in the preceding verse. This room is called the *sanctuary* because the word means "holy," a type of the church which is said to be holy (Ephesians 5: 27). The placing of the articles named is recorded in Exodus 40: 4.

Verse 3. *After the second vail.* The entrance to the tabernacle was enclosed with a vail (Exodus 26: 36). That makes the next one the *second* as it is called here, and it is described in Exodus 26: 31-33. The room of the *tabernacle* enclosed by this vail is called *Holiest of all.* It is so called because it contained the ark and was a type of Heaven, into which our High Priest (Christ) has gone (chapter 6: 19, 20). This service of Christ will be considered further when we come to verse 24 of this chapter.

Verse 4. *Golden censer.* According to Leviticus 16: 12 the high priest burned incense in the most holy place on the day of atonement. A censer is a vessel to be carried in the hand and used in the manner of fumigating. This instrument was necessary because the golden altar of incense was in the first room or holy place of the tabernacle. As proof of this we read in Exodus 40: 24 that the candlestick was placed in the "tent" of the congregation. Then in verse 26 it says the golden altar also was in the "tent" or the same place where the candlestick was. Hence, the golden altar of incense was in the holy place or first room of the tabernacle, making it necessary to have this censer in the most holy place. *Ark of the covenant* is so called because it contained the *tables of the covenant* (Deuteronomy 10: 1, 2). For the history of the pot of manna and Aaron's rod, see Exodus 16: 32-34 and Numbers 17:1-11.

Verse 5. The mercy seat was made of solid gold and served as a covering for the ark as well as a resting place for the cherubims. (See Exodus 25: 17-21.) *Cannot speak particularly* means he was not ready to enter into detail about the separate services of these parts.

Verse 6. *Ordained* signifies to be prepared or made ready, and refers to the articles in the two rooms of the tabernacle. The priests *went always* is said in the sense of going daily or frequently, in contrast with "once a year" as in the next verse. *First tabernacle* refers to the first room of the tabernacle, and the common priests might enter this place any time it was necessary, and they were the ones who did most of the service of that room.

Verse 7. *The second* means the most holy place which was "within the vail" (chapter 6: 19, 20), and no one but the high priest was permitted to enter this room while it was in service. *Once every year* means on the one day only, for he made more than one entrance into the most holy place on that day. (See Leviticus 16.) *Not without blood.* The passage just cited explains where and how he got the blood. *Offered for himself.* That was necessary because those priests were all erring creatures (contrary to our High Priest). *The people* signifies that the service performed in the most holy place by the high priest was for the sake of the nation as a whole. If any individual was personally indebted to the Lord because of his sin, he was required to attend to that as his own personal duty. (See Leviticus 4: 27-35.)

Verse 8. The Holy Ghost (or Spirit) inspired the writers of the Bible, and in the present case it signified something by the "setting" of things in the tabernacle. The thing signified was the idea that the *way into the holiest*—the way by which man could reach the holiest place, or Heaven— was still unrevealed. The vail is what kept the most holy place out of sight, for the high priest only was ever permitted to enter that room, and that on one day of the year only. As long as that tabernacle was standing the vail also was standing between. But the death of Christ and his resurrection, after which He entered Heaven, was equivalent to removing the vail to the extent at least of giving others a glimpse (by the eye of faith) into Heaven. That is why the vail was rent from top to bottom at the death of Christ (Matthew 27: 51). This vail is connected with the flesh of Christ in chapter 10: 19, 20.

Verse 9. *Which was a figure* means these things were types of the institutions of Christ. *Gifts and sacrifices* is explained at chapter 8: 3. *Not make him . . . perfect.* A popular notion is that sins were not forgiven under the Mosaic law. This subject will be dealt with fully when we come to chapter 10: 4.

Verse 10. *Meats and drinks* has reference to the regulations under the law of Moses concerning what they were to eat and drink. *Washings* is explained at chapter 6: 2 on the word "baptisms." *Carnal ordinances* refers to the outward ceremonies such as animal sacrifices and burning of incense, not that they were "carnal" in the sense of being sinful. *Imposed* is not used in the sense of forcing something unjustly upon them in the sense that we usually understand the word. Its meaning is that the ordinances were put in force over the people of that dispensation. *Time of reformation* means the institution of Christ. It is so called because Christ remodeled (reformed) the scheme of human redemption, by bringing into the world the last or final religious plan, of which those in force under the Mosaic system were types or figures, which were to be used until the Lord was ready to set up the completed form.

Verse 11. *Not made with hands* has the same meaning as "pitched" in chapter 8: 2. *Good things to come* signifies that the greatest values to be obtained from the New Testament institution will be enjoyed in the future. *This building* refers to the tabernacle all parts of which were on the earth, while that part called the holiest of all typified Heaven which is not on the earth. That is why the institution of Christ is called a *greater and more perfect tabernacle*.

Verse 12. This verse states another of the contrasts between the two dispensations. The first used the blood of dumb animals, while the second used that of the High Priest himself. *Eternal redemption* contains the special idea of spiritual benefits, and not those that pertain to bodily or fleshly ones. Since this redemption is *eternal* and hence is endless, it was necessary for Christ to provide it only *once*.

Verse 13. The cleansing of fleshly or bodily impurities (which might be either physical or "ceremonial" or both), is fully described in Numbers 19 which should be carefully read. With that ceremony as a background it will be easier to appreciate the argument of our verse and the next one.

Verse 14. The Hebrews admitted that the blood of animals could cleanse the bodies of men from outward impurity. That should enable them to believe in the greater sterilizing power of the blood of Christ. The animals used under the old law were required to be without spot. Likewise the sacrifice of Christ was perfect since He had no blemish either in body or mind or spirit. This sacrifice was made possible through the Spirit, which was necessary because the literal blood of Christ was poured out on the ground and never reclaimed. But the *spiritual* worth of it was taken into the Most Holy place (Heaven) by Him (verse 12). *From dead works* means to draw the Christians from the works of the law. (See comments at chapter 6: 1.) *To serve the living God* in this age can be done only by accepting the perfect sacrifice made through the Son.

Verse 15. The argument of this verse will receive further attention when we come to chapter 10: 4. For the present it is well to state that whenever a man was forgiven under the Mosiac exercises, the sins were charged up against the blood of Christ (not "rolled forward"). Hence when Jesus came into the world in the form of flesh, it was necessary for Him to make all of those instances good by His own blood. Thus Christ was not required merely to give "a pint of blood" but He was made to give it all, and thus assure the whole world of the possibility for *eternal inheritance*.

Verses 16, 17. This paragraph may be regarded as a companion passage of chapter 8: 4, in that the New Testament which is the covenant or will of Christ was not in force until after His death. This is a rule that is generally recognized concerning testaments (or wills) that men make, in that such wills are not in force during the lifetime of the men who make them.

Verse 18. *Death* is the central idea in this part of Paul's argument, hence he states that the first testament was *dedicated* (consecrated) with blood. Since the shedding of blood requires the death of the creature furnishing it, the circumstance makes the type and antitype complete. The animals died in order to dedicate (or put into force) the Old Testament or covenant, and Christ died and gave his blood to dedicate and render forceful His New Testament. (See Matthew 26: 28). Therefore the animals slain in sacrifice under the law constituted the *testator* of that system.

Verse 19. In keeping with the truth just referred to, Moses used blood to put into force the words of the law after he had spoken them. Regardless of the excellence of the words of that law, it required the blood of the testator (the animals) to render them valid. Likewise the words of Christ spoken in his personal ministry and to be spoken by the apostle afterwards, required the blood of Him who was to be the testator of the new law or new covenant.

Verse 20. This language is similar to that spoken by Jesus when he was instituting the ceremony that was to symbolize the dedicating virtue of the New Testament. (See Matthew 26: 28 and 1 Corinthians 11: 25.)

Verse 21. The passages in Exodus and Leviticus that record this use of the blood of animals are too numerous even to cite at this place.

Verse 22. Paul confirms the remark made in the preceding paragraph, by the general statement that *almost all things are by the law purged with blood*. He was therefore considering only the blood of animals when he said *without the shedding of blood there is no remission*. He had no reference to the blood of Christ in this statement. His blood is not even referred to until the latter part of the next verse, and then indirectly only. The statement is frequently quoted by brethren when presiding at the Lord's table and applied to the blood of Christ. Such a use of the passage is not only a perversion of it, but it destroys the interesting argument the apostle is making.

Verse 23. *It was therefore necessary*, etc. Paul is still speaking about the *patterns* or types in the Old Testament, that even they had to be purified or dedicated *by these*, meaning the blood of animal sacrifies. The blood of Christ has not been considered as yet. Then the apostle introduces by inference only the necessity of the blood of Christ. If the *patterns* or types of heavenly things required such blood (without the shedding of which there was *no remission* for the Hebrews), then the heavenly things themselves—the things pertaining to the New Testament—called for *better sacrifices*. This is Paul's introduction for the blood and sacrifice of Christ, which has not been the subject for several verses.

Verse 24. Christ never did any official or priestly services in the temple at Jerusalem while on earth, for the priests of the law were still in that service (chapter 8: 4). Hence He entered that place of which the one made with hands was a figure or type. He is there to be in the presence of God *for us* or on our behalf as our High Priest. This is another item in Paul's reasoning with the Hebrew Christians. He is showing them that in clinging to the service of the Levitical priesthood, the Judaizers are repudiating the One who has actually entered into the presence of God.

Verse 25. Another contrast is in the frequency with which the two priests performed their services in the most holy place. The high priests of the Levitical order had to repeat theirs often *(every year)*. *Blood of others* means that the high priest of that law used the blood of a victim and not his own blood.

Verse 26. If the sacrificial service of Christ was exactly like that of the Levitical priests, then He would have been required not to wait so long before beginning it. He would have needed to begin it at the same time the world (inhabitants of the earth) began to exist. Since one time only was necessary because the sacrifices of the old system were taking care of the sins for the time (to be explained at chapter 10: 4), He could wait until the *end of the world* to perform His. *World* in this place is from AIONION which means age or dispensation. Jesus died in the last weeks of the Jewish Dispensation; fifty days after His death the Holy Spirit came upon the apostles, thus cancelling the Old and ushering in the New Testament Dispensation. Unlike the high priests of the Levitical system, Christ performed his by the *sacrifice of himself*.

Verse 27. The preceding verse maintains that Christ needed to make his sacrifice only once. However, that is on the ground that man will go through death and the judgment but once. Hence this verse proceeds on that principle to affirm that it is appointed unto man to die *once*, and the judgment will come afterwards.

Verse 28. Having but one sacrifice to offer, Christ waited until the typical dispensation was at its end before He did it. *Bear the sins of many*. The sacrifice of Christ was for the sins of the whole world (John 1: 29). That means that by His one great sacrifice Christ made provision for the remission of sins for all men who will avail themselves of it under whatever dispensation they live. The rest of the verse is a beautiful likeness drawn from the procedure of the high priest of the Mosaic system. While he was in the tabernacle (or temple) performing the services for the people, they were on the outside waiting for him. After the services were completed he would come out and bless the waiting throng. (See Leviticus 9: 15-24; Numbers 16: 15-17; Luke 1: 9, 10.) Likewise faithful servants of God who are looking (with pleasure 2 Timothy 4: 8) for Christ, will see Him come to earth the second time. *Without sin* means He will not come to make another sacrifice for sin. (One offering was all that was necessary.) When He comes it will be *unto salvation;* that is to complete the salvation of those who will be faithfully looking for Him.

Hebrews 10

Verse 1. The difference between *shadow* and *very image* is the same as between type and antitype, or between form and substance. The sacrificial system under the law was a figure of the one under Christ. *Can never . . . make . . . perfect* which means complete. (See the comments at verse 4.)

Verse 2. Had those sacrifices been complete (of themselves or by their own virtue) they would have ceased to be offered. When a devoted Hebrew nation had made one full program of atonement for sin, it would have been permanent and would not have to be repeated. Such a conclusion is logical, and it should have convinced the Judaizers that something was to come in the place of those institutions.

Verse 3. *Remembrance again made.* But it does *NOT SAY* that the sins were remembered *against* them as it is so frequently expressed. Every year when the national atonement day arrived, the nation had a public and formal *reminder* of sin by the entrance of their high priest into the most holy place with the blood of atonement. Contrary to that, our High Priest entered once and forever into the presence of God with the blood of the New Covenant, and it has never had to be repeated.

Verse 4. *It is not possible that the blood of bulls and goats should take away sins.* Any explanation of a passage that contradicts another plain one is bound to be wrong, for the Bible does not contradict itself. To say that sins were not forgiven under the Old Testament is a contradiction of the following. Leviticus 4 describes the sin offerings under the Mosaic system that were required of various Hebrews who had sinned. Verses 20, 26, 31 and 35 state these persons are to offer these sacrifices for sin, and in each case after doing it the passage plainly declares, "And it shall be forgiven him." Perhaps someone replies that it does not say they were to be forgiven *then*. Well, we will consider another place in the Old Testament, namely, 1 Kings 8. After the temple was completed, Solomon offered a prayer on behalf of the people in which he asked God to forgive them upon their prayer to Him. Verse 30 makes it definite as to when the forgiveness was to take place, for it says, "When they shall pray toward this place; hear thou in heaven thy dwelling place, and *when thou hearest, forgive."* This is very definite; when they prayed was the time God was to hear and when He heard was the time the forgiveness was to be granted. But was this prayer of Solomon granted? Chapter 9 and verse 3 of that book says, "And the Lord said unto him, I have heard thy prayer and thy supplication that thou hast made before me." That settles the point that sins were actually forgiven under the Old Testament times.

This is another place where we should remember the main subject of this book. The Judaizers were insisting on the permanence of the old law and its ordinances of religious service. They thought that the benefits to be obtained from those performances were by reason of the virtue of those things and hence that they were good enough to be continued. Were Paul to write an epistle to many disciples and others today, he would use the same argument about baptism and the other items of service to Christ. He would say that it is impossible for baptism and the other formalities of the Gospel to take away sin. Indeed, the denominational world actually does see that and that only with reference to the ordinances. They will say "there is no salvation in water," and that is true in the same sense that the blood of animals could not take away sins. No, the saving virtue is in the blood of Christ and *it* is the purchasing power for salvation on behalf of mankind in whatever age he lives. But He will not apply that blood to any man unless he has enough faith in the Lord to do whatever he is told to do. That may be the command to offer animal sacrifices or be baptized, depending on what age he is under. Hence in any of the dispensations that God has placed among men, all who will do whatever they are told to do, will be forgiven on the strength of the blood of Christ. The virtue is in the blood is why it never had to be repeated.

Verse 5. The two pronouns *he* and the one *me* refer to Christ, and the two pronouns *thou* stand for God. When Christ was ready to come into the world He knew it was to fulfill the promise made to Abraham (Galatians 3: 16, 19), also that He was to make of himself a sacrifice to replace the animal sacrifices of the old law. Yes, Christ existed before he was born of the virgin (John 8: 58), and hence when God made the promise to Abraham, He made it also to Christ. (See the passages in Galatians referred to above.) The coming of Christ into the world by way of the virgin birth was therefore voluntary on His part, in the spirit of obedience to his Father. He also knew that a spiritual body could not die, and hence that a fleshly body would be needed. That is why it was said that God had prepared a body for Him, to be produced within the fleshly body of the virgin and consisting of one that could be made to die.

Verse 6. This verse represents Christ as explaining why the plan was needed referred to in the preceding verse, namely, that God no longer was pleased with burnt offerings offered under the law.

Verse 7. *Then said I* (Christ), *in the volume of the book it is written of me.* Christ knew that the Old Testamen predicted His coming into the world as a sacrifice for sins. The great respect Christ had for the Father, also for the majesty of the ancient writings, induced Him to cooperate in the great plan. That is why He said, *I come to do thy will, O God.*

Verse 8. This verse is mostly an explanation or repetition of the preceding ones, to the effect that the displeasure of God was concerning the sacrifices of the law. Of course it should be understood that such a condition of mind came after those sacrifices had served the divine purposes.

Verse 9. The forepart of this verse is a repetition of verse 7. The antecedent of *first* is *will*, referring to the old will or covenant consisting of the ordinances of the Mosaic law. God took away the first one that He might establish the second. He never had two systems of religion in force at the same time for the same people. This verse is a complete refutation of the Sabbatarian heresy even if there did not exist a single other passage on the subject.

Verse 10. *By the which will* means that by the *second* will or system of salvation, we are sanctified (or consecrated) through the body of Christ, (not that of animals).

Verse 11. This is explained by the comments at verse 4.

Verse 12. *This man* refers to Christ, and *for ever* means His sacrifice would be permanent and would not have to be repeated as did those of the old law.

Verse 13. *From henceforth expecting* signifies that He expects to remain *on the right hand of God till his enemies are made his footstool.* (1 Corinthians 15: 25, 26.)

Verse 14. This is equivalent to chapter 9: 26; and verse 12 in this chapter.

Verse 15. *Holy Ghost* (or Spirit) *also is a witness to us.* The prophets of the Old Testament and the apostles of the New were all inspired by this Spirit.

Verses 16, 17. This makes specific reference to one of the Old Testament predictions, and it is to be found in Jeremiah 31: 31-33, which is explained at chapter 8: 8-13.

Verse 18. See the comments at verse 3.

Verse 19. *Boldness* does not mean a spirit of forwardness but rather one of strong confidence. *Enter into the holiest.* Not literally but by faith through the merits of the blood of Jesus Christ.

Verse 20. *This new and living way . . . through the vail* is explained by the comments at chapter 9: 8. It is *living* in that it need not be repeated.

Verse 21. This verse shows one of the likenesses between the two systems in that each had the services of a high priest. The distinction is the truth that Christ is over the house of God which is said in the sense of the church and Heaven.

Verse 22. *Draw near.* The nearest the people of the first priesthood could get to the most holy place was by way of or near the vail. Likewise Christians may get very near the throne of God (by the *full assurance of faith*). The *heart* and *conscience* are the inner and invisible part of man, hence we know that *sprinkled* is used figuratively and means to be cleansed spiritually. The figure is drawn from the fact that the blood was actually sprinkled on men to consecrate them for the priesthood under the old law (Exodus 29: 21). Our bodies are literal and hence they are literally washed in the water of baptism. *Pure water* has no reference to the subject of sanitary conditions. The word means "unmixed" and is a contrast from the water of purification used under the law. That water was mixed with the ashes of an animal (Numbers 19).

Verse 23. *Hold fast* means to be faithful to the end. *He is faithful* denotes that the Lord is always true and makes His promises good.

Verse 24. To *provoke* means to induce or stimulate others to do that which is good. We should do this by exhortation and that will require the following verse.

Verse 25. *Forsaking is from* EGKATALEIPO, which Thayer defines, "To abandon, desert, to leave in straits, leave helpless; leave in the lurch." The word does not refer to those who are "irregular in attendance" or who "just come occasionally." (There are other scriptures which take care of such delinquents.) But it means those who remain away from the assemblies so long that they can no longer be considered as a part of the group. *Assembling of ourselves together*. This does not apply to any one of the public gatherings of Christians any more than it does to another. The assembling to have the Lord's Supper is included in the passage, but it does not apply to that any more than to any other scriptural gathering of the church. Malachi 3: 16 is clearly a prediction of conditions to exist in the dispensation of Christ, and it says "Then they that feared the Lord spake often one to another." They cannot do this unless they are together, and coming together once a week cannot truly be said to be "often." *The day* first refers to the day when the city of Jerusalem was to be destroyed, which was then near at hand. At that time a general disturbance was expected when many opportunities for assembling would be hindered and in some places would be completely impossible. Since that event is now past, *the day* means the judgment day when all opportunities for Christian assembling will be forever ended on earth. We can *see the day approaching* by faith, for each day brings us "One day nearer our Father's house than ever we've been before" (Romans 13: 11).

Verse 26. *Sin wilfully* means to sin deliberately or purposely, in contrast with that committed incidentally or through weakness. *No more sacrifice* does NOT SAY there is no more chance of forgiveness. Jesus taught that all manner of sins would be forgiven except that against the Holy Spirit. This passage is in the same class or principle as chapter 6: 4-6, in that it mentions that the persons had *received the knowledge of the truth*. The point is that Christ made one sacrifice for sin and will make no other. If this one is repudiated there is no other to which we can look as the Hebrews could in the Mosaic system. Those sacrifices were repeated over and over again and after every transgression the guilty ones could look forward to another sacrifice. If we reject the one in Christ there will be no one and nothing else to which we may look (Galatians 5: 4). But that does not say we cannot change our mind and return to the sacrifice that is still available for all who will receive it on the Lord's terms.

Verse 27. If we do not return to Christ then we must look for that which is fearful, namely, the judgment of God at which He will exhibit *fiery indignation*. *Devour* is from a word that literally means to eat. However, we do not eat that which we dislike, hence the thought is that God will dispose of these adversaries by abandoning them to the regions of endless destruction.

Verse 28. To *despise* means to disrespect and refuse to obey. The punishment for disobeying the law of Moses in extreme cases was death without mercy (Numbers 35: 30; Deuteronomy 17: 5, 6).

Verse 29. The law of Christ is so much more final and far-reaching that the violation of it deserves a much *sorer* (worse) punishment than an unmerciful death of the body. But since such a punishment as that is the most severe of any that can be imposed on a human being in this world, the *sorer* punishment will have to wait until the next world to be inflicted. That is why the unjust are to be "reserved unto the day of judgment to be punished"

(2 Peter 2: 9). All of the wrongs mentioned in the rest of this verse may be charged against the Judaizers, because they have *trodden under foot the Son of God*. They did so by rejecting Him and going back to the sacrifices that were offered under the law. *Blood of the covenant* refers to the blood of Christ because it was shed to make good all the promises God made to the descendants of Abraham. To reject it and go back to the sacrifices for salvation is equivalent to *counting it an unholy thing* in that it implies that it is no better than the blood of animals. *Spirit of grace* is a phrase signifying the New Testament since it is the final system under the favor of God, and it was given through the means of the Holy Spirit.

Verse 30. Paul cites a statement of God recorded in Deuterony 32: 34-36, in regard to the determination of God to *judge* (execute punishment) the people who reject His terms of mercy.

Verse 31. All men and all things are ever in the hands of God in a general sense, and hence cannot *fall into* His hands. The verse therefore has a special meaning which is related to the mediation of Christ. There is no being in the universe who is between God and man but Christ, by whom man may escape the judgment mentioned in the preceding verse. Hence if a man repudiates Christ (as the Judaizers were doing), he deprives himself of any intercessor, and must take his chances with an avenging God who has declared vengeance against all who are not pardoned by the blood of Christ.

Verse 32. *Illuminated* means to be enlightened by the Gospel. Soon after these people became Christians they were persecuted by the unbelivers of both Jews and Gentiles. Paul terms this experience with afflictions as a fight, and of course it would be a "fight of faith" (1 Timothy 6: 12).

Verse 33. *Made a gazingstock* denotes an exhibition of something for people to gaze at with contempt. By *reproaches* and *afflictions* the enemy drew attention to the Christians with the result that they were made light of. Some did not personally have this experience, but they associated with and showed friendship for those who did, and thus brought upon themselves the same kind of reproaches.

Verse 34. Paul was a prisoner in chains for the sake of the Gospel, but these disciples manifested sympathy for him and thus invited the darts of the enemies. As a punishment for their manifestation of faith, they were forced to submit to the *spoiling* (plundering) of their possessions. They did not even fret about such losses because they believed there were better riches awaiting them in Heaven.

Verse 35. *Confidence* means strong assurance which prompts one to face danger or affliction on behalf of the truth. The reward will be great in the end.

Verse 36. *Patience* is the same as perseverance, and it is manifested by those who continue to have confidence. We need not expect to receive the fulfillment of God's promises unless we first do the will of the Lord.

Verse 37. *Little while* is comparative, for the endless term of the reward will make even centuries of waiting seem but a short time.

Verse 38. *Live by faith* agrees with the idea of persevering on the strength of our faith. *Draw back* means to hesitate or shrink from going forward against afflictions.

Verse 39. *But we are not, etc.* In placing himself with them the apostle regards them in a favorable light. It is true that many of the Hebrews had remained true. However, many others had gone backward, and others were in danger of doing so on account of the Judaizers among them. That made it necessary for the apostle to warn them repeatedly against the disastrous results of faltering.

Hebrews 11

General remarks. The point has been frequently emphasized that the outstanding subject of this book is the disturbances of the Judaizers. There would seem to be a shift now to the subject of unbelief. And yet it is not so much of a change at the base. All failure to do that which is right may be charged up against unbelief. In 1 Corinthians 10 Paul enumerates a number of misdeeds that contributed to the overthrow of the Israelites in the wilderness. But in Hebrews 3: 19 where he has the same history in mind, the apostle says they could not enter in because of unbelief. By the same token, the mistake of rejecting Christ for the sake of going back to the old law may truly be attributed to unbelief. Much has been said against the denominational teaching of "faith alone," and justly so. At the same time we should be careful not to underestimate the importance of belief or faith. It is true that we cannot be saved by faith alone, neither can we be saved without it. We cannot be saved by "faith only," but we can be lost by unbelief only. That is because it requires all the items of the plan of salvation to please God, while the omission of one fundamental item is enough to displease Him. This is especially true of such a principle as faith which is the motive power of all our actions as the present chapter will show.

Verse 1. *Substance* is from a word that means basis or foundation on which something rests. *Faith* constitutes such a basis for our hope since it is produced by testimony. Even *things not seen* but desired may be expected and thus hoped for when we have the evidence of their truthfulness.

Verse 2. *Elders* is from PRESBUTEROS and Thayer defines it at this place as "forefathers." *Good report* is used in the sense that they obtained a good reputation by their faith that was "put into practice."

Verse 3. *Through faith* does not mean that the following things of this verse were accomplished by faith, for God does not have to act on faith, He knows what he can do. It is through faith that we understand about it. *Worlds* is defined by the lexicon at this place, "The worlds, the universe," and *framed* is defined, "To fit out, equip, put in order, arrange, adjust." *Are seen* and *do appear* are both in the present tense, and *made* is from a Greek word that means "caused to be." The sentence means that the universe which we see was not made out of anything else that appears to us. But that does not say that God "made something out of nothing." Such a notion is not taught in any scripture that I have read. Just because we cannot see what God made the universe of does not prove that He made it out of nothing. *Word* is from RHEMA, which Thayer defines at this place, "The word by which some thing is commanded, directed, enjoined." This agrees with Psalms 33: 9, which says, "He spake and it was done; he commanded and it stood fast." Also the phrase "and God said" occurs nine times in the first chapter of Genesis.

Verse 4. *By faith Abel.* Romans 10: 17 says faith comes by hearing the word of God. Hence Abel had been told by the Lord what to do or he could not have done it by faith. When he offered an animal *by faith*, therefore, it was because God had told him to do so. That made it a *more excellent* (superior) sacrifice than the one Cain offered, for God had not told him to offer the fruit of the ground. *Obtained witness* means that testimony was borne him that he was a righteous man. *Dead yet speaketh.* Although Abel is dead physically, yet the record of his righteous performance is preserved down to the present time, and it *speaks* or testifies to the good deed that was done through his faith in the word of God.

Verse 5. *Translated . . . not see death.* The last phrase explains the first word, and *was not found* any more on earth because he was taken to Heaven. *Had this testimony.* It is recorded in Genesis 5: 24 that *Enoch walked with God*, which means he walked or conducted himself according to the "word of God" which produces faith.

Verse 6. The apostle interrupts his line of special instances to state the general principle of faith. Regardless of whatever apparent good there might be in one's actions, it will not be pleasing to God unless he has authorized it. *Believe that He is* means to believe in the existence of God. *Furthermore,* unless a man believes that God will reward a diligent seeker, he will not make any effort to come to Him.

Verse 7. The flood of which Noah was warned was over a century in the future (Genesis 6: 3), yet he prepared an ark according to the Lord's instructions. That was because he believed what God told him and acted accordingly. *To the saving of his house* from the flood that destroyed the rest of mankind. *Condemned the world.* Thayer defines the first word at this place as follows: "By one's good example to render another's wickedness more evident and censurable." *Heir of righteousness.* The last word is what is done and not inherited, hence the phrase means to inherit the reward that comes to one whose faith leads him to seek a righteous life.

Verse 8. The main point that showed Abraham's faith was his obedience even when he did not know where he was going. But God promised that it was to be towards a place which he should some day inherit.

Verse 9. *Strange* means "belonging to another"; Abraham considered himself a sojourner which means a temporary dweller. That is why he lived

Hebrews 11: 10-21

in tabernacles (or tents) because he regarded himself as well as his immediate descendants as heirs only. He believed the land would sometime be actually possessed by the nations coming from him.

Verse 10. Abraham did not expect to possess personally the land of Canaan, hence he did not provide himself any permanent building for a home. He believed that his descendants would finally get possession of it. As for himself, he chose to be faithful to God while sojourning in the land, then finally enter the city with *foundations*, which means the permanence of the Eternal City or Heaven.

Verse 11. Being delivered of a child was not the miracle in this case, but it was the ability to conceive one to begin with. Sarah was ninety years old and thus was past the usual age of child-bearing. She also had been barren all her life so that she was not at any time able to conceive by the natural process of reproduction. Hence she would have felt no urge to cooperate with her husband in carrying out their part of God's plan. But on account of her faith in the promise of God she acted and was rewarded with the *strength* (ability) to conceive.

Verse 12. *As good as dead*. The second word is not in the original as a separate term. The phrase is used figuratively because all appearances were that way. We know Abraham's reproductive powers were not gone, for at least thirty-seven years later he married the second time and begat six sons (Genesis 23: 1; 25: 1, 2). There is no evidence that a miracle was performed to enable him to beget these sons. Besides, they were not needed to fulfill the promise made in the beginning. *Stars* and *sand* are used to indicate the vast number of his descendants.

Verse 13. *These* means Abraham and Isaac and Jacob, who never lived to see the fulfilment of the promises. *Died in faith* means that their faith remained with them as long as they lived. *Seen them afar off* (by the eyes of faith). Being *strangers and pilgrims* (temporary dwellers), they did not expect to possess the land personally, but they never doubted that their descendants would according to the promises.

Verse 14. The faith described in the preceding verse implies a belief in some other country than was then visible.

Verse 15. The country *from whence they came out* (Mesopotamia) was visible and would require no faith to realize it. Moreover, it was still obtainable and had they been *mindful of it* or cared for it, they could have returned to that place, although in so doing they would have lost their favor with God.

Verse 16. This verse expresses the same hope mentioned of Abraham in verse 10. God is pleased to own people who are trusting Him, and as a reward he will admit them into the heavenly city in the "sweet by and by." Such a home will be a *better country* than the one from which they came, or even than the one in which they were "sojourners."

Verse 17. *When he was tried* means when his faith was put to a test. *Offered up Isaac*. Abraham did not literally sacrifice his son, but he went as far as the Lord permitted him to go. Not knowing that God would change the order, Abraham was put to as strong a test of his faith as if he had slain his son. *His only begotten son* is mentioned to emphasize the severity of the test.

Verse 18. Regardless of how many other sons he might have had, that would not have lessened the severity of the test for the promise was restricted to Isaac.

Verse 19. Abraham never doubted God's ability and faithfulness in fulfilling the promise, even though his only son should die. The reason for that faith is explained in this verse in that he expected God to bring his son back to life. *Received him in a figure;* this may be regarded in two senses. The performance came so near to actual death for Isaac that the change in God's order was virtually the same to Abraham's mind as if the son had died. It was in the nature of a case where it is said that one "is snatched from the jaws of death." Another phase is the truth that it all was a figure or type of the restoration of the Son of God from death after having been slain and made an offering at the cross.

Verse 20. This blessing is recorded in Genesis 27, and it pertains to favorable experiences that were to come to his sons in the future. Being a patriarch, Isaac could speak as by a revelation from God, but he would not have done so had it not been for his faith in the declarations of God.

Verse 21. Jacob was another patriarch and could speak by the Lord's instruction. The favorable predictions he made for Joseph's sons are recorded in Genesis 48.

Verse 22. When Joseph was taken into Egypt it was said that "the Lord was with him" (Genesis 39: 2), and He continued to be with him all the time. Hence he was able to make the prediction (by faith) that is mentioned here and at Genesis 50: 24, 25.

Verse 23. It should be understood that it was the parents of Moses who had the faith. They were true servants of God and believed that He would protect their child if they did what they could to help him live. *Not afraid* means they were not frightened by what the king of Egypt had ordered to be done to the infants.

Verse 24. *Come to years* corresponds with "full forty years old" in Acts 7: 23. At that time he repudiated his relation to the daughter of Pharaoh in order to join himself with the Hebrews. The circumstance of becoming related to Pharaoh's daughter referred to here is recorded in Exodus 2: 5-10.

Verse 25. *Pleasures of sin* refers to the life he was connected with while a part of the royal family of Egypt. *A season* would be the comparatively short time in this world, for sinful pleasures will all cease at the judgment and endless punishment will follow. On the other hand the faithful people of God, though afflicted by the enemy in this life, will enjoy endless pleasure in the world to come.

Verse 26. *Reproach of Christ.* Moses did not yet know the full system of salvation of which Christ is the central figure, but Paul considers any suffering endured in service to God as also being for the sake of Christ. *Treasures in Egypt* were the luxuries experienced by the royal group of Egyptians. (See comments at verse 25.)

Verse 27. *Forsook Egypt.* This was forty years later than the preceding verse, referring to the time he led the Israelites out of the land. *Not fearing the wrath* means notwithstanding the wrath of the king. *Seeing* (by the eye of faith) *him who is invisible* to mortal eyes.

Verse 28. This event is recorded in Exodus 12, where the sprinkling of blood was to save them from death. Since such a means could not naturally prevent death, the observance of it was necessarily done *through faith* as an act of obedience.

Verse 29. There was no natural cause for the Red Sea to open up and stand as walls, hence the Israelites marched down between them because they believed God would hold them up until His people were passed over. Egyptians *assaying* (trying) to go through the same passage were drowned because God was not with them.

Verse 30. There was no physical force in the marching and shouting of the Israelites to bring down the walls of Jericho. The power of God brought them down, but it would not have been done had they not believed in God who told them (through Joshua) to march around. The power was in God as in other cases, but He would not have used it had the people lacked the faith to obey.

Verse 31. Joshua 6: 25 says that Rahab was preserved "because she hid the messengers whom Joshua sent to spy out Jericho." But she hid them because she believed the reports of the favorable things the Lord had done for His people. Acting on that faith she cooperated with the messengers in escaping the wrath of the king of Jericho. As a reward for her faith she was permitted to dwell with the Israelites, and was honored by being permitted to be in the line of ancestors of Christ. (See Joshua 6: 25; Matthew 1: 5.)

Verse 32. *What shall I more say?* Why go into details further in illustrating the fruits of faith by the lives of ancient worthies? *Time would fail me.* This is an accommodative expression, meaning that the time that would be used in going on into the same details concerning the following cases individually, would be more than is suitable to an epistle of the length of this one. Paul therefore groups a number of outstanding characters and also groups a list of things they did among them. The remainder of the chapter will be devoted to a description of heroic deeds performed through the incentive of faith. If the reader wishes to get the details of the particular persons named he may see Gideon at Judges 6: 11; Barak at Judges 4: 6; Samson at Judges 13: 24; Jephthah at Judges 11: 1; David at 1 Samuel 16: 1; Samuel at 1 Samuel 1: 20.

Verse 33. *Subdued kingdoms.* An instance of it is in 2 Samuel 8 where David overcame the Philistines; God gave him the victory because of his faithfulness. *Wrought righteousness* means to do righteous work through the motive of faith. *Obtained promises* means they obtained the fulfillment of them because they had the faith to comply with the conditions on which the promises were made. *Stopped the mouths of lions.* This was done directly by Samson in Judges 14: 5, 6, and by Daniel indirectly in Daniel 6. In each case God gave the victory because of the faith of the men.

Verse 34. *Quenched the violence of fire* occurred when the three companions of Daniel were cast into the fiery furnace (Daniel 3). *Escaped the edge of the sword.* Instances of this are too numerous to mention all, but a notable one is in 1 Samuel 20. *Out of weakness were made strong.* An outstanding instance was that of Samson in Judges 16: 28-30, where his strength was given back to him because of his returning faith and dependence upon God. *Waxed valiant* means the servants of God were strong and brave in their contests with the enemies of God. The unassisted strength of man is a failure when faced with the might of worldly hosts, but God rewards his faithful servants with victory when the attack is made. *Aliens* refers to those of another nation. Gideon routed the Midianites in connection with his war cry, "The sword of the Lord and Gideon" (Judges 7: 20-23).

Verse 35. The phrase *raised to life again* and the word *resurrection* are from the Greek word ANASTASIS, and the phrase is a good definition of the word. Two cases of such a favor shown to women are in 1 Kings 17: 17-24 and 2 Kings 4:18-37. *Were tortured.* This was done to force the servants of God to renounce their faith. They were promised relief from the torture if they would turn against the Lord, but they would *not accept* deliverance on such terms. Their motive for such resistance was that they might obtain a *better resurrection.* All mankind will be resurrected, but only those who are faithful till death will come forth to a happy life (Daniel 12: 2; John 5: 29.)

Verse 36. Not all the persecuted ones were put to death, but they were mistreated in various ways. Jeremiah was placed in prison (Jeremiah 37: 15-21), and afterward was put into the dungeon (Jeremiah 38: 1-6).

Verse 37. *They were stoned.* Two instances of this are recorded in 1 Kings 21: 1-14 and 2 Chronicles 24: 21, 22. *Sawn asunder.* This is a correct translation according to Thayer, and he says that an ancient tradition claims that the prophet Isaiah was put to death in that way. This was one manner in which the ancient worthies *were tempted* or put to a test of their faith. Others were put to death by having their head severed from their body, or by being thrust through the bowels. The reason for their wandering *in sheepskins and goatskins* is explained by the next phrase, namely, *being destitute.* Of course the condition of destitution was brought about by the cruelty of their enemies, who *afflicted* and *tormented* them in whatever way they could devise.

Verse 38. *Of whom the world was not worthy.* The world of mankind that mistreated those faithful servants of God was not fit to have their presence. They wandered in these places to escape their enemies. (See Judges 6: 2 and 1 Samuel 13: 6.)

Verse 39. *Good report* signifies they were well spoken of on account of their faith. The passage says they received not *the promise* which refers to the promise of the seed of Abraham who was to bless the nations of the world. It means they did not live to see the fulfillment of the promise, but their confidence in the promises of God was so strong that they maintained their faith until death.

Verse 40. The *better thing* is the New Covenant established on "better promises" (chapter 8: 6), that was to be brought into the world through Christ. God's purpose was to provide this institution for *us* (Christians). Because of such a plan He did not bring the fulfillment of the promise in the lifetime of those worthies. *Not be made perfect* or complete, denotes that the scheme that was started in their days could not be completed until the time of *us* (Christians).

Hebrews 12

Verse 1. This is an illustration drawn from the footraces that were popular in ancient times. There were always some witnesses whose business was to look on to see that the runners observed the "rules of the game." Knowing that they were being watched, the contestants would be more careful to do their best to run according to the regulations. The word *cloud* means a great throng, and the *witnesses* refers to the list of worthies who are described in the preceding chapter. Those persons were dead and hence could not actually be looking on as the Christians were running the race. The idea is that the examples of faith that were performed by those characters should serve as an incentive for us to do our best also. *Weight* is from a Greek word that is defined in the lexicon as anything that might be a hindrance. The contestants in the races would discard all extra clothing or whatever was attached to their bodies that would make it more difficult or uncertain in runing the race. Likewise the Christian should put off all practices or other conditions that would interfere with the service to Christ. Paul specifies one such hindrance which is the *sin which doth so easily beset us*. That sin is evidently unbelief, since the importance of belief (or faith) is the subject of the entire eleventh chapter. A lack of faith in the Lord would necessarily hinder anyone from rendering acceptable service. *Patience* means endurance or perseverance, and the Christian must not be irregular or unsteady in his service, but should continue steadfastly to the end. *Race* is from AGON which means any kind of contest in general use, but is here applied to the contest of the footrace. *Is set before us* denotes that the contest is open for us, but we must voluntarily enter it if we engage in it at all.

Verse 2. A runner would forget the things behind him and be looking toward the goal and what it would mean to reach it. Likewise the Christian should have his eyes on Jesus who has set the goal at the end of a faithful life. *Author* means one who sets an example for others to follow, and *finishr* is one who carries out that example by a faithful life unto the end. The pronoun *our* is not in the original and is not necessary to the thought in the mind of the apostle. The sentence denotes the faith of the Gospel as it is demonstrated by the life of Christ. The *joy* that was set before Jesus was that of being the Saviour of the world, even though it required Him to die on the cross. *Despising* means to belittle or count as nothing the *shame* of such a death. It was bad enough to die at all, the just for the unjust, but it was more humiliating to die by crucifixion because only the worst of criminals were usually executed by that means. That is why Paul makes the remark that Jesus obeyed his Father unto death, *"even* the death on the cross"* (Philippians 2: 8). Christ was rewarded for his humble service by being seated at the right hand of God, and those who fashion their lives after the pattern set by Jesus will be permitted to live with him and God.

Verse 3. Christians were persecuted for the sake of Jesus and often thought their sufferings were unnecessary. On this account they sought to avoid it by deserting Him and going back to Moses as their lawgiver. But Jesus also suffered for righteousness' sake, including mistreatment from sinners who were usually contradicting His teaching. Christians should consider this example and take courage for the conflict. *Faint in your minds* means to be discouraged on account of trials.

Verse 4. They had not suffered as much as Jesus did, for he was compelled to defend His faith to the extent of shedding his blood.

Verse 5. The *exhortation* referred to is in Proverbs 3: 11, 12. This exhortation by Solomon is based on a truth that is in force under all ages of the world, hence Paul cites it and applies it to the servants of God in the Christian Dispensation. *Despise not* denotes that they should not belittle or disrespect the correction. *Chastening* refers to the discipline that a righteous parent will exercise upon his son for disobedience. To *faint* means to become despondent over the rebukes of our Heavenly Father.

Verse 6. The Lord chastises his children because of His love for them, even to the extent of scourging (suffering them to be afflicted) for their training.

Verse 7. Paul is making his comparison to an earthly parent who is the proper kind, not one who fails in his duty of controlling his children. God chastens his children for their good as do fleshly fathers their sons. Christians are exhorted to submit humbly to the chastisement from God, on the principle that His love for them prompts the correction.

Verse 8. *Bastards and not sons.* Even so-called "illegitimate" boys are sons of men and women, and are brought forth by the same law of reproduction that is the source of all human beings. Hence the term as used in contrast with *sons* is employed in a technical or legal sense. The idea is that if a man refrained from using discipline on a boy it would be on the ground that he was not his son; that he belonged to another outside his own family. Likewise, if a professed Christian objects to being chastised by the Lord, it implies that he does not claim to be a son of the Lord.

Verse 9. All good persons remember with appreciation the punishment they received from their fathers in the days of their minority, for they realize that it was for their good. How much more should we accept with humility the correction from *the Father of spirits* (our spiritual Father) and live a life of uprightness.

Verse 10. *For a few days.* During the days when we were minors which was a comparatively short time in the light of the endless future. *Their own pleasure.* Not that the fathers obtained any enjoyment from the punishing of their children, but the word means that it was according to their best judgment. God is infinite in judgment and totally unselfish in His motive for chastising his children, and does it solely for their own advantage.

Verse 11. Punishment is always unpleasant to the body and cannot bring any enjoyment for the time being. The good done is to be realized in the form of a better line of conduct by having been corrected from a life of waywardness. Of course this is on condition that the children are *exercised thereby*, which means they take the correction properly and amend their ways.

Verse 12. Hands hanging down and feeble knees indicate a spirit of despair or aversion to the chastisement for the punishment of wrong. Such persons should take a different attitude in the matter and look upon the situation as one where they really have been favored.

Verse 13. *Make straight paths.* Christians are not permitted to devise their own plan of religious life; that has been done by the Lord. The meaning is that they should be careful to walk in the path that has been prepared for them. They should do this not only for their own sake, but for others who may be influenced by their example. Otherwise if they do that which is not right, those who have less knowledge or ability might be confused and caused to lose the way. Instead of such a result, their lives should be such that the *lame* or weaker ones may be *healed* or led aright.

Verse 14. *Follow peace* should be on the basis of James 3: 17 which requires the peace to be in harmony with the pure wisdom from above. Paul recognizes the necessity of this proviso in Romans 12: 18 where he says "if it be possible." *Holiness* is the same as righteousness and without it no man shall *see the Lord* which means to enjoy Him.

Verse 15. *Look diligently* denotes the idea of being careful how one conducts himself, otherwise he may get out of the right path and fall from the grace or favor of God. *Root of bitterness* means a feeling of hatred against others, which could be only a source of *trouble* among disciples that would spread defilement among them.

Verse 16. This verse specifies some of the things referred to in general terms in the preceding one. Fornicators should not be permitted to remain among the disciples because of their evil influence (1 Corinthians 5: 6, 7). A *profane* person is one who makes a temporal use of a sacred thing. That is what Esau did when he sold his *birthright* (a sacred possession) for a mess of food (a temporal article). In general practice it means any disciple who would try to obtain some earthly advantage out of his profession of faith in Christ.

Verse 17. *Found no place for repentance.* Repentance means more than sorrow or regret for a mistake, but also requires that it be corrected. Esau knew afterward that he had acted foolishly in selling his birthright, but he had no opportunity for getting it back, for Jacob would not give it up.

Verse 18. From here through several verses the apostle returns to the leading subject of the epistle, namely, the contrasts between the system under Moses and that under Christ. The mount that *might be touched* was Sinai because it was a literal one (Exodus 19: 12), and it was from this mount that the old law was given. The rest of the verse is descriptive of the conditions when the Israelites approached the area.

Verse 19. This continues the conditions at Sinai which are recorded in Exodus 20: 19 and other passages in connection therewith.

Verse 20. *Could not endure that which was commanded* sounds as if God required something that the people could not do, which we know was not the case. The meaning is that the conditions were so awe-inspiring that it overwhelmed them with terror. The things mentioned in the latter half of the verse are recorded in Exodus 19: 12, 13.

Verse 21. This remark of Moses is not recorded in Exodus, but Paul was inspired and was able to report this part of the circumstance for our information.

Verse 22. The preceding verses describe the mount to which Christians do *not come* (as the Israelites did); the apostle now will describe the mount to which they have come. He does so by a series of points of identity which apply to the one divine institution under Christ, which was set up in Jerusalem which is termed *Mount Zion*. Christians do not actually go to the city of Jerusalem, but they come to the institution that was set up in that city. In coming to this divine institution we are brought into near relation with other spiritual places and things, to be named in this and the next two verses. *City of the living God* is that one in which He lives and which is the one "which hath foundations" (chapter 11: 10). *Heavenly Jerusalem* is a contrast between Heaven above and the literal one below. The angels live in Heaven but are used in service for the people of God (chapter 1: 14). By coming into the church it brings us into the benefit of these holy services.

Verse 23. *General assembly* is from PANEGURIS, which means the same as a mass meeting, and refers to the universal membership of the church of Christ. The same institution is composed of the *firstborn* which is plural in the original Greek and also is in the possessive case. The members of the church are called *firstborn* in a figurative sense. In old times the firstborn child was heir to the possessions of his father. Since all faithful members of the church are heirs of the spiritual possessions of Christ, they are here called the *firstborn* (ones). The phrase *church of the firstborn* is not a scriptural title or name of the church as it is erroneously used often by our brethren. *Written in heaven.* The names of the faithful children of God are enrolled in heaven (Luke 10: 20; Revelation 21: 27). Membership in the church of Christ brings us into fellowship with God who is the *Judge of all*. It also makes us have relationship with the *spirits of just men made perfect*, meaning those who have reached the complete state under the providence of God, such as those described in Matthew 27: 53; Romans 8: 29; 1 Corinthians 15: 20; Ephesians 4: 8; Jude 14.

Verse 24. Jesus became the mediator of the new covenant by giving that law into the world to take the place of the law of Moses. *Blood of sprinkling* is so worded because under the system of Moses the blood of animals was literally sprinkled on the objects to be affected. The blood of Christ is sprinkled figuratively when men obey the Gospel which brings them into the benefits of that blood. (See 1 John 1: 7.) *Speaketh better things than that of Abel.* The blood of Abel cried for vengeance (Genesis 4: 10 and 15), while the blood of Christ calls for mercy (chapter 2: 17). The word *better* means "more useful or serviceable." The blood of Christ opened up a way of salvation for all mankind, which was not true of the blood of Abel.

Verse 25. *Him that speaketh* means Christ whose blood speaks better things than that of Abel. Judaizers would have the Christians *refuse* Jesus by going back to Moses for their law. Moses *spake* on earth (at Sinai) and even his law dared not be refused (chapter 2: 1, 2; 10: 29). Jesus spake *from heaven* when he sent the Holy Spirit down to the apostles in order to give them the new law. Paul asks how can we escape rejection from the Lord if we refuse His law.

Verse 26. *Whose voice* means that of God, speaking in conjunction with that of Christ who was always associated with God in all that was done (Genesis 1: 26; John 1: 3). *Then shook the earth* occurred at Sinai as described in verses 18-20. That shaking brought in a new system of religious practice, but it was one that was not destined to be permanent. Instead, God purposed to bring about one more shaking that was to be more extensive and would involve both heaven and earth; the event is predicted in Haggai 2: 5-9. The prediction refers to the time when the Lord was to bring in the New Covenant and thereby disannul all other systems that had been in use.

Verse 27. Paul explains that since there was to be but one more shaking, it signified that what would be left in force after the shaking would be so firm that it woul be useless to try the shaking again. Such was the case, for when the great shaking took place at Jerusalem on Pentecost, the Jewish and Patriarchal Dispensations were gone and only the kingdom of Christ was able to *remain* as our verse says.

Verse 28. *We* (Christians) *receiving a kingdom* takes place when people renounce the worldly life and come into the kingdom of Christ. *Cannot be moved* is explained in the preceding verse, and in Daniel 2: 44. With such an institution in which we may live, there is much reason for our serving God acceptably, and the apostle prays that divine grace may be had in the service. *Reverence* and *godly fear* are virtually the same, meaning profound regard for God and resolve to treat him with full devotion.

Verse 29. God is merciful to all those who will accept His mercy, but he is a revenging God upon those who do not respect His law (chapter 10: 28, 29; verse 25).

Hebrews 13

Verse 1. The main argument of this epistle is completed and the present chapter is given to various subjects pertaining to the church and individual duties. *Brotherly love* signifies the love extended to others by reason of the common relationship in the family of God.

Verse 2. *Entertain strangers* is from a Greek word that is defined in the lexicon as hospitality, especially toward those outside one's immediate personal acquaintances. *Entertained angels unawares* was done by Abraham in Genesis 18. However, Jesus taught the principle of discretion in the bestowal of favors (Matthew 7: 6), hence a Christian is not required to keep "open house" for all stragglers regardless of circumstances.

Verse 3. The *bonds* were the chains fastened upon disciples because of their devotion to Christ. Those who are fortunate enough not to be in chains as yet, should consider themselves as partakers of the same persecutions. *Also in the body* refers to the body of Christ (the church); being in the same body with the persecuted ones should create a feeling of brotherly sympathy.

Verse 4. *Marriage is honorable* because it is the Lord's arrangement for the perpetuation of the race, hence the marriage bed should be regarded as undefiled. As an inducement for man to cooperate with God in this plan, He has made the intimate relation a pleasurable one. All good things may be abused, hence there are people who use this relationship for the one purpose only. Such people should remember the case of Onan in Genesis 38: 8-10 and beware. The fact of having contracted legal marriage does not justify Christians in counteracting God's original purpose for the institution. *Whoremongers* refers especially to men who are immoral and *adulterers* to either sex.

Verse 5. *Conversation* means one's conduct or manner of life, and the sentence means that their lives should not be influenced by an overmuch desire for the wealth of this world. *To be content* does not deny one the right to "look out for a rainy day," or to acquire more of the good things of life than he needs for his own personal use; such a theory would contradict Ephesians 4: 28. The thought is that while we are making lawful efforts to produce the desirable things of life, we should not be fretting because we are not as successful as others or as much so as we had expected to be ourselves. We may always have the assurance that we will be cared for in some way.

Verse 6. We may *boldly* or confidently say that the Lord is our helper. Men may persecute us even to the extent of depriving us of the comforts of life, yet we should not fear about the outcome if we are faithful to Him.

Verse 7. *Remember* means to be mindful of these rulers which means the elders. They have spoken the word of God in their work as shepherds over the flock (Acts 20: 28). *Whose faith follow.* That is we should imitate the example of faithfulness in the discharge of their duties. Verse 17 is more direct in its requirements of the treatment of the rulers in association with the flock, hence the present verse has especial reference to the ones who have gone on out of life, but whose examples of faith were still worthy of imitation. The disciples are told to consider the object and outcome of those noble lives of faith.

Verse 8. This verse continues the thought begun in the preceding one, telling us what was the *end* or object or motive of the faithful lives of the rulers, namely, the Lord Jesus Christ. Since He is *the same yesterday, and today, and forever,* to have Him as the motive of one's life would insure a life of faithfulness till death.

Verse 9. The *divers* (different) and *strange* (from the outside) *doctrines* (or teachings) refers especially to the disturbances of the Judaizers. To be *carried about* indicates something that can be moved with the wind and hence having very little weight. Paul wishes them to be *established* or firmly set with the *grace* or favor of Christ, instead of relying on the regulations of the old law regarding meats. A few more verses are devoted to some contrasts and likenesses between the two dispensations.

Verse 10. The Mosaic system had a literal altar service on which animals were burned in sacrifice. Some parts of the beasts were reserved for food to be eaten by the priests who performed the service. We Christians also have an altar that is not a literal or temporal one; it is the sacrificial service of Christ. Those who accept the teaching of the Judaizers in going back to the old tabernacle, forfeit their right to the benefits of Christ's sacrifice; they have fallen from grace (Galatians 5: 4).

Verse 11. *The bodies of those beasts,* etc. (See Exodus 29: 14.) The blood of those beasts was used in the most holy place while the bodies were taken to the outside of the camp and burned as a sacrifice for sin.

Verse 12. There is a beautiful parallel drawn here between the bodies referred to and that of Christ. He was taken outside the city of Jerusalem to be put to shame by death on the cross as the worst of criminals.

Verse 13. But this humiliating treatment of Jesus was imposed upon him by his enemies, although it was a part of God's great plan of salvation to be accomplished through His only begotten Son. True followers of Him therefore will not be ashamed to "stand by" Him in his humiliation and will take joy in sharing in the reproach.

Verse 14. The material things of this world are all finally to pass away. Even the cherished city of Jerusalem in which was located the temple and center of the Mosaic worship, was then about to be destroyed by the Romans. Then why not give attention to the service under Christ which will prepare one for the city which is *to come* and which will never pass away.

Verse 15. Instead of the material incense that was used with the sacrifices of the Mosaic system, let us offer the kind that is spiritual. Instead of the fruit of the field or sheepfold, let it be the *fruit of our lips* in the form of praise to God for all the wonderful blessings which we have received.

Verse 16. Not that all physical or temporal services are to be dropped from our activities. We may still do good to others by *communicating* or sharing with them the good things necessary to their personal wellbeing. God is still pleased with that kind of sacrifices.

Verse 17. *Obey* is from PEITHO and Thayer defines it at this place as follows: "To listen to, obey, yield to, comply with." The definition agrees with the connection in which it is used here. The persons are said to *have the rule* which could not be accomplished unless they were obeyed. This thought is repeated by the word *submit* which is from HUPEIKO, which Thayer defines in the same passage as follows: "To give way, yield, to yield to authority and admonition, to submit." No institution can succeed without government, and that calls for governors or rulers. But such officers cannot govern unless they are obeyed, hence the members of the church are commanded to be obedient to the rulers which means the elders. *They watch for your souls.* Since the souls of men cannot be seen it follows that the elders must watch the actions of their bodies. The members sometimes resent their elders and seem to think they have a strong complaint when they say "we are being watched." But the elders are not doing their duty unless they watch the actions of the members. The elders will have to *give account* for the conduct of the flock, and if the members do not live in obedience to their rulers the account will not be a joyous one. If the facts require an unfavorable report to the Chief Shepherd, such an account will be unprofitable for the sheep for it will cause their souls to be rejected at the day of judgment.

Verse 18. *Pray for us.* Inspired apostles felt the need of fellowship and the benefit of the prayers of their brethren. Paul professes to have a good conscience which was doubtless suggested by the accusations that had been made against him, making him a prisoner in Rome. The original for *honestly* is really a stronger word than it, for a man could be honest while doing wrong. It truly means to live "so that there shall be no room for blame"—Thayer. In order for a man to have a *good conscience* in the sight of God, it is necessary that his life be right as measured by the will of God.

Verse 19. Evidently the Hebrew brethren to whom this epistle was written were principally those living in Judea. Paul was in Rome and detained as a prisoner on account of his testimony for Christ. He besought the brethren to pray for his deliverance so that he might again come among them and labor in the work of the Lord.

Verse 20. *God of peace* is said of Him because he is the source of all genuine peace that is in harmony with divine wisdom (James 3:17). He brought his Son from the dead in order to give the assurance of genuine peace to all true servants of righteousness. *Great shepherd of the sheep* is Christ who is called the "chief Shepherd" in 1 Peter 5:4. This emphasized title is given to Christ because elders are referred to as shepherds in that they are told to "feed the church of God" which is termed the flock (Acts 20:28). The things Paul wishes God to do for them in the next verse are to be accomplished *through the blood of the everlasting covenant*. It is called everlasting because it was not to be replaced by any other as was the Mosaic covenant.

Verse 21. *Make you perfect* means to equip them completely for every good work in doing His will. It is to be done through Jesus Christ which will make it *well-pleasing in his* (God's) *sight*.

Verse 22. *Exhortation* means to insist on doing one's known duty, and Paul has clearly made known to them their duty to serve under Christ and not Moses. *Few words* is a comparative term. The epistle to the Hebrews though consisting of several chapters, yet it embraces arguments covering the books of Exodus and Leviticus and parts of others in the Old Testament. That makes the book of Hebrews comparatively "few words."

Verse 23. This is the only place I have found that mentions the imprisonment of Timothy. Paul's confidence in the prospect of his own release (verse 19) was so strong that he planned on joining Timothy soon in going to meet with these brethren.

Verse 24. *Salute* means to give a friendly greeting which implies a wish for the wellbeing of the one saluted. This was to include the rulers (elders) as well as other saints (Christians). Others in Italy (of which Rome was the capital) joined Paul in his salutation for the brethren in Judea.

Verse 25. *Grace* means the unmerited favor of the Lord and it was the sincere wish of Paul that his brethren everywhere should so live as to receive that favor. *Amen* is from a Greek word that is spelled the same as English. In the King James Version it is rendered "amen" 50 times and "verily" 100 times.

James 1

Verse 1. I have consulted a number of works of reference such as commentaries, lexicons, dictionaries and histories, as well as the various passages in the New Testament that are related to to the subject, and my conclusion is that the author of this epistle is "James the Lord's brother" (Galatians 1:19). In the passage just cited he is called an apostle but not one of the twelve. He was an important man as may be seen by the following passages. Acts 12:17; 15:13-21; 21:18; Galatians 1:19; 2:9, 12. James calls himself a servant of God *and* of the Lord Jesus Christ. This is significant, for it indicates that both of these members of the Deity must be recognized as having divine authority. The epistle was especially written to Jewish Christians who were scattered among the Gentiles. The term *twelve tribes* is used figuratively only, for in Christ there are no tribal distinctions. It is used in the same sense as Paul used it in Acts 26:7, where we know he was speaking of them as Christians. The truth is that there were disciples of Christ made from all the twelve tribes. *Greeting* means a friendly salutation from one who wishes well for the one greeted.

Verse 2. *Count it all joy* cannot mean to pretend that they get enjoyment out of that which is disagreeable, for that would be an act of insincerity. The idea is they should regard it as something that would result in a benefit. *Temptations* refers to adversities or hardships such as might be imposed upon them by their enemies.

Verse 3. *Patience* means endurance and if the disciples remain true to Christ amidst the trials, it will demonstrate the genuineness of their faith.

Verse 4. Since the good result of trials that have been endured through faith is to demonstrate *patience*, the disciples are urged to "let the good work go on." The word *perfect* means complete, and if the good work is allowed to continue to the end, it will result in a life that is completely devoted to God or that is willing to go far enough that it will be *wanting* (lacking) *nothing*.

Verse 5. The word *wisdom* is from the Greek word SOPHIA which occurs 51 times in the New Testament. It has many shades of meaning concerning which Thayer makes the following statement: "Used of the knowledge of very diverse [different] matters, so that the shade of meaning in which the word is taken must be discovered from the context [connection] in every particular case." We are sure that God will not change the physical conditions of any man's brain, therefore the wisdom which James says He will give in answer to prayer cannot mean the natural gift colloquially called "horse sense." Hence the passage means to ask God to help us in our efforts to use our faculties in acquiring useful knowledge. *Upbraideth not* means God will never tire of hearing the requests of His children.

Verse 6. Regardless of what may be said as to how or when God answers prayer, we are sure He will not grant any petition that is not in harmony with His word. Therefore to *ask in faith* means to ask for such favors that are in harmony with that word since faith comes by hearing it (Romans 10: 17). Furthermore, we must believe that word after we hear it or else our attitude will be a wavering one. James likens such a mind to a wave that is unsteady because it changes its position every time the wind changes.

Verse 7. Again, regardless of how or when God answers prayer, He will not grant any petition made by a person such as the preceding verse describes.

Verse 8. *Double minded* means to be uncertain or doubting. Thayer defines it at this place as one who is "divided in interest." Since the passage says he is *unstable in all his ways* it puts him in the class described in verse six.

Verse 9. *Low degree*. Those in the humble or lowly walks of life may take satisfaction from the *exaltation* or honor of being a servant of Christ. That is the most dignified station or manner of life that any man can maintain.

Verse 10. *The rich* man who trusts in his wealth (Mark 10: 24) has no just cause for rejoicing unless he become *low* or humble. The uncertainty of the wealth of this world is likened to the flowers that are flourishing so briefly.

Verse 11. As the sun overcomes the beauty and show of the blossoms, so the test of time will finally put an end to the vanity of riches. *Ways* means purposes or schemes that a man has that have the accumulation of wealth as their chief motive. This does not condemn the lawful production of property that is intended to be used for doing good. (See Ephesians 4: 28.)

Verse 12. *Temptations* means trials same as in verse 2. They are bound to come especially to a man who is determined to serve Christ in the midst of sinful men. But such experiences are calculated to become a test of his faith. The test will not be completed until the end of life (Revelation 2: 10), and if the disciple is thus faithful he will receive the crown promised by the Lord.

Verse 13. The Bible does not contradict itself, so when it says for us to consider temptations as cause for joy (verse 2) then here tells us that God does not tempt any man, we know there is a difference between temptations. The key to the subject is in the word *evil* which is not the same as trials or adversities. It is from an original word that always means the opposite of good; is always morally bad. Of course God does not use such means to test His creatures in their religious life.

Verse 14. James uses the process of natural reproduction to illustrate the course of sin. First a man's lust (evil desire) entices the object or victim of wicked design.

Verse 15. With the consummation of the evil design, that is, when it has accomplished its gratification the conception takes place. After the conception the next step is the *bringing forth* of the creature that was conceived. The name of the creature so conceived and brought forth is *SIN*. The final destiny of such a creature is *death* or separation from God. The way to avoid such a regrettable reproduction is for a man to resist all of the enticements as a virtuous woman should resist all who would lure her into a life of shame.

Verse 16. In the preceding two verses the writer draws an illustration from the natural process of reproduction. In this and the following verse he makes one out of the motions of the heavenly bodies. *Err* is from the Greek word PLANAO, and it is the verb form of a noun in the same class which is "planet," coming from the Greek word PLANATES, which Jude 13 uses where he speaks of "wandering stars." Since these planets or stars were believed to wander from side to side, their action was adopted into

James 1: 17-25

language to describe men who stray from the straight path. The verse means that Christians should not imitate the action of those planets here translated by the word *err*.

Verse 17. We may rightly feel indebted to any thing or person that is the source of benefits to us. The planets are not such a source in the sense of being the giver, but instead are themselves a gift to us. The giver of them is God and James calls Him the *Father of lights*, the last word meaning the planets because they are luminous bodies. Since the Father (or creator) of these lights is the giver of all good things, we should imitate Him and not the planets which have the habit of *erring* or wandering about. God does not waver and as an indication of the steadiness of His example, James declares that He does not even produce a shadow by *turning*. The figure is drawn from the circumstance that at certain seasons and at particular places on the earth, when the sun is straight over the equator it cannot cause any shadow. But when it *turns* to go either north or south (as it seems to do), it will then cast a shadow. James thus describes God as more fixed in His characteristics than the sun.

Verse 18. The writer again uses the thought of reproduction for an illustration. A father begets his own children and they become of the same *kind* of creatures as himself. God begets men by the word of truth concerning Christ (1 John 5: 1). *Firstfruits* is used in the sense of seniority because Christians are the first creatures who are said to have been born to God through faith in Jesus who is the "only begotten" Son of the Father in the sense of personality of being.

Verse 19. *Wherefore* means because of such a truth, namely, that belief of the word concerning Christ begets one unto God, it is a great reason for giving respect to that word. *Swift* means eager or ready to hear the word of the Lord. No man can be too eager to hear the word of God, but he should be *slow* or discreet in what he says. Likewise he is not condemned for the mere fact of becoming angry (Ephesians 4: 26), but he should bring himself into control and not be inclined to fly into a rage at every provocation.

Verse 20. A man who controls himself may do right in spite of his anger, but no person will work the righteousness of God because he is worked up by wrath.

Verse 21. *Lay apart* signifies that a man must put his evil practices out of his life himself, and not expect God to work some special influence over him to purify him. *All filthiness* means any kind of impurity either of body or mind. *Naughtiness* is a stronger word than is usually attached to it, and means that which is injurious and wicked. *Superfluity* signifies something that is extra or that is useless as an item of a man's character. The sentence denotes that any evil principle is such an item when it is a part of a man's conduct. *Receive with meekness* means to accept the word in humility and not in the spirit of resentment. *Engrafted* signifies to be implanted or received in the heart with the spirit of obedience. If it is so received the word of the Lord will save the soul.

Verse 22. Even a good seed that is implanted in the soil will produce no fruit unless it becomes active. So the *engrafted* word will be fruitless unless the receiver of it becomes active and does what it directs. It is a matter of self-deception to imagine that hearing the word is all that is required to be acceptable to the Lord. Even men will not be deceived (much less the Lord) by such a character, for it will be apparent to all that such a person is not producing anything useful to others.

Verse 23. While a man is standing before a mirror he is seeing himself in reflection but no action is being shown. Likewise as long as a person is only hearing (or reading) the Bible he is seeing his duties portrayed but seeing nothing being done.

Verse 24. The moment he leaves the mirror the image disappears from his mind, and he will need to return to it again to "see himself as others see him." If he could remain constantly before the glass he would never forget the vision of his appearance. However, in a literal sense a man could not remain always in front of the mirror and also attend to his other business, but that is not the part of the subject James is illustrating.

Verse 25. In mental and spiritual matters it is possible to accomplish things that are impossible with material activities. Hence it is possible to be constantly in the view of the spiritual mirror and at the same time be actively engaged in the Lord's work as the writer now insists. It is called the *perfect law of liberty* because it makes us free from our sins and gives us the spiritual liberty that cannot be had from any other source. (See Romans 8: 2) It is necessary to look into the Bible in order to learn what kind of work the Lord desires, then what is done will be correct as to activity and such will bring the blessing of God.

Verse 26. Thayer defines the original for *religious* as "Fearing or worshipping God," and *religion* is the noun form of the same term. *Bridleth not his tongue* would violate verse 19, and such a person is considered self-deceived (verse 22). Such a religion is *vain* which means "without any force" according to Thayer's definition.

Verse 27. *Pure* means unmixed and *undefiled* denotes something that is unsoiled. There is not much difference between the two words, but the former has the idea of something not attached to another ingredient to begin with, while the latter denotes that it remains so afterward. *Visit.* One definition of the word is "To look upon in order to help or benefit"—Thayer. It has to do with one's actions toward others. *Unspotted from the world* means to be free from the vices commonly practiced by mankind.

James 2

Verse 1. *Have* is from ECHO which requires two full pages in Thayer's lexicon for definitions. The specific meaning of it in any given passage must therefore be determined by the way it is used. In this verse the writer discusses the subject of proper treatment for others and hence it means they are not to hold or exercise the faith as stated. *Respect of persons* comes from one Greek word that means "partiality." *The faith* is used as a term for the whole system of religious practice under Christ. Therefore the verse means they should not show partiality in the exercises that pertain to the public assembly. (See verse 4.)

Verse 2. This verse merely describes two men in different classes as to their possessions and personal appearance. Nothing is said of character or anything that pertains to actual merit.

Verse 3. This verse indicates they had the services of ushers, and they would seat the audience as they were coming in, showing a preference for the "well-dressed" ones by giving them the most desirable places.

Verse 4. Here the writer uses the very word of our definition by saying they are *partial. Judges of* is rendered "judges having" by The Englishman's Greek New Testament. The passage means those people had evil thoughts when they were judging or deciding on who should sit where.

Verse 5. A man will not be given any special credit in the kingdom of heaven by virtue of his being poor. The conditions of salvation are such that the poor have the same chance as the rich. Moreover, since the conditions require a great deal of humility and sacrifice, the poor generally are the more ready to accept it. In that sense the poor are *chosen* to be *rich in faith*. Such richness in faith is what makes them heirs or entitles them to the advantage of the kingdom. This is also according to the promise that has been made by Christ and the apostles.

Verse 6. To *despise* means to belittle or look down upon, and some of the disciples had been guilty of such an attitude toward people who were poor. It is usually the rich people who resort to the courts in suits of oppression in order to squeeze a little more money out of unfortunate debtors.

Verse 7. Thayer defines the original for *blaspheme* as follows: "To speak reproachfully, rail at, calumniate [accuse falsely]." The *worthy name* is Christ whom oppressors would be inclined to belittle because His teaching condemns their practices.

Verse 8. *Royal* means kingly and the greatest laws ever given to men have come from the King of heaven. Among those laws is the one which commands to "love thy neighbor as thyself." James says if we obey this we will do well.

Verse 9. No man who loves his neighbor as himself will mistreat him because he is poor. Hence he will not show *respect to persons* which we have seen is defined as "partiality." *Convinced of the law* denotes that the one who shows partiality is guilty under the law of being a transgressor of that law.

Verse 10. *Whole law* as James is using it refers to the ten commandments. Not that the decalogue is still the law of God as it once was, for it has been replaced by the law of Christ. But it is used to illustrate the point which the writer has under consideration, because it is formed into a certain number of separate commandments each of which is a complete unit of law. Thus if a man rejects a single one of these ten commands he is guilty of all because they all were given by one authority.

Verse 11. The command at the end of verse 8 is not in that exact form in the first account of the decalogue but it is so worded in Leviticus 19: 18. It is also virtually included in the last six of the ten, for if a man loves his neighbor as himself he will observe all those six. In our verse the writer mentions two of the original ten commandments. The point he is making is that since the same God who gave one of them gave the other also, therefore no matter which a person rejects he is rejecting God. So the verse has no application to the mistakes that all people are liable to make through forgetfulness or other weaknesses of the flesh. In other words, the whole matter that James is considering pertains to the question of the Lord's authority.

Verse 12. *Law of liberty* is the one named in chapter 1: 25 and refers to the New Testament. *So speak ye and so do.* Since that law is the one by which we will be judged, our lives should be regulated by it now.

Verse 13. Matthew 5: 7 says the merciful shall obtain merey, which is the affirmative side. The present verse deals with the negative and teaches that if a man shows no mercy to others, he likewise shall *have no mercy* given him at the day of judgment. *Mercy rejoices against judgment.* If a man is merciful to others he will not have any fears of the judgment day as far as this subject is concerned.

Verse 14. The writer is still treating the subject introduced in the early verses of the chapter which concerns the proper conduct toward the poor. This verse states a principle that has general application in the Christian life, but it will be used for a specific purpose at present with reference to those in need.

Verse 15. The conditions mentioned designate needs that are actual and not merely some imaginary ones, so that the persons deserve assistance of their brethren.

Verse 16. It is well to have sympathy for those in need if the expressed wishes are supplemented with actions. But the most touching sentiments that can be spoken will not put any clothing upon a naked body.

Verse 17. Faith is a grand principle and no man can be a Christian without it. Neither will he be regarded by the Lord as one unless he makes his faith a living one by good works, such as supplying the comforts of life to those in need and worthy.

Verse 18. The first sentence represents a man who seems to think that faith and works are two distinct virtues of equal worth, and that a person is at liberty to make his own choice of them and the reward from the Lord will be the same in either case. James replies with a remark that shows he will not endorse either without the other. *Show me thy faith without thy works* only states what the pretender claims to show, not that James is admitting that the claim is true. He does not ask anyone to take his word but proposes to prove his faith by actions.

Verse 19. It is well to believe there is one God if a man does not stop there; if he does he is no better than the devils (or demons). Matthew 8: 29 gives one account of the trembling of these beings. But while they trembled their expressions of terror did not bring them any benefit, which shows that trembling or belief is not enough.

Verse 20. *Vain* means empty or useless, and James so considers a man who makes a profession of faith but does not back it up with something helpful.

Verse 21. Hebrews 11: 17 says Abraham's faith was tried by the event about his son. The present verse says it was *works* that did it or that justified him. There is no disagreement between the passages. It was his faith that caused him to offer up his son; his works put his faith into a practical proof.

Verse 22. The word *perfect* means complete, and thus the works of Abraham completed or rounded out the character which was founded upon his faith.

Verse 23. *Scripture was fulfilled* or made good. This refers to Genesis 15: 6 where God had just assured Abraham that he would have a great many descendants. He knew that Abraham would finally prove his faith by his works, and hence he was regarded as a righteous man. Abraham is called the *friend of God* in 2 Chronicles 20: 7 and it is repeated by James. This is on the same principle that Jesus uses the word "friend" in John 15: 14. He says they are His friends "if ye do whatsoever I command you." There are people today who glory in calling themselves "friends," yet they stoutly disobey and even resist many of the commands of Christ. According to Jesus they are not His friends; if not friends then they must be considered enemies.

Verse 24. The *works* that James means consist of doing what the Lord commands. He is not considering the works of the law of Moses, for at the time of this epistle those were termed "dead works" (Hebrews 6:1; 9:14).

Verse 25. Rahab was justified by works in the same sense as that of Abraham. (See the comments at verse 21.)

Verse 26. The spirit or soul of a man does not operate in this world separate from his body. Neither can the body act without the spirit and hence when alone the body is dead. The circumstance is used to illustrate the difference between faith and works.

James 3

Verse 1. *Masters* is from DIDASKALOS, and it is the same word rendered "teachers" in Hebrews 5:12. In that place Paul says the brethren ought to be teachers, using the word in a good sense, while James says for the brethren not to have many of them. We must therefore consider the connection in which it is used in order to get the meaning in any given case. In our verse it is plain that James is writing of men who put themselves up as teachers who do not properly control their tongues. Such people are to be condemned all the more because they do harm by their words.

Verse 2. *For in many things*. If we do have too many of such professed teachers we will *offend all* or all (of us) will *offend* or stumble. The importance of our language is the subject in several verses. If a man does not *offend* (or stumble) with the improper use of his tongue he will prove to be a perfect or complete man, controlling even his body.

Verse 3. The great influence of apparently small things is the idea James is illustrating in this and the next verse. In size and weight a bridle bit is very small, yet with it we control the direction of the entire animal.

Verse 4. The same thing is true of the *helm* or rudder of a ship. It is but a few inches or feet long, yet it may guide a ship that is many hundreds of feet in length.

Verse 5. The application of the illustration is made to the *tongue*. The last word is from GLOSSA, which means as its first definition the literal organ that is a member of the fleshly body. The Greek term is used because the tongue is the instrument by which the speech or words of a person are produced. Actually it is the language of the individual that is being considered, although the form of the phrases is related to the physical organ of speech. James uses another illustration for the same purpose as that in verses 3 and 4. If a man wished to burn a structure as tall as a tower, he would need only to use a torch an inch long.

Verse 6. James calls the tongue a *fire* because he had just used the illustration of "a little fire." It is called a *world of iniquity* because the original word for *world* means mankind. The evil use of the tongue will affect mankind in general if it is not curbed. *Defiles the whole body*. Our organ of speech if allowed to work sinfully will result in evil conduct of the whole body. *Course* literally means "a wheel" according to Thayer, and *nature* means the procedure of human existence. The figure represents it as a wheel that is rolling onward. James means that the evil tongue sets this wheel on fire. *It is set on fire of hell* (GEHENNA); not literally, of course. But a torch has to be "lighted" from some source, and James regards a wicked tongue as so bad that he represents its owner as having applied to hell to "get a light."

Verse 7. The facts of controlling a horse with a bit, guiding a ship with a rudder or training a beast by man all have one thing in common, namely, the feat is accomplished by another party; the things controlled are acted upon by an outside force.

Verse 8. Such a feat cannot be accomplished upon the tongue because of its characteristic of poison which defies being subdued by another man than its owner. James does not say a man cannot subdue his own tongue; in truth he teaches that a man can and should bridle his own tongue (chapter 1:26).

Verse 9. The main point in this and the next verse is to show the inconsistency in the uncontrolled tongue. Man is made *after the similitude of God*, therefore He should be regarded with respect. Yet the evil tongue will bless one and curse the other.

Verse 10. This repeats the thought of the preceding verse in another form of expression. The words *same mouth* emphasize the inconsistency in a more direct way.

Verses 11, 12. James refers to the consistency of the things in the natural creation, to shame the man who is double-minded in the use of his tongue. The same God who made the inanimate things named also created man and gave him a tongue wherewith to express his intelligence. How inexcusable it is therefore in him to make such an evil use of the blessing of speech.

Verse 13. *Wise man* is one who has learned to exercise good judgment, and *knowledge* means information concerning which he may exercise that good judgment. James gives some specific suggestions on how such a man may manifest those traits in his *conversation*, which means conduct or manner of life. He is to do it with *meekness of wisdom;* a truly wise man will be *meek* or humble and not boastful of his knowledge.

Verse 14. *Bitter envying* denotes a mind that is resentful toward another person who is fortunate. The original word for *strife* means an attempt to outdo some other person by fair means or otherwise. Should such a person succeed he is admonished not to glory in it. *Lie not against the truth.* Certainly all lies are against the truth, but the special thought is that an envious person cannot oppose a righteous or fortunate one without contradicting the truth involved.

Verse 15. *Wisdom* is from a Greek word that has a great variety of meanings. Thayer comments on this phase of the subject as follows: "Used of knowledge of very diverse matters, so that the shade of meaning in which the word is taken must be discovered from the context [connection] in every particular case." In general the word refers to knowledge or information that a person may have (or claim to have), whether it be good or bad, true or false. This should prepare us to see why James calls something by the word *wisdom* when he is speaking of that which he disapproves. Earthly is used as a contrast to *above; sensual* pertains to the natural or animal part of our nature; *devilish* is an adjective and means something that has the character of demons.

Verse 16. James verifies his description of *this wisdom* (preceding verse) by repeating virtually the sentiments of verse 14. He emphasizes it by adding the results of such "wisdom," namely, *confusion and every evil work.*

Verse 17. In verses 14-16 James designates the kind of wisdom that does not come from above (or heaven); the present verse describes the kind that does come from the higher source. *First pure* signifies that it is of the most importance for a man's information to be *pure* or unmixed with anything false. *Then peaceable* indicates that peace is not to be desired unless it is according to the truth. That is why Paul placed it on condition in Romans 12: 18. *Gentle* means to be mild and fair in one's temperament even when insisting on truth as being preferable to peace. *Easy to be intreated* is all from one Greek word that means to be of a yielding disposition and not stubborn when the heavenly wisdom is presented. *Full of mercy* means that one's life is merciful toward those in difficulties whenever the occasion arises, and not only when it is the most convenient to be so. *Fruits* are the deeds that are performed and heavenly wisdom will prompt one to produce *good* deeds. *Without partiality* denotes an attitude that does not show respect of persons. (See chapter 2: 1-4.) *Without hypocrisy* means that our expressions of friendliness to others will be sincere and not a mere pretense. A tree is known by its fruit, hence if a man is being influenced by the wisdom that is from above, he will exhibit the characteristics that are described in this verse.

Verse 18. If a man possesses good fruit he usually wishes to reproduce it by sowing or planting it. Hence he will sow it righteously by conforming to the rules of peace that have been formed in harmony with the *pure* wisdom.

James 4

Verse 1. *Wars and fightings* are virtually the same except the first refers to a state of conflict in general and the second to the single battles of the war. James is writing of spiritual or moral things and not of warfare in its usual sense. *Lusts* refers to unrighteous pleasures and the strife after such gratifications is bound to bring conflicts between different *members* of the body of Christ.

Verse 2. *Lust and have not.* They had the unholy desires but were not always able to obtain what they craved, and that caused them to *kill* (have murderous thoughts, 1 John 3: 15) those who resisted their unrighteous desires. *Fight and war* is the same as *wars and fightings* in the first verse. In some cases they might have obtained things they had asked for had they asked for them in a lawful manner.

Verse 3. While they did not ask in the proper way, some did make unlawful demands but were refused because of the impure motive that prompted the requests. That unrighteous motive was that their personal cravings might be gratified and not that lawful benefits might be obtained. The passage as a whole (verses 1-3) pictures a group of professed disciples who were confused and unsettled in their lives, trying to partake of the same practices as those of the world, at the same time pretending to be serving the Lord in things spiritual.

Verse 4. In the temporal world a person who commits unlawful intimacy is guilty of immorality. Likewise in the realm of the family of God, those who are intimate with the sinful pleasures of the world are guilty of spiritual adultery because they are untrue to Christ, who is their lawful partner. This intimacy is here called *friendship* and James says it is *enmity* (at war) with God. On this principle James declares that a person cannot be a *friend* (be intimate with) of the world without being an enemy of the Lord. This is the same thing that Jesus teaches in Matthew 12: 30.

Verse 5. *Envy* and jealousy have some phases of meaning in common and hence are used to show God's great concern for the purity of His people. Exodus 20: 5 says He is a jealous God and Paul writes on behalf of the Lord and says he is jealous about his brethren (2 Corinthians 11: 2). In Genesis 6: 3 the Spirit of God is said to be striving with man, that is the same Spirit that our verse says *dwelleth in us*. James asked if they think that this concern of the Spirit is in vain or to no purpose. A negative answer is implied and means that the brethren should take the admonition seriously and not provoke the Lord too far.

Verse 6. James does not wish his brethren to become too downcast over the stern remarks of the preceding verses, hence the consoling remark that *he giveth more grace* (or favor) is made. In order to profit by His grace it is necessary to be submissive, so the statement is made concerning the *proud* and the *humble*.

Verse 7. *Submit yourselves* calls for a voluntary act on the part of man, else his pride will come up against the resistance of God. *Resist* requires more than a mere aversion to the devil; it calls for active opposition. If a disciple will put up that kind of fight he is assured of victory over the enemy.

Verse 8. This verse also indicates a voluntary action on the part of man. The Lord has made full provision for the spiritual welfare of the human creature, hence it is necessary for man to make the next move. *Cleanse your hands* specifies what is to be done, and *ye sinners* designates to whom the demand applies. No person is accused nor even specifically admonished except the guilty ones. To *purify* means to remove all mixture of evil desires, and the heart can be thus purified only "by [the] faith" Acts 15: 9. *Double minded* is explained at chapter 1: 8.

Verse 9. This verse is directed toward those who are unconcerned about their worldliness, and who are finding joy in such activities. They should reverse all of such false grounds of gratification, after which they will have something real and lasting in which to take joy.

Verse 10. This is virtually the same admonition as in verse 6.

Verse 11. *Speak not evil* means to say that which slanders another and injures his reputation. This bad use of the tongue is treated in several verses of the preceding chapter. *Speaketh evil of the law*. One of the commandments is not to bear false witness against another (Exodus 20: 16), and the same is taught in many places in the New Testament (Matthew 19: 18; Romans 13: 9). If a man claims the right to ignore this law he is thereby assuming that such a law is unnecessary. That is why James says such a person becomes a judge of the law instead of a doer.

Verse 12. *There is one lawgiver* who is the Lord, and no man should dare put himself up as a judge of His law. The author of the true law is able either to *save* or *destroy* ("To give over to eternal misery"—Thayer). *Who art thou*—why do you dare judge another or slander him?

Verse 13. *Go to* is from AGE, a Greek word that Thayer defines, "Come!

come now!" It is a pointed expression made to someone, calling attention to foolish presumptions. The things mentioned are not necessarily wrong in themselves, but the folly is in taking it for granted that nothing can prevent it.

Verse 14. The foolishness of the matter is in the uncertainty of human existence. Regardless of what one plans to do as to whether it is right or wrong, it cannot be carried out unless he lives. The comparison to a passing cloud by James shows this to be his principal thought.

Verse 15. *If the Lord will* has been much strained by many whose intentions were good toward God. The expression is made to mean if the Lord does not interfere with some "providential act" that will make the plan impossible. God is not doing such things as that in these days. During the formative centuries while the Bible was being revealed and God's dealings with man were not yet fully made known, He performed various miracles to demonstrate in the ears and before the eyes of man what it means to displease Him. That is all past now and no special act is theatened to show God's favor or disfavor for what man does; that has to be learned from the written word. The thought is, therefore, that we should make all our plans subject to two provisos, namely, that the Lord wills (that it is according to His will as revealed in the Bible), and that we live to do it. The additional conjunction "and" that is in the Greek text has been omitted by the King James Version. The Englishman's Greek New Testament renders this verse as follows: "Instead of your saying [the saying expressed in verse 13; the thing they should say is], if the Lord should will and we should live, also, we may do this or that." This shows the two conditions mentioned above, and rules out any need for "special providence."

Verse 16. *Rejoice in your boastings* denotes they first presumed they could do whatever they wished, then used the presumption as a basis of boasting. *Such rejoicing is evil* because it ignores the truths set forth in verse 14.

Verse 17. *Knoweth to do good* has special reference to the information offered in the preceding verses. We should first learn if what we plan is right, then also remember the frailty of human life and plan accordingly.

This is the way to do that which is good and not in the boastful manner as described. But the principle expressed for this special case would apply to all other relations of life.

James 5

Verse 1. *Go to* is the same phrase as that in chapter 4: 13. There it is a rebuke for those who are boastful of their expected gain, here it is against those who have obtained it by wrongful means which will be considered at verse 4. The *miseries* will come upon them at the day of judgment.

Verse 2. Wealth that is not needed and especially that has been accumulated in an evil manner, will deteriorate by the simple fact of hoarding.

Verse 3. *Witness against you* means that the fact of their cankering and rusting will prove they did not need them and that they had been hoarded. *For the last days* denotes that these treasures will be against them at the last great day of judgment.

Verse 4. The mere possession of wealth does not condemn one as may be seen from Matthew 27: 57; Mark 15: 43; Luke 23: 50, 51; Mark 10: 24; 1 Timothy 6: 17-19. The question is as to how a man obtains his wealth and the use he makes of it. In the present verse the men became rich by withholding the wages of their employees. This does not have any bearing on disputes about what should be the wages, but is considering only what was *kept back by fraud. Sabaoth* means "hosts" or armies, and the thought is that He who is able to command the armies of Heaven will be able to deal with all unjust men.

Verse 5. *Day of slaughter* signifies a day of great preparation for gratification of self at the expense of others. *Been wanton* means they had lived in luxury upon the things they had fraudulently taken from the poor.

Verse 6. This verse might seem to be a break into the line of thought but it is not. The poor people who had been imposed upon were not receiving their just dues, and they would naturally feel disturbed over the seeming neglect of the Lord. James mentions the fact of the condemnation and slaying of the Just One, meaning Christ, that even He did not resist. (See Isaiah 53: 7 and Acts 8: 32.)

Verse 7. James now addresses the poor brethren who had been unjustly treated, and on the basis of facts and truths just revealed, exhorts them to be patient unto the coming of the Lord when all wrongs will be adjusted. As an example of patience he refers to the *husbandman* or farmer as he proceeds in his business. *Early and latter rain* actually means the fall and spring rains. I shall quote from Smith's Bible Dictionary as follows: "In the Bible 'early rain' signifies the rain of the autumn, and 'latter rain' the rain of spring. For six months in the year, from May to October, no rain falls, the whole land becomes dry, parched and brown. The autumnal rains are eagerly looked for, to prepare the earth for the reception of the seed."

Verse 8. *Also patient* has reference to the patience of the husbandman commented upon in the preceding verse. Christians can well afford to be patient for their interests are far more valuable than those of a farmer. *Draweth nigh*. Whether James has reference to the destruction of Jerusalem which was then only a few years away, at which time the persecutions of the disciples were to be somewhat eased, or to the personal appearance on earth of Jesus for the judgment, the time would be comparatively short when the endless duration after the judgment is considered.

Verse 9. To *grudge* means to murmur against another because of oppression. Christians not only were told to be patient under the persecutions from enemies in the world, but to exhibit the same patience toward their brethren who are so unthoughtful as to mistreat them. *Lest ye be condemned* when Jesus comes to summon all before the judgment, at which time he will condemn all who did not maintain patience under difficulties as well as those who caused the difficulties. *Judge standeth at the door* is explained by the comments on the preceding verse.

Verse 10. A few verses above James refers to the farmer who sets an example of patience under times of anxiety. He now makes reference to the teaching prophets of old time for the same purpose of a lesson in patience.

Verse 11. Those who endure afflictions are to be *counted happy* because of what it indicates for them. (See chapter 1: 2, 3.) Just after using the word *endure* James makes mention of the *patience* of Job which verfies the definition often given of the word *patience*, namely, that it means endurance. *End of the Lord* means the outcome of the case under the blessing of the Lord. It shows that He is merciful even though he suffers a righteous man to be afflicted for a good purpose (Job 42: 12-17).

Verse 12. *Swear not*. Jesus taught that his disciples should not make oaths in Matthew 5: 34, 35, and the reader should see the comments at that place. Sometimes an attempt is made to justify making oaths by saying Jesus was only condemning false oaths. But James spoils that theory by his words *neither by any other oath*, which rules out every shade and grade of swearing. Besides, there is nothing that should urge the Christain to make oaths, for this is a case where he can obey the command of the Lord and satisfy the laws of the land also. Instead of making an oath the Christian can notify the officer saying "I will affirm," and his word will be taken for the same value as an oath. That is what the scripture here and at Matthew 5: 37 means by directing that your yea be yea and your nay be nay. The fundamental difference between an oath and an affirmation is that the latter does not use the name of God; also that one says "I affirm" instead of "I swear." *Lest ye fall into condemnation* is another way of saying that if a disciple makes an oath he will be condemned, because both Jesus and James have forbidden it.

Verse 13. *Afflicted* is from KAKO-PATHEO, and Thayer defines it, "To suffer evils; hardship, troubles." It does not refer to physical diseases which will come in the next verse. When a disciple is beset with these trials he should be in the frame of mind that would lead him to go to God in prayer for strength and encouragement. *Merry* does not mean to be gay or frivolous, for the original is defined to denote "Be of good cheer." The phrase *let him sing psalms* is from the noted Greek word PSALLO, and Thayer defines it as follows: "In the New Testament to sing a hymn, to celebrate the praises of God in song." There are times when a person is not in the "mood" for singing and James recognizes that truth in this verse. David also recognizes it in Psalms 137: 2-4. Solomon likewise had the thought in mind when he spoke of the inappropriateness of the man "that singeth songs to an heavy heart" (Proverbs 25: 20).

Verse 14. The word *sick* is from AS-THENEO, which Thayer defines at this place, "To be feeble, sick." Robinson defines it, "A sick person, the sick." It is the word that is used in the Greek text at Luke 7: 10; John 4: 46; 11: 3; Acts 9: 37 and other similar passages. From the above information we are sure the word in our passage has the regular sense of bodily disease, and not a figurative or spiritual condition as some teach. This verse should be regarded in the same light as Mark 16: 17, 18: 1 Corinthians chapters 12, 13, 14; Ephesians 4: 8-13; Hebrews 2: 3, 4 and all other passages dealing with the subject of spiritual gifts. In the early years of the church the Lord granted miraculous demonstrations to confirm the truth that had been preached while the New Testament was being completed. Among those miracles was that of healing the sick and since elders (or pastors, Ephesians 4: 11) were among those receiving such gifts, it is reasonable that they should be called in such a case. The use of oil does not signify anything contrary to these remarks, for Jesus sometimes used material articles in connection with His miraculous healing, such as clay in the case of the blind man in John 9: 6, 7. Just why such things were done in connection with the miracles we are not told and we need not speculate as to why.

Verse 15. *Prayer of faith* means miraculous faith which was one of the spiritual gifts discussed in the preceding paragraph (1 Corinthians 12: 9). The forgiveness of sins is mentioned in addition to the healing of sickness. This shows that sickness is not spiritual for that would be the same as guilt of sins. It would be meaningless to speak of healing spiritual sickness or a condition of sin and then add that the man's sins also would be forgiven. That would be equivalent to saying the Lord would heal a man of his sins (would forgive him) *and* would also forgive his sins. It would not alter the discussion to say that the sins were what caused the man to be sick, for that would still leave the truth that it refers to sickness of the body.

Verse 16. *Confess your faults* does not mean merely to confess that we have faults, but the faults themselves are to be acknowledged. *One to another* denotes that we are to confess the faults that we have committed against another; we are to confess such faults to him. Sins which are known to God only need only be confessed to Him. *That ye may be healed.* This is said in direct connection with the mention of faults, hence we know the last word is used figuratively or concerning a spiritual cure. No man can do another man's praying for him, but both can pray together for the forgiveness of the one at fault. *Effectual* means active or practical, and it is used to indicate a man who not only prays to God but who also makes it his business to serve Him. The prayers of such a man will be regarded by the Lord.

Verses 17, 18. The account of this event with Elias (Elijah in the Old Testament) is in 1 Kings 17: 1-7 and 18: 41-46. The prophet did not perform the feat merely to demonstrate his miraculous power, for such kinds of evidence were not necessary at that time. The connection shows that Ahab was a wicked king of Israel, and the Lord saw fit to punish him with a dearth by withholding the rain. The prayer of Elijah is not recorded, but he was a righteous man and realized that the wicked king would not be brought to repentance but by some severe judgment. Accordingly, when he prayed to the Lord on the subject his prayer was accepted as just and the chastisement was sent on the king and his country. It was therefore a miracle granted because of the righteousness of the request. Yet even at such a time, had he not been *a righteous man* his prayer would not have *availed* any, to say nothing about its availing *much*. *Subject to like passions* means he was only a human being, yet because of his good life his prayer was heard, since that was yet in the days of special providence.

Verse 19. To *err from the truth* means to wander to one side according to the comments at chapter 1: 16. To *convert* such a person means to induce him to turn and reenter the pathway of truth, since the word *convert* literally means to reverse a direction.

Verse 20. A *sinner* is any person who is doing wrong, whether he be a man of the world or an erring disciple. No man can repent for another but he may be able to persuade the guilty one to repent. If he succeeds he will *save a soul from death* because the one in error was going the way that leads to spiritual death. *Hide* is from KALUPTO, and both Thayer and Robinson explain it to mean that by reason of the repentance of the erring one, the Lord will overlook and not punish the one who had gone astray. This act of the Lord's mercy would be equivalent to hiding the sins because they would not be brought up to judgment afterward.

1 Peter 1

Verse 1. The various works of reference discuss the question whether the persons to whom this epistle is addressed were Jews or Gentiles. It is my belief that both were involved to some extent, but that generally speaking they were Gentiles according to the flesh. Chapter 2: 9, 10 clearly shows they were not Jews for the writer says they were not formerly a people of God, while we know the Jews were so. *Scattered* is from a Greek word that originally means Jews who were dispersed among the Gentiles in various parts of the Roman Empire. However, the term has been used in a more figurative way, so that it may include Christians of both races as it does in this epistle. *Strangers* is from PAREPIDEMOS, which literally means a person from the outside who temporarily lives in a place. The word also may be used figuratively to designate Christians who are regarded as citizens belonging to Heaven (Philippians 3: 20), but who are dwelling on earth for the time being. Thayer defines the word in this passage, "One who sojourns on earth." It is true the epistle specifies certain localities to which it is addressed and the writer's purpose is not revealed, yet that does not conflict with the idea that all Christians as well other servants of God are "strangers and pilgrims on the earth." (Hebrew 11: 13.) The places named were provinces of the Roman Empire located in what was known as Asia Minor.

Verse 2. *Elect*. The first or general definition of this word is "Picked out, chosen." The reason for and manner how the choosing is done must be determined by the connection in which the word is used. *Foreknowledge* denotes that He knew beforehand the needs of mankind and what it would take to meet those needs; they are indicated by the rest of this verse. *Sanctification* means consecration to God, and it is said to be accomplished by his Spirit. That is because the Spirit guided the apostles in giving the truth to mankind that would direct them in this consecration. (See John 16: 13.) *Unto obedience* denotes that a man will not become sanctified or consecrated except by obedience.

This shows that God does not predestinate a person to salvation independent of his proper conduct. *Sprinkling of the blood*. The meaning of this sprinkling is explained by the comments on Hebrews 12: 24. *Grace* is the unmerited favor of God and it brings genuine peace to those who obey the Gospel and thus become sanctified or consecrated to the Lord. *Multiplied* is a figurative term meaning the favor of God toward his faithful servants will be abundant.

Verse 3. *Blessed* means to be worthy of praise and it is ascribed to God. He is the Father of Christ which contradicts a theory that God and Christ are the same person; no one could be father of himself. *Abundant* means "much" and it is said of God's mercy for the children of men in that He did so much for their salvation. *Begotten us again* is equivalent to "born again" as in John 3: 3. *Lively hope* or living hope is thus described because it pertains to something that will never die. to be described in the next verse. This hope was made possible by bringing Christ from the dead.

Verse 4. This verse states the hope referred to in the preceding one to which disciples are begotten. An *inheritance* is something not yet possessed but looked forward to. It also is not that which a person produces for himself but what he receives by inheritance. It is so termed in this case because the preceding verse says they had been begotten of God, which makes them heirs of His eternal estate. *Incorruptible* means it cannot decay; *undefiled* denotes that it is pure or unsoiled, and *fadeth not away* means it will be perpetual. It will be unlike the earthly possessions that are with us today and gone tomorrow. To be *reserved* has the idea of being held in safe keeping and also that it is to be possessed at some future time. *In heaven* tells where the inheritance is kept and hence it is in a safe place. (See Matthew 6: 19-21.) In temporal matters when something is said to be "reserved," it is understood that only certain persons have a right to it. Such is true of the heavenly inheritance and the right persons will be described in the next verse.

Verse 5. Not only is the inheritance safely cared for, but the heirs are also assured that they will "live to see the estate settled" as the expression is often heard concerning an earthly estate. *Kept* is defined "being guarded" and it is by the power of God. However, the heirs must cooperate by being faithful until the time of the distribution. *Revealed in the last time.* On the day of judgment all intelligent creatures in the universe will see who are to be given the eternal riches.

Verse 6. *Temptations.* These disciples were in the midst of heathen people who made things bitter with persecution. They gave the people of God an opportunity to have their faith tested. But they could *greatly rejoice* in the hope they had of a better life to come, which made the *heaviness* of their trials seem only *for a season.*

Verse 7. It was their *faith* that was more precious than gold, even after the metal has withstood the test of the fire. The reason is that the very best of precious metals or any other like substance of earthly valuables, is subject to destruction when other earthly things shall cease to be. Also even while the earth remaineth, the joys that gold may procure for us are uncertain and often flee like the dew of morning. But the happiness that is obtained by an enduring faith will not pass away. Of course this is all on condition that the faith is found to be steadfast until the *appearing of Jesus Christ.*

Verse 8. We do not have to see Jesus to love him if we believe the multitude of evidences of His love for us. "We love him because he first loved us" (1 John 4: 19.) His faith in the unseen Christ enables us to have great joy. *Unspeakable* means it cannot be fully described by human speech. *Full of glory* means it is a joy that imparts to one a sense of dignity, not a feeling of outward show.

Verse 9. The word *receiving* means "to provide for," and that is what an abiding faith will do. It will provide for the faithful one *the salvation of his soul.*

Verse 10. The *prophets* refer to those in Old Testament times who were inspired to speak of the salvation to come through Christ. *Enquired and searched diligently* has reference to the interest they had in the predictions they were directed to make. Being inspired enabled them to make the prophecies accurately, even though they did not personally understand "what it was all about" as they wished to. We recall that Jesus spoke about these persons of old time who wished to know those truths in their final meaning but were not permitted to. (See Matthew 13: 17; Luke 10: 24.)

Verse 11. This repeats the thoughts of the preceding verse, with the addition of predictions concerning the personal sufferings of Christ which were necessary for the salvation of man. (See Psalms 22 and Isaiah 53.)

Verse 12. The only "inside information" that was offered those ancient servants of God, was that their ministry of prophecy was not for their sake, but was for those to come into the service of the Lord in the next age or Christian Dispensation. Those truths are now delivered to us by the preachers of the Gospel (the apostles) in fuller detail. They are enabled to do so by the Holy Ghost (or Spirit) that was sent down from heaven. *The angels desire to look into.* (See Exodus 25: 20; Ephesians 3: 10.)

Verse 13. *Gird up the loins of your mind.* The first two words are from the one Greek word ANAZONNUMI. Thayer gives the historical explanation of the term as follows: "A metaphor [illustration] derived from the practice of the Orientals, who in order to be unimpeded in their movements were accustomed, when about to start on a journey, or engage in any kind of work, to bind their long and flowing garments closely around their bodies and fasten them with a leathern girdle." Robinson gives the same definition and explanation. It explains "loins girded" in Exodus 12: 11, and "cast thy garment about thee" in Acts 12: 8. Peter uses the circumstance as an illustration on the use of the mind. The Christian is exhorted to "get himself together" and be unhampered for the service of the Lord. To *be sober* means to be calm and collected, and not driven to extremes by the difficulties that beset them. Such a frame of mind will enable one to maintain his hope to the end. This hope is looking for *the grace* or favor of God that will be given through Jesus Christ, to be realized at His *revelation* which means his appearance at the last day.

Verse 14. *As obedient children.* One becomes a child of another by having been begotten by him. Being *obedient* is another matter which depends on the child's own conduct. These disciples had formerly lived after the lusts of the flesh, and now they are admonished not to live any longer after that *fashion.* At that time it was *in their ignorance* that they followed such a course of life, but now the Gospel has shown them the folly of such a life, so that they cannot plead ignorance any more.

Verse 15. The Lord is the one who has called them into divine service. Such a call would have been fruitless had they not accepted the call, thereby acknowledging it to be a righteous invitation. Hence they should imitate the character of the One who called them, which would require that they live a life that is *holy* since He is holy, which is another word for righteousness. *Conversation* means manner of life.

Verse 16. This citation is in Leviticus 11:44 where God is admonishing the children of Israel to be holy and not like the heathen nations about them.

Verse 17. The Englishman's Greek New Testament renders the beginning of this verse, "And if as Father ye call on him," etc. The meaning is that if they approach God on the ground that He is their Father, they should have due regard for His character and act accordingly. God does not show any respect of persons in His judgments but acts according to their works. Accordingly His children should pass the time of their *sojourning* (see first verse) in *fear* or serious regard for the greatness of God and his impartial judgment to come.

Verse 18. What may be justly expected from servants who have been redeemed from bondage, will depend largely on what was exchanged for their freedom. These servants of God had formerly followed a *conversation* (manner of life) that was handed down by tradition from their heathen fathers. God did not procure their freedom by the use of silver and gold which are *corruptible* which means perishable.

Verse 19. They were redeemed, instead, with the precious blood of Christ. The reference to *a lamb without blemish* is from the requirement of that kind of animal sacrifices in former ages. The public life of Christ on earth showed one of spotless righteousness. "He did no sin, neither was guile found in his mouth" (1 Peter 2: 22).

Verse 20. *World* is from KOSMOS, which is used 188 times in the Greek New Testament, and in every place except one it is rendered by this word in the King James Version. It is given 8 different definitions in Thayer's lexicon, and the particular meaning in any given place must be gathered from the connection in which it is used. The definition that will most generally fit in with the passages where it is used is the fifth one as follows: "The inhabitants of the world; the inhabitants of the earth, men, the human race." Before the existence of the human race God (whose foreknowledge is infinite) saw what was going to be needed to save mankind, namely, a sacrifice that would have the redeeming virtue of a spotless victim. He decreed that his Son should be that victim, but did not even tell any person about it until He made the promise to Abraham (Galatians 3: 16). Nor was the full significance of the promise realized even by him. That great favor was reserved to be made *manifest in these last times,* meaning the Christian Dispensation.

Verse 21. This verse tells to whom Christ has been manifest, namely, to the believers. Not that any secrecy was kept from the world in general, for the Gospel was preached to every creature in all the world. But the manifestation was realized or recognized only by those who believed in His resurrection from the dead, and the glory that was afterward given Him. The purpose of all this grand scheme of human redemption was to show that all faith and hope has to be in God.

Verse 22. The writer of this epistle is the speaker in Acts 15: 9 where he declares that the heart is purified by faith. The thought of that passage is equivalent to the one in our verse, the *heart* and *soul* being virtually the same, likewise *faith* being according to *the truth.* *Through the Spirit* is stated because the truth which they had obeyed was given by the inspiration of the Holy Spirit. *Unto* means in order to love the brethren, meaning that was one of the objects to be attained by this purification. Having gone that far, the apostle means for them to carry out that purpose by loving each other with a *pure heart.* That denotes a heart that is not mixed up with unrighteous sentiments. *Fervently* means earnestly and denotes a love for the brethren that is warm and sympathetic.

Verse 23. *Born again* is rendered "begotten again" by the Englishman's Greek New Testament, which is more accurate because it pertains to the father's part of reproduction. *Not of corruptible seed* denotes that it is not by the fleshly reproductive germ. It is the spiritual new birth and hence the seed is *the word of God*. This is the same thought expressed in James 1: 18 which shows that God has begotten the spiritual creatures. For explanation of "born" and "begotten," see the comments at John 3: 5 in the first volume of the New Testament Commentary. *Liveth and abideth for ever* is said because the seed is the word of God which can never die.

Verse 24. This verse indicates the temporal nature of man as regards his flesh. It is material and subject to decay, even as the glory of vegetation is destined to pass away. The apostle is not underestimating the importance of man, for even his fleshly body is made in the likeness of God. The point is to impress upon the disciples the truth that their spiritual relation to Him is not subject to decay as the fleshly nature is. Having become a part of the Lord's spiritual race, they should honor that relationship by a righteous life.

Verse 25. The reader is not left in any uncertainty as to what is meant by the spiritual seed of reproduction. It is the word that was brought into the world by the Gospel, hence the new birth does not consist of some mysterious operation of God upon sinful man. It is the simple matter of believing and obeying the Gospel.

1 Peter 2

Verse 1. *Wherefore* (or therefore) indicates a conclusion; in view of the truths set forth in the preceding chapter, the readers are exhorted to do the following items. *Laying aside* denotes an action on the part of the individual, instead of expecting it to be done for him by the Lord. *Malice* means ill-will or the disposition to injure another. *Guile* is an effort to deceive another by some kind of trickery. *Hypocrisies* are the pretensions that one makes which he knows are false. *Envies* denotes a feeling of spite against one who is more favored in some way than himself. *Evil speaking* is that which would injure the good name of another.

Verse 2. The disciples to whom this epistle is addressed were not actually beginners in the service of Christ. Peter only means for them to be *as newborn babes* in that they were to be free from the evils named in the preceding verse. This is a very appropriate illustration seeing an infant would be free from such. Also *as newborn babes* in that they would show a desire for the nourishment provided for them.

Verse 3. *If so be ye have tasted.* Sometimes an infant just arrived in the world will seem disinclined to receive the milk that nature had provided. But if the attendant is patient and urges the babe until he gets a taste he will not require to be urged further. Frequently we observe disciples who seem indifferent about the spiritual food which has been provided for them. It is fair to conclude that such persons have not as yet even tasted of the *milk of the word*, and hence they do not realize how precious or agreeable to the spiritual palate such nourishment is.

Verse 4. The figure of infantile nourishment is now dropped and the apostle takes up another illustration. Christ is represented as a *living* stone which denotes that He is not a material one such as the temples of men use for their foundation. *Disallowed indeed of men* refers to the rejection of Christ at the hands of the Jewish leaders. Jesus thus spoke of himself when talking to those self-righteous men (Matthew 21: 42). Notwithstanding His rejection by the Jewish leaders, God accepted Him and showed him to be precious by revealing the eternal riches offered thereby.

Verse 5. Jesus is represented as a living stone for a foundation, and hence it is appropriate to consider the parts of the building upon it as *lively stones* also. The foundation of the building and its parts being spiritual, it follows that the whole structure is considered as a spiritual one. Every building of whatever kind is erected for some specific purpose, and this one is no exception to the rule. In the material building of the Mosaic system, there was a practice of offering sacrifices which also were of material character, namely, the bodies of animals. In this spiritual house the sacrifices are of a spiritual character, as they are composed of the religious services of the people of God. *An holy priesthood.* Under the old system the priests only officiated in the sacrifices, and they all came from just one of the tribes. By an interesting coincidence the performances under the new system are also conducted only by the priests. But since every disciple is a priest (verse 9 below; Revelation 1: 6), it means that each one is expected to participate in the service. The things offered in the old arrangement must be acceptable to God, and the same is required under the new which is authorized by *Jesus Christ*.

Verse 6. The apostle now quotes from Isaiah 28: 16 to show that even while the Mosaic service was in force, the Lord was planning on another one to come and made predictions concerning the same. *Lay in Sion* (or Zion). This literally refers to the city of Jerusalem as a whole, and sometimes to a particular portion of the city designated as the "city of David." The church was started in the city of Jerusalem and hence it is often referred to as "Mount Zion" (Hebrews 12: 22). A conclusion is given us therefore that the foundation stone (Christ) was to be laid in the church. *Chief corner stone*. The corner stone of a building was important because it served to unite the walls into one structure. Christ is called the *elect* because the word means "pointed or picked out, chosen." God chose his Son to be the chief corner stone of the final building to be erected in the Christian Dispensation. It is a *precious* stone because of the valuable benefits it will furnish those who will accept them. To *be confounded* is defined by Thayer "To be put to shame." On the day of judgement The Lord Jesus Christ will put to shame all those who refused to believe in Him in this world, since that unbelief indicates they are ashamed of Him (Luke 9: 26).

Verse 7. An unbeliver sees nothing precious or of special honor in Jesus for his interests are in the vain things of this world. That is why Paul says a man must become a believer before he can come to God (Hebrews 11: 6). Note that a *disobedient* person is placed opposite a *believer*, and that is because all disobedience is charged to unbelief. The various acts of disobedience that the Israelites committed in the wilderness kept them out of the land of Canaan, yet Paul sums it up with one word "unbelief" (Hebrews 3: 19). But the disobedience of unbelievers will not affect the authority of the stone which the Lord chose to be the head of the corner.

Verse 8. *Stone of stumbling and rock of offence*. No part of the Bible must be interpreted in a way that will contradict another part. God does not want the anyone to do wrong or be lost (2 Peter 3: 9); but man can be saved only through Christ, and therefore it was necessary that He be sent into the world. If His presence is so objectionable to some that they permit Him to be a stone over which they stumble the Lord cannot be blamed for it. *Stumble at the word* specifies in what way certain men stumble; it is at His word. People do not like to obey that which interferes with their sinful life and hence it becomes a stumbling stone to them. James Macknight translates a part of his verse as follows: "The disobedient stumble against the word, to which verily they were appointed." The thought is that they were not appointed to be disobedient, but to stumble at the word because of their disobedience.

Verse 9. The various things said in this verse about disciples of Christ, should cause them to exert themselves to the utmost to live up to the great honor and responsibility. *Generation* means race or kind, and the Lord has chosen them because they had been "born again" thus becoming another kind (John 3: 3). *Royal priesthood* means a kingly priesthood. Under the Mosaic law the same man could not be both king and priest (2 Chronicles 26: 18), but disciples of Christ are said to be both (Revelation 1: 6). Christians are kings (of a secondary order of course) in that they reign under Christ and the apostles (1 Corinthians 4: 8). *Nation* denotes a number of persons living together as a group, and Christians are such having become *holy* or consecrated to God by obedience to the Gospel. *Peculiar* is from a Greek word that means "purchased," and they are called that because they have been purchased with the blood of Christ (Acts 20: 28). When a man buys something and pays a great price for it, he expects to accomplish something of importance with it. Accordingly the Lord's object in purchasing the church was to have an institution equipped for an important work. It was that they should *show forth the praises* [virtues] *of him*. etc. This makes it plain that no institution of man has any business to engage in religious instruction. The church alone, which was obtained by the blood of Christ, has any right to such a glorious work (Ephesians 3: 21).

Verse 10. *Which in time past were not a people*. This clearly indicates that this epistle was not written to

1 Peter 2: 11-17

Jews since they in the past were the people of God. *Had not obtained mercy* as a people, although the families of the Gentiles were favored when they complied with the requirements of the Patriarchal Dispensation.

Verse 11. *Strangers and pilgrims* is explained at chapter 1: 1. *Fleshly* is defined by Thayer at this place, "Having the nature of flesh," and he explains it as follows: "Under the control of the animal appetites; governed by mere human nature and not by the Spirit of God." Peter confirms this definition and explanation by saying *which war against the soul*.

Verse 12. *Having your conversation* (conduct) *honest* (righteous) *among the Gentiles*. These disciples were Gentiles in the sense of not being Jews according to the flesh, but the word is from ETHNOS which means the heathen nations generally who had not accepted the Gospel. *Speak against you*. The heathen people were in the habit of speaking evil of the Christians because they would not mix with them in their sinful practices. (See chapter 4: 4). *Good works which they shall behold*. When the test comes upon these disciples in the form of persecutions *(the day of visitation)*, and the heathen see how they are patient and law abiding, it will disprove the false charges they have been making. It will then be evident that such a conduct is caused by their faith in God and as a result these heathen accusers will give God the glory.

Verse 13. *Submit yourselves*. The Lord wants his people to be law-abiding citizens of the nations in which they live. Paul teaches this obligation in Romans 13: 1-7. However, this command is subject to the proviso stated in Acts 5: 29; when the law of man conflicts with those of God then it is the duty of Christians to obey the latter. *Whether it be to the king, as supreme*. In some countries the highest temporal ruler is called a king, and if disciples live there it is their duty to respect him.

Verse 14. *Or unto governors* refers to the deputies or other executioners acting under the supreme ruler. In either case the obligation of obedience is the same on the part of the disciples. This verse shows two objects of government and they are summed up in the words *punishment* and *praise*. The first is classified as the penal code and is the one being considered in 1 Timothy 1: 9, 10. The second is for the encouragement of those who wish to be good citizens. The two parts of government are denoted also in Romans 13: 3. All this disproves a theory that we would not need any government if everybody lived righteously. The human family could not continue in an orderly manner without some form of government, and hence the Lord's people are required to respect that form under which they are living.

Verse 15. It was sometimes charged that the disciples of Christ were opposed to the rulers of the land. Such an accusation was made against Christ and Paul (Luke 23: 2; John 19: 12; Acts 17: 7). Such charges were *foolish* and showed the *ignorance* of those who made them, for there was nothing in the conduct of the accused that even hinted at rebellion against the laws of the land. Our verse means that such ignorance may be exposed if the disciples will practice *well doing*, showing that they are good and law-abiding citizens of the community.

Verse 16. To be *free* means they had been delivered from the bondage of sin, but that does not signify they had the license to ignore all manner of service. They should therefore not take undue advantage of their liberty from sin which they had received from Christ, and use it to cover up a feeling of *maliciousness* or ill-will toward the rulers of the land. On the other hand, they should let it be known that, being *servants of God*, they were all the more desirous of living quiet and obedient lives under the government. Such an example would have a tendency to make a favorable impression on those who represent the powers that be. That is why the apostle makes the remark in verse 13 that disciples are to submit themselves to the ordinances of man "for the Lord's sake." The same thought is expressed by Paul Colossians 3: 23. The apostle is writing of the obligation of disciples toward their masters, that they should do it "as to the Lord."

Verse 17. *Honor all men*. The same command is given by Paul in Romans 13: 7, but the connection shows that the honor is to be shown to those only to whom it is due. *Love the brotherhood*. This is the whole band of brethren in Christ, and we should love them all as being in the one body, and not be partial or show favoritism. *Fear God*. Not the kind of fear that is like being terrified, for if we love Him as we should it will cast out such fear (1 John 4:18). We should fear God in the sense of reverencing Him and being unwilling to grieve Him. *Honor the king.* (See verses 13 and 14.)

Verse 18. The subject of *servants* is commented upon at length at Ephesians 6:5 and the reader is asked to see that place. The masters were not all of the same temperament and they showed it in their treatment of their servants. *Froward* means to be unfair and surly, but whether they were thus or were gentle, the servant was told to obey them even though it cause them much unpleasantness.

Verse 19. To be *thankworthy* means to be entitled to thanks for something; to be commended for it. An instance of it is when a man is doing what is right and he is persecuted for it. If he has a clear conscience on the matter he will endure the mistreatment cheerfully.

Verse 20. To be *buffeted* means to be treated roughly for one's wrong doing. If that is done to a man who is guilty he has no room to complain. He should *take it patiently* on the ground that "it was coming to him." On the other hand, if a man is mistreated for doing what is right it should be regarded as a persecution. Christians are taught to endure persecutions, and hence if such a person is patient under the mistreatment he will be deserving of commendation.

Verse 21. *Hereunto were ye called.* The disciples of Christ are called upon to endure sufferings for His sake. (See Acts 14:22; Romans 8:17; Philippians 1:29; 2 Timothy 3:12.) Jesus does not require his followers to bear any burden that is greater than He carried himself, hence He set an example by going through the severest of sufferings. Now the disciples are called upon to *follow his steps* in that they cheerfully accept the trials that are forced upon them for His sake.

Verse 22. Jesus *did no sin* in the conduct of his own body, *neither was any guile* (deceitful language) *found in his mouth.* If Jesus who was sinless had to suffer persecution, surely His imperfect followers should expect to endure such treatment.

Verse 23. *Reviled not again.* When vile and disrespectful things were said to Jesus, he did not "answer back" but bore it meekly (Matthew 27:39; Hebrews 12:3). Even while Jesus was on the cross he did not make any remarks about the cruelty of his enemies but rather prayed for them (Luke 23:34). *Committed himself.* Jesus confided in the mercy and wisdom of his Father and left the case in His hands (Luke 23:46).

Verse 24. *Bare our sins.* Jesus never sinned and hence none were literally attached to Him at any time. But something had to be done and some one had to "take the blame" in order to satisfy the vengence of a just God. No mere man was good enough and no angel was human enough to accomplish the purpose, hence the Son was called upon to make the sacrifice. Thayer's first definition of the original for *tree* is "that which is made of wood . . . a gibbet, a cross." When Jesus died on the tree of the cross He became a perfect sacrifice that provided for the remission of sins for all who will accept it on the Lord's terms. Those terms require that man become *dead to sins* which denotes that he separate himself from a life of sin, then follow up with a life of righteousness. *Stripes* is from MOLOPS which Thayer defines, "a bruise, wale, wound which trickles with blood." Since it is the blood of Christ that brings salvation from sin, we can understand why Peter says *by whose stripes ye were healed.*

Verse 25. *As sheep going astray.* All mankind went astray from God and were lost in the wilderness of sin. Continuing the language belonging to the business of a shepherd and the flock, the apostle represents these disciples as the wandering sheep who heard the voice of the Shepherd and returned to him. Jesus is not only a *shepherd* in that He attends to the feeding, but also is their Bishop in that he inspects and governs them.

1 Peter 3

Verse 1. One definition of *likewise* is "moreover," denoting that the writer has something more to say, but not necessarily on the same subject he has been considering. The wives addressed are disciples who have husbands not members of the church. Wives are expected to be in subjection to their husbands regardless of their religious profession. But if the Christian wives show that they can live in obedience to their companions in marriage notwithstanding their religion, it will speak well for their profession. *Be won without the word.* A man might not be interested directly by the written word, but when he sees the principles of that word as practiced by his Christian wife, he may thereby be led into obedience to the truth.

Verse 2. This continues the thought in the preceding verse. *Chaste* means pure and *conversation* refers to the general life or conduct. *Fear* is used in the sense of a person who has respect for another and who is unwilling to do anything improper toward him. If a husband observes that his wife is that kind of woman, and that the religion she professes prompts her unto such an attitude toward him, he may become a disciple also as a result of such godly influence.

Verse 3. One definition of *adorning* is "decoration," and means the general appearance of one that is arranged for the observation of another. One of the items that Peter forbids is *putting on of apparel*. He does not specify any certain kind of dress (as Paul does in 1 Timothy 2: 9). However, we know the wife is not forbidden the putting on of clothing, hence the unavoidable conclusion is that she must not depend on the display of articles mentioned in this verse to interest her husband. Instead of a gaudy display of jewelry or showy garments, she will restrict herself within reasonable and modest bounds in her use of such feminine dainties, and rely on the better attractions named in the preceding verses and some others to follow. (See the comments on this subject at 1 Timothy 2: 9, 10.)

Verse 4. It is right for a woman to display a proper attraction for the opposite sex, but it is much more important that she appear as she should in the eyes of God; the things that will please Him are described in this verse. *Hidden man of the heart* is a figure of speech to denote the opposite of the outward body that may receive material adornment. *Not corruptible* means something not subject to decay as is the material of bodily dress. *Meek* and *quiet* are virtually the same in effect. The first indicates a mind of humbleness and the second denotes the conduct that such a spirit manifests. In God's sight such qualities are of *great price* which signifies they are of much value. That is because they are durable and destined to outlast all temporal ornaments such as those made of gold and silver.

Verse 5. The phrases *holy women* and *trusted in God* are expressed as being related, and account for the other statement that they adorned themselves according to the principles that are discussed in the preceding verses of the chapter. It should not be overlooked that the kind of women here described will be *in subjection to their own husbands* as those were in old time called "holy."

Verse 6. *Obeyed* and *lord* are related in this verse, for both in the Old Testament and the New where this circumstance is recorded, the word *lord* means "ruler." It is therefore not used as a title of rank under royalty as the term is used in the East. *Not afraid with any amazement.* This means the wife must not obey her husband because she is "scared" or frightened into it, but should do it from a motive of modesty and respect. Such women are called daughters of Sara (Sarah in the Old Testament) because they are a generation of faithful wives like the wife of Abraham.

Verse 7. *Dwell with them according to knowledge* means for the husband to act intelligently toward his wife. That will cause him to remember that she is the *weaker vessel* in that she belongs to the "weaker sex" physically, and therefore is not as rugged as he. But while there is this difference in their strength, yet they are equal heirs to the *grace of life*, which means the favors that the Lord has promised to those who live for Him. *Prayers be not hindered*. This phrase indicates that where husbands and wives are both disciples, they will engage in mutual prayer services in their homes. Yet such services would be hindered were their love not mutual also.

Verse 8. The instructions are now directed more generally and apply to Christians in the various walks of life. To be *of one mind* means to be united upon the matters that pertain to the service of Christ, especially those which have to do with their treatment of each other. *Having compassion one of another* all comes from one Greek word which Thayer defines in part as "sympathetic." *Love as brethren* denotes the love one has for another because he is a brother in Christ. *Pitiful* is virtually the same as tender hearted, and *courteous* means to be friendly and kind.

Verse 9. The first half of this verse means not to return evil for evil, but to return good for evil. It is the same thought that Paul teaches in Romans

12: 19-21. *Ye are thereunto called.* When the Gospel call was made to them it was with the understanding they would conduct themselves after this manner. Disciples must be willing to bless (do good) their brethren in Christ if they expect to *inherit a blessing* from Him.

Verse 10. This is a quotation from Psalms 34: 12 and is made a part of the apostle's letter to Christians. It is presented as a higher basis for an enjoyable life than the popular standards of the world. An evil tongue is one that speaks to the injury of another's good name, and to speak guile is to use speech that is deceitful.

Verse 11. *Eschew evil* denotes that one avoids it and does that which is good instead. *Seek peace* expresses the mere desire for it while *ensue it* is a stronger term and means to take active steps to accomplish it.

Verse 12. The Lord sees everything at all times and in all places, hence the word *over* is used in a special sense here. The connection shows it means He has his eyes upon the righteous for their good, even as a faithful guardian keeps watch over his charge. On the same principle His ears are ready to listen to the prayers of His righteous servants. But the Lord will not even look toward the doers of evil; He will "turn his back to them." An ancient prophet expresses the same thought (on the favorable side) by the words, "To this man will I look, even to him that is poor and of a contrite spirit, and trembleth at my word" (Isaiah 66: 2).

Verse 13. This verse is similar in thought to Galatians 5: 23. It does not mean that nobody will oppose those who do good, for they will. They might even do a person some bodily damage which would be considered as harmful. However, in the end the true servant of God will be the victor and hence no actual harm will result. Jesus taught this in Matthew 10: 28 where he showed that real harm is that which affects the soul. Our verse means therefore that if we do that which is good, nothing harmful can happen to us even if we do lose our temporal lives.

Verse 14. This is virtually like the preceding verse as to the security of the righteous; they have much for which to be thankful. Enemies may threaten us but we need not be afraid of them. At the worst they can only kill the body while the soul may continue to live and be with "God who gave it."

Verse 15. *Sanctify* is from HAGIAZO and Thayer's first definition is, "To render or acknowledge to be venerable [sacred], to hallow." The reader should carefully note that the word has a twofold meaning, namely, either to cause another to become holy (which can be done to man by the Gospel), or to recognize another to be already that way (which can be done only to the Lord who is the author of the Gospel). The passage instructs disciples to recognize the Lord as holy and entitled a permanent place in their hearts. The way this can be done is made clear in Ephesians 3: 17 by the words, "That Christ may dwell in your hearts by faith." Add to this the statement as to the source of faith (Romans 10: 17) and the subject is complete. We should make ourselves so familiar with the word of God that He will be in our hearts (minds) all the time. If all this is done we will be prepared to comply with the rest of the verse. *Answer* means an explanation that shows the basis for believing anything that might be called in question. When any man asks us to show that basis we must be prepared to do so. Neither is this to be done at stated times only or after we have "brushed up" our memory on it, but we are to be ready *always*. This will be possible if we have obeyed the first part of the verse which will have made us acquainted with the word of God. *With meekness and fear.* We should be humble and not overbearing when someone asks us to defend our position. We should have great respect for the subject and answer the questions according to Him who is living in our hearts and whom we *fear* or reverence.

Verse 16. This verse implies that at least some who call for an explanation of our faith may be unfriendly. They may approach us with a "chip-on-the shoulder" attitude, which explains why the preceding verse instructs us to be meek and respectful; if we observe all these instructions we can have a good conscience. When the critics make their approach with the questions, they often imply that no good reason can be given for the conduct of the disciples because they (the disciples) are *evildoers* so they will say. But when the reasons are shown to be well founded in the word of God it will put to shame the false accusers. *Good conversation* means their conduct or manner of life is good and in harmony with the word of God.

Verse 17. If a person suffers for well doing it may be considered as a persecution, and such an experience will be something in which to rejoice. The early disciples found joy in suffering shame for the sake of Christ (Acts 5: 41). But if one suffers on account of his evil doing it is to be regarded as a chastisement, and in such a case the guilty one may well be ashamed of himself.

Verse 18. No unjust person could suffer and die on behalf of another like him, hence it was necessary for the just Christ to do this. *Put to death in the flesh.* In order to die it was necessary for Christ to take on a fleshly body. He was quickened or returned to life *by the Spirit.* The italicized phrase is an important key to the passage of several verses. The Deity or Godhead is composed of three persons, the Father, Son and Holy Spirit. These are all equal as being divine and pure, but the Father and Son are the makers and preservers of all things. They accomplish their wonderful works through the services of the Spirit. It should therefore be understood that the leading thought in this and the following verse is what was accomplished for Christ through the instrumentality of the Spirit.

Verse 19. *By which* (Spirit). The services of the Spirit is still the subject that was introduced in the preceding verse. Christ (in cooperation with his Father) did some preaching through the agency of the Spirit. But since the Spirit never speaks directly to sinful man concerning his personal duty, it is necessary to have also the services of a human preacher. That preacher was Noah, for 2 Peter 2: 5 says he was "a preacher of righteousness," which would mean he did the right kind of preaching. The connection shows that the ones to whom he preached were disobedient persons, hence the preaching consisted in exhortation and call to repentance. *In prison.* This is a figure of speech drawn from the direct preaching that Jesus did in person to sinners while He was on earth. In Isaiah 42: 7 and 49: 9 it is predicted that Jesus would preach to people in prision (of sin), and by that same figure the ones to whom Noah preached might be called "spirits in prison."

Verse 20. The preceding verse tells *what* was done—that some preaching was done to people in the prison house of sin. The present verse tells *when* it was done, namely *in the days of Noah.* The reason given for the preaching is that they were disobedient. A fuller description is given in Genesis 6: 5 which says "every imagination [purpose] of the thoughts of his heart was only evil continually." The length of time during which God labored or "strived" with man (through Noah) is explained by *the longsuffering* of Him. The period of longsuffering included the time necessary for the building of the ark. One of Thayer's definitions of the original Greek word for *soul* is, "That in which there is life; a living being," hence it is used in this passage to mean the eight members of Noah's family. *Saved by water.* Being heavier than the ark and its contents, the water bore them on its bosom and thus kept them safe from the revages of the flood.

Verse 21. *Like figure.* The only comparison the apostle makes is between the water of the flood and that of baptism. No writer in the New Testament ever refers to the ark as a type of the church. The fact that Peter does specify the one item and call it a figure, but makes no mention of any other comparison shows it was not because he was so far away from the subject. There are too many items that are against the theory. The people are said to have been saved by water, yet that element came after the people entered the ark, while baptism is necessary before people can enter the church. Again, there were unclean beasts taken into the ark, while only those who are saved or clean are added to the church (Acts 2: 47). *Not the putting away of the filth of the flesh.* This statement indicates that baptism is a washing of the whole body. No one would have formed the erroneous idea that baptism was intended as a cleaning bath for the body had the rite been performed by sprinkling, for all would know that such an act would not cleanse anything. The explanation is suggested by the practice in Old Testament times of washing the bodies of animal sacrifices in water. *Answer* is from EPEROTEMA and Thayer defines it at this place as follows: "A demand; earnest seeking, i.e. a craving, an intense desire, to long for something." That which is desired is a good conscience toward God. When a sinner is taught that he must be baptized for the remission of sin, and he has the desire to do right, he will not have a good conscience until he obeys this command. The above explanation is inserted to avoid an erroneous idea about baptism, after which the writer resumes the subject of salvation by baptism. The information is added that the salvation is accomplished *by the resurrestion of Jesus Christ*. Had He not come from the dead it would not have availed anything for a man to be baptized.

Verse 22. After Jesus accomplished his work on earth for the redemption of man, He ascended to heaven as the great Conqueror. Just before He left the earth he told his apostles that "All power [authority] is given unto me in heaven and in earth." That truth is here repeated by the apostle, and suggests the beautiful language of David in Psalms 24: 7-10.

1 Peter 4

Verse 1. *Forasmuch then* refers back to chapter 3: 18 which mentions the suffering and death of Christ in the flesh which He underwent for our sins. *Arm yourselves likewise with the same mind*. Prepare yourselves for the trials that will come upon you for being faithful disciples of Him, by a mind that expects such experiences. *He that hath suffered . . . ceased from sin*. Christ suffered in the flesh in order to make atonement for sin. The true disciple who wishes to profit from the example of Christ, will cease his life of sin even though he must suffer persecution for it.

Verse 2. This continues the thoughts of the preceding verse. It is not enough to make a break in one's life of sin, but he should practice sin *no longer*. *Lusts of men* means the lusts that men of the world practice, while *the will of God* will direct the disciple in a pathway of righteousness.

Verse 3. It is a popular notion that every person should have the privilege of some worldly enjoyment. The apostle does not endorse that idea, yet even if such a claim were allowed, the writer shows that they have had their full opportunity along that line. *Will of the Gentiles* means the manner of the nations who are still in heathendom. *Walked in lasciviousness* means to continue in the way of filthy desires. *Lusts* is repeated from the preceding verse; it especially means "desire for what is forbidden"—Thayer. *Excess of wine*. A little wine for the stomach's sake (1 Timothy 5: 23) will not make a man drunk, hence the excessive use of it would be that amount that will intoxicate. *Revellings, banquetings*. These words are similar in meaning according to the definitions of Thayer. The first he defines, "A revel, carousal," and the second is, "A drinking, carousing." The overall meaning of the two words is a reference to any disorderly or riotous conduct, including dancing and late "night parties." *Abominable idolatries*. There are no forms of idolatry that are right; the first word is used to intensify the extreme objectionable character of such practices to the loathing of God.

Verse 4. *They* means the Gentiles or unconverted nations referred to in verse 3. *Think it strange* means to be surprised at something as though a novelty had been introduced from the outside. It would especially have the idea of something very unexpected. This describes the impression that was being made on these Gentiles by the conduct of the Christians. The heathen thought there was much reason for indulging in the worldly practices because it brought them gratification for their fleshly lusts. They thought their standard of life was correct and that all normal people should follow it. When they observed the Christians' opposite way of life they concluded that something was wrong with them and expressed themselves with evil accusations. *Excess of riot;* an extreme degree of loose and disorderly conduct.

Verse 5. *Give account* denotes that these people who persecute Christians in this world, will have to answer for it to the Lord Jesus Christ, he being *ready* (authorized and qualified) to judge the *quick* (living) and the dead. There will be men living when Jesus comes (1 Corinthians 15: 51), and they will have to stand before the judgment of Christ, as well as the ones not living. (See Acts 10: 42; 17: 31.)

Verse 6. *For this cause*. For the reason that is about to be stated. This verse does not teach that people will be preached to after they die. Why give the Gospel to dead people when they will not have any opportunity of obeying it then? This is clearly taught in the story of the rich man and Lazarus in Luke 16: 19-31. It is important to observe that the words *was* and *are* do not have the same tense; the one is past and the other is present. The Gospel *was* preached at some time before Peter was writing, but the ones who received that preaching afterward died. Hence at the time the apostle was writing this epistle he would say they *are* dead. *Judged according to men in the flesh.* At the last day men will be judged according to the way they lived while in the flesh or before they died (2 Corinthians 5: 10). If they have been falsely accused notwithstanding their obedience to the Gospel, they will be permitted to live *according to God;* will live with Him *in the spirit* or in the spirit world. This grand truth should be comforting to all the true servants of Christ who are persecuted for righteousness' sake.

Verse 7. *End of all things is at hand* or near comparatively speaking, for "our life on earth is but a span." With the day of judgment an assured event and not far away, it behooves us to be *sober* or serious minded. *Watch unto prayer* is the same as "watch and pray" as Jesus taught while here (Matthew 26: 41).

Verse 8. The original word for *charity* means such love for the brethren as causes one to have a genuine interest in their welfare. To *cover* the sins does not mean to shield another in wrong, for that would make the two equally guilty. But there are countless instances where the sins are not positively proved, or where there might be some question as to the extent of the wrong done, if any. In such cases we should exercise that charity that will give the other person the "benefit of the doubt." If that is done the sins will be *covered* in that they will not be held against the other person nor be spread out publicly.

Verse 9. *Hospitality one to another.* This is the treatment to be shown by the brethren toward each other, and is different from that which pertains to "strangers" (Hebrews 13: 2). Since the disciples of Christ have a common relation to Christ, they ought to feel "at home" when in each other's company. *Without grudging* denotes that it will be without murmuring or complaining. When brethren extend the hospitality of their homes to each other, it should not be in the attitude of "have-to" duty, as if they were dealing with "objects of charity."

Verse 10. *Received the gift.* The preceding verse deals with hospitality, hence the present one has that subject principally under consideration, so that the *gift* has special application to the good things of life with which one can manifest hospitality. He should not be selfish with the favors he has in possession since they all came from God and the disciple is but a *steward* (agent) under Him. Of course the principle of this passage will logically apply to any talent a man may possess.

Verse 11. *Speak as the oracles of God.* In old times certain persons were consulted who were supposed to have special or superhuman knowledge. Those who believed in them would go there for information, then *speak* or deliver that information to others. The persons thus consulted were referred to as "oracles." Myers Ancient History says the following on this subject: "The Romans, like the Greeks, thought that the will of the gods was communicated to men by means of oracles, and by strange sights, unusual events, or singular coincidences." Peter therefore means for the disciples to speak as the oracles of God (the Bible) and not those of superstition. *If any man minister* or serve, let him do whatever his ability under God will enable him to do. By such performances the glory will go to God who is the giver of all talents, and all will be accomplished through Christ. *Dominion* (rule or authority, Matthew 28: 18) *for ever and ever* signifies that Jesus is to reign until he has put all foes beneath His feet (1 Corinthians 15: 25).

Verse 12. To *think strange* has the same meaning that the word does in verse 4; disciples should not be surprised if trials and persecutions come upon them. (See verse 1.)

Verse 13. They would not rejoice in the sufferings as though they are things that give pleasure in themselves. To pretend to find such to be enjoyable would be affectation. The rejoicing is over the thought of being a *partaker* or partner with Christ. If His disciples share with his suffering they may expect to have a part in His glory when the day of redemption arrives.

Verse 14. To *be reproached* means to be reviled or have belittling things said of one. If that kind of treatment is given to a man because of his connection with Christ, he then will have much reason to rejoice on the principle set forth in the preceding verse. Such enemies unconsciously recognize the *glory* (honor) of God that has been bestowed upon His servants by the Spirit. It should be observed that no specific wrong is charged against the disciple, only he is reproached just because of his profession of faith in Christ. *Their part* refers to the enemies who revile the disciples because of their devotion to Christ. *Your part* means that the persecuted disciples feel *glorified* or honored by such treatment, because it is an acknowledgement that the worst that can be said of them is that they are believers in Christ.

Verse 15. *Suffer* is from the Greek word PASCHO, and Thayer defines it at this place (and many others) as follows: "To suffer, to undergo evils, to be afflicted." Peter applies his instruction to specific actions that are wrong, and hence to things that the disciples could commit but should not. They are forbidden to act in such a way that they could justly be made to *suffer* for it. The apostle is not expecting his readers to prevent such mistreatment being unjustly forced upon them, for that would be requiring what might be impossible. He means for them not to be guilty and thus bring suffering upon themselves as a punishment for the deeds now to be mentioned. *Murderer* and *thief* are specific and it would be proper for them to be made to suffer were they guilty of being such persons. *Evildoer* seems more general yet it refers to any violation of law and in any given instance the accusation could be made specific. *Busybody in other men's matters* all comes from one Greek word ALLOTRIOEPISKOPOS, and Thayer defines it as follows: "One who takes the supervision of affairs pertaining to others and in no wise to himself, a meddler in other men's affairs." He then gives the following explanation of the origin of the word: "The writer seems to refer to those who, with holy but intemperate zeal, meddle with the affairs of the Gentiles—whether public or private, civil or sacred—in order to make them conform to the Christian standard." The lexicons of Robinson and Strong give virtually the same definition and explanation of the word, which is not in any other passage in the New Testament.

Verse 16. *Any man suffer.* These words are not in the Greek text in this verse, but they are justified by the language in the preceding verse. To suffer *as a Christian* is the same as to suffer *for the name of Christ* as in verse 14. For the significance of the name Christian, see the comments at Acts 11: 26 in the first volume of the New Testament Commentary. To suffer as a Christian does not specify any wrong-doing on the part of the accused, but only means persecution for being a follower of Christ. A man need not be ashamed for being a follower of Him and of having such an experience, for it promises him the recognition of Christ before his Father in heaven (Matthew 10: 32); for this reason he may *glorify God* or give God the glory. *On this behalf* means in this respect or because of this great honor.

Verse 17. *Is come* has been supplied by the King James Version, but the words are inserted in square brackets by the Englishmen's Greek New Testament, and they are included also in three other translations that I have examined. It is an important item in explaining this passage, for it shows that whatever Peter meant by *judgment* was not to wait until the last day of the world. Hence the word refers to the persecutions that God will let come on His people in this life, to test their faith whether they are genuine children of God. With this thought in mind I will ask the reader to see the following passages. (1 Corinthians 11: 19; 2 Timothy 3: 12; Hebrews 12: 6-11; James 1: 2-4.) *Us* and *house of God* are used in the same connection which shows who is to receive the *judgment* mentioned; it means the Christians. If good people like Christians deserve the unpleasant experiences in the form of persecutions in order to keep them in the line of obedience, then certainly those who make no profession at all will come to a sad end afterward.

Verse 18. *Righteous scarcely be saved.* The salvation of the righteous is no uncertain matter, and the Bible in no place indicates any doubt about it. As to whether a man becomes and remains righteous is another subject, and he is warned all through the word of God to be watchful and not become slack in his service to the Lord. But our passage is speaking only of the faithful and so far as the salvation of them is concerned the scriptures are definite. (See John 10: 28; 11: 26: 2 Timothy 2: 19; 2 Peter 1: 10, 11; Revelation 20: 6.) The word for *scarcely* is defined "with difficulty" by Thayer, hence we should have no trouble in understanding the statement. The trials that will be forced upon Christians by the foe will make the conflict difficult, but if they will be faithful to the end in spite of the difficulties (which is something that all who will can do), then their salvation is as sure as that the Lord lives. If the words *ungodly* and *sinner* are used separately they mean virtually the same. Peter uses them in one sentence hence he recognizes a distinction. *Ungodly* his direct reference to a man's deliberate disrespect for God, while *sinner* has more reference to the kind of personal life he is following without any special consideration of what he thinks of God. Of course both men described are wrong and will not be saved unless they repent. The question about where they shall appear is an implied declaration that they will appear or show up at the day of judgment on the left side of Him before whom all nations will be gathered (Matthew 25: 31-33).

Verse 19. This verse is the grand and consoling conclusion from the truths that have been considered in the preceding three chapters. To *suffer according to the will of God* means to suffer persecutions for having lived in harmony with His will. *Commit the keeping of their souls.* Man can kill the body but not the soul (Matthew 10: 28). This commitment must be done *in well doing*, and since God created that soul He is the one who can and will keep it safely.

1 Peter 5

Verse 1. *Elders which are among you.* This phrase harmonizes with the form of government that was established for the church by the apostles. To be *among* the brethren means to be in their midst and a part of the same community. Elders have no authority over disciples among whom they are not residing. That is why we read that they "ordained them elders in every church" (Acts 14: 23; Titus 1: 5). *Also an elder* is defined "a fellow-elder" by Thayer. As an apostle Peter would have more authority than an elder, but he humbly leaves out that dignity and makes his exhortation as one of them. His experience as a witness of the sufferings of Christ would add weight to his plea. *Partaker of the glory.* As Peter not only witnessed the sufferings of Jesus, but also endured much of the same kind of persecution, he expected to share in the glory that will come at the last day.

Verse 2. *Feed* is from POIMAINO which Thayer defines, "To feed, to tend a flock, keep sheep; to rule, govern." This is all logical, for if a shepherd is to attend to the proper feeding and keeping of a flock, he should have the right to rule or govern it. *Which is among you.* The same word *among* is used that is used in the preceding verse in relation to the elders and the members. In other words, both the elders and the members under their rule must be *among* or in the midst of each other. These fundamental principles disprove a popular notion that a person can be a member of a congregation even though he is too far away to be *among* the elders and the other members. The idea that a person can live in one community and "have his membership" in another has no scriptural authority. If he is so far away or is otherwise so situated that he cannot attend the services of a congregation, then he cannot be considered a member of it, and the elders can have no jurisdiction over him.

Taking the oversight is from a Greek word that means "To look upon, inspect, oversee, look after, care for"—Thayer. It should be understood that the phrase applies to men who have been placed into the eldership according to the scriptural procedure that is shown in 1 Timothy 3 and Titus 1. *Not by constraint.* They should not have to be forced into the office but should accept it willingly. *Not for filthy lucre* is translated "not for base gain" by The Englishman's Greek New Testament. This refers to the temporal support that was given to elders who devoted their time to the care of the congregation. See the comments at 1 Timothy 5: 17, 18 where it is evidently shown that it is right to support an elder so he can give his entire attention to the flock in spiritual matters. But our verse warns that a man should not use the office for the sake of his personal support. He should have *a ready mind* which means he accepts the work because his mind is concerned for the spiritual welfare of the flock.

Verse 3. *Neither as being lords over God's heritage.* There have been elders dealt with on the charge that they "lorded it over God's heritage," using this statement as the basis for the action. Such an action is a misuse of the passage even though it had been properly translated, which it had not, and further because it entirely leaves out the very point the writer is making. One meaning of *lord* is "ruler," and 1 Timothy 3: 5; 5: 17; Hebrews

13: 7, 17 shows that elders are to rule. Therefore the elders are to be lords over God's heritage. Peter is not objecting to the manner of anyone's rule itself, but to the motive some might have who rule. The men who wrote the Authorized Version knew there was no original word in this passage for the name of God, hence they put it in italics. And because they misunderstood the main point the apostle was making they erred in the rendering of the original. *Heritage* is possessive and in the 2nd person as the inflection denotes. The passage, therefore, should have been rendered as follows: "Not as being lords over your own heritage." The Englishman's Greek New Testament renders it, "Not as exercising lordship over your possessions." The manner of the ruling is not the subject, but the motive or attitude of the rulers. If a man considers the church as his own, then he is indeed likely to rule in an improper manner. And so if an elder will keep in mind that the heritage or church is not his own, he will not have the incentive to bear the wrong kind of rule, which is the point the apostle is making. The wording of the passage as we have it in the King James Version not only inserts a word (the name of God) not authorized by the original, and also erroneously renders the word for *heritage*, but gives a thought that is positively contrary to that of the apostle. *Being examples to the flock*. If an elder will back up his instructions with his own example of right living his word will have more weight with the members of the flock. Such elders will win the respect of the members so that they will be led "to esteem them very highly in love for their work's sake" (1 Thessalonians 5: 13).

Verse 4. The writer continues the subject of a shepherd and his flock. *Chief Shepherd* is Christ who calls himself the "good shepherd" in John 10: 11. When He is included in the parable it represents the elders of congregations as shepherds who are acting on behalf of the Chief who owns all of the groups of sheep wherever they may be in the world. If these under shepherds perform their work faithfully they will be rewarded when the chief Shepherd appears. *Fadeth not away*. The phrase is used in contrast with the crowns bestowed by men; being composed of material substances they soon fade and lose their glory or beauty.

Verse 5. The duties and authority of elders have been considered, now the *younger* or other members of the flock are to *submit* themselves to the elders. *All of you be subject one to another*. This instruction is not based upon any definite authority that one has for another, but rather pertains to the respect that each member should have for the others. Since the Bible does not contradict itself, we know this does not mean to ignore the rule of the elders which the other members are to observe. But every member of the body of Christ should wish to please his fellow-member in whatever is right, and should be willing to grant such requests that he might make. This will show the true spirit of humility and will receive the grace or favor of God who resists the proud.

Verse 6. *Humble yourselves*. When it is said that God gives grace to the humble (preceding verse), it means those who become such of their own accord. The proud will finally be made humble by the Lord (Matthew 23: 12), but such humility will bring only shame to the victim. The exaltation that is promised to the ones who willingly become humble is to come *in due time*, which means at the judgment day.

Verse 7. *Casting all your care upon him* means upon God, for the preceding verse says He is the one who will exalt the humble. Not that we are to be thoughtless about the stern realities of life, for the next verse will contradict that. It means that we should believe that our interests are His interests and that we should not always be fretting about the future. Jesus taught that we should not be overanxious about the morrow (Matthew 6: 25-34), and our present verse declares that *he careth for you*. Then let us go on our pilgrim journey with abiding faith in Him who holds the universe in the hollow of his hand.

Verse 8. To be *sober* means to be serious minded and *vigilant* denotes that the one is watchful—is on his guard, and the reason for this exhortation is next stated. The English word *devil* in the King James Version comes from the Greek words which are DIABOLOS and DAIMONION. The first refers to Satan the chief of devils, the second is a name for the evil spirits in Hades or the unseen world. The reader should see the extended description of these evil spirits or demons, at Matthew 8: 28, 29 in the first volume of the New Testament Commentary. The word in our verse is from the first Greek word and means Satan or *the devil*. We know that Satan does not literally walk about among men, for he does not have a material or visible body and hence could not be seen by human eyes. Yet Peter exhorts the disciples to be vigilant which means watchful. But it would be useless to be on the lookout for a being whom no one can see. Matthew 25: 41 speaks of the devil and his angels. The last word means messengers of any kind, so that any being who carries messages or has communication on behalf of Satan may be said to be one of his angels. We know the Bible teaches that he has various agencies among mankind who are working for him. *Roaring lion* is said because a lion roars when he is hungry and prowling around looking for food.

Verse 9. This verse will throw more light on the preceding one. The pronoun *whom* refers to the devil, and Christians are exhorted to resist him. Then in direct connection with the subject they are told that their brethren have been experiencing the *same afflictions*. This makes it plain that when Christians are tempted and persecuted by evil men, as these disciples had been, the apostle would say it is the work of the devil, and in that way he goes about like a roaring (ravenous) lion. The reference to *your brethren* is for the purpose of encouraging them in their conflicts with the enemy. When they know that these afflictions are *accomplished* (endured to the end) by their brethren in Christ elsewhere, they may conclude they can do the same since what one can do (under Christ) another can accomplish by endurance.

Verse 10. *God of all grace.* Since grace means the unmerited favor of God, it is fitting that all such favors should be attributed to Him. This is especially true since it pertains to the favor of saving mankind from his sins, when strict justice would demand that he be condemned. God alone through his Son has the power to bestow such a favor on human beings. An item of this unmerited favor is the calling of man into the eternal glory of serving God in this world and of enjoying His presence in the world to come. This call is made *by Christ Jesus* and the instrument with which it is accomplished is the Gospel. *After that ye have suffered a while.* The last word is used in a comparative sense, and has the same thought as Paul's remarks in 2 Corinthians 4: 17 and Romans 8: 18. The last part of the verse is a wish on behalf of the brethren for certain blessings to be given to them by the *God of all grace. Perfect* means to be complete in Christ; *stablish* denotes being confirmed in the faith; *strengthen* is general and means to enable them to be strong in the Lord; to *settle* signifies giving one a firm and definite position in the service of Christ.

Verse 11. The antecedent of *him* is the "God of all grace" in the preceding verse. *Glory* means honor and respect, and *dominion* has the idea of authority and rulership. Peter ascribes these qualities to God and declares they are to belong to Him for ever. For the meaning of *amen* see the comments at Romans 16: 24 in the first volume of the New Testament Commentary.

Verse 12. Both Thayer and Robinson say that *Silvanus* is another form for Silas. It was by him that Peter sent this epistle to the brethren designated in chapter 1: 1. *As I suppose* is not an expression of doubt, but as Peter had only lately become acquainted with Silvanus, he concluded (one meaning of *suppose*) that he was a faithful brother, basing his conclusion on commendations of the brethren from whom he had recently come. *Written briefly* is another comparative phrase, considering the vast amount of subject matter covered in the epistle. *Exhorting* pertains to the urging that the writer does for the brethren to discharge their duties, and *testifying* refers to the evidences he had as proof of his declarations. The conclusion that is reached from the truths set forth in the epistle, is that the brethren were standing in the *true grace of God*.

Verse 13. *Church that is at Babylon.* There is so much uncertainty in the discussions to be found in the histories, lexicons and commentaries on this phrase, that I shall be careful to avoid speculation. The word *church* is not the original at all but has been supplied by the translators. The Greek words at this place are as follows in the composition; HE EN BABULONI, and the literal rendering of them by the Englishman's Greek New Testament is, "she in Babylon." A number of other translations render it in the same way, which seems reasonable since the other salutations are from individuals also. As to what person is meant the matter is equally indefinite, except that it is some Christian woman who had been *elected* or chosen by the Lord the same as the ones to whom the epistle is written. (See the word explained at chapter 1: 1.) We know that ancient Babylon was completely destroyed never to be rebuilt, according to both prophecy and history, hence the term is used figuratively and that also is subject to some uncertainty. *Marcus my son* refers to John Mark, and Peter calls him his son because he had converted him, hence he was his "son in the faith" as Paul called the evangelist (1 Timothy 1: 2).

Verse 14. *Kiss of charity* or love refers to the salutation of the kiss as was customary in old times. The custom as it is related to Christians is explained at 1 Corinthians 16: 20. The peace that Peter wishes for the brethren is on condition that they *are in Christ Jesus*. That is equivalent to the peace that is "first pure" set forth in James 3: 17.

2 Peter 1

Verse 1. Peter designates himself both as a *servant* and an *apostle* but mentions the servant first. The epistle is addressed to the same kind of people as his first one only it is stated differently. The first calls them the "elect" or chosen of God which was according to His prearranged plan. This epistle is addressed to those of *like precious faith* with the apostle. This faith was *obtained* (not born with them at infancy), but the means of obtaining it is clearly stated to have been the *righteousness of God*. Romans 1: 16, 17 states that this righteousness is revealed in the Gospel. Hence the conclusion is clear that men receive faith through the Gospel, which agrees with Romans 10: 17 which declares that faith comes by hearing the word of God. Note that our verse includes the righteousness of our Savior Jesus Christ.

Verse 2. This virtually repeats the thoughts of the preceding verse. The favor of God is to come through knowledge of God, and the preceding paragraph shows that such knowledge is to be obtained through the word of God in the Gospel.

Verse 3. Inasmuch as salvation is the subject under consideration, the phrase *his divine power* refers to the Gospel for Romans 1: 16 declares that it is the *power of God unto salvation*. Our verse states that this power (which is the Gospel) hath given *all things that pertain unto life and godliness*. The negative thought would be therefore that any doctrine or practice that is not authorized by the Gospel does not have anything to do with life and godliness. The terrible conclusion that is unavoidable is that when men practice anything in their religious life that is not authorized by the Gospel, they are guilty of that which will result in death to them because it is classed with ungodliness. The offering of these life-giving items is done through knowledge of the Lord since he is the one who has made the call herein mentioned. *Glory* means honor and dignity and *virtue* means excellence or a condition of completeness. The word *to* is from DIA and its leading meaning is "by means of." The statement about the call should then be worded as follows: "Knowledge of him who hath called us by his glory and virtue." Such a rendering is also in line with the connection which shows that the Gospel, in which these qualities are contained, is the means by which men are called into the service of Christ.

Verse 4. *Whereby* means that by the kind of life that is designated in the preceding verse, we may claim the *exceeding great and precious promises*. The things promised are *great* because no one but the Lord can grant such favors, and they are *precious* because all the wealth of the universe could not purchase them. The antecedent of *these* is the *glory* and *virtue* mentioned in the preceding verse. In addition to enjoying the precious promises offered in the Gospel, we may become partakers of the *divine nature*. Divine means godlike and nature refers to the qualities that distinguish that which is godlike from that which is not. The man who attains this personality through the Gospel is that much like God. The *corruption that is in the world* is brought about *through lust* of sinful men. When one obeys the Gospel he escapes from that corruption in the sense that he has been cleansed therefrom by the "divine power." He is then prepared to proceed with the kind of life that such a person is expected to follow in his service for Christ.

Verse 5. *And beside this*. It is not enough to obey the commands that cause one to become a Christian, but he must add to his faith the practices and qualities that are to be named in this and other verses following. *Diligence* is from SPOUDE and the definition of Thayer is, "earnestness, diligence." He explains the word as follows: "Universally earnestness in accomplishing, promoting, or striving after anything." A brief and workable definition of the word would be "thoughtful activity." Peter directs that it be used in the work of adding these necessary things to one's faith. *Virtue* is the same term that is used in verse 3. The outstanding word in the definition is "excellence," which means the quality of excelling or going beyond one's present attainments. A Christian should never be satisfied with his present growth, but should be determined to increase more and more. *Knowledge*. The general meaning of this word is "information," and the particular kind of information that is meant in any case must be determined by the connection. Colossians 2: 3 states that all treasures of wisdom and knowledge are hid (contained) in the Lord. Then the verses in the beginning of our chapter clearly show that such knowledge is to be learned through the Gospel. Thus the instruction of the apostle is for the Christian to study the Gospel (the New Testament) and add such knowledge to the faith he had that caused him to become a servant of Christ.

Verse 6. The lexicon defines the Greek word for *temperance* with the single word "self-control." A practical illustration of the subject is shown in James 3: 2, 3. In general the word means for Christians to use moderation in the various things of life. Of course the word applies only to things that are not wrong in themselves, but wrong only when carried to excess. Therefore is has no place in the subject of intoxicating liquor as a beverage, for that is wrong regardless of the degree of indulgence. *Patience*. The leading idea of this word may be stated by the words "constancy" and "endurance." The first term denotes a steadiness of one's activities for the Lord and the second means that he will continue it to the end. "Be thou faithful unto death, and I will give thee a crown of life" (Revelation 2: 10). *Godliness* is from EUSEBEIA which Thayer defines as follows: "Reverence, respect; piety towards God, godliness." The word not only requires that a man will live as he should, but that his motive for such a life will be his respect for God.

Verse 7. The two words *brotherly kindness* come from the one Greek word PHILADELPHIA. Thayer's definition of the word is, "The love of brothers (or sisters), brotherly love; in the New Testament the love which Christians cherish for each other as brethren." The disciples of Christ should feel a nearness for each other that is stronger even than their love for flesh-and-blood relatives. *Charity* is from AGAPE which is one of the Greek words translated "love" in the New Testament. The principal meaning of the word in the present passage is to have a sincere interest in the welfare of others. The subject of love is often misunderstood by students of the Bible, due partly to the circumstance that the word comes from different Greek originals which have different meanings. There is a complete page devoted to the subject made up from the authoritative quotations from the lexicons of Thayer and Strong. The comments are at Matthew 5: 43 which I urge the readers to see and study carefully; they are in the first volume of the New Testament Commentary.

Verse 8. *In you and abound*. Thayer defines the original for the last word, "To superabound; to exist in abundance; to increase, be augmented." It is one of the outstanding principles of the teaching in the Bible that the life of a servant of God should be one of growth. Hence the Christian should determine to make these "seven graces" increase in his life as the days go by. If he will do so it will assure him that he will be neither *barren nor unfruitful*. These words have about the same meaning and are used together as a matter of emphasis. The first specifically means "idle or inactive," and that condition would necessarily result in absence of fruit-bearing. The particular kind of fruit just here being considered is worded *knowledge of our Lord Jesus Christ*. If a tree fails to bear fruit it may be attributed to a lack of moisture and other ingredients necessary to produce fruit, or to the failure of the plant to absorb those materials that are near it. Likewise if a disciple is inactive in the matter of acquiring the knowledge of Christ that is within his reach in the Gospel (verses 2, 3), it can only result in a life that bears no fruit unto God. Such a state is dangerous for Jesus declares that all such trees will be hewn down and cast into the fire (Matthew 7: 19).

Verse 9. *Blind*. Not "stone-blind" for

then he could not see at all whereas this person can see a little. The idea is as if a smoke was raised making the vision dim. *Cannot see afar off* all comes from MUOPAZO which Thayer defines, "To see dimly, see only what is near," and the Englishman's Greek New Testament renders it "short sighted." We have all seen persons who were afflicted with this defect regarding their bodily eyes and can have only pity for them. But in the case of those who are spiritually "near sighted" there is not much reason for pity, since it is a defect that they can help if they will. *Hath forgotten.* Not that his memory has become a blank, for that would be impossible as long as he maintains his faculties at all. The meaning is that he ceases to hold in grateful remembrance the glorious time when he was washed from his sins by the blood of Christ in baptism.

Verse 10. *Wherefore the rather* denotes that the disciple should not make the mistake just described, but instead he should do the following. Again the apostle advises the use of *diligence* which is explained at verse 5. By using this "thoughtful activity" the disciple may accomplish a very desirable result which certainly every person would welcome. *Calling and election.* When a man hears the Gospel and obeys it he is called into the service, and by a proper walk in life he will be "elected" or chosen of God as one of His own. It is up to the disciple to make that relationship with God permanent or sure. Such a thing is possible else the apostle would not exhort the brethren to do so. He explains how it is done, namely, *if ye do these things* which means the duties outlined in the preceding verses, and if they do he says *ye shall never fall*. While this language gives a disciple an assurance of salvation that no man can take from him, yet the condition on which the assurance is given just as clearly shows that it is possible for a man to fall even after having been "purged from his old sins." This is disproof of the Calvinistic heresy that says "once in grace, always in grace." If that notion were taught in the word of God, then a Christian could do nothing that would cause him to fall. Neither could he do anything to assure himself of final salvation were he one of the "non-elect."

Verse 11. An *abundant entrance* is a phrase of emphasis, meaning that the disciple who is faithful till death will receive all of the glory accompanying the entrance into the delightful place. *Everlasting kingdom* does not mean the church on earth, for one has to be in that institution first before he can begin to plan for this kingdom. It means the kingdom after Christ has delivered it up to God. (1 Corinthians 15: 24).

Verse 12. *Put you always in remembrance.* Much of the writing and preaching of the New Testament times was done on the principle stated in this phrase. (See chapter 3: 1.) The human mind is inclined to forget what it has learned; that is, in the sense of the word as explained at verse 9. Paul has such a thought in mind in Hebrews 2: 1. Therefore the teachers of the present day find it necessary to repeat the same warnings and exhortations over and over again. It is not necessarily for the purpose of imparting new information, but in order to jog the memory on information already made known. Peter implies that if he should fail to do this reminding of his brethren he would be guilty of *negligence*. Let elders and evangelists and all other public workers take a lesson from this and not become impatient in their labors with indifferent disciples. *Present truth* means the information that they had received up to the present time. The New Testament had not been completed and additional inspired truth was to come as the time went by, but these disciples were pretty well fixed in their belief of the truth already received. Hence another phase of the duty of a teacher is indicated by this. He should constantly exhort his brethren who may actually be somewhat faithful, lest they should later become unmindful and fall into a state of carelessness concerning their duty.

Verse 13. *Think it meet* or suitable to continue the reminding. *Stir you up* means to rouse them to further activities by approaching them and appealing to their memory. *In this tabernacle* means as long as he is in the flesh. Paul refers to the mortal body as a tabernacle in 2 Corinthians 5: 1-6. The word is from SKENOS and Thayer defines it, "A tabernacle, a tent," and he explains that it is "used figuratively of the human body, in which the soul dwells as in a tent, and which is taken down at death." This is another suggestion of the temporary nature of our stay upon this earth, and of the folly of men in acting as if they expected to live on the earth for ever.

Verse 14. *Shortly I must put off*, etc. Peter means he was to die before long; it is stated in Smith's Bible Dictionary that Peter wrote this epistle near the close of his life. *As our Lord Jesus Christ hath showed me.* This evidently refers to the conversation recorded in John 21: 18, 19 in which Jesus predicts that Peter would die a violent death at the hands of his enemies. No definite date is given for the tragic event, only he was told that it would happen *when thou shalt be old*. At the time of this epistle Peter was an old man and hence he could say knowingly that this death was near, based on the prediction of Christ.

Verse 15. *After my decease.* There is an interesting item in this phrase. The last word is from EXODUS which Thayer defines, "Exit, i. e. departure; departure from life, decease." We know by the connection that Peter is writing about his death but calls it by a word that means "departure" or going out. The meaning of this word is what gives the second book of the Bible its name, because the "going out" of the children of Israel from Egypt is the main event of that book. But the passage is fatal to the doctrine of soulsleepers and other materialists. They teach that nothing leaves the body at death; that all there is of man goes to the grave at that time. The statement of Peter about his death belies the heresy for we know that his body did not depart when he died. *Have these things always in remembrance.* By putting the teaching in writing with assurances of its truthfulness, the brethren would have the reminder before them even after the soul of Peter had "put off its tabernacle" and had made its exit from this world.

Verse 16. *Cunningly devised fables.* Certain speculators among the Jews joined with others in those days in delivering myths (here translated *fables*) to listeners, and many of them were so tricky in their wording that the uninformed were deceived. The apostles found it necessary to give warnings against heeding s u c h speeches (1 Timothy 1: 4; 4: 7; 2 Timothy 4: 4; Titus 1: 14). Peter declares that he was not depending on such stories in his revealing of the things concerning Christ. What a man sees is a matter of positive knowledge and does not require any ingenious wording to make the report acceptable. *We* is literal and means actually that more than one were witnesses, not just the "editoral I" as is sometimes used for the sake of modesty. If one inspired witness makes a declaration it is as true as if a hundred would say it, yet if more than one witness the same thing it will be strengthened on the basis of corroboration. *Power and coming.* The last word is elsewhere defined "presence," and since we know Peter has direct reference to the scenes of the transfiguration, the word is used in that sense and applies especially to the *majesty* (greatness) of Christ. However, the very visible demonstration of His greatness of which Peter and others were witnesses, would give evidence of the reasonableness of the predictions of the second coming of Christ to earth.

Verse 17. *He received* means Christ when he received *honor and glory* in the mount of transfiguration (Matthew 17: 1-5). *Such a voice* refers to the voice of God that was heard by Peter, James and John who were taken by Christ up into the mount. The *honor and glory* consisted in the acknowledgement of Christ as the Son of God, and also the announcement that the Father was *well pleased* in his Son.

Verse 18. This is called the *holy mount* because of the sacred things that transpired there, not that any physical change was made in the spot. The first definition of the word for *holy* is, "worthy of veneration" or great respect. Certainly a place where such an awe-inspiring scene took place as the transfiguration is worthy of the most profound respect and in that sense it was holy.

Verse 19. *More sure* is from the one Greek word BEBEIOS which Thayer defines, "Stable, fast, firm; sure, trusty." The word *more* is unnecessary because no comparison is being made, but only some additional information that corroborates the report that Peter just made of his own personal knowledge; nothing could be surer than it. No particular prediction is cited but the fact of there having been such statements made by the prophets of old time is the point Peter is making. The apostle advises his readers to take heed unto those prophecies. He compares them to a light penetrating the *dark place* meaning the (then) future. *Until the day dawn* means the day of the fulfillment of those prophecies, at which the *day star* (morning star) who is Christ (Revelation 22: 16) will *arise in your hearts.* The study of the many prophecies of Christ in the Old Testament (too numerous to cite here), will bring one up to the fuller report in the history as given in the New Testament, and it will be like the morning star that announces to the world that a new day has dawned. In the words of the wise king of Israel, such a procedure of the study will be like the "shining light, that shineth more and more unto the perfect day" (Proverbs 4:18).

Verse 20. *Knowing this first* is Peter's introduction to a further explanation of why the "word of prophecy" is to be considered "sure" as stated in the preceding verse. *No prophecy of the scripture.* The last word means the Old Testament because the New Testament had not been completed when Peter was writing, and besides it would not make a prophecy of the kingdom of Christ since that institution already existed while the New Testament was in the making. *Private interpretation.* The Romish church leaders make much of this phrase because they think it supports their heresy about reading the Bible. The pressure of popular sentiment has induced that institution to relax its restrictions against the reading of the Holy Book by the masses. They are now given certain limited privileges of reading it, but they are forbidden to "interpret" it on the strength of the mentioned phrase. The first definition of the original for *interpretation* is, "A loosening, unloosing," and for that of *private* it is, "Pertaining to one's self, one's own." Hence it is clear that Peter is not writing about anyone's interpreting the scripture in the sense of explaining it. He is considering the prophecies in the Old Testament and says that they were not just something that the prophets thought about. It was not their own personal production or something that was their own "brain child." A similar use of language is in John 11:51 where Caiaphas is making a prediction. The writer explains that Caiaphas did not say it "of himself," but spoke with the inspiration possessed by the high priests.

Verse 21. The thoughts of the preceding verse are continued. *Will of man* is used in the sense of "private interpretation," meaning that the prophecies were not the production of mere human beings. Instead, they spoke as by inspiration of the Holy Ghost.

2 Peter 2

Verse 1. All good things can be abused and that which is true will always have pretenders or imitators. In old times the Lord had faithful prophets and many people learned to love them for their work's sake. Profiting by the respect that was rightly had for the true prophets, others attempted to put over some unrighteous schemes in the name of prophecy. Among the people of Israel were many false prophets and the number of instances is too great to enumerate, but the one in 1 Kings 18 is a noted case. Likewise in the time of the New Testament Peter says there will be false *teachers* (one name for prophets). *Damnable heresies* means false doctrines that will condemn all who accept them. The apostle specifies one of the false doctrines, namely, a denial of the divinity of the Lord notwithstanding that He has bought them with his own blood. *Privily* means secretly; false prophets or teachers are not usually open with their wicked works for fear of being exposed by someone who knows the truth. (John 3:19-21.) *Swift destruction* means the condemnation that God will bring on these false teachers; it will be swift in that it will be sure and the Lord will not hesitate to inflict the punishment when the time comes.

Verse 2. The leading thought in *pernicious* is something that is destruction of the truth. That definition is confirmed by the rest of the verse, for it says the way of truth shall be evil spoken of by the ones who follow the false teachers.

Verse 3. *Through covetousness* indicates the motive of the false teachers. *Feigned words* means those so formed as to deceive the hearer. *Make merchandise* denotes that they were so successful in imposing their false theories on the people that they could make a gain off of them. There are so many things that could be conducted on this principle that it would be useless to try specifying. We understand that many people are conscientious regarding the propagation of religious principles. If they can be made believe that people are working in the interest of truth, they will be willing to give liberal support to a man engaged in it. *Whose judgement now of a long time.* God has always condemned the false teacher and evil worker. *Lingereth not.* The leading definition of the first word is "to be idle." The passage means that the judgement or condemnation of such characters is of long standing, but that God has not changed his mind about it nor even tempered His wrath against them. Thayer explains the definition as follows: "Whose punishment has long been impending and will shortly fall." However, the word "shortly" must be understood in a compartive sense, because the apostle proceeds at once to illustrate his declaration by referring to the unjust to be reserved unto the day of judgement to be punished.

Verse 4. *For if*. This phrase will be taken up with comments when we get to verse 9. *God spared not the angles that sinned*. We occasionally meet people who are troubled over the idea of angels sinning since they are in heaven. They are overlooking the truth that neither angels nor man have reached the judgement day, and until that time both classes are capable of sinning. Were that not the case there would not now be such a creature as "the devil," for he was once in heaven and was thrust out because of his pride (1 Timothy 3: 6; Luke 10: 18). But after the judgement no more changes will take place either for better or for worse. (See Revelation 22: 10, 11.) That means after that all wicked men and angels will be in the place of everlasting punishment where they can never reform, and the righteous men and angels will be in heaven where they can never sin because the divine decree is that the righteous shall "be righteous still." The English word "hell" in the King James Version comes from three different Greek words that have different meanings. In our present passage it comes from TARTAROO which means that part of the intermediate state where the wicked go at death. This whole subject of "hell" is explained in detail at Matthew 5: 30, in the first volume of the New Testament Commentary. *Into chains of darkness* is figurative and refers to the regions of the wicked dead, because that place was thought of as one of midnight darkness. *Reserved unto judgement*. These fallen angels have no prospect of deliverence but must await the final judgement day. The only relief that any of them ever had was when some of them were released temporarily to enter into men in the time of Christ and the apostles. See the long note on this at Matthew 8: 28-31 in the first volume of the New Testament Commentary.

Verse 5. *Spared not the old world* refers to the people that were living in the days of Noah, because the last word is from KOSMOS which is defined "the inhabitants of the earth." They were wicked and God did not spare them from the flood; Noah was spared because he was a man of faith. *Noah the eighth*. This could not mean that Noah was number eight in the genealogy for he was tenth. The lexicons and various translations prefer to word this place, "Noah and seven others." He is called *a preacher of righteousness* because he preached what was right and what pertained to the needs of the day. The people were wicked and living after their evil imaginations, and the situation required teaching directing them to reform. *World of the ungodly* is the same as *old world* in the beginning of the verse.

Verse 6. The history of Sodom and Gomorrha is in Genesis 19. *Into ashes* states the result of the *overthrow* which was sent on them in the *condemnation* from God. *An example*. The punishment of evildoers is not only for their own sakes, but also that the example may be a lesson for warning to others. (See 1 Timothy 5: 20.)

Verse 7. *Just Lot*. This statement is made by an inspired writer and must be accepted as true. Much criticism has been made of Lot because of the choice he made in the time of Abraham. The criticism is unjust because it is contrary to the facts of the circumstance. The reader may see a full explanation of this subject at Genesis 13: 9-12, in Volume 1 of Bible Commentary. *Vexed with the filthy conversation* (conduct) *of the wicked*. This has special reference to their gross immorality, for the account that is given in Genesis 19: 4-11 shows them to have been worse than dumb beasts.

Verse 8. This is the same as the preceding verse.

Verse 9. This verse resumes the thought that was introduced at verse 4, but was interrupted with a list of facts set forth as a basis for the present passage. The argument is that *if* God was able and also disposed to do all the things referred to, He is able and determined also to do the following. *Deliver the godly out of temptation*. God does not promise to work a miracle to keep the trials from coming, but if a disciple is faithful He will care for him and help him overcome them (1 Corinthians 10: 13). *Reserve the unjust* indicates that the punishment of the unjust is to be at a future time. This spoils a wishful-thinking notion that "a man will get all of his 'hell' in this life." Wicked men as well as wicked angels will not be given their final sentence until the judgement at the last day.

Verse 10. *Chiefly* has no reference to the kind of punishment that is to be meted out to these sinners for all will receive the same doom. In Matthew 25: 31-46 we see that those whose only sin mentioned is a failure to relieve the needy, will receive the same punishment that was "prepared for the devil and his angels." The word *chiefly* means that Peter is making particular mention of these characters. *Walk after the flesh*. The connection shows they were living after the lowest desires similar to the Sodomites. *Despise government* means they belittled the laws that would curb their immoral lives. *Presumptuous* and *self-willed* mean virtually the same, referring to people who are determined to have their own way, regardless of whether it is right or wrong. *Speak evil of dignities*. The last word means any thing or any being that is glorious, but the connection shows Peter is writing of angels because of their dignity and glory.

Verse 11. The angels of whom the mentioned "presumptuous" persons are not afraid to speak evil, show more courtesy toward their inferior accusers than the accusers show to them. *Power* and *might* have virtually the same degree of importance in the lexicon definition, hence their use is for the sake of emphasis. *Bring not railing accusation* which means blasphemous charges. A specific instance of this kind of angelic mildness is shown in Jude 6.

Verse 12. *These* refers to the ungodly people described in verse 10. The Englishman's Greek New Testament translates the next four words, "as natural irrational animals," and it is these creatures that Peter says were *made to be taken and destroyed*. He compares the wicked men to these in that they act as if they were as irrational as they. He is expressing the situation as one that is surprisingly foolish, that human beings would behave no better than creatures that were not intended to be any more important than to be taken and slain. But the comparison is just, since they *speak evil of the things that they understand not*. Certainly men who thus speak do not show much better intellect than the brute beasts. *Utterly perish in their own corruption*. This is said as a contrast to the case of the dumb animals. They are taken by others and slain, while these will be self-destroyed; perish in their *own* corruption.

Verse 13. *Reward of unrighteousness* means they will be treated as an unrighteous man should be treated; they will "reap what they have sowed." *Pleasure to riot in the day time*. It is wrong to riot at any time, but the usual practice is to use the night for it. "For they that be drunken are drunken in the night" (1 Thessalonians 5: 7). But these characters are brazen and take pleasure in flaunting their evil conduct at a time when everyone can see it. *Spots and blemishes*. Paul says the church was desired to be without spot (Ephesians 5: 27), but the conduct of these wicked men puts a terrible blemish on the institution. *Sporting themselves* is defined by Thayer, "To live in luxury," and it was done *while they feast with you*. This has reference to the love feasts that the Christians conducted in the early times. Such feasts were intended only as an expression of good will and were put on for the special benefit of the poorer Christians. But they were often abused as most good things may be, and evil persons attended the assemblies merely to indulge themselves in the good things provided by the brethren for the help of the poor. (See Jude 12.)

Verse 14. *Adultery* is from a Greek word that is defined by Thayer, "An adulteress." He explains about eyes being full of her as follows: "Eyes always on the watch for an adulteress, or from which adulterous desire beams forth." *That cannot cease from sin*. We know the Lord will not condemn a man for something he actually cannot avoid, hence we must look for the meaning of this phrase. In Thayer's definition of the Greek (the words in italics), he says, "Not quieted, that cannot be quieted," and he explains it as follows: "Eyes not quieted with sin, i. e. which they commit with adulterous look." Hence it does not mean these men cannot cease looking at an adulteress (for they could), but they cannot satisfy themselves just by looking;

they will desire to obtain gratification. Doubtless that is why Jesus said "Whosoever looketh on a woman to lust after her hath committed adultery with her already in his heart" (Matthew 5: 28). *Beguiling unstable souls.* These men looking round for an adulteress may not find one with such intentions, but if they are *unstable* (not firm in character), these evil men may entice them into sin. *Covetous practices.* In addition to being immoral they are grasping and try to take undue advantage of the free provisions that were intended as an expression of brotherly fellowship. *Cursed children.* The first word is an adjective and describes *children* which means a certain class of individuals. These people are under the curse of the Lord because He has pronounced condemnation upon all such characters who do not repent before death.

Verse 15. *Forsaken the right way* indicates these men had once been righteous, but had *gone astray* which means to step aside from the pathway of righteousness. *Bosor* is the same as Beor, the father of Balaam. Balaam pretended that all the wealth of Balak could not entice him to come to him, but he finally yielded and went in the direction of sin (Numbers 22-24).

Verse 16. This verse continues the case begun in the preceding one, and the record is included in the chapters in Numbers cited. The point is that the false prophet was rebuked even though no other was at hand through whom God could speak. Yet since He was able to give speech to the dumb brute to chastise the prophet, it is made sure that the Lord will be able to give wicked men their proper punishment when the time comes for the judgement of evildoers.

Verse 17. *Wells without water* are places that are supposed to furnish water but have gone dry. *Clouds carried with a tempest* are those without much moisture and hence are so light they are driven about with the wind. Both figures are used to illustrate men who make the pretense of service for the Lord but who are empty of real worth. *Mist of darkness is reserved.* Since these pretenders are like a mist without rainfall, they deserve to go into another form of mist or gloom, and that is eternal darkness which is being reserved for them.

Verse 18. The principal subject of this verse is the influence these evil men have over **those** who would desire to be good if left alone. They accomplish their wicked designs by means of *great swelling words of vaity.* This means they use deceptive language that causes others to expect certain enjoyments. They make their contact with the victims at the point of *wantonness* (impure desires) and *lusts of the flesh,* that being the place in the nature of a human being where he is the most apt to be influenced. These wicked pretenders are so successful that they *allure* (draw aside) those who were *clean escaped* from a life of error. Some translations render this as if the victims were only in the process of being brought out of error, but the word for *clean* is defined by Thayer, "Truly, in reality, in point of fact." This definition agrees also with the reasoning in verses 20-22 below.

Verse 19. A man cannot truly impart something to another he does not have himself, especially when it concerns moral or spiritual principles. These evil workers held out the prospect of a life free from the restraints of law. Yet while emphasizing the good fortune of being "free men," they were themselves a group of slaves. Not to temporal or literal masters it is true, but to the harsh master of sin. Peter proves his assertion by the self-evident truth that if a man is overcome by any person or thing he is the slave of that thing; Paul teaches the same in Romans 6: 16.

Verse 20. The words *latter end* are from a Greek word that is defined "last state" in the lexicon. It does not mean that he has come to the end of his oportunity; that there is nothing he can do about it. The only point the apostle is making at this place in the man's life, is a comparison between his state at the two periods of his experience. They are the one where he escaped from error and the one after he went back to it; of the two the second is worse.

Verse 21. *For it had been better*, etc. It is sometimes argued from this verse that it would be wise not to become a Christian in the first place, then one can avoid what Peter says is the worse of two states. The apostle had no such idea in mind when he wrote this passage, and the theory does him an injustice. Besides, the one who makes such a proposition assumes that only two states are possible and everyone must take one or the other of them. Such is not true for it is not necessary to decide on either, namely, either remain unconverted or go back into sin afterward. The thing he can do and should do is to know and enter *the way of righteousness*, then remain in it. The reason a backslider is in worse state than the alien sinner, is that his heart has been hardened by the experience and will be less favorable to the truth.

Verse 22. The proverb about the dog is in Proverbs 26: 11, but I have no information about the one concerning the sow. The two proverbs are stated only as an illustration of what men did, not that they had to do it. If we apply the reasoning and my comments of the preceding verse to this one, it will say that the sick dog did not have to retain the objectionable matter in his stomach, nor did he have to return to it afterward. Likewise, it was proper to wash the sow after her mire and then for her to stay away from the place of filth. It is not so strange that dumb animals would act as here described, but men may be expected not to imitate them. If they do they will duplicate the saying in verse 12 where men are shown to act like the "brute beasts that were made to be taken and destroyed," and certainly no person would wish to place himself in that class.

2 Peter 3

Verse 1. In calling this his *second epistle* which he says he writes *unto you*, it shows that the persons he addresses in 1 Peter 1: 1 and 2 Peter 1: 1 are the same brethren though he designates them in different language. He is still calling attention to the motive in each epistle, namely, to stir up their memory. *Pure minds* denotes that their minds were sincerely interested in the truth.

Verse 2. The *holy prophets* refers to those of the Old Testament times and the *apostles* pertain to the New. The truthfulness of each is the same, because the former "spake as they were moved by the Holy Ghost or Spirit (chapter 1: 21), and the latter spoke "as the Spirit gave them utterance" (Acts 2: 4). The particular things in their sayings being considered were predictions of complainers that were to show up. Peter wishes his brethren not to be confused and hence he is reminding them about it.

Verse 3. *Knowing this first.* They had first-hand information because it came from inspired prophets and apostles. *Last days.* Some of the things to which Peter refers were being said at the time he was writing, for in verse 5 he speaks in the present tense when he says *"are* ignorant." Therefore the last days is a general reference to the Christian Dispensation. *Scoffers* means men who mock or make light of things they do not like but cannot refute. Robinson says the word was "spoken of impostors, false prophets, deceivers." The motive of these objectors is revealed by the words *walking after their own lusts.* It is a common practice of men who do not wish to be disturbed in their sinful ways, to make light of any authorities that threaten their punishment. They would naturally take that attitude toward the second coming of Christ, because it was predicted that He would judge the world when he comes (Matthew 25: 31-46; Acts 17: 31).

Verse 4. *Promise* is from a word that is somewhat general and includes the idea of "announcement." It is that feature of the term that was worrying the scoffers, because it was announced that when Jesus comes he will condemn the wicked. *Where is the promise.* What has become of this promise that was predicted? *The fathers* comes from a word with so various a meaning that the connection will need be considered in each passage. One of the definitions of Thayer is, "The founder of a race or tribe, progenitor of a people, forefather." This is the sense Peter uses and hence it refers to the patriarchs in the beginning, because he mentions the flood as coming after these fathers *fell asleep.* The scoffers asserted that since that happened there have been no interruptions into the course of things that were arranged in the creation. Their point is to poohpooh such "pessimism" as that any change will ever take place.

Verse 5. *Willingly are ignorant* because it is recorded in the Scriptures, and these scoffers could have known about it had they wanted to know the truth. It was *by the word of God* that the "heavens and earth" were created (Genesis 1: 1), and by which also the *earth* and *water* were separated from each other (Genesis 1: 9, 10).

Verse 6. *World* is from KOSMOS, which means the inhabitants of the earth, and that is the world that perished in the flood. The account of the flood is in the book that the scoffers did not deny being true, but their interest in lustful practices had kept them from learning about it.

Verse 7. *Heavens and earth* are the same that are in verse 5 which were created *by the word of God*. After the people living on the earth were destroyed by the flood (except Noah and family), it left the heavens and earth still in existence and again was covered with inhabitants. The *same word* that created them is keeping them *in store*, being reserved against (until) the destruction by fire. That will be done on the same day that the ungodly men will be judged and sent into perdition. The earth will be permitted to remain until the day of judgment because man is to live on it that long.

Verse 8. Having made his exposure of the scoffers and their wilful ignorance, the apostle devotes the rest of the epistle to the good brethren. They have been advised against being misled by the false statements of the scoffers, yet they doubtless wished sincerely to have information concerning the seeming delay of the second coming of Christ. Peter will take up that matter and explain it for the sake of them and other readers of the epistle. *One day is with the Lord as a thousand years*. It should be noted the apostle does not say a day is as long as a thousand years with us for that would not be true. When the earth revolves once man has been given a day. It must make such a revolution 365 times to give him one year and that must be multiplied a thousand times to amount to the period of the italicized statement. But with the Lord no such measurements are necessary for He inhabits eternity (or time, which is the same), and as there is no limit or end to it, He can prolong the earth's existence through hundreds of such revolutions as easily as through one. To man it seems like a drawn-out delay and hence the apostle gives the explanation herein.

Verse 9. To be *slack* means to delay or be slow in doing something that has been promised or predicted. *As some men count slackness*. What would be regarded as tardiness by men does not apply to the Lord. That is, the seeming delay in bringing the earth to an end is not due to that cause as the scoffers implied. It is rather due to the *longsuffering* or patience that He is manifesting toward humanity. *Not willing that any should perish*. This statement is another proof that no chance of being saved will be given after the earth is destroyed. If men are delievered from their sins at all, it must be before the end of the world or before their death. In contrast with *perish* the apostle sets the phrase *come to repentance*, which shows that all who do not repent will perish. Jesus taught the same truth in person as recorded in Luke 13: 3, 5. But the longsuffering of God is not endless; it was not in the days of Noah (Genesis 6: 3; 1 Peter 3: 20). When God in his infinite wisdom decides that His longsuffering has served its full purpose He will bring about the end.

Verse 10. The Lord is nowhere compared to *a thief*, but the time of His coming is where the likeness is. That is because a thief makes no announcement of his approach but comes in by surprise, usually selecting the time of night for the event. There are three *heavens* spoken of in the Bible, the third one being the dwelling place of God (2 Corinthians 12: 1-4), and of course that will never pass away. The other two are in the material universe, comprising the region of the atmosphere for the first and that of the planets for the second. These shall pass away *with a great noise*. The italicized words come from one Greek word which Strong defines, "Whizzingly, i. e., with a crash." The original for *elements* is defined by Thayer as follows: "The elements from which all things have come, the material causes of the universe." These materials will become liquefied by the intense heat that the Creator will send upon them. The *earth* is a part of the same material universe mentioned in the quoted definition, but it is given special mention because it is where man lives at the present, thus giving him serious warning of the fateful event.

Verse 11. *All these things*. The things of the material universe named in the preceding verse are all to be *dissolved* or melt. That will be the end of man's existence on the earth and hence the end of his opportunity to prepare for the judgment. Such is the reason for the exhortation to be *holy* (righteous) in *conversation* (conduct) by living according to *godliness;* live as God has directed us to live.

Verse 12. *Hasting* means "to desire earnestly" for the *coming of the day of God*. And this notwithstanding the day will bring the dissolving of this earth on which we have lived and enjoyed the blessings of God. But this seeming contradiction in our attitude will be explained in the next verse.

Verse 13. The promise referred to is in Matthew 5: 5 where the meek are promised to inherit the earth. The future state of the saved will be spiritual, hence the only way man can be given a foresight of it is by likening it to what he understands and enjoys while living in a material home. The present abode is on the earth with its two heavens, the atmosphere and starry region. Genesis 1: 14-16 says the planets were made to give light upon the earth, hence it is proper to mention those heavens in connection with the earth when referring to the home of mankind. But while the form of language is based upon man's present abode, in reality his eternal home will be spiritual and one wherein shall dwell righteousness.

Verse 14. With such a prospect as this it should be an incentive for us to live in view of it. To do so we should be diligent (thoughtfully active) and maintain ourselves in the peace that is according to the wisdom from above (James 3: 17). Since that wisdom is pure (unmixed) it will make those *without spot* who follow it.

Verse 15. *Longsuffering is salvation* is the same as mentioned in verse 9, hence Christians should not fret over the seeming delay of His coming. Peter says that Paul wrote to these people on the same matters as the present epistle. Peter wrote both of his epistles to the same brethren for he calls this one the second one he had written to them (verse 1). In the first epistle he mentions brethren in Galatia and Asia, and we know that Paul wrote to brethren in those same regions (Galatians and Ephesians). Peter says that Paul wrote *according to the wisdom given unto him.* This refers to his inspiration for he tells us himself that his preaching was "In demonstration of the Spirit and of power" (1 Corinthians 2: 4).

Verse 16. Peter here makes a more general reference to the epistles of Paul, and says that in all of them he speaks of the same things that the present letter treats. This shows that Peter was familiar with the Pauline writings and that he had great respect for them. Since both apostles wrote about so many items that pertain to the kingdom of God, it would be unnecessary to try pointing out which Peter means by *these things.* All of the words *hard to be understood* are from the one Greek word DUSNOETOS, which Thayer defines with the same four words. Robinson defines it, "difficult of perception." We should note it does not say that it is impossible to understand them, hence the expression does not contradict the general idea of the simplicity of the Gospel. Moreover, it merely says there are *some things* like this, which would not be surprising in documents that have to do with performances of both God and man and of both bad men and Satan. Besides, the only ones who had any serious trouble were those who were *unlearned* (uninformed) and *unstable* (unsettled in their convictions). But even these are not to be excused for they could do better, since they *wrest* (twist) the scriptures which means to force them out of their obvious meaning. And since they wilfully misuse the sacred writings Peter says it will be *unto their own destruction.*

Verse 17. The foregoing remarks are said for the warning of the better class of disciples to whom Peter is sending this epistle. They should beware and not be led astray by designing false teachers who are "walking after their own lusts." No person can be on both sides of a subject at the same time, hence in order to be stedfast in the faith one must turn away from such evil characters.

Verse 18. *Grow in grace* means to grow (or increase) in the favor of the Lord. Note that this exhortation is coupled with the *knowledge* of Him. Hence our favor with the Lord will increase as our knowledge of Him increases, which we may obtain only by becoming familiar with the Gospel. *To him be glory* means that all honor and dignity should be ascribed to the Lord, and that such respect will be due Him for ever. *Amen* is ascribed as an expression of emphasis; its uses and meaning are explained in the comments at Romans 16: 24 in first volume of the New Testament Commentary.

1 John 1

Verse 1. This verse is equivalent to the first verse of John's account of the Gospel. When the words *the beginning* are used as an abstract term, that is one without any qualifying context, they always have the same meaning. The popular notion is that they mean "the beginning of time." That is wrong because time (which merely means duration) had no beginning and of course will have no end. The means by which we measure time, such as the movements of the earth and other planets, will come to an end, but that does not mean that time will end then. It would be like saying that if the clocks all stopped that time would stop also. Not so; the means we were using to measure it only have stopped. The term *the beginning* means the beginning of the material creation. The reader should see the comments on this subject at John 1: 1 in the first volume of the New Testament Commentary. In our present verse John comes to a later period and refers to the circumstance when the word took upon himself that form which could be seen and handled by fleshly man.

Verse 2. This verse gives some more details of the general truths that are stated in the preceding one. *The life* is the same as "Word of life" above which was with the Father before the inhabitants of the earth ever heard about it. It was manifested to the extent that it could be seen with human eyes as well as be "handled" as stated in the first verse. The manner in which this was done is expressed somewhat more directly by this same writer in John 1: 14 which says that "the Word was made flesh." Everyone will understand this refers to the fact of the life of Christ in a fleshly body on the earth. *Show unto you that eternal life.* Such a life is spiritual and thus cannot literally be shown, but John means that when a man sees Christ he is seeing eternal life in that He is the one who gives us the hope of eternal life.

Verse 3. John was especially concerned with the divinity of Christ, that although He dwelt among men in the flesh (in order that they might see and hear Him), yet he was (and is) the divine Son of God. *Have fellowship with us* denotes having a share in or being partakers with the apostles in the relationship between God and Christ and their faithful disciples.

Verse 4. *That your joy may be full.* The last word is where the emphasis of thought should be placed. Small or partial joy may be possible from many different sources, but the joy that can come from a faith in the only divine Son of God is *full* both in the sense of being complete in its extent, and perfect in its quality. It will leave nothing that can reasonably be desired further by a firm believer.

Verse 5. The message which *we* (the apostles and others through them) have heard of *him* (the Son of God). The subject of the message is *light*, brought into the world by Christ which he received from his Father. God not only has light (spiritual truth) but He has nothing else; no darkness at all. Good men and angels have some light but it is limited, while with God it is light unmodified.

Verse 6. The Lord is all light and truth which is the opposite of darkness. For this reason no man can possibly be a partaker (have fellowship) with Him whose life is one of darkness which is a figurative name for that which is not the truth. Hence it is a logical conclusion that if a man claims to be on both sides of this proposition at the same time he is lying.

Verse 7. *Walk in the light.* No man lives who does not make some mistakes and commit sin incidentally. But this phrase means a man whose general life is one of godliness and whose motive principle is the light of the New Testament. This man can truly be said to be walking with the Lord because he is in the pathway that Jesus laid out for him. Being in the fellowship with God the source of all light, is like being constantly in the stream of the blood of His son. That blood is constantly flowing (figuratively) through the body or church of the Lord Jesus Christ. In the natural body of a man whose blood stream is healthy, if germs slip into the person that blood, being always present, will be like a disinfectant that will destroy the germ. Likewise the blood of Christ is ever present to cleanse away the mistakes and incidental sins that a true Christian does. Hence if a man is a worker in the Lord's vineyard and his life as a whole is one of obedience to the law of Christ, he does not need to worry about the mistakes he might make which he does not realize, for the blood of Christ will take care of it and wash them away. They will be cleansed by the "fountain opened to the house of David . . . for sin and for uncleanness" (Zechariah 13: 1). "There is a fountain filled with blood, drawn from Immanuel's veins; And sinners plunged beneath that flood, lose all their guilty stains."

Verse 8. This verse does not contradict the preceding one or the comments made on it. To say we *have no sin* would be like saying we do not have any need for the blood of Christ. Hence even a faithful disciple should admit his weaknesses and understand his dependence upon the blood of Christ for his cleansing.

Verse 9. *Confess our sins.* This does not say that we are to confess that we have sins for that would be so general that it would be virtually no confession at all; the sins themselves is what we are to confess. Sometimes persons will come forward in a meeting saying they wish to make a confession, and when given the opportunity will say, "I have not been living as I should." That does not confess any sin as our verse requires. It may be replied that David made that sort of confession to the prophet because all he said was, "I have sinned." That is true but it was after his sin had been pointed out so that his statement was an acknowledgment of the specific sin. It was like the action of a jury that says, "We find the defendant guilty as charged" without naming any particular misdeed. If a disciple does not know of anything wrong he has done then he has none to confess. Should he have some faults of which he is not aware, verse 7 of this chapter will take care of them. If he has committed sins which only he and the Lord know about, then he needs only to make his confession to Him. *Faithful and just.* The first word means He will keep his promise to forgive the sins of the penitent, and it is *just* for Him to do so since the sacrifice of Christ makes it possible for God to be merciful and just at the same time (Romans 3: 26).

Verse 10. *Have not sinned* differs from *have no sin* in verse 8 because it goes back over the past of our lives. When the two are considered together they mean that there never has been a time since we were old enough to be responsible, that we were "as free from sin as the angels" as it is sometimes expressed; hence man has needed a Saviour all the years of his life. *Make him a liar.* If a person makes an assertion that contradicts what another has said, it is equivalent to calling him a liar even though no direct reference is made to him. God has said in his word that all men are sinners (Ecclesiastes 7: 20), therefore if a man says he has not sinned he contradicts the Lord and that is why John says such a man will *make him a liar. His word is not in us* because that word declares that all men have sinned.

1 John 2

Verse 1. *My little children* is a fatherly address to the disciples since John was an old man when he wrote this epistle. Furthermore, notwithstanding his strong language when treating of definite sins, he is known in history to have been a man of tender sentiments, so much so that he won a like feeling from Jesus, for it is said that he was the disciple "whom Jesus loved" John 13: 23; 19: 26; 20: 2, 21: 7, 20, 24). Thus we have a number of endearing terms in the writings of this apostle. *That ye sin not; if any man sin.* These phrases do not conflict with each other although they may seem to. The disciples of Christ are expected to oppose sin and be constantly "striving against sin" (Hebrews 12: 4), and to help them in their struggles the apostles have written instructions on the right ways of life. But in spite of all this they are going to make mistakes. (See the comments on verses 6-8 in the preceding chapter.) Hence the second phrase *if any man sin* is inserted to explain why the provision has been made for an *advocate.* That is from PARAKLETOS, which Thayer defines as follows: "One who pleads another's cause with one, an intercessor."

Verse 2. *Propitiation* means something that appeases or satisfies one who is (justly) making strong demands. God is violated by the sins of mankind and His justice demands the eternal condemnation of the offenders. Man was unable to furnish what was rightly required to pay the debt, but Jesus was able and willing to do so. That is what he did when He shed his blood as was shown in chapter 1: 7. *Not for ours only but also,* etc. The pronoun stands for disciples who have already made use of the cleansing blood by obedience to the Gospel. But the blood is sufficient to cleanse the whole world if all will accept it on the same terms as the present disciples. (See the familiar passage in John 3: 16.)

Verse 3. *Know* is not used in view of some technical distinction between faith and knowledge. The thought is that *if we keep his commandments* (and we may *know* whether we have done so or not), then we may be sure or have the assurance that we have a saving knowledge of Him.

Verse 4. A knowledge of having kept the commandments is necessary to a knowledge of Him (see preceding verse). Therefore if a man asserts that he knows the Lord when he has not kept the commandments (and he may know whether he has or not), he is rightly classed with liars as the apostle here states.

Verse 5. *The love of God perfected* has virtually the same thought as Jesus expressed in John 14: 21. To be perfected means to be made complete, and that will be accomplished when a man proves his love for God by keeping the commandments. On the same principle a man cannot truly claim to love the Lord who does not obey His word, even though he may sing "O how I love Jesus" as vigorously as anyone. *Know that we are in him.* For comments on the word *know* see those at verse 3.

Verse 6. To abide in Christ is equivalent to walking with Him, for Christ is an active being and no person can continue with Him and not walk in the same way. "Can two walk together except they be agreed?" (Amos 3: 3.)

Verse 7. The word *new* may mean with reference to its age or date. In that sense the divine law is not new because God has placed governing law before man ever since he has existed. On that basis it is *the old commandment* and they had heard it *from the beginning.*

Verse 8. The commandments of the Lord are *new* in the sense of being fresh and vigorous (not infirm as with old age). The newness or liveliness of the laws of the Lord is manifested in their being able to dispel the darkness of ignorance, and shed the light of knowledge in the Lord.

Verse 9. This is the same in thought as several preceding verses, namely, that true love is manifested by showing an obedient spirit toward the law of God, and that law requires a disciple to love his brother.

Verse 10. *Occasion of stumbling* denotes being the cause of another's stumbling or committing error. If a man loves his brother he will not put any stumbling block in his way (Romans 14: 13).

Verse 11. *Darkness is figurative* and means the absence of truth. The truth of God requires that the brethren love each other, hence if one brother hates another he is not walking according to the word of God but is *walking in darkness.*

Verse 12. In this and the two verses following the writer uses the different age groups in a natural family to compare the ones with different talents and experiences in the family of God. *Little children*, therefore, cannot mean those usually designated by the term, since they do not have sins to be forgiven. It is used in view of some of them who were recent additions to the divine family by the spiritual birth.

Verse 13. As *fathers* in the natural family would be mature and ripe with the experience of age, so there are those in the church who have that qualification over other brethren. *Young men* are more mature than little children and have lived long enough to have demonstrated their strength in the contests of life. In the preceding verse the *little children* are given mention because of their purification from sins. Now they are named because of their knowledge of the Father from whom they have received the forgiveness of their sins.

Verse 14. This verse adds no special thoughts to the preceding two, except to indicate their importance by the repetition for emphasis.

Verse 15. *World* is from a word that means the inhabitants of the earth. Other passages require us to love our enemies and John 3: 16 says God loved the world. The apparent difficulty is explained by the words *things that are in the world.* We should understand that Christians are not to love the things that the people in the world possess and use for their lustful pleasures. Of course no man can love such things and love the Father also, for He has condemned them and commanded His children to "abstain from fleshly lusts which war against the soul" (1 Peter 2: 11).

Verse 16. The things named in this verse the apostle says are *all that is in the world.* That is not merely an arbitrary declaration made just because the apostle chose to sum it all up that way, but upon examination it will be seen that it is historically and logically true. In Genesis 3: 6 we read: "When the woman saw that the tree was good for food [lust of the flesh], and that it was pleasant to the eyes [lust of the eyes], and a tree to be desired to make one wise [pride of life]," etc. Next we shall consider Luke 4: 1-13. Satan suggested to Jesus a way to get food, which was an appeal to the lust of the flesh. (The obtaining of food was no sin if done by lawful means.) Satan showed Christ the kingdoms of the world which was an appeal to the lust of the eyes. Next he challenged Him to cast himself from the roof of the temple to show the greatness of His power, which was an attempt to get Jesus to yield on a point that would have shown the spirit of pride. Luke says after these three items that "the devil had ended all the temptations," which agrees with John that the three classes of evil are *all that is in the world.*

Verse 17. *World* is still from the word that means the inhabitants of the earth, and the *lusts* are the practices of the same which confirms the comments on the preceding verse. Since this world and its practices are to pass away, it is great folly for a disciple to let his affections be attached thereto. But the doer of God's will *abideth for ever* and hence that is the proper subject to receive our sincere interests.

Verse 18. *Little children* is used in the sense that is explained at the first verse of the chapter. *Last time* could have a number of definitions on account of the second word, hence the thought must be gathered from the use that is made of it. The doctrine of Christ is not directly taught in the Old Testament while He is the central figure in the New. The verse speaks of *antichrists* (which means against Christ) so we understand John means we are living in the last Dispensation. Such is a logical conclusion because the basis of the whole system is belief in Christ (not Moses).

Verse 19. *Went out from us* signifies the antichrists were once associated with the true believers but apostatized from the faith. All this pertains to their outward movements only, for John says that *they were not of us.* Church workers are not mind readers, and if unconverted persons go through the motion of obedience to the Gospel there is no way to detect or avoid it. They obeyed the *form of doctrine* but not "from the heart" (Romans 6: 17). Such persons will wait until some pretext appears when they will show their true sentiments by turning against the church and making false accusations. It is true that John is writing directly about *antichrists* which means those who oppose Christ. The principle is the same, for whoever opposes the church of Christ is an enemy of Him. At heart they are disbelievers in Christ but show their spite against Him by turning against his church.

Verse 20. *Unction* is used figuratively from the ancient custom of pouring oil on the heads of those who were to act in the service of the Lord. In its spiritual sense it refers to the enlightening that the Lord bestowed on the apostles, enabling them to impart the necessary information to the members of the body of Christ. *Ye know all things* means they know all that pertains to life and godliness (2 Peter 1: 3).

Verse 21. Not all inspired writing was done to give new information but also to supplement what had been given (2 Peter 1: 12, 13; 3: 1). Another consideration is that people who have already shown an interest in the truth are glad to have it repeated to them. *No lie is of the truth.* Anything that denies a truth is bound to be a lie, and John was particularly concerned about the truth of the divinity of Christ.

Verse 22. This verse is virtually the same as verse 18.

Verse 23. God and Christ are two distinct persons but are one in divinity, hence to reject the one is the same as rejecting the other. The last half of this verse is not found in some copies of the Greek text and for that reason some translations leave it out. However, it does not add anything that disagrees with the rest of the New Testament, hence no harm is done by retaining it at least to the extent of endorsing it.

Verse 24. *Heard from the beginning* refers to the truth given to the world through Him who is "from the beginning" (chapter 1: 1). If this truth remains in us we will be in fellowship with both the Father and the Son.

Verse 25. The reward for being in fellowship with God and his Son is not of a temporal nature; it is eternal life. That reward will be given to those who are faithful until death, since it will not come in this world but in the next which will be "when earthly things have ceased to be."

Verse 26. To *seduce* a person means to mislead him or cause him to stray from the truth. There were many deceivers in the world who were so expert in their false reasoning that the uninformed were easy victims. For this reason the apostle was writing the warning information to the disciples.

Verse 27. *Anointing* is from the same word as "unction" in verse 20. *Need not that any man should teach you.* This means that no uninspired man should be depended upon for teaching on the great story of Christ. They had the enlightening that had come to them from Christ through the inspired teachers. With such divine guidance they were able to *abide in him* who is Christ.

Verse 28. *Little children* is general and is the same endearing term that

John uses in the beginning of the chapter. With the advantage of the spiritual enlightenment the disciples are exhorted to *abide in him*. This means more than merely being in Christ at times but it should be always. No man knows when Jesus is coming hence it is important always to be in His favor. In that case the disciple will not be taken unawares and be made ashamed, but will be confidently looking for Him.

Verse 29. The Lord is righteous and hence can beget righteous offspring only. The exhortation is for the disciples to honor their family reputation by being righteous.

1 John 3

Verse 1. *Behold* is a term used as a call to attention, directing the minds of the readers to a matter the apostle regards as of special importance. It is the *manner* (sort, kind or quality) of love that the writer wishes to emphasize. God's love was so great that He was willing to demonstrate it by giving us the highest possible honor, namely, taking us into the divine family as children. It is like a very wealthy king who takes a poor man from the depths of poverty and humility, and makes him an heir to the royal estate, only the illustration but faintly compares the circumstance. Since the world knew not the Father it would not recognize those who have been redeemed from the regions of sin, and adopted into the family of the Heavenly King.

Verse 2. In beginning this verse with the word *beloved*, the apostle does so in the same sentiment that caused him to use the term *little children;* it is a term of endearment. *Now* signifies he is speaking of the condition in this life before *he shall appear*. Being a son of God is a spiritual relationship which does not make any change in our personal appearance. That is because we must retain our fleshly body while we live in this world. *What we shall be* pertains to what can be seen as the connection in the verse shows, and John is referring to what our appearance will be after the coming of Christ. He says what that will be *doth not yet appear*. Yet he does know (by inspiration) that when Jesus comes *we shall be like him*. But the apostle did know even as he was writing, what the appearance of Jesus was when he was on the earth, for he appeared as a man with a fleshly body. Hence He will be changed and John was not instructed as to what the new form would be in appearance. Another thing of which he was certain was that *when he shall appear we shall be like him*. If that is the case then we shall be alike since "things equal to the same thing are equal to each other." Then if the saved ones are all alike there will be no distinction between them. This is fatal to the carnal notion that we will recognize our "loved ones" (family relations) in heaven. There will be no male nor female nor other personal distinctions and hence no recognition of one person as to whether he is my father or your brother or the husband of this or that woman: all bodily or personal distinctions are for this life only.

Verse 3. *Hath this hope* means the hope of seeing Jesus and being like him. With such an incentive it is expected that all who have become the sons of God will cleanse themselves of impurity in life and strive to be like his Son.

Verse 4. Since *committeth* is a key word in verse 9 I shall leave my comments on it until that verse is reached. *Sin is the transgression of the law.* It should be observed that John does not say transgression is the only thing that constitutes sin; it is the only phase of the subject being considered at this place.

Verse 5. *In him is no sin.* This is what is meant in John 14: 30 where Jesus says the prince of this world (Satan) cometh "and hath nothing in me." No sacrifice could have atoned for the sins of the world if attempted by a person who was himself tainted with sin.

Verse 6. *Abideth* signifies a continuous life in Christ and not a wavering from side to side. Such a person *sinneth* not which is akin to the word *committeth* as to its ending which will be explained at verse 9. A person cannot *abide in Christ* until he first comes into Him, then if he continues in that relation it can be said that he is abiding in Him. By the same token if a man *sinneth* it is proof that such a person has not yet made his acquaintance with Christ.

Verse 7. *Little children* is general and is used as explained at chapter 2: 1. They are again warned against being deceived which evidently refers to the antichrists who are mentioned in the preceding chapter. The first *he* stands for the faithful follower of Christ and the second *he* means Christ himself. *Doeth* and *is righteous* are related and will receive some more light at verse 9.

Verse 8. **Committeth** and *sinneth* will be explained by the comments on the next verse. *Is of the devil* refers to the practice of sin which was introduced into the world by the devil. *From the beginning* means the beginning of mankind on the earth. Not that he had not sinned before that, for he had, by reason of which he was cast out of heaven (Luke 10: 18). But John is here concerned only with the devil's first attack upon man as the rest of the verse indicates. We know that the Son of God *was manifested* in the world to destroy the works of the devil, therefore the word *beginning* can apply only to the beginning of man on the earth.

Verse 9. The two key words in this verse are *commit* and *cannot*. Words, like people, "Are known by the company they keep," which is another way of saying that the meaning of words may be learned by their connection or by the use that is made of them. The first word is from POIEO and Thayer uses three pages of his lexicon with definitions and explanations, which indicates the wide scope of its meaning. Among his comments on the word are, "To follow some method in expressing by deeds the feelings and thoughts of the mind; carry on; describing a plan or course of action." Robinson gives as one explanation, "What one does repeatedly, continuedly, habitually." One of Webster's definitions is, "To pledge; to bind; as, to commit oneself to a certain course." The Englishman's Greek New Testament translates the word by "practice." All of these definitions and translations show the word has no reference to what a man does occasionally or incidentally, but it means what he makes a practice of. The term "practicing physician" does not mean a man who occasionally gives a dose of medicine to a friend. If a man "retires" from the occupation of a carpenter he may occasionally drive a nail or saw a board, yet we would not say he has gone into the occupation again. Likewise a man who becomes a child of God ceases to *commit* sin as a "practice," but that does not mean he will never do anything that is wrong. (See the comments at chapter 1: 7, 8.) We are certain an inspired man would not contradict himself, so John would not use the word *commit* in this verse to mean an occasional sin, when he taught in chapter 1: 7 that even a man who "walks in the light" needs to be cleansed from sin by the blood of Christ.

Cannot is from OU-DUNAMAI, which means morally unable and not that it is physically impossible. We will consider some other passages where the same word is used. Matthew 5: 14 says "A city that is set on a hill cannot be hid." Yet all of us know that during the war many cities and other important places were actually hid by camouflage. In Mark 2: 19 Jesus says of certain persons that "they cannot fast"; does this mean they actually could not refrain from eating? Luke 11: 7 says the man who had retired but was asked to give a friend some bread replied, "I cannot rise and give thee." We know the man did not lack the physical ability of getting out of bed. And so the word in our verse does not mean that the child of God has come to the place where he is physically unable to do any wrong, but that he is morally restrained from it, just as a good man who is asked to join another in some crime would reply, "O no, I couldn't do anything like that." Besides, to say a man has reached a condition where it is impossible for him to do anything wrong, would be like taking from him the necessity of watching his step, and would also make it unnecessary for him to seek the services of the Intercessor. The principle on which all these things are said of the child of God is the truth that he is born (begotten) of God. He has been conceived and born of a parentage that is spiritual and hence that holy characteristic is constantly in his spiritual person to urge him in the right course of life.

Verse 10. *In this* refers to the practice of sin as explained in the preceding verse. *Doeth* is used in the same sense as the word *commit* (or committeth), meaning the continual or general manner of life. The children of the devil may occasionally perform some act that is good in itself but their life as a whole is devoted to the service of Satan.

Verse 11. *From the beginning* means from the start of man's existence on the earth. The message is the teaching that we should love each other.

Verse 12. This verse confirms the comments on the preceding one as to when *the beginning* occurred. The case of Cain and Abel is the first one in the divine record that pertains to the subject of love. Cain would not have slain his brother had he loved him. John's explanation of the cause of the lack of love is that his own works were evil while those of his brother were righteous. It seems strange that such a circumstance would cause the hatred. The basic or remote cause actually was envy which gave him a feeling of spite.

Verse 13. *Marvel not* means not to be surprised or wonder at it, because such an attitude is to be expected. Jesus taught the same thing as recorded in John 15: 18, 19, and it is also taught in 1 Peter 4: 12. The world will hate a faithful disciple of Christ on the same principle that Cain hated his brother. The righteous life is a constant rebuke to the unrighteous ways of the world and causes it to hate the righteous people.

Verse 14. The absence of love for the brethren is proof of one's being still out of the body of Christ. Those who actually enter the spiritual body will necessarily have a fellow feeling for the members. The act of entering the body is equivalent to passing from death unto life. John says *we know* in the sense that we have the direct evidence, namely, our mutual relation to each other in Christ. The last sentence of the verse is merely the reverse of the forepart. With this verse before us we may conclude that genuine evidence of brotherly love is not just the sentimental feeling, but it can be claimed only after a person has passed from death unto life. There will be more said on this subject when we come to chapter 5: 2.

Verse 15. Cain slew his brother because he hated him, so that the poison of murder was in his mind before he talked with him. Others may have the same kind of hatred in their heart but do not have the opportunity of carrying it out. The Lord can read such a mind and hence will regard that man as a murderer. *Ye know that no murderer*, etc. The Old Testament condemned a murderer and required that he be punished with death (Genesis 9: 6 and many other passages). John is repeating the same condemnation except that he applies it to murderous intent as well as the actual deed.

Verse 16. The words *of God* have been supplied by the translators. The passage means that the Lord gave direct evidence of His love in that he laid down his life for us. This is a beautiful contrast with the man who hates his brother. Such a person not only does not make any sacrifice for another, but takes the other man's life from him. *We ought to lay down our lives for the brethren.* This cannot necessarily mean that we can literally die for the sake of another, except where the other person's life is in danger and we might lose ours in protecting him. The passage refers to the interest or devotion we would manifest for our brethren even to the extent of making great and trying sacrifices. (See Romans 16: 4.)

Verse 17. In this verse the apostle gives a simple example (on the negative side) of what it means to be devoted to the interests of others. *Bowels* is used figuratively because people in old times thought that was the seat of the finer sentiments of the mind. John uses it to mean that when a man closes his sentiments of compassion against such an unfortunate creature as this, he cannot truly claim the love of God.

Verse 18. This verse means for our love to go farther than words; to be proven by our actions. It is a summing up of the preceding verse.

Verse 19. Nothing can give a disciple any stronger confidence than to know that he is proving his love by actions that benefit the brethren. He thereby manifests his relationship with the truth of the Lord which requires us to show practical love.

Verse 20. *Our heart* refers to our mind with its various attributes. Having been instructed to show our love by helpful works, if we do so we will feel assured in connection with the subject. If we fail to do our known duty we will have "a guilty conscience" and be self-condemned. If our own knowledge of neglect causes us to feel condemned, we may be sure that God will condemn us also because He knows our hearts.

Verse 21. This verse is virtually a repetition of the preceding one, except that it is considering a person who has carried out the teaching of practical love.

Verse 22. *Because we keep his commandments* is the condition on which we will receive what we ask. Keeping the commandments includes the obligation of consulting the scriptures to learn what would be right for us to receive. It also includes our doing the things that please Him.

Verse 23. Believing on Christ and loving the brethren (with practical love) sums up the qualities of an obedient child of God. That is because belief in Christ means more than a mere profession. It includes a working faith that will carry out the teaching in James 2: 18, to show our faith by our works.

Verse 24. *Dwelleth in him, and he in him.* The matter of dwelling is a mutual affair between the Lord and his people. Since the subject is a spiritual one it is possible for "two persons to be at the same place at the same time"; it means they are dwelling with each other. *Spirit which he hath given us* enabled the apostles to speak with knowledge on the affairs of the kingdom.

1 John 4

Verse 1. The *spirits* means those men who profess to be speaking by inspiration, such as John mentions in the closing verse of the preceding chapter. The false teachers used that claim to obtain attention from the uninformed. The brethren are warned not to believe every man who makes such a claim, but first *try* them which means to test and examine them by the rule that is given in the next verse.

Verse 2. Nobody denied that a person lived on earth by the name of Jesus Christ, but some denied that He was divine in a body of flesh. That was equivalent to saying that He was not the divine Son of God. That would also mean that Christ had no authority or saving virtue. It was generally known that a person was predicted to come into the world to fulfill the law and the prophets, and to effect a plan of salvation on the merits of His blood. But it was denied by some that the person known as Jesus Christ was the expected one. Hence if a man acknowledged the divinity of Christ it was evidence that he was inspired by the Holy Spirit. Paul teaches this also in 1 Corinthians 12: 3 where he says, "No man can say Jesus is the Lord, but by the Holy Ghost" or Spirit.

Verse 3. This verse merely sets forth the opposite of the preceding one, and completes the rule by which the brethren may *try the spirits*, thus avoiding the misfortune of being misled by the antichrists and other false teachers.

Verse 4. The disciples had *overcome them* (the antichrists) because they were the children of God. He will care for those who trust in Him, and that will insure them the victory over the enemy because God who is in them is greater than the "wise men" of the world who were trying to seduce them.

Verse 5. *They* (the antichrists) *are of the world*, which means they are interested in worldly practices. That is why they are opposing Christ because he condemns their evil ways. But the people of the world will hear their false teaching because it encourages their unrighteous life.

Verse 6. *We* has special reference to John and the other apostles because they had been inspired to write the truth. To *know God* means to have come into close fellowship with Him by obedience to the word that was given by the Spirit. All such persons would logically be inclined to hear the apostles. The conflict between truth and error still is the concern of the apostle. That conflict is determined by whether a man is of God or of the world.

Verse 7. The apostle again comes to the subject of love which seems to have been very near to him. He has a sound reason for such interest in that subject, namely, love and God are inseparable. For that reason if a man is born (begotten) of God he is sure to exhibit love also since it is the family trait of God's children.

Verse 8. On the basis of the affirmative as shown in the preceding verse, if a man does not have love as a predominant factor in his life, it is proof that he has not yet become acquainted with God.

Verse 9. This verse corresponds with John 3: 16.

Verse 10. The example of love was set by the Father and not by man. That is why we have the brief but comprehensive statement in verse 19.

Verse 11. If God was willing to love us first even when we were in sin, we ought to love each other since no one of us is any more worthy than another.

Verse 12. *No man hath seen God* literally, but we may exhibit evidences of spiritual knowledge of Him by having love for the brethren. If we do so it will cause God to *dwell in us* or in our midst spiritually. His love is *perfected* or made complete in us when we follow His example of loving the children of God.

Verse 13. This is the same in thought as chapter 3: 24; see the comments there.

Verse 14. John and the other apostles could testify, because they *had seen* the evidences that the Father has sent the Son to be the Saviour of the world.

Verse 15. See the comments at verses 1-3.

Verse 16. *Known* and *believed*. There is no conflict between these words as might be concluded because of the difference technically between them. The things that were *known* were the evidences, and what they *believed* was based on those evidences, namely, that God had a great love for man. The latter part of the verse has been explained in a number of the preceding verses.

Verse 17. *Love made perfect* means it is complete, and God made it possible for man to have that perfect (or complete) love, to give them *boldness* in view of the judgment day. *As he is, so are we.* To be confident with reference to the judgment, we must be on good terms with God in this world. That can be accomplished only by manifesting that unselfish love that was first shown by the Lord for us.

Verse 18. The Bible does not contradict itself, and when it appears that it does there is always an explanation for it. We know we are commanded to fear God (1 Peter 2: 17), but our present verse says that perfect love will cast out fear. The explanation is very simple which depends on the meanings of the original Greek word *phobos*. Thayer gives us two definitions of the word as follows: "1. fear, dread, terror," and "2. reverence, respect." As we have seen frequently before, the particular meaning of any word must be determined by the connection in which it is used. The connection here shows John is using it in its bad sense which would made it read, "There is no dread or terror in love." If we love God and manifest it by loving our brother, we will not have any dread at the thought of meeting God in the judgment.

Verse 19. This is commented on at verse 10.

Verse 20. John has previously made this same charge, but he adds a logical reason for it here. It certainly is as easy to love a brother who is with us and whose fellowship we can enjoy, as it is to love God whom we cannot see now and must love on the basis of faith.

Verse 21. On the basis of the reasoning in the preceding verse, John commands the disciples not to attempt loving God it they will not love the brethren also, for their profession of love will be rejected.

1 John 5

Verse 1. In the New Testament there is only one original word for either *born* or *begotten* which is *gennao*, hence the connection has to be depended upon in each case to determine which is the proper translation. Since the act of begetting is that of the father, it should be the proper translation in passages where the connection shows that he is the parent being spoken of. On that ground the word *born* in this verse should have been translated "begotten" just as it is in the others. The seed of reproduction is the word of God and it tells us that Jesus is the Christ. Whenever a man believes that truth, he is begotten of the Father. Therefore it says that everyone who loves him who begat (who is the Father) loveth him also who is begotten (and that is the child). All this is logical, for if we love a man we should love his children.

Verse 2. In chapter 3: 14 it is stated that we know we have passed from death unto life because we love the brethren. But that passage does not deal with the question of how to know that we actually do love the brethren, while the present verse does tell us how, namely, that we love God *and keep his commandments*. And so a man's mere assertion that he loves the brethren is not to be accepted. He cannot truthfully make the claim unless he has obeyed the commandments, including repentance, baptism and the others which God has given in the New Testament.

Verse 3. Our love for God is proved only by keeping His commandments. *Grievous* means heavy or burdensome and it certainly should not seem burdensome to obey the commands of the One whom we love.

Verse 4. The *world* means the evil practices of mankind. (See the comments on chapter 2: 15.) If a man truly loves God of whom he was *begotten*, the love he has for his Father will induce him to overcome the evil practices of the world. That is because his love is directed by his faith that was produced by the word of God.

Verse 5. This is the same as the preceding verse except it states how and when one is *born* (begotten) of God. That is when he believes in Jesus as the Son of God as was stated in verse 1.

Verse 6. The pronouns *this* and *he* refer to Jesus as the Son of God. The verse deals with three items that testified to that claim. *He came* means his introduction to the world especially into the public ministry. The *water* refers to his baptism because it was then John the Baptist said he learned that Jesus was the one who was to come after him. The *Spirit* also is mentioned because he appeared in the form of a dove in connection with the voice of God that acknowledged the Son. The *blood* was in evidence when Jesus shed it on the cross, thus concluding the long blood line that began with Adam and ran down through the ages. (Read Luke chapter 3.)

Verse 7. Most translations omit this verse on the ground that it is not in the oldest Greek manuscripts. I will make remarks similar to what were said at chapter 2: 23. The passage does not add anything that is different from the other passages on the same subject, nor will anything be lost if it is left out. With these comments I shall proceed with the next verse.

Verse 8. This verse differs from verse 6 as to date only; each has to do with the threefold testimony for the divinity of Christ. However, verse 6 pertains to the time of His stay on the earth, while this one is continuous and applies to what has been going on since Christ left the earth. The testimony of the *Spirit* is that which is recorded in the New Testament and written by the inspired men. The *water* is in evidence every time a person is baptized, because there is no way to account for the continuation of this plain ordinance other than the fact that it originated in the time of Christ. The *blood* testifies every time the Lord's supper is observed in which is the fruit of the vine, for Paul says (1 Corinthians 11: 26), "As often as ye eat this bread and drink this cup, ye do show the Lord's death till he come." *Three agree in one* means they all bear testimony to one fact, namely, Jesus is the divine Son of God.

Verse 9. *If we receive the witness of men* means that we do receive such witness. It is as if he said "since we receive such witness," etc. It is true that human testimony when confirmed is an established rule of mankind in dealing with each other. The apostle is making the point that we should receive the testimony of God, for it is much greater than mere human testimony. That which God gives establishes the fact that Jesus is His Son.

Verse 10. *Hath the witness in himself*. Not that he produced it by his own mind, but it is testimony that can be received by the mind and hence can be retained there. (See Hebrews 8: 10.) *Made him a liar*. When a man rejects a statement made by another he thereby makes that man out a liar. Otherwise if the other person is not regarded as a liar, there would be no pretext for the first one to disbelieve him. All of this pertains to the declaration of God that Christ is his Son.

Verse 11. *Record* is from the same word as "evidence." John means that in giving to us the evidence of the Sonship of Christ, we are thereby given assurance that we may have eternal life through Him.

Verse 12. The foregoing important truths are summed up in the conclusion that to have life one must have the Son by sincere belief in Him as the source of that life.

Verse 13. *Written unto you that believe* again sets forth the idea that not all of the apostolic writings are given as new information. The purpose for repeating it is stated *that ye may know* or that they may have their faith for eternal life confirmed.

Verse 14. The proviso *according to his will* is important and shows that we are not at liberty to make just any kind of wild request and expect God to grant it.

Verse 15. This verse explains what it means to be heard for our prayers. When we *have the petitions* (granted) then we know that they were scriptural or God would not have granted them.

Verse 16. *Sin unto death*. Not that the man has reached the state of eternal death but is headed *unto* it; his conduct is in that direction. The condition described in Hebrews 6: 4-6 is a clear case of this kind of sin; let the reader see the comments at that place. Paul says it is impossible for another person to renew that kind of sinner to repentance. It would therefore be inconsistent to engage in a prayer service with a brother who has gone so far in deliberate sin that he could not be induced to repent by anyone else,

John says he would not ask anyone to pray for such a brother. The kind of sin that is *not unto death* would be like that mentioned in Galatians 6: 1 where the brethren are told to work for the restoration of the one overtaken. *He shall ask* sounds as if John means for the brother discovering sin in another to do the praying for him, when Peter told Simon to pray for himself. That it true but it is also true that brethren can pray together on behalf of the erring one. Then if he repents the Lord will grant him *life* (forgiveness) for his sins. (See James 5: 15, 16.) The pronouns may be a little confusing the way they are used. The first *he* means the man who sees his brother sin, and the second *he* means the Lord from whom all forgiveness must come. (See Ephesians 4: 32 as to the source of forgiveness.)

Verse 17. *All unrighteousness is sin.* (See the comments at chapter 3: 4.) John makes this statement that it might not seem he is underestimating the seriousness of any sin. He wishes only to show that not all sins are as fatal as others; that there is such a sin *not unto death.*

Verse 18. See the comments at verse 1 for the meaning of *born* and *begotten.* For the verse in general see the comments on chapter 3: 9.

Verse 19. *We* means those who have been begotten of God. *Whole world lieth in wickedness.* World means the inhabitants of the earth as it does in chapter 2: 15. The italicized words mean the same as "all that is in the world" in chapter 2: 16, which explains why the world is said to lie in wickedness.

Verse 20. The word *know* is frequently used by inspired writers to mean a strong assurance, not that it is intended to take the place of faith. It is true that the apostle John could use the word in its technical sense concerning Christ. That is because he was with Him in person during all of his personal ministry. He also knew that Christ had given him the (inspired) understanding which he promised, for just before leaving this world Jesus told his apostles he would send the Spirit upon them which would guide them into all truth (John 16: 13). The *true God* is said in contrast with the false ones that were worshiped by many people. He also is the source of eternal life in that He gave his only begotten Son into the world for that purpose.

Verse 21. *Little children* is explained at chapter 2: 1. Even the best of disciples need to be cautioned against evils that we would not ordinarily expect them to commit. John tells his readers to *keep themselves from idols* which is one of such warnings. Paul told the brethren in Corinth to "flee from idolatry" (1 Corinthians 10: 14).

2 John

Verse 1. John and Peter each called himself an elder. It is not merely an allusion to their age, because they both use an article before it which would make a noun out of the word. *Lady* is from the Greek word KURIA, which Thayer says means "Cyria," and then gives us the explanation, "A Christian woman to whom the second epistle of John is addressed." Robinson defines it, "Mistress, lady," and then adds an explanation much like that of Thayer. In the early days of the Gospel the church in some localities was contained in one family and had its regular assemblies in their house. This woman named Cyria and her children constituted the group to which John wrote this epistle. She is called *elect* which means a person chosen of the Lord through obedience to the Gospel. *Love in the truth* is said because John is using his favorite subject from a religious standpoint. *All they that have known the truth* indicates further that the apostle is speaking of "brotherly love."

Verse 2. *For the truth's sake* denotes that John loves this woman and her children because of their devotion to the truth. This truth *shall be with us for ever,* hence a love that is based on it will be permanent.

Verse 3. This is a form of friendly salutation which many of the writers of the New Testament used. Aside from the brotherly sentiments it expresses, the important principle is set forth that such blessings as grace, mercy and peace are to come from God and Christ if they are to be lasting.

Verse 4. *I found of thy children.* We do not have definite information as to how many of her children John had seen nor just where it was. The important thing is that in conversing with them he found them devoted to the truth for which he greatly rejoiced. This truth in which her children were walking had come by commandment from the Father, so that their lives were not moulded by their own sentiments.

Verse 5. *Lady* is the same as that used in the first verse. *Not . . . new commandment.* (See the comments at 1 John 2: 7, 8 as to why it was not a new commandment.) It pertains to the subject of love which is a precious one especially to John.

Verse 6. Love, like faith, is to be shown by works, hence this verse says that to walk after the commandments *is love;* to walk means to keep moving onward.

Verse 7. This verse corresponds with 1 John 4: 1.

Verse 8. *Look to yourselves* means for them to watch and not let the deceivers get in their evil work of leading souls astray. John had converted them to the Gospel and he did not want to have the disappointment of seeing them perverted by false teachers. That is what he means by *lose not those things which we have wrought.* He did not wish to lose the work he had accomplished in leading them to Christ. *Full reward.* No worker for Christ is to be rewarded with eternal life on the basis of his success in converting people nor on the faithfulness of his converts. But the reward consists in the joy (at the present time) of seeing them faithful. This is virtually the meaning of his statement in 3 John 4 regarding his "children."

Verse 9. This and the following verse is written in view of the warning expressed in verse 8. John is giving this group some instructions on how to detect false teachers. Of course the principles laid down are general in their application and should be observed by churches today. To *transgress* means to go beyond something, or go farther than it indicates. The particular thing that John means is expressed by the words *doctrine of Christ*. The word "to go beyond" offered above as a definition of *transgress* is confirmed by the words in this verse, namely, *abideth not in;* the man who does this *hath not God.* This is logical and consistent with other passages in the New Testament. God is to be found in His word only as far as salvation is concerned, hence if a man leaves the word it necessarily follows that he leaves God. The *doctrine of Christ* cannot be restricted to the teaching that He gives in person, for he is not on the earth now and was not when John was writing. In John 13: 20 Jesus says: "He that receiveth whomsoever I send receiveth me; and he that receiveth me receiveth him that sent me." This shows that the *doctrine of Christ* includes the teaching of the apostles and all others who are inspired.

Verse 10. *This doctrine* refers to the *doctrine of Christ* in the preceding verse where it is explained. A man coming unto the disciples who does not remain true to that doctrine is to be rejected. *Not into your house.* The question is often asked whether this means our personal home or the church building. It means either where the services are being conducted Of course in this particular instance it means the personal home because the church was contained in that place, but the same principle applies with reference to the regular church house. It should be understood this means not to receive him as a teacher. No man can be barred from coming into a church house as a spectator as long as he behaves himself, because it is a public place to which the laws of the land admit all people. And the same applies to the family home when it is used for church services. That is because all gatherings claiming to be by the church must be made public in order to be scriptural, regardless of where they are conducted. This verse requires the church to forbid all false teachers to speak to the assemblies, and if that instruction had always been observed the cause of Christ would have been preserved in many places.

Verse 11. This verse extends the remarks at the close of the preceding one. It shows that we have no right to encourage false teachers even to the degree of expressing our good wishes. If we do we are *partakers* (having fellowship) of his evil deeds and thus become his partner in heresy.

Verse 12. *Not write with paper and ink.* This does not mean that he was thinking of writing by some other method, but that he would not depend upon writing at all. There were so many needed instructions in his mind that he preferred to impart them personally. This is understandable as we know that personal conversations have many advantages.

Verse 13. *Elect* has the same meaning here as elsewhere, namely, a person chosen of the Lord through obedience to the truth (1 Peter 1: 2). I can find no dependable information as to the identity of this *sister,* but since John calls her *elect* we understand she was a faithful disciple and that she had children also interested in the Lord. Friendly salutations were common in those times, and it was natural for these children who evidently were with John to join in friendly greetings to their mother's sister.

3 John

Verse 1. *The elder.* This term is explained at verse 1 of 2 John. There are several persons named Gaius in the New Testament. Thayer notes them in connection with certain passages, and at our verse he says the following: "An unknown Christian, to whom the third epistle of John is addressed." Robinson's Lexicon, Funk and Wagnalls New Standard Bible Dictionary all favor the same identity. He was evidently John's convert, for in verse 4 he is included in "my children." *Whom I love in the truth* is the same thing he says of the "lady" in the preceding book. It means his love for them is because of their devotion to the truth.

Verse 2. This verse is similar to many passages where the grace of God is wished for the disciples. However, in this the writer is first expressing a wish for the physical health of his convert. He is interested in his spiritual welfare, of course, but he seems to know that Gaius is in satisfactory condition in that respect, which is indicated by the words *as thy soul prospereth.*

Verse 3. Some brethren had brought a report of the conduct of Gaius which was favorable. That is the basis of his remark about his soul prospering.

Verse 4. The *joy* over the faithfulness of his convert is the kind of "reward" that he means in 2 John 8. Being one of his converts John speaks of him as being among his children. (See explanation of this subject at 1 Timothy 1: 2.)

Verse 5. *Doest faithfully* denotes that whatever Gaius did he was in earnest about it; not halfhearted. He did his good deeds for others "heartily, as to the Lord, and not unto men" (Colossians 3: 23). To *brethren* and to *strangers* is in keeping with Galatians 6: 10. Paul there says for disciples to "do good unto all men, especially to them who are of the household of faith."

Verse 6. *Have borne witness* was done by the brethren mentioned in the preceding verse. They seem to have been traveling from place to place, or some of them were, which gave them an opportunity for making the report to John referred to. Gaius assisted these travelers in some way for their journey. *After a godly sort* means it was in the name of God and because of their work for Him.

Verse 7. These traveling brethren were evidently engaged in spreading the Gospel, for the next verse speaks about being fellowhelpers to the truth. The Lord has "ordained that they which preach the gospel should live of the gospel" (1 Corinthians 9: 14). Yet Paul refrained from such support in order that he might relieve the brethren of that pressure. The brethren of our verse did something similar, except they evidently made that concession to the people of the nations (Gentiles).

Verse 8. Because of the aforesaid sacrifice John insists that the disciples should voluntarily assist them. *Fellowhelpers to the truth.* A man may not be able to preach the Gospel, but if he supports the man who does so he becomes a partner with him in the work and will be blessed of the Lord for his contribution.

Verse 9. *I wrote unto the church* means the church of which Gaius was a member. This is indicated by some following statements in the book. John insists that he will come to the place to which he wrote the letter referred to, and at the same time trusts to see Gaius face to face. The fact that John wrote unto the church but that Diotrephes ignored the letter, indicates that the epistle was sent to this man as an elder of the congregation. That would be usual to send an official document to the officers, or at least in their care, as we read that Paul addressed his epistle to the church at Philippi to "the bishops and deacons" (Philippians 1: 1). The epistle had something to do with John's proposed visit to the church, since he declares or implies that he is going to make the journey notwithstanding the opposition of Diotrephes. This may raise a question in the mind of the reader whether it is right to visit a congregation against the authority of an elder. It is proper for an apostle to do so, for they were in the church before the elders. (See 1 Corinthians 12: 28 where "governments" stands for the eldership.) *Loveth to have the preeminence.* This thirst for power among the elders is what resulted in the great falling away and development of the Church of Rome. Paul said in 2 Thessalonians 2:7 that the mystery of this iniquity was already at work when he was writing, and he evidently was referring to such characters as Diotrephes. (See "General remarks at 2 Thessalonians 2:)

Verse 10. John expects to come and when he does he will consider the deeds of Diotrephes, namely, his opposition to the apostle. *Prating* means to use false accusations against John in an effort to defend himself. *Malicious words* are the kind uttered with the intent of doing harm. *Not content therewith* is said because he not only opposed John, but opposed the brethren whom he sent to the church as messengers. He also forbade others who would have accepted the messengers, and if they showed friendship for the apostolic messengers, they were excluded from the church.

Verse 11. This whole verse is a kindly exhortation for Gaius to continue in the good life that he is now following which will demonstrate that he *is of God*.

Verse 12. This Demetrius is not found in any other place that I have seen. He was a disciple well spoken of by all who knew him. *Of all, and of the truth itself*. A man could have a good name without deserving it, but the report for Demetrius was a truthful one. John adds his testimony for the good name of this brother by saying *we also bear record*. It is probable that he was to be the bearer of this epistle.

Verse 13. This has the same meaning as 2 John 12.

Verse 14. The usual friendly salutation from *friends*, just another affectionate title from the mind of the loving John. *Greet the friends by name*. This denotes a personal recognition of the faithful messengers who are coming to see the congregation.

Jude

Verse 1. The writer of this epistle calls himself *brother of James*, no doubt because of the prominence of James in the Jerusalem church, the man who wrote the epistle of that name. Neither of these men was one of the twelve apostles as is shown in remarks at James 1:1. This epistle is addressed to *them that are sanctified* which means Christians. (See the comments at 1 Peter 1:1.)

Verse 2. To be *multiplied* means the blessings are to be very abundant.

Verse 3. The definition "thoughtful activity" has been offered the readers for the word *diligence*. Jude says he used it in writing this epistle which indicates its importance, also the trustworthiness of him as an author. *Common salvation* means a plan of salvation that is offered to all people alike, whether they be Jews or Gentiles. *Earnestly contend*. Both words are from EPAGONIZOMAI, which Thayer defines with the single word "contend"; it means that Christians should "face the foe" wherever he is met. *The faith* means the New Testament in which the *common salvation* is revealed. *Once delivered to the saints*. This denotes that the plan was put into the hands of men (who are saints; Christians) and that once is as often as it had to be revealed.

Verse 4. *Crept in unawares* means they came in some underhanded manner to get advantage over the disciples. *Ordained* is from a Greek word that means they were predicted in old times, that they would do the things that would bring *this condemnation*. They misused the grace (favor) of God by making it seem to support their *lasciviousness* (filthy desires). It would be expected that such characters would deny Jesus Christ because he would condemn their wicked deeds.

Verse 5. The importance of reminders is again indicated, for these brethren had known of the history of the Israelites. The point is that it is not enough to start serving the Lord, but it must be continued or He will judge his people.

Verse 6. This has the same point as the preceding verse. These angels had a favorable *estate* at first, but left their *own habitation* (their proper domain). These are the angels that *sinned* in 2 Peter 2:4, and they are kept in *everlasting chains under darkness* which means Hades; they will be judged at the last day.

Verse 7. *Even as* denotes that the people of Sodom and Gomorrha will also be punished at the last day. *Suffering the vengeance* refers to the future judgment day. The last word means a sentence unto punishment the same as 2 Thessalonians 1:9. The destruction of those cities was for this world only and did not constitute the *eternal fire*, for that is to come at the day of judgment. But their destruction in Genesis was intended as an example for the warning of others, and when that calamity came upon them they were given this sentence to be carried out at the last day. *Strange flesh* refers to their filthy immorality as described in Romans 1: 27.

Verse 8. *Filthy dreamers* means they had visions of depraved indulgencies which defiled the flesh. *Speak evil of dignities* is explained at 2 Peter 2: 10.

Verse 9. The reference to Michael is for a contrast on the same principle as 2 Peter 2: 11. *Devil disputed about the body of Moses.* All we know about this dispute is what is said here, but we learn from Deuteronomy 34: 6 that no *man* knew his burying place; that does not say the devil and the angels did not know. We are not told what was the point in their discussion; the important thing is the mildness of Michael in contrast with the false teachers.

Verse 10. This means they act more like beasts than men. (See 2 Peter 2: 12).

Verse 11. *Way of Cain* refers to his life of wicked selfishness, and they are compared to Balaam because of his willingness to be bribed. *Gainsaying* means contention for one's personal desires. Such a person is like Core (Korah in Numbers 16).

Verse 12. *Spots* is a figure of speech drawn from a hidden rock in the sea that wrecks the vessels. Jude says they will come to the feasts of charity (love feasts, 2 Peter 2: 13) for the purpose of *feeding themselves. Clouds without water* is explained at 2 Peter 2: 17. *Trees . . . twice dead* is another figure, indicating something utterly useless; the same is meant by being *plucked up by the roots.*

Verse 13. *Raging waves* is used because such things make great disturbances but accomplish nothing but threatening appearances. *Wandering stars* refers to the planets that seem to have no fixed position and these men are like that. *Blackness of darkness* refers to the "outer darkness" awaiting the wicked.

Verse 14. The Bible does not record this prophecy of Enoch, but Jude was an inspired man and knew what he was talking about. *Seventh from Adam* means he was in that numerical place in the genealogy of Christ. The *ten thousand saints* include those mentioned in Matthew 27: 52, 53. For complete comments on this subject see those at Romans 8: 29, 30 in the first volume of the New Testament Commentary.

Verse 15. This verse describes some of the work Jesus will do when he comes at the last day. *Convince* means to convict and punish these ungodly persons. All their *ungodly deeds* and *hard speeches* are considered as being *against Him.*

Verse 16. *Murmurers and complainers* are usually those who wish to walk *after their own lusts.* They speak *great swelling words* for their effect upon those whom they think they can deceive. Having men's *persons* (desirable appearances) in admiration. That is, they become "respecter of persons" for their own personal advantage. The whole passage describes people extremely selfish.

Verse 17. Another reminder, but this time it is of things spoken before by the apostle. In referring to those who spoke before and mentioning *apostles* with them, it strengthens the conclusion that Jude was not one of them.

Verse 18. A *mocker* is one who makes fun of that which he cannot meet otherwise. The motive they have is their desire to *walk after their own ungodly lusts.*

Verse 19. *Separate themselves.* They put themselves in a different class from the faithful disciples by their wicked deeds. *Sensual* denotes being interested only in things that gratify the senses whether good or bad. *Having not the Spirit* because its teaching is against the kind of life they are following.

Verse 20. *Building up* means to edify themselves by the word which is the source of the *most holy faith* (Romans 10: 17). *Praying in the Holy Ghost* (or Spirit) means to pray according to its teachings in the scriptures.

Verse 21. All who *keep* the commandments will have the love of God, and such persons may expect the mercy of the Lord when he comes to judge the world.

Verse 22. People should be dealt with according to their ability, and also their opportunity for knowing right from wrong. (See Galatians 6: 1.)

Verse 23. *Save with fear* denotes a feeling of terror over the wilful doing of wrong by others. Those deserve no mercy especially and should be dealt with sternly in the hopes they may possibly be rescued, just as we would snatch a person from drowning even if we had to grasp him by the hair of his head. *Hating even the garment* denotes that we should abhor anything that has been near fleshly sin. James 1: 27 says that pure religion consists in one's *keeping himself unspotted from the world.*

Verse 24. This and the next verse are a form of praise to the Lord that is most impressive. *Keep you from falling* will be done according to 2 Peter 1: 10. Christ will present us faultless if we serve him in this life (Luke 12: 8), and He will do this *with exceeding joy* to Him and us.

Verse 25. Transferring the praise to God directly Jude says He is *only wise.* That means that God is the First Cause of wisdom as He is of all things. *Glory* means grandeur and *majesty* means greatness. *Dominion* means domain and *power* means authority. Jude ascribes these dignities to God to last *now and ever.*

Revelation 1

General remarks. In approaching this book for the purpose of writing comments thereon, I am resolved not to resort to speculation or guesswork. True that should be one's purpose regarding every part of the Bible. But the various extremes to which so many would-be interpreters have gone make it especially important to observe this safety principle with this book. One extreme has the position that the book is a deep mystery that the Lord never intended to be understood. The fact that it is a part of the Sacred Volume and that He pronounces a blessing on those who *read* and *hear* and *keep* the things written therein (chapter 1: 3) shows the error of this position. An opposite extreme is that it is "just as simple and easy as any other part of the Bible." At first thought one might not realize the evil of the statement, but it will be manifest by the manner of reasoning that is resorted to, in order to carry out what is thought to be required by the law of consistency. In pursuing such a course it is claimed that the prophecies of the book are literal and attempts are made to find such facts in the history of the world. This theory ignores the statement in chapter 1: 1 which says the book was revealed by being "signified" or by signs and symbols, which rules out literalism in explaining the book as a whole.

We should avoid both extremes mentioned above and seek an explanation that will be consistent with the facts and other truths that are available to us. A sign or symbol must stand for something that is literally true or else its use can accomplish nothing. We should understand, therefore, that the ones in this book point forward to facts that were destined to occur literally in the then future years of the world. Since God knows the future as well as the present or past (Isaiah 46: 9, 10) it was possible for Him to look forward from the time of John and see the events that would occur in the world, including those of the religious and political domains of human activities. It would be unreasonable to suppose that He would direct a man to write a book with symbols which were not in harmony with the facts of history. The business of the student, therefore, is to read the symbols and then seek the explanation in the statements of authentic history. That is the task I have set for myself in writing a commentary on this book.

I shall here write a brief outline of the facts of history, to show the general program that has been and is now and will be carried out, in fulfillment of the predictions that John was told to write in the language of symbols. Many of the specific and detailed incidents of history will be reserved to be cited as the particular passages are reached in our studies. Among the sources of my information are the following: *Ancient Monarchies,* by George Rawlinson; Mommsen's *History of Rome;* Josephus' *History of the Jews;* Myers' *Ancient History;* Decline and Fall of the Roman Empire, by Edward Gibbon; *Mosheim's Ecclesiastes History;* Jones' *Church History;* Eusebius' *Church History;* and many others. Due to the wide field of historical material, it will not be expected that I can cite the actual text of the sources except in particular cases. The Roman Empire was at the height of its power in the time of Christ and the apostles, and continued so through several centuries. Religion was a state affair, being protected and regulated by the government under the direction of the emperor. That of Rome was the pagan or heathen and its worship was in devotion to idolatry. Other religions were tolerated as long as they did not become too conspicuous and did not show signs of interference with the state religion.

Among the religions tolerated was Christianity, started by Christ and propagated by the apostles. At first it was regarded as an insignificant movement and little attention was paid to it by the leaders in Rome. But as it grew in numbers and influence the Empire began to fear for its effect on the state and tried to counteract it by persecution. After a few centuries the church or leaders therein began to grow corrupt, and they sought to concentrate their power with a view to reaching a condition where one man would dominate the entire brotherhood. This ambition for power was held back by the power of Rome whose religion was the pagan or heathen. But a change took place in this Empire that removed the hindrance. In the beginning of the fourth century the emperor was Constantine the Great. He finally professed to be converted to the Christian religion and accordingly gave it the endorsement of the Empire. That resulted in the union of church and state so that the emperor over the government and the bishop over the church, both of whom resided in the city of Rome, were joined in a mutual interest and hence took away the rights or privileges of both the local leaders in the congregations, and those of kings and governors over smaller sections of the Empire. There is a lengthy note under "General remarks" at 2 Thessalonians 2 which the reader should see again.

After the union of church and state was formed there followed a period of twelve centuries known as the apostasy or Dark Ages. During that time the Bible was virtually taken from the common people and everyone both in religious and civil matters had to bow to the dictates issued at Rome by the joint power of the emperor and bishop (who finally took the title of pope). This condition continued until the time of Martin Luther and the other Reformers, who gave the Bible back to their respective countries in the language of their people, resulting in the dissolving of the union of church and state. The preceding paragraphs give a general picture of what actually occurred according to history, and of course the symbols of the book of Revelation should be interpreted in a way that agrees with the facts of history. Various details and specific instances will be related as occasion arises in our study of the book. Before taking up the chapters and verses on the plan that has been followed throughout the Commentary, it should be noted that the symbolical part of the book of Revelation is included in chapters 4 through 20. The three in the beginning and the two at the close of the book will be considered very much like the rest of the New Testament.

Verse 1. The word *revelation* occurs 12 times in the King James Version. It is from APOKALUPSIS and Thayer defines it as follows: "An uncovering; 1. properly a laying bare, making naked." The revelation is said to be of or from Jesus Christ and God gave it unto him. It was to show things that were to come to pass or that were in the future. *Shortly* is a comparative term, for while some things predicted did take place in a short time literally, some of them were hundreds of years in the future. *Signified* is from SE-MAINO, which Thayer defines, "To give a sign, to signify, indicate." (See the comments on "symbols" in General remarks at the beginning of the chapter.) The revelation was sent to John and the bearer of it was an angel of the Lord. The writer is one of the twelve apostles but he uses the term *servant* which indicates his attitude of modesty. In a later verse he refers to himself as a brother to his readers in the kingdom of the Lord Jesus Christ.

Verse 2. *Who* is a pronoun that stands for *John* in the preceding verse and he is the writer of this book. *Bare record* means he is making a record of what he saw, which was according to the testimony of Jesus Christ. It is also the word of God because he gave Christ the authority to make the revelation known to John by an angel.

Verse 3. *Blessed* means happy and it is said of those who read the words of this *prophecy* or book. But the blessing is not on those who read it only, but they also must *hear* it which means to give heed to it. The writer does not stop there but adds the condition that they shall *keep* ("observe"—Thayer) them. These three significant terms certainly do not agree with the notion that the book of Revelation is one to be ignored by Bible students. *Time is at hand*. That is, the general program that was to extend down through the centuries was soon to begin.

Verse 4. Let the reader note the statements at the close of General Remarks, which show that the three chapters will be given before the symbolical part of the book begins. They will consist of letters or epistles sent to a group of churches not far from where John was in exile. *The seven churches* does not mean there were no others in that territory for there were several. It means as if it said "write to the seven that will be named." The number seven was regarded as of special significance in old times, so that it came to be used as a symbol of completeness in many instances. Smith's Bible Dictionary says it was so regarded even among the Persians, Greeks, Indians and Romans. Doubtless the seven churches selected were representative of the general condition in the brotherhood at large, and hence the letters written to them may serve as important instruction for the congregations everywhere and at all times. *Asia* is a small province in what was known as Asia Minor until late years. It was one of the districts to which Peter addressed his first epistle (1 Peter 1: 1). The familiar salutation of grace and peace is given and it is from the same source. However, it is stated in different words, namely, from the One who *is, was* and *is to come*. This means that God always was and always will be. *Seven Spirits*. Paul says there is "one Spirit" (Ephesians 4: 4), so the term is figurative and used in the sense of completeness as symbolized by the number seven. This unit of seven Spirits is *before the throne* because the Spirit has always been an agency of God and Christ in carrying out the divine plans, and it would be appropriate for it to be always near at hand to receive orders.

Verse 5. *The faithful witness* does not imply there are no other witnesses who tell the truth since we know there are many. We therefore must take this to mean that Jesus was the bearer of testimony for God in a preeminent degree. *First begotten of the dead* to die no more (Romans 6: 9). *Prince of the kings of the earth*. All power in heaven and in earth was given to Christ (Matthew 28: 18) thus making Him a prince above all. Jesus showed his love for men by giving his blood for their cleansing.

Verse 6. Made us *kings* and *priests*. The word *kings* is from BASILEUS and I shall quote the definitions of a number of lexicons as follows: Greenfield, "A king, monarch, one possessing regal authority." Robinson, "A king." Thayer, "Leader of the people, prince, commander, lord of the land, king." Groves, "A king, monarch, sovereign, prince, chieftain." Donnegan, "A king." Hickie, "A king." I have quoted thus extensively because there is a tendency upon the part of some to deny that Christians should be called kings since Christ only is king. Yet it is freely admitted that Christians are priests although Christ is our priest also. There should be no difficulty on this point, for Jesus is High Priest, while Christians are inferior priests under Him. Likewise they are inferior kings under Christ who is "King of kings and Lord of lords." Peter says Christians are a royal (kingly) priesthood (1 Peter 2: 9), and Paul told the Corinthians they had "reigned as kings" and furthermore he would that they "did reign" (1 Corinthians 4: 8). Since Christ accomplishes all His spiritual work through the church (Ephesians 3: 10, 12; 1 Timothy 3: 15), it is logical that if He is to be a king his servants are to cooperate in the work. That would make them secondary kings acting under their Chief. *Glory* means grandeur and *dominion* denotes scope or domain; John ascribes them to Christ to be everlasting.

Verse 7. *Behold* is a call to attention because something of great importance is about to be said. *He cometh with clouds*. The two men in white apparel (Acts 1: 9-11) announced the same thing, and Jesus also made the announcement before leaving the earth (Matthew 24: 30; 26: 64). *Every eye shall see him*. The fact that the writer next specifies the executioners of Christ as among those who *shall see him* proves that it will not be restricted to His faithful followers. That explodes the arrogant heresy taught by a group of materialists that Jesus came but that only they have seen Him, and that is because they are Jehovah's Witnesses. *All kindreds shall wail* because they will realize that Christ has come to judge the world. But John and all other faithful servants will not wail because they will "love His appearing" (2 Timothy 4: 8). That is why he exclaims *even so, Amen;* both terms mean virtually the same in effect.

Verse 8. The pronoun *I* refers to Christ because he is the one who is to come in the clouds. *Alpha* and *Omega* are the first and last letters of the Greek alphabet (the language in which the New Testament was written). It is a figure to indicate completeness, similar to saying a man knows his business "from A to Z." *Beginning and ending* denotes the same idea as the other figure, the particular words being selected because Christ was present at all of the works of God from the beginning (John 1: 1-3; Ephesians 3: 9). *Is, was* and *is to come* has the same meaning as in verse 4. *The Almighty.* This phrase belongs primarily to God the Father, but since God is a name for the Deity or Godhead, and Christ is a member of that family, it is proper to ascribe the title to Him also. He is called "The everlasting Father" in Isaiah 9: 6, and it can be understood only because of His relation to the Deity.

Verse 9. John says he is *in the kingdom and patience of Jesus Christ.* It is impossible to be in something that does not exist, hence the kingdom of Christ was in existence in John's day; that disproves the heresy of premillennialists. *Patmos.* A number of reference works give a description of this place which agrees in substance. I shall quote from the Rand-McNally Bible Atlas as follows: "Patmos, to which the apostle John was banished. This lies 20 miles south of the island of Samos, 24 miles west of Asia Minor, and about 70 miles southwest of Ephesus. It is about 20 miles in circumference, and is rocky and barren. Its loneliness and seclusion made it a suitable place for the banishment of criminals; and to it the apostle John was banished by the emperor Domitian, near the close of the first Christian century." John says he was in this isle *for the word of God, and for the testimony of Jesus Christ.* The word *for* is from DIA, which the Englishman's Greek New Testament translates "because of." In other words, John was banished to this lonely spot as a punishment by the Roman emperor, because of his preaching the word of God.

Verse 10. *In the Spirit* means he was in a spiritual rapture in which he could hear and see things that could not ordinarily be heard and seen. *Lord's day.* The New testament religion has no holy days as did that of the Old. However, the Lord arose from the dead on the first day of the week (Mark 16: 9), the church was started on the first day of the week (Leviticus 23: 16; Acts 2), the disciples met on the first day of the week to break bread (Acts 20: 7), and the congregational collection of money was made on the first day of the week (1 Corinthians 16: 1, 2). These facts would give the first day of the week some distinction that is said of no other day. The conclusion is clear that the same day is what is meant by the *Lord's day* in our verse. *As of a trumpet.* The comparison is made because that kind of instrument had a vibratory sound that was intense in quality and far-reaching in volume. John does not mean he thought he heard a trumpet, for verse 12 says he turned to "see the voice." But the voice was so impressive that John likened it to a trumpet. *Heard behind me* is significant. By coming up behind John he could hear the voice before seeing the tremendous display of spiritual imagery accompanying it.

Verse 11. Before turning round the voice delivered the names of the churches to which he said in verse 4 he was writing. The remarks were repeated that are at the beginning of verse 8. *What thou seest, write.* This did not mean only what his eyes would behold, but also what he would hear, for later he is told what to put in the letters to the seven churches.

Verse 12. *Turned to see the voice.* That is he turned to see the source from which the voice was coming, and when he did he saw something more than the speaker. Candlesticks (or lampstands) for the purpose of light were used in the tabernacle services (Exodus 25: 31-37), but in that case there was only one unit that had seven parts to it. In the present the candlesticks are separate pieces, the reason for which will be seen in the next chapter.

Verse 13. *Like unto the Son of man.* Much of the language addressed to John is worded as if Christ did the talking personally. That is not the case, for He has been on his throne in heaven since his ascension and will remain there until He comes to judge the world (Hebrews 10: 12, 13). All that is said as coming from and concerning Christ is done through the instrumentality of an angel. (See chapter 22: 8.) The long garments were worn by the priests, and the girdle of gold around the breast betokened a king. All this was very appropriate because Christ is both High Priest and King (Zechariah 6: 13), and this angel was representing Him.

Verse 14. When *white* is used as a symbol, it indicates purity and glory. *Flame of fire.* The first word indicates that the eyes are active and penetrating. *Fire* will consume dross and rid a situation of that which is objectionable.

Verse 15. The original for *brass* is defined by Thayer as follows: "Some metal, like gold if not more precious." *As if they burned in a furnace* is said to indicate the brightness of the appearance. When used figuratively *many waters* means great numbers of people. The significance of this and the preceding verse is to show the dignity and authority of Christ as represented by this person.

Verse 16. *Had in his right hand* denotes the ability to grasp and support the things named. It is similar to a familiar saying that "God holds all things in the hollow of His hand." We will learn in verse 20 what the seven stars represent. *Sharp twoedged sword* is the word of God (Hebrews 4: 12). The original for *countenance* means the appearance in general, but in this passage Thayer defines it, "Face, countenance." In comparing this person's face to the shining sun (a condition when the sun is not obscured by clouds), the purpose is to indicate the penetrating brilliance of the Lord's face.

Verse 17. The sight and sound of this wonderful being so overcame John that he was prostrated with fear. Not that he was rendered unconscious for then he could not have been benefited by encouraging words which were spoken to him. *Fear not* indicates that John was affected with a feeling that perhaps something was about to happen for which he was not prepared. Hence he was given this assurance that the one who was before him was He that was *the first and the last.* Verse 8 tells us that the phrase refers to the Lord who is being represented by this angel.

Verse 18. This verse gives further items of the dignity and power of the person speaking to John. *Liveth, and was dead* identifies him as Christ since the Father was never dead. *Alive for evermore* is further proof that it is Christ because that is declared of him (Romans 6: 9). The person who holds a group of *keys* has the power or authority to open and shut. The places where Christ can use these *keys* will next be named. *Hell* is from HADES, which is the abode of departed spirits. *Death* is from THANATOS, which is the state of the body after the spirit leaves it. The passage as a whole means the Lord has the power or control over the bodies and souls of men. That is why Jesus said what he did in Matthew 10: 28.

Verse 19. The subject matter of what John is to write is divided into three parts, namely, what he *hast seen, are,* and *shall be;* past, present and future. However the past goes back only to the things he had seen since coming as an exile to Patmos.

Verse 20. A *mystery* is anything not revealed or understood, and it is here applied to some of the things which John *hast seen* and which until now had not been explained to him. The seven stars are the angels of the seven churches and the seven candlesticks represent the churches. Since the angel is telling John what are represented by the stars and candlesticks it is foolish for men to offer speculations on the subject. *Angels of the seven churches.* The word for *angel* in the New Testament is AGGELOS, which means primarily "a messenger." But it has several shades of application and each case must be considered separately. We should adhere to what the text says and then we will be on safe ground. The angels of these churches are spoken of in the singular number for each church. The churches were establshed ones and hence had elders who are always spoken of in the plural. Therefore all we know and all we need to know is that these angels were not elders but were persons who were responsible for getting the letters before the respective congregations. For that reason John was instructed to write the letters to these angels, and they in turn would see that the documents would be delivered to the churches in the proper way to make them responsible for the admonition and/or encouragement contained therein.

Revelation 2

Verse 1. See the comments on last verse of the preceding chapter for explanation of *the angel.* This letter is written to the same church at Ephesus to which Paul wrote his epistle bearing that name. The beginning of this church is recorded in Acts 18: 19. Before John wrote his letter to it the congregation had been placed under elders (Acts 20: 17). The Authority for this letter identifies himself by repeating chapter 1: 13, but adding the significant fact that he *walketh in the midst of the seven golden candlesticks.* This signifies that Christ is present (in spirit) and knows what is going on in the churches of the brotherhood.

Verse 2. This and the following verse will name a number of things in the conduct of the church that are favorable. By doing that the Lord sets a good example of giving due credit which would be well for disciples to follow in their treatment of others. *I know thy works*. The Greek for the first word has many shades of meaning but they are classified under virtually two groups only, namely, to know in the sense of being aware of, and to know in the sense of acknowledging or approving; the connection must determine which is used. In our verse the Lord means he approves of the works which are mentioned. *Labor* and *patience* means they were persistent in their labors. They were very good negatively in that they could *not bear them which are evil*. They were faithful in detecting and exposing false teachers. (See 1 John 4: 1.)

Verse 3. *Borne* and *patience* are virtually the same as labor and patience in the preceding verse. The main idea is that they had followed such a course for a long time. They had likewise done these things for the Lord's *name's sake*, which denotes a proper motive technically for their *labors*. *Have not fainted* means they had been unfaltering in their religious activities.

Verse 4. *Nevertheless*. This single word conveys a very important truth, namely, while the Lord does not fail to see all the good a disciple does, yet that will not cause Him to accept the service unless it is correct as a whole. *Left thy first love*. This phrase may be illustrated by the warmth of feeling that exists in the first part of the relation of husband and wife. The word *love* is from AGAPE and its chief meaning is to have that regard for another that will cause one to be interested in his welfare and happiness. Such a love will prompt one even to "go out of his way" to do things to please the other. Likewise a Christian should have such a feeling for his brother and for Christ who is the bridegroom of the church. This going "out of his way" does not mean to go beyond the lawful regulations, for that would not be pleasing to a bridegroom regardless of its motive. But there are countless instances where a Christian can make a special exertion to show his love for the Lord. The church at Ephesus had fallen into the frame of mind where it performed its services from the legal standpoint only, and it had ceased to be a "labor of love" as Paul mentions in 1 Thessalonians 1: 3.

Verse 5. *From whence thou art fallen*. They had fallen from a condition of fervent love for Christ and his cause to one of legal or technical formality. *Repent*. They have not been charged with doing anything wrong; everything they did was right as far as the acts themselves were concerned. It was what they were *not* doing that made up the Lord's objection to them; they were right affirmatively but wrong negatively. Yet they were told to repent, which shows a disciple may be condemned for what he is not doing. (See Hebrews 2: 3.) *Do the first works* means those extra acts of love they did in the beginning of their service to Christ, not that they must repeat the first principles of the Gospel. *I will come quickly*. He was already walking round midst all the churches, but this means He will come specifically to this particular church to judge it. *Will remove thy candlestick*. Now we can see the reason for the remarks at chapter 1: 12 about the seven candlesticks being separate items. That makes it possible to remove one without disturbing the others. Another important thought is signified in this circumstance, namely, the churches of Christ are independent units as to their government and have no official connection with each other. It should be noted further that notwithstanding the complaints the Lord had against the church, He did not threaten to remove its candlestick (which would be His way of rejecting this church) unless it failed to repent. In connection with this case it is well to consider Matthew 11: 20 where Jesus upbraids some wicked cities "because they repented not." In Luke 13: 3, 5 He declares certain ones will perish "except they repent." In 2 Peter 3: 9 the wicked need not perish if they will "come to repentance." This group of kindred passages gives us an insight into the principle on which God deals with mankind. A church (or individual) does not forfeit its standing with God at the mere point of doing wrong (else we all would be falling daily), but it is when it does wrong and refuses to repent of it.

Verse 6. *Nicolaitanes*. There is little definiteness in the treatment of this subject by the histories and lexicons and other works of reference. Thayer merely comments that they were "the followers of Nicolaus," a heretic in the time of the apostles. Robinson makes similar remarks about the subject. We note that both the deeds and the doctrine of this sect are condemned. It had something to do with a life of fleshly indulgencies. The church at Ephesus rejected this sect which was one other point in its favor stated in the letter written by John.

Verse 7. *He that hath an ear* does not imply that some people are without ears literally, but this is a solemn call upon all to give profound attention to what is being said to the churches. *What the Spirit saith* is the same as what the Lord says for He uses the Spirit to direct John in writing the letters. *To the churches.* There is no indication that the seven letters were to be circulated generally among the seven churches. Instead in each separate instance the instruction is to write a certain letter to a particular church. Therefore the phrase *to the churches* signifies that what the Spirit says to any certain church that may be named among the seven, the Lord intends to be for the instruction of the churches of Christ everywhere. This "call to attention" is made in connection with each of the seven letters and will not be commented upon after this one. But the promises that are made are different each time, hence that part of the letters will be commented upon as we come to them. *Tree of life... paradise of God.* The phrasing about the tree is based on the one that was in the garden of Eden. Man lost that tree by sinning, but it may be regained in a spiritual form by proper conduct, namely, by *overcoming* his sins while in this life. *Paradise* comes from a word that may mean any place of bliss or happiness. That is why it is used in reference to the abode of the righteous after death (Luke 23: 43), and to the place where God dwells and will be the abode of the righteous after the judgment. Paul calls it both by "paradise" and "third heaven" in 2 Corinthians 12: 2, 4. John had a vision of the tree of life as he describes it in chapter 22: 2. The reader may see a fuller description of the original word for *paradise* at Nehemiah 2: 8 in Volume 2 of Bible Commentary.

Verse 8. See the comments on last verse of the preceding chapter for an explanation of *the angel.* Smyrna is one of the places that received a letter John was told to write. The description of the One who was dictating the letter is the same as in chapter 1: 18; the same who was walking in the midst of the churches. This is one of the two that received no rebuke from the Lord in the letters to the seven churches.

Verse 9. *I know thy works.* See comments at verse 2 for the general definition of this phrase which is used at the beginning of each of the seven letters; in this place it means the Lord approves of their conduct. *Tribulation* refers to the oppression being put upon this church by the enemy. A part of this resulted in the loss of their possessions which brought upon them a condition of poverty. *But thou art rich.* They were poor as far as this world's goods was concerned but were "rich in faith" (James 2: 5). *Say they are Jews, and are not.* They belonged to the Jewish race but were not true to their religious profession; such people frequently joined with the heathen in persecuting the Christians. *Synagogue of Satan* means they really were serving the interests of Satan and hence were to be classed with his agents. Such insincere Jews would assemble in their synagogues for their pretended services to God, but due to their hypocrisy the Lord considered it a synagogue of Satan.

Verse 10. Imprisonment as a persecution was to be one feature of their tribulation which will be credited to the devil. *Ten days* is a figurative reference to a series of persecutions that were heaped upon the church under the opposition from the Roman government. This was to become a trial of their faith, and the Lord consoles them with the assurance that they need *fear none of those things. Faithful unto death.* Even death cannot defraud a true disciple of his reward. *Crown of life.* A crown is a decoration for being victor over a foe and such a token is worthy those who remain true to the Lord in the presence of death. Their body may die in His service but it will not deprive them of eternal life. (See Luke 12: 4.)

Verse 11. *He that overcometh* means the one who is "faithful unto death." The *second death* means the lake of fire (chapter 20: 14) which cannot hurt the faithful.

Verse 12. The author identifies himself in this place by His possession of the *sharp sword with two edges.* This refers to the word of God which is described in Hebrews 4: 12. The Lord says he *hath* this sword or that He originated it and has a perfect knowledge of the proper use of it. *And to the angel* is explained at chapter 1: 20.

Verse 13. *I know thy works.* (See comments at verse 2.) *Know* is used in the sense of approval with regard to the *works* in this verse. *Where Satan's seat is.* Pergamos was in one of the worst centers of idolatry, making the temptation all the greater. This church as a whole withstood the influence of heathendom, holding fast to the name of Christ as the true person to worship. *Not denied my faith* denotes that they maintained the basis of that faith or system of religion which was the Gospel. Not much is said elsewhere about this Antipas further than what is said here. He is referred to as a "martyr" even as it is in our passage. However, the reason for so classifying him is an error, namely, because it is said that he *was slain* for his faith. He was a martyr before being slain because death is not what makes a man a martyr; it only proves that he was a martyr. That term is from the same Greek word as "witness" and it means the same. It is the word for "witness" in Hebrews 12: 1 where we know Paul is speaking about the faithful servants of God enumerated in the preceding chapter. We also know that some of those "witnesses" (martyrs) did not die, for they "wandered in deserts and in mountains." Hence a martyr is one who is true to the testimony of the Lord come what may, whether it be death or loss of goods or banishment like the case of John. Accordingly in the case of Antipas; he went to his death because he had been a true and *faithful martyr* for Christ.

Verse 14. *Thou hast there* means the church was holding within its fellowship these characters. *Hold the doctrine* denotes that they believe and retain and endorse it. The *doctrine of Balaam* is briefly stated in direct connection with this passage. It pertains to the advice that Balaam gave Balac after the four speeches that he (Balaam) made under the control of the Lord. The historical account of it is quoted from Josephus in connection with Numbers 25: 1-5 in Volume 1 of Bible Commentary. The persons in the church at Pergamos were endorsing the same practices which were a mixture of idolatry and immorality.

Verse 15. See the comments at verse 6 on the Nicolaitanes.

Verse 16. *Repent.* (See comments at verse 5 on this subject.) *Fight against them* means a spiritual war since the weapon is the *sword of my mouth.* It means these guilty members will be exposed and condemned by this sword which is the word of God.

Verse 17. *He that hath an ear* is commented upon at verse 7. *Him that overcometh* signifies one who is faithful to the Lord until death. *Eat of the hidden manna.* This is a figure of speech formed from the circumstance recorded in Exodus 16: 32-34; it is referred to by Paul in Hebrews 9: 4. This manna was in the ark in the Most Holy Place where none were permitted to enter and partake. It is used here to represent the exclusive spiritual blessings that the Lord will bestow only on His faithful servants. *A white stone* alludes to some practices of old in which a favored contestant was given this kind of stone as a badge of distinction, on much the same principle as a soldier's decorations. This *new name* also signifies the special relation between a faithful servant and his Lord. *No man knoweth* in the sense that no man can realize or appreciate what it means to be thus blessed of the Lord.

Verse 18. See comments at chapter 1: 20 for the explanation of *the angel.* In this letter the author states his personal name before giving a description of himself and it is the Son of God. Comparing His eyes and feet to *fire* and *brass* is explained at chapter 1: 14, 15.

Verse 19. *I know thy works* is commented upon at verse 2. After naming the works He immediately uses the word *notwithstanding,* which shows that the *works* to which He refers are the things named in our present verse. Since they are all good we understand the word *know* is used in the sense of approval. *Charity* means an interest in the welfare of others, and *service* means the doing of something to assist in that welfare. *Faith* is produced by the word of God (Romans 10: 17) and with the assurance that the divine word is leading them aright, it would cultivate *patience* or endurance in their activities. In the beginning of the verse the word *works* is used as a general reference to their manner of life. It now is used to bring out the fact that they performed good deeds for the welfare of others. *Last to be more than the first.* This is as it should be, for Christians are expected not only to produce the fruits of righteousness but to increase therein (2 Corinthians 9: 10).

Verse 20. Having given the church credit for the good things it was doing the Lord next makes his complaints. *Thou sufferest.* When a church retains a bad character in its fellowship, it becomes a partaker of the evil deeds of that person and will be condemned by the Lord. (See verses 14, 15.) The church at Thyatira was doing so concerning a false prophetess named *Jezebel.* Thayer defines this word, "A second Jezebel," then gives us the following historical statement. "The symbolic name of a woman who pretended to be a phophetess, and who, addicted to antinomianism [the doctrine of faith alone], claimed for Christians the liberty of eating things sacrificed to idols." This statement of Thayer's agrees with the language of the verse.

Verse 21. *Gave her space* (of time) *to repent* indicates the longsuffering of God toward evildoers. *Repent of her fornication.* Doubtless those whose religion was so materialistic as to worship dumb idols also indulged themselves in fleshly fornication. However, it is evident from many passages that idolatry was classed as spiritual fornication in Bible times; one such passage is Jeremiah 3: 9.

Verse 22. This verse indicates that spiritual adultery (idolatry) is what is meant through most of these verses. The Lord here threatens to punish this wicked woman by casting her and her customers into a bed together. That would not be any punishment for a woman who was a literal adulteress. But the form of language is used that indicates something unpleasant was to be inflicted, for it refers to the bed as a place of tribulation. Of course in a case of literal adultery the Lord would regard an impure woman and her patrons as being guilty together. Likewise if a woman entices the professed servants of God to commit idolatry, the whole group would be held as partners in the guilt. (See Matthew 15: 14.)

Verse 23. *Kill her children with death.* This may sound strange to us if we try to be technical, for if a person is killed at all it would mean death. It is what is known as a Hebraism which means an expression peculiar to the speech of the Hebrews and used by others for the purpose of emphasis. The idea is to make the hearer realize the certainty that death is to be inflicted. It is similar to "thou shalt surely die" (Genesis 2: 17), or not to "die the common death of all men" (Numbers 16: 29). *All the churches shall know.* Whatever was going to be done was to be of such a public character as to make it an example. *Searcheth the reins and hearts.* The Lord is able to penetrate the innermost thoughts and expose the evil to the shame of the guilty. *Will give unto every one of you according to your works.* Those who are personally responsible for the conditions will be called to account.

Verse 24. *Unto you I say . . . as many as have not this doctrine.* In every condition of evil there are some who have not endorsed the evils of others, and they are not held responsible for that which they could not prevent. *Not known the depths of Satan.* Not been mixed up in these evil things of Satan who is prompting Jezebel and her partners. *As they speak* refers to the false teaching of this wicked woman and those being influenced by her. *Put upon you none other burden.* The Lord will not condemn them for what they cannot prevent, but He will "burden" them with the duty of abstaining from the evil practices that he has been condemning.

Verse 25. *Hold fast*, or maintain their disconnection with these evil things. *Till I come* is equivalent to saying "until death."

Verse 26. Figurative language must be based on some literal fact or possible fact. Christians are not to exercise any temporal rule over the world on the basis of their religious profession, but they are to be joint rulers with Christ as to spiritual conduct that will please the Lord. (See the comments at chapter 1: 6.) This partnership with Christ is on condition that the disciple is faithful *unto the end*, which means until death if such should be imposed upon him.

Verse 27. An iron rule does not always mean one of harshness, but that metal should also be thought of as being unyielding and strong and enduring under a strain. All the phrases of this verse should be understood in this figurative sense.

Verse 28. *Morning star.* Jesus calls himself the "morning star" in chapter 22: 16. The significance of this phrase is due to its brightness as it precedes the sun in rising, thus announcing that a new day is dawning. (See 2 Peter 1: 19.) The present verse means that the faithful disciple will be given the spiritual brightness of Christ.

Verse 29. *He that hath an ear.* (See verse 7.)

Revelation 3

Verse 1. The Lord identifies himself as the one who has the seven *spirits of God*. Robinson says the following about this numeral: "The number *seven* was often put by the Jews for an indefinite round number. Likewise as a sacred number, of good omen, as also among the Egyptians, Arabians, Persians, etc." (See the comments at chapter 1: 4.) *I know thy works* is used in the sense of disapproval for it is directly followed by something that is bad. This church was alive as far as its profession and reputation were concerned, but in reality as the Lord saw it the church was dead.

Verse 2. The aforesaid charge of being dead is relative for dead people cannot do anything. Yet these people are exhorted to do something about that which is *ready to die*, which shows that some prospect of life was in sight. *Not found thy works perfect.* The church as a whole had some good qualities but it was not as good as it could and should be considering its opportunities.

Verse 3. *Remember ... received and heard.* God holds men responsible according to the information and other advantages they have received (Luke 12: 47, 48). The church at Sardis had been given Gospel instruction and ought to have known better than think that a mere profession is sufficient. That is why it is warned to *hold fast* which means to preserve the talents that were given to it and also to develop them (Matthew 25: 16). *Repent.* This is another instance where disciples are exhorted to repent of a negative wrong. These people were guilty of not rising above a mere profession or reputation. They must bestir themselves and prove their right to such a name by more spiritual activity. Furthermore if a person does not make the progress or growth he should, he is sure to go the other way and become tainted with the evil things around him and thus *defile his garments* as most of these disciples had done. *Come on thee as a thief.* The Lord does not compare himself to a thief, only the hour of His coming is likened to one; for that reason it is important to be watchful.

Verse 4. *Hast a few names* means there were a few persons in Sardis who had not become defiled. We have already seen that God does not hold anyone responsible for what he cannot prevent (chapter 2: 24); so it was with these *few names* in Sardis. *Walk with me in white.* White is an emblem of purity and is always so used in the Bible when taken figuratively (Psalms 51: 7; Isaiah 1: 18; Revelation 19: 8). This promise looks beyond the day of judgment to the eternal association with Jesus in the home of the soul. However, it does not wait until then for its fulfillment in every sense. It also includes the fellowship with Christ that a faithful disciple may claim and enjoy in this life. "When we walk with the Lord in the light of His word; What a glory He sheds on our way!" (See 1 John 1: 7.) *They are worthy.* We sometimes hear brethren criticize a familiar phrase "save us if worthy," and they will object that "none of us can ever be worthy." Jesus says we can, but he does not say that it is through the merits of our deeds. The worthiness consists in our relationship with the Lord as shown in the passage cited in 1 John above.

Verse 5. *He that overcometh* is the same as being faithful until death. *Clothed in white raiment* is explained at the preceding verse. *Not blot out his name out of the book of life.* It is a universal practice for institutions that consist of individual membership to keep a record of its names in a book. The fact is a basis for the figurative idea of a *book of life* in which the Lord keeps a list of his people (Malachi 3: 16; Luke 10: 20; Hebrews 12: 23; Revelation 20: 15). The point is that all whose names are there may be considered as those who are in good standing with the Lord. But their names are not put there with "indelible ink" but they may and will be *blotted out* if they are not faithful. *Will confess his name* is the same promise that Jesus made while on earth (Matthew 10: 32).

Verse 6. *He that hath an ear* is commented upon at chapter 2: 7.

Verse 7. The church in Philadelphia was another that did not receive any rebuke in the letters (the one at Smyrna being the other). The most of this verse is used in describing the One who is authorizing this letter. *Holy* and *true* may be said of all true servants of God but it is true of Christ in a complete sense. *Key of David* refers to the authority that was predicted for Christ because he was to come into the world as the most noted descendant of that great ancestor. (See comments at chapter 1: for meaning of *key*.) That explanation will show why the opening and shutting are mentioned as pertaining to Christ and not to any mere man.

Verse 8. *I know thy works* is said in the sense of approval since everything said about this church is good. The *open door* is figurative and means the door of opportunity to advance the Gospel as it is expressed at 1 Corinthians 16: 9; 2 Corinthians 2: 12; Colossians 4: 3. *No man can shut it.* Man can hinder and persecute the disciples but he cannot actually prevent them from carrying out the Gospel life in the world. *Hast a little strength.* They are commended for being faithful even though their strength is not great, a condition which they cannot help. *Kept my word* means they had been true to the commandments in the word of God. *Not denied my name* means they were not ashamed to confess the name of Christ as explained at verse 5.

Verse 9. *Synagogue of Satan* is commented upon at chapter 2: 9; *say they are Jews and are not* is explained at the same place. *Worship.* This term comes from about 12 different Greek words and has a variety of meanings. A complete extract from the lexicon on the subject may be seen at Matthew 2: 2 in the first volume of the New Testament Commentary. At our present passage the word refers to an act of courtesy or admiring respect, as if to congratulate another over some favor that has been granted him. That favor is expressed by the words *to know that I have loved thee.*

Verse 10. *Word of my patience* denotes that they had endured according to His word. As a reward for their patience the Lord will *keep them* or preserve them when the *hour of temptation* (or trial) comes. Such a promise is so far-reaching, that it could refer to the specific siege of persecution that the pagan government was about to wage against the church, or to tribulations from the world in general.

Verse 11. *Behold* is an expression to arouse attentive interest. *I come quickly* would apply to the personal coming of Christ to judge the world, or to the close of their life at which time all opportunity for service will cease. In either case the important thing is to *hold that fast which thou hast* which means to maintain their present life of faithfulness. *That no man take thy crown.* Not that one man can literally get possession of a crown that belongs to another. But if a disciple suffers the enemy to mislead him it will cause him to lose his crown.

Verse 12. *Him that overcometh* is equivalent to being faithful until death. *Make a pillar* is a figure of speech signifying a fixed or permanent place in the favor of God, and *go no more out* emphasizes the same thought. *Write upon him . . . name of the city.* Another figure meaning the faithful servant will be recognized as a citizen of the celestial city. (See Philippians 3: 20.) *My new name* means a name that will signify a victorious life for Christ. (See comments at chapter 2: 17.)

Verse 13. *He that hath an ear* is explained at chapter 2: 7.

Verse 14. See the comments at chapter 1:20 for significance of *Angel*. The *Amen* is given special meaning here by the words *the faithful and true witness.* This is logical since the word *amen* means "so be it" or is an endorsement of some stated or implied fact. A true witness would not endorse any declaration that was not correct. *The beginning of the creation of God.* This is equivalent to the statement in Colossians 1: 15 that Christ is "the firstborn of every creature." The reader will do well to see the comments at that place also on a number of verses following it. The "beginning of the creation" coincides with John 1: 1-3 where Christ is said to have been "in the beginning," then explains it with the declaration that "all things were made by Him."

Verse 15. *I know thy works.* Again this is used in the sense of disapproval for it is followed immediately with something that is bad. *I would thou wert cold or hot.* The figure is based upon the idea of food and its agreeableness to the taste. Some articles are supposed to be eaten hot and others cold. If either kind becomes neutral on the subject of temperature it will be objectionable. Also there are some articles of food that are suitable in either condition, but it is not desired that they be between the two states. On that basis as an illustration the Lord desires his disciples not to be neutral.

Verse 16. No parable or illustration should be strained in the application. This one does not teach that God would be pleased at all with one who is cold in his religious practices—that point is not being considered in the least in this illustration. The only idea is with the comparative preference for something cold over a lukewarm article. When we make the application the reason for this preference is evident. If a professed disciple is cold it will be clearly recognized by the world, and he will not have much influence in keeping others from the service of Christ through his example. On the other hand, a lukewarm disciple may be a tolerably good man so that others may admire him. Yet he is not urgent in advising them to be busy in the Master's service and consequently his influence will be detrimental to the cause of Christ and for that reason he will be rejected. Retaining the same subject matter for his figure, the Lord threatens to treat this church as a man would a piece of food that he took into his mouth and found it had become lukewarm; he will *spew* (spit) it out of his mouth.

Verse 17. The outstanding thought in this verse is to show how much a church can be self-deceived as to its real condition. Doubtless it possessed all of the things named of a temporal nature. One of the evil effects of earthly riches is to mislead their owners into a feeling of independence or self-sufficiency. That is why Jesus speaks of "the deceitfulness of riches" in Matthew 13: 22. The condition of this church was the opposite to that of Smyrna which was poor in this world's goods but was rich in faith. Our present case is one of complete deception, for the church had concluded that it had *need of nothing*. We often hear the remark that some man "is independently rich," which is just the state of mind the church at Laodicea was cherishing. The Lord admits that those people did not know (or realize) what their actual condition was from a spiritual standpoint. *Wretched* is defined by Thayer, "Enduring trials and troubles." They had a good many conflicts because of their lack of spiritual worth, but their confidence in their wealth gave them a false sense of triumph over them all. *Miserable* virtually refers to the same condition as being wretched and their deception covered their situation also. *Poor* in faith while rich in the perishable things of this world. *Blind* means their eyes of faith had become entirely afflicted with a spiritual cataract developed from their corroding wealth, and hence they could not see that they were naked.

Verse 18. *Gold tried in the fire* is a figurative name for faith (1 Peter 1: 7.) *White raiment* consists of the righteousness of the Lord's people (chapter 19: 8), and the people could have such raiment to wear if they would follow a life of righteous conduct. *Anoint thine eyes.* In 2 Peter 1: 9 the man who lacked the qualities named in that chapter is said to be "blind," and on that basis the church at Laodicea needed to use the anointment of those virtues to remove the cataract from their eyes.

Verse 19. *Love* in this place is from the word that signifies the warmest sentiments of affection. It makes a strong and unusual situation to say that such treatment of loved ones is the very proof of that love. Yet that is a principle that is true whether a human or divine Parent is being considered. (See Hebrew 12: 6, 9.) *Be zealous therefore.* Since these stern rebukes are evidence of the Lord's love for them, it should induce them to repent with zeal which means to be active about it. The fundamental meaning of repentance is a change from one condition to another for the better. These people were relying on their temporal wealth for gratification and were poor in faith. They now should take on a sincere interest in the spiritual things of Christ and begin serving him by righteous living.

Verse 20. The specific subject matter for the various churches seems to have been completed. This verse represents the general attitude of the Lord toward all human beings. The door is that of the heart into which Jesus will enter if given a welcome. He will not force an entrance into a man's life, for the only kind of service that will be pleasing to Him is a willing service. Hence the human heart must respond to the call of the Lord. *Sup with him and he with me.* In old times it was one of the surest indications of hospitality for a man to eat with another. It also was a token of recognition and endorsement. (See Mark 2: 16; 1 Corinthians 5: 11.) This mutual supping between Christ and his host is a figure of speech to indicate the great intimacy that He offers to share with a human being if permitted to do so.

Verse 21. *Him that overcometh* means one who is faithful under all trails and difficulties. *Sit with me in my throne* is another figurative expression, meaning that such a person will be regarded as having right to that fellowship with Christ in the kingdom, that is stated in 1 Corinthians 4: 8 and 1 Peter 2: 9.

Verse 22. *He that hath an ear* is commented upon at chapter 2: 7.

Revelation 4

Verse 1. With this chapter we start into the symbolic part of this book. I urge the reader to turn back to the "General remarks" at the introduction of chapter 1, and carefully read through the paragraphs, especially for the purpose of being prepared to appreciate what will be said relative to the symbolic and literal features of the book. Bear in mind that literally John is on the isle of Patmos and will be there all through the book. When the langauge seems to take him to some other place it is only figuratively so. When he speaks about going somewhere or of seeing something that we know is not actually out there on that isle, we must understand that he had a vision of such things and is only writing a description of what he sees. *Door opened in heaven* signifies that John was to be admitted into the confidences of the Lord and be told things not known by other men. A voice like a trumpet indicates that it was strong and filled with the characteristic of authority. *Things which must be hereafter* has direct reference to events in the future. However, we should not forget the overall scope of his vision as stated in chapter 1: 19. That passage says he was to write of things pertaining to the past, present and future. That explains why he here tells us of conditions then existing, which will be involved in many of the future events of the book.

Verse 2. *In the spirit* means the vision was opening up before him. The first thing he saw was a throne in heaven and the throne was not vacant; *one sat on the throne.* That indicated that heaven had an occupant who had authority to give rule over the earth as well as over other persons in heaven.

Verse 3. These precious stones are used to indicate the worth and also the brilliance of the one on the throne. The *rainbow* refers to the arched halo that is generally pictured over the head of one occupying a place of authority. *Like unto an emerald.* This is another precious stone that is used to signify the glory about the head of the person occupying the throne.

Verse 4. God has had two organic systems of religion in the world, the Mosaic and the Christian. The former was arranged under twelve tribes (with their heads) and the latter is administered under twelve apostles (Matthew 19: 28). The four and twenty elders represent the two systems of religion. *Clothed in white raiment* signfies a life of righteousness, because all men who live righteously before God, whether they were in the days of the Mosaic system or in those of the Christian, will be permitted to surround the throne in heaven as victors over the world. These elders are in the vision to represent all the saved under the two systems.

Verse 5. *Lightnings and thunderings and voices* symbolize authority issuing from the throne and it is coming from some being whose voice is as penetrating as ligthning and as impressive as a roll of thunder. *Seven lamps* denote complete illumination and the *seven Spirits of God* are explained at chapter 1: 4.

Verse 6. A *sea* is deep and *crystal glass* is clear and pure, symbolizing the beauty of the scene around the throne. *Four beasts* is an unfortunate translation, for we always think of a "beast" as an animal of the lower world, and hence not a fitting symbol of something enjoying the dignity of these in this verse; the proper rendering of the original word is, "living creatures." *Full of eyes before and behind* symbolizes the ability to look in a universal direction.

Verse 7. In comparing one living creature with another it is intended only to consider one or two points of similarity, because there might be some characteristics common to all of them. A *lion* is bold and strong; a *calf* represents meekness; a *man* signifies more intelligence than other creatures; an *eagle* denotes exaltation and fleetness. The identity of these creatures and the reason why there were just four of them will be shown in the next chapter.

Verse 8. *Had each of them six wings.* Had it said that they had four wings even, it would have aroused our inquiry since a flying creature normally uses only two wings. We must conclude, therefore, that these wings were not all for the purpose of flying. A similar figure is given in Isaiah 6: 2 where the creatures that stood near the throne had each six wings. We may obtain some suggestions for our verse by reading the use Isaiah said these creatures made of their six wings. Each one used two of his wings to *cover his face* (indicating humility in the presence of God); with two of them he *cover his feet* (indicating m o d e s t y before the throne); with two *he did fly* (denoting a readiness to go on any errand desired by the Lord). *Full of eyes within* denotes that they could make an intelligent application of the things they could see outwardly or around them. *Rest not* means they did not pause day or night in ascribing praise to the Lord. *Was and is and is to come* is commented upon at chapter 1: 4.

Verse 9. These beasts (living creatures) not only ascribed glory and honor to the Lord, but also gave *thanks* to Him who sat on the throne continuously. That for which they were thankful will be understood when we study the next chapter.

Verse 10. The *four and twenty elders* are explained at verse 4. *Cast their crowns* is not a movement as if discarding the crowns for all the circumstances are against anything that unfavorable. It was a gesture of respect, recognizing the Lord as the one to whom they owed all the honor that was being enjoyed in possessing crowns.

Verse 11. *Thou art worthy* is not an overture of flattery, for they immediately give their reasons for the expression of praise, namely, He was the Creator of all things.

Revelation 5

Verse 1. *Him that sat on the throne* was God, for he is said to be the creator of all things, in the last verse of the preceding chapter. What was called a *book* in old times is the same as we call a roll; something like a long strip of paper and rolled up from one end. Let us remember we are in a book of signs or symbols. This *book* or roll is a symbol of the future events, and being sealed signifies that the future is unrevealed to all unless the seals can be broken so that the writing can be read. There were seven seals which is the complete number again, signifing that the future is hidden from the world. If the seals can be broken and the writing read, each one will reveal a part of the events that are to come in the future.

Verse 2. *Strong angel proclaiming.* He was asking a question *with a loud voice* which signifies a general call in order to give all a chance. The call was to the task of opening the book which means to make predictions of the coming events.

Verse 3. *Heaven* (where God dwells), *earth* (the abode of living human beings), *under the earth* (the abode of departed spirits). These three regions take in all intelligent creatures in the universe. Note that no man in any place was able to respond, which signifies that the future is a sealed book as far as uninspired beings are concerned, whether they be in heaven or on earth.

Verse 4. Since the loud request had been made by a strong angel the importance of the subject was evident, which explains why John wept when *no one* (the word for man is not in the original) was able to respond. *Read the book, neither to look thereon* signifies that unless the seals can be broken, no uninspired person can even see the writing much less read (understand and interpret) it.

Verse 5. *One of the elders* means one of the four and twenty who represent the two great systems of religion. He was able to console John and bid him refrain from weeping, because there was one available who would be able to open the book. *Lion of the tribe of Juda* (Judah). In Genesis 49: 9, 10 this lion is predicted and Hebrews 7: 14 tells us that Christ came from the tribe of Juda. *Root of David* means that Christ was the very important descendant of David the son of Jesse (Isaiah 11: 1, 10). This conversation represents the leaders of the two organized systems of religion as understanding that the great plans in which they were only agents in the service of God, were made good through the merits of this Lion.

Verse 6. *In the midst*, etc. Thayer gives us the rendering as follows: "And I saw between the throne and the four living creatures and the elders." He then offers his explanation as follows: "In the vacant space between the throne and the living creatures (on one side) and elders (on the other side), accordingly nearest the throne." *As it had been slain.* A lamb may be slain and then come back to life still bearing the marks of its death wounds. Thus Jesus was permitted to retain the wound marks until He had completed the great work with His apostles. (See John 20: 20.)

Horns in symbolic language means authority, and *seven* of them means complete authority. (See Matthew 28: 18.) *Seven eyes* signifies a perfect vision which would be necessary in order to see into the future. *Seven Spirits* is explained at chapter 1: 4.

Verse 7. *He* (this Lion and Lamb) came to the throne to get the book. *Him that sat upon the throne* means God, and in giving the book to the Lamb signifies that God gave his Son the ability to reveal the future events. This fact is stated literally in the first verse of the book of Revelation.

Verse 8. When God gave to his Son the right to open the book it caused rejoicing of all concerned in the great plans. The verse symbolizes this by telling of the actions of the *four beasts* (living creatures) and the *four and twenty elders*. They all fell down before the Lamb which is the usual practice of manifesting homage and recognition to a superior. *Harps* in symbolic language signify instruments of praise, and the next verse will tell us that these instruments were the human voice because they were used by which to sing. *Odors* in literal performances refers to incense offered to God in the services to Him (Exodus 30: 7, 8), but John interprets it as *prayers of saints*. This denotes that under whatever system of God's religions a man has lived, he is regarded as a *saint* (righteous person) and has the privilege of praying to God. This explains why it was said to Cornelius, "Thy prayers and thine alms are come up for a memorial before God" (Acts 10: 4), he having lived under the Patriarchal Dispensation, the unorganized system of religion. And it also accounts for the fact that Saul of Tarsus spent the time praying in Acts 9: 11. It is true the system under which he was brought up was done away but he had not realized it as yet.

Verse 9. It is important to note that the pronoun *they* means the *four beasts* (living creatures) and the *four and twenty elders* of the preceding verse. Also that the connection shows the word *saints* (righteous persons) applies to those who have lived under the systems designated by these *four* and *four and twenty*. After their performance of homage to Christ these creatures state their reasons for it, that He was worthy to be the one to open the book. In stating their reasons they will give their identity to which reference was made in the comments at chapter 4: 7. They say, *Thou wast slain, and hast redeemed us to God by thy blood out of every kindred, and tongue, and people, and nation.* We know that human beings only are the subjects of salvation, therefore these living creatures represent the redeemed human beings of the earth. The reason there are just four of the creatures in the one group is the fact that the surface of the earth has just four directions, and hence the saved would all come within the scope of those four areas. The four and twenty could join in the identifying declaration on the principle that both of the organized systems of religion were conducted in a way that was looking toward the universal salvation of mankind. *Sang a new song.* It was new in that they could not sing the praises of Christ as the actual Redeemer until he had qualified by being *slain* and giving His blood.

Verse 10. See the comments on chapter 1: 6 for the explanation of this verse.

Verse 11. The several phrases in the end of this verse are represented by only two Greek words in the original which The Englishman's Greek New Testament renders "thousands of thousands." Whichever translation we adopt, we should understand it to be a figurative statement to indicate a very great number of the heavenly host. They were joining in the praises of the four creatures and the four and twenty elders.

Verse 12. The praises of these angels were along the same line as those that were given by the creatures in verse 9 and for the same reason. The favors named in the verse do not refer to any specific blessings. As a group they signify that the Lamb of God is entitled to every blessing that God can bestow, and that they will rejoice in the great honors thus given to Him.

Verse 13. *Heaven, earth* and *under the earth* is explained at verse 3. *In the sea and all that are in them.* This cannot mean the men who had lived on the waters for they are included in the creatures *on the earth*. It means the living creatures of that domain which constitutes three fourths of the surface of the earth. Of course those dumb things cannot intelligently praise the Lord, but their very existence and service to humanity under the supervision of Him is a form of praise and an evidence of the existence and wisdom and power of the Almighty. (See Psalms 148: 1-10.) *Him that sitteth upon the throne* is God the Father and *the Lamb* is God the Son.

Verse 14. The four creatures and the four and twenty elders had already expressed their admiration (verses 8, 9), and when all these other beings uttered their praises it caused the creatures and elders to voice their pleasure by an *amen* of approval.

Revelation 6

Verse 1. The Lamb began to open the book (or roll), and when the first seal was broken John heard a voice like thunder. That indicated a powerful voice was sounding that would demand attention. Accordingly one of the four creatures called to John to come and see.

Verse 2. Horses were used in war and it could mean either spiritual or carnal war depending upon the connection in which it is used. The rider on the horse had both a *crown* and a *bow*, which signified that he was a person of authority and that he would engage in war. The rider represents Christ who was fighting for the truth through the instrumentality of His disciples. The white horse agrees with the phrase *conquering and to conquer*, for the Gospel won many battles over the foe in the first years of the church.

Verse 3. At the breaking of each of the first four seals the event was announced by one of the four beasts (or creatures). *Come and see* means to call the attention of John to what was about to be revealed.

Verse 4. The next horse was red which denotes bloodshed. Accordingly the rider was given power to take peace from the earth. This was fulfilled by the persecutions the Roman Empire began to wage against the Christians when their teaching began to show up with greater success.

Verse 5. The third seal was broken and the announcement was made for John to come and see. This time he saw a black horse which symbolized a condition of famine or shortage of food. The same subject was further indicated by the *pair of balances* that the rider held in his hand. It denoted that the necessities of life would be measured out to the people.

Verse 6. *Wheat and barley* are necessities of life, and the great price that is indicated by the figures shows that it was to be a time of scarcity, which is generally the case after a siege of warfare. *Oil and wine* are not necessary as articles of food, but are helpful as agencies of relief in times of distress. In the midst of the hardships the Lord predicted some relief would be afforded through these articles.

Verse 7. No description is given of the voice of the beasts (living creatures) after the first one. But in each case (up to the fourth) the call to attention is made to John that he would be sure to see what was about to be revealed.

Verse 8. When the fourth seal was broken John saw a pale horse which indicates death. That calmity would come first as a result of the terrible famine which the war had brought about, and it was made worse by the persecutions that were fostered by the Pagan Roman Empire. *Death* and *hell* are named in the order they would observe in their occurrence. The word *hell* is from *Hades* which is the abode of departed spirits. It was logical therefore to name them in the order as stated. *Power . . . over the fourth part of the earth.* God never did suffer the enemy to exterminate completely the victims attacked. The general purpose of the enemy was *to kill*. The means by which it might be accomplished were various, such as with the *sword* and *hunger*. With either of these the death would be a direct result of the means used. *With death* might seem a meaningless phrase unless it is understood that it refers to some indirect means such as a pestilence. Another means of causing the death of the Lord's people was to expose them to vicious beasts as was done in the arenas of Rome.

Verse 9. This verse brings to the fifth seal but nothing is said by either of the four creatures. Evidently by this time John's interest had been so centered on the drama being enacted before him that it was not necessary to call his attention. He was shown an altar because this is a book of symbols that are used to denote some literal facts. The present symbol is drawn from the temple of the Jews in which the altar was the center of their worship. At the bottom of the altar the blood of the sacrifices was poured, the bodies having been laid on the altar to be burned. (See Leviticus 4: 7.) From this imagery it was fitting to represent the Christians as victims that had been sacrificed to the cruelty of their persecutors, and also to picture their souls as being poured out at the foot of the altar. It is interesting to note that the bodies only had been put on the altar which left the souls still alive and able to speak intelligently. (See Matthew 10: 28.) The word *for* is used twice which is from the Greek word DIA. The Englishman's Greek New Testament renders this word "because of." The point is that these Christians had been killed "because of" their defense of the word of God. It is the same word that is used in chapter 1: 9 where John was banished to the isle of Patmos "for" (because of) the word of God. Hence both John and these Christians who had been slain were martyrs, because the word means one who is faithful to the word of God regardless of threatened consequences.

Verse 10. The witnesses whose souls John saw (he was able to see a soul because he himself was "in the Spirit" —chapter 1: 10) were calling for vengeance to be put on the ones who had caused their mistreatment.

Verse 11. Before replying to their cry with the explanation of the situation, they were given present consolation in the form of *white robes*. That indicated their standing of favor with God for chapter 3: 4 shows white as a symbol of worthiness in His sight. It was then told them that they would be avenged after a while, namely, when some of their brethren should be killed. *As they were* means they would be killed "for" (because of) the word of God. This was fulfilled as reported in chapter 20: 4 which will be commented upon when we come to that passage.

Verse 12. Following the opening of the fifth seal John saw some of the results of persecution, and it had been brought against Christians by Pagan (heathen) Rome. But there came a change in the general conditions. The emperor Constantine professed to be converted to Christianity, and it caused him to make many reverses in the activities of men in high places. The statements through the rest of this chapter are worded as if John saw the works of creation undergo radical changes. Such is to be expected in a book written with symbols. Hence the earthquake and darkening of the heavenly lights are tokens of the disturbances in the government.

Verse 13. *Stars of heaven* refer to men in high places who lost much of their power by the changes that Constantine was making. *Untimely figs* means fruit that is not ripe, yet it was shaken loose by the revolution going on in the government.

Verse 14. The *heaven* refers to the region that covers the earth, used here as a symbol of the great domain in which important men ruled with selfish interests. The disappearance of this reign of selfishness is likened to a *scroll* that is rolled up and laid away. *Mountains* and *isles* in symbolic language means seats of government, and these began to be altered by the revolutionary work of Constantine.

Verse 15. The various great persons named in this verse are the men in high position who had been holding uninterrupted sway over their people. As they began to see the fading of their domination it filled them with terror. Such an attitude is symbolized by an attempt to find hiding places in dens and among the rocks.

Verse 16. In their state of fear they would prefer being put out of the conflict, even if the mountains would tumble down upon them. *Hide us . . . from the face of the Lamb*. These men who had held sway for so long were made to realize that the change was brought about by the influence of the religion their emperor had espoused.

Verse 17. *Great day of his wrath* does not refer to the last great day of judgment, for the book is not that far along in the world drama. It is the day in which these overbearing men in high places in the pagan government of Rome, came to realize the effects that the religion of Christ was bringing as a punishment upon them.

Revelation 7

Verse 1. After the altar scene in chapter 6: 9-11, the vision opens the sixth seal to give a view of the consternation that came upon the men in high places, because of their mistreatment of Christians and because they were faced with the reverses that the emperor had forced upon them. The present chapter extends the consideration that God had for the "martyrs," at the same time He was bringing the siege of consternation upon the persecutors of His people. The *four angels* are so numbered because of the *four corners* or four points of the earth's compass. *Holding the four winds* symbolizes the blowing of the wrath of God over the realm of the persecutors, and these angels were holding this wind ready to be released whenever they were so ordered.

Verse 2. As the four angels were "standing at attention" ready to turn the winds loose upon *the earth* (referring to the domains of the Roman Empire), another angel was seen coming with a special message to the four. *From the east* is figurative and means it was from the throne of God, because he is the source of all spiritual light, even as the sun which brings material light to the world, first appears in the east. *Hurt the earth* is referring back to the conditions of consternation and destruction described in the closing verses of chapter 6.

Verse 3. They were told to hold back the winds until the faithful ones had been accounted for. A seal is a stamp of ownership and is placed on the proper persons to indicate the approval of the authority behind it. (See the comments at 1 Corinthians 9: 2.) This seal was to be placed in the forehead which indicates they would be visible to the public. Whatever was the exact fulfilling of this symbol, there was something that would tell the world of God's approval of them. Hence when the wicked men of power were undergoing their terrors, they could realize how much they had failed in their wicked designs. Right while they were trembling in the terrors of their crumbling dominions, they could see the victims of their cruelty with the marks of approval from their God.

Verse 4. The number of those who were sealed is given in exact and equal figures, which makes us know that it is all another expression of figurative speech and that the meaning is that great numbers of true Christians had won the stamp of approval from the Lord. *Tribes of the children of Israel.* It is known that after the conversion of Cornelius in the first four years of the Gospel, the Gentiles furnished many converts to Christ. Hence there were many of those who were persecuted as well as of the Jews. The reference to the twelve tribes is therefore accommodative, similar to the instance in James 1: 1.

Verses 5-8. Having explained the significance of the tribal classification, and since the same thing is said of each tribe, I am combining these verses into one paragraph to conserve time and space.

Verse 9. This verse verifies the comments at verse 4, for here we have the same kind of persons referred to in other numerical terms. They also are said to be from *all nations*, etc., which would prevent us from restricting the "twelve tribes" to the Jews. *White robes* signified a life of righteousness and *palms* are medals betokening their victory over "great tribulation" (verse 14).

Verse 10. *Salvation to our God* means to ascribe salvation to Him, *and unto the Lamb* is combined in the praise because God perfects all plans through the Son.

Verse 11. The angels stood round about the throne and in the presence of the elders and the four living creatures as a mark of respect. But when they performed their homage of worship it was before the throne unto God.

Verse 12. *Saying, Amen.* Thayer says that at the beginning of a discourse the word means, "Surely, of a truth, truly." Thus the angels were announcing that they were about to utter something that would surely be the truth, namely, that all the good qualities mentioned in the verse should truly be ascribed to God. The declaration was made emphatic still more by closing it with *Amen.*

Verse 13. The elder put his statement in the form of a question to gain the attention of John. The ones *arrayed in white robes* were those in chapter 6:11 and those of the twelve tribes in this chapter.

Verse 14. John understood that such was the purpose of the question, for he replied *thou knowest.* The elder then gave the answer which confirms the idea that they were the persecuted servants of God already referred to. *Came out of great tribulation* denotes their triumph over their persecutors. Not that they escaped death, for John had seen their souls outside of their bodies. But if a servant of God is faithful even in the midst of persecution then death cannot rob him of victory. *Washed their robes* is a figurative reference to their being cleaned by the blood of Christ.

Verse 15. All of the statements in this verse are figurative, for the purified saints had lost their lives for testifying on behalf of the word of God. But they were being held in honored remembrance and were destined to be always "welcome callers" in the intimacies of the Father.

Verse 16. Shall not *hunger* nor *thirst* because those are wants that pertain to this life, and they have become citizens of a region where physical wants are unknown. The light and heat of the sun are things of the past for the same reasons.

Verse 17. *Lamb shall feed them* with delicacies that are unknown to men living in the flesh. *Living fountains of waters* are among the blissful objects to be enjoyed by those who overcome by faith in the Lamb. *Wipe away all tears* by preventing anything that could cause tears.

Revelation 8

Verse 1. The seventh and last seal was opened but nothing took place for half an hour. In the march of events it frequently happens that a lull will come between different campaigns. That is described here as being a silence of half an hour. We recall that when the four angels in chapter 7: 1-3 were prepared to continue the action of God's judgments against the persecutors of His people, they were told to hold the winds back until the sealing of the faithful had been completed. This half hour silence represents the lull in the judgments while the sealing was being done.

Verse 2. The events of the seventh seal will include several verses, for there are seven angels involved in the events and all that transpires in connection with them is what was revealed when the seventh seal was broken. The angels were given each a trumpet but they will not all be used in the same series. Four of them will sound one after the other, then will come a halt after which the remaining three will sound. (See verse 13.) Doubtless the first four angels correspond with the four that were holding the four winds that were to bring consternation upon the persecutors of God's people, which is the reason why the seven angels are divided into separate groups, four and three.

Verse 3. Incense is a symbol of prayer, and while the judgments of God against the persecutors were preparing, the faithful servants of God were engaged in their devotions to Him. That is why the incense and prayer are combined in this verse.

Verse 4. The odor of incense was pleasing to God in the days when such services were required (Exodus 30: 7-9; Leviticus 16: 12, 13). and likewise the prayers of faithful servants in the Christian Dispensation are acceptable (1 Peter 3: 12).

Verse 5. *Filled it with fire off the altar.* In the Mosaic system the priest obtained the fire from the brazen altar with which to burn the incense. The angel followed the same pattern in the symbolical performance, except that after having used some fire for the burning of incense before the golden altar, he got some more fire which he put in the censer (a portable fumigator) and cast it into the earth. This aroused voices like the sound of thunderings which were the complaints of the foes of truth at the prospect of God's judgment about to come upon them. So mighty and widespread were these murmurings that John likened them to an earthquake.

Verse 6. The half hour silence is about to end and the four winds are about to be released; the first four angels with trumpets are about to sound.

Verse 7. It should be remembered through verse 12 that the plagues symbolized represent the reverses that came upon the Roman Empire which finally resulted in the downfall of the government. The items mentioned are figurative or symbolic, but they are worded as if literal calamities were being imposed. That is because in a book where certain facts of an immaterial character are predicted in symbols, the events have to be reported as if they were happening literally. Thus we have a hail and electrical storm that causes bloodshed and scorching of much of the vegetation.

Verse 8. The judgments of God against the Empire continue as the second angel sounds his trumpet. *Great mountain burning* signifies the downfall of some unit of the government. *Cast into the sea* symbolizes the people (represented by the sea) as feeling the effects of this political downfall. *Sea became blood* signifies that much bloodshed was suffered among the people caused by the internal disturbances.

Verse 9. All of this is figurative because the literal sea and its vessels of traffic were unharmed by the political confusion. But it gives a picture of what did occur, and in stating an exact percentage as dying we will understand that a great portion suffered but the government was not exterminated.

Verse 10. No change in the general drama takes place, but some special incident is predicted to affect the people unfavorably. A *star* in symbolical language denotes some leader, and he is here likened to a meteor that falls to the earth, selecting as its landing place the rivers and fountains of water. That is attacking a vital portion of a country because of the necessity of water.

Verse 11. The name of this star was *Wormwood*. That is from the Greek word APSINTHOS, which Thayer defines, "wormwood, absinthe." Webster's definition of the word is as follows: "A green alcoholic liquor containing oils of wormwood and anise, and other aromatics. Its continued use causes nervous derangement." It is no wonder, then, that *many men died of the waters*.

Verse 12. *Third part* is commented upon at verse 9. This angel gave a sound that resulted in throwing all the luminaries out of order, pitching the country into a state of semi-darkness. It was another shake-up among the leaders of the empire.

Verse 13. The things which happened to the country, when the four winds were turned loose or when the angels sounded, seemed bad enough if that was to be the end of the troubles. But it was not, for there came another angel flying through *the midst of heaven*, which denotes that he came into the region of the political heavens of the Roman Empire. He pronounced a triple woe on the people to come when the remaining three angels sound their trumpets. Let us bear in mind that we are still reading of things that were revealed when the seventh seal was broken.

Revelation 9

Verse 1. It is fair to my readers to state that a number of commentators connect this chapter with Mohammed. In reasoning upon the subject some of them will mention certain things that could not have been true of any persons but the soldiers of Mohammed. But in their reasoning I note that the chief basis of their argumant is the idea that the literal characteristics of locusts and horses and soldiers, etc., will not agree with any interpretation except to apply the predictions to Mohammed. But we are in a book of symbols where it does not count for a conclusion to rely on the literal nature of things. On the principle of "giving others the benefit of the doubt," I am sure there were many facts and truths about Mohammedanism that correspond with the language of the several verses. Yet that could truly be said of some other noted impostors who have come into the world to poison the minds of men. The scope of history is so wide that one might find incidents to correspond with various characters he would select for the comparison. Against all of the above considerations I am keeping in mind that the Lord was concerned principally with the experiences of His people in connection with the Roman Empire, and the great apostasy that was formed by the corruption of His system with its union of church and state. In view of the aforesaid remarks I shall devote my comments to the items that were and are being fulfilled by the doings of the institution of Rome. *Star fall from heaven* is rendered "out of heaven fallen" by The Englishman's Greek New Testament. It denotes that John saw a star (symbol for a leader among men) that was in fallen condition, not that he saw it fall. That would be true of the head of Rome; he had fallen from the spiritual purity that exists in heavenly things. *Bottomless pit* is from ABUSSOS, which is explained at Luke 8: 31 in the first volume of New Testament Commentary.

Verse 2. We have learned that the bottomless pit is the abode of demons (usually translated "devils" in the King James Version). These demons were suffered to come into the world at one time and afflict mankind. After that period was gone it was easy to refer to such a performance as a symbol of other activities in the politico-religious world, namely, the institution in which the church and state were united. Since this great apostate organization served the interests of Satan so much, it was appropriate to represent the Roman bishop as having a joint interest with him in opposing the true servants of God. Paul verifies this conclusion in 2 Thessalonians 2: 9 where he says: "Even him, whose coming is after the working of Satan with all power and signs and lying wonders." Literally we would think of smoke coming out of a place where there is a flame of fire (Luke 16: 24), but it is used symbolically which will be developed as the chapter proceeds.

Verse 3. We still have symbols but they are more definite. The smoke proves to have been a "smoke screen" that enclosed a swarm of locusts. That explained why the sun was darkened by the "smoke" in the preceding verse. It has been known many times that this insect comes in such great numbers as to have the effect of a cloud that obscures the sun. In selecting a symbol the Lord would call attention to some literal fact that would truly represent some other fact or truth that is not literal. This swarm of locusts was the clergy of Rome acting on behalf of the apostate church, otherwise called Babylon the Great. As the swarm of locusts obscured the sun so the clergy of Rome would prevent the people from having the full benefit of the "Sun of Righteousness" (Malachi 4: 2). *Scorpions* is described by Thayer as follows: "The name of a little animal, somewhat resembling a lobster, which in warm regions [such as Hades, E.M.Z.] lurks especially in stone walls; it has a poisonous sting in its tail."

Verse 4. Here we have another instance where the Lord uses a literal object to symbolize a fact that is not literal, except that He uses the symbol contrary to its usual behavior. This is not the only instance where a performance in nature is used "contrary" to its usual manner. (See Romans 11: 24.) The natural thing is for the locusts to eat the very things this verse says they did not hurt. They were to hurt men only and not all of them even. Their destructive work was to be against the *men which have not the seal of God in their foreheads*. Such men were true servants of God and no kind of oppression could actually hurt them. But on the principle that "evil sometimes works its own rebuke," the Lord suffers the workers of iniquity to be scourged by their own leaders. It is a historical fact that the dupes of Rome often suffer many hardships at the hands of the clergy. The writer of this paragraph knew a family in which a small son was compelled to earn money, half of which was taken from him by the clergy though his widowed mother was much in need of it.

Verse 5. *Not kill them.* The clergy needed to retain their dupes that they might further exploit them for their own selfish interests. *Five months* is a definite period of time if taken literally, but in actual history we do not find such processes as have been described being so exact in their beginning and ending. The figure refers to some particular period in the history of the apostate church when the oppression by the clergy was active to an extraordinary degree.

Verse 6. *Seek death and shall not find it.* There are some things worse than death (Jeremiah 8: 3). I once heard a lecture by a woman who had escaped from the clutches of Rome. In that lecture the speaker related the experiences of a woman who was being tortured as a result of self-inflicted wounds induced by the heresies of Rome. This victim moaned and sighed as if death at once would have been a relief.

Verse 7. It was fitting that these locusts were in the form resembling war horses, for the apostate institution has not hesitated at using carnal warfare for its defense whenever it was thought necessary. *Crown of gold* indicates both authority and wealth, and the clergy of Rome have ever been equipped with both, in order to carry out the schemes of the headquarters of the corrupt organization. *Faces of men* is an important identification also, because while the use of war horses is necessary in the program of Rome, it also requires the scheming trickery of human intelligence.

Verse 8. *Hair of women . . . teeth of lions;* this is a very interesting combination. In 1 Corinthians 11: 15 it is shown that women are expected to have long hair (that being the only distinction between the hair of women and that of men as far as the appearance is concerned.) Women are supposed to be milder and less harmful in their natural disposition. Hence when these creatures first appear they are regarded as women and thus would not be suspected as being such as needed to be avoided. But they had teeth like those of lions which indicates that they were in reality a dangerous group of creatures. That is a true picture of the clergy of Rome, including all from the pope down to the humblest priest.

Verse 9. A *breastplate* is a piece for the protection of the vital parts of the body. The apostate church stood behind its clergy and gave them all the protection necessary. *Sound of their wings.* The locusts have wings literally and since the symbolism is still drawn from those insects it is appropriate to mention that part of their anatomy. Yet we know it is not to be taken literally, for the rest of the verse represents them sounding like war chariots drawn by horses going into battle.

Verse 10. This is the same as verses 3 and 4.

Verse 11. See the remarks at verse 1 for the meaning of *bottomless pit*.

The angel of this place would mean some outstanding character who was in partnership with the influences of that domain. The capitalized words of this verse are used by John as proper nouns, but in Bible times most names of persons had special meaning. That of the ones in this verse means "destroyer," and it is certainly an appropriate name in view of the destructive work and tendencies of the leaders of Rome. This *king* or *angel* would be either the pope or some special member of the clergy who had unusual success in controlling the others. It is noteworthy that John connects this evil arrangement with the *bottomless pit* which is the abode of fallen angels called demons.

Verse 12. *Two woes more* is a reference to the statement of the angel in chapter 8: 13, who announced that three woes more were to be pronounced against the inhabitants of the earth. One of them has been announced and two more are waiting to be sounded.

Verse 13. The golden altar was in the first room of the tabernacle and placed by the vail that separated the second room. Just through the vail was the ark where God met with the high priest to speak to him. Hence the voice John heard was coming from the presence of God.

Verse 14. The voice was giving instructions to the sixth angel. The river Euphrates is a significant subject in connection with God's people. The ancient city of Babylon was situated on its banks, which was the capital of the first of the four world empires. The word "babylon" came to mean confusion and was finally applied to the great institution of the apostate church, concerning which we are now reading in our studies. It was fitting, therefore, that these four angels should be represented being located in this river. The particular events which they were to announce are not named, but the train of happenings is not interrupted. It means that the disciplinary treatment which the dupes of Rome were suffered to have come upon them was continuing. It will be well now to read the comments at 2 Thessalonians 2: 11, 12. There it will be seen that God sent certain judgments upon the citizens of the apostate institution, using their own people and practices as the instrument by which judgments were to be sent. That is what is going on in our chapter, and the four angels are merely some of the specific agencies within the corrupt institution for this epoch in the punishments.

Verse 15. The *hour, day, month* and *year* are exact periods of time when literally considered, but they are to be understood in the same light as "five months" in verse 5 which the reader should see. Likewise he should see the comments at chapter 8: 9 for the meaning of *third part*.

Verse 16. The number of the army is another exact figure if taken literally, but the meaning is that a great army was serving the interests of the evil institution. *And I heard the number of them.* The conjunction *and* is not in all copies and it is unnecessary, for the sentence means that John was not sizing up the army personally but the number was announced to him.

Verse 17. Some commentators see an invasion of heathen armies into the domain of the Roman Empire. No doubt things of that nature took place at certain times through the centuries. However, the fundamental background of the vision being shown to John has not been changed, hence I believe all these descriptive phrases are symbolical of the fierceness of the judgments which the dupes of Rome brought upon themselves. For that reason I shall not attempt any further comments on the descriptions.

Verse 18. See the comments at chapter 8: 9 for the significance of *third part*.

Verse 19. These creatures were invested with powers at the two extremities of their bodies, which indicates how complete was the agency that God suffered to come upon the citizens of the corrupt organization.

Verse 20. The worship of devils and other forms of idolatry that are mentioned refers to the worship of dead "saints" that was practiced by the members of the apostate church. They also introduced images into their churches and they would fall down before them (even as they do in our day) which constituted the idol worship condemned here. *Repented not.* Notwithstanding all the hardships that had been brought upon the leaders and many of their followers by their corrupt practices, the others (*rest of the men*) did not "learn their lesson" so as to be induced to repent.

Verse 21. These are literal crimes which doubtless many of them committed, for it is well established that the apostate church deals in all of such means to further the interests of the corrupt institution.

Revelation 10

Verse 1. The drama of the book of Revelation is proceeding down through the centuries, until we are about to arrive at the revolution known in history as the Reformation. But the full development of that mighty movement will be preceded by some items preparatory to it. Now is another time when the reader should again read carefully the "General remarks" at the beginning of this book. But the oppression from the power that was created through the union of church and state has exhausted the patience of the Almighty and he will soon inaugurate the work that is destined to dissolve the unrighteous monster and return to the people their right to act upon their own responsibility. The preliminary events necessary for the main performance are due to begin soon, which will be indicated by some of the symbols of this chapter. The angel in this verse came down from heaven and the description shows he was coming on behalf of the Lord to impart some predictions about to be carried out. *Clothed with a cloud* agrees with the fact that he was from the courts of heaven, because the clouds are frequently used in connection with heavenly events (chapter 1: 7; 14: 14; Matthew 24:30; Acts 1: 9; 1 Thessalonians 4: 17). *Rainbow upon his head* signifies the dignity and grandeur of his mission. His face like the sun denotes great light which was especially appropriate since his mission was to announce the shedding of Gospel light on those who had been deprived of it because of the Dark Ages. *Pillars of fire*. Thayer explains this to mean. "Flames rising like columns." It denotes a penetrating brilliance that belongs only to heavenly beings.

Verse 2. The angel had a *little book* which indicated that the events about to be predicted would not take long and hence would not require a large book to record them. The book was *open* which signified that the things about to happen were to be made known; that their account was not a sealed book as the one in chapter 2. It denoted further that the Bible which had been closed to the people by Rome would soon be opend again so that all might read. The *sea* and *earth* comprise the entire surface of the globe and the symbol means that all the world would be affected by what was soon to occur and which would be announced presently.

Verse 3. The angel's voice was like that of a lion in that it was strong and itself heard far and near. We know from the context that the angel's cry was the announcement that the Bible was again to be given to the people. Of course that would be unwelcome news to the heads of the apostate church and it was natural for them to protest. That called for *seven thunders* from the "seven-hilled" city of Rome.

Verse 4. Not realizing the deception there was in the protests, John was about to write down what the thunderous voices said. (We remember he was told in chapter 1: 19 to write the things that should be thereafter.) But the Lord understood the motive of the seven voices coming from the headquarters of the "man of sin," and He caused a voice to instruct John not to record them but to seal them up.

Verse 5. In lifting up his hand the angel mentioned before (in verse 2) was preparing to make an oath. (There is no inconsistency in this, for he was al an angel of God and man only is forbidden to make oaths.)

Verse 6. *Should be time no longer*. Much misuse has been of this passage. It is not uncommon to hear a preacher making an earnest plea to his audience to obey the Gospel while the time is here. That soon the angel of God would place one foot on land and the other on the sea and declare that "time shall be no longer." They thus make the phrase mean that the last day of the earth has come and hence it will be "the end of time." In the first place the events concerning which the angel uttered the phrase were several centuries prior to the second coming of Christ. In the second place the Bible does not teach there will ever be an end of time, for the word means the same as the word "eternity," and both words simply mean "duration" which is something that had no beginning and will never have an end. The word in our passage does not mean "time" as being the opposite of "eternity," but it has the same meaning the word would have if a moderator announced to the speaker that his time was up. The Englishman's Greek New Testament renders the word "delay." The passage means that the events being predicted—the events getting ready for the Reformation—were about due to start and that there would be no longer delay in the matter.

Verse 7. *The mystery of God* refers to the work of the Reformation that was to restore the Bible to the people. The seventh angel has not yet sounded, but he soon will because the preceding verse says there was not to be any further delay. By the time this seventh angel gets his message sounded the complete work of the Reformation will be done, that is, the prediction will be completed. Of course an inspired prophet speaks of things in the present tense even though he is speaking of events long in the future. John was seeing this vision in the first century and the Reformation came in the sixteenth, but an inspired angel can speak of such an event as having taken place. Such is the meaning of this verse when it says that *when he shall begin to sound, the mystery of God should be finished.* (See chapter 11: 15.)

Verse 8. This *little book* is the one mentioned in verse 2 which contains predictions of things about to begin. John was the human agency of God for delivering the message to the world, and hence it was appropriate for him to receive the book at the bidding of the angel. We note two angels are involved in this episode, the one that held the book and the other one that sounded the instructions to John.

Verse 9. In obedience to the instructions of the angel John went and requested the other angel to give him the little book. As the angel delivered it to him he told him to *eat it up.* This was a symbol and indicated that John was to be inspired to report to the people. A similar instance of such a symbolic inspiration of a prophet is in Ezekiel 3: 1-3. The book produced two opposite effects upon the prophet although he had only one body to absorb it. There was nothing inconsistent in John's personal attitude toward the word of God, but the world would not take the same stand in view of the unpleasant things it contains in its teachings. Therefore John was required to have a bodily experience that represented both his and the people's reaction to the word. See the note about "prophets acting" at 1 Kings 20: 35 in Volume 2 of Bible Commentary.

Verse 10. John took the book and ate it with the results that he was told what would happen within his body.

Verse 11. We are sure that the effects of eating the book included the reactions of the world, for this verse refers to the subject in direct connection with his eating it. The instruction explains why he was to eat the book, and why it had the mentioned effects, namely, that he was to *prophesy* again before many peoples, etc. Incidentally, this last statement shows that the one in verse 6 that there should *be time no longer,* does not mean that the end of the world had come.

Revelation 11

Verse 1. The reed given unto John was a measuring rule and is a symbol of the word of God. This is clear from the fact that the angel gave it to John who was one of the apostles. We know the word of God is the divine standard for it is required in 1 Peter 4: 11 that, "If any man speak, let him speak as the oracles of God." At the time predicted by this chapter the apostasy ("falling away") was an established fact. The Bible was virtually taken from the people and the religious lives of men and women were judged by the decrees of Rome instead of by the word of God. This verse is a symbol of the true standard of the measurement as the apostles were given the authority to execute (Matthew 19: 28). The *temple of God* means the church (1 Corinthians 3:16, 17). The altar was the center of worship in the Mosaic system, and it is referred to here as a symbol of the worship under that of Christ. *Them that worship therein* means Christians, whose personal lives must be measured (regulated) by the word of God and not by the decrees of Rome.

Verse 2. The *court* in the old temple was the part that was open to the people generally. It is referred to in our passage as a symbol of the treatment that was imposed upon the institution of God by its enemies. Under the Mosaic system the temple was under the jurisdiction of the Jews, and that is why those on the outside were called Gentiles. But in the fulfillment of the symbol the word refers to the enemies of the true church, namely, the leaders in the church of Rome. It must be borne in mind that all through this part of the book of Revelation, when reference is made either to Rome, or Babylon, or church and state, the same institution is always meant (if no exception is stated). That is because it was by the union of church and state that such a complete control was obtained over all the lives of the people. That is what is meant by the prediction that they were to *tread under foot* these arrangements of God. It is important to note that they did not tread under foot the temple nor the altar. That is because all through the Dark Ages there was a true church in existence in spite of the corruptions of Rome, although it was obscured more or less from the full public view. *Forty and two months.* This is the first time this unit of time has appeared in this book, but it will reappear many times under various figures. It refers to the period of the apostasy or Dark Ages as it is familiarly termed by the teachers in the brotherhood. In literal terms it means 1260 years and the various forms in which it is stated will all sum up to that figure by observing the rule in prophetic language that the month has 30 days. The exact number of years that requires the 60 is reached by the dates on which the full rule of Rome began and ended. Some of the details of that subject are not available to me at present, but we may be sure that the figure is correct from the fact that each of the various forms in which it is stated brings out the same 1260. And as to the correctness of the calculation we have historical verification of the round number in the words of Edward Gibbon, author of The Decline and Fall of the Roman Empire. He was an infidel and would have no motive for verifying the word of God, but he was an authentic historian whose ability and accuracy were unquestioned and I shall quote from him as follows: "In the long period of twelve hundred years, which elapsed between the reign of Constantine and the reformation of Luther, the worship of saints and relics corrupted the pure and perfect simplicity of the Christian model; and some symptoms of degeneracy may be observed even in the first generation which adopted and cherished this pernicious innovation."—Volume 2, Chapter 28, Page 615. The *forty and two months* of our verse gives us the 1260 by multiplying forty-two by thirty.

Verse 3. The word *power* is not in the Greek and is not necessary for the thought, which is that God would see that His two witnesses could speak. The two witnesses are the Old and New Testaments, the documents that Rome took away from the people. To *prophesy* is from PROPHETEUO and Thayer's general definition is, "Speak forth by divine inspiration." Hence it includes the making of predictions and any form of speech that will impart information that is in harmony with the will of God. The word in our passage means that the Old and New Testaments would continue to exist and offer their information through the period designated. In symbolic language a day stands for a year (Ezekiel 4: 6), hence the number of days named with words corresponds with the 1260 years. *Clothed in sackcloth* symbolizes a condition of mourning, and it is used in this verse to refer to the mistreatment the word of God would receive all through the Dark Ages.

Verse 4. Olive oil was the chief source of artificial light in Bible times (Exodus 27: 20; Leviticus 24: 2). Olive oil requires olive trees and hence since the word of God is the only source of spiritual light directly available to man, it is symbolized by olive trees. The phraseology in the last part of the verse is drawn from Zechariah 4: 11-14.

Verse 5. *If any man will hurt them, fire proceedeth, etc.* Both sentences of this verse mean the same. We know that no one was ever literally injured by the Bible, hence we must understand this to be a symbol. Its meaning is that God is jealous for his word and will inflict vengeance upon all who oppose it. In times of "special providence" He caused various judgments to come upon men who mistreated the divine word. Otherwise the time will come when eternal punishment will be inflicted upon all who have not given the word of God the respect it deserves.

Verse 6. This verse is to be understood in the light of the preceding one. God is so jealous of his word that if He deems it called for he will inflict such judgments as these upon those who mistreat His word.

Verse 7. *Finished their testimony* does not mean they quit testifying for they will not do that while the world stands. It means when their testimony has been made complete—when the New Testament is all written. When John was writing it had not all been composed yet, for the book he was writing was to be a part of that Volume. About the time the whole Bible was composed and confirmed, which was after all the apostles had passed from life, was the time that

Rome became alarmed at the influence of the Bible. Also that was near the time that the union of church and state arrived at its great height, in which it obtained such power as to control all the people under its dominions. We understand the *beast* to be Satan operating through the power of Rome. Shall *kill them* is figurative because the Bible never was actually killed, but as far as its opportunity for control over the lives of men was concerned the Book was slain. Let the reader remember that it is the two witnesses of verse 3 that the present verse is dealing with.

Verse 8. *Dead bodies* must be understood in the light of the comments on the preceding verse. We know the literal truth is that Rome was the institution that mistreated the Bible and took it away from the people. For that reason the symbols in this verse must be interpreted accordingly. The city is the domain of the apostate church, and the reference to Sodom and Egypt is made because of the wickedness that was in those places and their enmity against the Lord. The Lord's crucifixion also is laid to the same kind of elements that plotted the attack upon the Bible.

Verse 9. The Bible continued to be a prohibited book all through the Dark Ages or the 1260 years. That is the period represented here by *three days and a half*. The term is obtained by reducing three and a half years to days (1260), then remembering that a day in symbolic language stands for a year. *Not suffer . . . put in graves.* A refusal to give burial to a body that has been slain would indicate much disrespect for the body. The figure is used to denote the low esteem the church of Rome had for the word of God.

• Verse 10. The teaching of the Bible stands in the way of the evil desires of men who wish to profit by a misuse of the religion of Christ which they profess to follow. It torments them as the verse states it, and therefore it would be a cause for rejoicing among such people to have it put out of the way. *Two prophets* are other terms for the Old and New Testament. It was a custom to exchange gifts upon occasions of special rejoicing which was a form of mutual congratulations. (See Nehemiah 8: 12 and Esther 9: 22.)

Verse 11. *After three days and a half* means after the Dark Ages of 1260 (verse 9). *Spirit of life* is figurative on the same principle as being dead in verse 7. The apostate church took the Bible away from the people and "slew" it. Luther and his co-workers gave it back to the people which put "life" back into it.

Verse 12. This is another symbolical passage for in fact the Bible was already in heaven. "For ever, O Lord, thy word is settled in heaven" (Psalms 119: 89). The passage gives a symbolical performance that was to notify the enemies of the word of God that the forces of Heaven were recognizing it and were ready to welcome its renewed power on the earth. We know that such is the purpose of the verse for the closing statement is *and their enemies beheld them.*

Verse 13. *Earthquakes* in symbolic language stand for revolutions in governments and the powers that be. When the work of the reformers got underway it caused many disturbances among the rulers of the world, who had been holding undisputed sway over the people through the past centuries. The numerical units that are mentioned—*tenth part* and *seven thousand*—are too exact to be taken literally. The meaning is that a great part of the former tyrannies was overthrown. *Remnant . . . gave glory to God.* When the work of the reformers became an established fact, it convinced some of the leaders that they had been in the wrong and were thus led to acknowledge their mistake. *Were affrighted* means they were compelled to feel a greater respect for God and his Book than they had before.

Verse 14. *Second woe is past.* The first was the scourge of the Dark Ages, the second was the dissolving of the union of church and state which was connected with the giving of the Bible back to the people. The third woe (not to God's people but to the enemies) is the resumption of power by the several kings and rulers, who had been deprived of their royal rights by the dominating power in Rome, that forced all people to be subject to its dictates.

Verse 15. Kingdoms of the world are not asked to become part of the kingdom of Christ. That would be virtually another union of church and state. What happened was a change in the attitude of the earthly kingdoms. Before the Reformation the kings on those thrones could not reign as Christ would have wished them to and as they personally would have been inclined.

They had to take their instructions from Rome and rule their subjects as that head dictated. After the delusion was lifted by the insight into the scriptures that was afforded them through the work of the reformers, they learned that they could permit their subjects to regulate their own religious life as they believed Christ wished them to. It is in that sense that the kingdoms *of this world are become the kingdoms of our Lord.* Such a revolution was a woe to the "man of sin" in Rome for it meant the end of his arrogant rule. It is the third woe already predicted and now announced by the sounding of the seventh angel. *He shall reign for ever and ever.* Christ never ceased to be a king from the time He ascended to his Father's right hand (1 Peter 3: 22), and will continue to be king until the time of His second coming (1 Corinthians 15: 24, 25). But He was not recognized as king by these earthly rulers while they were under the control of Rome.

Verse 16. These are the four and twenty elders of chapter 4: 4. They rejoiced to see the triumph of Him who was and is the saving virtue of both of the organized systems of religion given into the world by the Lord.

Verse 17. *Taken to thee thy great power* refers to the triumph of righteousness over evil when the word God was given back to the people of the various kingdoms.

Verse 18. *Nations were angry.* That is that part of them that still wished to profit by the deception of the people. *Thy wrath is come* means that God's vengeance had come upon the apostate church for abusing His word. *The time of the dead* also hath come, meaning the dead whose souls John saw under the altar (chapter 6: 9). They cried for vengeance or judgment and were told that "their time" would come. Now that time has come and God has *judged* the apostate church by separating her from the advantages of temporal power. At the same time He *gave reward* to his faithful servants by having His word placed again in their hands. *Destory them which destroy the earth* refers to the same evil men described before who planned to destroy (corrupt in the margin) the earth.

Verse 19. This verse is a symbol that is very significant. The Bible had been denied the people for 1260 years but is now restored to them. That is like letting the servants of God "in" on a great intimacy with the Lord. The original law was laid up by the ark in the Most Holy Place (Exodus 25: 16; Deuteronomy 10: 2). The people were never permitted to see into that place where the book of God was deposited. Likewise the people under Rome were shut off from seeing the Book through the years of the apostasy. But the work of the Reformation broke through that and forced open the privacy and gave them another view of the law. As an illustration of such a privilege John was given a view into the place where the ark was which he calls the *ark of his testament* or holy law. The *lightnings* and other things named refer to the commotions that were caused by the Reformation.

Revelation 12

Verse 1. As an aid in identifying this *woman* we will learn that she is the one who lived through the 1260 years of the apostasy (verse 6). That was not true in any sense of Mary the mother of Jesus. Besides, Mary was a literal woman and we are studying in a book of symbols. We should also remember that the apostate church as opposed to the Lord's institution is the outstanding subject of this book, and of course that of necessity is the church of Christ. *Clothed with the sun* symbolizes the light of divine truth with which the church has been entrusted (Ephesians 3: 10; 1 Timothy 3: 15). As the moon is a lesser light than the sun, so there are those in the church who are light bearers *under* the jurisdiction of the church. *Crown of twelve stars* evidently refers to the apostles. A crown indicates a position of rulership or judgeship. Accordingly we read of Jesus saying to his apostles, "Ye also shall sit upon twelve thrones, judging the twelve tribes of Israel" (Matthew 19: 28).

Verse 2. This verse describes the mother, but the literal facts are symbols of something that is not literal.

Verse 3. When a birth is expected in a family the members thereof are generally hovering near, impatiently waiting for the happy event. But in the case of this woman there is a being waiting near who is not friendly toward the event. This being is called *a great red dragon.* He is called Satan in other places and that is because he works through agencies that belong to this world. The dragon of our verse, then, is Rome. Some commentators designate that it means Pagan Rome but I do not believe it is to be restricted to that. However, since both Pagan and Papal Rome had their headquarters in the city of Rome, it will not make any difference as far as this verse is concerned, which angle of the subject we take. The description of the dragon in this verse agrees with the government of Rome with the leading European kingdoms that were connected with it and formed a part of the institution as a whole. The seven heads are so numbered because the city of Rome literally has seven hills on which it is situated. But those seven hills are not important except as symbols of something else not literal or at least not material. They represent the sevenfold power of that mighty institution in opposing the works of God. The ten horns are the same that Daniel saw (Daniel 7: 7), and they correspond to the ten toes of the giant image in Nebuchadnezzar's dream.

Verse 4. *Third part of the stars* means the men in positions of importance. The reason why only a portion of them was drawn is the same as other similar passages, namely, God has never suffered the enemy to annihilate completely that which he attacks. This dragon is standing by expecting to destroy the child as soon as it is born.

Verse 5. When the child was born it was a *man child*. In preceding chapters we have seen that the outstanding feature of Rome, as well as of other despotic governments, is the hatred of people who wish to have a voice in their own government. As long as the people can be kept in ignorance of their personal rights, they will meekly submit and be ruled over. But the Bible in its clear method of showing people their personal responsibility in determining their manner of conduct, has taught them the truth about it and led them to notify Rome to keep hands off. But the Bible is not a self-propagating document, hence the church was the Lord's instrument for bringing that great truth into the world. In symbolizing that revolutionary event the Lord gave the vision to John of a woman nearing the time of delivery of a child so near in fact that the pains of the event had started. The child may conveniently and truly be called "self-determination" in the light of what has been just shown on the subject of personal responsibility and the right to discharge it without the interference of a dictatorial monarchy. The church as Christ and the apostles set it up, taught men not to call any man "father" upon earth (Matthew 23: 9). It taught that all men were to consult the word of God for their guidance (James 1: 25). That the Lord's servants are to speak as the oracles of God (1 Peter 4: 11), and that means that every man will be able to read and "interpret" the word for himself and not have to take dictation from some supreme authority independent of his own responsibility. When men learned these truths they rebelled at the idea of world monarchies. That is the reason Daniel predicted that the stone cut out of the mountain—the kingdom set up by the God of heaven—was to put an end to world power. Daniel 2: 44.) It is no wonder, then, that the dragon wanted to kill this man child. *Rule with a rod of iron.* This may sound severe but iron is not necessarily harsh or cruel, it means it is strong and durable. *Child was caught up* is another symbol. If a babe was born that was at once surrounded with dangerous conditions so that the mother would have to flee to some place for safety, some kind hearted friends would take care of the infant. Accordingly, when the church was driven into the wilderness, her child "self-determination," was watched over by the kind Father in heaven to see that it would live through all those years of the apostasy.

Verse 6. This *wilderness* was the period of the Dark Ages where the length of it is given in words and which is the same 1260 that the other computations give. All through that period the true church was alive but was in comparative obscurity because of the oppressive domination of the institution of Rome with its union of church and state. But her child—the spirit of self-determination—was alive and tenderly watched over by an infinite Guardian, and was destined some day to "make his mark in the world" upon the return of his mother from the wilderness.

Verse 7. *War in heaven.* We must keep in mind that everything being described is symbolic and shown to John right there on that isle of Patmos. But also we should not forget that inspired symbols stand for actual facts and truths. This war was not the first conflict that the forces of heaven had had with Satan for Jesus said he saw him fall from heaven (Luke 10: 18). And Paul tells us what was the cause of the first conflict, namely, his pride (1 Timothy 3: 6). Ever since that event he has been the bitter enemy of heaven and all that pertains thereto, never losing an opportunity of getting in his evil work. Now when he sees this expectant mother in heaven (verse 1) he is determined to start a war over it. Just why or how the devil could be present in the vicinity of the angels is not told us in detail, but we know from Job 1: 6 and 2: 1 that he has been suffered in the past to be present at gatherings of the angels before God. But the time Jesus saw him fall as cited in Luke was not on the occasion of this war, for the angels who won in the war ascribed the victory to the blood of the Lamb, and when Jesus said he saw Satan fall from heaven was before He had shed his blood. Hence this war was just another attempt of Satan to get in his wicked work and head off the plan of the Lord to give to the world a religion free from the entanglements of worldly despotism, and the selfish ambition of wicked men. It was fitting that Michael should be the angel to lead the forces of heaven against Satan, for he is called "one of the chief princes" in Daniel 10: 13, and chapter 12: 1 of that same book says that he is the prince that "standeth for the children of thy people."

Verse 8. Satan was defeated and *neither was their place found any more in heaven.* This means that the enemy not only was vanquished but driven from the field.

Verse 9. Satan was cast out *and his angels were cast out with him.* This agrees with 2 Peter 2: 4 and Jude 6, and also explains why Jesus speaks of the devil's angels in Matthew 25: 41. Satan is called *that old serpent* because he used that beast as his agent in Genesis 3: 1-4. *Deceiveth the whole world* does not mean that every person in the world is deceived for there are exceptions. The thought is that all deception that is in the world is to be attributed to him.

Verse 10. It was perfectly logical that the righteous persons should rejoice over the defeat of Satan. *Now is come* is their way of saying that the *kingdom of our God* was given another victory through the *power of his Christ. Accuser of our brethren.* The specific accusation is not stated, but since it was a daily performance we may conclude that it refers to the general opposition that Satan has always waged against the Lord and his faithful servants.

Verse 11. The pronoun *they* stands for "our brethren" in the preceding verse, who are said to have overcome Satan in the *war* that was fought in heaven. Verse 7 says that Michael and his angels fought against the dragon. There is no conflict in the statements which show that the forces of heaven are always ready to join in any battle with the forces of evil. This recalls the statement of Paul in Hebrews 1: 14 that the angels are "ministering spirits, sent forth to minister for them who shall be heirs of salvation." *Overcame him by the blood of the Lamb.* The blood had brought them the hope of salvation and that hope gave them the courage to fight Satan. *By the word of their testimony.* They persisted in their defence of the testimony of Jesus and that helped to put Satan to flight. James 4: 7 says, "Resist the devil and he will flee from you." *Loved not their lives unto death.* Their faith in the righteousness of their Master's cause was so strong that even the threat or presence of death could not dampen their zeal. (See Matthew 10: 28.) An army of such soldiers can rout the fiercest attacks of Satan.

Verse 12. These happy victors are bidding all the domain of intelligent creatures to rejoice over the situation. However, while the devil has lost this battle, he has not been put out of existence but will use every opportunity that appears for opposing the friends of truth. For this reason the inhabitants of *earth and sea* are given warning of what to expect. There are literally no creatures in the sea in which Satan is interested. The phrase is a figure of speech that means all creatures everywhere will be the victims of Satan's hatred. *Hath but a short time.* Whatever Satan accomplishes against the spiritual interests of mankind must be done while the world stands. After that he and his angels will be cast into the lake of eternal fire from which they will never escape even temporarily.

Verse 13. *Was cast unto the earth.* The attempts of Satan against the forces of heaven were completely overthrown. That left only the territory of the earth for future operations, and as a persistent general he began at once to carry out his wicked strategy. His objective was to persecute the woman (the church) who had given birth to the man child, namely, the principle of "self-determination."

Verse 14. This is a repetition of verse 6 with the additional information about the *two wings* that were given her. They are symbols and refers to the Old and New Testament, for it is the word of God that sustains the church in all the trying scenes of this world. It is by this word the woman (the church) was to be *nourished* (given spiritual food) while she is in the wilderness. The length of her exile in the wilderness is the same actual period that has been stated elsewhere, only it is indicated with different figurative terms. The word "time" in figurative language means "year;" this is indicated in Daniel 4: 16; 7: 25; 12: 7. Our verse calls for *time* (one), *times* (two) and *half a time*. It sums up three and a half times or years. Multiply 360 by three and a half and you have 1260, the period of the Dark Ages.

Verse 15. Sometimes when specific temptations do not make the desired "dent" in the character of a Christian, he may be finally overcome by an avalanche of afflictions. The devil (in the form of a serpent) tried this last method on the church. It was symbolized by having the devil cast a flood of water out of his mouth, hoping to engulf the woman in it there being no way to escape due to its volume. The Roman Empire used both methods in opposing the Lord's people. Sometimes an outstanding instance would be used such as burning a man at the stake or nailing some disciple to a cross. Then again the government would let loose a wholesale sweep of persecutions.

Verse 16. In the case of a flood there would appear to be no possible way of escape. But an unexpected opening in the earth let the water down and the woman was thereby saved. Likewise it happens that when matters seem to be at a crisis, and when "no earthly help is nigh," something will occur to defeat the enemy and rescue the would-be victim.

Verse 17. If the devil fails to make a wholesale destruction of the church, he will work on as many of the individual members as he can contact. This is the only explanation I can see that will harmonize the parts of this verse which might seem to be in difficulty. The woman (the church) is made up of individual disciples, and to attack one is to attack the other. Yet there is a distinction between the church as a whole and the individual members thereof. Paul said "ye are the body of Christ, and member in particular" (1 Corinthians 12: 27).

Revelation 13

Verse 1. It is very important that the reader take the time to read carefully the "general remarks" at the beginning of this book. He should note especially the information concerning the changes that took place in the Roman Empire due to its different state religions. A brief mention of them is all the space that can be used here, namely, Pagan Rome means the empire while its religion was the pagan or heathen. Papal Rome means when the state religion was the Papal or that under the pope. There is another item that should be stated in order to avoid confusion. The events that are described in the book of Revelation are not all given in the strict order of their occurrence. For instance, the present chapter opens with a vision of Pagan Rome which we know was before the days of Constantine. That means also that it was before the beginning of the Dark Ages of 1260 years. Yet we have already had a vision of that period even down to and including the Reformation of Luther, which is shown in chapter 11. This style of composition will be noticed in various places in this book. The vision will perhaps take the reader down the years through some important happenings, then go back many centuries and start all over again but with different symbols.

The *sea* is a symbol of humanity because all governments are products of human formation. The *beast* that John saw in this verse is Pagan Rome. The *seven heads* are explained at chapter 12: 3, referring to the literal or geographical fact that the city of Rome is situated upon seven hills. There is little or no importance attached to that except as a means of identification as to what city may be meant in the writings of some prophet or historian. If any political significance has been attached to the seven hills it would not affect the general plan of the book of Revelation. I believe that the Lord was concerned only with the outstanding subject of His church in its relation to both Pagan and Papal Rome, hence I have restricted my general considerations to that line. *Ten horns*. The Roman Empire was the fourth and last of the "four world empires" as they are familiarly termed. Its head was in the city of Rome and the emperor was the ultimate ruler of the entire government. However, the various nations were subdivided into smaller kingdoms with their own local administration under a king, whose authority was only one in name for he was subject to the head in the city of Rome. The ten horns symbolize the outstanding ones in the domain of the Empire. The names that I have are England, Germany, Italy, France, Holland, Belgium, Austria, Switzerland, Portugal and Spain. *Name of blasphemy.* All of these kings were under the control and influence of Pagan Rome which was in opposition to the authority of the Lord, hence their language would be that of blasphemy (evil speaking) against Him.

Verse 2. There are some distinctive characteristics between a leopard, bear and lion, but they all have in common that of fierce destructiveness. Such a symbolism would be appropriate to represent the attitude of Pagan Rome against Christianity. *The dragon* (Satan, chapter 12:9) *gave him his power* means the devil used his influence in favor of the beast of Rome. Satan has always been interested in supporting any institution that is an enemy of God.

Verse 3. There is much uncertainly among the commentators that I have consulted concerning the interpretation of this verse. The question is raised whether it means one of the ten horns, or that some part of the city was weakened, or that some one of the prominent emperors is meant. With such a state of variation among the able historians and commentators, I will offer only what I am sure will at least not conflict with the facts of history. In some way the government of Rome received a stroke that threatened to be fatal, until something was done that closed the breach and the threatened disaster was avoided. It must have been rather unusual for all the world wondered at the recovery from the wound.

Verse 4. *They* means the people of the world who worshipped the dragon (Satan) who gave his power to the *beast* (Pagan Rome). *Worship* is from a Greek word that means to do homage, not that any formal services were rendered. They *worshipped* the beast (Pagan Rome) which explains why they worshipped the dragon. They were admirers of the beast and naturally would feel kindly toward any being that would give him some support. With all this background in favor of the beast, they asked in the spirit of challenge who was able to make war with him.

Verse 5. *There was given unto him.* When something is given there must be a giver either directly or indirectly. The preceding verse tells of the people of the world worshipping the beast, and hence it is reasonable to conclude that this power or permission to speak blasphemies was his by common consent. These are the same kind of blasphemous words that are mentioned in verse 1. *Continue forty and two months.* We recognize this to be the same period that is elsewhere mentioned and that it is the Dark Ages. An apparent difficulty may present itself here. It is well known that the Dark Ages of 1260 years was the result of the union of church and state, at which time the apostate church was come to power. But our present verse is still under the time of Pagan Rome, and hence the period of the forty two months should not be started yet. It is one of the cases where God charges the fruits of a thing to that thing itself. Pagan Rome started the work of persecuting the Christians, and when the apostate church came into power it formed another beast (the Papal) which "retired from active service" the other beast. But the new beast just followed after the pattern set by the first one—"exerciseth all the power of the first beast" (verse 12). John was enabled to look ahead and see this conduct of the second beast, and hence laid the blame of the forty and two months at the door of the first beast, considering him as morally responsible for it, even though the apostasy did not actually get under way until the first beast was "taken out of the way" (2 Thessalonians 2:7).

Verse 6. To blaspheme means to speak evil against that which is disliked. The leaders in Pagan Rome did not like the name of God nor the services of His *tabernacle* (the church), because He taught men they should not worship idols. Therefore they spoke against the divine institution that was on the earth, and against the beings in heaven who were servants of God.

Verse 7. *Was given unto him* has virtually the same meaning as a like phrase in verse 5. Also the Lord suffered these things to go on for the time being. *Overcome them;* this was true in two senses. He overpowered the faithful disciples with his ability to persecute them, even putting some of them to death. And he overcame some of them morally, such as were not steadfast in the faith. He also exercised a controlling influence over the lives of men in *all kindreds, and tongues, and nations,* because the Roman Empire was in power in all the so-called civilized world.

Verse 8. *All . . . shall worship him* except those *whose names are not written in the book of life of the Lamb.* In this passage the effect is named before the cause. These names were written in the book because they refused to worship the beast. It is another way of saying that the faithful servants of God refused to worship the Beast. *Slain from the foundation of the world.* The last word is from a Greek term that means the inhabitants of the earth, especially when they became a fixed order of intelligent beings composing a social world. Before that state of affairs came into existence, God saw the necessity for a plan of human redemption. Accordingly He devised one that was to be made effective through the sacrifice of his Son.

Verse 9. This language is a solemn call upon all to give profound attention. The things having been said and that are still to be said are of great importance to all mankind.

Verse 10. *He that leadeth . . . shall go,* etc. The verse is a statement of principle that is true in whatever domain of human activity it is considered. It is the rule of moral law and it is also true on the basis of cause and effect. It is the rule that Paul has in mind where he says, "Whatsoever a man soweth that shall he also reap" (Galatians 6: 7). *Here is the patience and faith of the saints.* This means that when all these commotions are taking place under the wicked powers of the world, the saints (Christians) will have an opportunity of proving their faith and patience by remaining steadfast and true to the Lord.

Verse 11. The word *earth* like *sea* in verse 1 is used figuratively, referring to the people of the world because all governments on earth must be composed of human beings. *Another beast* is Papal Rome or the apostate church in connection with the state A few words of explanation of the term "pope" which means "universal father" according to the members of the apostate church. They regard the pope as their father or papa. When the letter l is added we have papal, making it an adjective meaning "of the pope." After Constantine adopted the religion professed by the bishop of the church (who later assumed the title of pope), the whole institution was thereafter known as Papal Rome. The beast of this verse had two horns which refers to the two parts of the empire, namely, church and state. *Spake as a dragon.* The apostate institution made the profession of Christianity but its decrees and communications to the people were prompted by the dragon (Satan). This is what Paul predicts in 2 Thessalonians 2: 9 where he describes the pope as follows: "Whose coming is after the working of Satan, with all power and signs and lying wonders."

Verse 12. *Exerciseth all the power of the first beast* is commented upon in the remarks at verse 5. *Causeth . . . to worship the first beast.* Papal Rome was composed of church and state, and the two parts of that institution supported each other. The pope instructed his subjects that they must obey the orders of the state in all matters of conduct, even including their religious activities. *Whose deadly wound was healed.* (See the comments at verse 3.) The pope had a grateful remembrance of that episode in the affairs of state. Had the wound not been healed and the state had gone down, he would not then have the powerful support of the government to back him up in his wicked control over the lives of his people. So it is not strange that he directed them to *worship* that beast. That could not mean any formal ceremonies, the beast was not in existence in reality any way. It means for them to pay homage to the memory of the beast.

Verse 13. This verse is a statement of the false claims of the church of Rome, not that it actually performed the wonders mentioned. (See next verse.)

Verse 14. *And deceiveth them* is the key to the preceding verse. Paul has the same subject in mind in 2 Thessalonians 2: 9 where he calls it "signs and lying wonders." Bible students know that since the days of the apostles, no man has been able to perform any supernatural acts. The word *mi-*

racle means generally anything wonderful or out of the ordinary. *He ... do ... in the sight of the beast* means the pope performed the deceptive tricks with the leaders of state looking on and approving. *Make* means to "form or fashion," and *image* means an imitation or repetition. The pope required his people to imitate the characteristics of the first beast in his opposition to the worship of the true God. We should not lose sight of the dependence the pope felt he had upon the support of the secular power. That is why the church of Rome would have church and state united today if it could.

Verse 15. The *image* of the beast is something that is a figure or is like it. The predominating characteristic of Pagan Rome with regard to her treatment of Christianity, was her persecution of the disciples and even to the extent of slaying the true worshipers of God. Therefore any person or group of persons that imitated that character would have the support of Papal Rome, and in that sense would receive *life* therefrom. The closing words of this verse verify the above statement by saying that those who would not worship (pay homage to and show respect) *should be killed*.

Verse 16. *Mark* is from CHARAGMA, which Thayer defines, "a stamp, an imprinted mark," then explains it to mean, "of the mark stamped on the forehead or the right hand as a badge of the follower of Antichrist." Of course the branding which John saw was symbolical of something that would not be seen with natural eyes. The invisible fact concerning those who imitated the beast was their guilt. God could see it and the detectives of the pope had some way of recognizing it.

Verse 17. The pope restricted the privileges and rights of all who would not submit to his dictation. If a man gave evidence of having the mark (the stain of guilt), and who *had* (knew and endorsed) the *number of his name* was given permission to proceed with his own interests.

Verse 18. *The number of the beast* and *the number of a man* are declared to be the same. Also according to the preceding verse these phrases are both equivalent to the *number of his name*. John tells us the number of his name which is 666, but he does not tell us what the name is. Remember the beast now being cited is the first one or Pagan Rome. Well, the government is not what has this number, for John says it is the number of a man. So we need to find a man who was outstanding at the head of Pagan Rome the letters of whose name will give us the number (numerical values being indicated with letters in those times). In the Greek it is CHXS and Thayer gives us the following comments on the term. "A mystical number the meaning of which is clear when it is written in Hebrew letters . . . i. e., Nero Caesar." The question might arise why this particular one of the Caesars or Roman Emperors was selected for the symbol. The reason is that he was one of the most notorious and infamous of the emperors. He was the one who had Paul slain and his inhuman treatment of Christians set the pattern after which other rulers followed in their opposition to the true church.

Revelation 14

Verse 1. The preceding chapter took us back to the first century of the Christian Era and dealt with the years of Pagan Rome, then came on to the time of Papal Rome and predicted the Dark Ages of 1260 years. The present chapter will continue down through that period and through the days of the Reformation, finally reaching the last great day of judgment and the separation of the saved from the unsaved. The Lamb is Christ and Zion is the true church which has been persecuted all through the Dark Ages. In the course of that period there were multitudes of faithful Christians who would not receive the mark of the beast, but instead they had the name of the Father written in their foreheads.

Verse 2. *Voice of many waters* symbolizes that great numbers had resisted the temptations of Rome, and *thunder* is a symbol denoting that the sound of triumph is strong and of great volume. *Voice of harpers* means the organs of song in the bodies of the redeemed, for the next verse says they were singing with the harps.

Verse 3. *A new song*. The saints of God always have the same story to tell and the same song to sing, and that is about redemption through the blood of the Lamb. But that story has a new significance whenever the faithful have another victory over the forces of evil through faith in Christ Jesus, and in that sense it becomes *a new song*. At the present time they had gained a victory over the apostate institution and hence they had great reason to rejoice and sing. The four *beasts* (living creatures) and the four and twenty elders are among the grateful listeners to the song. The hundred and forty and four thousand are the same ones we read about in chapter 7. *No man could learn that song.* Men of the world can sing any kind of song that is written as far as the literal execution of it is concerned, but they cannot realize what it means to express themselves in song as can those who have been redeemed from sin in the blood of the Lamb, and then again experienced the joy of winning out in a battle against the hosts of wickedness as these had. The corrupt institution of Rome had tried to overcome them by its abominable allurements but had failed.

Verse 4. In figurative language heathenism, paganism or idolatry, likewise any other form of unlawful worship is used to symbolize adultery and other forms of immorality. The persons of this verse were disciples who had remained true to the service of Christ though often tempted to commit spiritual adultery with paganism and other practices of Rome. *Follow the Lamb whithersoever he goeth* covers much more than is often realized. It means to follow Him through sorrow as well as joy; through evil report as well as good, and through the valley of death if the enemy drives that affliction upon the servant of the Lord. Incidentally this verse gives us some information on the subject of virgins. The common idea is that only women can be virgins but these are called such because they had not been defiled with women, and men only could be defiled in that way. True the writer is considering spiritual adultery, but the language would not have been used were it not understood that either sex may be a virgin. *Firstfruits* is figurative in the sense of quality, and the word is based on the requirements of the Mosiac law. The Jews were commanded to give the first of all their flocks and herds and the products of the field unto the Lord. The word finally came to mean the best service that one could render to Him. The disciples of this verse had performed such excellent devotions that the word *firstfruits* is used denoting something especially dear to the Lord.

Verse 5. *Guile* means deceit and these faithful disciples had no desire nor occasion to try deceiving anyone. That evil trait was one of the prominent ones of the "man of sin." *Fault* means blemish or spot in one's conduct or manner of life. Hence this verse represents persons who are correct in both word and deed. That would indicate that their hearts were right also because "out of the abundance of the heart the mouth speaketh" (Matthew 12: 34), and from the heart come "murders, adulteries," etc. (Matthew 15: 19). These saints were free from all these products of an evil heart so we may conclude they were pure in heart. That explains why they were allowed to be *before the throne of God,* for Matthew 5: 8 says the pure in heart shall see God. These brave soldiers of the cross had been strengthened in their fight of faith by the very trials that were intended to destroy them.

Verse 6. *Everlasting gospel* is what had been kept from the people during the Dark Ages. As long as Rome could hold her subjects in ignorance of the Bible she was able to continue the dictatorial rule over them. Even the kings and other rulers over the various nations and countries were held back because they were not permitted to make their own application of the scriptures either for the lives of their subjects or for themselves. They were told that the scriptures were "not of any private interpretation" (making a perverted use of 2 Peter 1: 20), and that they must leave that to the church. Not only were they forbidden to interpret what they might have been able to read, but the Bible was kept in the Latin language so that they could not even read it. But Martin Luther and his associates gave the Book to the people in their native tongue so they could read for themselves. Concerning this great work I shall make a quotation from Edward Gibbon the English historian: "By their hands the lofty fabric of superstition, from the abuse of indulgencies to the intercession of the Virgin, has been levelled with the ground. Myriads of both sexes of the monastic profession [that of the secluded monks] were restored to the liberty and labors of social life. A hierarchy of saints and angels, of imperfect and subordinate deities, were stripped of their temporal powers, and reduced to the enjoyment of celestial happiness; their images and relics were banished from the church; and the credulity [blind readiness to believe] of the people was no longer nourished with the daily repetition of miracles and visions." — Volume 4, Page 608.

Verse 7. The angel is announcing the glorious work of giving the word of God back to the people, and bidding them rejoice over it and give Him glory for it. *Hour of his judgment* means the time is come when the great apostate institution is to be judged by having her power broken through the work of the reformers. *Worship him that made heaven and earth*, instead of the superstitious objects held before them by Rome.

Verse 8. A result of the *everlasting gospel* which the preceding angel announced is then stated by *another angel*, namely, *Babylon is fallen*. The reader is reminded that the term *Babylon* in this part of the great drama means the institution that was formed by the union of church and state. It is here called *that great city* because its head was the city of Rome where both the emperor and pope resided. *Wine of the wrath of her fornication* is a figurative phrase combining the false teaching and idolatrous practices of Rome. As long as the people were kept in ignorance of the Bible, they could be *made to drink* of this wine. The announcement that *Babylon is fallen* means that the union of church and state was dissolved as a result of the information brought to the people through the Bible, translated in their native language so they could read it for themselves, and form conclusions independent of Rome.

Verse 9. A third angel appeared to give a warning for all who might still persist in following after the evil pattern set by Rome. He mentions the three phases of the subject that were treated at chapter 13: 14-17. Concerning the *image* I shall make another quotation from Edward Gibbon which follows that which is quoted at verse 6. 'The imitation of Paganism was supplied [replaced] by a pure and spiritual worship of prayer and thanksgiving, the most worthy of man, the least unworthy of the Deity."

Verse 10. The false worshippers are told that if they persist in drinking of this wine of the wrath of Rome, they will be punished by having to drink of another supply of wine; that will be the *wine of the wrath of God*. Wine has been used figuratively for centuries to symbolize wrath and anger and other intense conditions of the intellect. (See Psalms 60: 3; Proverbs 4: 17; Jeremiah 25: 15; 51: 7.) *Without mixture* means it will not be diluted nor weakened, but they shall get the full effect of the wrath of God upon those who have been devoted to Rome. *Shall be tormented with fire and brimstone* refers to the lake of fire into which the wicked will be cast at the day of judgment. *In the presence . . . of the Lamb*. This denotes that the sentence of this punishment will be pronounced in the presence of Christ and his angels. (See Matthew 25: 31-46; 2 Thessalonians 1: 7-9.) The sentence will be pronounced then but it will be served according to the next verse.

Verse 11. *Smoke of their torment* refers to that which will arise from the fire in the lake into which the wicked will have been cast. *Ascendeth up for ever and ever*. If the smoke is to ascend for ever it follows that the torment will continue for ever. It will come from the lake of fire which has been created for the purpose of tormenting the unsaved. The particular unsaved persons named in this place are those who have guilty relations with the beast, the image or the mark (chapter 13: 14, 15). But all the unsaved will be in this place for Matthew 25: 41 says they will be told: "Depart from me, ye cursed, into everlasting fire, prepared for the devil and his angels." *No rest day nor night* is another way of saying that the punishment of the unsaved will be endless. Terrible thought!!

Verse 12. This has the same meaning as chapter 13: 10.

Verse 13. *Blessed are the dead who die in the Lord*. That can be said of every person who is faithful until death, but it is said here especially with reference to those who have died under persecution. It is peculiarly appropriate to make the statement in view of the thousands who had been slain by Pagan and Papal Rome through the past centuries. Also after the Reformation had stirred up the anger of the "die-hards" of Babylon many others were put to death in their struggles. *From henceforth*. Some commentators say this means from the judgment day and thereafter. It is true that all righteous people will be blessed (happy) after that day, but I do not believe the Spirit was applying the blessing to that date in this verse. There will be saints living when Christ comes who will never die, yet they will be happy for ever. But our verse is about those who *die* in the Lord, and they are especially mentioned for the reason described in the first part of this paragraph. And since these who died in the Lord had the experience some time before the end of the world, the passage gives us the grand information that when a righteous person dies he is happy from that moment onward. This all agrees with Paul's remarks in Philippians 1: 21-23. *Their works do follow them.* The Greek for *follow* means both to accompany a person and to come along afterwards. Both senses of the word apply to a faithful servant of God. The good deeds he performs will still linger behind to be an influence for others. ("By it he being dead yet speaketh," Hebrews 11: 4.) Also the record of faithfulness will be with him in principle to recommend him before God.

Verse 14. The rest of the chapter is a vision of the day of judgment. Clouds are often used as symbols of glory and power especially white clouds. The person sitting on the cloud is *like* the Son of man because he is but a symbol. Yet we must think of Christ, who is being symbolized by the vision. *Golden crown* signifies a king and we are told in 1 Corinthians 15: 25 that He is to reign until the end. *Sharp sickle* is an instrument for gathering the fruits of a harvest. Jesus is king in his own right, but he is generally represented as accomplishing the work of His kingdom in cooperation with the angels. Especially is this true of the work to be performed at his second coming. (See Matthew 25: 31; 1 Thessalonians 4: 16; 2 Thessalonians 1: 7.)

Verse 15. *Another* angel is said because angels have been named previously in this chapter, and because those heavenly beings are so often employed to act as attendants upon the Lord or sometimes upon other angels as will be done yet in this chapter. There are to be two kinds of crops gathered on the day of judgment as generally happens after any growing season. One kind is the good and the other is the bad, and they are always separated one from the other and different dispositions made of them. In the present case the good is represented in the ordinary phraseology of a good harvest which implies sheaves of grain. The bad is represented by grapes which we have just seen above symbolize the wrath of God upon the wicked. The attending angel signalled to Him who was on the cloud to use his sickle to gather the ripe harvest.

Verse 16. The One on the white cloud did as requested and gathered the grain. The reader will understand this represents the good among mankind.

Verse 17. The other sickle was in the hands of an angel instead of Him who was on the cloud. This also agrees with the language of Christ in Matthew 13: 39 where he says "the angels are the reapers." Notice these angels are said to come *out of the temple.* That is because it is in heaven from where the authority of God is issued.

Verse 18. The next attending angel came out from the *altar.* That article was also at the temple and it was the piece that was used for burning certain victims. The symbol is very appropriate since this sickle is to be used for gathering the grapes; grapes for the wrath of God. This angel gave the signal to the one holding the second sickle to use it for gathering in the clusters. The reason assigned by him for the order was *her grapes are fully ripe.* God is never premature in his operations. He explained to Abraham in Genesis 15: 16 that the reason for waiting until the fourth generation for attacking the land of promise was that "the iniquity of the Amorites is not yet full." In 2 Peter 3: 15 it says that the longsuffering of God in delaying the destruction of the earth "is salvation." Whenever God in his infinite wisdom sees that the time is *fully ripe* for the harvest He will send forth the reapers and bring an end to the earth and its contents.

Verse 19. As a literal fact a winepress is a large vat in which grapes are placed for extraction of the juice. In Bible times mechanical means had not been invented for pressure, and the result was accomplished by man power. A lattice-like platform was laid on top of the grapes and a number of men walked round and round over it until the juice was forced out, being received below through a trough running from the vat to a receiving vessel. The symbolic feature is in the fact that the desired result was accomplished by a treading under foot. The operation is used to symbolize the act of the Lord in trampling under his feet the wicked people of the earth. The flowing of the wine signifies the flowing of the wrath of God against men's unrighteousness.

Verse 20. The symbol continues with the same significance but with some added specifications. Being done *with-*

out the city denotes that the punishment of the wicked will be outside the holy city in the eternal world. In computing the amount of blood (of the grape) that came out we must not forget that the whole performance is symbolic, and the volume is given in order to furnish us some idea of the terrible fate of those whose unrighteous lives have brought upon them the wrath of God. To be conservative I suppose *unto the horse bridles* would be about four feet. The amount was enough to flood the ground for a distance of a thousand and six hundred furlongs or two hundred miles. Nothing is said about any kind of retainer on the sides, hence to be wide enough to flow freely that far and that deep (if only in the center) would require a considerable width. It all should give us a profound impression of the fate of those who die out of Christ.

Revelation 15

Verse 1. The preceding chapter describes the vision before John that came down to the day of judgment and to the final assignment of all mankind to their eternal destinations. The present chapter goes back some distance (as the book has done before), and will again take up the judgments of God that were poured out upon the apostate church for her worship of idols and her persecution of the faithful servants of God. *Seven* angels are seen as a symbol of the completeness of God's system for executing his wrath upon the wicked of the earth.

Verse 2. Clear glass and fire are symbols of opposite facts and yet are appropriately used. The verse tells of several persons who had won a victory of a spiritual nature over the forces of Rome. The fire symbolizes their conflicts in which they were victorious, and the clear glass signifies their calmness of mind after the victory. The beast, the image and the mark were all involved in the conflict. The faithful servants resisted the direct attacks of Rome, also avoided imitating her in their lives, and as a consequence had escaped receiving the mark of guilt. *Over the number of his name.* The man whose number is stated in the text is Nero Caesar. Getting the victory over the number of his name is an indirect way of saying their victory was over Nero. That is significant since he was the emperor who was chief among the heads of Rome that tried to force the Christians to sin.

Verse 3. The song of Moses and of the Lamb was especially appropriate. It is to be associated with the four and twenty elders who have been mentioned a number of times. Twelve of them represent the Mosaic system and twelve stand for that under Christ. The song John heard these happy persons singing was about the lawgivers of those great institutions. But while the subject matter of the song was concerning them as the lawgivers, they ascribed the credit to works of God because they are marvelous, and to Christ as a King who is true and just in his ways.

Verse 4. The occasion for this great rejoicing is the prospect of judgments that are soon to be inflicted upon the powers of Rome whose hold upon the people has just been broken by the effects of the Reformation. That is why they exclaim about the worthiness of the Lord to be glorified. *All nations shall come and worship before thee.* Their worship will consist in doing homage to God as the true object of praise, for the light of truth that the Bible shed on them since it was given back to them. Through that channel of information they have been informed that God's judgments are just.

Verse 5. This verse has the same significance as chapter 11: 19.

Verse 6. Much of what is said and is to happen in many of the chapters to come has been considered before. It will pertain to God's judgments against the corruptions of Rome and for her mistreatment of the faithful servants of Christ. Seven angels were clothed in white linen which means purity and the golden girdles signify the splendor of the place.

Verse 7. It is important to keep constantly in mind that we are studying in a book of symbols or signs. Many of the things John saw in the vision have reference to the severe denunciations that were made in the days of the Reformation. Those statements were sounded into the ears of kings and other leaders of the apostate church. A *vial* is used in the symbolic picture because it is a vessel out of which something can be poured, and the judgments of God are said to be *poured* out. That would indicate a large and continuous stream of His judgments. One of the *beasts* (living creatures) gave the vials to the angels; that was appropriate. The beasts were the saved in the Lord who had been the victims of the rage of the beast of Rome. They had won a victory through faith, and it was fitting that they should have the honor of handing the vials to the angels.

Verse 8. *Temple was filled with smoke*. This was not the smoke of incense as is sometimes mentioned, for that occurs only when righteous servants are performing worship, and that is not what is going on now. It is the smoke of God's wrath against the corruptions of the beast. Those guilty of the corruptions are under judgment and God is about to execute wrath upon them. It is too late for them to expect mercy from God, hence no one will be permitted to enter the temple to plead for it.

Revelation 16

Verse 1. The great voice was out of the temple. That means it was from God, for we have learned in the preceding chapter that no man was able to be in the temple at this time. The seven angels have been given the vials of divine wrath, now the voice bids them empty their contents in the places deserving such treatment.

Verse 2. *Noisome and grievous* indicates something extremely objectionable and damaging. It should be remarked that the judgments against the wicked leaders in the corrupt institution were suffered immediately. They felt it through the humiliation of seeing their places of evil rulership brought down through the effects of the Reformation. But this was destined to be only a foretaste of the final judgment that will be pronounced upon them at the last day. The *mark* and *image* of the beast have been explained at chapter 13: 14.

Verse 3. *Blood of a dead man*. When a man dies his blood dies with him and becomes poisonous. That which would come in contact with it would be killed. The blood of Christ was dead when it was poured out, hence it will kill the sins of the world if brought into contact with them. (See 1 John 1: 7.)

Verse 4. The mention of the earth and other parts of the creation are to represent them as symbols, denoting the completeness of God's judgments against evil men. That is why rivers and water fountains are named in this verse.

Verse 5. *Angel of the waters* is the one in the preceding verse. These angels form a unit (seven) and hence any principle held by one goes for all of them. The angel commended the action of the Lord for the righteous judgments inflicted upon the servants of the beast. *Art*, and *wast* and *shalt be* is the same as saying that God had no beginning and will have no end. Such a Being cannot do wrong hence his judgments against His enemies are bound to be just.

Verse 6. The first part of this verse is literal, for the agencies of both Pagan and Papal Rome caused many righteous servants of God to shed their blood. *Given them blood to drink* is figurative and refers to the legal executions imposed on the wicked.

Verse 7. This angel repeated the same commendation of God's judgments that was expressed by the one in verses 5 and 6.

Verse 8. The sun is a part of the creation which was commented upon at verse 4. It is specified in the present group of symbols because of the particular item it contributes to the welfare of humanity when it is used normally. It is the source of light and heat without which man could not live. But it is now used as a symbol of torment of fire by increasing the volume of the rays upon men. In Malachi 2: 2 the Lord was making threats against some of His ancient people for their wickedness in which he says "I will curse your blessing." The thought is similar to the one of our verse. The sun is normally a blessing to the people of the earth, but it is used as a symbol of cursing.

Verse 9. The intense heat caused men to blaspheme the name of God because of their suffering; that was because they recognized Him as being the cause of the affliction. But the very motive that caused them to blaspheme Him, should have had the effect of making them repent, for they must have known that a Being who can bring such tremendous revolutions in the universe is worthy to be feared and served.

Verse 10. *The seat of the beast* means his throne or headquarters. The *darkness* is figurative and refers to some confusion or disarrangement of the affairs of the government. To gnaw the tongues for pain would be a natural or literal performance, but it is another one of the many symbols used in this book, and represents the intense disappointment and humiliation of the leaders in Rome when they see their structure of oppressive power tumbling about them.

Verse 11. This is similar to verse 9 and shows the effect that pride can have upon men. *Repented not* can be accounted for only by thinking of their stubbornness which is a form or manifestation of pride.

Verse 12. The great river Euphrates has played an important part in God's dealing with his people in their relation with the nations. The city of Babylon was situated upon its banks. When the time came for the overthrow of the first of the "four world empires" (the Babylonian), it was accomplished by diverting the stream from its regular channel. When that was done the water was lowered (was *dried up)* so that the soldiers of Cyrus *(kings of the east)* could march into the city and slay the man on the throne. All of this describes a literal event in history, but it is used to form the phraseology for the overthrow of another Babylon ("Mystery Babylon the Great"), which had been brought into existence by the union of church and state.

Verse 13. Frogs are slimy, loathsome creatures and are used to represent three very loathsome powers and individuals. They are the *dragon* (Satan, chapter 12:9), the *beast* (Rome) and *the false prophet*. The last phrase is singular in grammatical form but does not refer to any particular one of the false prophets. It means the group of evil workers who used their deceptive tactics to mislead the people all over the domain or the dominions of Rome.

Verse 14. *Devils* means the demons by which the apostate church imposed upon the victims of their treachery. *Working miracles* is explained at chapter 13:14, and it is the same that Paul predicts in 2 Thessalonians 2:9 as follows: "Whose coming is after the working of Satan with all power and signs and lying wonders." *Gather them to the battle* means the battle will continue until the great day.

Verse 15. This verse is in the nature of a parenthesis because it speaks of the coming of Christ, at which time all things on the earth will end. But the preceding verse mentions a battle that is to continue until that event, and the verse following our present one will go back to the beginning of that battle as to its coverage of time.

Verse 16. *Armageddon* is the Greek word of the original text spelled with English letters. The literal meaning of the word as defined in Thayer's lexicon is "destruction." It is the action referred to by "battle" in verse 14 which means war in general, not merely a single fight. This will be commented upon at length at chapter 20.

Verse 17. The *seventh angel* was the last of the group that was to pour the vials out upon the earth. The voice came out of the temple which signifies that it was a voice of authority. The voice made the brief announcement that *it is done*, meaning that the revolution signified by the "seven last plagues" was accomplished. The great revolution thus symbolized was the Reformation of Luther and his fellow workers that resulted in breaking up the union of church and state.

Verse 18. *Thunder, lightnings* and *earthquake* in symbolic language refers to great commotions in the public affairs. Such a mighty movement as the dissolving of church and state was enough to bring forth these demonstrations about the temple, for it meant so much to the interests of the cause of God who occupies the temple.

Verse 19. The *great city* means the institution composed of the union of church and state, as it is used here and some other places, not merely church or state singly. It is in that sense that the name Babylon is used in this verse, because the literal city of Babylon had been destroyed centuries before (Isaiah 13:19-22), and the apostate church of Rome as a religious institution is not to be destroyed until Jesus comes again (2 Thessalonians 2:8). But Babylon as the union of church and state was dissolved by the Reformation never to be restored. *Divided into three parts.* This partial destruction has been indicated a number of times and has been explained to mean that God does not completely extinguish every institution He condemns. *Came in remembrance before God* means he remembered the evils that city had done to His people. *Give unto her the cup*, etc., is the same figurative sense of wine that has been commented upon in chapter 14:19, 20.

Verse 20. *Island* in symbolic language means inhabited spots and *mountains* denotes units of government. John saw these *flee away* in the vision which was symbolical, and the meaning is on the same subject that has been under consideration through many of the passages, namely, the downfall of the political power of Rome.

Verse 21. Weight of *talents* varied according to the different standards and they were at least fifty pounds on an average. To drop a hail stone of that weight as a symbol of God's wrath would give some impression of the greatness of that wrath. *Blasphemed God* means they spoke very evil words against Him, because of their disappointment and humiliation over the loss of their political power.

Revelation 17

Verse 1. This chapter (like some others) goes back to the time just before the Reformation, and will make symbolic predictions of that revolution. It should be stated that while the institution of church and state (which has not yet been dissolved as to the start of this chapter), is regarded as Babylon the Great and an enemy of God, the church part of the combination will seem to receive the more attention from the Lord in his condemnations. That is because it deals with the affairs of the soul which are more important than those of the secular government. Yet because the apostate church was supported by the political power of Rome and her Empire, much of the language in the symbols will be based upon the geographical and political features of that city. *Show unto thee the judgment* or give John a prediction of God's judgments in a vision. The *great whore* is said of the apostate church because false religions of all kinds are likened to immorality in figurative language. *Sitteth upon many waters.* Waters in symbolic language means people upon whom the corrupt institution pressed down with her desolating weight of intolerance and persecution.

Verse 2. The *kings of the earth* means the rulers over the various divisions of the political empire, such as the ones named at chapter 13:1. In their devotion to the spiritual harlot they were guilty of fornication. The *inhabitants of the earth* refers to the subjects under these kings who submitted to their adulterous ruling. *Wine of her fornication.* In literal practice we find "wine and women" often associated, hence they are so considered in the symbolic vision that John saw.

Verse 3. *Carried me away in the spirit* is significant, and reminds us again of the truth that John never did leave the isle of Patmos literally while in the vision of this book. It was a part of the symbolical vision to be taken away into the wilderness and see the things that shall be described. The *woman* is the apostate church of Rome symbolized by the city of Rome because the church rested on the government of that city for support. The literal reason for using a beast in the symbol that was scarlet, was the fact that scarlet was one of the royal colors of the Empire. *Seven heads and ten horns* is explained at chapter 13:1, and it will appear in this chapter with a slight variation in the application.

Verse 4. Since the state color of the beast (Rome) was scarlet and purple, it was appropriate that the rider of the beast should be robed to match. It is literally true that the clergy of the church of Rome wear these colors in their church ceremonies. It is also appropriate that such colors be used in the symbols of that church, in view of the faithful people of God who had their blood taken from them in the persecution at the hands of that wicked institution. Being decked with precious stones and pearls also was appropriate because the church of Rome possesses and uses great wealth in her ceremonies. The symbolic cup represents the corrupt practices that the church of Rome forced upon her subjects. It is symbolized in the form of a person filling a cup with vile and abominable materials then forcing some helpless person to drink it.

Verse 5. The name that John saw written on the forehead of this woman was put there by the Lord to designate to the apostate her true character, not that she had taken to herself such an inscription. In truth the leaders of the church of Rome of today deny that this applies to their "holy mother church." *Mystery* is a part of her characteristics; Thayer's definition of the word at this place is, "The mystic or hidden sense." The apostate church has always thrived most when she could keep her people in ignorance of what was going on. *Babylon the great.* There are many ways in which anything can be great both good and bad. Babylon was great in a bad sense and that is because she was the most extensive and powerful influence for evil that Satan ever devised. *Mother of harlots.* A bad woman can be the mother of pure daughters and they would not need to participate in the wickedness of their mother; but this woman's daughters also are harlots. Of course as we have previously learned, harlotry in figurative language means any false religion or unscriptural organization. The conclusion is that the religious denominations in the world are the harlot daughters of Rome, because they obtained the principal tenets that make up their creeds from the doctrines put out by that apostate church. *Abominations of the earth* is a general summing up of the evil doctrines and practices of the church of Rome throughout the world.

Verse 6. *Saints* and *martyrs* refer to the same people although the words have a different (but not conflicting) meaning. *Saint* means a holy or righteous person which applies to all Christians. *Martyr* means witness and all Christians are martyrs because they are faithful to the testimony of the Gospel regardless of what may be the result. The fact that both *saints* and *martyrs* had shed their blood in defence of the testimony of Jesus, shows the latter word is not applied to some on the simple ground that they died for Christ. *Saw the woman drunken.* To be drunk literally requires that a person be under the influence of alcohol. The term has come to be used figuratively, as when it is said that a man is "drunk with a craze for money; or for pleasure." Rome had shed so much blood of righteous people she is said to be drunk with the desire to slay the Christians. *Wondered with great admiration.* The last word usually has the sense of approval, but it is not restricted to that meaning. The phrase means the vision John saw was so unusual and vast that he could only gaze at it.

Verse 7. *Wherefore didst thou marvel?* This question indicates that the amazed expression on the face of John was mixed with that of being puzzled over the whole phenomenon. The angel promises to explain to him all about the mystery involving the *woman*, the *beast* and the *seven heads* and *ten horns* that the beast had. The passage deviates from the usual manner of the book. When the symbols are described we are generally left to figure out (by the help of history) what the interpretation is. This time the angel will tell to what institutions and persons the symbols refer. Not that he will specify the personal items of application, but he will describe it so that a student of the Bible and history should have no uncertainty about it.

Verse 8. *Was and is not* refers to Pagan Rome which ceased to be such an institution (on the surface) after the time of Constantine. *Ascend out of the bottomless pit.* The last two words mean that part of the intermediate state where evil men and angels are kept until the judgment day. It is the place where the wicked rich man went as recorded in Luke 16:23 where the word is "hell" but comes from a different Greek term. Since the members of Pagan Rome were wicked it was necessary to show them as ascending from this pit. But we should take notice that the vision leaps across all the intervening years for the moment to predict the final destiny of those members of the beast that had been in the bottomless pit. After the intermediate state is no longer needed, these wicked persons will ascend out of that pit and *go into perdition,* which means they will be cast into the lake of fire. Having shown a brief picture of the fate of this beast, the vision at once resumes the events and appearances that are to take place before the final day of *perdition.* The vision is so unusual that the uninformed shall *wonder* at it. That is the same word used in verse 6 which was seen to mean that one is puzzled with amazement, and it would have that meaning especially with the uninformed. By that word I mean the ones described by John as those *whose names are not written in the book of life.* Chapter 13:8 shows this italicized statement means those who are not faithful servants of Christ. Their names (of the faithful) are said to have been written in the book *from the foundation of the world* or before the human family had become an orderly group of human beings. The beast that *was* and *is not* and *yet is* was that which caused the astonishment spoken of above. The beast *was* Pagan Rome outwardly until the time of Constantine, who caused the union of church and state to take place. That put an end to Pagan Rome as far as outward profession was concerned, and it is in that sense that John says the beast *is not.* But in reality Papal Rome retained so much of the doctrines and wicked practices of the original empire, that it could truly be said of Papal Rome that it was Pagan Rome in disguise or in another form. It is in that sense that John says the institution *yet is,* which caused the uninformed of the world to be amazed and puzzled. But the righteous did not have to be in such a state of mind because they had always been respectful hearers of what inspired men had said. For instance, if they had only read and considered what Paul wrote in 2 Thessalonians 2, they would have expected such revolutions to take place as these affairs of Rome.

Verse 9. The *seven mountains* have no special significance except as an item of geography and history by which to identify the city of Rome. *On which the woman sitteth* means that the apostate church rested upon the government of Rome for support.

Verse 10. In some previous verses and in verse 12 below the text plainly says the ten horns represent ten kings or kingdoms that were inferior units of the Roman Empire. Hence the *seven kings* of this verse must have another meaning, and I believe they refer to important men who were leaders in the affairs of state right in the capital city. It is merely a coincidence that the Lord had seven of those prominent men in mind which is also the number of the geographical hills or "mountains" that comprised the city of Rome. It is clearly shown in Roman history that leading men in the Empire often vied with each other for power and the vision shows such a conflict.

Verse 11. The beast that *was* has been already shown to be Pagan Rome. The apostle says this beast is the eighth; not merely one more beast that would count up to eight, but it was the eigh*th* and *of the seven*. This denotes that it was in the same line, or bore some fact in common with the others. And the phrase *goeth into perdition* strengthens that conclusion, for we learned in verse 8 that it was Pagan Rome that was to go into perdition. (Not that Papal Rome will escape perdition, but that is not under consideration at present.) The vision means that Pagan Rome as a whole must take her place in the count with all those individual "kings" or chief men in the corrupt institution, and all go down as a unit into the lake of perdition.

Verse 12. These *ten kings* (or small kingdoms) are named at chapter 13: 1. It says they had received no kingdom *as yet*. The meaning is they were not in rightful control of their kingdoms although they were acting as kings. But the phrase also indicates that they will finally be kings in their own right after Papal Rome has been put down even as Pagan Rome was, then each nation will have its own chosen form of government. But for the time being they may only act *as kings*. *One hour with the beast* is a figure of speech meaning that the time for continued oppression of Rome was to be comparatively short. The reader should bear in mind that the vision goes from the days of Pagan Rome in verse 11 to those of Papal Rome in the present verse. On that basis the beast now is Papal Rome in conjunction with the state.

Verse 13. *These* means the ten kings of the preceding verse and until they have had their eyes opened by receiving the Bible back again, they will not know any better than to give their power and strength unto the beast (church and state).

Verse 14. *These* again means the ten kings just mentioned. While they were still under the control of Papal Rome and blinded by the false doctrines of that corrupt beast, they were opposed to the Lamb of God and made (religious) war with Him. *The Lamb shall overcome them*. This will be accomplished by the Reformation, for that movement will give the Bible back to the people in their native tongue. When that is done the Lamb shall *overcome them* which means He will subdue their opposition to the word of God and to the true church that is regulated by that word. *Lord of lords* puts Christ above all other rulers, and *King of kings* means He is greater than the ten kings who fought against Him. Christ does not conduct the conflict directly but does it by His great army. The army is composed of those who are *called* (by the Gospel), and they are *chosen* because they have qualified themselves by being *faithful*.

Verse 15. The angel now begins to give John the interpretation of the vision as was mentioned at verse 7. The first verse says the corrupt woman sits upon many waters, and this verse explains it to mean peoples and nations, etc. That is because the Roman Empire was one of the "four world empires" which contained all the so-called civilized people of the earth.

Verse 16. The ten horns are the kings or kingdoms which are named in the comments at chapter 13: 1. *Shall hate the whore* is literal, for when the kings and people of the smaller units of the Empire come to realize how deeply they have been deceived by her they can have no other feeling toward her. The rest of the verse is a symbolical vision of the resistance that will be put up by these ten kings and their people when they "get their eyes open."

Verse 17. *God hath put in their hearts.* God never directly causes any person to do wrong who wants to do right. But when a man or group of men shows a persistence toward wrong, then He gives them up to carry out their own ways until they have learned their lesson. (See the comments at 2 Thessalonians 2: 11.) It had been predicted (in such passages as that just cited) that such conduct would be practiced by these kings, hence in doing so they were carrying out the divine prediction. But they will be suffered to operate in that way only *until the words of God shall be fulfilled.* This means until the time for them to be enlightend by the work of the Reformation.

Verse 18. Since the Reformation has not occurred yet, at the point of the great drama applying to this verse, the *woman* and *great city* refers to Babylon as the union of church and state.

Revelation 18

Verse 1. The angel had great *power* which is from EXOUSIA, the leading meaning of which is "authority." The possession of that qualification is explained by the fact that he *came down from heaven* which is the seat of all authority. It is understandable also why his glory would light up the earth, for everything that pertains to that celestial region is glorious.

Verse 2. The preceding chapter pictures conditions just prior to the revolution of the Reformation. The present chapter will extend the vision on through that period, showing the effects it will have among the nations of the world, and will predict the permanent end of the union of church and state. We should keep clearly in mind the truth that we are studying a book of symbols, and therefore we will not try to make a literal application of the symbols. However, even political and religious advantages may sometimes bring material gains to men of selfish character, hence we should not be surprised to see indications of that in some instances. The angel cried with a *strong voice*, which signified that his announcement was of interest to many. *Babylon* here means the institution formed by the union of church and state. That body had been in control since the time of Constantine, but now it is destined to be dissolved by the work of the Reformation. *Babylon is fallen, is fallen;* the repetition is for emphasis. The *fall* refers to the disolving of church and state through the influence of the Bible that had been given to the people by Luther and his fellow workers. *Is become the habitation,* etc. This is symbolic and the language is formed from what literally happened to the ancient city of Babylon after it was destroyed by its conqueror. The description of that destruction from which our verse gets its symbols may be seen in Isaiah 13: 19-22 and Jeremiah 50: 35-40.

Verse 3. *Wine of the wrath of her fornication.* This combines several symbolical thoughts. Wine suggests drunkenness and that is used figuratively sometimes to mean being beside oneself through the influence of false doctrine, which certainly was an outstanding characteristic of Rome. It also stands for the wrath of God upon evildoers, and fornication refers to intimacy with unlawful organizations. Kings and merchants all reaped personal advantages from their subjects and customers, because they were duped into thinking they should submit to the wishes of their superiors.

Verse 4. *Come out of her my people.* Even after the work of the reformers was well under way, and the institution of Babylon as a body had fallen, there were still some individuals connected with the church part of the former institution who were honest and at heart were desirous of serving God. They are the ones who are called *my people* because the Lord considered them true to the testimony of Christ as far as they had been permitted to learn it. Now if they will heed the call to *come out* and line up with the workers of the Reformation they will be received by Him. If they refuse to heed this call they will have to *receive of her plagues.*

Verse 5. *Sins have reached unto heaven* means the corruptions of Rome were an offense to heaven, and also had become notoriously public so that God *remembered* (took unfavorable notice of) her iniquities.

Verse 6. The pronoun *you* refers to "my people" in the preceding verse. Human beings cannot bring judgment upon a universal body of corruption by mere human strength. But if they will *come out* and then use their influence to expose the harlot (which many people did as shown in various histories of the Reformation), they will bring about a chastisement of her that is figuratively described as making her drink a double measure of her own wine.

Verse 7. The leaders in Rome or Babylon had been living a selfish life at the expense of their helpless dupes. Now that they have been undeceived by the workers in the Reformation, they are urged to make their condemnation all the more severe upon her. A *queen* would be in good circumstances in that she would have one on whom to depend for support and would have no *sorrow* or anxiety.

Verse 8. *One day* cannot be restricted to a period of 24 hours, but the things predicted of her will come on the same day or by the same cause. That will be the effects of opening the eyes of the nations that have been oppressed by her. The *mourning* will be literal and it will be over the loss of her former power. *Utterly burned with fire* denotes that the fire of God's jealousy will bring utter (complete) destruction to the combination of church and state—not to each separately, but the combination will be dissolved for ever.

Verse 9. *Kings of the earth* had been protected in their defrauding of the uninformed people. *Committed fornication*. Rome has been called a harlot hence those who have been intimate with her are guilty of fornication. It is natural for them to lament seeing her burning (under the fiery judgments of God.)

Verse 10. The symbols are changed from a woman to a city. But it means the same thing for the mother of harlots had her seat where she carried on her adulterous practices in the city of Babylon. Of course to see her "red light district" going up in smoke means the end of her trade. *One hour* is used here to mean the same period as *one day* in verse 8.

Verse 11. *The merchants* were the prominent leaders in Rome who had been reaping much gain (both political and material) by imposing their false doctrines on them. There will now be no demand for such "wares" for the customers will have learned that they had been defrauded.

Verse 12, 13. All of the articles named in this paragraph are literal products, and doubtless the leaders in the corrupt institution dealt in such property for their own selfish enjoyment, but the literal articles are used as symbols of the selfish enjoyments they had by being able to extract the services of the dupes under them.

Verse 14. This virtually continues the same prediction that is made in the preceding verses, but I will call attention to the words about these gains that *thou shalt find them no more at all*. That means the advantages once enjoyed by Babylon (church and state) were never again to be enjoyed by her as before because she will never exist again to enjoy them.

Verse 15. This is virtually the same lament that is described in verse 9, 10, because of their loss of unlawful privileges at the expense of the people. *For the fear of her torment* denotes that the sight of such a burning will give them a feeling of horror. Lest the reader gets lost in all this array of figurative judgments, I shall again state that it is a symbolical picture of the political and religious revolution that came upon the old wicked institution of Rome, after the work of the Reformation broke up the great conspiracy.

Verse 16. The items mentioned are used symbolically, but there is some special appropriateness in the materials named. The formalities of the old Pagan Roman ceremonies were copied by the clergy of Papal Rome. Linen was used for the official robes in the services, and purple and scarlet were the royal colors. The garments were decked literally with gold and precious stones. The city is said to have all these decorations because the scarlet woman was located in the city for her corrupt practices.

Verse 17. *One hour* calls for the same comments that are offered at verse 10. The chapter as a whole is a vision in symbolic form, yet the institution of Babylon or Rome was so widespread, that it was logical to include many of the activities of the members of it. Hence the people interested in the traffic of the sea are brought into the picture, among those whose selfish practices were to be cut off by the downfall of the city.

Verse 18. *What city is like* means a general statement of her greatness as of the past, for now she is very low and worthless since she is being destroyed by fire.

Verse 19. There is not much change in the significance of the symbols of this verse. Casting dust on their heads was an ancient custom to give expression to feelings of mourning and dismay (Joshua 7: 6; Job 2: 12; Lamentation 2: 10). *One hour* is the same figurative phrase that is in verse 10. *Made desolate* means that Babylon the Great as the union of church and state was to be deserted and cease to be.

Verse 20. The speaker is still the *voice from heaven* (verse 4) which is bidding the apostles and prophets to rejoice over the downfall of Babylon (union of church and state). It was especially appropriate to congratulate these great servants of God, because they had been foremost in defending the lawful church of the Lord against the encroachments of the apostate church. Now that the conspiracy formed by the union of church and state was thrust down, they had great and just reason to rejoice.

Verse 21. *Mighty angel* is said to indicate the size or weight of the stone that was to be handled. The stone was *like* great millstones which were heavy, and their weight was such that if they were thrown into the water they would most assuredly sink; nor would such an object float back up to the surface. That is doubtless why Jesus used it in his comparison of the irreparable fate of certain sinners (Matthew 18: 6). After this mighty angel had cast the stone into the sea he made his explanation of the symbol; it represented the casting down of Babylon. We know it does not mean literal Babylon for that city had not been in existence for centuries (Isaiah 13: 19-22). We know also it does not apply to the religious part of the corrupt institution (though it also was known as Babylon), for that apostate church is not to be destroyed until Jesus comes (2 Thessalonians 2: 8). Hence this can apply only to the Babylon that was composed of church and state. When the stone that represented it was cast into the sea, the angel said that it *shall be found no more at all.* From the foregoing evidences we are given the divine assurance that there will never be another world-wide union of church and state.

Verse 22, 23. The enterprises and activities of human interest that are mentioned in these verses have all been considered in this chapter and understood to have a symbolical meaning. In this paragraph they may be used in both symbolical and literal senses. In either sense the announcement is made that they will never be done again. However, this is not true until we apply it in the light of a proviso that is stated as follows. The phrase *in thee* is used five times in these two verses, and that is the key to the subject. There is not an interest mentioned that will not continue to be practiced as long as the world stands. But they will not be done "in thee" (Babylon as the union of church and state), for that institution will have gone down never to rise again.

Verse 24. This short verse is merely a summing up of the crimes that have been committed by Babylon, on account of which she was doomed to complete overthrow.

Revelation 19

Verse 1. For several verses the vision will show the heavenly hosts rejoicing together over the victory that has been won over Babylon by the work of the Reformation. *Alleluia* means "praise ye the Lord," and the exclamation is made in view of His great works. *Salvation* is to be ascribed to the Lord because no other has the power to save, and for that reason we should give all *honor* to Him and acknowledge that all power belongs to Him.

Verse 2. The *great voice* is still speaking and acknowledging the righteousnes of God's judgments. Those acknowledgements are general and now they will become specific. *Judged the great whore* refers to the overthrow of Babylon which was accomplished by the Reformation. *Hath avenged the blood of his servants.* This fulfilled the promise made to the souls under the altar (chapter 6: 11).

Verse 3. *Her smoke arose up for ever and ever.* "Where there is smoke there is fire." If the smoke ascends for ever the fire will be of the same continuance. Of course this is first applied figuratively to Babylon, meaning her downfall is to be permanent. It is next applied to the individuals who were leaders and supporters of the corrupt beast, who are destined to go into perdition where the fire is endless.

Verse 4. The four beasts (living creatures) felt happy over the victory of Christ because it was through His blood that they had been redeemed from sin. And the four and twenty elders had the same motive for praising God, because they represented the two organized systems of salvation that had produced the four living creatures.

Verse 5. The voice thus far in these verses seems to have come from the people in general who respect the Lord. Now the voice comes *out of the throne* as if to acknowledge the congratulations just offered to God, and endorsing the idea that all servants of whatever degree or rank should praise Him.

Verse 6. So many people of the civilized world had suffered under the oppression of Rome through the Dark Ages, that it explains why the *voice of a great multitude* was heard praising God. *Voice of many waters* is the same except it is in symbolic form, waters in figurative language being used to represent human voices in action. *Omnipotent* means almighty; God can do anything that is right. The difficulty of conquering the giant influence of the beast in Rome was regarded so great, that it brought to their attention the might of God and called forth these words of praise, and caused the declaration that *He reigneth*.

Verse 7. *Marriage of the Lamb is come.* The subject of marriage is spoken of in the Bible from two different angles, and unless this is understood we may think there are some contradictions. For instance, Christians are said to be married to Christ at the present time (Romans 7: 4), and now our verse says the marriage is about to take place. In old times an engagement was regarded in the light of marriage as far as the moral obligation is concerned. That is why Genesis 19: 14 speaks of the men who had "married his [Lot's] daughters" when they were engaged to them. And in Matthew 1: 18 it says that Mary was espoused to Joseph, while the next verse calls him her husband. So Christians are actually only espoused (engaged) to Christ now. That is why Paul says "I have espoused you to one husband, that I may present you as a chaste virgin to Christ" (2 Corinthians 11: 2). But the actual marriage is what is meant in our verse. *His wife hath made herself ready.* This remark is based on the common practice that causes a woman to prepare her garments for the important occasion.

Verse 8. This verse names the kind of raiment that is to be worn by the bride, namely, clean and white linen. Since that is figurative the apostle explains that it means *righteousness*, so the making of herself ready mentioned in the preceding verse, means she has followed a righteous life in preparation for her marriage.

Verse 9. This will be one marriage and accompanying "refreshments" at which there will be no human guests but the bride. Hence the blessing pronounced on those who are called to the supper, means in reality the people should become a part of the espoused bride by becoming Christians. Before going further in the comments it will be well to make some explanatory remarks as to the "hour of the ceremony." Verse 7 says the marriage *is come*, when we know we will find that the work of the Reformation is to be gone over again by the vision. There will be no difficulty if the reader recalls that the book has more than once departed from the chronological order of events to take up some other period of the Christian Dispensation. Hence these preceding verses brought us down to the last day and announced the final marriage of Christ to his bride (the church). The vision will now take up some principles of a general character, then bring us again to the work just preceding the Reformation.

Verse 10. The pronouns *his* and *him* refer to the angel who was sent to show the vision to John (chapter 1: 1). It was natural for John to have this inclination toward worship of the angel, for the great vision shown made the apostle have a feeling of inferiority. There are some conditions when even a man may receive some form of worship from others (Luke 14: 10), but under the present circumstances it would have been improper. The reader may see a complete explanation of the word worship at Matthew 2: 2 in the first volume of the New Testament Commentary. *I am thy fellowservant* reminds us of Hebrews 1: 14. *Of thy brethren that have the testimony of Jesus.* This is equivalent to describing the ones for whom the angels are sent forth to minister. To *have* the testimony does not merely mean to have access to it (everyone has that), but it is those who hold themselves faithfully to it. *The testimony of Jesus is the spirit of prophecy.* This means that the subject of Jesus as the Saviour of mankind is the main thought running through all the prophetic writings.

Verse 11. *White horse* symbolizes a war animal that is to engage in a war for purity. The rider was Christ who is described as *Faithful and True*. That is because the war in which He is about to engage (the Reformation) is a righteous one.

Verse 12. Eyes of fire would signify that which is bright and penetrating. *Many crowns*. Actually no king wears more than one crown as far as the article as a unit is concerned, but in some way the ornamentations on it showed that Christ had won over all others. *Name no man knew* does not indicate some dark or mysterious secret, for verse 16 gives a great description of His name as written on his clothing. But no mere man can appreciate the name of Christ until he becomes His disciple.

Verse 13. *Vesture dipped in blood* is because Christ shed his blood for the sake of mankind. *The Word of God* is the name which all men can read and hence is not a secret, but they cannot realize what it means unless they appropriate that name to themselves by wholehearted obedience to its commandments. (See the name at John 1: 1.)

Verse 14. This is a symbolic picture of the war that is about to be fought against the beast that has been defying Heaven's authority for 1260 years.

Verse 15. The *sharp sword* is the *sword of the Spirit* (Ephesians 6: 17; Hebrews 4: 12). *Smite the nations* with this Word by the work of the Reformation. *Rule with a rod of iron*. Iron is both firm and severe, and it will be used in the latter sense against the wicked nations who have been supporting Babylon. *Treadeth the winepress* is explained at chapter 14: 10.

Verse 16. *King of kings and Lord of lords*. *King* indicates supreme authority and lord means one who governs the conduct of others. Jesus was given these two titles because He had overcome all who opposed him. Having the title attached to his *vesture* (clothing) was on the principle of decorations given men who have distinguished themselves in the service of their country.

Verse 17. When a man makes a great "killing" he often invites his friends to come and share the feast with him. The effects of the Reformation are symbolized in this and the following verse. It is especially appropriate to base the imagery on the fowls of the heaven, for they are generally thought to prefer feeding on the flesh of animals that have been slain and left on the field. (See Matthew 24: 28.) The present case is one where the beasts were not killed and dressed as would be done ordinarily. They were to be killed to get them out of the way, and the birds might as well get the benefit of it since that is the kind of food they prefer. *Standing in the sun* was the appropriate place for the angel to stand where he could make his invitation to the creatures that live above the earth.

Verse 18. Of course this is symbolical of the defeat and destruction that is about to be imposed upon Babylon (church and state). Yet it is appropriate to use the symbols named because the conflict is actually to be with *kings* and their *captains* and *mighty men*, and these made use of *horses* in their warfare.

Verse 19. *Beast* is Babylon and the *kings* are the inferior rulers under her. All mustered their forces to resist the attack of Christ through the Reformation.

Verse 20. The *lake of fire* for the present is the destruction of Babylon, but in the day of judgment it will be the lake of fire that is unquenchable. The *false prophet* and *miracles* are explained at various passages preceding this.

Verse 21. The *remnant* means the straggling individuals who were left as "die-hards" after the beast of Babylon as a unit had been given a death blow by the Reformation.

Revelation 20

General remarks. We have come to the climax of the book of Revelation as far as the symbolic predictions are concerned. The last two chapters have figurative language of the same kind that is frequently used all through the Bible, but they pertain to conditions that are to exist after the world comes to its end. The events still in the future (as of the place where this chapter belongs in the great drama of the book) will be predicted symbolically in this chapter, which starts at the time of the great Reformation. Before taking up the chapter verse by verse, I will offer a general note that will deal with the chapter in a more condensed form. Some of the verses will be enlarged upon as occasion suggests, but I urge that my readers make themselves familiar with this note as references may be made to it at certain places.

Revelation 20 — General Remarks

On Revelation 20: One of the keys to the understanding of this noted chapter is the fact that Satan was to be bound away from the *nations* and not from any individual. There never was a time when it was predicted that he was to be chained away from any individual: it was from *nations*. He always has had and still has access to individuals and the only thing that will keep him away from such is his individual faith in the Scriptures. By reason of the union of church and state the nations had been led to think they could not legislate nor decide on religious questions as they might have seen fit, but must take their cue from Rome. But when the Reformation broke and gave the Bible to various peoples in their own language so that they could read for themselves they saw, to their surprise, that they had been deceived all these years—that they did not need to depend on Rome. Since this truth became known to various kings, and the people under them, they turned their back against Rome, which resulted in the break-up of the union of church and state, and thus the deception that caused the *nations* to think they must ask Rome all about it was banished. Thus the devil by the chain of truth in the Reformation, was chained away from the *nations*, and the Reformation period was allowed to go on. This situation explains the statement in the forepart of the fourth verse that tells us of the "thrones and they sat upon them, their judgment was given unto them," meaning that now they have learned of their own right to do their own judging instead of asking Rome about it. This was made possible by the facts just stated. Now about this time when Rome saw what it was about to amount to, she began to oppress the reformers and made life so bitter for some of them that it required the same fortitude and courage in facing Rome that had been required in the beginning of the Christian religion to face the oppression of Pagan Rome. These martyrs were equal to the occasion. They defied death and everything like it, and so nearly did they reenact the very spirit of the martyrs. As we sometimes say, that a certain individual though dead yet now speaks, meaning that someone has risen reproducing the same spirit and fortitude as the other person. So these reformers and co-workers in their courage and defiance of death, showed the spirit that the martyrs had shown and in this way we could say that the martyrs were living again. Not that any individual who had really been dead had come to life. But they who loved the truth so much were willing to die rather than go back to Rome. In this way they were reenacting the spirit of the first martyrs and so could be said to be "living" again. And since through faith and courage those who are true to the Book have been said by Paul and others to be reigning with Christ, this explains why these people are said to be reigning with Christ. The arbitrary statement of a thousand years is one instance in the Bible where a definite amount is stated when the writer refers to an indefinite one. In this case the thousand years is just an expression referring to the bright period of the Reformation when those who loved the truth had been of Christ and reigned with him during that time.

This brings us to understand the statement in verses 5 and 6 about the first resurrection as follows: "Now this is the first resurrection." The pronoun "this" instead of having an antecedent is a prospective pronoun and means the same as if the writer had said "I am going to tell you something of the first resurrection." The man that has part in the first resurrection will not be hurt of the second death, which we understand from other scripture is the lake of fire. This is taught especially in the language expressed by Christ in his conversation with Martha (John 11: 25, 26). The expression "first resurrection" does not have any numerical significance, but is used to indicate its importance. It is the first resurrection in importance and not in numerical order since there will be but one resurrection numerically. If Christ is *the* resurrection, that would make it the first; and we note that the passage does not say "blessed and holy is he that" is in the first resurrection, but he that "hath part in" the first resurrection. And since Christ is the first resurrection, it follows that having part in the first resurrection means to have part in Christ, and hence this noted passage means simply the same that John 11: 25, 26 meant, the same as Christ meant when he said to the sister "I am the resurrection and the life" and also stated that those who continue in that faith in Him would never die. So the expression "shall never die" to Martha is equivalent to the expression "not hurt of the second death" here. And hence this passage has no reference whatever to some visionary theory about reigning on this earth.

The expression in the forepart of verse 5, "rest of the dead" is explained to mean those people who did not have enough confidence in the truth to have died for it, as the martyrs had. Of course during this bright period of the Reformation their characteristics would not be in evidence so that is why it says they will not live again until the thousand years are finished, which means until the best part of the Reformation and its effects have run their course. And since the chaining of the devil meant to undeceive the *nations*, by the same token turning the devil loose again means he will again operate in a national and public manner. Not necessarily through the same nations of course, but it means that he will not be satisfied with his individual influence over men and women, but will wish to poison the public streams of thought and in so doing will raise a great conflict between the friends of truth and the friends of error. The "little season" referred to in this chapter is elsewhere called the battle of Armageddon. That battle is now going on and has been ever since the Reformation period began to lose its good effects. If one were to doubt what the devil is doing in a public wholesale manner, we cite the fact that in the state of New York a few years ago, the state chartered an institution whose avowed purpose was to advance atheism in all the schools and colleges in the United States, and thus such a charter authorized by the state is similar to the idea of the devil working through the nations. Almost every state in the Union is supporting and authorizing the teaching of evolution in the name of education which is another means of the devil to operate publicly; and all other like influences such as the support and endorsement of several nations and states and lawmakers authorizing things that have always heretofore been regarded as not even moral, much less according to the Bible, all go to the conclusion that the devil is now, as he was before the Reformation, working through public wholesale channels by influencing legislatures and kings and lawmakers in the direction of infidelity, thus producing the great battle of Armageddon. Trusting the reader has carefully read the foregoing note and will be able to make proper reference to it when it is suggested, I shall take up this chapter by verses as has been done with others.

Verse 1. *Bottomless pit* is from ABUSSOS which means the place in Hades where angels are cast when they sin and where wicked men go when they die.

Verse 2. In this verse the four words *serpent, dragon, Devil* and *Satan* are applied to the same being, so that we need have no doubt as to the one who is meant. *Thousand years* is a figurative expression that is not bound by the calendar. In symbolic language the Bible does not restrict itself to exact mathematical values of the numbers mentioned. Sometimes the period will be longer and at others it will be shorter. I shall cite one or two examples by way of illustration on the matter of this use of figurative time. In Daniel 9: 24 a prediction is made of seventy weeks and we know it actually means 490 years. In chapter 6: 11 of our book the phrase *little season* really was to be until the Reformation which was several centuries in the future. The angel bound Satan with the chain mentioned in the preceding verse, and the chain was the Bible that was to be given back to the people in their own language. That chain bound him from the *nations*, which means the heads of the nations were able to see their rights by the information of the Book and realized that the devil had been deceiving them. When that occurred they resisted him and that chained him from them.

Verse 3. *Cast him into the bottomless pit* is symbolical of the restrictions that were placed upon Satan as to his influence over *nations*, for he has been there personally all the time. The restrictions were caused by the chain of the Bible that had been placed in the possession of the national leaders. (See again the note at beginning of this chapter.) These restrictions were to continue as long as the leaders of nations and other heads of the channels of thought continued their active defense of the Book. Knowing that human weakness would assert itself causing a letting down of the activities for the truth, the Lord saw the advantage it would give Satan and that he would again come out in his fight against the Bible. Hence it is stated that after the thousand years were expired—after the restrictions of the Bible had weakened due to the loss of activities of the professed friends of truth—Satan would be *loosed a little season. This little season* is the same as the "battle" of verse 8 which will be discussed at that place.

Verse 4. *And I saw thrones . . . given unto them.* This is the same vision that is described at chapter 17: 12 and the reader should see the comments at that passage. The pronoun *they* means the kings who had occupied their thrones in form only, but who really had not been free to use their own judgment in their ruling. *Sat upon them* denotes that they were occupying their thrones in fact and not merely in name. *Judgment was given unto them* signifies they were allowed to render their own judgment in matters pertaining to their kingdoms. *Saw the souls . . . a thousand years.* Before reading further at this place, let the reader reexamine very carefully the first paragraph of the note referred to previously. That is especially necessary to get the significance of the thousand years of reign with Christ. The souls John saw were of those who were beheaded by Papal Rome because they refused to submit to her false demands. Their death recalls a like experience recorded in chapter 6: 9 of those who had been slain by Pagan Rome. These whom John saw in our present verse resisted the *beast* (Babylon), his *image* (those who imitated the beast) and the *mark* (those who brought upon themselves the guilt of doing the things originally incited by Nero.)

Verse 5. *Rest of the dead* is symbolical or figurative and refers to people who did not "have enough life" or interest to be active in defense of the truth. *Until the thousand years were finished.* When that bright period of the Reformation (here called the thousand years) was over and the former defenders of truth began to lag, then the enemies of the Bible "came to life" and became active in opposition to the word of God, acting under the influence of Satan who was now *loosed* in that the Bible was not binding him as it did. Such a movement stimulated the former "dead" ones to action and then was begun the conflict between the friends of truth and its enemies, a conflict that has continued to our day. *This is the first resurrection.* The pronoun does not refer directly to what has been said but to what is yet to be said, and it refers to the subject as a whole. John 11: 25, 26 should be considered in connection with the *first resurrection*, also read the note to which reference was made.

Verse 6. The *first resurrection* is that mentioned in the preceding verse of which John said he was going to speak. He is doing so now and telling us of the blessing that will be for those who have part in this *first resurrection*. In John 11: 25 Jesus says "I am the resurrection and the life." Jesus was the first one to be resurrected never to die again (Acts 13: 34). To have part in the *first resurrection* means to have part in Christ. And to get the spiritual benefits of the resurrection of Christ as the bodily benefits, it is necessary to be faithful after coming into Him. That is what is meant in John 11: 26 by "liveth and believeth in me." That person "shall never die" according to Christ's statement to Martha, which means the same as *on such the second death hath no power* in our present verse. This *second death* is the punishment in the lake of fire and brimstone according to chapter 21: 8 of our present book. *Shall reign with him a thousand years.* This period is the same that is explained at verse 2. Of course the word *reign* is not literal because Christ is the sole King on the throne. Thayer's explanation of the word as it is used here is as follows: "Paul transfers the word to denote the supreme moral dignity, liberty, blessedness, which will be enjoyed by Christ's redeemed ones." The principle expressed will apply to the faithful in Christ of all ages. However, the present application is made to those who had been faithful to Christ under the persecutions of Babylon. This spirit of devotion in the presence of death was a reenactment of the spirit of the first martyrs (chapter 6: 9-11), and they lived (were in evidence) all through this bright period of the Reformation. It is in that sense only that they were to be resurrected and reign with Christ through the thousand years. There was no prediction of any literal resurrection of some while others were to remain in their graves. There will be but one bodily resurrection (and it is still future), and at that same hour all human beings, both good and bad, will be brought to life (Daniel 12: 2; John 5:28, 29). It is plainly taught in other passages that when Jesus comes again it will mark the end of the kingdom and all things on the earth. (1 Corinthians 15: 24, 25; 2 Peter 3: 10). All statements of a resurrection that is to occur before the second coming of Christ are figurative only.

Verse 7. This is a repetition of verse 3.

Verse 8. The *nations* here are the same as in verse 3 as to the meaning of the word. But the identical groups of men who had been deceived by Satan before the Reformation would not be available to him in the same manner, for they still have the Bible in their own languages, and will always know better than to surrender their rights as nations with their kings again. But having found by experience the great advantage of working through the various headquarters, so as to effect a broad-scale opposition to the truth, he determined to direct his efforts along that line. Of course his objective is the destruction of the Bible or the faith of the people in it. That is why this great and long conflict is called Armageddon in chapter 16: 16, for one of the terms in Thayer's definition of the word is "destruction." Satan's strategy in this war was to use any means he could command that would destory men's faith in the Book. *Gog* and *Magog* were ancient peoples and countries that were numerous, savage and at enmity with civilization. The words are used symbolically here to indicate the kind of forces and means that Satan would use in his war against the Bible. In the note referred to at the beginning of this chapter, it is shown that a phase of Satan's public attacks upon the Bible is in the form of evolution, seeing that it is taught in the public schools, also be chartered and endorsed by states and educational headquarters. The same objective is now being attempted in the form of communism. In proportion as a man believes in this doctrine he will not believe in the Bible and Satan knows it. That is why he is pressing its tenets upon the people through every channel possible. It accounts for the number of communists among the school teachers of our free school system. Also for the presence of communists and their sympathizers in the three branches of our government; the legislative, executive and judicial. I am sometimes asked if I believe the present conflict with Russia and her satellites was predicted. My answer is yes as the whole picture is considered. Communism is just the present objective in the war, the conflict being either for or against it. In that sense it was predicted for it is a continuation of the *battle* (war) of Armageddon, which was begun after Satan was loosed and is destined to continue until Christ comes. As in most other wars, there are spies and sympathizers who pretend to be on the right side, but whose heart is in favor of the enemy. Such traitors either deny being communists or even refuse to say whether they are or not. We know that when a man refuses to answer questions on this subject when propounded by a proper person, that person is a communist at heart and should be regarded as one of Satan's soldiers in the war of Armageddon.

Verse 9. The pronoun *they* stands for the hostile forces of Satan symbolically mustered from the regions of Gog and Magog. This is the army of Satan that is described in the preceding paragraph. They will fight under his directions with the object of destroying men's faith in the Bible. The apostate church of Rome taught that the religious conduct of men should be regulated according to the pope and his college of cardinals. The teaching of Christ is that men's lives should be regulated by the Bible (1 Peter 4: 11; 1 John 1: 7), that the sole institution for making that Book known is the church (Ephesians 3: 10, 21; 1 Timothy 3: 15). Hence the army of Satan was to compass the *camp of the saints*. This means the church when considered as a group of individuals, and *the beloved city* means the church if spiritual Jerusalem is used as a symbol. So here is where the issue is joined in this great battle of Armageddon. The church of Christ is on one side, and everything else is on the other in all controversies that involve moral and religious interests, and where belief in or opposition to the Bible is at stake. The first two thirds of this brief verse covers the entire period of the war of Armageddon, beginning when Satan was *loosed* and extending to the coming of Christ. The last sentence of the verse marks the end of the war. Not that it tells of the date (no passage does), but it names the event that will bring the conflict to a close, namely, the consuming fire out of heaven. We are told in 2 Thessalonians 2: 8 that the pope will be destroyed at the coming of Christ. It is very fitting that the war of Armageddon should be destroyed at the same time, since the pope and Satan have been allies arrayed against the forces of Christ for centuries. And with this verse the prophetic symbols of the book of Revelation bring us to the judgment day for the final showing. At various places in our study we have been brought to that event, then taken back to some earlier period and started all over again. But the rest of the chapter will describe the events on the day of judgment and not go back.

Verse 10. *Devil that deceived them* refers to the vast hordes who comprised the army of Satan. This verse says nothing about the fate of the deceived ones; that will be shown later. This is the lake of fire and brimstone that is mentioned in chapter 21: 8. Tormented *day and night* is figurative as to the parts of the time for there will be no recurrence of day and night literally. The expression is used to give emphasis to the literal part of the sentence, namely, *for ever and ever.* In other words there will be no "breathing spell" or even brief intermission for the sake of relief; it will be continuous and endless.

Verse 11. *Great white throne* signifies purity and justice. *From whose face . . . fled away . . . no place for them.* This agrees with the next chapter that will tell us of the new heaven and earth.

Verse 12. *Small and great.* In God's eyes there are no "big I and little you," so the phrase is used only to denote that all human beings will be brought before the judgment. This conclusion also agrees with the literal statements of scripture in other passages (2 Corinthians 5: 10). *Books* occurs twice in this verse and it is stated that the judgment will be rendered according to the *works* that are written in the books. Hence the *books* means God's books of remembrance. (See Psalms 56: 8; Malachi 3: 16.) God does not literally need the mechanical use of books, but the words are used symbolically to impress us with the truth that none of the things we do will escape His knowledge. The *other* book is described as the *book of life.* It is referred to in the last verse as containing the names of the faithful servants of the Lord. This same thought is expressed in chapter 21: 27; Luke 10: 20; Philippians 4: 3. Upon the basis of this information we may conclude that the *books* were the records of men's actions, and the *book of life* contained a list of those whose conduct had caused their names to be written in this book, and whose continued good deeds had prevented their names from being *blotted out* (chapter 3: 5).

Verse 13. The preceding verse makes a general statement of the persons to be summoned before the judgment. "Small and great" would virtually include all human beings that ever lived. The present verse gives particulars, doubtless to impress us with the completeness of the resurrection of all persons regardless of where their bodies and spirits had been, even including the sea with its millions of ravenous creatures to feed upon the bodies of the dead. *Death* refers to the dead bodies and *hell* (from HADES), is the place where the spirits had been. Both will be reunited and brought before the judgment.

Verse 14. *Death* (of the body) and *hell* (HADES), will not be needed any longer, hence they will be consigned to the lake of fire. Not all men, of course, but the ones who will be designated in the next verse.

Verse 15. This explains who is meant in the preceding verse to be cast into the lake of fire. In order to avoid such a doom it behooves us all to get our names written in the book of life, then live so that they will not be blotted out.

Revelation 21

General remarks. When this and the next chapter are being considered, it is usually asked if the statements are literal or figurative. And as a rule no distinction is made between the righteous and the wicked when asking the question. Evidently a distinction should be made since the conditions of the persons themselves will not be the same. At any rate we do not have the specific information concerning that of the wicked that we do of the righteous. Therefore I believe it will be well to offer some remarks on this matter before taking up the verses. It is known that the Bible uses both literal and figurative language all through the volume, which is true of most compositions of literature. It is also true that a statement might be made of some truth or fact that could be correctly applied in either way, depending on how the statement is worded. For instance it might be declared of a certain thing that it is dead. But that might be said of its personal being and mean that it is dead because the life has actually gone out of it. Or it might be declared to be dead because the whole being is separated from something else, the word "death" meaning a separation. But if the statement is made from the former standpoint the meaning would be literal, and if from the other the figurative sense should be understood.

It will be necessary, therefore, to consider the context in specific passages in determining which form of language is used.

There is no direct information nor promise for the wicked to have a spiritual or glorious body after the resurrection. Any positive affirmation that may be made on this matter must be done in the absence of any declaration in the Bible. As far as the promises or information are concerned, the wicked will go into the next world with the same kind of bodies they had when they left this world. That is not so concerning those who die in Christ, for there are many passages that promise them a body that will be changed from a fleshly to a spiritual character. Hence it is an unavoidable conclusion that the future circumstances of the righteous must be the kind that can be experienced and enjoyed by a person who is wholly spiritual. Then a logical question may be asked as to why the Lord would use language that is apparently literal if it must be understood figuratively. It is in order to bring the divine thoughts to within the human understanding. Isaiah 55: 9 says of God: "For as the heavens are higher than the earth, so are my ways higher than your ways, and my thoughts than your thoughts." If the thoughts of God are that much higher than those of man, had He clothed his thoughts in language correspondingly high, then man never could have comprehended them. For that reason the heavenly thoughts are expressed in human terms. Accordingly Paul says, "I speak after the manner of men because of the infirmity of your flesh" (Romans 6: 19).

Man would have no other way of appreciating a description of the future after this life except by such a form of speech. Even the inspired apostle John did not know what we will be in the next life (1 John 3: 2). Hence in giving man a description of the eternal state of the righteous, it is often contrasted with things we dislike and compared with what we enjoy. And even such illustrations may be relative only, for a thing may be desirable from one standpoint and undesirable from another. To cite a single instance we are told that "there shall be no night there." That is said from the standpoint that we prefer the daylight to darkness. And yet from another we might think favorably of the night because it brings us the cooling atmosphere and the time of rest. And so all of these thoughts should be observed when considering the two chapters now before us. I will offer another suggestion before starting into the comments on the verses. God never exaggerates the truth, and in giving us a description of the future condition of mankind, He has not made it look any stronger than it actually will be. If the description of the fate of the lost is figurative only, then what will be the literal state? Likewise, if the home of the soul as described in these chapters is pictured in figurative language only, then how wonderful the real situation will be! In the words of the song: "We speak of the realms of the blest, that country so bright and so fair; and oft are its glories confessed, but what must it be to be there! We speak of its pathways of gold, of its walls decked with jewels so rare; of its wonders and pleasures untold, but what must it be to be there!" And thus on the basis of the foregoing paragraphs, I shall try to explain the various descriptions given in these closing chapters of the great Book.

Verse 1. *New heaven and a new earth.* The heavens means the atmospheric region surrounding the earth and is a part of the same unit in creation. The home of the redeemed is called by the phrase "heaven and earth" because that is the present kind of home man lives in. If we were birds instead of men the vision would have showed John a "new nest." This new heaven and earth is what Jesus means in Matthew 5: 5 where He says, "Blessed are the meek for they shall inherit the earth." It is the one Peter is looking for when he says, "We, according to his promise, look for new heavens and a new earth, wherein dwelleth righteousness" (2 Peter 3: 13). *No more sea.* This is an instance of a kind referred to in the general remarks, where the application must be made upon the basis of the context. In some respects we can think of the sea in a favorable light, with its wondrous treasures and submarine plants, and the innumerable varieties of food to gratify our appetites. But we know the vision is to show something desirable on the basis of contrast, and that makes us think of the ceaseless unrest and destructive billows that engulf men and ships.

Verse 2. *Holy city new Jerusalem* means the church that is to be united at the last day in the final marriage of Christ as the bridegroom. (See the comments at chapter 19:7.) Paul speaks of the church as the "heavenly Jerusalem" in Hebrews 12:22, and he also speaks of it as the city that is above and is free and "the mother of us all" (Galatians 4:26). *Prepared* refers to the condition a bride brings to herself in view of her approaching marriage.

Verse 3. *Tabernacle* is used figuratively to represent the place where a person resides. It is used here as a symbol of the close association that will exist between God and his people in the eternal age. He will not merely honor the saved of men by making a call upon them but will come and *dwell* with them. That does not mean that God will descend from his lofty condition so that man would think of having a guest that is his equal in rank. He will still be God and the redeemed of men will still compose a people, but notwithstanding this great difference He will be a gracious Friend to give the honor of divine "company" to the creatures made in His image.

Verse 4. *God shall wipe away all tears from their eyes.* Upon hearing this read once a little girl was caused to exclaim, "God must have a large handkerchief." I report this because she was making the same erroneous interpretation of the passages that many older people make. That is because they forget that they are reading in a book that was written on the basis of symbols. The significance of the statement is that the tears will be wiped away by removing or preventing anything that could cause tears; the next words of the verse agree with this explanation. *There shall be no more death.* The Saviour went down into the depths of death and came out again, bringing with Him the eternal victory over it, thus removing the possibility for the "grim monster" ever again to overcome those who are accounted worthy of the "better resurrection" with either physical or spiritual death. This will prevent *sorrow, crying* and *pain*, which explains how God will wipe away all tears. *Former things are passed away* will be true at that period beyond the resurrection of the righteous.

Verse 5. *He that sat upon the throne* is the same as was shown in chapter 20:11. He is the one who created all things that exist, but all the items that were made in the first creation pertaining to the material universe will be replaced with a new order of things that will be eternal, and adapted to the needs and enjoyment of the glorified part of humanity. The pronoun *he* means the angel who has been John's companion and exhibitor all through the vision of this book. Having taken a view of these wonderful objects the angel tells John to write the description in his book, and assures him that all that he has seen and heard is *true and faithful*, which means the vision and the words are a faithful report of the truth.

Verse 6. *It is done* is the same thing that was said as reported at chapter 16:17. The expression signifies that everything planned by the Lord and predicted for the period up to the point at hand has been accomplished. *Alpha* and *Omege* are the first and last letters of the Greek alphabet and the phrase is used symbolically, signifying that Jesus has been connected with all things done by his Father throughout. The same truth is meant by the following phrase, *the beginning and the end. I will give*, etc. Having completed everthing necessary for the redemption and glorification of man, He is prepared to offer the benefit of the plan to humanity. It will be *freely* means not only that it is not something that can be purchased with silver and gold, but also that it will be supplied in abundance. Another condition that should be noticed is the offer is made to those who are *athirst*. The Lord's favors have always been offered on such a condition. Jesus said (Matthew 5:6), "Blessed are they which do hunger and thirst after righteousness for they shall be filled." He also specified in the great invitation to "come unto me" that He meant those who were "heavy laden." There is nothing selfish or arbitrary about this, for only those who sincerely desire the water of life would relish its taste if they even attempted to drink it.

Verse 7. *He that overcometh* is another of the principles that distinguish the favor of God from what is generally offered by man. It is not to the strongest and successful ones, for then there would be many worthy people who would lose out, for few if any can be successful when that word is used in its ordinary sense. But the reward is to those who *overcome*, and 1 John 5:4 states that faith is the means by which we may overcome. That brings the blessings of God within reach of all men since all can have faith whether they are those of one or five talents. *Inherit all things* logically has to mean the things to which reference has just been made concerning the new creation. *Be his God . . . be my son* is the same close association that is mentioned and commented upon at verse 3.

Verse 8. *Fearful* is from DEILOS, which Thayer defines, "timid, fearful," and he then explains it to denote "Christians who through cowardice give way under persecutions and apostatize [deny their Lord]. This definition or explanation is justified by the next word in the text, namely, the *unbelieving. Abominable* is from BDELUSSO, and Thayer's definition is "to render foul, to cause to be abhorred." It is a word that would have a general meaning, hence the apostle follows up with a number of specifications. *Whoremongers* are men who do not merely commit adultery on some specific occasion (which of itself would be wrong), but who are regular patrons of women whose business is to receive men either for lust or money. *Sorcerers* is from PHARMAKENS, and Thayer's lexicon defines it, "one who prepares or uses magical remedies; a sorcerer." It could well be classed with the "dope" trade of our day. *Idolaters* is defined, "A worshipper of false gods." That is its literal meaning and makes it apply to any conduct where a man shows a perference for something over the true God. Hence Paul declares in Ephesians 5: 5 that a covetous man is an idolater. *All liars* is rendered "liars of all kinds" by Moffatt. That rendering is evidently correct for it would be unnecessary to state that every liar is meant in the sense of not allowing some of them to escape; that would be taken for granted. But it means to include not only those who in the direct sense make positive statements that are false, but also everyone who says or does anything for the purpose of making a false impression. When Ananias and his wife deposited some money before Peter there is no evidence that they actually said anything about it until Peter forced them to speak. But yet he accused them of lying because they intended to make a false impression upon the apostle. Therefore we should understand that all deliberate attempts to deceive another will be regarded as lies. It can be done even by stating a part of the truth in such a way as to make a false impression. Paul doubtless was thinking of this when he declared he was not "handling the word of God deceitfully" (2 Corinthians 4: 2). *Have their part.* They will not receive any part of the good things that have just been promised to the faithful. Their fate will be to be cast into the lake of fire and brimstone, which is the place designated by the Greek word GEHENNA. *Which is the second death.* It is called this because all mankind are bound to die physically (Hebrews 9: 27) on account of the sin of Adam. But the wicked will die (be separated) from God for ever and have to remain in this lake of fire away from God.

Verse 9. The original angel who came to John at the beginning of the vision has not left the isle, but occasionally there will be an extra conversation permitted for some one or more of the other persons introduced from time to time. For instance, one of the elders (chapter 5: 5), the beasts or living creatures (chapter 6: 1, 3, 5, 7), the voice from heaven (chapter 10: 8), one of the seven angels (chapter 17: 1) and the one in our verse. John heard many other voices from time to time, but the ones to which reference is made talked *to* him. This angel of our verse invited John to see a vision of the bride, the Lamb's wife.

Verse 10. *He carried me away* was not literal because John never actually left the isle any time through the scenes of this book. The sense in which it was done is signified by the words *in the spirit*. These extra visions injected into the over-all picture of this book, may be illustrated by certain special items called "insets" that are often seen within the scope of some large picture. They serve as explanations of some outstanding feature. In this special vision John saw a mountain from the top of which he could get a good view of what the angel wished him to see. The angel told John he would show him the bride, the Lamb's wife, and when he looked he saw a city instead. That is because the bride is the church (Ephesians 5: 25-33), and also the church is likened to a city (Hebrews 12: 22, 23). Having transferred the imagery from a woman to a city, the following passages will be a description of a beautiful city. It is called *holy Jerusalem* because that title is attached to the church "which is the mother of us all" (Galatians 4: 26). *Descending out of heaven from God.*

That was very appropriate because while the church is composed of men and women on the earth, the design and origin of it were from the dwelling place of God.

Verse 11. *Having the glory of God* is understandable because anything that comes from heaven would be adorned with the glory of God. The glory of the city was so great that John likens it to the rays of a precious stone. There is something most significant about using precious stones as symbols in describing the splendors of the celestial city. We have all beheld diamonds and other precious jewels and admired their glittering brilliance. However, we have observed also that the greatest degree of their beauty is caused by the light that is reflected upon them from some outside source. So with these precious stones that bedeck the city of God; they obtain their glow from the light that radiates from the throne of God. The one named in this verse is only referred to for a comparison, but the actual use of the stones themselves will be described in a later place in this chapter. The jasper that is used to compare the brilliant light is described as being *clear as crystal*. That is a description of a diamond which is among the most attractive of stones.

Verse 12. The dimensions of the wall will be noticed at verses 16 and 17, but here they are briefly stated to be *great and high*. In old times the most important cities were surrounded with walls, hence it is a desirable asset to say this city was walled. It is significant that it was great and high. That would indicate good protection from the enemies, since the wall was too high to be scaled and too great or strong to be penetrated or beaten down. Among the numerical symbols that have been very prominent in this book are four and its multiples, twelve and four and twenty. Four was the number of the living creatures that represented the redeemed from the four corners of the earth. Twelve was used if the organized systems that God has had are being considered from one dispensation alone, either the Mosaic or the Christian. That is because there were twelve tribes in the one and twelve apostles in the other. Hence it is appropriate that John should see the twelve gates to this city representing the twelve tribes of Israel. The twelve apostles will be pointed out later, but it was in order to show the twelve tribes first because the Mosaic system was first given.

Verse 13. The tabernacle of the Mosaic system had much beauty in its formation, and also in the garments of the priestly service. That was not as an encouragement to vanity or doing something for mere show. But God is the designer and maker of all things, and those that are seen in the universe that are beautiful are not so by accident. Among the items that contribute to the beauty of any structure is the symmetry of its arrangement. A city that is foursquare should not have a varying number of gates in its walls. There are twelve gates to this city and the equal distribution of them in sets of three is very appropriate. It might have seemed sufficiently clear to say that the gates were equally divided amidst the four sides of the city. However, this is supposed to be a somewhat poetical or picturesque description of a very superb spot, and it is fitting to go into these details.

Verse 14. This completes the full representations corresponding to the four and twenty elders. The twelve gates stand for the tribes of Israel, and here are the twelve original apostles of Christ. There is nothing said about angels in connection with the twelve apostles as there was with the twelve gates. That is doubtless because gates call for guards at the entrance of an important city, while a foundation is a more fixed part of a structure and does not call for supervision. In literal architecture there would be actually only one foundation to a building. Yet it might be built of several stones as was this one, and each stone is spoken of as a foundation. In literal language it would be one foundation but composed of a number of stones. In truth that is the way Paul speaks of the church in Ephesians 2: 20 where he says Christians are built upon the foundation (singular) of the apostles and prophets. It is common to see important names engraved on stones composing a building. It generally is of persons who have made valuable contributions to the structure. From that standpoint it is significant to have the names of the apostles on these stones.

Verse 15. *He that talked with me* means the angel who had been sent to give John the vision. This angel had the measuring reed and he did the measuring. A *reed* in nature is produced on the banks or near the edge of bodies of water and the stems are used for various purposes. The one the angel had was an artificial one and was made of bright and precious metal. Such an instrument was proper for the important matter of measuring divine things. We are not told the capacity of this measuring rule as we might do in the case of a literal measuring stick, such as a yardstick or foot measure. We have only the computation after the angel did the measuring.

Verse 16. The city was a cube, the length and breadth and height being equal. The measurement was twelve thousand furlongs, which is fifteen hundred miles. For an approximate estimate to help us visualize the size of that city, let us think that if a man were to start at the Gulf of Mexico and travel to the Great Lakes, he would have made the journey along one side only of the city. It is true that the eternal city will not be restricted to miles as we measure distances, but the figures are intended to give us some impression of the abundant provision that God has made for the saved of all ages.

Verse 17. In the preceding verse the angel measured the *city* which gave the length of it. In this verse he *measured the wall* which necessarily means the thickness of it. The measurement was a hundred and forty and four cubits, another multiple of one of our prominent numbers, twelve. *Measure of a man, that is, of the angel.* This unusual language only means that the angel used the same action in measuring the wall that a man would use in such a situation. The usual length of a cubit is eighteen inches, hence this wall was two hundred and sixteen feet thick. Such would be a proper thickness to be proportionate to such a height.

Verse 18. The body of the wall was of jasper, which we are told in verse 11 is a substance that is "clear as crystal" thus describing a diamond. Let us try to see with our mind's eye a diamond that is fifteen hundred miles in diameter and we will have a mental picture of one side of this city. *City was pure gold* means the street of it according to verse 21. Gold is a metal (not a stone), hence the likeness to *clear glass* is explained in verse 21 as of *transparent* glass. Literal gold is one of the most condensed of metals and hence would naturally be the opposite of transparent. So we should understand that the metal was so pure and the texture so fine that it would take on a very high polish. It was so much that way that in looking upon it one would really seem to see a substance that his eyes were penetrating (as if they were performing the action of an X-ray), when in reality he was beholding something with an incomprehensibly high gloss.

Verse 19. The foundation stones of the wall were garnished (decorated) with *all manner* of precious stones, which means with stones of various descriptions. The first was *jasper* which we have previously learned is like a diamond. *Sapphires* are of several varieties and no special one is named, but the general description in the English dictionaries shows them to be brilliant gems inclined to be transparent. A *chalcedony* is a stone with a blue tint and a glossy surface. *Emerald* is a stone with rich coloring of green and very much prized as a precious stone.

Verse 20. A *sardonyx* is described by Thayer as follows: "A precious stone marked by the red color of the carnelian (sard) and the white of the onyx." A *sardius* is a flesh-colored stone. Thayer says a *chrysolyte* is "a precious stone of a golden color," and he says a *beryl* is "a precious stone of a pale green color." A *topaz* is a stone of a greenish-yellow color as given by Thayer. *Chrysoprasus.* Thayer defines this as follows: "A precious stone in color like a leek, of a translucent [transparent] golden-green." A *jacinth* is also the name of a flower (commonly called a hyacinth). The color of it and the stone by the same name is dark-blue, almost black. Thayer says an *amethyst* is a precious stone of a violet and purple color.

Verse 21. *Every several gate was of one pearl.* There is nothing said nor intimated that the gates resembled pearls or were merely as beautiful as pearls. No, the first phrase is, *the twelve gates were twelve pearls.* And we should take for granted that the Lord would not use any but genuine pearl, but He would also use the best of it for the construction of a city to be the eternal home of the redeemed, where they are to share the glory with Him and all the celestial beings that He has created. I will quote from Smith's Bible Dictionary some information about pearls: "The finest specimens of the pearl are yielded by the pearl oyster . . . the oysters grow in clusters on rock in deep water, and the pearl is found inside the shell, and is the result of a diseased secretion caused by the introduction of foreign bodies, etc., between the mantle and the shell . . . The size of a good Oriental pearl varies from that of a pea to about three times that . . . Pearls have been valued as high as $200,000 apiece." Now let us do some calculating and try to form some idea of the beauty and value of just the gates to the celestial city. Everything thus far has been in the proportions that would be required for beauty, hence these gates would be of the width and height that would not be out of proportion. In a wall fifteen hundred miles high and two hundred and sixteen feet thick, any opening of ordinary dimensions would look like a tunnel more than an entrance to a city of residence. We are not given the actual dimensions of the gates, but in order to bring them near enough for us to do some kind of calculating, we know they would not have been less than a hundred feet wide and two hundred feet high. If a pearl three times the size of a pea is worth two hundred thousand dollars, then one pearl as large as I have suggested (and doubtless these gates were larger) would be worth many times more than all the wealth of the world, and besides this, there were twelve of these costly gems. I would be willing to give a year or more of the severest kind of service just to see one of those gates.

Verse 22. *I saw no temple.* John was thinking of the temple that was in the literal city of Jerusalem, and was contrasting that situation with what he saw in the vision. Even that temple which was built for the service to God was not good enough nor big enough to contain Him (1 Kings 8: 27; Acts 7: 47-50), much less would He need a temple to confine him when He is already occupying the whole city.

Verse 23. The sun, moon and stars were necessary to give light upon the earth, but that planet will have passed away. The light that would be adapted to glorified residents of the eternal city would need to be more brilliant than a multitude of suns such as we now see. But the city will not be without light for the glory of God and the Son will lighten it. Think of a Being so bright and glorious that its rays would reach from wall to wall in a city 1,500 miles wide. No wonder Moses was not permitted to come within the rays of that glory.

Verse 24. *Nations* and *kings* of the earth will not come into the city literally, for those relationships are of a temporal nature. This verse is based on the practice in ancient times that required a captive city to pay tribute to a city that had overcome it. Doubtless there will be men who had been kings, and others who were citizens of the nations ruled by these kings, who will have become servants of God and who will be among the many thousands who will throng that city.

Verse 25. *The gates shall not be shut at all by day* (or day by day). This also is based upon the practice of ancient cities closing their gates at the approach of night (Joshua 2: 5). John says there will not be any need for such a performance, for *there shall be no night there.* It is his way of emphasizing the absence of night, for there will be no enemy who could enter the city any way.

Verse 26. This is the same as verse 24.

Verse 27. The evils named have been fully described previously, but I will cite the remarks at verse 8 about liars. Those whose names are in *the book of life* is explained at chapter 20: 15.

Revelation 22

Verse 1. The pronoun *he* refers to the angel who has been with John all through the vision of this book. There is nothing more pleasing to the eye than a flowing body of water. It signifies something that is constant and moving with majestic procedure. But many rivers are attractive from these standpoints only, while within them may be vicious creatures that would devour helpless victims that came within reach. Also there may be much that is vile and foul, carrying with them the waste materials of the cities. But the river John saw had nothing of that kind because it had not been in contact with any place containing filth. Instead, its source is the throne of God and the Lamb where there can be nothing vile. For this reason the river is pure and also clear as crystal because there are no materials to becloud the stream. It is called *water of life* because it is always moving (never stagnant) and because of the quality and purity described in the foregoing comments.

Verse 2. *In the midst of the street of it* means the street of the city, and the river of life flowed down the center of the street. This description will give us no difficulty if we will think of the "divided highways" that grace our country in many places. Let us think of a river flowing from an inexhaustible fountain and proceeding on through a beautiful city. On each bank is a row of fruit trees that serve a double purpose, namely, furnish ornamentation for the crystal stream, and a source of food for those who are walking upon the section of the "divided highway" that one may be using. To clarify the description we think of it in this manner. First is a section of the street, next a row of trees, next the river, next another row of trees and then the other section of the street. *Tree of life.* This tree is promised to all who overcome the contests of life (chapter 2: 7). The phraseology is based on the tree of life that was in the garden of Eden. It will be well for us again to remember we are still in a book of symbols, where the Lord is giving us a picture of Heaven in as strong terms as our human mind can grasp. The tree is spoken of in the singular number because there was but one in the garden. But the varieties are not limited to one, because this tree is pictured in connection with spiritual things. Here we have another instance of the numeral that has been so prominent throughout this book. That is twelve which is a multiple of four (the four creatures), and the number each of the two organized systems of salvation that God has given the world. The special significance of the twelve here is to show the fruit-bearing season is continuous and perennial, but a different kind of fruit will be produced each month, so that no occasion will exist for longing after a change; there will be one coming each month. Many kinds of fruit trees not only produce fruit, but also their leaves have medicinal value in them. Thus we are told that the leaves of this tree will have healing qualities. Not that any citizens will become sick, but it is on the same principle of wiping away all tears (chapter 21: 4). The leaves of ths tree will heal the people by keeping them in such a condition that sickness will be impossible.

Verse 3. *No more curse* is an allusion to the curse pronounced upon the ground because of the sin of Adam (Genesis 3: 17). Instead of a curse there will be endless blessings because not only will the tree of life be in the city (as it was in the garden), but God and the Lamb will themselves be there. Also all creatures who would tempt the righteous will have been consigned to their eternal place in the lake of fire. *Servants shall serve him.* It is sometimes asked if the saved are to be entirely free in that city, since it is spoken of as the place of rest for God's people. The word *serve* does not necessarily mean labor or toil. The word is from LATREUO and at this place Thayer's definition (the words in italics) is as follows: "To render religious service or homage, to worship." It certainly will be only unspeakable pleasure to engage in such employment as worshipping God in his immediate presence, when faithful disciples have taken real happiness from their worship of Him while in the world. In the words of one of the old songs of the church, it will be a service in a time and place "Where congregations ne'er break up, and rest days have no end."

Verse 4. *Shall see his face* is mentioned to indicate the great intimacy that will exist between God and the creatures that have been redeemed by the blood of the Lamb. Persons spending some time in a city where many others are present, may be seen with pennants attached to their clothing for the purpose of identification. In this celestial city the name will be on the person, on the most conspicuous part of it, the forehead. How different this is from the condition of the members of the apostate church; they had the mark of the beast in their forehead (chapter 14: 9).

Verse 5. *Shall be no night there.* (See the comments at chapter 21: 25.) *Need no candle neither light of the sun.* This is one of the most significant symbols used in this series, because it includes the two extremes on the subject. A candle is an artificial light and the weakest that man has devised. The sun is God's own direct work and is the strongest light in all the natural creation. In saying that neither will be needed in the celestial city, John is giving us the greatest possible picture of the strength of the light that will radiate from the throne of God; although he was to be the lawgiver, Moses was a natural man. And 1 Timothy 6: 16 says God is "dwelling in the light which no man can approach unto; whom no man hath seen, nor can see." *They shall reign for ever and ever,*

The word *reign* may raise a question in connection with the truth that even Jesus is said to reign only until death has been conquered (1 Corinthians 15: 25, 26). The explanation lies in the definitions of the original word. The Greek original is BASILEUO, which means "to reign," but in our passage Thayer explains it to mean "to denote the supreme moral dignity, liberty, blessedness, which will be enjoyed by Christ's redeemed ones." Hence the word does not necessarily mean to rule as a king. It is a figurative term and denotes a situation where a certain condition prevails. It is like saying that "all difficulties were removed and peace again reigned." We have the blessed assurance from the apostle that the condition of such a reign will continue *for ever and ever*.

Verse 6. *He said* means the angel said it to John. *Faithful and true*. These words are virtually the same in their fundamental meaning, and either could properly be used in place of the other for general purposes. Technically they mean the words or sayings just delivered by the angel are worthy of being relied on because they are true. *Of the holy prophets* is referred to as an evidence that His sayings are worthy of being relied on, for the predictions that God enabled the prophets to make were fulfilled in the proper time. For that reason there should be no doubt concerning the predictions that He has authorized his servants to make in the present book. *Sent his angel*. This refers to the angel who has been with John from the beginning of his vision on the isle. *Must shortly be done*. The Englishman's Greek New Testament renders this phrase, "must come to pass soon." The word in question is a relative term, for even a number of centuries would be short when compared with the endlessness of what will come after the judgment day. However, since this period in the vision of John is at the near approach of the last day (as to the events predicted), the end is literally close at hand.

Verse 7. *Quickly* is from the same word as "shortly" in the preceding verse. *Blessed* means happy, denoting a condition entirely satisfactory. *Keepeth* is from TEREO and in the King James Version it is translated hold fast 1 time, keep 57, observe 4, preserve 2, reserve 8, watch 2. It is a word with many shades of meaning which must be determined in each place according to the connection. If it is used in relation to things a man is required to do, then it means he must understand and do them. If used only of things stated as truths, whether they are predictions or otherwise, then the word means we are to believe them and keep them in respectful remembrance. The present verse applies the word to the prophecy of this book, hence it has the meaning just described. However, it would imply some activities on the part of man, for among the things predicted is the judgment day on which men will be judged according to their deeds. Hence if a man believes and respects that prediction, he will not forget it but will fashion his life in such a way as to be adjudged worthy of everlasting life. This explains why the angel said those were *blessed* or happy who *keepeth the sayings*.

Verse 8. *These things* refer to the vision of the celestial city and what the angel said about it. In chapter 19: 10 John attempted to worship the angel but was prevented. Hence the *things* of our verse would have to apply to what had come before him since that time. The word *worship* is one of the terms in the Greek New Testament that have many shades of meaning, because it is from a dozen original words with about that many different definitions. Hence not every form or kind of worship would be condemned. The word as used in our verse and the following one, also in chapter 19: 10, means to prostrate oneself before another as a recognition of superiority in rank. Such an attitude is due only to God and his Son. Angels are not superior to men as to their personal merit nor even in authority. In the great sphere of service to God the angels are only some of His servants. That is the reason that the angel assigned for his instructions to John in this place and also in chapter 19: 10 refused to be worshipped. And it is the same reason why Peter refused the worship from Cornelius in Acts 10: 25, 26 saying, "Stand up; I myself also am a man." This does not condemn the acts of homage that are paid to kings or other dignitaries as was the custom in old time and is yet in some countries. Those performances pertain to matters of social or legal standing, while the word under consideration in our passages has to do with authority in religion. For a complete analysis of this word according to the lexicon and concordance, see the comments at Matthew 2: 2 in the first volume of the New Testament Commentary.

Verse 9. Many comments that would be suggested on this verse were made on the preceding one. There were two phases of devotion to God in which John and the angel were in the same class, namely, *fellowservant* and *prophet*. The first will apply to all of the Lord's disciples while the second pertains to their work in predicting future events. But neither of these services entitles a man to receive worship from another, so the angel told John to *worship God*.

Verse 10. *Seal* is from SPHRAGIZO, which Thayer defines at the passage, "keep in silence, keep secret." In the beginning of our study of this book, we were told that the future experiences of the church in its relations with the governments were unrevealed. That was indicated by a book (containing visions of the future) that was sealed, and it required the inspiration of Christ to reveal it. At some time before the Christian Dispensation (we know not how long) God composed the subject matter that makes up the book of Revelation, but since the events were not to be fulfilled "for many days" as Daniel was told (Daniel 12: 1-4), He sealed them up in the book we are studying. When the time came to begin making them known He enabled the "Lion of the tribe of Judah" to break the seals. But at the point reached by us in the vision there is nothing depending on future developments—*the time is at hand*—hence there is no reason for sealing it up.

Verse 11. The preceding verse must be remembered in connection with this one in order to get the full meaning of the passage—it is very vital. We are arrived at the judgment day (in the vision) when the final and eternal lot of all intelligent creatures will be announced for good. After this there will never be any change either for better or worse with anyone. The *unjust* and *filthy* will always be so, and the *righteous* and *holy* likewise will remain so. That is why there will never be any sin committed in Heaven by angel or man after the judgment. Neither will there be any chance for reformation on the part of the creatures in the lake of fire.

Verse 12. *I come quickly* is explained at verse 7. *My reward is with me.* When Jesus comes again it will not be for the purpose of setting up another reign on the earth, for all of His reign will then come to a close (1 Corinthians 15: 24-26). The lot of both just and unjust will have been decided at that time, and Christ will be coming to bestow the reward according to that decision. It is in that sense that the reward will be *with Him*—not coming merely to announce what it is going to be. He will at that time recompense either "tribulation" or "rest" upon mankind (2 Thessalonians 1: 6, 7), which is the meaning of the present passage. The basis on which the rewards will be distributed is *according as his work shall be*.

Verse 13. This is virtually the same as chapter 1: 8; see those comments.

Verse 14. *Blessed* is from MAKARIOS, and in the King James Version it has been rendered "blessed" 43 times and "happy" 6 times. The reason for their blessedness or happiness is their *right* to the tree of life. The word *right* is from the word EXOUSIA, which also means power or authority. It is a very serious passage in view of the notions of many people as to the lot of the unsaved. As an outburst of sentiment or emotion it is said, "How could God refuse to admit any person to the eternal happiness when He has it within his power to grant it." But the last part of the statement is not true, for God cannot do that which is not right. (Titus 1: 2; 2 Timothy 2: 13.) If those who do the commandments are the ones who have the *right* to the tree of life, then it would not be right for others to have access to it. And if they would not have a right to it, it would be wrong for them to have it. And since God cannot do wrong it follows that He cannot admit any person to the city who has not done the commandments. It is clear that having right to the tree of life requires the right for entrance into the city, for we learned at verse 2 that the tree is growing inside the city.

Verse 15. *Without* means on the outside of the eternal city. The preceding verse reveals who will be permitted to enter the city and this one tells some of the kind that will not enter. *Dogs.* It would be foolish to think this is used with reference to the dumb brute, for it would not be more true of the dog than of all others of the animal kingdom. 2 Peter 2: 12 informs us that the beasts are destined to be destroyed; there will be no "hereafter" for them. The word is from KUON and Thayer says that some authorities define it to mean "sodomites." The word corresponding to it in the Old Testament is *keleb* which Strong defines, "A dog; hence (by euphemism) [substitution of a milder word as being less offensive to the ear] a male prostitute." In Deuteronomy 23: 18 the word is used in that sense where it is associated with an immoral woman in designating "tainted money." The "hire of a whore" means money an immoral woman receives from her male patrons. While on that subject it was appropriate to name another immoral person and that is a man who practices unnatural immorality for money, and that is what is meant by "the price of a dog." It seems very fitting to call a Sodomite a dog, for that animal is the only creature of the brute creation that is inclined to gratify his lust on one of his own sex. And we have the same appropriateness of the two kinds of immoral characters that the Old Testament passage showed, namely, the *dogs* and very soon the *whoremongers*. The dogs are men who have immoral relations with other men, and whoremongers are men who patronize women who are immoral as an occupation.

Thayer says a *sorcerer* is "one who prepares or uses magical remedies." It is similar to those who are engaged in the "dope" business today. The scriptures tell us that medicine does good (Proverbs 17: 22), but any kind of drugs or narcotics that produce unnatural feelings of gaiety, or the opposite one of abandonment to lasciviousness, will damage the body and that will bring the curse of God upon the guilty. (1 Corinthians 6: 18-20.) The first sin committed by man against man was murder (Genesis 4: 8). That crime is so great that God finally gave the decree of capital punishment against all who commit it (Genesis 9: 6). But literal murder is not the only kind that can be committed. 1 John 3: 15 says a man who hates his brother is a murderer, and of course all such persons will be on the outside of the holy city. *Idolaters* are those who worship anything or any person besides the true God. It may be images made with hands or the works of creation such as the planets or animals, etc. Also Paul says that covetousness is idolatry (Colossians 3: 5), hence there will be no covetous persons in Heaven. Chapter 21: 8 shows that liars of all kinds will be cast into the lake of fire. Our verse expresses the same thought as to its comprehensiveness by taking in all who love the liars.

Verse 16. This book starts out by telling us that it is the revelation of Jesus Christ (not of "Saint John the Divine" as the heading title erroneously states), and this verse reveals Him introducing himself directly. However, He does not overlook the services of the angel, but faithfully backs up his work by saying that He sent him. *To testify* means to transmit the testimony to the churches. That is, to bear testimony to the things that have been showed him throughout the vision of this book. *Root and offspring of David.* This means that Jesus was in the direct line of genealogy that came down from Abraham through David. That great man was not the only prominent Hebrew in the line, but there was a distinction in his case. David had two sons by the same woman, Bathsheba, and those sons were Solomon and Nathan (1 Chronicles 3: 5). At this place the blood line divides and on Solomon's side it comes down to Joseph the husband of Mary. On Nathan's side it comes down to Mary the mother of Jesus. (See Matthew 1 and Luke 3.) There is another fact that makes David of special importance. He was the first king of the Israelites from the tribe of Judah, and it had been predicted (Genesis 49: 10) that the tribe of Judah was to give law to God's people in latter times. The Mosaic law was of the tribe of Levi (Exodus 2: 1-10). David was the first king of the tribe of Judah to sit upon the throne of God's ancient people. That kingdom was destined to be set aside and replaced by another. But God assured David that his throne would not always be vacant. There was to be one of his descendants who would reign on the throne, only by that time it would be spiritual and not one with temporal government as its purpose. Such a king was worthy of coming to John with an authoritative commission such as this vision. *Bright and morning star* is what He says of himself in chapter 2: 28. The significance of this phrase is due to its brightness as it precedes the sun in rising, thus announcing that a new day is beginning. (See 2 Peter 1: 19.) And truly did the rising of Jesus come as a star to announce that a new day was about to come, the day of the Christian Dispensation.

Verse 17. The subject running through this verse is along the line of invitations. It has been stated more than once that as to the relative place of the items in the over-all vision of this book, the time of the judgment has been reached. From that standpoint there would be no reason to give anyone an invitation to come for salvation—that opportunity has passed. Yet in reality, aside from the symbolized feature of the book, the basic purpose of the book of Revelation is to give the world a final document from Heaven as an incentive for preparing to meet the day of all days, the second coming of Christ and the judgment of the world. Otherwise there would be no point in inviting men to come and drink of the water of life. Nor would there be any call for the warning sounded in the two verses following this. Hence we shall consider the important phrases of this combined invitation. The bride is the (espoused) church (2 Corinthians 11: 2) and the Spirit is in the church (Ephesians 2: 22). The church of Christ has a standing invitation to people of the world, wishing them to accept the salvation offered so freely. In truth, it is the only organization that has any right to make such an offer (Ephesians 3: 21 and 1 Timothy 3: 15). But others as individuals have the right to repeat the invitation, hence the verse says for those who hear to repeat the call. That makes it the duty of every individual to be active in the salvation of souls. *Let him that is athirst come.* This is in line with the statement of Jesus in Matthew 5: 6 that they who hunger and thirst after righteousness shall be filled. That is logical, for unless a man is thirsty he will not be interested in the opportunity to drink. *Whosoever will* signifies the same as the preceding comment, that unless a man is willing it would do him no good to go through the formality of obeying the Gospel. Let it be observed also that the blessing is to those who *come.* Man must come to the fountain for it will not be moved towards him for his convenience. The *water of life* is the same that Jesus made known to the woman of Samaria (John 4: 10-14). This water is the word of God and it will be in man "a well of water springing up into everlasting life." It is offered freely which means abundantly and without the price such as silver and gold.

Verse 18. It is asked if the phrase *this book* refers to the book of Revelation or to the whole Bible. Its direct application is to this book for it is the one that John was engaged to write. But the principle applies to the entire word of God, for 1 Peter 4: 11 commands "any man" who speaks to do so as the oracles of God. That would not be done were he to make any change in the Sacred Text, either by adding to it or by taking from it. To *add unto these things* would not be done only by literally writing some uninspired words to the document; no person is apt to do that. But when a man assumes the privilege of practicing things not authorized in the book, he thereby adds to it in principle. The *plagues* were symbolized and were repeated in various forms. The idea is that such a man will be plagued as severely as those described.

Verse 19. There is nothing put in the book of God that is not necessary, therefore it is sinful to take any of it out. That would be done by rejecting any of its requirement. (See Hebrews 2: 2.) *Take away his part.* No man actually has possession of any part of the things in the holy city, but God has prepared a part for each person who will prepare himself for it by faithfulness to the word.

Verse 20. *He which testifieth these things* means Christ according to the statement in chapter 1: 1. *I come quickly* is also stated in verses 7 and 12 and explained in connection with those passages. The word *surely* is added at this place for the sake of emphasis. The attitude of John to that announcement is that which every faithful disciple will have. In 2 Timothy 4: 8 the apostle Paul is speaking of the crown to be given him at the coming of Christ. He says it will be for him but not for him only; it will *be unto all them also that love his appearing.* If a man is living a righteous life he will not dread to think either of death or the judgment.

Verse 21. The grace of the Lord is the favor that is bestowed upon all who are living in faithful service to Him. All can be faithful regardless of human weaknesses, hence no reason exists why anyone should be rejected when He comes. John lovingly thinks of his brethren to whom he is to commit this book and wishes for the favor of Christ to be with them. When *Amen* is used at the close of a sentence or composition, it means "so be it, may it be fulfilled." John has no regrets about anything he has been told to write, and hence closes the great book with the sincere endorsement.

www.ingramcontent.com/pod-product-compliance
Lightning Source LLC
Chambersburg PA
CBHW050513170426
43201CB00013B/1936